A history of the French Novel

(To the close of the 19th century)

(Volume II)

From 1800 to 1900

George Saintsbury

Alpha Editions

This edition published in 2019

ISBN : 9789353705008

Design and Setting By
Alpha Editions
email - alphaedis@gmail.com

A HISTORY OF THE FRENCH NOVEL

MACMILLAN AND CO., Limited
LONDON · BOMBAY · CALCUTTA · MADRAS
MELBOURNE

THE MACMILLAN COMPANY
NEW YORK · BOSTON · CHICAGO
DALLAS · SAN FRANCISCO

THE MACMILLAN CO. OF CANADA, Ltd.
TORONTO

A HISTORY

OF THE

FRENCH NOVEL

(TO THE CLOSE OF THE 19TH CENTURY)

BY

GEORGE SAINTSBURY

M.A. AND HON. D.LITT. OXON. ; HON. LL.D. ABERD. ; HON. D.LITT. DURH. ;
FELLOW OF THE BRITISH ACADEMY ; HON. FELLOW OF MERTON COLLEGE, OXFORD ;
LATE PROFESSOR OF RHETORIC AND ENGLISH LITERATURE IN THE UNIVERSITY OF EDINBURGH

VOL. II

FROM 1800 TO 1900

MACMILLAN AND CO., LIMITED
ST. MARTIN'S STREET, LONDON

1919

Sólo á veces, con un dejo
de zozobra y de ansiedad,
tímido tiembla en sus labios
un viejo y triste cantar,
copla que vibre en el aire
como un toque funeral :
La Noche Buena se viene,
la Noche Buena se va !
Y nosotros nos iremos
y no volveremos más.

CARLOS FERNANDEZ SHAW,
La Balada de los Viejos.

PREFACE

" THE second chantry " (for it would be absurd to keep
" temple ") of this work " is not like the first " ; in one
respect especially, which seems to deserve notice in its
Preface or porch—if a chantry may be permitted a porch.
In Volume I.—though many of its subjects (not quite all)
had been handled by me before in more or less summary
fashion, or in reviews of individual books, or in other
connections than that of the novel—only Hamilton,
Lesage, Marivaux, and the minor " Sensibility " men and
women had formed the subjects of separate and somewhat detailed studies, wholly or mainly as novelists. The
case is altered in respect of the present volume. The
Essays on French Novelists, to which I there referred, contain a larger number of such studies appertaining to the
present division—studies busied with Charles de Bernard,
Gautier, Murger, Flaubert, Dumas, Sandeau, Cherbuliez,
Feuillet. On Balzac I have previously written two
papers of some length, one as an Introduction to Messrs.
Dent's almost complete translation of the *Comédie*, with
shorter sequels for each book, the other an article in the
Quarterly Review for 1907. Some dozen or more
years ago I contributed to an American edition [1] of translations of Mérimée by various hands, a long " Intro-

---

[1] It is perhaps worth while to observe that I did not " edit " this, and that I had
nothing whatever to do with any part of it except the *Introduction* and my earlier translation of the *Chronique de Charles IX*, which was, I believe, reprinted in it.

duction " to that most remarkable writer, and I had, somewhat earlier, written on Maupassant for the *Fortnightly Review*. One or two additional dealings of some substance with the subject might be mentioned, such as another Introduction to *Corinne*, but not to *Delphine*. These, however, and passages in more general *Histories*, hardly need specification.

On the other hand, I have never dealt, substantively and in detail, with Chateaubriand, Paul de Kock, Victor Hugo, Beyle, George Sand, or Zola[1] as novelists, nor with any of the very large number of minors not already mentioned, including some, such as Nodier and Gérard de Nerval, whom, for one thing or another, I should myself very decidedly put above minority. And, further, my former dealings with the authors in the first list given above having been undertaken without any view to a general history of the French novel, it became not merely proper but easy for me to " triangulate " them anew. So that though there may be more previous work of mine in print on the subjects of the present volume than on those of the last, there will, I hope, be found here actually less, and very considerably less, *réchauffé*—hardly any, in fact (save a few translations[2] and some passages on Gautier and Maupassant)—of the amount and character which seemed excusable, and more than excusable, in the case of the " Sensibility " chapter there. The book, if not actually a " Pisgah-sight reversed," taken from Lebanon

[1] In very great strictness an exception should perhaps be made for notice of him, and of some others, in *The Later Nineteenth Century* (Edinburgh and London, 1907).

[2] There will, for pretty obvious reasons, be fewer of these than in the former volume. The texts are much more accessible ; there is no difficulty about the language, such as people, however unnecessarily, sometimes feel about French up to the sixteenth century ; and the space is wanted for other things. If I have kept one or two of my old ones it is because they have won approval from persons whose approval is worth having, and are now out of print : while I have added one or two others—to please myself. Translations —in some cases more than one or two—already exist, for those who read English only, of nearly the whole of Balzac, of all Victor Hugo's novels, of a great many of Duma's, and of others almost innumerable.

instead of Pisgah after more than forty years' journey, not in the wilderness, but in the Promised Land itself, attempts to be so ; and uses no more than fairly " reminiscential " (as Sir Thomas Browne would say) notes, taken on that journey itself.

It was very naturally, and by persons of weight, put to me whether I could not extend this history to, or nearer to, the present day. I put my negative to this briefly in the earlier preface : it may be perhaps courteous to others, who may be disposed to regret the refusal, to give it somewhat more fully here. One reason— perhaps sufficient in itself—can be very frankly stated. I do not *know* enough of the French novel of the last twenty years or so. During the whole of that time I have had no reasons, of duty or profit, to oblige such knowledge. I have had a great many other things to do, and I have found greater recreation in re-reading old books than in experimenting on new ones. I might, no doubt, in the last year or two have made up the deficiency to some extent, but I was indisposed to do so for two, yea, three reasons, which seemed to me sufficient.

In the first place, I have found, both by some actual experiment of my own, and, as it seems to me, by a considerable examination of the experiments of other people, that to co-ordinate satisfactorily accounts of contemporary or very recent work with accounts of older is so difficult as to·be nearly impossible. The *foci* are too different to be easily adjusted, and the result is almost always out of composition, if not of drawing.

Secondly, though I know I am here kicking against certain pricks, it does not appear to me, either from what I have read or from criticisms on what I have not, that any definitely new and decisively illustrated school of novels has arisen since the death of M. Zola.

Thirdly, it would be impossible to deal with the subject, save in an absurdly incomplete fashion, without discussing living persons. To doing this, in a book, I have an unfashionable but unalterable objection. The productions of such persons, as they appear, are, by now established custom, proper subjects for " reviewing " in accordance with the decencies of literature, and such reviews may sometimes, with the same proviso, be extended to studies of their work up to date. But even these latter should, I think, be reserved for very exceptional cases.

A slight difference of method may be observed in the treatment of authors in Chapter X. and onwards, this treatment being not only somewhat less judicial and more " impressionist," but also more general and less buckrammed out with abstracts of particular works.[1] There appeared to me to be more than one reason for this, all such reasons being independent of, though by no means ignoring, the mechanical pressure of ever-lessening space. In the first place, a very much larger number of readers may be presumed to be more or less familiar with the subjects of discussion, thus not only making elaborate " statement of case " and production of supporting evidence unnecessary, but exposing the purely judicial attitude to the charge of " no jurisdiction." Moreover, there is behind all this, as it seems to me, a really important principle, which is not a mere repetition, but a noteworthy extension, of that recently laid down. I rather doubt whether the absolute historico-critical verdict and sentence can ever be pronounced on work that is, even in the widest sense, contemporary. The " firm perspective of the past " can in very few instances be acquired : and those few, who by good luck have acquired something of it, should not presume too much

---

[1] The chief exceptions are Dumas *fils*, the earliest, and Maupassant, the greatest except Flaubert and far more voluminous than Flaubert himself.

on this gift of fortune. General opinion of a man is during his lifetime often wrong, for some time after his death almost always so : and the absolute balance is very seldom reached till a full generation—something more than the conventional thirty years—has passed. Meanwhile, though all readers who have anything critical in them will be constantly revising their impressions, it is well not to put one's own out as more than impressions. It is only a very few years since I myself came to what I may call a provisionally final estimate of Zola, and I find that there is some slight alteration even in that which, from the first, I formed of Maupassant. I can hardly hope that readers of this part of the work will not be brought into collision with expressions of mine, more frequently than was the case in the first volume or even the first part of this. But I can at least assure them that I have no intention of playing Sir Oracle, or of trailing my coat.

The actual arrangement of this volume has been the subject of a good deal of " pondering and deliberation," almost as much as Sir Thomas Bertram gave to a matter no doubt of more importance. There was a considerable temptation to recur to the system on which I have written some other literary histories—that of " Books " and " Interchapters." This I had abandoned, in the first volume, because it was not so much difficult of application as hardly relevant. Here the relevance is much greater. The single century divides itself, without the slightest violence offered, into four parts, which, if I had that capacity or partiality for flowery writing, the absence of which in me some critics have deplored, I might almost call Spring, Summer, Autumn, and Winter. There is the season of little positive crop but important seed-sowing,—the season in which the greater writers, Chateaubriand and Mme. de Staël, perform their office.

Here, too, quite humble folk—Pigault-Lebrun complet-
ing what has been already dealt with, Ducray-Duminil
and others doing work to be dealt with here, and Paul
de Kock most of all, get the novel of ordinary life ready
in various ways : while others still, Nodier, Hugo, Vigny,
Mérimée, and, with however different literary value,
Arlincourt, implant the New Romance. There is the
sudden, magnificent, and long-continued outburst of all
the kinds in and after 1830. There is the autumn of
the Second Empire, continuing and adding to the fruits
and flowers of summer : and there is the gradual decadence
of the last quarter of the century, with some late blossoming and second-crop fruitage—the medlars of the novel—
and the dying off of the great producers of the past.
But the breach of uniformity in formal arrangement
of the divisions would perhaps be too great to the eye
without being absolutely necessary to the sense, and
I have endeavoured to make the necessary recapitula-
tion with a single " halt " of chapter-length [1] at the exact
middle. It will readily be understood that the loss of
my own library has been even more severely felt in this
volume than in the earlier one, while circumstances,
public and private, have made access to larger collections
more difficult. But I have endeavoured to "make good "
as much as possible, and grumbling or complaining
supplies worse than no armour against Fate.

I have sometimes, perhaps rashly, during the writing
of this book wondered " What next " ? By luck for
myself—whether also for my readers it would be ill
even to wonder—I have been permitted to execute all

---

[1] The most unexpected chorus of approval with which Volume I. was received by
reviewers, and which makes me think, in regard to this, of that unpleasant song of the
Koreish " After Bedr, Ohod," leaves little necessity for defending points attacked. I
have made a few addenda and corrigenda to Volume I. to cover exceptions, and the
" Interchapter " or its equivalent should contain something on one larger matter—the
small account taken here of French *criticism* of the novel.

the literary schemes I ever formed, save two. The first of these (omitting a work on " Transubstantiation " which I planned at the age of thirteen but did not carry far) was a *History of the English Scholastics*, which I thought of some ten years later, which was not unfavoured by good authority, and which I should certainly have attempted, if other people at Oxford in my time had not been so much cleverer than myself that I could not get a fellowship. It has, strangely enough, never been done yet by anybody; it would be a useful corrective to the exoteric chatter which has sometimes recently gone by the name of philosophy; and perhaps it might shake Signor Benedetto Croce (whom it is hardly necessary to say I do *not* include among the " chatterers ") in his opinion that though, as he once too kindly said, I am a *valente letterato*, I am sadly *digiúno di filosofia*.[1] But it is "too late a week" for this. And I have lost my library.

Then there was a *History of Wine*, which was actually commissioned, planned, and begun just before I was appointed to my Chair at Edinburgh, and which I gave up, not from any personal pusillanimity or loss of interest in the subject, but partly because I had too much else to do, and because I thought it unfair to expose that respectable institution to the venom of the most unscrupulous of all fanatics—those of teetotalism. I could take this up with pleasure : but I have lost my cellar.

What I should really like to do would be to translate *in extenso* Dr. Sommer's re-edition of the Vulgate Arthuriad.

---

[1] I wonder whether he was right, or whether the late Edward Caird was when he said, " I don't think I ever had a pupil [and he was among the first inter-collegiate-lecturers] with more of the philosophical *ethos* than you have. But you're too fond of getting into logical coaches and letting yourself be carried away in them." I think this was provoked by a very undergraduate essay arguing that Truth, as actually realised, was uninteresting, while the possible forms of Falsehood, as conceivably realisable in other circumstances, were of the highest interest.

But I should probably die before I had done half of it; no publisher would undertake the risk of it; and if any did, " Dora," reluctant to die, would no doubt put us both in prison for using so much paper.   Therefore I had better be content with the divine suggestion, and not spoil it by my human failure to execute.

And so I may say, for good, *Valete* to the public, abandoning the rest of the leave-taking to their discretion.[1]

GEORGE SAINTSBURY.

1 Royal Crescent, Bath,
  Christmas, 1918.

---

[1] I have to give, not only my usual thanks to Professors Elton, Ker, and Gregory Smith for reading my proofs, and making most valuable suggestions, but a special acknowledgment to Professor Ker, at whose request Miss Elsie Hitchcock most kindly looked up for me, at the British Museum, the exact title of that striking novel of M. H. Cochin (*v. inf.* p. 554 *note*).   I have, in the proper places, already thanked the authorities of the *Reviews* above mentioned; but I should like also to recognise here the liberality of Messrs. Rivington in putting the contents of my *Essays on French Novelists* entirely at my disposal.   And I am under another special obligation to Dr. Hagbert Wright for giving me, of his own motion, knowledge and reading of the fresh batch of seventeenth-century novels noticed below (pp. xiv-xvi).

ADDENDA AND CORRIGENDA FOR VOL. I

P. 13.—" The drawback of explanations is that they almost always require to be explained." Somebody, or several somebodies, must have said this ; and many more people than have ever said it—at least in print—must have felt it. The dictum applies to my note on this page. An entirely well-willing reviewer thought me " piqued " at the American remark, and proceeded to intimate a doubt whether I knew M. Bédier's work, partly on lines (as to the *Cantilenae*) which I had myself anticipated, and partly on the question of the composition of the *chansons* by this or that person or class, in this or that place, at that or the other time. But I had felt no " pique " whatever in the matter, and these latter points fall entirely outside my own conception of the *chansons*. I look at them simply as pieces of accomplished literature, no matter how, where, in what circumstances, or even exactly when, they became so. And I could therefore by no possibility feel anything but pleasure at praise bestowed on this most admirable work in a different part of the field.

P. 38, l. 27.—A protest was made, not inexcusably, at the characterisation of *Launfal* as "libellous." The fault was only one of phrasing, or rather of incompleteness. That beautiful story of a knight and his fairy love is one which I should be the last man in the world to abuse *as such*. But it contains a libel on Guinevere which is unnecessary and offensive, besides being absolutely unjustified by any other legend, and inconsistent with her whole character. It is of this only that I spoke the evil which it deserves. If I had not, by mere oversight, omitted notice of Marie de France (for which I can offer no excuse except the usual one of hesitation in which place to put it and so putting it nowhere), I should certainly have left no doubt as to my opinion of Thomas Chester likewise. Anybody who wants this may find it in my *Short History of English Literature*, p. 194.

P. 55, l. 3.—*Delete* comma at "French."

P. 60, l. 6.—Insert "and " between "half" and "illegitimate."

P. 72, l. 4.—I have been warned of the "change-over" in "Saracen" and "Christian "—a slip of the pen which I am afraid I have been guilty of before now, though I have known the story for full forty years. But Floire, though a "paynim," was not exactly a "Saracen."

P. 75, l. 2 from bottom.—*For* "his" *reaa* "their."

Pp. 158-163.—When the first proofs of the present volume had already begun to come in, Dr. Hagbert Wright informed me that the London Library had just secured at Sotheby's (I believe partly from the sale of Lord Ellesmere's books) a considerable parcel of early seventeenth-century French novels. He also very kindly allowed me perusal of such of these as I had not already noticed (from reading at the B. M.) in Vol. I. Of some, if not all of them, on the principle stated in the Preface of that vol., I may say something here. There is the *Histoire des Amours de Lysandre et de Caliste ; avec figures*, in an Amsterdam edition of 1679, but of necessity some sixty years older, since its author, the Sieur d'Audiguier, was killed in 1624. He says he wrote it in six months, during three and a half of which he was laid up with eight sword-wounds—things of which it is itself full, with the appurtenant combats on sea and land and in private houses, and all sorts of other divertisements (he uses the word himself of himself) including a very agreeable ghost-host—a ghost quite free from the tautology and grandiloquence which ghosts too often affect, though not so poetical as Fletcher's. "They told me you were dead," says his guest and interlocutor, consciously or unconsciously quoting the *Anthology*. "So I am," quoth the ghost sturdily. But he wants, as they so often do, to be buried. This is done, and he comes back to return thanks, which is not equally the game, and in fact rather bores his guest, who, to stop this jack-in-the-box proceeding, begins to ask favours, such as that the ghost will give him three days' warning of his own death. "I will, *if I can*," says the Appearance pointedly. The fault of the book, as of most of the novels of the period, is the almost complete absence of character. But there is plenty of adventure, in England as well as in France, and it must be one of the latest stories in which the actual tourney figures, for Audiguier writes as of things contemporary and dedicates his book to Marie de Medicis.

Cléon ou le Parfait Confidant (Paris, 1665), and *Hattigé ou Les Amours au Roy de Tamaran* (Cologne, 1676), the first anonymous, the second written by a certain G. de Brimond, and dedicated to an Englishman of whom we are not specially proud—Harry Jermyn, Earl of St. Albans —are two very little books, of intrinsic importance and interest not disproportioned to their size. They have, however, a little of both for the student, in reference to the extension of the novel *kind*. For *Cléon* is rather like a "fictionising" of an inferior play of Molière's time ; and *Hattigé*, with its privateering Chevalier de Malte for a hero and its Turkish heroine who coolly remarks "L'infidélité a des charmes," might have been better if the author had known how to make it so. Both these books have, as has been said, the merit of shortness. Puget de la Serre's *La Clytie de la Cour* (2 vols., Paris, 1635) cannot plead even this ; for it fills two fat volumes of some 1500 pages. I have sometimes been accused, both in France and in England, of unfairness to Boileau, but I should certainly never quarrel with him for including La Serre (not, however, in respect of this book, I think) among his herd of dunces. Like most of the novels of its time, though it has not much actual *bergerie* about it, it suggests the *Astrée*, but the contrast is glaring. Even among the group, I have seldom read, or attempted to read, anything duller. *Le Mélante du Sieur Vidal* (Paris, 1624), though also somewhat wordy (it has 1000 pages), is much more Astréean, and therefore, perhaps, better. Things do happen in it : among other incidents a lover is introduced into a garden in a barrow of clothes, though he has not Sir John Falstaff's fate. There are fresh laws of love, and discussions of them ; a new debate on the old Blonde *v.* Brunette theme, which might be worse, etc. etc. The same year brought forth *Les Chastes Amours d'Armonde* by a certain Damiron, which, as its title may show, belongs rather to the pre-Astréean group (*v. sup.* Vol. I. p. 157 *note*), and contains a great deal of verse and (by licence of its title) a good deal of kissing ; but is flatly told, despite not a little *Phébus*. It is a sort of combat of Spiritual and Fleshly Love ; and Armonde ends as a kind of irregular anchorite, having previously "spent several days in deliberating the cut of his vestments."

Les Caprices Héroïques (Paris, 1644) is a translation, by Chateaunières de Grenaille, from the Italian of Loredano. It consists of variations on classical stories, treated rather in the declamation manner, and ranging in subject from Achilles to "Friné." How many readers (at least among those who read with their eyes only) will affirm on their honour that they identified "Friné" at first reading ? In Italian there would, of course, be less hesitation. The book is not precisely a novel, but it has merits as a collection of rhetorical exercises. Of a somewhat similar kind, though even further from the strict novel standard, is the *Diverses Affections de Minerve* (Paris, 1625) of the above-mentioned Audiguier, where the heroine is *not* the goddess, and all sorts of places and personages, mythological, classical, historic, and modern, compose a miraculous *macédoine*, Brasidas jostling Gracchus, and Chabrias living in the Faubourg Saint-Martin. This *is* a sort of story, but the greatest part of the volume as it lies before me is composed of *Lettres Espagnoles, Épîtres Françaises, Libres Discours*, etc.

We can apparently return to the stricter romance, such as it is, with the *Histoire Asiatique* of the Sieur de Gerzan (Paris, 1633), but it is noteworthy that the title-page of this ballasts itself by an " Avec un Traité du Trésor de la Vie Humaine et La Philosophie des Dames." I confess that, as in the case of most of the books here mentioned, I have not read it with the care I bestowed on the *Cyrus*. But I perceive in it ladies who love corsairs, universal medicines, poodles who are sacrificed to save their owners, and other things which may tempt some. And I can, by at least sampling, rather recommend *Les Travaux du Prince Inconnu* (Paris, 1633) by the Sieur de Logeas. It calls itself, and its 700 pages, the completion of two earlier perform-ances, the *Roman Historique* and the *Histoire des Trois Frères Princes de*

Constantinople, which have not come in my way. There is, however, probably no cause to regret this, for the author assures us that his new work is "as far above the two former in beauty as the sun is above the stars." If any light-minded person be disposed to scoff at him for this, let it be added that he has the grace to abstract the whole in the *Avis au Lecteur* which contains the boast, and to give full chapter-headings, things too often wanting in the group. The hero is named Rosidor, the heroine Floralinde ; and they are married with "la réjouissance générale de toute la Chrétienté." What can mortals ask for more ?

Polémire ou l'Illustre Polonais (Paris, 1647), is dedicated to no less a person than Madame de Montbazon, and contains much piety, a good deal of fighting, and some verse. *L'Amour Aventureux* (Paris, 1623), by the not unknown Du Verdier, is a book with *Histoires*, and I am not sure that the volume I have seen contains the whole of it. *L'Empire de l'Inconstance* (Paris, 1635), by the Sieur de Ville, and published "at the entry of the little gallery of Prisoners under the sign of the Vermilion Roses," has a most admirable title to start with, and a table of over thirty *Histoires*, a dozen letters, and two "amorous judgments" at the end. *Les Fortunes Diverses de Chrysomire et de Kalinde* (Paris, 1635), by a certain Humbert, blazons "love and war" on its very title-page, while *Célandre* (Paris, 1671), a much later book than most of these, has the rather uncommon feature of a single name for title. Thirty or forty years ago I should have taken some pleasure in "cooking" this batch of mostly early romances into a twenty-page article which, unless it had been unlucky, would have found its way into some magazine or review. Somebody might do so now. But I think it sufficient, and not superfluous, to add this brief sketch here to the notices of similar things in the last volume, in order to show how abundant the crop of French romance—of which even these are only further samples—was at the time.

P. 231, l. 9 from bottom.—*Add* 's (Herman sla lerman's).

P. 237, *note* 2, l. 1.—*For* "revision" *read* "revisal."

P. 241, 2nd par., last line but two.—*For* "But" *read* "Still."

P. 278, l. 7 from bottom.—Delete comma at "Thackeray's."

P. 286, l. 18.—It occurred to me (among the usual discoveries which one makes in reading one's book after it has passed the irremeable press) that I ought to have said "Planchet's" horse, not "D'Artagnan's." True, as a kindly fellow-Alexandrian (who had not noticed the slip) consoled my remorse by saying, the horse was D'Artagnan's *property* ; but the phrase usually implies riding at the moment. And Aramis, brave as he was, would have been sure to reflect that to play a feat of possibly hostile acrobatism on the Gascon, without notice, might be a little dangerous.

P. 304, ll. 4 and 7.—Shift "with his wife and mistress" to l. 4, reading "the relations with his wife and mistress of that Henri II.," etc.

P. 314, l. 12 from bottom.—*For* "usual" *read* "common" (common norm.)

P. 338, l. 21.—Delete "in" before "among."

P. 381.—One or two reviewers and some private correspondents have expressed surprise at my not knowing, or at any rate not mentioning, the late Professor Morley's publication of *Rasselas* and a translation of *Candide* together. I cannot say positively whether I knew of it or not, though I must have done so, having often gone over the lists of that editor's numerous "libraries" to secure for my students texts not overlaid with commentary. But I can say very truthfully that no slight whatever was intended, in regard to a scholar who did more than almost any other single man to "vulgarise" (in the wholly laudable sense of that too often degraded word) the body of English literature. Only, such a book would not have been what I was thinking of. To bring out the full contrast-complement of these two strangely coincident masterpieces, both must be read in the originals. Paradoxically, one might even say that a French translation of Johnson, with the original of Voltaire, would show it better than the converse presentment. *Candide* is so intensely French—it is even to such an extent an embodiment of one side of Frenchness—that you cannot receive its virtues except through the original tongue. I am personally fond of translating; I have had some practice in it; and some good wits have not disapproved some of my efforts. But, unless I knew that in case of refusal I should be ranked as a Conscientious Objector, I would not attempt *Candide*. The French would ring in my ears too reproachfully.

P. 396, last line.—Shift comma from after to before "even."

P. 399, l. 10.—*For* "Rousseau" *read* "his author."

P. 424, *note*, first line.—Delete quotes before "The."

P. 453, l. 15.—*For* "Courray" *read* "Couvray."

P. 468, l. 17.—*For* "France has" *read* "France had."

P. 477.—In the original preface I apologised—not in the idle hope of conciliating one kind of critic, but out of respect for a very different class—for slips due to the loss of my own library, and to the difficulty (a difficulty which has now increased owing to circumstances of no public interest, in respect of the present volume) of consulting others in regard to small matters of fact. I have very gratefully to acknowledge that I found the latter class very much larger than the former. Such a note as that at Vol. I. p. xiii, will show that I have not spared trouble to ensure accuracy. The charge of *in*accuracy can always be made by anybody who cares to take "the other authority." This has been done in reference to the dates of Prévost's books. But I may perhaps say, without *outrecuidance*, that there is an *Art de négliger les dates* as well as one *de les verifier*. For the purposes of such a history as this it is very rarely of the slightest importance, whether a book was published in the year one or the year three : though the importance of course increases when units pass into decades, and becomes grave where decades pass into half-centuries. Unless you can collate actual first editions in every case (and sometimes even then) dates of books as given are always second-hand. In reference to the same subject I have also been rebuked for not taking account of M. Harrisse's correction of the legend of Prévost's death. As a matter of fact I knew but had forgotten it, and it has not the slightest importance in connection with Prévost's work. Besides, somebody will probably, sooner or later, correct M. Harrisse. These things pass : *Manon Lescaut* remains.

ADDENDA AND CORRIGENDA FOR VOL. II

P. 65.—A reviewer of my first volume, who objected to my omission there of Madame de Charrières, may possibly think that omission made more sinful by the admission of Madame de Montolieu. But there seems to me to be a sufficient distinction between the two cases. Isabella Agnes Elizabeth Van Tuyll (or, as she liked to call herself, Belle de Zuylen), subsequently Madame de Saint-Hyacinthe de Charrières (how mellifluously these names pass over one's tongue !), was a very interesting person, and highly characteristic of the later eighteenth century. I first met with her long ago (see Vol. I. p. 443) in my "Sensibility" researches, as having, in her maturer years, played that curious, but at the time not uncommon, part of "Governess in erotics " to Benjamin Constant, who was then quite young, and with whose uncle, Constant d'Hermenches, she had, years earlier and before her own marriage, carried on a long and very intimate but platonic correspondence. This is largely occupied with oddly businesslike discussions of marriage schemes for herself, one of the *prétendants* being no less a person than our own precious Bozzy, who met her on the Continental tour for which Johnson started him at Harwich. But— and let this always be a warning to literary lovers—the two fell out over a translation of the Corsica book which she began. Boswell was not the wisest of men, especially where women were concerned. But even he might have known that, if you trust the bluest-eyed of gazelles to do such things for you, she will probably marry a market-gardener. (He seems also to have been a little afraid of her superiority of talent, *v.* his letters to Temple and his *Johnson*, pp. 192-3, Globe Ed.)

Besides these, and other genuine letters, she wrote not a few novels, concocted often, if not always, in epistolary form. Their French was so good that it attracted Sainte-Beuve's attention and praise, while quite recently she has had a devoted panegyrist and editor in Switzerland, where, after her marriage, she was domiciled. But (and here come the reasons for the former exclusion) she learnt her French as a foreign language. She was French neither by birth nor by extraction, nor, if I do not mistake, by even temporary residence, though she did stay in England for a considerable time. Some of these points distinguish her from Hamilton as others do from Madame de Montolieu. If I put her in, I do not quite see how I could leave Beckford out.

P. 400, ll. 2, 3.—*For* " 1859 . . . 1858 " *read* " 1857—a year, with its successors 1858 and 1859,"

CONTENTS

CHAPTER I

CHAPTER II

xxi

CHAPTER VI

CHAPTER VII

CHAPTER VIII

CHAPTER IX

CHAPTER X

CHAPTER XI

CHAPTER XII

CHAPTER XIII

CHAPTER XIV

PAGE

CHAPTER I

MADAME DE STAËL AND CHATEAUBRIAND

IT has often been thought, and sometimes said, that the period of the French Revolution and of the Napoleonic Reasons for beginning with Mme. de Staël. wars—extending as it does strictly to more than a quarter of a century, while four decades were more than completed before a distinct turn of tide—is, for France, the least individual and least satisfactorily productive time in all her great literature. And it is, to a large extent, true. But the loss of individuality implies the presence of indiscernibility; and not to go out of our own department, there are at least three writers who, if but partially, cancel this entry to discredit. Of one of them—the lowest in general literature, if not quite in our division of it—Pigault-Lebrun—we have spoken in the last volume. The other two—much less craftsmanlike novelists merely as such, but immeasurably greater as man and woman of letters—remain for discussion in the first chapter of this. In pure chronological order Chateaubriand should come first, as well as in other " ranks " of various kinds. But History, though it may never neglect, may sometimes overrule Chronology by help of a larger and higher point of view: sex and birth hardly count here, and the departmental primes the intrinsic literary importance. Chateaubriand, too, was a little younger than Madame de Staël in years, though his actual publication, in anything like our kind, came before hers. And he reached much farther than she did, though curiously enough some of his worst faults were more of the eighteenth century than hers. She helped to finish " Sensibility " ; she transformed " Philosophism " into something more modern ; she borrowed a good deal (especially in the region of aesthetics) that was to be importantly germinal from Germany. But she had practically nothing of that sense of the past and of the strange which was to rejuvenate all literature, and which he had ; while she died before the great French Romantic outburst began. So let us begin with her.[1]

" This dismal trash, which has nearly dislocated the jaws of every critic who has read it," was the extremely *Delphine.* rude judgment pronounced by Sydney Smith on Madame de Staël's *Delphine.* Sydney was a good-natured person and a gentleman, nor had he, merely as a Whig, any reason to quarrel with the lady's general attitude to politics—a circumstance which, one regrets to say, did in those days, on both sides, rather improperly qualify the attitude of gentlemen to literary ladies as well as to each other. It is true that the author of *Corinne* and of *Delphine* itself had been rather a thorn in the side of the English Whigs by dint of some of her opinions, by much of her conduct, and, above all, by certain peculiarities which may be noticed presently. But Sydney, though a Whig, was not " a *vile* Whig," for which reason the Upper Powers, in his later years, made him something rather indistinguishable from a Tory. And that blunt common sense, which in his case cohabited with the finest *un*common wit, must have found

---

[1] Although, except in special cases, biographical notices are not given here, the reader may be reminded that she was born in 1766, the daughter of Necker and of Gibbon's early love, Susanne Curchod ; married at twenty the Swedish ambassador, Baron of Staël-Holstein ; sympathised at first with the Revolution, but was horrified at the murder of the king, and escaped, with some difficulty, from Paris to England, where, as well as in Germany and at Coppet, her own house in Switzerland, she passed the time till French things settled down under Napoleon. With him she tried to get on, as a duplicate of himself in petticoats and the realm of mind. But this was clearly impossible, and she had once more to retire to Coppet. She had separated, though without positive quarrel, from her husband, whom, however, she attended on his deathbed ; and the exact character of her *liaisons* with others, especially M. de Narbonne and Benjamin Constant, is not easy to determine. In 1812 she married, privately, a young officer, Rocca by name, returned to Paris before and after the Hundred Days, and died there in 1817.

itself, in this instance, by no means at variance with its housemate in respect of Anne Germaine Necker.

There are many *worse* books than *Delphine*. It is excellently written ; there is no bad blood in it ; there is no intentional licentiousness ; on the contrary, there are the most desperate attempts to live up to a New Morality by no means entirely of the Higgins kind. But there is an absence of humour which is perfectly devastating : and there is a presence of the most disastrous atmosphere of sham sentiment, sham morality, sham almost everything, that can be imagined. It was hinted in the last volume that Madame de Staël's lover, Benjamin Constant, shows in one way the Nemesis of Sensibility ; so does she herself in another. But the difference ! In *Adolphe* a coal from the altar of true passion has touched lips in themselves polluted enough, and the result is what it always is in such, alas ! rare cases, whether the lips were polluted or not. In *Delphine* there is a desperate pother to strike some sort of light and get some sort of heat ; but the steel is naught, the flint is clay, the tinder is mouldy, and the wood is damp and rotten. No glow of brand or charcoal follows, and the lips, untouched by it, utter nothing but rhetoric and fustian and, as the Sydneian sentence speaks it, "trash." [1]

In fact, to get any appropriate metaphorical description of it one has to change the terminology altogether. In a very great line Mr. Kipling has spoken of a metaphorical ship—

> With a drogue of dead convictions to keep her head to gale.

Madame de Staël has cast off not only that drogue, but even the other and perhaps commoner floating ballast and steadier of dead *conventions*, and *The tone.* is trying to beat up against the gale by help of all sorts of jury-masts and extemporised try-sails of other new conventions that are mostly blowing out of

---

[1] I never can make up my mind whether I am more sorry that Madame Necker did not marry Gibbon or that Mademoiselle Necker did not, as was subsequently on the cards, marry Pitt. The results in either case—both, alas ! could hardly have come off—would have been most curious.

the bolt-ropes. We said that Crébillon's world was an artificial one, and one of not very respectable artifice. But it worked after a fashion ; it was founded on some real, however unrespectable, facts of humanity; and it was at least amusing to the naughty players on its stage to begin with, and long afterwards to the guiltless spectators of the commonty.   In *Delphine* there is not a glimmer of amusement from first to last, and the whole story is compact (if that word were not totally inapplicable) of windbags of sentiment, copy-book headings, and the strangest husks of neo-classic type-worship, stock character, and hollow generalisation.   An Italian is necessarily a person of volcanic passions ; an Englishman or an American (at this time the identification was particularly unlucky) has, of equal necessity, a grave and reserved physiognomy.   Orthodox religion is a mistake, but a kind of moral-philosophical Deism (something of the Wolmar type) is highly extolled.   You must be technically " virtuous " yourself, even if you bring a whole second volume of tedious tortures on you by being so ; but you may play Lady Pandara to a friend who is a devout adulteress, may force yourself into her husband's carriage when he is carrying her off from one assignation, and may bring about his death by contriving another in your own house.   In fact, the whole thing is topsy-turvy, without the slightest touch of that animation and interested curiosity which topsy-turviness sometimes contributes.   But perhaps one should give a more regular account of it.

Delphine d'Albémar is a young, beautiful, rich, clever, generous, and, in the special and fashionable sense, extravagantly " sensible " widow, who opens *The story.* the story (it is in the troublesome epistolary form) by handing over about a third of her fortune to render possible the marriage of a cousin of her deceased husband. This cousin, Matilde de Vernon, is also beautiful and accomplished, but a *dévote*, altogether well-regulated and well-conducted, and (though it turns out that she has strong and permanent affections) the reverse of "sensible "—in fact rather hard and disagreeable—in manner.   She has a scheming mother, who has run herself deeply, though privately, into debt, and the intended husband and son-in-law, Léonce de Mandeville, also has a mother, who is half Spanish by blood and residence, and wholly so (according to the type-theory above glanced at) in family pride, personal *morgue*, and so forth. A good deal of this has descended to her son, with whom, in spite or because of it, Delphine (she has not seen him before her rash generosity) proceeds to fall frantically in love, as he does with her.   The marriage, however, partly by trickery on Madame de Vernon's part, and partly owing to Delphine's more than indiscreet furthering of her friend Madame d'Ervin's intrigue with the Italian M. de Serbellane, does take place, and Mme. de Staël's idea of a nice heroine makes her station Delphine in a white veil, behind a pillar of the church, muttering reproaches at the bridegroom.   No open family rupture, however, is caused; on the contrary, a remarkable and inevitably disastrous " triple arrangement " follows (as mentioned above), for an entire volume, in which the widow and the bridegroom make despairing love to each other, refraining, however, from any impropriety, and the wife, though suffering (for she, in her apparently frigid way, really loves her husband), tolerates the pro- ceeding after a fashion.   This impossible and pre- posterous situation is at last broken up by the passion and violence of another admirer of Delphine—a certain M. de Valorbe.   These bring about duels, wounds, and Delphine's flight to Switzerland, where she puts up in a convent with a most superfluous and in every way unrefreshing new personage, a widowed sister of Madame de Mandeville.   Valorbe follows, and, to get hold of Delphine, machinates one of the most absurd scenes in the whole realm of fiction.   He lures her into Austrian territory and a chamber with himself alone, locks the door and throws the key out of the window,[1] storms,

---

[1] The most obvious if not the only possible reason for this would be intended outrage, murder, and suicide; but though Valorbe is a robustious kind of idiot, he does not seem to have made up such mind as he has to this agreeable combination.

rants, threatens, but proceeds to no *voie de fait*, and merely gets himself and the object of his desires arrested by the Austrians ! He thus succeeds, while procuring no gratification for himself, in entirely demolishing the last shred of reputation which, virtuous as she is in her own way, Delphine's various eccentricities and escapades have left her ; and she takes the veil. In the first form the authoress crowned this mass of absurdities with the suicide of the heroine and the judicial shooting of the hero. Somebody remonstrated, and she made Delphine throw off her vows, engage herself to Léonce (whose unhappy wife has died from too much carrying out of the duty of a mother to her child), and go with him to his estates in La Vendée, where he is to take up arms for the king. Unfortunately, the Vendéans by no means " see " their *seigneur* marrying an apostate nun, and strong language is used. So Delphine dies, not actually by her own hand, and Léonce gets shot, more honourably than he deserves, on the patriot-royalist side.

Among the minor characters not yet referred to are an old-maid sister-in-law of Delphine's, who, though tolerably sensible in the better sense, plays the part of confidante to her brother's *mijaurée* of a widow much too indulgently ; a M. Barton, Léonce's mentor, who, despite his English-looking name, is not (one is glad to find) English, but is, to one's sorrow, one of the detestable " parsons-in-tie-wigs " whom French Anglomania at this time foisted on us as characteristic of England ; a sort of double of his, M. de Lerensei, a Protestant free-thinker, who, with his *divorcée* wife, puts up grass altars in their garden with inscriptions recording the happiness of their queer union ; an ill-natured Mme. du Marset and her old cicisbeo, M. de Fierville, who suggest, in the dismallest way, the weakest wine of Marmontel gone stale and filtered through the dullest, though not the dirtiest, part of Laclos.

Yet the thing, " dismal trash " as Sydney almost justly called it, is perhaps worth reading once (nothing but the sternest voice of duty could have made me read it twice) because of the existence of *Corinne*, and because also of the undoubted fact that, here as there, though much more surprisingly, a woman of unusual ability was drawing a picture of what she would have liked to be—if not of what she actually thought herself.[1] The borrowed beauty goes for nothing—it were indeed hard if one did not, in the case of a woman of letters, " let her make her dream All that she would," like Tennyson's Prince, but in this other respect. The generosity, less actually exaggerated, might also pass. That Delphine makes a frantic fool of herself for a lover whose attractions can only make male readers shrug their shoulders— for though we are *told* that Léonce is clever, brave, charming, and what not, we see nothing of it in speech or action — may be matter of taste; but that her heroine's part should seem to any woman one worth playing is indeed wonderful. Delphine behaves throughout like a child, and by no means always like a very well-brought-up child; she never seems to have the very slightest idea that " things are as they are and that their consequences will be what they will be "; and though, once more, we are *told* of passion carrying all before it, we are never *shown* it. It is all " words, words." To speak of her love in the same breath with Julie's is to break off the speech in laughter; to consider her woes and remember Clarissa's is to be ready to read another seven or eight volumes of Richardson in lieu of these three of Madame de Staël's.

And yet this lady could do something in the novel way, and, when the time came, she did it.

Between *Delphine* and *Corinne* Madame de Staël had, in the fullest sense of a banal phrase, " seen a great
Corinne.   deal of the world." She had lost the illusions which the Duessa Revolution usually spreads among clever but not wise persons at her first appearance,

---

[1] I forget whether other characters have been identified, but Léonce does not appear to have much in him of M. de Narbonne, Corinne's chief lover of the period, who seems to have been a sort of French Chesterfield, without the wit, which nobody denies our man, or the real good-nature which he possessed.

and had *not* left her bones, as too many [1] such persons
do, in the *pieuvre*-caves which the monster keeps ready.
She had seen England, being "coached" by Crabb-
Robinson and others, so as to give some substance to
the vague *philosophe-Anglomane* flimsiness of her earlier
fancy. She had seen Republicanism turn to actual
Tyranny, and had made exceedingly unsuccessful attempts
to captivate the tyrant. She had seen Germany, and
had got something of its then not by any means
poisonous, if somewhat windy, "culture"; a little
romance of a kind, though she was never a real Romantic;
some aesthetics; some very exoteric philosophy, etc.
She had done a great deal of not very happy love-making;
had been a woman of letters, a patroness of men of
letters, and—most important of all—had never dis-
mounted from her old hobby "Sensibility," though she
had learnt how to put it through new paces.

A critical reader of *Corinne* must remember all this,
and he must remember something else, though the
reminder has been thought to savour of brutality. It is
perfectly clear to me, and always has been so from
reading (in and between the lines) of her own works, of
Lady Blennerhassett's monumental book on her, of M.
Sorel's excellent monograph, and of scores of longer and
shorter studies on and references to her—English and
German and Swiss and French—from her own time downwards, that the central secret, mainspring, or whatever
any one may choose to call it, of Madame de Staël's life
was a frantic desire for the physical beauty which she
did not possess,[2] and a persistent attempt, occasionally
successful, to delude herself into believing that she had
achieved a sufficient substitute by literary, philosophical,
political, and other exertion.

This partly pathetic, partly, alas! ridiculous, but
on the whole (with a little charity) quite commiserable
endeavour, attained some success, though probably with

---

[1] Perhaps, after all, *not* too many, for they all richly deserve it.
[2] Eyes like the Ravenswing's, " as b-b-big as billiard balls " and of some brightness,
are allowed her, but hardly any other good point.

not a little extraneous help, in *De l'Allemagne,* and the posthumous *Considérations* on the Revolution ; but these Its improved books do not concern us, and illustrate only conditions. part of the writer's character, temperament, and talent, if not genius. *Corinne* gives us the rest, and nearly, if not quite, the whole. The author had no doubt tried to do this in *Delphine,* but had then had neither art nor equipment for the task, and she had failed utterly. She was now well, if not perfectly, equipped, and had learnt not a little of the art to use her acquisitions. *Delphine* had been dull, absurd, preposterous ; *Corinne,* if it has dull patches, saves them from being intolerable. If its sentiment is extravagant, it is never exactly preposterous or exactly absurd ; for the truth and reality of passion which are absent from the other book are actually present here, though sometimes in unintentional masquerade.

In fact, *Corinne,* though the sisterhood of the two books is obvious enough, has almost, though not quite, all the faults of *Delphine* removed and some merits added, of which in the earlier novel there is not the slightest trace. The history of my own acquaintance with it is, I hope, not quite irrelevant. I read it—a very rare thing for me with a French novel (in fact I can hardly recollect another instance, except, a quaint contrast, Paul de Kock's *André le Savoyard*)—first in English, and at a very early period of life, and I then thought it nearly as great " rot " as I have always thought its predecessor. But though I had, I hope, sense enough to see its faults, I had neither age nor experience nor literature enough to appreciate its merits. I read it a good deal later in French, and, being then better qualified, *did* perceive these merits, though it still did not greatly " arride " me. Later still—in fact, only some twenty years ago—I was asked to re-edit and " introduce " the English translation. It is a popular mistake to think that an editor, like an advocate, is entitled, if not actually bound, to make the best case for his client, quite apart from his actual opinions ; but in this instance my opinion of the book mounted considerably. And it has certainly not declined since, though this *History* has necessitated a fourth study of the original, and though I shall neither repeat what I said in the Introduction referred to, nor give the impression there recorded in merely altered words. Indeed, the very purpose of the present notice, forming part, as it should, of a connected history of the whole department to which the book belongs, requires different treatment, and an application of what may be called critical "triangulation" from different standpoints.

By an odd chance and counter-chance, the edition which served for this last perusal, after threatening to *An illus-* disserve its text, had an exactly contrary result. *trated edition* It was the handsome two-volume issue of *of it.* 1841, copiously adorned with all sorts of ingenious initial-devices, *culs-de-lampe*, etc., and with numerous illustrative " cuts " beautifully engraved (for the most part by English engravers, such as Orrin Smith, the Williamses, etc.), excellently drawn and composed by French artists from Gros downwards, but costumed in what is now perhaps the least tolerable style of dress even to the most catholic taste—that of the Empire in France and the Regency in England—and most comically " thought." [1] At first sight this might seem to be a disadvantage, as calling attention to, and aggravating, certain defects of the text itself. I found it just the reverse. One was slightly distracted from, and half inclined to make allowances for, Nelvil's performances in the novel when one saw him—in a Tom-and-Jerry early chimneypot hat, a large coachman's coat flung off his shoulders and hanging down to his heels, a swallow-tail, tight pantaloons, and Hessian boots —extracting from his bosom his father's portrait and expressing filial sentiments to it. One was less likely to accuse Corinne of peevishness when one beheld the delineation of family worship in the Edgermond house-

---

[1] I never pretended to be an art-critic, save as complying with Blake's negative injunction or qualification " not to be connoisseured out of my senses," and I do not know what is the technical word in the arts of design corresponding to διάνοια in literature.

hold from which she fled. And the faithful eyes remonstrated with the petulant brain for scoffing at excessive
sentiment, when they saw how everybody was always
at somebody else's feet, or supporting somebody else in
a fainting condition, or resting his or her burning brow
on a hand, the elbow of which rested, in its turn, on a
pedestal like that of Mr. Poseidon Hicks in *Mrs. Perkins's
Ball.* The plates gave a safety-valve to the letterpress
in a curiously anodyne fashion which I hardly ever
remember to have experienced before. Or rather, one
transferred to them part, if not the whole, of the somewhat
contemptuous amusement which the manners had excited,
and had one's more appreciative faculties clear for the
book itself.

The story of *Corinne,* though not extraordinarily
" accidented " and, as will be seen, adulterated, or at
The story. least mixed, with a good many things that are
not story at all, is fairly solid, much more so
than that of *Delphine.* It turns—though the reader is
not definitely informed of this till the book is half over—
on the fact of an English nobleman, Lord Edgermond
(dead at *temp.* of tale), having had two wives, the first
an Italian. By her he had one daughter, whose actual
Christian name (unless I forget) we are never told,
and he lived with them in Italy till his wife's death.
Then he went home and married a second wife, an
English or Scotch woman (for her name seems to have
been Maclinson—a well-known clan) of very prudish
disposition. By her he had another daughter, Lucile—
younger by a good many years than her sister. To that
sister Lady Edgermond the second does not behave
exactly in the traditionally novercal fashion, but she is
scandalised by the girl's Italian ways, artistic and
literary temperament, desire for society, etc. After Lord
Edgermond's death the discord of the two becomes
intolerable, and the elder Miss Edgermond, coming of
age and into an independent fortune, breaks loose and
returns to Italy, her stepmother stipulating that she
shall drop her family name altogether and allow herself

to be given out as dead.   She consents (unwisely, but perhaps not unnaturally), appears in Italy under the name of " Corinne," and establishes herself without difficulty in the best Roman society as a lady of means, great beauty, irreproachable character, but given to private displays of her talents as singer, improvisatrice, actress, and what not.

But before she has thus thrown a still respectable bonnet over a not too disreputable mill, something has happened which has, in the long run, fatal consequences. Lord Edgermond has a friend, Lord Nelvil, who has a son rather younger than Corinne.   Both fathers think that a marriage would be a good thing, and the elder Nelvil comes to stay with the Edgermonds to propose it.   Corinne (or whatever her name was then) lays herself out in a perfectly innocent but, as he thinks, forward manner to please him, and he, being apparently (we never see him in person) not a little of an old fool, cries off this project, but tells Edgermond that he should like his son to marry Lucile when she grows up.

Without an intolerable dose of "argument," it is only possible to say here that Nelvil, after his father's death, journeys to the Continent (where he has been already engaged in a questionable *liaison*), meets Corinne, and, not at first knowing in the least who she is, falls, or thinks he falls, frantically in love with her, while she really does fall more frantically in love with him.   After a sojourn, of which a little more presently, circumstances make him (or he thinks they make him) return home, and he falls, or thinks he falls,[1] out of love with Corinne and into it (after a fashion) with Lucile.   Corinne undertakes an incognito journey to England to find out what is happening, but (this, though not impossible in itself, is, as told, the weakest part of the story) never makes herself known till too late, and Nelvil,

---

[1] I hope this iteration may not seem too damnable.   It is intended to bring before the reader's mind the utterly *willowish* character of Oswald, Lord Nelvil.   The slightest impact of accident will bend down, the weakest wind of circumstance blow about, his plans and preferences.

partly out of respect for his father's wishes, and
partly, one fears, because Lucile is very pretty and
Corinne seems to be very far off, marries the younger
sister.

It would have greatly improved the book if, with or
even without a "curtain," it had ended here. But Madame
de Staël goes on to tell us how Nelvil, who is a soldier
by profession,[1] leaves his wife and a little daughter,
Juliette, and goes to "Les Iles" on active service
for four years ; how Lucile, not unnaturally, suspects
hankering after the sister she has not seen since her
childhood ; how, Nelvil being invalided home, they all
go to Italy, and find Corinne in a dying condition ; how
Lucile at first refuses to see her, but, communications
being opened by the child Juliette, reconciliations
follow ; and how Corinne dies with Nelvil and Lucile
duly kneeling at her bedside.

The minor personages of any importance are not
numerous. Besides Lady Edgermond, they consist of
the Comte d'Erfeuil, a French travelling companion of
Nelvil's ; the Prince of Castel-Forte, an Italian of the
highest rank ; a Mr. Edgermond, who does not make
much appearance, but is more like a real Englishman
in his ways and manners than Nelvil ; an old Scotch
nincompoop named Dickson, who, unintentionally, makes
mischief wherever he goes as surely as the personage
in the song made music. Lady Edgermond, though
she is neither bad nor exactly ill-natured, is the evil
genius of the story. Castel-Forte, a most honourable
and excellent gentleman, has so little of typical Italianism
in him that, finding Corinne will not have him, he actually
serves as common friend, confidant, and almost as
honourable go-between, to her and Nelvil.

On the other hand, French critics have justly com-
plained. and critics not French may endorse the complaint, that the Comte d'Erfeuil is a mere caricature of

---

[1] That he seems to have unlimited leave is not perhaps, for a peer in the period, to
be cavilled at ; the manner in which he alternately breaks blood-vessels and is up to
fighting in the tropics may be rather more so.

the " frivolous " French type too commonly accepted
out of France.   He is well-mannered, not ill-natured,
and even not, personally, very conceited, but utterly
shallow, incapable of a serious interest in art, letters, or
anything else, blandly convinced that everything French
is superlative and that nothing not French is worthy of
attention.   Although he appears rather frequently, he
plays no real part in the story, and, unless there was
some personal grudge to pay off (which is not unlikely),
it is difficult to imagine why Madame de Staël should
have introduced a character which certainly does her
skill as a character-drawer very little credit.

It is, however, quite possible that she was led astray
by a will-o'-the-wisp, which has often misled artists not
The character of the very first class—the chance of an easy
of Nelvil. contrast.   The light - hearted, light - minded
Erfeuil was to set off the tense and serious Nelvil—a
type again, as he was evidently intended to be, but a
somewhat new type of Englishman.   She was a devotee
of Rousseau, and she undoubtedly had the egregious
Bomston before her.   But, though her sojourn in England had not taught her very much about actual Englishmen, she had probably read Mackenzie, and knew that
the " Man of Feeling " touch had to some extent affected
us.   She tried to combine the two, with divers hints
of hearsay and a good deal of pure fancy, and the result
was Oswald, Lord Nelvil.   As with that other curious
contemporary of hers with whom we deal in this chapter,
the result was startlingly powerful in literature.   There
is no doubt that the Byronic hero, whose importance
of a kind is unmistakable and undeniable, is Schedoni,
René, and Nelvil sliced up, pounded in a mortar, and
made into a rissole with Byron's own sauce of style in
rhetoric or (if anybody will have it so) poetry, but with
very little more substantial ingredients.   As for the
worthy peer of Scotland or England, more recent estimates have seldom been favourable, and never ought to
have been so.   M. Sorel calls him a " snob "; but
that is only one of the numerous and, according to

amiable judgments, creditable instances of the inability
of the French to discern exactly what " snobbishness "
is.[1] My Lord Nelvil has many faults and very few
merits, but among the former I do not perceive any
snobbishness. He is not in the least attracted by
Corinne's popularity, either with the great vulgar or the
small, and his hesitations about marrying her do not
arise from any doubt (while he is still ignorant on the
subject) of her social worthiness to be his wife. He *is*
a prig doubtless, but he is a prig of a very peculiar
character—a sort of passionate prig, or, to put it in
another way, one of Baudelaire's " Enfants de la lune,"
who, not content with always pining after the place
where he is not and the love that he has not, is
constantly making not merely himself, but the place
where he is and the love whom he has, uncomfortable
and miserable. There can, I think, be little doubt
that Madame de Staël, who frequently insists on his
" irresolution " (remember that she had been in Germany
and heard the Weimar people talk), meant him for a
sort of modern Hamlet in very different circumstances
as well as times. But it takes your Shakespeare to
manage your Hamlet, and Madame de Staël was not
Shakespeare, even in petticoats.

The absurdities of the book are sufficiently numerous.
Lord Nelvil, who has not apparently had any special
experience of the sea, " advises " the sailors,
and takes the helm during a storm on his
passage from Harwich to Emden; while these
English mariners, unworthy professional descendants of
that admirable man, the boatswain of the opening scenes
of *The Tempest*, are actually grateful to him, and when
he goes ashore " press themselves round him " to take
leave of him (that is to say, they do this in the book ; what

And the book's absurdities.

---

[1] As I may have remarked elsewhere, they often seem to confuse it with " priggishness," " cant," and other amiable *cosas de Inglaterra*. (The late M. Jules Lemaître, as Professor Ker reminds me, even gave the picturesque but quite inadequate
description : " Le snob est un mouton de Panurge prétentieux, un mouton qui saute à la
file, mais d'un air suffisant.") We cannot disclaim the general origin, but we may
protest against confusion of the particular substance.

in all probability they actually *said* would not be fit for
these pages).   He is always saving people—imprisoned
Jews and lunatics at a fire in Ancona ; aged lazzaroni
who get caught in a sudden storm-wave at Naples ; and
this in spite of the convenient-inconvenient blood-vessels
which break when it is necessary, but still make it quite
easy for him to perform these Herculean feats and
resume his rather interim military duties when he pleases.
As for Corinne, her exploits with her " schall " (a vest-
ment of which Madame de Staël also was fond), and her
crowning in the Capitol, where the crown tumbles off—
an incident which in real life would be slightly comical,
but which here only gives Nelvil an opportunity of
picking it up—form a similar prelude to a long series
of extravagances.   The culmination of them is that
altogether possible-improbable visit to England, which
might have put everything right and does put everything
wrong, and the incurable staginess which makes her, as
above related, refuse to see Oswald and Lucile *together*
till she is actually *in articulo mortis*.

And yet—" for all this and all this and twice as much
as all this "—I should be sorry for any one who regards
Corinne as merely a tedious and not at all brief subject
for laughter.   One solid claim which it possesses has
been, and is still for a moment, definitely postponed ;
but in another point there is, if not exactly a defence, an
immense counterpoise to the faults and follies just mentioned.   Corinne to far too great an extent, and Oswald
to an extent nearly but not quite fatal, are loaded (*affublés*,
to use the word we borrowed formerly) with a mass of
corporal and spiritual wiglomeration (as Mr. Carlyle
used expressively and succinctly to call it) in costume
and fashion and sentiment and action and speech.   But
when we have stripped this off, *manet res*—reality of truth
and fact and nature.

There should be no doubt of this in Corinne's own
case.   It has been said from the very first that she is,
as Delphine had been, if not what her creatress was, what
she would have liked to be.   The ideal in the former

case was more than questionable, and the execution was
very bad. Here the ideal is far from flawless, but it is

Compen-
sations—
Corinne
herself. greatly improved, and the execution is improved
far more than in proportion. Corinne is not
" a reasonable woman " ; but reason, though
very heartily to be welcomed on its rare occur-.
rences in that division of humanity, when it does not
exclude other things more to be welcomed still, is very
decidedly not to be preferred to the other things themselves. Corinne has these—or most of them. She is
beautiful ; she is amiable ; she is unselfish ; without the
slightest touch of prudery she has the true as well as
the technical chastity ; and she is really the victim of in-
auspicious stars, and of the misconduct of other people—
the questionable wisdom of her own father ; the folly of
Nelvil's ; the wilfulness in the bad sense, and the weakness of will in the good, of her lover ; the sour virtue
and *borné* temperament of Lady Edgermond. Almost
all her faults and not a few of her misfortunes are due to
the "sensibility" of her time, or the time a little before her ;
for, as has been more than hinted already, *Corinne*, though
a book of far less genius, strength, and concentration than
Adolphe, is, like it, though from the other side, and on
a far larger scale, the history of the Nemesis of Sensibility.

But Nelvil ? He is, it has been said, a deplorable
kind of creature—a kind of creature (to vary Dr. John-

Nelvil again. son's doom on the unlucky mutton) ill-*bred*,
ill-educated, ill- (though not quite in the
ordinary sense) natured, ill-fated to an extent which he
could partly, but only partly, have helped ; and ill-
conducted to an extent which he might have helped
almost altogether. But is he unnatural ? I fear—I
trow—not. He is, I think, rather more natural than
Edgar of Ravenswood, who is something of the same
class, and who may perhaps owe a very little to him.
At any rate, though he has more to do with the theatre,
he is less purely theatrical than that black-plumed Master.
And it seems to me that he is more differentiated from
the Sensibility heroes than even Corinne herself is

from the Sensibility heroines, though one sympathises with her much more than with him. *Homo est*, though scarcely *vir*. Now it is humanity which we have been always seeking, but not always finding, in the long and often brilliant list of French novels before his day. And we have found it here once more.

But we find also something more; and this something more gives it not merely an additional but even to some extent a fresh hold upon the history of the novel itself. To say that it is in great part a "guide-book novel," as indeed its second title [1] honestly declares, may seem nowadays a doubtful testimonial. It is not really so. For it was, with certain exceptions in German, the *first* "guide-book" novel: and though some of those exceptions may have shown greater literary genius than Madame de Staël's, the Germans, though they have, in certain lines, had no superiors as producers of tales, have never produced a good novel yet.[2] Moreover, the guide-book element is a great set-off to the novel. It is not—or at any rate it is not necessarily—liable to the objections to "purpose," for it is ornamental and not structural. It takes a new and important and almost illimitably fresh province of nature and of art, which is a part of nature, to be its appanage. It would be out of place here to trace the development of this system of reinforcing the novel beyond France, in Scott more particularly. It is not out of place to remind the reader that even Rousseau (to whom Madame de Staël owed so much) to some extent, Bernardin de Saint-Pierre and Chateaubriand to more, as far as what we may call scenery-guide-booking goes, had preceded her. But for the "art," the aesthetic addition, she was indebted only to the Germans; and almost all her French successors were indebted to her.[3]

Its aesthetics.

[1] *Corinne, ou l'Italie.*

[2] If anybody thinks *Wilhelm Meister* or the *Wahlverwandtschaften* a good novel, I am his very humble servant in begging to differ. Freytag's *Soll und Haben* is perhaps the nearest approach; but, on English or French standards, it could only get a fair second class.

[3] Corinne "walks and talks" (as the lady in the song was asked to do, but without requiring the offer of a blue silk gown) with her Oswald all over the churches and palaces and monuments of Rome, "doing" also Naples, Venice, etc.

Although, therefore, it is hardly possible to call Madame de Staël a good novelist, she occupies a very important position in the history of the novel. She sees, or helps to see, the "sensibility" novel out, with forcible demonstration of the inconveniences of its theory. She helps to see the aesthetic novel—or the novel highly seasoned and even sandwiched with aesthetics—in. She manages to create at least one character to whom the epithets of "noble" and "pathetic" can hardly be refused; and at least one other to which that of "only too natural," if with an exceptional and faulty kind of nature, must be accorded. At a time when the most popular, prolific, and in a way craftsmanlike practitioner of the kind, Pigault-Lebrun, was dragging it through vulgarity, she keeps it at any rate clear of that. Her description is adequate: and her society-and-manners painting (not least in the *récit* giving Corinne's trials in Northumberland) is a good deal more than adequate. Moreover, she preserves the tradition of the great *philosophe* group by showing that the writer of novels can also be the author of serious and valuable literature of another kind. These are no small things to have done: and when one thinks of them one is almost able to wipe off the slate of memory that awful picture of a turbaned or "schalled" Blowsalind, with arms[1] like a "daughter of the plough," which a cruel tradition has perpetuated as frontispiece to some cheap editions of her works.

The author's position in the History of the Novel.

There is perhaps no more difficult person to appraise in all French literature—there are not many in the literature of the world—than François René, Vicomte de Chateaubriand. It is almost more difficult than in the case of his two great disciples, Byron and Hugo, to keep his personality out of the record: and it is a not

Chateaubriand—his peculiar position as a novelist.

---

[1] She was rather proud of these mighty members: and some readers may recall that not least Heinesque remark of the poet who so much shocks Kaiser Wilhelm II., "Those of the Venus of Milo are not more beautiful."

wholly agreeable personality. Old experience may perhaps attain to this, and leave to ghouls and large or small coffin-worms the business of investigating and possibly fattening on the thing. But even the oldest experience dealing with his novels (which were practically all early) may find itself considerably *tabusté*, as Rabelais has it, that is to say, " bothered " with faults which are mitigated in the *Génie du Christianisme*, comparatively (not quite) unimportant in the *Voyages*, and almost entirely whelmed in the *Mémoires d'Outre-Tombe*. These faults are of such a complicated and various kind that the whole armour of criticism is necessary to deal with them, on the defensive in the sense of not being too much influenced by them, and on the offensive in the sense of being severe but not too severe on them.

The mere reader of Chateaubriand's novels generally begins with *Atala* and *René*, and not uncommonly stops there. In a certain sense this reader is wise in his generation. But he will never under- stand his author as a novelist if he does so; and his appreciation of the books or booklets themselves will be very incomplete. They are both not unfrequently spoken of as detached episodes of the *Génie du Christianisme*; and so they are, in the illus- trative sense. They are actually, and in the purely con- stitutive way, episodes of another book, *Les Natchez*, while this book itself is also a novel " after a sort." The author's work in the kind is completed by the later *Les Martyrs*, which has nothing to do, in persons or time, with the others, being occupied with the end of the third century, while they deal (throwing back a little in *Atala*) with the beginning of the eighteenth. But this also is an illustrative companion or reinforcement of the *Génie*. With that book the whole body of Chateaubriand's fiction [1] is thus directly connected; and the entire collec-

And the remarkable interconnec- tion of his works in fiction.

---

[1] Including also a third short story, *Le Dernier Abencerage*, which belongs, construct- ively, rather to the *Voyages*. It is in a way the liveliest (at least the most " incidented ") of all, but not the most interesting, and with very little *temporal* colour, though some local. It may, however, be taken as another proof of Chateaubriand's importance in the germinal way, for it starts the Romantic interest in Spanish things. The contrast with the dirty rubbish of Pigault-Lebrun's *La Folie Espagnole* is also not negligible.

tion, not a little supported by the *Voyages*, constitutes a
deliberate "literary offensive," intended to counter-work
the proceedings of the *philosophes*, though with aid drawn
from one of them—Rousseau,—and only secondarily
designed to provide pure novel-interest. If this is
forgotten, the student will find himself at sea without
a rudder ; and the mere reader will be in danger of exagger-
ating very greatly, because he does not in the least understand, the faults just referred to, and of failing altogether
to appreciate the real success and merit of the work as
judged on that only criterion, "Has the author done
what he meant to do, and done it well, on the lines he
chose ?" Of course, if our reader says, "I don't care
about all this, I merely want to be amused and interested,"
one cannot prevent him. He had, in fact, as was hinted
just now, better read nothing but *Atala* and *René*, if not,
indeed, *Atala* only, immense as is the literary importance
of its companion. But in a history of the novel one is
entitled to hope, at any rate to wish, for a somewhat
better kind of customer or client.

According to Chateaubriand's own account, when
he quitted England after his not altogether cheerful
experiences there as an almost penniless *émigré*, he left
behind him, in the charge of his landlady, exactly 2383
folio pages of MSS. enclosed in a trunk, and (by a combination of merit on the custodian's part and luck on his
own) recovered them fifteen years afterwards, *Atala*,
René, and a few other fragments having alone accompanied him. These were published independently, the
Génie following. *Les Martyrs* was a later composition
altogether, while *Les Natchez*, the *matrix* of both the
shorter stories, and included, as one supposes, in the
2383 waifs, was partly rewritten and wholly published
later still. A body of fiction of such a singular character
is, as has been said, not altogether easy to treat ; but,
without much change in the method usually pursued
in this *History*, we may perhaps do best by first giving a
brief argument of the various contents and then taking
up the censure, in no evil sense, of the whole.

Atala is short and almost entirely to the point. The heroine is a half-breed girl with a Spanish father and for mother an Indian of some rank in her tribe, who has subsequently married a benevolent chief. She is regarded as a native princess, and succeeds in rescuing from the usual torture and death, and fleeing with, a captive chief of another " nation." This is Chactas, important in *René* and also in the *Natchez* framework. They direct their flight northwards to the French settlements (it is late seventeenth or early eighteenth century throughout), and of course fall in love with each other. But Atala's mother, a Christian, has, in the tumult of her early misfortunes, vowed her daughter's virginity or death; and when, just before the crucial moment, a missionary opportunely or inopportunely occurs, Atala has already taken poison, with the object, it would appear, not so much of preventing as of avenging, of her own free will, a breach of the vow. The rest of the story is supplied by the vain attempts of the good father to save her, his evangelising efforts towards the pair, and the sorrows of Chactas after his beloved's death. The piece, of course, shows that exaggerated and somewhat morbid pathos of circumstance which is the common form of the early romantic efforts, whether in England, Germany, or France. But the pathos *is* pathos; the unfamiliar scenery, unlike that of Bernardin de Saint-Pierre (to whom, of course, Chateaubriand is much indebted, though he had actually seen what he describes), is not overdone, and suits the action and characters very well indeed. Chactas here is the best of all the " noble savages," and (what hardly any other of them is) positively good. Atala is really tragic and really gracious. The missionary stands to other fictitious, and perhaps some real, missionaries very much as Chactas does to other savages of story, if not of life. The proportion of the whole is good, and in the humble opinion of the present critic it is by far Chateaubriand's best thing in all perhaps but mere writing.

Atala.

And even in this it is bad to beat, in him or out of
him. The small space forbids mere surplusage of
description, and the plot—as all plots should do, but,
alas ! as few succeed in doing—acts as a bellows to kindle
the flame and intensify the heat of something far better
than description itself—passionate character. There are
many fine things—mixed, no doubt, with others not so
fine—in the tempestuous scene of the death of Atala,
which should have been the conclusion of the story.
But this, in its own way, seems to me little short of
magnificent :

" I implored you to fly ; and yet I knew I should die if you were
not with me. I longed for the shadow of the forest ; and yet I
feared to be with you in a desert place. . Ah ! if the cost had only
been that of quitting parents, friends, country ! if—terrible as it
is to say it—there had been nothing at stake but the loss of my own
soul.[1] But, O my mother ! thy shade was always there—thy shade
reproaching me with the torments it would suffer. I heard thy
complaints ; I saw the flames of Hell ready to consume thee. My
nights were dry places full of ghosts ; my days were desolate ; the
dew of the evening dried up as it touched my burning skin. I
opened my lips to the breeze ; and the breeze, instead of cooling me,
was itself set aglow by the fire of my breath. What torment,
Chactas ! to see you always near me, far from all other human-
kind in the deepest solitude, and yet to feel that between us there
was an insuperable barrier ! To pass my life at your feet, to serve
you as a slave, to bring you food and lay your couch in some secret
corner of the universe, would have been for me supremest happiness ; and this happiness was within my touch, yet I could not
enjoy it. Of what plans did I not dream ? What vision did not
arise from this sad heart ? Sometimes, as I gazed on you, I went
so far as to form desires as mad as they were guilty : sometimes I
could have wished that there were no living creatures on earth
but you and me ; sometimes, feeling that there was a divinity
mocking my wicked transports, I could have wished that divinity
annihilated, if only, locked in your arms, I might have sunk from
abyss to abyss with the ruins of God and of the world. Even now—
shall I say it ?—even now, when eternity waits to engulf me, when
I am about to appear before the inexorable Judge—at the very

---

[1] For the mother, in a fashion which the good Father-missionary most righteously
and indignantly denounces as unchristian, had staked her own salvation on her daughter's
obedience to the vow.

moment when my mother may be rejoicing to see my virginity devour my life—even now, by a terrible contradiction, I carry with me the regret that I have not been yours!"

At this let who will laugh or sneer, yawn or cavil. But as literature it looks back to Sappho and Catullus and the rest, and forward to all great love-poetry since, while as something that is even greater than literature— life—it carries us up to the highest Heaven and down to the nethermost Hell.

René[1] has greater fame and no doubt exercised far more influence ; indeed in this respect *Atala* could not do much, for it is not the eternal, but the temporal, which "influences." But, in the same humble opinion, it is extremely inferior. The French Werther[2] (for the attempt to rival Goethe on his own lines is hardly, if at all, veiled) is a younger son of a gentle family in France, whose father dies. He lives for a time with an elder brother, who seems to be " more kin than kind," and a sister Amélie, to whom he is fondly, but fraternally, attached. René has begun the trick of disappointment early, and, after a time, determines to travel, fancying when he leaves home that his sister is actually glad to get rid of him. Of course it is a case of *coelum non animum.* When he returns he is half-surprised but (for him) wholly glad to be at first warmly welcomed by Amélie ; but after a little while she leaves him, takes the veil, and lets him know at the last moment that it is because her affection for him is more than sisterly, that this was the reason of her apparent joy when he left her, and that association with him is too much for her passion.[3] *She* makes an exemplary nun in a seaside

René.

---

[1] Its author, in the *Mémoires d'Outre-Tombe*, expressed a warm wish that he had never written it, and hearty disgust at its puling admirers and imitators. This has been set down to hypocritical insincerity or the sourness of age : I see neither in it. It ought perhaps to be said that he "cut" a good deal of the original version. The confession of Amélie was at first less abrupt and so less effective, but the newer form does not seem to me to better the state of René himself.

[2] There had been a very early French imitation of *Werther* itself (of the end especially), *Les dernières aventures du sieur d'Olban,* by a certain Ramond, published in 1777, only three years after Goethe. It had a great influence on Ch. Nodier (*v. inf.*), who actually republished the thing in 1829.

[3] This " out-of-bounds " passion will of course be recognised as a Romantic trait,

convent, and dies early of disease caught while nursing others. *He*, his wretchedness and hatred of life reaching their acme, exiles himself to Louisiana, and gets himself adopted by the tribe of the Natchez, where Chactas is a (though not *the*) chief.

Now, of course, if we are content to take a bill and write down Byron and Lamartine, Sénancour and *Jacopo Ortis* (otherwise Ugo Foscolo), Musset, Matthew Arnold, and *tutti quanti*, as debtors to *René*, we give the tale or episode a historical value which cannot be denied ; while its positive aesthetic quality, though it may vary very much in different estimates, cannot be regarded as merely worthless. Also, once more, there is real pathos, especially as far as Amélie is concerned, though the entire unexpectedness of the revelation of her fatal passion, and the absolute lack of any details as to its origin, rise, and circumstances, injure sympathy to some extent. But that sympathy, as far as the present writer is concerned, fails altogether with regard to René himself. If his melancholy were traceable to *mutual* passion of the forbidden kind, or if it had arisen from the stunning effect of the revelation thereof on his sister's side, there would be no difficulty. But, though these circumstances may to some extent accentuate, they have nothing to do with causing the *weltschmerz* or *selbst-schmerz*, or whatever it is to be called, of this not very heroic hero. Nor has Chateaubriand taken the trouble—which Goethe,

Marginal note: Difference between its importance and its merit.

---

though it had Classical suggestions. Chateaubriand appears to have been rather specially "obsessed" by this form of it, for he not merely speaks constantly of René as *le frère d'Amélie*, but goes out of his way to make the good Father in *Atala* refer, almost ecstatically, to the happiness of the more immediate descendants of Adam who were *compelled* to marry their sisters, if they married anybody. As I have never been able to take any interest in the discussions of the Byron and Mrs. Leigh scandal, I am not sure whether this *tic* of Chateaubriand's has been noticed therein. But his influence on Byron was strong and manifold, and Byron was particularly apt to do things, naughty and other, because somebody else had done or suggested them. And of course it has, from very early days, been suggested that Amélie is an experience of Chateaubriand's own. But this, like the investigations as to time and distance and possibility in his travels and much else also, is not for us. Once more I must be permitted to say that I am writing much about French novels, little about French novelists, and least of all about those novelists' biographers, critics, and so forth. Exceptions may be admitted, but as exceptions only.

with his more critical sense of art, *did* take—to make
René go through the whole course of the Preacher, or
great part of it, before discovering that all was vanity.
He is merely, from the beginning, a young gentleman
affected with mental jaundice, who cannot or will not
discover or take psychological calomel enough to cure
him. It does not seem in the least likely that if Amélie
had been content to live with him as merely " in all good,
all honour " a loving and comforting sister, he would
have really been able to say, like Geraldine in Coleridge's
original draft of *Christabel*, " I'm better now."

He is, in fact, what Werther is not—though his own
followers to a large extent are—mainly if not merely
a Sulky Young Man : and one cannot help imagining that
if, in pretty early days, some one had been good enough
to apply to him that Herb Pantagruelion, in form not
exactly of a halter but of a rope's end, with which O'Brien
cured Peter Simple's *mal de mer*, his *mal du siècle* would
have been cured likewise.

Of course it is possible for any one to say, " You are
a Philistine and a Vulgarian. You wish to regard life
through a horse-collar," etc., etc. But these reproaches
would leave my withers quite ungalled. I think *Ecclesiastes* one of the very greatest books in the world's literature, and *Hamlet* the greatest play, with the possible
exception of the *Agamemnon*. It is the abysmal sadness
quite as much as the *furor arduus* of Lucretius that makes
me think him the mightiest of Latin poets. I would not
give the mystical melancholy of certain poems of Donne's
for half a hundred of the liveliest love-songs of the time,
and could extend the list page-long and more if it
would not savour of ostentation in more ways than
one. But mere temperamental ἑωλοκρασία or κραιπάλη
(next-day nausea), without even the exaltation of a
previous orgy to ransom it,—mere spleen and sulks and
naughty-childishness,—seem to me not great things at all.
You may not be able to help your spleen, but you can
" cook " it ; you may have qualm and headache, but in
work of some sort, warlike or peaceful, there is always

small beer, or brandy and soda (with even, if necessary, capsicum or bromide), for the ailment. The Renés who can do nothing but sulk, except when they blunder themselves and make other people uncomfortable in attempting to do something, who " never do a [manly] thing and never say a [kind] one," are, I confess, not to my taste.[1]

Both these stories, as will have been seen, have a distinctly religious element; in fact, a distinctly religious *Les Natchez.* purpose. The larger novel-romance of which they form episodes, as well as its later and greater successor, *Les Martyrs*, increase the element in both cases, the purpose in the latter; but one of the means by which this increase is effected has certainly lost—whether it may or may not ever recover—its attraction, except to a student of literary history who is well out of his novitiate. Such a person should see at once that Chateaubriand's elaborate adoption, from Tasso and Milton, of the system of interspersed scenes of Divine and diabolic conclaves and interferences with the story, is an important, if not a wholly happy, instance of that general Romantic *reversion* to earlier literary devices, and even atmospheres, of which the still rather enigmatic personage who rests enisled off Saint-Malo was so great an apostle. And it was probably effectual for its time. Classicists could not quarrel with it, for it had its precedents, indeed its origin, in Homer and Virgil; Romanticists (of that less exclusive class who admitted the Renaissance as well as the Dark and Middle Ages) could not but welcome it for its great modern defenders and examples. I cannot say that I enjoy it; but I can tolerate it, and there is no doubt at all, odd as it may seem to the merely twentieth-century reader, that it did something to revive the half-extinct religiosity which had been starved and poisoned in the later days of the *ancien régime*, forcibly suppressed under the Republic,

---

[1] I once had to fight it out in public with a valued and valiant friend for saying something like this in regard to Edgar of Ravenswood—no doubt, in some sort a child of René's or of Nelvil's; but I was not put to submission. And Edgar had truer causes for sulks than his spiritual ancestor had—at least before the tragedy of Amélie.

and only officially licensed by the Napoleonic system. In *Les Martyrs* it has even a certain "grace of congruity,"[1] but in regard to *Les Natchez*, with which we are for the moment concerned, almost enough (with an example or two to come presently) has been said about it.

The book, as a whole, suffers, unquestionably and considerably, from the results of two defects in its author. He was not born, as Scott was a little later, to get the historical novel at last into full life and activity; and it would not be unfair to question whether he was a born novelist at all, though he had not a few of the qualifications necessary to the kind, and exercised, coming as and when he did, an immense influence upon it. The subject is too obscure. Its only original *vates*, Charlevoix, though always a respectable name to persons of some acquaintance with literature and history, has never been much more, either in France or in England. The French, unluckily for themselves, never took much interest in their transatlantic possessions while they had them; and their dealings with the Indians then, and ours afterwards, and those of the Americans since, have never been exactly of the kind that give on both sides a subject such as may be found in all mediaeval and most Renaissance matters; in the Fronde; in the English Civil War; in the great struggles of France and England from 1688 to 1815; in the Jacobite risings; in La Vendée; and in other historical periods and provinces too many to mention. On the other hand, the abstract "noble savage" is a faded object of exhausted *engouement*, than which there are few things less exhilarating. The Indian *ingénu* (a very different one from Voltaire's) Outougamiz and his *ingénue* Mila are rather nice; but Celuta (the ill-fated girl who loves René and whom he marries, because in a sort of way he cannot help it) is an eminent example of that helpless kind of quiet misfortune the unprofitableness of which Mr. Arnold has confessed and registered

---

[1] Not in the strict theological meaning of this phrase, of course; but the misuse of it has aesthetic justification.

in a famous passage. Chactas maintains a respectable
amount of interest, and his visit to the court of Louis
XIV. takes very fair rank among a well-known group
of things of which it is not Philistine to speak as old-
fashioned, because they never possessed much attraction,
except as being new- or regular-fashioned. But the
villain Ondouré has almost as little of the fire of Hell as
of that of Heaven, and his paramour and accomplice
Akansie carries very little " conviction " with her. In
short, the merit of the book, besides the faint one of having
been the original framework of *Atala* and *René*, is almost
limited to its atmosphere, and the alterative qualities
thereof—things now in a way ancient history—requiring
even a considerable dose of the not-universally-possessed
historic sense to discern and appreciate them.

Outside the " Histoire de Chactas " (which might,
like *Atala* and *René* themselves, have been isolated with
great advantage), and excepting likewise the passages
concerning Outougamiz and Mila—which possess, in
considerable measure and gracious fashion, what some
call the " idyllic " quality—I have found it, on more
than one attempt, difficult to take much interest in *Les
Natchez*, not merely for the reasons already given, but
chiefly owing to them. René's appearances (and he is
generally in background or foreground) serve better than
anything in any other book, perhaps, to explain and
justify the old notion that *accidia*[1] of his kind is not
only a fault in the individual, but a positive ill omen and
nuisance [2] to others. Neither in the Indian characters

---

[1] *I.e.* not mere " sloth," but the black-blooded and sluggish melancholy to which
Dante pays so much attention in the *Inferno*. This deadly sin we inadequately translate
" sloth," and (on one side of it) it is best defined in Dante's famous lines (*Inf.* vii. 121-3) :

> Tristi fummo
> Nell' aer dolce che dal sol s' allegra,
> Portando dentro accidioso fummo.

Had Amélie sinned and not repented she might have been found in the Second circle,
flying alone ; René, except *speciali gratia*, must have sunk to the Fourth.

[2] For instance, he goes a-beaver-hunting with the Natchez, but his usual selfish
moping prevents him from troubling to learn the laws of the sport, and he kills females—
an act at once offensive to Indian religion, sportsmanship, and etiquette, horrifying to
the consciences of his adopted countrymen, and an actual *casus belli* with the neighbouring
tribes.

(with the exceptions named) nor among the French and creole does one find relief: and when one passes from them to the " machinery " parts—where, for instance, a " perverse couple," Satan and La Renommée (*not* the ship that Trunnion took), embark on a journey in a car with winged horses—it must be an odd taste which finds things improved. In Greek verse, in Latin verse, or even in Milton's English one could stand Night, docile to the orders of Satan, condescending to deflect a hatchet which is whistling unpleasantly close to René's ear, not that he may be benefited, but preserved for more sufferings. In comparatively plain French prose— the qualification is intentional, as will be seen a little later—with a scene and time barely two hundred years off now and not a hundred then, though in a way un- familiar—the thing won't ·do. " Time," at the orders of the Prince of Darkness, cutting down trees to make a stockade for the Natchez in the eighteenth century, alas ! contributes again the touch of weak allegory, in neither case helping the effect; while, although the plot is by no means badly evolved, the want of interest in the characters renders it ineffective.

The defects of *Les Martyrs* [1] are fewer in number and less in degree, while its merits are far more than *Les Martyrs.* proportionally greater and more numerous. Needing less historical reinforcement, it enjoys much more. *Les Natchez* is almost the last, certainly the last important novel of savage life, as distinguished from " boys' books " about savages. *Les Martyrs* is the first of a line of remarkable if not always successful classical novels from Lockhart's *Valerius* to Gissing's *Veranilda*. It has nothing really in common with the kind of classical story which lasted from *Télémaque* to *Belisarius* and later. And what is more, it is perhaps

---

[1] Its second title, *ou Le Triomphe de la Religion Chrétienne*, connects it still more closely than *Les Natchez* with *Le Génie du Christianisme*, which it immediately succeeded in composition, though this took a long time. No book (it would seem in consequence) exemplifies the mania for annotation and " justification " more extensively. In vol. i. the proportion of notes to text is 112 to 270, in vol. ii. 123 to 221, and in vol. iii., in- cluding some extracts from the Père Mambrun, 149 to 225

better than any of its followers except Kingsley's *Hypatia*,
which is admittedly of a mixed kind—a nineteenth-
century novel, with events, scenes, and *décor* of the fifth
century. If it has not the spectacular and popular
appeal of *The Last Days of Pompeii*, it escapes, as that does
not, the main drawback of almost all the others—the
" classical-dictionary " element : and if, on the other,
its author knew less about Christianity than Cardinals
Wiseman and Newman, he knew more about lay
" humans " than the authors of *Fabiola* and *Callista*.

It is probably unnecessary to point out at any great
length that some of the drawbacks of *Les Natchez* disappear almost automatically in *Les Martyrs*. The supernatural machinery is, on the hypothesis and at the time
of the book, strictly congruous and proper ; while, as a
matter of fact, it is in proportion rather less than more
used. The time and events—those of the persecution
under Diocletian—are familiar, interesting, and, in a
French term for which we have no exact equivalent,
dignes. There is no sulky spider of a René crawling
about the piece ; and though history is a little strained
to provide incidents,[1] " that's not much," and they are
not in themselves improbable in any bad sense or degree.
Moreover, the classical-dictionary element, which, as
has been said, is so awkward to handle, is, at least after
the beginning, not too much drawn upon.

The book, in its later modern editions, is preceded
not merely by several Prefaces, but by an *Examen* in the
old fashion, and fortified by those elaborate citation-
notes [2] from authorities ancient and modern which were
a mania at the end of the eighteenth and the beginning
of the nineteenth century, and which sometimes divert
and sometimes enrage more modern readers in work so
different as *Lalla Rookh* and *The Pursuits of Literature*,
while they provided at the time material for immortal
jokes in such other work as the *Anti-Jacobin* poems. In

---

[1] Such as Eudore's early friendship at Rome, before the persecution under Diocletian,
with Augustine, who was not born till twenty years later.
[2] See note above.

the Prefaces Chateaubriand discusses the prose epic, and puts himself, quite unnecessarily, under the protection of *Télémaque* : in the *Examen* he deals systematically with the objections, religious, moral, and literary, which had been made against the earlier editions of the book.   But these things are now little more than curiosities for the student, though they retain some general historical importance.

The book starts (after an " Invocation," proper to its scheme but perhaps not specially attractive " to us ") with an account of the household of Demodocus, a Homerid of Chios, who in Diocletian's earlier and unpersecuting days, after living happily but for too short a time in Crete with his wife Epicharis, loses her, though she leaves him one little daughter, Cymodocée, born in the sacred woods of Mount Ida itself.   Demodocus is only too glad to accept an invitation to become high priest of a new Temple of Homer in Messenia, on the slopes of another mountain, less, but not so much less, famous, Ithome.   Cymodocée becomes very beautiful, and receives, but rejects, the addresses of Hierocles, proconsul of Achaia, and a favourite of Galerius.   One day, worshipping in the forest at a solitary Altar of the Nymphs, she meets a young stranger whom (she is of course still a pagan) she mistakes for Endymion, but who talks Christianity to her, and reveals himself as Eudore, son of Lasthenes.   As it turns out, her father knows this person, who has the renown of a distinguished soldier.

The story.

From this almost any one who has read a few thousand novels—almost any intelligent person who has read a few hundred—can lay out the probable plot.   Love of Eudore and Cymodocée ; conversion of the latter ; jealousy and intrigues of Hierocles ; adventures past and future of Eudore ; transfer of scene to Rome ; prevalence of Galerius over Diocletian ; persecution, martyrdom, and supernatural triumph.   But the " fillings up " are not banal ; and the book is well worth reading from divers points of view.   In the earliest part there

is a little too much Homer,[1] naturally enough perhaps.
The ancient world changed slowly, and we know that
at this particular time Greeks (if not also Romans) rather
played at archaising manners. Still, it is probably not
quite safe to take the memorable, if not very resultful,
journey in which Telemachus was, rather undeservedly,
so lucky as to see Helen and drink Nepenthe[2] and to
reproduce it with guide- and etiquette-book exactness,
c. A.D. 300. Yet this is, as has been said, very natural;
and it arouses many pleasant reminiscences.

The book, moreover, has two great qualities which
were almost, if not quite, new in the novel. In the first
place, it has a certain *panoramic* element which
admits—which indeed necessitates—pictur-
esqueness. Much of it is, almost as neces-
sarily, *récit* (Eudore giving the history of his travels and
campaigns); but it is *récit* of a vividness which had
never before been known in French, out of the most
accomplished drama, and hardly at all in prose. The
adventures of Eudore require this most, of course, and
they get it. His early wild-oats at Rome, which earn
him temporary excommunication; his service in the wars
with the Franks, where, for almost the only time in literature, Pharamond and Mérovée become living creatures;
his captivity with them; his triumphs in Britain and his
official position in Brittany, where the entrance of the
Druidess Velléda and the fatal love between them provide
perhaps the most famous and actually one of the most
effective of the episodes of the book—all " stand out
from the canvas," as the old phrase goes. Nor is the
mastery lost when *récit* becomes direct action, in the scenes
of the persecution, and the final purification of the hero
and crowning of the heroine in the amphitheatre. " The
work burns "; and, while it is practically certain that the
writer knew the Scudéry romances, the contrast of this

Margin note: Its "panoramic" quality.

---

[1] There cannot be too much Homer in Homer; there may be too much outside
Homer.

[2] If one had only been Telemachus at this time! It would have been a good " Declamation " theme in the days of such things, " Should a man—for this one experience—
consent to be Telemachus for the rest of his life—and after ? "

"burning" quality becomes so striking as almost to justify, comparatively if not positively, the accusations of frigidity and languor which have been somewhat excessively brought against the earlier performances. There is not the passion of *Atala*—it would have been out of place: and there is not the soul-dissection of *René*, for there is nothing morbid enough to require the scalpel. But, on the other hand, there is the bustle—if that be not too degrading a word—which is wanting in both; the vividness of action and of change; colour, variety, suspense, what may perhaps best be called in one word "pulse," giving, as a necessary consequence, life.

And this great advance is partly, if not mainly, achieved by another—the novelty of *style*. Chateaubriand had set out to give—has, indeed, as far as his intention goes, maintained throughout—an effort at *le style noble*, the already familiar rhetoric, of which, in French, Corneille had been the Dryden and Racine the Pope, while it had, in his own youth, sunk to the artifice of Delille in verse and the "emphasis" of Thomas in prose. He has sometimes achieved the best, and not seldom something that is by no means the worst, of this. But, consciously or unconsciously, he has more often put in the old bottles of form new wine of spirit, which has not only burst them, but by some very satisfactory miracle of literature shed itself into new receptacles, this time not at all leathery but glass of iridescent colour and graceful shape. It was almost inevitable that such a process, at such a time, and with such a language—for Chateaubriand did not go to the real "ancient mother" of pre-*grand siècle* French—should be now and then merely magniloquent, that it should sometimes fall short of, or overleap, even magniloquence and become bombast. But sometimes also, and not so seldom, it attains magnificence as well; and the promise, at least the opportunity, of such magnificence in capable followers can hardly be mistaken. As in his younger contemporary, compatriot, and, beyond all doubt, disciple, Lamennais, the results are often

And its remarkable advance in style.

crude, unequal, disappointing; insufficiently smelted
ore, insufficiently ripened and cellared wine. But the
quantity and quality of pure metal—the inspiriting
virtue of the vintage—in them is extraordinary: and
once more it must be remembered that, for the novel,
all this was absolutely new. In this respect, if in no other,
though perhaps he was so in others also, Chateaubriand
is a Columbus of prose fiction. Neither in French nor
in English, very imperfectly in German, and, so far as
I know, not in any other language to even the smallest
degree, had "prose-poetry" been attempted in this
department. "Ossian" perhaps must have some of
the credit: the Bible still more. But wherever the capital
was found it was Chateaubriand who put it into the
business of novel-writing and turned out the first specimens of that business with the new materials and plant
procured by the funds.

Some difficulties, which hamper any attempt to
illustrate and support this high praise, cannot require
much explanation to make them obvious. It has
not been the custom of this book to give large
untranslated extracts: and it is at least the
opinion of its author that in matters of style,
translation, even if it be of a much higher quality than
he conceives himself able to offer, is, if not quite worthless, very inadequate. Moreover, it is (or should be)
well known that the qualities of the old French *style
noble*—which, as has been said, Chateaubriand deliberately adopted, as his starting-point if nothing more—
are, even in their own language, and still more when
reproduced in any other, full of dangers for foreign
appreciation. The no doubt largely ignorant and in
any case mistaken contempt for French poetry and poetic
prose which so long prevailed among us, and from which
even such a critic and such a lover (to some extent) of
French as Matthew Arnold was not free, was mainly
concerned with this very point. To take a single instance, the part of De Quincey's "Essay on Rhetoric"
which deals with French is made positively worthless

*Chateau-
briand's
Janus-position
in this.*

by the effects of this almost racial prejudice. Literal translation of the more *flamboyant* kind of French writing has been, even with some of our greatest, an effective, if a somewhat facile, means of procuring a laugh. Furthermore, it has to be remembered that this application of ornate style to prose fiction is undoubtedly to some extent an extraneous thing in the consideration of the novel itself. It is "a grand set off" (in the old phrase) to tale-telling; but it is not precisely of its essence. It deserves to be *constaté*, recorded and set to the credit of those who practise it, and especially of those who first introduced it. But it is a question whether, in the necessarily limited space of a book like this, the consideration of it ought to occupy a large room.

Still, though the warning, "Be not too bold," should never be forgotten, it should be remembered that it was given only once and its contrary reiterated : so here goes for one of the most perilous of all possible adventures— a translation of Chateaubriand's own boldest undertaking, the description of the City of God, in which he was following not only the greatest of the Hebrew prophets, but the Vision of Patmos itself.

("*Les Martyrs,*" *Book III., opening. The Prayer of Cyril, Bishop of Lacedaemon, has come before the Throne*)

At the centre of all created worlds, in the midst of innumerable stars which serve as its bastions as well as avenues and roads to it, there floats the limitless City of God, the marvels whereof no mortal tongue can tell. The Eternal Himself laid its twelve foundations, and surrounded it with the wall of jasper that the beloved disciple saw measured by an angel with a rod of gold. Clothed with the glory of the Most High, the unseen Jerusalem is decked as a bride for her bridegroom. O monumental structures of earth ! ye come not near these of the Holy City. There the richness of the matter rivals the perfection of the form. There hang, royally suspended, the galleries of diamond and sapphire feebly imitated by human skill in the gardens of Babylon. There rise triumphal arches, fashioned of brightest stars. There are linked together porticoes of suns extended across the spaces of the firmament, like the columns of Palmyra over the sands of the desert. This architecture is alive. The City of

Illustrated.

God has a soul of its own. There is no mere matter in the abiding places of the Spirit; no death in the locality of eternal existence. The grosser words which our muse is forced to employ deceive us, for they invest with body that which is only as a divine dream, in the passing of a blissful sleep.

Gardens of delight extend round the radiant Jerusalem. A river flows from the throne of the Almighty, watering the Celestial Eden with floods of pure love and of the wisdom of God. The mystic wave divides into streams which entwine themselves, separate, rejoin, and part again, giving nourishment to the immortal vine, to the lily that is like unto the Bride, and to all the flowers which perfume the couch of the Spouse. The Tree of Life shoots up on the Hill of Incense; and, but a little farther, that of Knowledge spreads on all sides its deep-planted roots and its innumerable branches, carrying hidden in the golden leafage the secrets of the Godhead, the occult laws of Nature, the truths of morality and of the intellect, the immutable principles of good and of evil. The learning which intoxicates *us* is the common food of the Elect; for in the empire of Sovereign Intelligence the fruit of science no longer brings death. Often do the two great ancestors of the human race come and shed such tears as the Just can still let flow in the shadow of the wondrous Tree.

The light which lightens these abodes of bliss is compact of the rose of morning, of the flame of noon, of the purple of even; yet no star appears on the glowing horizon. No sun rises and no sun goes down on the country where nothing ends, where nothing begins. But an ineffable clearness, showering from all sides like a tender dew, maintains the unbroken [1] daylight in a delectable eternity.

Of course any one who is so minded may belittle this as classically cold; even as to some extent *neo*-classically bedizened; as more like, let us say, Moore's *Epicurean* than like our greater " prose-poets " of the seventeenth and the nineteenth centuries. The presence in Chateaubriand of this dose of the style that was passing, and that he helped to make pass, has been admitted already: but I confess I think it is only a dose. Those who care to look up the matter for themselves might, if they do not

---

[1] In the original the word which I have translated " unbroken " is *éternel*, and with the adjacent *éternité* illustrates (as do *tonnerre* and *étonnante* in Bossuet's famous passage on the death of " Madame ") one of the minor but striking differences between French and English rhetoric. Save for some very special purpose, we should consider such repetition a jingle at best, a cacophony at worst: they think it a beauty.

choose to read the whole, turn to the admirable picture of camp-life on the Lower Rhine at the opening of Book VI. as a short contrast, while the story is full of others.   Nor should one forget to add that Chateaubriand can, when he chooses, be epigrammatic as well as declamatory.   " Such is the ugliness of man when he bids farewell to his soul and, so to speak, keeps house only with his body " is a phrase which might possibly shock La Harpe, but which is, as far as I remember, original, and is certainly crisp and effective enough.

Reassembling, then, the various points which we have endeavoured to make in respect of his position as novelist, it may once more be urged that if not precisely a great master of the complete art of novel-writing, by actual example, he shows no small expertness in various parts of it: and that, as a teacher and experimenter in new developments of method and indication of new material, he has few superiors in his own country and not very many elsewhere.   That in this pioneer quality, as well as in mere contemporaneousness, he may, though a greater writer, be yoked with the authoress of *Corinne* need hardly be argued, for the accounts given of the two should have sufficiently established it.

CHAPTER II

THE mediocre poet has had a hard fate pronounced against him of old; but the minor novelist, perhaps

The fate of popular minor novelists. because he is much more likely to get some good things in his own time, has usually a harder lot still, and in more than one way, after physical or popular death. In fact it may be said that, the more popular he is in the one day, the more utterly forgotten he is likely to be in the other. Besides the obvious facts that his popularity must always have been gained by the adoption of some more or less ephemeral fashion, and that plenty of his own kind are always ready to take his place—doing, like the heir in the old story, all they can to substitute *Requiescat in Pace* for *Resurgam* on his hatchment—there is a more mechanical reason for his occultation. The more widely he or she has been read the more certain either has been of being "read to pieces."

These fates, and especially the last, have weighed upon the minor French novelists of the early nineteenth

Examples of them. century perhaps even more heavily than upon our own: for the circulating library was an earlier and a more widely spread institution in France than in England, and the lower and lowest middle classes were a good deal more given to reading, and especially to "light" reading, there than here. Nor can it be said that any of the writers to be now mentioned, with one possible and one certain exception,

39

is of importance to literature as literature. But all have their importance to literary—and especially departmental-literary—history, in ways which it is hoped presently to show: and there is still amusement in some. The chief, though not the only, names that require notice here are those of Mesdames de Montolieu and (again) de Genlis, of Ducray-Duminil, born almost as early as Pigault-Lebrun, even earlier a novelist, and yoked with him by Victor Hugo in respect of his novel *Lolotte et Fanfan* in the sneer noted in the last volume;[1] the *other* Ducange, again as much " other " as the other Molière;[2] the Vicomte d'Arlincourt; and—a comparative (if, according to some, blackish) swan among these not quite positive geese—Paul de Kock. The eldest put in his work before the Revolution and the youngest before Waterloo, but the most prolific time of all was that of the first two or three decades of the century with which we are dealing.

With these, but not of them—a producer at last of real " letters " and more than any one else except Chateaubriand (more " intensively " perhaps even than he was) a pioneer of Romanticism—comes Charles Nodier.

Major Pendennis, in a passage which will probably, at least in England, preserve the name of the author Paul de mentioned long after his own works are even Kock. more forgotten with us than they are at present, allowed, when disparaging novels generally, and wondering how his nephew could have got so much money for one, that Paul de Kock " certainly made him laugh." In his own country he had an enormous vogue, till the far greater literary powers and the wider range of the school of 1830 put the times out of joint for him, and even much later. He actually survived the Terrible Year: but something like a lustrum earlier, when running over a not small collection of cheap novels in a French country inn, I do not remember coming across anything of his. And he had long been classed as " not a serious person " (which, indeed, he certainly was not) by French

---

[1] Vol. I. pp. 458, 472, *notes*.   [2] Vol. I. p. 161.

criticism, not merely of the most academic sort, but of
all decidedly literary kinds.   People allowed him *entrain*,
a word even more difficult than *verve* to English exactly,
though " go " does in a rough sort of way for both.
They were of course not very much shocked at his in-
decorums, which sometimes gave occasion for not bad
jokes.[1]   But if any foreigner made any great case of
him they would probably have looked, if they did not
speak their thoughts, very much as some of us have
looked, if we have not spoken, when foreigners take
certain popular scribes and playwrights of our own time
and country seriously.[2]

Let us see what his work is really like to the eyes of
impartial and comparative, if not cosmopolitan, criticism.

Paul de Koçk, whose father, a banker, was a victim,
but must have been a late one, of the Terror, was born
L'Enfant de in 1794, and took very early to letters.   If
ma Femme. the date of his first book, *L'Enfant de ma
Femme*, is correctly given as 1812, he must
apparently have written it before he was eighteen.   There
is certainly nothing either in the quantity or the quality
of the performance which makes this incredible, for it
does not fill quite two hundred pages of the ordinary
18mo size and not very closely packed type of the
usual cheap French novel, and though it is not unreadable,
any tolerably clever boy might easily write it between
the time when he gets his scholarship in spring and
the time when he goes up in October.   The author
had evidently read his Pigault and adopted that writer's
revised picaresque scheme.   His most prominent character (the hero, Henri de Framberg, is very " small

---

[1] When he published *Le Cocu*, it was set about that a pudibund lady had asked her
bookseller for " Le Dernier de M. Paul de Kock."   And this circumlocution became for
a time popular, as a new name for the poor creature on the ornaments of whose head our
Elizabethans joked so untiringly.

[2] A short essay, or at least a " middle " article, might be written on this way of regarding a prophet in his own country, coupling Béranger with Paul de Kock.   Of course
the former is by much a *major* prophet in verse than Paul is in prose.   But the attitude
of the superior French person to both is, in different degrees, the same.   (Thackeray
in the article referred to below, p. 62 *note*, while declaring Paul to be *the* French writer
whose works are best known in England, says that his educated countrymen think him
pitoyable.—*Works*, Oxford edition, vol. ii. p. 533.)

doings "), the hussar-soldier-servant, and most oddly
selected " governor " of this hero as a boy, Mullern,
is obviously studied off those semi-savage " old mous-
taches " of whom we spoke in the last volume, though
he is much softened, if not in morals, in manners.   In
fact this softening process is quite obvious throughout.
There is plenty of " impropriety " but no mere nastiness,
and the impropriety itself is, so to speak, rather indicated
than described.   As nearly the last sentence announces,
" Hymen hides the faults of love " wherever it is possible,
though it would require a most complicated system of
polygamy and cross-unions to enable that amiable
divinity to cover them all.   There is a villain, but he is
a villain of straw, and outside of him there is no ill-nature.
There seems to be going to be a touch of " out-of-
boundness " when Henri, just about to marry his beloved
Pauline, is informed that she is his sister, and when the
pair, separating in horror, meet again and, let us say,
forget to separate.   But the information turns out to be
false, and Hymen duly uses the not uncomfortable
extinguisher which, as noted above, is supplied to him
as well as the more usual torch.

To call the book good would be ridiculous, but a very
large experience of first novels of dates before, the same
as, and after its own may warrant allotment to it of possibilities of future good gifts.   The history, such as it is, runs
currently ; there are no hitches and stops and stagnations,
the plentiful improbabilities are managed in such fashion
that one does not trouble about them, and there is an
atmosphere, sometimes of horseplay but almost always of
good humour.

The matter which, by accident or design, goes with
this in mid-century reprints of Paul, is of much later
Petits   date, but it shows that, for some time, its author
Tableaux de had been exercising himself in a way valuable
Mœurs.   to the novelist at any time but by no means
as yet frequently practised.   *Petits Tableaux de Mœurs*
consists of about sixty short sketches of a very few pages
each (usually two or three) and of almost exactly the

same kind as those with which Leigh Hunt, a little earlier
in England, transformed the old *Spectator* essay into
the kind of thing taken up soon afterwards by "Boz"
and never disused since. They are sketches of types of
men, of Parisian cafés, gardens, and restaurants; fresh
handlings of old subjects, such as the person who insists
on taking you home to a very bad "pot-luck" dinner,
and the like. Once more, there is no great brilliance in
these. But they are lightly and pleasantly done; it
must be obvious to every one that they are simply invaluable training for a novelist who is to leave the beaten
track of picaresque adventure and tackle real ordinary
life. To which it may be added, as at least possible, that
Thackeray himself may have had the creation of Woolsey
and Eglantine in *The Ravenswing* partly suggested by a
conversation between a tailor and a hairdresser in Paul's
" Le Banc de Pierre des Tuileries." As this is very short
it may be worth giving :

To finish our observations, my friend and I went and sat
behind two young men dressed in the extreme of the fashion, who,
with their feet placed on chairs as far as possible from those in which
they were sitting, gracefully rocked themselves, and evidently
hoped to attract general attention.

In a minute we heard the following conversation :

" Do you think my coat a success ? " " Superb ! delicious !
an admirable cut ! " " And the pantaloons ? " " Ravishing !
Your get up is really stunning." " The governor told me to spend
three hours in the Grand Alley, and put myself well forward.
He wants people to take up this new shape and make it fashionable.
He has already one order of some consequence." " And, as for
me, do you think my hair well done ? " " Why, you look like
a very Adonis. By the way, *my* hair is falling off. Do give me
something to stop that." " You must give it nourishment. You
see hairs are plants or flowers. If you don't water a flower, you
can see it withering." " Very true. Then must I use pom-
made ? " " Yes, but in moderation ; just as a tree too much
watered stops growing. Hair is exactly like vegetables." " And
both want cutting ? " " Why, yes ; it's like a plantation ; if
you don't prune and thin the branches it kills the young shoots.
Cutting helps the rise of the sap." " Do you hold with false
fronts ? " " I believe you ! Why, I make them ; it's just like

putting a new roof on a house." "And that does no harm to one's head ?" "Impossible ! neither glue nor white of egg, which needs must hinder growth, are used. People who wear them mix their own hair with the front. They are two flocks, which unite to feed together, as M. Marty says so well in the *Solitaire.*"[1] "Two torrents which join in the valley : that is the image of life ! "

We had heard enough, and so we left the tailor's young man and the romantic hairdresser to themselves.

In *Gustave ou Le Mauvais Sujet*, a book still early but some years later than *L'Enfant*, Paul de Kock got nearer to his proper or improper subject—bachelor life *Gustave.* in Paris, in the sense of his contemporary Pierce Egan's *Life in London.*[2] The hero may be called a French Tom Jones in something (but not so much as in the original phrase) of the sense in which Klopstock was allowed to be a German Milton. He has his Allworthy in a benevolent uncle-colonel, peppery but placable ; he is far more plentifully supplied than even Tom was with persons of the other sex who play the parts of Black George's daughter and Mrs. Waters, if not exactly of Lady Bellaston. A Sophia could hardly enter into the Kockian plan, but her place in that scheme (with something, one regrets to add, of Lady Bellaston's) is put in commission, and held by a leash of amiable persons —the erring Madame de Berly, who sacrifices honour and beauty and very nearly life for the rascal Gustave ; Eugénie Fonbelle, a rich, accomplished, and almost wholly desirable widow, whom he is actually about to marry when, luckily for her, she discovers his *fredaines*, and " calls off " ; and, lastly, a peasant girl, Suzon, whom he seduces, whom he keeps for six weeks in his uncle's house, after a fashion possibly just not impossible in a large Parisian establishment ; who is detected at last by the uncle ; who runs away when she hears that Gustave is going to marry Eugénie, and who is at the end produced,

[1] A gibe at the Vicomte d'Arlincourt's very popular novel, to be noticed below. I have not, I confess, identified the passage : but it may be in one of the plays.

[2] It would *not* be fair to compare the two as makers of literature. In that respect Theodore Hook is Paul's Plutarchian parallel, though he has more literature and less life.

with an infant ready-made, for Paul's favourite " curtain "
of Hymen, covering (like the curtain) all faults.   The
book has more " scabrous " detail than *L'Enfant de ma
Femme*, and (worse still) it relapses into Smollettian-
Pigaultian dirt ; but it displays a positive and even large
increase of that singular readableness which has been
noticed.   One would hardly, except in cases of actual
novel-famine, or after an immense interval, almost or
quite involving oblivion, read a book of Paul's twice,
but there is seldom any difficulty in reading him once.
Only, beware his moral moods !   When he is immoral
it is in the bargain ; if you do not want him you leave
him, or do not go to him at all.   But when, for instance,
the unfortunate Madame de Berly has been frightfully
burnt and disfigured for life by an act of her own, intended
to save—and successful in saving—her *vaurien* of a lover,
Paul moralises thus at the end of a chapter—

Julie perdit en effet tous ses attraits : elle fut punie par où
elle avait pêché.   Juste retour des choses ici-bas.

there being absolutely no such *retour* for Gustave—one
feels rather inclined, as his countrymen would say, to
" conspue " Paul.[1]   It is fair, however, to say that these
accesses of morality or moralising are not very frequent.

But there is one thing of some interest about *Gustave*
which has not yet been noticed.   Paul de Kock was
certainly not the author,[2] but he must have been
one of the first, and he as certainly was one of
the most effective and continuous, promoters
of that curious caricature of Englishmen which everybody knows from French draughtsmen, and some from
French writers, of the first half of the nineteenth century.
It is only fair to say that we had long preceded it by
caricaturing Frenchmen.   But they had been slow in
retaliating, at least in anything like the same fashion.
For a long time (as is again doubtless known to many

*The cari-
catured
Anglais.*

----

[1] Charity, outrunning knowledge, may plead "Irony perhaps ?"   Unfortunately
there is no chance of it.

[2] I really do not know who was (see a little below).   Parny in his absurd *Goddam !*
(1804) has something of it.

people) French literature had mostly ignored foreigners. During the late seventeenth and earlier eighteenth centuries few, except the aristocracy, of either country knew much of the other, and there was comparatively little (of course there was always some) difference between the manners and customs of the upper classes of both. Prévost and Crébillon, if not Marivaux,[1] knew something about England. Then arose in France a caricature, no doubt, but almost a reverential one, due to the *philosophes*, in the drawing whereof the Englishman is indeed represented as eccentric and splenetic, but himself philosophical and by no means ridiculous. Even in the severe period of national struggle which preceded the Revolutionary war, and for some time after the beginning of that war itself, the scarecrow-comic *Anglais* was slow to make his appearance. Pigault-Lebrun himself, as was noted in the last volume, indulges in him little if at all. But things soon changed.

In the book of which we have been speaking, Gustave and a scapegrace friend of his determine to give a dinner to two young persons of the other sex, but find themselves penniless, and a fresh edition of one of the famous old *Repues Franches* (which date in French literature back to Villon and no doubt earlier) follows. With this, as such, we need not trouble ourselves. But Olivier, the friend, takes upon him the duty of providing the wine, and does so by persuading a luckless vintner that he is a " Milord."

In order to dress the part, he puts on a cravat well folded, a very long coat, and a very short waistcoat. He combs down his hair till it is quite straight, rouges the tip of his nose, takes a whip, puts on gaiters and a little pointed hat, and studies himself in the glass in order to give himself a stupid and insolent air, the result of the make-up being entirely successful. It may be difficult for the most unbiassed Englishman of to-day to recognise himself in this portrait or to find it half-way somewhere about 1860, or even, going back to actual " *temp*. of tale,"

---

[1] And *he* knew something of it through Addison.

to discover anything much like it in physiognomies so different as those of Castlereagh and Wellington, of Southey and Lockhart, nay, even of Tom and Jerry.[1] But that it is the Englishman of Daumier and Gavarni, *artistement complet* already, nobody can deny.

Later in the novel (before he comes to his very problematical " settling down " with Suzon and the ready-made child) Gustave is allowed a rather superfluous scattering of probably not final wild oats in Italy and Germany, in Poland and in England. But the English meesses are too *sentimentales* (note the change from *sensibles*) ; he does not like the courses of horses, the combats of cocks, the bets and the punches and the plum-puddings. He is angry because people look at him when he pours his tea into the saucer. But what annoys him most of all is the custom of the ladies leaving the table after dinner, and that of preferring cemeteries for the purpose of taking the air and refreshing oneself after business. It may perhaps diminish surprise, but should increase interest, when one remembers that, after Frenchmen had got tired of Locke, and before they took to Shakespeare, their idea of our literature · was largely derived from " Les Nuits de Young " and Hervey's *Meditations among the Tombs.*

Another bit of copy-book (to revert to the Pauline moralities) is at the end of the same very unedifying novel, when the benevolent and long-suffering colonel, joining the hands of Gustave and Suzon, remarks to the latter that she has proved to him that " virtues, gentleness, wits, and beauty can serve as substitutes for birth and fortune." It would be unkind to ask which of the " virtues " presided over Suzon's original acquaintance

---

[1] The straight hair is particularly curious, for, as everybody who knows portraits of the early nineteenth century at all is aware, Englishmen of the time preferred brushed back and rather " tousled " locks. In Maclise's famous " Fraserians " there is hardly a straight-combed head among all the twenty or thirty. At the same time it is fair to say that our own book-illustrators and caricaturists, for some strange reason, did a good deal to authorise the libels. Cruikshank was no doubt a wonderful draughtsman, but I never saw (and I thank God for it) anything like many, if not most, of his faces. " Phiz " and Cattermole in (for example) their illustrations to *The Old Curiosity Shop* and *Barnaby Rudge* sometimes out-Cruikshank Cruikshank in this respect.

with her future husband, or whether the same or another
undertook the charge of that wonderful six weeks'
abscondence of hers with him in this very uncle's house.

But no doubt this capacity for "dropping into"
morality stood Paul in good stead when he undertook
Edmond et (as it was almost incumbent on such a universal
sa Cousine. provider of popular fiction to do) what the
French, among other nicknames for them, call *berquinades*—stories for children and the young person, more or
less in the style of the *Ami des Enfants*. He diversified
his *gauloiseries* with these not very seldom. An example
is bound up with *Gustave* itself in some editions, and
they make a very choice assortment of brimstone and
treacle. The hero and heroine of *Edmond et sa Cousine*
are two young people who have been betrothed from
their youth up, and neither of whom objects to the
situation, while Constance, the "She-cosen" (as Pepys
puts it) is deeply in love with Edmond. He also is
really fond of her, but he is a bumptious and superficial
snob, who, not content with the comfortable [1] income
which he has, and which will be doubled at his marriage,
wants to make fame and fortune in some way. He
never will give sufficient scope and application to his
moderate talents, and accordingly fails very plumply in
music, playwriting, and painting. Then he takes to
stock-exchange gambling, and of course, after the usual
"devil's *arles*" of success, completely ruins himself,
owes double what he has, and is about to blow out his
somewhat unimportant brains. But Constance, in the
truest spirit of melodrama, and having long sought him in
vain under the guidance of a *quarta persona*, of whom
more presently, realises almost the whole of her
fortune, except a small pittance, dashes it down before
him in the nick of time, and saves him for the moment.

Perhaps the straitest sect of the Berquinaders would

---

[1] Paul's ideas of money are still very modest. An income of 6000 francs (£240)
represents ease if not affluence ; with double the amount you can "aspire to a duchess,"
and even the dispendious Irish-French Viscount Edward de Sommerston in *La Fille aux
Trois Jupons* (*v. inf.*) starts on his career with scarcely more than three thousand a year.

have finished the story here, made the two marry on
Constance's pittance, reconciled Edmond to honest
work, and so on.   Paul, however, had a soul both above
and below this.   Edmond, with the easy and cheap
sham honour of his kind, will not " subject her to priva-
tions," still hopes for something to turn up, and in
society meets with a certain family of the name of Bringuesingue—a father who is a retired mustard-maker with
some money and no brains, a mother who is a nonentity,
and a daughter Clodora,[1] a not bad-looking and not
unamiable girl, unfortunately dowered with the silliness
of her father and the nullity of her mother combined
and intensified.   There is some pretty bad stock farce
about M. Bringuesingue and his valet, whom he pays
to scratch his nose when his master is committing sole-
cisms ; and about Edmond's adroitness in saving the
situations.   The result is that the Bringuesingues throw
their not unwilling daughter at Edmond's head.   To
do him the only justice he ever deserves, he does not like
to give up Constance ; but she, more melodramatic than
ever, contrives to imbue him with the idea that she is
false to him, and he marries Clodora.   Again the thing
might have been stopped ; but Paul once more goes
on, and what, I fear, must be called his hopeless bad
taste (there is no actual bad *blood* in him), and the precious
stage notion that " Tom the young dog " may do anything and be forgiven, make him bring about a happy
ending in a very shabby fashion.   Edmond is bored
by his stupid though quite harmless and affectionate
wife, neglects her, and treats his parents-in-law with
more contempt still.   Poor Clodora dies, but persuades
her parents to hand over her fortune to Edmond, and with
it he marries Constance.   " Hide, blushing honour !
hide that wedding-day."   But, you see, the Paul-de-
Kockian hero was not like Lord Welter.   There was
hardly anything that *this* " fellow couldn't do."

[1] Paul's scholarship was very rudimentary, as is shown in not a few scraps of un-
grammatical Latin : he never, I think, ventures on Greek.   But whether he was the
first to *estropier* the not ugly form " *Cleodora*," I know not.   Perhaps he muddled it with
" Clotilde."

Paul, however, has kept his word with his subscribers by shutting out all sculduddery, even of the mildest kind, and has, if not reconciled, partly conciliated critics by throwing in some tolerable minor personages. Pélagie, Constance's lively friend, has a character which he could somehow manage without Richardsonian vulgarity. Her amiable father, an orchestra musician, who manages to find *des jolies choses* even in a damned piece, is not bad ; and, above all, Pélagie's lover, and, till Edmond's misconduct, his friend, M. Ginguet—a modest Government clerk, who adores his mistress, is constantly snubbed by her, but has his flames crowned at last,—is, though not a particularly novel character, a very well-played part.

One of the author's longer books, *André le Savoyard*, is a curious blend of the *berquinade* with what some
André le Savoyard. English critics have been kind enough to call the "candour" of the more usual French novel. The candour, however, is in very small proportion to the berquinity. This, I suppose, helped it to pass the English censorship of the mid-nineteenth century ; for I remember a translation (it was the first book of the author's I ever read) far away in the 'fifties, among a collection of books where nothing flagrantly scabrous would have been admitted. It begins, and for the most part continues, in an almost completely Marmontelish or Edgeworthian fashion. A selfish glutton and *petit-maître* of a French count, M. de Francornard, loses his way (with a postilion, a valet, and his little daughter, whom he has carried off from her mother) in the hills of Savoy, and is rescued and guested by a good peasant, whom he rewards with a *petit écu* (three *livres*, not five or six). The peasant dies, and his two eldest boys set out for Paris as chimney-sweeps. The elder (eleven-year-old) André himself is befriended by a good Auvergnat water-carrier and his little daughter Manette ; after which he falls in with the Francornards—now, after a fashion, a united family. He is taken into their household and made a sort of protégé by the countess, the child

Adolphine being also very fond of him; while, though in another way, their *soubrette* Lucile, a pretty damsel of eighteen, is fonder still. Years pass, and the fortunate André distributes his affections between the three girls. Manette, though she ends as his wife, is more of a sister at first; Adolphine is an adored and unhoped-for idol; while Lucile (it is hardly necessary to say that it is in the scenes with her that " candour " comes in) is at first a protectress, then a schoolmistress of the school of Cupid, in process of time a mistress in the other sense, and always a very good-natured and unselfish helper. In fact, Manette is so preternaturally good (she can't even be jealous in a sufficiently human way), Adolphine so prettily and at last tragically null, that one really feels inclined to observe to André, if he were worth it, the recondite quotation

Ne sit ancillae tibi amor pudori,

though perhaps seven years *is* a long interval in the first third of life.

A still better instance of the modified *berquinade*—indeed, except for the absence of riotous fun, one of the best of all Paul de Kock's books—is *Jean*, *Jean.* also an example of his middle and ripest period. If translated into English it might have for second title, " or, The History of a Good Lout." The career of Jean Durand (one of the French equivalents for John Brown or Jones or Robinson) we have from the moment of, and indeed a little before, his birth to that crowning of a virtuous young Frenchman's hopes, which consists in his marrying a pretty, amiable, sensible, and well-to-do young widow.[1] Jean is the son of a herbalist

---

[1] This cult of the widow might form the subject of a not uninteresting excursus if we were not confining ourselves to the literary sides of our matter. It has been noticed before (Vol. I. p. 368), and forms one of the most curious differences between the two countries. For, putting Mr. Weller out of the question, I have known far from sentimental critics who thought Trollope's best book by no means improved by the previous experience of Eleanor Bold. Cherolatry in France, however, is not really old : it hardly appears before the eighteenth century. It may be partly due to a more or less conscious idea that perhaps the lady may have got over the obligatory adultery at the expense of her " dear first " and may not think it necessary to repeat. A sort of " measles over."

father who is an eccentric but not a fool, and a mother who is very much of a fool but not in the least eccentric. The child, who is born in the actual presence (result of the usual farcical opening) of a corporal and four fusiliers, is put out to nurse at Saint-Germain in the way they did then, brought home and put out to school, but, in consequence of his mother's absurd spoiling, allowed to learn absolutely nothing, and (though he is not exactly a bad fellow) to get into very bad company. With two of the choicest specimens of this he runs away (having, again by his mother's folly, been trusted with a round sum in gold) at the age of sixteen, and executes a sort of picaresque journey in the environs of Paris, till he is brought to his senses through an actual robbery committed by the worst of his companions. He returns home to find his father dead : and having had a substantial income left him already by an aunt, with the practical control of his mother's resources, he goes on living entirely à sa guise. This involves no positive debauchery or ruination, but includes smoking (then, it must be remembered, almost as great a crime in French as in English middle-class circles), playing at billiards (ditto), and a free use of strong drink and strong language. He spends and gives money freely, but does not get into debt ; flirts with grisettes, but falls into no discreditable entanglement, etc., etc.

His most characteristic peculiarity, however, is his absolute refusal to learn the rudiments of manners. He keeps his hat on in all companies ; neglects all neatness in dress, etc. ; goes (when he *does* go) among ladies with garments reeking of tobacco and a mouth full of strange oaths, and generally remains ignorant of, or recalcitrant to, every form of conventional politeness in speech and behaviour.

The only person of any sense with whom he has hitherto come in contact, an old hairdresser named Bellequeue (it must be remembered that this profession or vocation is not as traditionally ridiculous in French literature as in ours), persuades his mother that the one chance of reforming Jean and making him like other people is to marry him off. They select an eligible *parti*, one Mademoiselle Adelaide Chopard, a young lady of great bodily height, some facial charms, not exactly a fool, but not of the most amiable disposition, and possessed of no actual accomplishment (though she thinks herself almost a " blue ") except that of preserving different fruits in brandy, her father being a retired liqueur manufacturer. Jean, who has never been in the least "in love," has no particular objection to Adelaide, and none at all to the preserved cherries, apricots, etc., and the scenes of his introduction and, after a fashion, proposal to the damsel, with her first resentment at his unceremonious behaviour and later positive attraction by it, are far from bad. Luckily or unluckily—for the marriage might have turned out at least as well as most marriages of the kind—before it is brought about, this French Cymon at last meets his real Iphigenia. Walking rather late at night, he hears a cry, and a footpad (one of his own old comrades, as it happens) rushes past him with a shawl which he has snatched from two ladies. Jean counter-snatches the shawl from him and succours the ladies, one of whom strikes his attention. They ask him to put them into a cab, and go off—grateful, but giving no address. However, he picks up a reticule, which the thief in his fright has dropped, discovers in it the address he wants, and actually ventures to call on Madame Caroline Derville, who possesses, in addition to viduity, all the other attractions catalogued above.

Another scene of farce, which is not so far short of comedy, follows between the lout and the lady, the fun being, among other things, caused by Jean's unconventional strolling about the room, looking at engravings, etc., and showing, by his remarks on things—" The Death of Tasso," " The Marriage of Peleus and Thetis," and the like—that he is utterly uneducated.

There is about half the book to come, but no more abstract can be necessary. The way in which Jean is delivered from his Adelaide and rewarded with his Caroline, if not quite probable (for Adelaide is made to blacken her own character to her rival), is not without ingenuity. And the narrative (which has Paul de Kock's curious "holding" quality for the hour or two one is likely to bestow on it) is diversified by the usual duel, by Jean's noble and rather rash conduct, in putting down his pistols to bestow sacks of five-franc pieces on his two old friends (who try to burgle and—one of them at least—would rather like to murder him), etc., etc.[1] But the real value—for it has some—of the book lies in the vivid sketches of ordinary life which it gives. The curious Cockneydom, diversified by glimpses of a suburban Arcadia, in which the French *bourgeois* of the first half of the nineteenth century seems to have passed his time ; the humours of a *coucou* journey from Paris to Saint-Germain ; all sorts of details of the Durand and Chopard households—supply these. And not the least of them is given by the bachelor ménage of Bellequeue with his eighteen-year-old *bonne* Rose, the story whereof need not sadden or shock even Mrs. Grundy, unless she scents unrecounted, indeed not even hinted at, improprieties. Bellequeue, as noted above, is by no means a fool, and achieves as near an approach to a successful "character" as Paul de Kock has ever drawn ; while Rose plays the same part of piebald angel as Lucile in *André*, with a little more cleverness in her espièglerie and at least no vouched-for unlawfulnesses.

But perhaps if any one wants a single book to judge Paul de Kock by (with one possible exception, to follow this), he cannot do better than take *La Femme, le Mari et l'Amant*, a novel again of his middle period, and one which, if it shows some of his less desirable points, shows them characteristically and with comparatively little offence, while it exhibits what the shopkeepers would, I believe, call " a range of his best lines." The autobiographic hero,

La Femme, le Mari et l'Amant.

---

[1] He also improves his neglected education in a manner not unsuggestive of Prince Giglio. In fact, I fancy there is a good deal of half-latent parody of Paul in Thackeray.

Paul Deligny, is one of his nearest approaches to a gentleman, yet no one can call him insipid or priggish ; the heroine, Augustine Luceval, by marriage Jenneville, is in the same way one of his nearest approaches to a lady, and, though not such a madcap as the similarly situated Frédérique of *Une Gaillarde* (*v. inf.*), by no means mawkish. It is needless to say that these are " l'Amant " and " la Femme," or that they are happily united at the end : it may be more necessary to add that there is no scandal, but at the same time no prunes and prism, earlier. " Le Mari," M. Jenneville, is very much less of a success, being an exceedingly foolish as well as reprobate person, who not only deserts a beautiful, charming, and affectionate wife, but treats his lower-class loves shabbily, and allows himself to be swindled and fooled to the *n*th by an adventuress of fashion and a plausible speculator. On the other hand, one of this book's rather numerous grisettes, Ninie, is of the more if not most gracious of that questionable but not unappetising sisterhood. Dubois, the funny man, and Jolivet, the parsimonious reveller, who generally manages to make his friends pay the bill, are not bad common form of farce. One of the best of Paul's own special scenes, the pancake party, with a bevy of grisettes, is perhaps the liveliest of all such things, and, but for one piece of quite unnecessary Smollettism or Pigaulterie, need only scandalise the " unco guid." The whole has, in unusual measure, that curious *readableness* which has been allowed to most of our author's books. Almost inevitably there is a melodramatic end ; but this, to speak rather Hibernically, is made up for by a minute and curious account, at the beginning, of the actual presentation of a melodrama, with humours of pit, box, and gallery. If the reader does not like the book he will hardly like anything else of its author's ; if he does, he will find plenty of the same sort of stuff, less concentrated perhaps, elsewhere. But if he be a student, as well as a consumer, of the novel, he can hardly fail to see that, at its time and in its kind, it is not so trivial a thing as its subjects and their treat-

ment might, in the abstract, be pronounced to be by the
grave and precise.

Yet somebody may say, " This is all very well, but
what was it that made Major Pendennis laugh ? "
Mon Voisin Raymond. Probably a good many things in a good many
books ; but I do not know any one more likely
to have received that crown than the exception above
mentioned, *Mon Voisin Raymond*, which also bears (to
me) the recommendation of a very competent friend of
mine. My experience is that you certainly do begin
laughing at the very beginning, and that the laughter
is kept up, if not without cessation, with very few intervals, through a remarkable series of comic scenes.
The book, in fact, is Paul de Kock's *Gilbert Gurney*,
and I cannot sink the critic in the patriot to such an
extent as to enable me to put Theodore, even in what
is, I suppose, his best long story, above, or even on a
level with, Paul here.

The central point, as one sees almost at once, is that
this Raymond (I think we are never told his other name),
a not entirely ill-meaning person, but a *fâcheux* of almost
ultra-Molièresque strength, is perpetually spoiling his
unlucky neighbour's, the autobiographic Eugène Dorsan's, sport, and, though sometimes paid out in kind,
bringing calamities upon him, while at last he actually
capots his friend and enemy by making him one of
the *derniers* already mentioned ! This is very bold of
Paul, and I do not know any exact parallel to it. On
the other hand, Eugène is consoled, not only by Raymond's death in the Alps (Paul de Kock is curiously
fond of Switzerland as a place of punishment for his
bad characters), but by the final possession of a certain
Nicette, the very pearl of the grisette kind. We
meet her in the first scene of the story, where Dorsan,
having given the girl a guiltless sojourn of rescue in
his own rooms, is detected and exposed to the malice
of a cast mistress by Raymond. I am afraid that Paul
rather forgot that final sentence of his own first book;
for though Pélagie, Dorsan's erring and unpleasant

wife, dies in the last chapter, I do not observe that an actual Hymen with Nicette " covers the fault " which, after long innocence, she has at last committed or permitted. But perhaps it would have been indecent to contract a second marriage so soon, and it is only postponed to the unwritten first chapter of the missing fifth volume.[1]

The interval between overture and finale is, as has been said or hinted, uncommonly lively, and for once, not only in the final retribution, Paul has distributed the *peine du talion* pretty equally between his personages. Dorsan has already lost another grisette mistress, Caroline (for whose sake he has neglected Nicette), and a *femme du monde*, with whom he has for a short time intrigued ; while in both cases Raymond, though not exactly the cause of the deprivation, has, in his meddling way, been mixed up with it. In yet other scenes we have a travelling magic-lantern exhibition in the Champs Élysées ; a night in the Tivoli Gardens ; an expedition to a party at a country house, which, of course, Raymond's folly upsets, literally as well as metaphorically ; a long (rather too long) account of a musical evening at a very lower-middle-class house ; a roaringly farcical interchange of dinners *en cabinet particulier* at a restaurant, in which Raymond is the victim. But, on the whole, he scores, and is a sort of double cause of the hero's last and greatest misfortune. For it is a lie of his about Nicette which determines Dorsan to make a long-postponed visit to his sister in the country, and submit at last to her efforts to get him married to the exaggeratedly *ingénue* Pélagie, and saddled with her detestable aunt, Madame de Pontchartrain. The end of the book is not quite equal to some other parts of it. But there is abundance of excellent farce, and Nicette might reconcile the veriest sentimentalist.

At one time in England—I cannot speak for the

---

[1] There might have been fifteen or fifty, for the book is more a sequence of scenes than a schematic composition : for which reason the above account of it may seem somewhat *décousu*.

times of his greatest popularity in France—Paul de
Le Barbier Kock's name, except for a vague knowledge
de Paris. of his grisette and *mauvais sujet* studies, was
very mainly connected with *Le Barbier de Paris.* It was
an instance of the constant mistakes which almost all
countries make about foreign authors. I imagine, from
a fresh and recent reading of it, that he probably did
take more trouble with it than with most of his books.
But, unfortunately, instances of lost labour are not confined to literature. The subject and the author are very
ill matched. It is a romance of 1632, and so in a way
competing with the most successful efforts of the great
Romantics. But for such a task Paul had no gifts,
except his invariable one of concocting a readable story.
As for style, imagination, atmosphere, and such high
graces, it would be not so much cruel as absurd to
" enter " the book with *Notre-Dame de Paris* or the
Contes Drolatiques, Le Capitaine Fracasse or the *Chronique
de Charles IX.* But even the lower ways he could not
tread here. He did not know anything about the time,
and his wicked Marquis de Villebelle is not early Louis
Treize at all, but rather late Louis Quinze. He had not
the gift (which Scott first showed and Dumas possessed
in no small measure) of writing his conversations, if
not in actual temporal colour of language, at any rate
in a kind of *lingua franca* suitable to, or at the worst
not flagrantly discordant with, *any* particular time
and *any* particular state of manners. He could throw
in types of the kind so much admired by no less a
person than Sir Philip Sidney—a garrulous old servant, an innocent young girl, a gasconading coward,
a revengeful daughter of Italy, a this and that and the
other. But he could neither make individual character nor vivid historical scene. And so the thing
breaks down.

The barber-hero-villain himself is the most " unconvincing " of barbers (who have profited fiction not
so ill in other cases), of heroes (who are too often unconvincing), and even of villains (who have rather a

habit of being so).[1] Why a man who is represented as
being intensely, diabolically, wicked, but almost diabolically shrewd, should employ, and go on employing, as
his instrument a blundering poltroon like the Gascon
Chaudoreille, is a question which recurs almost throughout the book, and, being unanswered, is almost sufficient
to damn it. And at the end the other question, why
M. le Marquis de Villebelle—represented as, though also
a villain, a person of superior intelligence—when he has
discovered that the girl whom he has abducted and
sought to ruin is really his daughter ; when he has run
upstairs to tell her, has knocked at her locked door, and
has heard a heavy body splashing into the lake under
her window,—why, instead of making his way at once
to the water, he should run about the house for keys,
break into the room, and at last, going to the window,
draw from the fact that " an object shows itself at intervals
on the surface, and appears to be still in a state of agita-
tion," the no doubt quite logical inference that Blanche
is drowning — when, and only then, he precipitates
himself after her,—this question would achieve, if it were
necessary, the damnation.

The fact is, that Paul had no turn for melodrama,
history, or tragic matter of any kind. He wrote nearly
The Pauline a hundred novels, and I neither pretend to
grisette.   have read the whole of them, nor, if I had done
so, should I feel justified in inflicting abstracts on my
readers. As always happens in such cases, the feast
he offers us is " pot-luck," but, as too seldom happens,
the luck of the pot is quite often good. With the grisette,
to whom he did much to give a niche (one can hardly
call it a shrine) in literature, whom he celebrated so
lovingly, and whose gradual disappearance he has so
touchingly bewailed, or with any feminine person of
partly grisettish kind, such as the curious and already

---

[1] I think I have commented elsewhere on the difficulty of villains. It was
agreeable to find confirmation, when this book was already in the printer's hands,
given at an exemption tribunal by a theatrical manager. For six weeks, he said, he
had advertised and done everything possible to supply the place of a good villain, with
no success. And your bad stage villain *may* be comic : while your bad novel villain is
only a bore.

briefly mentioned heroine of *Une Gaillarde*,[1] he is almost invariably happy. The above-mentioned Lucile is not technically a grisette (who should be a girl living on her own resources or in a shop, not in service) nor is Rose in *Jean*, but both have the requirements of the type— *minois chiffonné* (including what is absolutely indispensable, a *nez retroussé*), inexhaustible gaiety, extreme though by no means promiscuous complaisance, thorough good-nature—all the gifts, in short, of Béranger's *bonne fille*, who laughs at everything, but is perfectly capable of good sense and good service at need, and who not seldom marries and makes as good a wife as, "in a higher *spear*," the English "garrison hack" has had the credit of being. Quite a late, but a very successful example, with the complaisance limited to strictly legitimate extent, and the good-nature tempered by a shrewd determination to avenge two sisters of hers who had been weaker than herself, is the Georgette of *La Fille aux Trois Jupons*, who outwits in the cleverest way three would-be gallants, two of them her sisters' actual seducers, and extracts thumping solatia from these for their victims.[2]

On the other hand, the older and, I think, more famous book which suggested the title of this—*L'Homme aux Trois Culottes*, symbolising and in a way giving a history of the times of the Revolution, the Empire, and the Restoration, and finishing with "July"—seems to me again a failure. As I have said, Paul could not manage history, least of all spread-out history like this ; and the characters, or rather personages, though of the lower and lower-middle rank, which he *could* manage best, are to me totally uninteresting. Others may have been, or may be, more fortunate with them.

Others.

So, too, *Le Petit Fils de Cartouche* (which I read before

---

[1] Frédérique, Madame Dauberny (who has, without legal sanction, relieved herself of a loathsome creature whom she has married, and lives a free though not at all immoral life), was not very easy to do, and is very well done.'

[2] This, which is short and thoroughly lively, is, I imagine, the latest of Paul's good books. It is indeed so late that instead of the *jupons*, striped and black and white, of which Georgette has made irreproachable but profitable use, she appears at the *denouement* in a crinoline !

coming across its first part, *Les Enfants du Boulevard*)
did not inspire me with any desire to look up this earlier
novel ; and *La Pucelle de Belleville*, another of Paul's
attempts to depict the unconventional but virtuous
young person, has very slight interest as a story, and is
disfigured by some real examples of the " coarse vulgarity " which has been somewhat excessively charged
against its author generally. *Frère Jacques* is a little
better, but not much.[1]

Something has been said of " periods " ; but, after
all, when Paul has once " got into his stride " there is
little difference on the average. I have read, for instance,
in succession, *M. Dupont*, which, even in the Belgian
piracy, is of 1838, and *Les Demoiselles de Magazin*,
which must be some quarter of a century later—so late,
indeed, that Madame Patti is mentioned in it. The
title-hero of the first—a most respectable man—has an
ingénue, who loves somebody else, forced upon him,
experiences more recalcitrance than is usually allowed
in such cases, and at last, with Paul's usual unpoetical
injustice, is butchered to make way for the Adolphe of the
piece, who does not so very distinctly deserve his Eugénie.
It contains also one Zélie, who is perhaps the author's
most impudent, but by no means most unamusing or
most disagreeable, grisette. *Les Demoiselles de Magazin*
gives us a whole posy of these curious flower-weeds of
the garden of girls—pretty, middling, and ugly, astonishingly virtuous, not virtuous at all, and *couci-couci* (one
of them, by the way, is nicknamed " Bouci-Boula,"
because she is plump and plain), but all good-natured,
and on occasion almost noble-sentimented ; a guileless
provincial ; his friend, who has a mania for testing his
wife's fidelity, and who accomplishes one of Paul's
favourite fairy-tale or rather pantomime endings by
coming down with fifteen thousand francs for an old
mistress (she has lost her beauty by the bite of a parrot,

---

[1] The most interesting thing in it is a longish account by Jacques of his association
with a travelling quack and fortune-teller, which at once reminds one of *Japhet in Search
of a Father*. The resemblances and the differences are almost equally characteristic.

and is the mother of the extraordinarily virtuous Marie) ; a scapegrace " young first " or half-first ; a superior ditto, who is an artist, who rejects the advances of Marie's mother, and finally marries Marie herself, etc. etc. You might change over some of the personages and scenes of the two books ; but they are scarcely unequal in such merit as they possess, and both lazily readable in the fashion so often noted.

If any one asks where this readableness comes from, I do not think the answer is very difficult to give, and it will of itself supply a fuller explanation (the words apology or excuse are not really necessary) for the space here allotted to its possessor. It comes, no doubt, in the first place, from sheer and unanalysable narrative faculty, the secret of the business, the mystery in one sense of the mystery in the other. But it also comes, as it seems to me, from the fact that Paul de Kock is the very first of French novelists who, though he has no closely woven plot, no striking character, no vivid conversation or arresting phrases, is thoroughly *real*, and in the good, not the bad, sense *quotidian*. The statement may surprise some people and shock others, but I believe it can be as fully sustained as that other statement about the most different subject possible, the *Astrée*, which was quoted from Madame de Sévigné in the last volume. Paul knew the world he dealt with as well almost as Dickens [1] knew his very different but somewhat corresponding one ; and, unlike Dickens, the Frenchman had the good sense to meddle very little [2] with worlds that he did not know. Of course it would be simply *bête* to take it for granted that the majority of Parisian shop- and work- and servant-girls have or had either the beauty or the amiability or the less praiseworthy qualities of his grisettes. But somehow or other one feels that the general *ethos* of the class has been caught. [3] His *bourgeois* interiors

---

[1] Of course I am not comparing him with Paul on any other point.

[2] Except in regard to the historical and other matters noticed above, hardly at all.

[3] For a picture of an actual grisette, drawn by perhaps the greatest master of artistic realism (adjective and substantive so seldom found in company !) who ever lived, see that *Britannia* article of Thackeray's before referred to—an article, for a long time, unre-

and outings have the same real and not merely stagy
quality; though his melodramatic or pantomimic endings
may smack of "the boards" a little.   The world to
which he holds up the mirror may be a rather vulgar
sort of Vanity Fair, but there are unfortunately few places
more real than Vanity Fair, and few things less unreal
than vulgarity.

The last sentence may lead to a remark of a graver
kind than has been often indulged in here.   Thackeray
defined his own plan in *Vanity Fair* itself as at least
partly an attempt to show people "living without God
in the world."   There certainly is not much godliness
in the book, but he could not keep it out altogether;
he would have been false to nature (which he never
was) if he had.   In Paul de Kock's extensive work, on
the other hand, the exclusion is complete.   It is not that
there is any expressed Voltairianism as there is in Pigault.
But though the people are married in church as well as
at the *mairie*, and I remember one casual remark about a
mother and her daughter going to mass, the whole
spiritual region—religious, theological, ecclesiastical, and
what not—is left blank.   I do not remember so much
as a *curé* figuring personally, though there may be one.
And it is worth noting that Paul was born in 1794,
and therefore passed his earliest childhood in the time
when the Republic had actually gagged, if not stifled,
religion in France—when children grew up, in some
cases at any rate, without ever hearing the name of God,
except perhaps in phrases like *pardieu* or *parbleu*.   It is
not my business or my intention to make reflections or
draw inferences; I merely indicate the fact.

Another fact—perhaps so obvious already that it
hardly needs stating—is that Paul de Kock is not exactly
the person to "take a course of," unless under such

---

printed, and therefore, till a comparatively short time ago, practically unknown.   This
and its companion articles from the *Britannia* and the *Corsair*, all of 1840–41, but sum-
marising ten or twelve years' knowledge of Paris, form, with the same author's *Paris
Sketch Book* (but as representing a more mature state of his genius), the best commentary on Paul de Kock.   They may be found together in the third volume of the
Oxford Thackeray edited by the present writer.

conditions as those under which Mr. Carlyle took a
course of a far superior writer, Marryat, and was (one
regrets to remember) very ungrateful for the good it
did him. He is (what some of his too critical countrymen
have so falsely called Dumas) a mere *amuseur*, and his
amusement is somewhat lacking in variety. Nevertheless, few critical readers [1] of the present history will,
I think, consider the space given to him here as wasted.
He was a really powerful schoolmaster to bring the
popular novel into still further popularity ; and he made
a distinct advance upon such persons as Pigault-Lebrun
and Ducray-Duminil—upon the former in comparative
decency, if not of subject, of expression ; upon the latter
in getting close to actual life ; and upon both in what may
be called the *furniture* of his novels—the scene-painting,
property-arranging, and general staging. This has been
most unfairly assigned to Balzac as originator, not merely
in France, but generally, whereas, not to mention our
own men, Paul began to write nearly a decade before
the beginning of those curious efforts, half-prenatal, of
Balzac's, which we shall deal with later, and nearly
two decades before *Les Chouans*. And, horrifying as
the statement may be to some, I venture to say that his
mere *mise en scène* is sometimes, if not always, better than
Balzac's own, though he may be to that younger contemporary of his as a China orange to Lombard Street in
respect of plot, character, thought, conversation, and all
the higher elements, as they are commonly taken to be,
of the novel.

It has been said that the filling-up of this chapter,
as to the rank and file of the novelists of 1800–1830,
The minors has been a matter of some difficulty in the
before 1830. peculiar circumstances of the case. I have,
however, been enabled to read, for the first time or afresh,

---

[1] Unless they start from the position that an English writer on the French novel
is bound to follow—or at least to pay express attention to—French criticism of it.
This position I respectfully but unalterably decline to accept. A critical tub that has
no bottom of its own is the very worst Danaid's vessel in all the household gear of
literature.

examples not merely of those writers who have preserved
any notoriety, but of some who have not, and to assure
myself on fair grounds that I need not wait for further
exploration. The authors now to be dealt with have
already been named. But I may add another novelist on
the very eve of 1830, Auguste Ricard, whose name I
never saw in any history of literature, but whose work
fell almost by accident into my hands, and seems worth
taking as " pot-luck."

Isabelle de Montolieu—a Swiss by birth but a French-
woman by extraction, and Madame de Crousaz by her
first marriage—was a friend of Gibbon's friend Georges Deyverdun, and indeed of Gibbon himself, who, she says, actually offered to father her novel. Odd as this seems, there really is in *Caroline de Lichtfield*[1] not merely something which distinguishes it from the ordinary " sensibility " tale of its time (it was first printed at Lausanne in 1786), but a kind of crispness of thought now and then which sometimes does suggest Gibbon, in something the same way as that in which Fanny Burney suggests Johnson. This is indeed mixed with a certain amount of mere " sensibility " jargon,[2] as when a lover, making a surprisingly honest confession to his beloved, observes that he is going " to destroy those sentiments which had made him forget how unworthy he was of them," or when the lady (who has been quite guiltless, and has at last fallen in love with her own husband) tells this latter of her weakness in these very engaging words : " Yes ! I did love Lindorf; *at least I think I recognise some relation between the sentiments I had for him and those that I feel at present !* "

A kind of affection was avowed in the last volume for

[1] The scene and society are German, but the author knows the name to have been originally English.
[2] Such, perhaps, as Gibbon himself may have used while he " sighed as a lover " and before he " obeyed as a son." It should perhaps be said that Mme. de Montolieu produced many other books, mostly translations—among the latter a French version of *The Swiss Family Robinson*.

the " Phoebus " of the " heroics," and something similar
may be confessed for this " Jupiter Pluvius,"
this mixture of tears and stateliness, in the
Sentimentalists.   But Madame de Montolieu
has emerged from the most *larmoyante* kind of " sensible "
comedy.   If her book had been cut a little shorter, and if
(which can be easily done by the reader) the eccentric
survival of a *histoire*, appended instead of episodically
inserted, were lopped off, *Caroline de Lichtfield* would not
be a bad story.   The heroine, having lost her mother,
has been brought up to the age of fifteen by an amiable
canoness, who (to speak rather Hibernically) ought to
have been her mother but wasn't, because the actual
mother was so much richer.   She bears no malice, however, even to the father who, well preserved in looks,
manners, and selfishness, is Great Chamberlain to
Frederick the Great.

That very unsacred majesty has another favourite,
a certain Count von Walstein, who is ambassador of
Prussia at St. Petersburg.   It pleases Frederick, and of
course his chamberlain, that Caroline, young as she is,
shall marry Walstein.   As the girl is told that her
intended is not more than thirty, and knows his position
(she has, naturally, been brought up without the slightest
idea of choosing for herself), she is not displeased.   She
will be a countess and an ambassadress ;   she will have
infinite jewels ;   her husband will probably be handsome
and agreeable ;   he will certainly dance with her, and may
very possibly not object to joining in innocent sports
like butterfly-catching.   So she sets off to Berlin quite
cheerfully, and the meeting takes place.   Alas !   the
count is a " civil count " (as Beatrice says) enough, but
he is the reverse of handsome and charming.   He has
only one eye ;   he has a huge scar on his cheek ;   a wig
(men, remember, were beginning to " wear their own
hair "), a bent figure, and a leaden complexion.   Caroline,
promptly and not unnaturally, " screams and disappears
like lightning."   Nor can any way be found out of
this extremely awkward situation.   The count (who is

a thoroughly good fellow) would give Caroline up, though he has taken a great fancy to her, and even the selfish Lichtfield tries (or *says* he tries) to alter his master's determination.   But Frederick of course persists, and with a peculiarly Frederician enjoyment in conferring an ostensible honour which is in reality a punishment, sees the marriage ceremony carried out under his own eye. · Caroline, however, exemplifies in combination certain old adages to the effect that there is " No will, no wit like a woman's."   She submits quite decently in public, but immediately after the ceremony writes a letter [1] to her husband (whose character she has partly, though imperfectly, gauged) requesting permission to retire to the canoness till she is a little older, under a covert but quite clearly intelligible threat of suicide in case of refusal.   There are of course difficulties, but the count, like a man and a gentleman, consents at once ; the father, *bon gré mal gré*, has to do so, and the King, a tyrant who has had his way, gives a sulky and qualified acquiescence. . What follows need only be very rapidly sketched.   After a little time Caroline sees, at her old-new home, an engaging young man, a Herr von Lindorf ; and matters, though she is quite virtuous, are going far when she receives an enormous epistle [1] from her lover, confessing that he himself is the author of her husband's disfigurement (under circumstances discreditable to himself and creditable to Walstein), enclosing, too, a very handsome portrait of the count *as he was*, and but for this disfigurement might be still.   What happens then nobody ought to need, or if he does he does not deserve, to be told.   There is no greatness about this book, but to any one who has an eye for consequences it will prob- ably seem to have some future in it.   It shows the break- ing of the Sensibility mould and the running of the materials into a new pattern as early as 1786.   In 1886 M. Feuillet or M. Theuriet would of course have clothed the story-skeleton differently, but one can quite imagine

[1] In dealing with " Sensibility " earlier, it was pointed out how extensively things were dealt with by *letter*. In such cases as these the fashion came in rather usefully.

either making use of a skeleton by no means much altered. M. Rod would have given it an unhappy ending, but one can see it in his form likewise.[1]

Of Stéphanie Félicité, Comtesse de Genlis, it were tempting to say a good deal personally if we did bio-
Madame graphies here when they can easily be found
de Genlis elsewhere.   How she became a canoness at
iterum. six years old, and shortly afterwards had for her ordinary dress (with something supplementary, one hopes) the costume of a Cupid, including quiver and wings ; how she combined the offices of governess to the Orleans children and mistress to their father ; how she also combined the voluptuousness and the philanthropy of her century by taking baths of milk and afterwards giving that milk to the poor ;[2] how, rather late in life, she attained the very Crown - Imperial of governess-ship in being chosen by Napoleon to teach him and his Court how to behave ; and how she wrote infinite books—many of them taking the form of fiction —on education, history, religion, everything, can only be summarised.   The last item of the summary alone concerns us, and that must be dealt with summarily too. *Mlle. de Clermont*—a sort of historico-" sensible " story in style, and evidently imitated from *La Princesse de Clèves*—is about the best thing she did as literature ; but we dealt with that in the last volume[3] among its congeners.   In my youth all girls and some boys knew *Adèle et Théodore* and *Les Veillées du Château*.   From a later book, *Les Battuécas*, George Sand is said to have said that she learnt Socialism : and the fact is that Stéphanie Félicité had seen so much, felt so much, read so much, and done so much that, having also a quick feminine wit, she could put into her immense body of work all sorts of crude second-hand notions.   The two last things that I read of hers to complete my idea of her were *Le Comte*

---

[1] The treatment of the authors here mentioned, *infra*, will, I hope, show that the introduction of their names is not merely " promiscuous."

[2] I am quite prepared to be told that this was somebody else or nobody at all.   " Moi, je dis Madame de Genlis."

[3] P. 436.

de Corke and *Les Chevaliers du Cygne*, books at least
possessing an element of surprise in their titles.   The
first is a collection of short tales, the title-piece inspired
and prefaced by an account of the Boyle family, and all
rather like a duller and more spun-out Miss Edgeworth,
the common relation to Marmontel accounting for this.
The concluding stories of each volume, " Les Amants
sans Amour " and " Sanclair," are about the best.   *Les
Chevaliers du Cygne* is a book likely to stir up the Old
Adam in some persons.   It was, for some mysterious
reason, intended as a sort of appendix—for " grown-
ups "—to the *Veillées du Château*, and is supposed to have
incorporated parabolically many of the lessons of the
French Revolution (it appeared in 1795).   But though
its three volumes and eleven hundred pages deal with
Charlemagne, and the Empress Irene, and the Caliph
" Aaron " (Haroun), and Oliver (Roland is dead at
Roncevaux), and Ogier, and other great and beloved
names; though the authoress, who was an untiring picker-
up of scraps of information, has actually consulted (at
least she quotes) Sainte-Palaye; there is no faintest
flavour of anything really Carlovingian or Byzantine
or Oriental about the book, and the whole treatment is
in the *pre*-historical-novel style.   Indeed the writer of
the *Veillées* was altogether of the *veille*—the day just
expired—or of the transitional and half-understood
present—never of the past seen in some perspective, of
the real new day, or, still less, of the morrow.

The batch of books into which we are now going to
dip does not represent the height of society and the
The minor interests of education like Madame de Genlis ;
popular novel nor high society again and at least strivings
—Ducray-
Duminil—*Le* after the new day, like the noble author of the
Petit Caril- Solitaire who will follow them.   They are, in
lonneur. fact, the minors of the class in which Pigault-
Lebrun   earlier   and   Paul   de   Kock   later   represent
such " majority " as it possesses.   But they ought not
to be neglected here : and I am bound to say that the
very considerable trouble they cost me has not been

wholly vain.[1] The most noted of the whole group, and one of the earliest, Ducray-Duminil's *Lolotte et Fanfan*, escaped[2] a long search; but the possession and careful study of the four volumes of his *Petit Carillonneur* (1819) has, I think, enabled me to form a pretty clear notion of what not merely *Lolotte* (the second title of which is *Histoire de Deux Enfants abandonnés dans une île déserte*), but *Victor ou L'Enfant de la Forêt, Cœlina ou L'Enfant du Mystère, Jules ou le Toit paternel*, or any other of the author's score or so of novels would be like.

The book, I confess, was rather hard to read at first, for Ducray-Duminil is a sort of Pigault-Lebrun *des enfants*; he writes rather kitchen French; the historic present (as in all these books) loses its one excuse by the wearisome abundance of it, and the first hundred pages (in which little Dominique, having been unceremoniously tumbled out of a cabriolet[3] by wicked men, and left to the chances of divine and human assistance, is made to earn his living by framed-bell-ringing in the streets of Paris) became something of a *corvée*. But the author is really a sort of deacon, though in no high division of his craft. He expands and duplicates his situations with no inconsiderable cunning, and the way in which new friends, new enemies, and new should-be-indifferent persons are perpetually trying to find out whether the boy is really the Dominique d'Alinvil of Marseilles, whose father and mother have been foully made away with, or not, shows command of its own particular kind of ingenuity. Intrigues of all sorts—violent and other (for his wicked relative, the Comtesse d'Alinvil, is always trying to play Potiphar's wife to him, and there is a certain Mademoiselle Gothon who would not figure as she does here in a book by Mr. Thomas Day)—beset

---

[1] The kind endeavours of the Librarian of the London Library to obtain some in Paris itself were fruitless, but the old saying about neglecting things at your own door came true. My friend Mr. Kipling urged me to try Mr. George Gregory of Bath, and Mr. Gregory procured me almost all the books I am noticing in this division.

[2] The British Museum (see Preface) being inaccessible to me.

[3] Readers will doubtless remember that the too wild career of this kind of vehicle, charioteered by wicked aristocrats, has been among the thousand-and-three causes assigned for the French Revolution.

him constantly ; he is induced not merely to trust his
enemies, but to distrust his friends ; there is a good deal
of underground work and of the explained supernatural ;
a benevolent musician ; an excellent curé ; a rather
" coming " but agreeable Adrienne de Surval, who,
close to the end of the book, hides her trouble in the bosom
of her aunt while Dominique presses her hand to his
heart (the aunt seems here superfluous), etc., etc.   Altogether the book is, to the historian, a not unsatisfactory
one, and joins its evidence to that of Pigault as showing
that new sources of interest and new ways of dealing
with them are being asked for and found.   In filling up
the map of general novel-development and admitting
English examples, we may assign to its author a place
between Mrs. Radcliffe and the *Family Herald* : confining
ourselves to French only, he has again, like Pigault,
something of the credit of making a new start.   He may
appeal to the taste of the vulgar (which is not quite the
same sort of thing as " a vulgar taste "), but he sees
that the novel is capable of providing general pastime,
and he does his best to make it do so.

" The other Ducange," whose patronymic appears
to have been Brahain, and who perhaps took the name
V. Ducange.   of the great scholar [1] for the sake of contrast,
was even more famous for his melodramas [2]
than for his fiction, one piece especially, " Trente Ans,
ou La Vie d'un Joueur," having been among the triumphs
of the Porte-Saint-Martin and of Frédérick Lemaître.
As a novelist he did not write for children like Ducray-
Duminil, and one of his novels contains a boastful preface
scoffing at and glorying in the accusations of impropriety
brought against him. I have found nothing very
shocking in those books of his which I have read, and I
certainly have not thought it necessary to extend my
acquaintance in search of it.   He seems to have been a

---

[1] Of course the author of the glossaries himself was, by actual surname, Dufresne,
Ducange being a seignory.

[2] It should be observed that a very large number of these minor novels, besides those
specially mentioned as having undergone the process, from Ducray's downwards, were
melodramatised.

quarrelsome sort of person, for he got into trouble not only with the moralists, not only with the Restoration government, but with the Academy, which he attacked ; and he is rather fond of " scratchy " references such as " On peut mériter encore quelque intérêt sans être un Amadis, un Vic-van-Vor [poor Fergus !], un Han, ou un Vampire." But his intrinsic merit as a novelist did not at first seem to me great. A book worse

L'Artiste et le Soldat. charpenté than that just quoted from, *L'Artiste et le Soldat,* I have seldom read. The first of its five volumes is entirely occupied with the story (not badly, though much too voluminously told) of a captain who has lost his leg at Waterloo, and though tended by a pretty and charming daughter, is in great straits till helped by a mysterious Black Nun, who loves *les militaires,* and has been entrusted with money to help them by the Empress Josephine. The second, " without with your leave or by your leave " of any kind,[1] jumps back to give us, under a different name for a long time, the early history of this captain, which occupies two whole volumes and part of a third (the fourth of the book). Then another abrupt shift introduces us to the " artist," the younger brother, who bears a *third* name, itself explained by another jump back of great length. Then a lover turns up for Suzanne, the captain's daughter, and we end the fifth volume with a wedding procession in ten distinct carriages.

Ludovica ou Le Testament de Waterloo, a much later book, was, the author tells us, finished in June 1830

Ludovica. under the fiendish tyranny of " all-powerful bigots, implacable Jesuits, and restored marquises " ; but the glorious days of July came ; a new dynasty, " jeune, forte, sincère " (Louis Philippe " young and sincere " !), was on the throne ; the ship of state entered the vast sea of liberty ; France revived ; all Europe seemed to start from its shroud—and *Ludovica* got published. But the author's joy was a little dashed

---

[1] That is to say, in the text : the second title of the whole book, " *ou Les Enfants de Maître Jacques,*" does in some sort give a warning, though it is with Maître Jacques rather than with his children that the fresh start is made.

by the sense that, unlike its half-score of forerunners, the book had not to battle with the bigots and the Jesuits and the " restored marquises "—the last a phrase which has considerable charms of suggestion.

All this, of course, has its absurd side ; but it shows, by way of redemption, that Ducange, in one of the many agreeable phrases of his country, " did not go to it with a dead hand." He seems, indeed, to have been a thoroughly " live " person, if not a very wise one : and *Ludovica* begins with a rousing situation—a crowd and block in the streets of Paris, brought about by nobody quite knows what, but ending in a pistol-shot, a dead body, the flight of the assassin, the dispersal of the crowd by the *gendarmes*, and finally the discovery by a young painter, who has just returned from seeing his mother at Versailles, of a very youthful, very pretty, and very terrified girl, speaking an unknown tongue, and not understanding French, who has fled for refuge into a dark alley ending in a flight of cellar-steps. It is to the point that among the confused cries attending the disturbance have been some about a girl being carried off.

It must be admitted that this is not unpromising, and I really think *Ludovica* (with a caution as to the excessive prolixity of its kind and time) might be recommended to lovers of the detective novel, of which it is a rather early sample. I have confessed, in a later chapter, that this particular " wanity " is not my favourite ; but I found myself getting through M. Victor Ducange's six volumes—burdened rather than ballasted as they are by political outbursts, rather " thorn-crackling " attempts at humour, and the like—with considerably less effort than has sometimes attended similar excursions. If they had been three instead of six I hardly think I should have felt the collar at all. The superiority to *L'Artiste et le Soldat* is remarkable. When honest Jules Janin attributed to Ducange " une érudition peu commune," he must either have been confusing Victor with Charles, or, which is more probable, exhibiting his own lack of the quality he refers to. Ducange does quote tags of Latin : but erudition which makes Proserpine the daughter of *Cybele*, though certainly *peu commune* in one sense, is not so in the other.   The purposes and the jokes, as has been said, may bore ; and though the style is better than Ducray's, it would not of itself " over-stimulate."   But the man is really almost prodigal of incident, and does not manage it badly.

Here, you have Ludovica's father and mother (the former of whom has been crimped to perform a marriage under the impression that he is a priest, whereas he is really a colonel of dragoons) escaping through a hole at the back of a picture from a skylighted billiard-room.   There, an enterprising young man, " sitting out " at a ball, to attend which he has disguised himself, kisses his partner,[1] and by that pleasing operation dislodges half his borrowed moustache.   It falls, alas ! on her hand, she takes it for a spider, screams, and so attracts an unwelcome public.   Later in the same evening he finds himself shut up in the young lady's bedroom, and hears her and her mother talking secrets which very nearly concern him.   The carrying off of Ludovica from Poland to Paris is very smartly managed (I am not sure that the great Alexander or one of his " young men " did not borrow some details from it for the arrest of D'Artagnan and Porthos after their return from England), and the way in which she and a double of hers, Trinette van Poupenheim, are mixed up is really clever. So is the general cross-purposing.   Cabmen turn up just when they should ; and though letters dropped out of pockets are as common as blackberries, I know few better excuses for such carelessness than the fact that you have pulled the letter out with a silk wrapper, which you proceed to fold tenderly round the beautiful neck of a damsel in a cab somewhere about midnight.   A holograph will made on the eve of Waterloo and preserved for fifteen years by the faithful depositary ; a good

---

[1] He has, though unknown and supposed to be an intruder, carried her off from an English adorer—a sort of Lovelace-Byron, whose name is Lord Gousberycharipay (an advance on Paul de Kock and even Parny in the nomenclature of the English peerage), and who inserts h's before French words !

doctor, of course ; many bad Jesuits, of course ; another,
and this time virtuous, though very impudent, carrying-
off of the *other* young woman from the clutches of the
hated *congréganistes* ;[1] a boghei ;[2] a jokei ; a third
enlèvement of the real Ludovica, who escapes by a cellar-
trap ; and many other agreeable things, end in the complete defeat of the wicked and the marriage of the good
to the tune of *four* couples, the thing being thus done to
the last in Ducange's usual handsome manner.[3] I do
not know whether *Ludovica* was melodramatised. *Le
Jésuite* of the same year by Ducange and the great Pixéré-
court looks rather like it ; and so does *Il y a Seize Ans*
of a year later, which he seems to have written alone.
But if it was not it ought to have been. The half-mous-
tache-spider-kissing-screaming scene, and the brilliant
youth retreating through the laughing crowd with the
other half of his decoration, might have reconciled even
me to the theatre.

A short account of the last novel (except *Le Solitaire*)
mentioned above must stand for sample, not merely of
the dozen other works of its author, Auguste
Ricard, but for many more advertised on
the fly-leaves of this time, and long since
made "alms for oblivion." Their titles,
Le Portier, *La Grisette*, *Le Marchand de Coco*, by Ricard
himself, on one side, *L'Homme des Ruines*, *Bleack-*
(sic) *Beard*, *La Chambre Rouge* (by a certain Dinocourt)
on the other, almost tell their whole story—the story of
a range (to use English terms once more) between the
cheap followers of Anne Radcliffe and G. W. M. Reynolds. *L'Ouvreuse de Loges*, through which I have
conscientiously worked, inclines to the latter kind, being

*Auguste
Ricard—
L'Ouvreuse
de Loges.*

---

[1] If novels do not exaggerate the unpopularity of these persons (strictly the lay
members of the S.J., but often used for the whole body of religious orders and their lay
partisans), the success of "July" needs little further explanation.

[2] That is to say, not a bogey, but a buggy.

[3] Here is another instance. Ludovica's father and a bad Russo-Prussian colonel
have to be finished off at Waterloo. One might suppose that Waterloo itself would
suffice. But no : they must engage in single combat, and even then not kill each other,
the Russian's head being carried off by some kind of a cannon-ball and the Frenchman's breast pierced by half a dozen Prussian lances. This is really "good measure."

anti-monarchic, anti-clerical, anti-aristocratic (though it admits that these aristocrats are terrible fellows for behaving in a way which the *roturier* cannot imitate, however hard he tries), and anti-things-in-general. Its title-heroine is a bad old woman, who " keeps the door " in the Elizabethan sense as well as theatrically. Its real hero is a *ci-devant* duke ; malversator under the Republic ; supposed but not real victim of the September-briseurs ; atheist ; winner and loser of several fortunes ; and at last *particulier* of Paris under a feigned name, with an apartment full of *bric-à-brac*, a drawer full of little packets of money, after the expenditure of the last of which he proposes to blow his brains out ; tall man of stature and of his hands, etc., etc. The book is in a way one of purpose, inculcating the danger of wooing opera-girls, and instancing it with three very weak young men, another duke, a rich young *parvenu*, and a musician. Of these the first and the last are, with their wives, rather arbitrarily saved from the clutches into which they have fallen, by the mysterious " M. Luc," while the other comes to a very bad end. The novel, which is in five volumes, is, like most of those mentioned in this section, not of the kind that one would read by preference. But it is a very fair specimen of the " below stairs " romance which sometimes prepares the way for others, fit to take their places above stairs. And so it has its place here.[1]

It has been pointed out more than once that though neglect of such books as these may be perfectly natural and probable in the average reader, such

The import-ance of these minors not inconsider-able.

neglect—and still more any contempt of them —is, though it may not be unnatural, utterly unscholarly and uncritical from the point of view of history. Their authors themselves learnt something from their own mistaken experiments, and their

---

[1] Ousting others which deserved the place better ? It may be so, but one may per-haps " find the whole " without particularising everything. Of short books especially, from Fiévée's *Dot de Suzette* (1798), which charmed society in its day, to Eugénie Foa's *Petit Robinson de Paris* (1840), which amused *me* when I was about ten years old, there were no end if one talked.

successors learnt a good deal more. They found that
" sculduddery " was not a necessary attraction. Ducray
does not avail himself of it, and Ducange seems to have left
it off. They did not give up, but they came less and less
to depend upon, extravagant incident, violent peripeteias, cheap supernaturalities, etc. But the most important thing about them perhaps is the evidence they
give of learning what has been called their " business."
Already, to a great extent if not wholly, that earliest
obsession and preoccupation of the novelist—the idle
anxiety to answer the question, " How do you know all
these things ? "—has begun to disappear. This is rather
less the case with another foolish fancy—the belief that it
is necessary to account not merely for what we call the
consequents, but for the antecedents of all the characters
(at least those of any importance) that you introduce.
There can be no doubt that this was one of the objects,
as it was part of the original cause, of the mistaken *Histoire*
system, which made you, when or soon after you introduced a personage, " tell us all about it," as the children
say, in a separate inset tale. You did not now do this,
but you made, as in the capital instance of Victor Ducange,
huge diversions, retrospects, episodes, in the body of the
story itself. This method, being much less skippable
than the inset by those who did not want it, was not likely
to continue, and so applied the cure to its own ill. And
yet further, as novels multiplied, the supposed necessity
of very great length tended to disappear. The seven or
eight volumes of the eighteenth century, which had replaced the twelves and twenties of the seventeenth, shrank
to six (*Ludovica*), five (*L'Artiste et Le Soldat* and *l'Ouvreuse de Loges*), four (*Le Petit Carillonneur*), and then
three or two, though later the historical kind swelled
again, and the almost invariable single volume did not
establish itself till the middle of the century. As a consequence again of this, the enormous delay over single
situations tended, though very slowly, to disappear.
It is one of the merits of Pigault-Lebrun that he is not
a great sinner in verbosity and prolixity : his contem-

porary minors of this volume are far more peccant in this kind.

Le Solitaire is a book which I have been " going to read " for some fifty years, but by some accident did not till the present occasion.   I knew it generally as one of the vedettes of Romanticism, and as extremely popular in its own day : also as having been, with its author's other work in poem and play and prose fiction, the subject of some ridicule.   But till I read it, and some things about it, I never knew how well it deserved that ridicule and yet how very popular it was, and how really important is its position in the history of the Romantic movement, and so of the French novel and French literature generally. It was published at the end of January 1821, and at the end of November a seventh edition appeared, with an elaborate *Io Triumphe !* from the publisher.   Not only had there been those seven editions (which, it must be remembered in fairness, represent at least seventy at the other end of the century [1]), but it had been translated into four foreign languages ; *fourteen* dramas had been based on it, some half of which had been at least conditionally accepted for performance ; painters of distinction were at work on subjects from it ; it had reached the stages of Madrid and of London (where one critic had called it " a very beautiful composition "), while French approval had been practically unanimous.   Nay, a game had been founded thereon, and—crowning, but perhaps rather ominous honour—somebody had actually published a burlesque imitation.

I have seldom read greater rubbish than *Le Solitaire*. It is a historical-romantic story (the idolatrous preface refers both to Scott and to Byron), and bears also strong, if sometimes distinctly unfortunate, resemblances to Mrs. Radcliffe, the Germans, and Chateaubriand.   The scene is that of Charles the Bold's defeat at Morat : and the " Solitary " is Charles himself—the identification of his body after the decisive overthrow at Nancy *was* a

The
Vicomte
d'Arlincourt
—*Le Solitaire.*

---

[1] *V. inf.* on M. Ohnet's books.

little doubtful—who has hidden there partly to expiate, by good deeds, his crime of massacring the monks of the adjoining Abbey of Underlach, and partly to avail himself of a local tradition as to a *Fantôme Sanglant*, who haunts the neighbourhood, and can be conveniently played by the aid of a crimson mantle. The slaughter of the monks, however, is not the only event or circumstance which links Underlach to the crimes of Charles, for it is now inhabited by a Baron d'Herstall (whose daughter, seduced by the Duke, has died early) and his niece, Elodie de Saint-Maur, whose father, a former favourite of the Burgundian, that prince has killed in one of his fits of rage. Throw in a local priest, Anselm, and you have what may be called the chief characters; but a good Count Ecbert de Norindall, a wicked Prince of Palzo, and divers others figure. Everybody, including the mysterious Bleeding-Phantom-Solitary-Duke him- self, falls in love with Elodie,[1] and she is literally " carried off " (that is to say, shouldered) several times, once by the alarming person in the crimson shroud, but always rescued, till it is time for her to die and be followed by him. There are endless " alarums and excursions "; some of the *not* explained supernatural; woods, caves, ruins, underground passages—entirely at discretion. Catherine Morland would have been perfectly happy with it.

It is not, however, because it contains these things that it has been called " rubbish." A book might contain them all—Mrs. Radcliffe's own do, with the aggravation of the explained wonders—and not be that. It is because of the extraordinary silliness of the style and sentiments. I should imagine that M. d'Arlincourt was trying to write like his brother viscount, the author of *Les Martyrs*, and a pretty mess he has made of it. " Le char de la nuit roulait silencieux sur les plaines du ciel " (p. 3). " L'entrée du jour venait de s'élancer

---

[1] Many people have probably noticed the frequency of this name—not a very pretty one in itself, and with no particular historical or other attraction—in France and French of the earlier nineteenth century. It was certainly due to *Le Solitaire*.

radieuse du palais de l'Aurore." " L'amante de l'Érèbe et la mère des Songes [1] avait achevé la moitié de sa course ténébreuse," etc., etc. The historic present is constantly battling with the more ordinary tenses—the very same sentence sometimes contains both. And this half-blown bladder of a style conveys sentiments as feebly pompous as itself. The actual story, though no great thing, is, if you could strip it of its froth and fustian, not so very bad : as told it is deplorable.

At the same time its mere existence—much more the fury of acceptance which for the moment greeted it—shows what that moment wanted. It wanted Romance, and in default of better it took *Le Solitaire*.

An occasional contrast of an almost violent kind may be permitted in a work requiring something more than merely catalogue-composition. It can hardly be found more appropriately than by concluding this chapter, which began with the account of Paul de Kock, by one of Charles Nodier.

To the student and lover of literature there is scarcely a more interesting figure in French literary history,

Nodier. though there are many greater. Except a few scraps (which, by one of the odd ways of the book-world, actually do not appear in some editions of his *Œuvres Choisies*), he did nothing which had the quality of positive greatness in it. But he was a considerable influence : and even more of a " sign." Younger than Chateaubriand and Madame de Staël, but far older than any of the men of 1830 proper, he may be said in a way to have, in his single person, played in France that part of schoolmaster to Romanticism, which had been distributed over two generations and many personalities in England ; and which Germany, after a fashion, did without, at the cost of a few undisciplined and quickly overbloomed master-years. Although he was born in

---

[1] If any proper moral reader is disturbed at this conjunction of *amante* and *mère*, he will be glad to know that M. d'Arlincourt elsewhere regularises the situation and calls Night "*l'épouse* d'Érèbe."

1780, nine years before the Revolution itself, he under-went German and English influences early, " took " Wertherism, Terrorism,[1] and other maladies of that *fin de siècle* with the utmost facility, and produced divers ultra-Romantic things long before 1830 itself. But he had any number of literary and other avocations or distractions. He was a kind of entomologist and botanist, a kind of philologist (one is a little astonished to find that rather curious and very charlatanish person and parson Sir Herbert Croft, whose secretary Nodier was for a time, dignified in French books by the name of " *philologue* Anglais "), a good deal more than a kind of bibliographer (he spent the last twenty years of his life as Librarian of the Arsenal), and an enthusiastic and stimulating, though not exactly trustworthy, critic. But he concerns us here, of course, for his prose fiction, which, if not very bulky, is numerous in its individual examples, and is animated in the best of them by a spirit almost new in French and, though often not sufficiently caught and con-centrated, present to almost the highest degrees in at least three examples—the last part of *La Fée aux Miettes*, *La Légende de Sœur Béatrix*, and, above all, *Inès de las Sierras*.

For those who delight in literary filiations and genealo-gies, the kind of story in which Nodier excelled (and in which, though some of his own were written after 1830, he may truly be considered as " schoolmaster " to Mérimée and Gautier and Gérard de Nerval and all their fellows), may be, without violence or exaggeration, said to be a new form of the French fairy-tale, divested of common form, and readjusted with the help of the German *Märchen* and fantasy-pieces. *Le Diable Amoureux* had, no doubt, set the fashion of this kind earlier ; but that story, charming as it is, is still scarcely " Ro-mantic." Nodier is so wholly ; and it is fair to remember that Hoffmann himself was rather a contemporary of his, and subject to the same influences, than a predecessor.[2]

---

[1] In the Radcliffian-literary not the Robespierrean-political sense. For the Wer-therism, *v. sup.* on Chateaubriand, p. 24 note.

[2] He was four years older than Nodier, but did not begin to write fiction nearly so early.

The best collection of Nodier's short tales contains nine pieces : *Trilby, Le Songe d'Or, Baptiste Montauban,* His short *La Fée aux Miettes, La Combe de l'Homme* stories. *mort, Inès de las Sierras, Smarra, La Neuvaine de la Chandeleur,* and *La Légende de Sœur Béatrix.* Of these I believe *Trilby, La Fée aux Miettes,* and *Smarra* have been the greatest favourites, and were pretty certainly the most influential in France. My own special delights are *Le Songe d'Or, Inès de las Sierras,* and *Sœur Béatrix,* with part of the *Fée.* But none is without its attractions, and the Preface to the *Fée aux Miettes,* which is almost a separate piece, has something of the quintessential in that curious quality which Nodier possesses almost alone in French or with Gérard de Nerval and Louis Bertrand only. English readers may " perceive a good deal of [Charles] Lamb in it," with touches of Sterne and De Quincey and Poe.

It is much to be feared that more people in England nowadays associate the name of " Trilby " with the late *Trilby.* Mr. Du Maurier than with Nodier, and that more still associate it with the notion of a hat than with either of the men of genius who used it in literature.

> So mighty Byron, dead and turned to clay,
> Gave name to collars for full many a day ;
> And Ramillies, grave of Gallic boasts so big,
> Found most perpetuation in a wig.[1]

The original story united divers attractions for its first readers in 1822, combining the older fashion of Ossian with the newer one of Scott, infusing the supernatural, which was one great bait of the coming Romanticism, and steeping the whole cake in the tears of the newer

---

The *Phantasiestücke* are of 1814, while Nodier had been writing stories, under German influence, as early as 1803. It is, however, also fair to say that all those now to be noticed are later than 1814, and even than Hoffmann's later collections, the *Elixiere des Teufels* and *Nachtstücke.*

[1] The prudent as well as judicious poet who wrote these lines provided a variant to suit those who, basing their position on " Ramillies *cock,*" maintain that it was a hat, not a wig, that was named after Villeroy's defeat. For " grave—big " read " where Gallic hopes fell flat," and for " wig " " hat " *simpliciter,* and the thing is done. But Thackeray has " Ramillies *wig,*" and Scott implies it.

rather than the older " Sensibility."   " Trilby, le Lutin
d'Argaïl " [1] (Nodier himself explains that he alters the
spelling here with pure phonetic intent, so as to keep the
pronunciation for French eyes *and* ears [2]), is a spirit
who haunts the cabin of the fisherman Dougal to make a
sort of sylph-like love to his wife Jeannie.   He means
and does no harm, but he is naturally a nuisance to the
husband, on whom he plays tricks to keep him away
from home, and at length rather frightens the wife.
They procure, from a neighbouring monastery, a famous
exorcist monk, who, though he cannot directly punish
Trilby, lays on him sentence of exclusion from the home
of the pair, unless one of them invites him, under penalty
of imprisonment for a thousand years.   How the story
turns to Jeannie's death and Trilby's duress can be
easily imagined, and may be read with pleasure.   I
confess that to me it seems pretty, but just a little mawkish.[3]
Perhaps I am a brute.

   Le Songe d'Or, on the other hand, though in a way
tragic, and capable of being allegorised almost *ad in-*
Le Songe *finitum* in its sense of some of the riddles of
d'Or.   the painful earth, is not in the least sentimental,
and is told, till just upon the end, with a certain tender
irony.   The author called it " Fable Levantine," and the
venerable Lo[c]kman is introduced in it.   But I have
read it several times without caring (perhaps this was
reprehensible) to ascertain whether it is in the recognised
Lokman bunch or not.   All I know is that here Nodier
and not Lokman has told it, and that the result is delightful.   First a beautiful " kardouon," the prettiest of
lizards, all azure and ruby and gold, finds in the desert
a heap of gold-pieces.   He breaks his teeth on them,

---

[1] Nodier, who had been in Scotland and, as has been said, was a philologist of the
better class, is scrupulously exact in spelling proper names as a rule.   Perhaps Loch
Fyne is not exactly " Le Lac Beau " (I have not the Gaelic).   But from Pentland to
Solway (literally) he makes no blunder, and he actually knows all about " Argyle's
Bowling Green."

[2] If phonetics had never done anything worse than this they would not be as loathsome to literature as they sometimes are.

[3] On the other hand, compared with its slightly elder contemporary, *Le Solitaire*
(*v. sup.*), it is a masterpiece.

but is sure that such nice-looking things must be good to eat—probably slices of a root which some careless person has left too long in the sun—and that, if properly treated, they will make a famous winter provision. So he conveys them with much care and exertion, one by one, to a soft bed of fresh moss, just the thing to catch the dew, under the shadow of a fine old tree. And, being naturally tired, he goes to sleep beside them. And this is the history of the kardouon.

Now there was in that neighbourhood a poor wood-cutter named Xaïloun—deformed, and not much more than half-witted, but amiable—who had taken a great fancy to the kardouon as being a beautiful beast, and likely to make a charming friend. But the kardouon, after the manner of shy lizards, had by no means recipro-cated this affection, and took shelter behind stones and tree-stumps when advances were made to him. So that the children, and even his own family, including his mother, used to jeer at Xaïloun and tell him to go to his friend. On this particular occasion, the day after the kardouon's *trouvaille*, Xaïloun actually found the usually wide-awake animal sleeping. And as the place, with the moss and the great tree-shadow and a running stream close by, was very attractive, Xaïloun lay down by the lizard to wait till he should wake. But as he himself might go to sleep, and the animal, accustomed to the sun, might get a chill in the shade, Xaïloun put his own coat over him. And he too slept, after thinking how nice the kardouon's friendship would be when they *both* woke. And this is the history of Xaïloun.

Next day again there came a fakir named Abhoc, who was on a pretended pilgrimage, but really on the look-out for what he might get. He saw a windfall at once, was sure that neither of its sleeping guardians could keep it from him, and very piously thanked the Almighty for rewarding his past devotion and self-sacrifice by opening a merry and splendid life to him. But as, with such custodians, the treasure could be " lifted " without the slightest difficulty, he too lay down by it, and went to sleep, dreaming of Schiraz wine in golden cups and a harem peopled with mortal houris. And this is the history of the fakir Abhoc.

A day and a night passed, and the morrow came. Again there passed a wise doctor of laws, Abhac by name, who was editing a text to which a hundred and thirty-two different interpretations had been given by Eastern Cokes and Littletons. He had just hit upon the hundred and thirty-third—of course the true one—when the sight described already struck him and put the discovery quite out of his head, to be lost for ever. As became a jurist, he was rather a more practical person than the woodcutter or the fakir, if not than the lizard. His human predecessors were, evidently, thieves, and must be brought to justice, but it would be well to secure " pieces of conviction." So he began to wrap up the coins in his turban and carry them away. But there were so many, and it was so heavy, that he grew very weary. So he too laid him down and slept. And this is the history of the doctor Abhac.

But on the fifth day there appeared a much more formidable person than the others, and also a much more criminous. This was the " King of the Desert "—bandit and blackmailer of caravans. Being apparently a bandit of letters, he reflected that, though lizards, being, after all, miniature dragons, were immemorial guardians of treasure, they could not have any right in it, but were most inconveniently likely to wake if any noise were made. The others were three to one—too heavy odds by daylight. But if he sat down by them till night came he could stab them one by one while they were asleep, and perhaps breakfast on the kardouon—said to be quite good meat. And he went to sleep himself. And this is the history of the King of the Desert.

But next day again the venerable Lokman passed by, and *he* saw that the tree was a upas tree and the sleepers were dead. And he understood it all, and he passed his hand through his beard and fell on his face, and gave glory to God. And then he buried the three covetous ones in separate graves under the upas itself. But he put Xaïloun in a safer place, that his friends might come and do right to him ; and he buried the kardouon apart on a little slope facing the sun, such as lizards love, and near Xaïloun. And, lastly, having stroked his beard again, he buried the treasure too. But he was very old : and he was very weary when he had finished this, and God took him.

And on the seventh day there came an angel and promised Xaïloun Paradise, and made a mark on his tomb with a feather from his own wing. And he kissed the forehead of Lokman and made him rise from the dead, and took him to the seventh heaven itself. And this is the history of the angel. It all happened ages ago, and though the name of Lokman has lived always through them, so has the shadow of the upas tree.

And this is the history of the world.

Only a child's goody-goody tale ? Possibly. But for my part I know no better philosophy and, at least as Nodier told it, not much better literature.

Baptiste Montauban and *La Combe de l'Homme mort* are, though scarcely shorter than *Le Songe d'Or*, slighter.

Minors. The first is a pathetic but not quite consummate story of " love and madness " in a much better sense than that in which Nodier's eccentric employer, Sir Herbert Croft, used the words as his title for the history of Parson Hackman and Miss Ray.[1] The second (" combe," the omission of which from the official French dictionaries Nodier characteristically denounces, is our own " combe "—a deep valley ; from, I suppose, the Celtic Cwm ; and pronounced by Devonshire folk in a manner which no other Englishman, born east of the line between the mouths of the Parret and the

---

[1] Two little passages towards the end are very precious. A certain bridegroom (I abridge a little) is " perfectly healthy, perfectly self-possessed, a great talker, a successful man of business, with some knowledge of physics, chemistry, jurisprudence, politics, statistics, and phrenology ; enjoying all the requirements of a deputy ; and for the rest, a liberal, an anti-romantic, a philanthropist, a very good fellow—and absolutely intolerable." This person later changes the humble home of tragedy into a " school of mutual instruction, where the children learn to hate and envy each other and to read and write, which was all they needed to become detestable creatures." These words " please the soul well."

Axe, can master) is a good but not supreme *diablerie* of
a not uncommon kind. *La Neuvaine de la Chandeleur*
is longer, and from some points of view the most pathetic
of all.   A young man, hearing some girls talk of a much-
elaborated ceremony like those of Hallowe'en in Scotland
and of St. Agnes' Eve in Keats, by which (in this case)
both sexes can see their fated lovers, tries it, and discerns,
in dream or vision, his ideal as well as his fate.   She
turns out to be an actual girl whom he has never seen,
but whom both his father and her father—old friends—
earnestly desire that he should marry.   He travels to
her home, is enthusiastically greeted, and finds her even
more bewitching than her wraith or whatever it is to be
called.   But she is evidently in bad health, and dies the
same night of aneurism.   Not guested in the house,
but trysted in the morning, hè goes there, and seeing
preparations in the street for a funeral, asks of some one,
being only half alarmed, " *Qui est mort ?* "   The answer
is, " Mademoiselle Cecile Savernier."

     Had these words terminated the story it would have
been nearly perfect.   Two more pages of the luckless
lover's progress to resignation from despair and pro-
jected suicide seem to me to blunt the poignancy.   .

     In fact, acknowledging most humbly that I could
not write even the worst and shortest of Nodier's
stories, I am bound to say that I think he
was not to be trusted with a long one.   *La
Fée aux Miettes* is at once an awful and a delightful
example.   The story of the mad shipwright Michel,
who fell in love with the old dwarf beggar—so unlike
her of Bednal Green or King Cophetua's love—at the
church door of Avranches ; who followed her to Greenock
and got inextricably mixed between her and the Queen
of Sheba ; who for some time passed his nights in making
love to Belkis and his days in attending to the wisdom
of the Fairy of the Crumbs (she always brought him his
breakfast after the Sabaean Nights) ; who at last identified the two in one final rapture, after seeking for a Singing Mandrake ; and who spent the rest (if not, indeed,

La Fée aux Miettes.

the whole) of his days in the Glasgow Lunatic Asylum ;—
is at times so ineffably charming that one is almost afraid
oneself to repeat the refrain—

> C'est moi, c'est moi, c'est moi !
> Je suis la Mandragore !
> · La fille des beaux jours qui s'éveille à l'aurore—
> Et qui chante pour toi !

though, after all, every one whose life has been worth
living has listened for the song all that life—and has
heard it sometimes.

To find any fault with the matrix of this opal is
probably blasphemous. But I own that I could do
without the Shandean prologue and epilogue of the
narrator and his man-servant Daniel Cameron. And
though, as a tomfool myself, I would fain not find any
of the actions of my kind alien from me, I do find some
of the tomfoolery with which Nodier has seasoned
the story superfluous. Why call a damsel " Folly Girl-
free " ? What would a Frenchman say if an English
story-teller christened some girl of Gaul " Sottise Libre-
fille " ? " Sir Jap Muzzleburn," the Bailiff of the Isle
of Man, and his black poodle-equerry, Master Blatt,
amuse me but little ; and Master Finewood, the ship-
builder,—whose rejected six sons-in-law, lairds of high
estate, run away with his thirty thousand guineas, and
are checkmated by six sturdy shipwrights,—less. I have
no doubt it is my fault, my very great fault, but I wish
they would *go*, and leave me with Michel and La Fée,
or rather allow me to *be* Michel *with* La Fée.

Smarra—which made a great impression on its contemporaries and had a strong influence on the Romantic

Smarra and movement generally—is a fantasia of night-
Sœur Béatrix. mare based on the beginning of *The Golden
Ass*, with, again, a sort of prologue and epilogue
of modern love. It is undoubtedly a fine piece of work
of its kind and beautifully written. But in itself it seems
to me a little too much of a *tour de force*, and its kind a little
rococo. Again, *mea maxima culpa* perhaps. On the
other hand, *Sœur Béatrix* is a most charmingly told

version of a very wide-spread story—that of Our Lady
taking the place of an erring sister during her sojourn in
the world, and restoring her to it without any scandal
when she returns repentant and miserable after years
of absence. It could not be better done.

But the jewel of the book, and of Nodier's work, to
me, is *Inès de las Sierras*—at least its first and larger part;
Inès de las for Nodier, in one of those exasperatingly
Sierras. uncritical whims of his which have been
noticed, and which probably prevented him from ever
writing a really good novel of length, has attached an
otiose explanation *à la* Mrs. Radcliffe, which, if it may
please the weakest kind of weak brethren, may almost
disgust another, and as to which I myself exercise the
critic's *cadi*-rights by simply ignoring and banishing
what I think superfluous. As for what remains, once
more, it could not be done better.

Three French officers, at the moment of disturbance
of the French garrisons in the north of Spain, owing to
Napoleon's Russian disasters (perhaps also to more local
events, which it was not necessary for Nodier to mention),
are sent on remount duty from Gerona to Barcelona,
where there is a great horse-fair on. They are delayed
by bad weather and other accidents, and are obliged to
stop half-way after nightfall. But the halting-place is
choke-full of other travellers on their way to the same
fair, and neither at inn nor in private house is there any
room whatever, though there is no lack of " provant."
Everybody tells them that they can only put up at " the
castle of Ghismondo." Taking this for a Spanish folk-
word, they get rather angry. But, finding that there *is*
a place of the name close by in the hills—ruinous, haunted,
but actual—they take plenty of food, wine, and torches,
etc., and persuade, with no little difficulty, their *arriero*
and even their companion and the real hirer of the vehicle
(a theatrical manager, who has allowed them to accompany him, when they could get no other) to dare the night
adventure. On the way the *arriero* tells them the legend,
how, centuries before, Ghismondo de las Sierras, ruined

by debauchery, established himself in this his last possession, with one squire, one page (both of the worst characters), his beautiful niece Inès, whom he has seduced, and a few desperate followers, who help him to live by brigandage. Every night the three chiefs drank themselves senseless, and were regularly dragged to bed by their men. But one Christmas Eve at midnight, Inès, struck with remorse, entered the hall of orgies, and implored them to repent, actually kneeling before Ghismondo, and placing her hand on his heart. To which the ruffian replied by stabbing her, and leaving her for the men-at-arms to find, a corpse, among the drunken but live bodies. For a whole twelvemonth the three see, in dreams, their victim come and lay a burning hand on their hearts; and at its end, on the same day and at the same hour, the dream comes true—the phantom appears, speaks *once*, " Here am I ! " sits with them, eats and drinks, even sings and dances, but finally lays the flaming hand of the dream on each heart; and they die in torture—the men-at-arms entering as usual, only to find *four* corpses. (Now it is actually Christmas Eve—the Spanish *Noche Buena*—at " *temp.* of tale.")

So far the story, though admirably told, in a fashion which mere summary cannot convey, is, it may be said, not more than " as per usual." Not so what follows.

The four travellers—the unnamed captain who tells the story; his two lieutenants, Boutraix, a bluff Voltairian, with an immense capacity for food and drink, and Sergy, a young and romantic Celadon, *plus* the actor-manager Bascara, who is orthodox—with the *arriero*, arrive at last at the castle, which is Udolphish enough, and with some difficulty reach, over broken staircases and through ruined corridors, the great banqueting-hall.[1]

Here—for it is less ruinous than the rest of the

---

[1] The description is worth comparing with that of Gautier's *Château de la Misère* —the difference between all but complete ruin and mere, though extreme, disrepair being admirably, and by the later master in all probability designedly, worked out.

building and actually contains furniture and mouldering
pictures — they make themselves tolerably comfortable
with their torches, a huge fire made up from broken
stairs and panels, abundance of provisions, and two
dozen of wine, less a supply for the *arriero*, who prudently
remains in the stables, alleging that the demons that
haunt those places are fairly familiar to him and not very
mischievous.   As the baggage has got very wet during
the day, the dresses and properties of Bascara's company
are taken out and put to air.   Well filled with food and
drink, the free-thinker Boutraix proposes that they shall
equip themselves from these with costumes not unsuit-
able to the knight, squire, and page of the legend, and
they do so, Bascara refusing to take part in the game,
and protesting strongly against their irreverence.   At
last midnight comes, and they cry, " Where is Inès de
las Sierras ? " lifting their glasses to her health.   Suddenly
there sounds from the dark end of the great hall the
fateful " Here am I ! " and there comes forward a figure
in a white shroud, which seats itself in the vacant place
assigned by tradition to Inès herself.   She is extraordinarily beautiful, and is, under the white covering,
dressed in a fashion resembling the mouldering portrait
which they have seen in the gallery.   She speaks too,
half rallying them, as if surprised at *their* surprise ; she
calls herself Inès de las Sierras ; she throws on the table
a bracelet with the family arms, which they have also
seen dimly emblazoned or sculptured about the castle ;
she eats ; and, as a final piece of conviction, she tears her
dress open and shows the scar on her breast.   Then
she drinks response to the toast they had in mockery
proposed ; she accepts graciously the advances of the
amorous Sergy ; she sings divinely, and she dances
more divinely still.   The whole scene is described
supremely well, but the description of the dance is one
of the very earliest and very finest pieces of Romantic
French prose.   One may try, however rashly, to translate it :

(She has found a set of castanets in her girdle)

She rose and made a beginning by grave and measured steps, displaying, with a mixture of grace and majesty, the perfection of her figure and the nobility of her attitudes.   As she shifted her position and put herself in new aspects, our admiration turned to amazement, as though another and another beautiful woman had come within our view, so constantly did she surpass herself in the inexhaustible variety of her steps and her movements.   First, in rapid transition, we saw her pass from a serious dignity to transports of pleasure, at first moderate, but growing more and more animated; then to soft and voluptuous languors; then to the delirium of joy, and then to some strange ecstasy more delirious still.   Next, she disappeared in the far-off darkness of the huge hall, and the clash of the castanets grew feeble in proportion to the distance, and diminished ever till, as we ceased to see, so we ceased to hear her. But again it came back from the distance, increasing always by degrees, till it burst out full as she reappeared in a flood of light at the spot where we least expected her.   And then she came so near that she touched us with her dress, clashing the castanets with a maddening volubility, till they weakened once more and twittered like cicalas, while now and then across their monotonous racket she uttered shrill yet tender cries which pierced to our own souls.   Afterwards she retired once more, but plunged herself only half in the darkness, appearing and disappearing by turns, now flying from our gaze and now desiring to be seen,[1] while later still you neither saw nor heard her save for a far-off plaintive note like the sigh of a dying girl.   And we remained aghast, throbbing with admiration and fear, longing for the moment when her veil, fluttering with the dance-movement, should be lighted up by the torches, when her voice should warn us of her return, with a joyful cry, to which we answered involuntarily, because it made us vibrate with a crowd of secret harmonies.   Then she came back; she spun round like a flower stripped from its stalk by the wind; she sprang from the ground as if it rested only with her to quit earth for ever; she dropped again as if it was only her will which kept her from touching it at all; she did not bound from the floor—you would have thought that she shot from it—that some mysterious law of her destiny forbade her to touch it, save in order to fly from it.   And her head, bent with an expression of caressing impatience, and her arms, gracefully opened, as though in appealing prayer, seemed to implore us to save her.

---

[1] *Et fugit ad salices et se cupit ante videri.*

The captain himself is on the point of yielding to the temptation, but is anticipated by Sergy, whose embrace she returns, but sinks into a chair, and then, seeming to forget the presence of the others altogether, invites him to follow her through tortuous and ruined passages (which she describes) to a sepulchre, which she inhabits, with owls for her only live companions. Then she rises, picks up her shroud-like mantle, and vanishes in the darkness with a weird laugh and the famous words, " *Qui m'aime me suive.*"

The other three have the utmost difficulty in preventing Sergy (by main force at first) from obeying. And the captain tries rationalism, suggesting first that the pretended Inès is a bait for some gang of assassins or at least brigands, then that the whole thing is a trick of Bascara's to " produce " a new cantatrice. But Boutraix, who has been entirely converted from his Voltairianism by the shock, sets aside the first idea like a soldier, and Bascara rebuts the second like a sensible man. Brigands certainly would give no such warning of their presence, and a wise manager does not expose his prima donna's throat to cohabitation in ruins with skeletons and owls. They finally agree on silence, and shortly afterwards the three officers leave Spain. Sergy is killed at Lutzen, murmuring the name of Inès. Boutraix, who has never relapsed, takes the cowl, and the captain retires after the war to his own small estate, where he means to stay. He ends by saying *Voilà tout.*

Alas ! it is not all, and it is not the end. Some rather idle talk with the auditors follows, and then there is the above-mentioned Radcliffian explanation, telling how Inès was a real Las Sierras of a Mexican branch, who had actually made her début as an actress, had been, as was at first thought, murdered by a worthless lover, but recovered. Her wits, however, were gone, and having escaped from the kind restraint under which she was put, she had wandered to the castle of her ancestors, afterwards completely recovering her senses and returning to the profession in the company of Bascara himself.

Now I think that, if I took the trouble to do so, I could point out improbabilities in this second story sufficient to damn it on its own showing.[1]   But, as has been said already, I prefer to leave it alone.   I never admired George Vavasour in Trollope's *Can You Forgive Her?*   But I own that I agree with him heartily in his opinion that " making a conjurer explain his tricks " is despicably poor fun.

Still, the story, which ends at " Voilà tout " and which for me does so end " for good and all," is simply magnificent.   I have put it elsewhere with *Wandering Willie's Tale*, which it more specially resembles in the way in which the ordinary turns into the extraordinary.   It falls short of Scott in vividness, character, manners, and impressiveness, but surpasses him in beauty[2] of style and imagery.   In particular, Nodier has here, in a manner which I hardly remember elsewhere, achieved the blending of two kinds of " terror "—the ordinary kind which, as it is trivially called, " frightens " one, and the other[3] terror which accompanies the intenser pleasures of sight and sound and feeling, and heightens them by force of contrast.   The scene of Inès' actual appearance would have been the easiest thing in the world to spoil, and therefore was the most difficult thing in the world to do right.   But it is absolutely right. In particular, the way in which her conduct in at once admitting Sergy's attentions, and finally inviting him to " follow," is guarded from the very slightest suggestion of the professional " comingness " of a common courtesan, and made the spontaneous action of a thing divine or diabolic, is really wonderful.

---

[1] Note, too, a hint at a never filled in romance of the captain's own.

[2] I must ask for special emphasis on " beauty." Nothing can be *finer* or *fitter* than the style of Steenie's ghostly experiences.   And the famous Claverhouse passage *is* beautiful.

[3] As Rossetti saw it in " Sibylla Palmifera " :

" Under the arch of Life, where Love and Death,
Terror and Mystery guard her shrine, I saw
Beauty enthroned."

At the same time, the adverse criticism made here, with that on *La Fée aux Miettes* and a few other foregoing remarks, will probably prepare the reader for the repeated and final judgment that Nodier was very unlikely to produce a good long story. And, though I have not read *quite* all that he wrote, I certainly think that he never did.

In adding new and important masterpieces to the glittering chain of short cameo-like narratives which Nodier's form the peculiar glory of French literature, special he did greatly. And his performance and quality. example were greater still in respect of the *quality* which he infused into those best pieces of his work which have been examined here. It is hardly too much to say that this quality had been almost dormant—a sleeping beauty among the lively bevies of that literature's graces—ever since the Middle Ages, with some touches of waking—hardly more than motions in a dream—at the Renaissance. The comic Phantasy had been wakeful and active enough; the graver and more serious tragic Imagination had been, though with some limitations, busy at times. But this third sister—Our Lady of Dreams, one might call her in imitation of a famous fancy—had not shown herself much in French merriment or in French sadness : the light of common day there had been too much for her. Yet in Charles Nodier she found the magician who could wake her from sleep : and she told him what she had thought while sleeping.[1]

---

[1] Perhaps there are few writers mentioned in this book to whose lovers exactly the same kind of apology is desirable as it is in the case of Nodier. "Where," I hear reproaching voices crying, "is *Jean Sbogar*? Where is *Laure Ruthven ou les Vampires* in novel-plural or *Le Vampire* in melodrama-singular? Where are a score or a hundred other books, pieces, pages, paragraphs, passages from five to fifty words long?" They are not here, and I could not find room for them here. "But you found more room for Paul de Kock?" Yes : and I have tried to show why.

CHAPTER III

At the present day, and perhaps in all days hitherto, the greatest writer of the nineteenth century in France
Limitations. for length of practice, diversity of adminis-tration of genius, height of ˙intention, and (for a long time at least) magnitude and altitude of fame, enjoys, and has enjoyed, more popular repute in England for his work in prose fiction than for any other part of it. With the comparative side of this estimate the present writer can indeed nowise agree; and the reasons of his disagreement should be made good in the present chapter. But this is the first opportunity he has had of considering, with fair room and verge, the justice of the latter part of Tennyson's compliment " Victor *in Romance* "; and it will pretty certainly be the last. As for a general judgment of the positive and relative value and qualities of the wonderful procession of work—certainly deserving that adjective whatever other or others may be added—which covers the space of a full half-century from *Han d'Islande* to *Quatre-Vingt-Treize*, it would, according to the notions of criticism here followed, be improper to attempt that till after the procession itself has been carefully surveyed.

Nor will it be necessary to preface, to follow, or, except very rarely and slightly, to accompany this survey with remarks on the non-literary characteristics of this French Titan of literature. The object often of frantic political and bitter personal abuse; for a long time of almost equally frantic and much sillier political

and personal idolatry; himself the victim—in consequence partly of his own faults, partly of ignoble jealousy
of greatness, but perhaps most of all of the inevitable
reaction from this foolish cult—of the most unsparing
rummage into those faults, and the weaknesses which
accompany them, that any poet or prose writer, even.
Pope, has experienced—Victor Hugo still, though he
has had many a *vates* in both senses of *sacer*, may
almost be allowed *carere* critico *sacro*,[1] in the best sense,
on the whole of his life and work. I have no pretensions
to fill or bridge the whole of the gap here. It will be
quite task enough for the present, leaving the life almost
alone, to attempt the part of the work which contains
prose fiction. Nothing said of this will in the least
affect what I have often said elsewhere, and shall hold
to as long as I hold anything, in regard to the poetry—
that its author is the greatest poet of France, and one of
the great poets of the world.

To deal with Hugo's first published, though not
first written, novel requires, in almost the highest degree,
Han   what Mr. Matthew Arnold called "a purged
d'Islande. considerate mind." There are, I believe,
some people (I myself know at least one of great excellence) who, having had the good luck to read *Han
d'Islande* as schoolboys, and finding its vein congenial
to theirs, have, as in such cases is not impossible, kept
it unscathed in their liking. But this does not happen
to every one. I do not think, though I am not quite
certain, that when I first read it myself I was exactly
what may be called a schoolboy pure and simple (that
is to say, under fifteen). But if I did not read it in upper
school-boyhood (that is to say, before eighteen), I
certainly did, not much later. I own that at that time,
whatever my exact age was, I found it so uninteresting
that I do not believe I read it through. Nor, except in
the last respect, have I improved with it—for it would
be presumptuous to say, "has it improved with me"—

---

[1] Mr. Swinburne's magnificent pæans are "vatical" certainly, but scarcely critical,
save now and then. Mr. Stevenson wrote on the Romances, but not on "the whole."

since.   The author apologised for it in two successive
prefaces shortly after its appearance, and in yet another
after that of *Notre-Dame de Paris*, ten years later.   None
of them, it is to be feared, " touches the spot."   The
first, indeed, is hardly an apology at all, but a sort of
goguenard " showing off" of the kind not uncommon
with youth ; the second, a little more serious, contains
rather interesting hits[1] of again youthful jealousy at
the popularity of Pigault-Lebrun and Ducray-Duminil ;
the third and much later one is a very early instance of
the Victorian philosophising.   " There must be," we
are told with the solemnity which for some sixty years
excited such a curious mixture of amazement and amusement, " in every work of the mind—drama or novel—
there must be many things felt, many things observed,
and many things divined," and while in *Han* there
is only one thing felt—a young man's love—and one
observed—a girl's ditto—the rest is all divined, is " the
fantastic imagination of an adolescent."

One impeticoses the gratility of the explanation, and
refrains, as far as may be, from saying, " Words !
words ! "   Unluckily, the book does very little indeed
to supply deeds to match.   The feeling and the observation furnish forth a most unstimulating love-story ; at
least the present critic, who has an unabashed fondness
for love-stories, has never been able to feel the slightest
interest either in Ordener Guldenlew or in Ethel Schumacker, except in so far as the lady is probably the first
of the since innumerable and sometimes agreeable
heroines of her name in fiction.   As for the " divining,"
the " intention," and the " imagination," they have been
exerted to sadly little purpose.   The absurd nomenclature, definitely excused in one of the prefaces, may have
a slight historic interest as the first attempt, almost a
hopeless failure, at that *science des noms* with which Hugo
was later credited, and which he certainly sometimes
displayed.   It is hardly necessary to say much about
Spladgest and Oglypiglaf, Musdaemon and Orugix.

---

[1] See note in Vol. I. p. 472 of this *History*, and in the present volume, *sup.* p. 40.

They are pure schoolboyisms. But it is perhaps fair to relieve the author from the reproach, which has been thrown on him by some of his English translators, of having metamorphosed "Hans" into "Han." He himself explains distinctly that the name was a nickname, taken from the grunt or growl (the word is in France applied to the well-known noise made by a paviour lifting and bringing down his rammer) of the monster.

But that monster himself! A more impossible improbability and a more improbable impossibility never conceived itself in the brain of even an as yet failure of an artist. Han appears to have done all sorts of nasty things, such as eating the insides of babies when they were alive and drinking the blood of enemies when they were not dead, out of the skulls of his own offspring, which he had extracted from *their* dead bodies by a process like peeling a banana : also to have achieved some terrible ones, such as burning cathedrals and barracks, upsetting rocks on whole battalions, and so forth. But the only chances we have of seeing him at real business show him to us as overcoming, with some trouble, an infirm old man, and *not* overcoming at all, after a struggle of long duration, a not portentously powerful young one. His white bear, and not he, seems to have had the chief merit of despatching six surely rather incompetent hunters who followed the rash "Kenny-bol": and of his two final achievements, that of poniarding two men in a court of justice might have been brought about by anybody who was careless enough of his own life, and that of setting his gaol on fire by any one who, with the same carelessness, had a corrupt gaoler to supply him with the means.

It would be equally tedious and superfluous to go through the minor characters and incidents. The virtuous and imprisoned statesman Schumacker, Ethel's father, excites no sympathy : his malignant and finally defeated enemy, the Chancellor Ahlefeld, no interest. That enemy's most *un*virtuous wife and her paramour

Musdaemon—*the* villain of the piece as Han is the
monster—as to whom one wonders whether he could
ever have been as attractive as a lover as he is unattractive
as a villain, are both puppets. Indeed, one would hardly
pay any attention to the book at all if it did not hold a
position in the work of a man of the highest genius
partly similar to, and partly contrasted with, that of
Zastrozzi and *St. Irvyne*. But *St. Irvyne* and *Zastrozzi*
are much shorter than *Han d'Islande*, and Shelley, whether
by accident, wisdom (*nemo omnibus horis insanit*), or the
direct intervention of Apollo, never resumed the task
for which his genius was so obviously unsuited.

Still, it must be said for Hugo that, even at this time,
he could have—in a manner actually had—put in evidence
of not absolute incompetence for the task.

Bug-Jargal was, as glanced at above, written, according to its author's own statement, two years before *Han*,
Bug-Jargal. when he was only sixteen; was partially
printed (in the *Constitutionnel*) and (in fear of
a piracy) rewritten in fifteen days and published, seven
years after its composition, and almost as many before
Notre-Dame de Paris appeared. Taking it as it stands,
there is nothing of the sixteen years or of the fifteen
days to be seen in it. It is altogether superior to *Han*,
and though it has not the nightmare magnificence and
the phantasmagoric variety of *Notre-Dame*, it is, not
merely because it is much shorter, a far better told,
more coherent, and more generally human story. The
jester-obi Habibrah has indeed the caricature-grotesquery
of Han himself, and of Quasimodo, and long afterwards
of Gwynplaine, as well as the devilry of the first named
and of Thénardier in *Les Misérables*; but we do not see
too much of him, and nothing that he does is exactly
absurd or utterly improbable. The heroine—so far as
there is a heroine in Marie d'Auverney, wife of the part-
hero-narrator, but separated from him on the very day
of their marriage by the rebellion of San Domingo—is
very slight; but then, according to the story, she is not
wanted to be anything more. The cruelty, treachery,

etc., of the half-caste Biassou are not overdone, nor is the tropical scenery, nor indeed anything else. Even the character of Bug-Jargal himself, a modernised Oroonoko (whom probably Hugo did not know) and a more direct descendant of persons and things in Rousseau, Bernardin de Saint-Pierre, and to some extent the " sensibility " novelists generally (whom he certainly did know), is kept within bounds. And, what is perhaps most extraordinary of all, the half-comic interludes in the narrative where Auverney's comrades talk while he makes breaks in his story, contain few of Hugo's usually disastrous attempts at humour. It is impossible to say that the book is of any great importance or of any enthralling interest. But it is the most workmanlike of all Hugo's work in prose fiction, and, except *Les Travailleurs de La Mer* and *Quatre-Vingt-Treize*, which have greater faults as well as greater beauties, the most readable, if not, like them, the most likely to be re-read. .

Its merits are certainly not ill set off by the two shorter pieces, both of fairly early date, but the one a little before *Le Dernier* and the other a little after *Notre-Dame de Paris, Jour d'un* which usually accompany it in the collected *Condamné.* editions. Of these *Le Dernier Jour d'un Condamné* is, with its tedious preface, almost two-thirds as long as *Bug-Jargal* itself; the other, *Claude Gueux*, contents itself with thirty pages. Both are pieces with a purpose—manifestos of one of Hugo's most consistent and most irrational crazes—the objection to capital punishment.[1] There is no need to argue against this, the immortal " Que MM. les assassins," etc., being, though in fact the weakest of a thousand refutations, sufficient, once for all, to explode it. But it is not irrelevant to point out that the two pieces themselves are very battering-rams against their own theory. We are not told—the objection to this omission was made at the time, of course, and Hugo's would-be lofty waving-off of this is one of the earliest of many such—what the

---

[1] These crazes were not in origin, though they probably were in influence, political : Hugo held more than one of them while he was still a Royalist.

condemned person's crime was. But the upshot of his lucubrations during these latest hours of his is this, that such hours are almost more uncomfortable than the minutes of the actual execution can possibly be. As this is exactly one of the points on which the advocates of the punishment, whether from the point of view of deterrence or from that of retribution, chiefly rely, it seems something of a blunder to bring it out with all the power of a poet and a rhetorician. We *want* " M. l'Assassin," in fact, to be made very uncomfortable—as uncomfortable as possible—and we want M. l'Assassin, in intention or deliberation, to be warned that he will be so made. " Serve him right " sums up the one view, " De te fabula " the other. In fact cheap copies of *Le Dernier Jour*, supplied to all about to commit murder, would be highly valuable. Putting aside its purpose, the mere literary power is of course considerable if not consummate ; it hardly pretends to be a " furnished " *story*.

The piece, however, is tragic enough : it could hardly fail to be so in the hands of such a master of tragedy, just as it could hardly fail to be illogical in the hands of such a paralogician. But *Claude Gueux*, though it ends with a murder and an attempt at suicide and an execution, is really, though far from intentionally, a farce. The hero, made (by the " fault of society," of course) a criminal, though not a serious one, thinks himself persecuted by the prison director, and murders that official. The reader who does not know the book will suppose that he has been treated as Charles Reade's wicked governor treated Josephs and Robinson and the other victims in *It is Never too Late to Mend*. Not at all. The redoubtable Claude had, like the great Victor himself and other quite respectable men, an equally redoubtable appetite, and the prison rations were not sufficient for him. As he was a sort of leader or prison shop-steward, and his fellow-convicts looked up to him, a young fellow who was not a great eater used to give Claude part of his allowance. The director, discovering

Claude Gueux.

this, removed the young man into another ward—an action possibly rather spiteful, possibly also only a slight excess, or no excess at all, of red-tapeism in discipline. Claude not merely asks reasons for this,—which, of course, even if respectfully done, was an act of clear insubordination on any but anarchist principles,—but repeats the enquiry. The director more than once puts the question by, but inflicts no penalty. Whereupon Claude makes a harangue to the shop (which appears, in some astounding fashion, to have been left without any supervision between the director's visits), repeats once more, on the director's entrance, his insubordinate enquiry, again has it put by, and thereupon splits the unfortunate official's skull with a hatchet, digging also a pair of scissors, which once belonged to his (left-handed) wife, into his own throat. And the wretches actually cure this hardly fallen angel, and then guillotine him, which he takes most sweetly, placing at the last moment in the hand of the attendant priest, with the words *Pour les pauvres*, a five-franc piece, which one of the Sisters of the prison hospital had given him ! After this Hugo, not contented with the tragedy of the edacious murderer, gives us seven pages of his favourite rhetoric in *saccadé* paragraphs on the general question.

As so often with him, one hardly knows which particular question to ask first, " Did ever such a genius make such a fool of himself ? " or " Was ever such an artist given to such hopeless slips in the most rudimentary processes of art ? "

But it is, of course, not till we come to *Notre-Dame de Paris* that any serious discussion of Hugo's claims as a novelist is possible. Hitherto, while in novel at least he has very doubtfully been an *enfant sublime*, he has most unquestionably been an *enfant*. Whatever faults may be chargeable on his third novel or romance proper, they include no more childishness than he displayed throughout his life, and not nearly so much as he often did later.

The book, moreover, to adopt and adapt the language

of another matter, whether disputably or indisputably great in itself, is unquestionably so " by position." It is one of the chief manifestos—there are some who have held, and perhaps would still hold, that it is *the* chief manifesto and example—of one of the most remarkable and momentous of literary movements—the great French Romantic revolt of *mil-huit-cent-trente*. It had for a time enormous popularity, extending to many who had not the slightest interest in it as such a manifesto ; it affected not merely its own literature, but others, and other arts besides literature, both in its own and other countries. To whatever extent this popularity may have been affected —first by the transference of interest from the author's " letters " to his politics and sociology, and secondly, by the reaction in general esteem which followed his death— it is not very necessary to enquire. One certainly sees fewer, indeed, positively few, references to it and to its contents now. But it was so bright a planet when it first came into ken ; it exercised its influence so long and so largely ; that even if it now glows fainter it is worth exploring, and the analysis of the composition of its light is worth putting on record.

In the case of a book which, whether it has or has not undergone some occultation as suggested, is still kept *The story* on sale not merely in the original, but in cheap *easy to* translations into every European tongue, there *anticipate.* is probably no need to include an actual " argument " in this analysis. As a novel or at least romance, *Notre-Dame de Paris* contains a story of the late fifteenth century, the chief characters of which are the Spanish gipsy [1] dancing-girl Esmeralda, with her goat Djali ; Quasimodo, the hunchbacked dwarf and bell-ringer of the cathedral ; one of its archdeacons, Claude Frollo, theologian, philosopher, expert in, but contemner of, physical and astrological science, and above all, alchemist, if not sorcerer ; the handsome and gallant, but " not intelligent " and not very chivalrous soldier Phœbus de Chateaupers, with minors not a few, " supers " very

---

[1] She is of course not really Spanish or a gipsy, but is presented as such at first.

many, and the dramatist Pierre Gringoire as a sort of half-chorus, half-actor throughout. The evolution of this story could not be very difficult to anticipate in any case ; almost any one who had even a slight knowledge of its actual author's other work could make a guess at the *scenario*. The end must be tragic ; the *beau cavalier* must be the rather unworthy object of Esmeralda's affection, and she herself that of the (one need hardly say very different) affections of Frollo and Quasimodo ; a charge of sorcery, based on the tricks she has taught Djali, must be fatal to her ; and poetic justice must overtake Frollo, who has instigated the persecution but has half exchanged it for, half-combined it with, later attempts of a different kind upon her. Although this *scenario* may not have been then quite so easy for any schoolboy to anticipate, as it has been later, the course of the romantic novel from Walpole to Scott in English, not to mention German and other things, had made it open enough to everybody to construct. The only thing to be done, and to do, now was, and is, to see, on the author's own famous critical principles,[1] how he availed himself of the *publica materies*.

Perhaps the first impression of any reader who is not merely not an expert in criticism, but who has not yet
Importance learnt its first, last, and hardest lesson, shirked
of the actual by not a few who seem to be experts—to
title. suspend judgment till the case is fully heard—may be unfavourable. It is true that the title *Notre-Dame de Paris*, so stupidly and unfairly disguised by the addition-substitution of " *The Hunchback* of Notre Dame " in English translations—quite honestly and quite legitimately warns any intelligent reader what to expect. It is the cathedral itself, its visible appearance and its invisible *aura*, atmosphere, history, spirit, inspiration which gives the author—and is taken by him as giving—his real subject. Esmeralda and Quasimodo,

---

[1] Stated in the Preface to *Cromwell*, the critical division of his fourfold attack on neo-Classicism, as *Les Orientales* were the poetical, *Hernani* was the dramatic, and *Notre-Dame* itself the prose-narrative.

Frollo and Gringoire are almost as much minors and supers in comparison with It or Her as Phœbus de Chateaupers and the younger Frollo and the rest are in relation to the four protagonists themselves. The most ambitious piece of *dianoia*—of thought as contrasted with incident, character, or description—is that embodied in the famous chapter, *Ceci tuera cela*, where the fatal effect of literature (at least printed literature) on architecture is inculcated. The situation, precincts, construction, constitution of the church form the centre of such action as there is, and supply by far the larger part of its scene. Therefore nobody has a right to complain of a very large proportion of purely architectural detail.

But the question is whether, in the actual employment, and still more in what we may call the administration, of this and other diluents or obstruents of story, the artist has or has not made blunders in his art; and it is very difficult not to answer this in the affirmative. There were many excuses for him. The " guide-book novel " had already, and not so very long before, been triumphantly introduced by *Corinne*. It had been enormously popularised by Scott. The close alliance and almost assimilation of art and history with literature was one of the supremest articles of faith of Romanticism, and "the Gothic" was a sort of symbol, shibboleth, and sacrament at once of Romanticism itself. But Victor Hugo, like Falstaff, has, in this and other respects, abused his power of pressing subjects into service almost, if not quite, damnably. Whether out of pure wilfulness, out of mistaken theory, or out of a mixture [1] of these and other influences, he has made the first volume almost as little of a story as it could possibly be, while remaining a story at all. Seventy mortal pages, pretty well packed in the standard two-volume edition, which in all contains less than six

The working out of the one under the other.

---

[1] It is scarcely excessive to say that this mixture of wilful temper and unbridled theorising was the Saturnian influence, or the " infortune of Mart," in Hugo's horoscope throughout.

hundred, dawdle over the not particularly well-told business of Gringoire's interrupted mystery, the arrival of
the Flemish ambassadors, and the election of the Pope
of Unreason. The vision of Esmeralda lightens the
darkness and quickens the movement, and this brightness and liveliness continue till she saves her unlucky
dramatist from the murderous diversions of the Cour
des Miracles. But the means by which she does this—
the old privilege of matrimony—leads to nothing but a
single scene, which might have been effective, but which
Hugo only leaves flat, while it has no further importance
in the story whatsoever. After it we hop or struggle
full forty pages through the public street of architecture
pure and simple.

At first sight " Coup d'œil impartial sur l'Ancienne
Magistrature " may seem to give even more promise
The story of November than of May. But there *is*
recovers itself action here, and it really has something to do
latterly. with the story. Also, the subsequent treatment of the recluse or anchoress of the severest type in
the Place Notre-Dame itself (or practically so), though
it is much too long and is lengthened by matters with
which Hugo knows least of all how to deal, has still
more claim to attention, for it leads directly on not merely
to the parentage of Esmeralda, but to the tragedy of her
fate. And almost the whole of the second volume is,
whether the best novel-matter or not, at any rate genuine
novel-matter. If almost the whole of the first had been
boiled down (as Scott at his best would have boiled it)
into a preliminary chapter or two, the position of the
book as qualified to stand in its kind could not have been
questioned. But its faults and merits in that kind would
still have remained matters of very considerable question.

In respect of one fault, the side of the defence can
surely be taken only by generous, but hardly judicious
But the or judicial devotees. Hugo's singular affec-
characters ? tion for the monster—he had Stephano to
justify him, but unfortunately did not possess either the
humour of that drunken Neapolitan butler or the power

of his and Caliban's creator—had made a mere grotesque of *Han*, but had been reduced within more artistic limits in *Bug*. In *Le Dernier Jour* and *Claude Gueux* it was excluded by the subjects and objects alike.[1] Here it is, if not an *intellectus*, at any rate *sibi permissus*; and, as it does not in the earlier cases, it takes the not extremely artistic form of violent contrast which was to be made more violent later in *L'Homme Qui Rit*. If any one will consider Caliban and Miranda as they are presented in *The Tempest*, with Quasimodo and Esmeralda as *they* are presented here, he will see at once the difference of great art and great failure of art.

Then, too, there emerges another of our author's persistent obsessions, the exaggeration of what we may call the individual combat. He had probably intended something of this kind in *Han*, but the mistake there in telling about it instead of telling it has been already pointed out. Neither Bug-Jargal nor Habibrah does anything glaringly and longwindedly impossible. But the one-man defence of Notre-Dame by Quasimodo against the *truands* is a tissue not so much of impossibilities—they, as it has been said of old, hardly matter—as of the foolish-incredible. Why did the numerous other denizens of the church and its cloisters do nothing during all this time? Why did the *truands*, who, though they were all scoundrels, were certainly not all fools, confine themselves to this frontal assault of so huge a building? Why did the little rascal Jean Frollo not take some one with him? These are not questions of mere dull common sense; it is only dull absence of common sense which will think them so. Scott, who, once more, was not too careful in stopping loose places, managed the attacks of Tillietudlem and Torquilstone without giving any scope for objections of this kind.

Hugo's strong point was never character, and it certainly is not so here. Esmeralda is beautiful, amiable, pathetic, and unfortunate; but the most uncharitable

---

[1] Unless anybody chooses to say that the gallows and the guillotine are Hugo's monsters here.

interpretation of Mr. Pope's famous libel never was more justified than in her case. Her salvage of Gringoire and its sequel give about the only situations in which she is a real person,[1] and they are purely episodic. Gringoire himself is as much out of place as any literary man who ever went into Parliament. Some may think better of Claude Frollo, who may be said to be the Miltonic-Byronic-Satanic hero. I own I do not. His mere specification—that of the ascetic scholar assailed by physical temptation—will pass muster well enough, the working out of it hardly.

His brother, the *vaurien* Jean, has, I believe, been a favourite with others or the same, and certainly a Villon-esque student is not out of place in the fifteenth century. Nor is a turned-up nose, even if it be artificially and prematurely reddened, unpardonable. But at the same time it is not in itself a passport, and Jean Frollo does not appear to have left even the smallest *Testament* or so much as a single line (though some snatches of song are assigned to him) reminding us of the " Dames des Temps Jadis " or the " Belle Heaulmière." Perhaps even Victor never presumed more unfortunately on victory than in bringing in Louis XI., especially in one scene, which directly challenges comparison with *Quentin Durward*. While, though Scott's *jeunes premiers* are not, as he himself well knew and frankly confessed, his greatest triumphs, he has never given us anything of the kind so personally impersonal as Phœbus de Chateaupers.

Per contra there are of course to be set passages which are actually fine prose and some of which might have made magnificent poetry; a real or at least—what is as good as or better than a real—a fantastic resurrection of Old Paris ; and, above all, an atmosphere of " sunset and eclipse," of night and thunder and levin-flashes, which no one of catholic taste would willingly surrender. Only, ungrateful as it may seem, uncritical as some may

---

[1] The failure of the riskiest and most important scene of the whole (where her surrender of herself to Phœbus is counteracted by Frollo's stabbing the soldier, the act itself leading to Esmeralda's incarceration) is glaring.

deem it, it is impossible not to sigh, " Oh ! why were
not the best things of this treated in verse, and why were
not the other things left alone altogether ? "

For a very long stretch of time—one that could hardly
be paralleled except in a literary life so unusually extended as his—it might have seemed that one
of those *voix intérieures*, which he was during
its course to celebrate in undying verse, had
whispered to Hugo some such warning as that conveyed
in the words of the close of the last paragraph, and that
he, usually the most indocile of men, had listened to it.
For all but three decades he confined his production—
at least in the sense of substantial publication [1]—to
poetry almost invariably splendid, drama always grandiose
and sometimes grand, and prose - writing of a chiefly
political kind, which even sympathisers (one would
suppose) can hardly regard as of much value now if they
have any critical faculty. Even the tremendous shock
of disappointment, discomfiture, and exile which resulted
from the success of Napoleon the Third, though it
started a new wave and gust of oceanic and cyclonic
force, range, and volume in his soul, found little prose
vent, except the wretched stuff of *Napoléon le Petit*, to
chequer the fulgurant outburst of the *Châtiments*, the
apocalyptic magnificence of the *Contemplations*, and the
almost unmatched vigour, variety, and vividness of the
Légende des Siècles.

At last, in 1862, a full decade after the cataclysm,
his largest and probably his most popular work of fiction
made its appearance in the return to romance-writing,
entitled *Les Misérables*. I daresay biographies say
when it was begun ; it is at any rate clear that even
Victor Hugo must have taken some years, especially in
view of his other work, to produce such a mass of matter.[2]

The thirty years' interval.

---

[1] *Le Beau Pécopin* in his *Rhine*-book is, of course, fairly substantial in one sense, but
it is only an episode or inset-tale in something else, which is neither novel nor romance.

[2] It must be four or five times the length of Scott's average, more than twice that
of the longest books with which Dickens and Thackeray used to occupy nearly
two years in monthly instalments, and very nearly, if not quite, that of Dumas'
longest and most " spun-out " achievements in *Monte Cristo*, the *Vicomte de Bragelonne*
and *La Comtesse de Charny*.

Probably not very many people now living, at least in England, remember very clearly the immense effect it produced even with us, who were then apt to regard Hugo as at best a very chequered genius and at worst an almost charlatanish rhetorician.

It was no doubt lucky for its popularity that it fell in with a general movement, in England as well as elsewhere, *Les* which had with us been, if not brought about, *Misérables.* aided by influences in literature as different as those of Dickens and Carlyle, through Kingsley and others downwards,—the movement which has been called perhaps more truly than sympathetically, " the cult of the lower [not to say the criminal] classes."   In France, if not in England, this cult had been oddly combined with a dash of rather adulterated Romanticism, and long before Hugo, Sues and Sands, as will be seen later, had in their different manner been priests and priestesses of it.   In his own case the adoption of the subject " keyed on " in no small degree to the mood in which he wrote the *Dernier Jour* and *Claude Gueux*, while a good deal of the " Old Paris " mania (I use the word nowise contumeliously) of *Notre-Dame* survived, and even the " Cour des Miracles " found itself modernised.

Whether the popularity above mentioned has kept itself up or not, I cannot say.   Of one comparatively recent edition, not so far as I know published at intervals, I have been told that the first volume is out of print, but none of the others, a thing rather voiceful to the understanding.   I know that, to me, it is the hardest book to read through of any that I know by a great writer.   *Le Grand Cyrus* and *Clélie* are certainly longer, *Clarissa* and *Sir Charles Grandison* are probably so.   *Le Vicomte de Bragelonne* is almost as long.   There are finer things in it than in any of them (except the deaths of Lovelace and Porthos and the kidnapping of General Monk) from the pure novel point of view, and not a few passages which ought to have been verse and, even prose as they are, soar far over anything that Mademoiselle de Scudéry or Samuel Richardson or Alexandre Dumas could possibly have written in either harmony. The Scudéry books are infinitely duller, and the Richardson ones much less varied.

But none of these others besets the path of the reader with things to which the obstacles interposed by Quilp in the way of Sampson Brass were down-pillows, as is the case with *Les Misérables*. It is as if Victor Hugo had said, "You shall read this at your peril," and had made good the threat by dint of every blunder in novel-writing which he could possibly commit. With his old and almost invariable fault (there is a little of it even in *Les Travailleurs de la Mer*, and only *Quatre-Vingt-Treize* avoids it entirely), he delays any real interest till the book, huge as it is, is almost half way through. Twenty pages on Bishop Myriel—that rather piebald angel who makes the way impossible for any successor by his fantastic and indecent "apostolicism" in living; who tells, *not* like St. Athanasius, an allowable equivocation to save his valuable self, but a downright lie to save a worthless rascal; and who admits defeat in argument by the stale sophisms of a moribund *conventionnel*—might have been tolerable. We have, in the compactest edition I know, about a hundred and fifty. The ruin and desertion of Fantine would have been worth twenty more. We have from fifty to a hundred to tell us the story of four rather impossibly beautiful *grisettes*, and as many, alas ! too possible, but not interesting, rascals of students. It is difficult to say how much is wasted on the wildly improbable transformation of Jean Valjean, convict and pauper, into " M. Madeleine," *maire* and (*nummis gallicis*) millionaire, through making sham jet. All this, by any one who really knew his craft, would have been sketched rapidly in fluent preliminary, and subsequent piecemeal retrospect, so as to start with Valjean's escape from Thénardier and his adoption of Cosette.

The actual matter of this purely preliminary kind extends, as has been ascertained by rough but sufficient calculation of the sort previously employed, to at least three-quarters of an average novel of Sir Walter's : it would probably run to two or three times the length of a modern " six-shilling." But Hugo is not satisfied with it. A point, an important point, doubtless, but one that could have been despatched in a few lines, connects the novel proper with the Battle of Waterloo. To that battle itself, even the preliminary matter in its earliest part is some years posterior : the main action, of course, is still more so. But Victor must give us *his* account of this great engagement, and he gives it in about a hundred pages of the most succinct reproduction. For my part, I should be glad to have it " mixed with much wine," even if the wine were of that luscious and headachy south-of-France character which he himself is said to have preferred to Bordeaux or Champagne, Sauterne or even Burgundy. Nay, without this I like it well enough and quarrel with nothing in it, though it is in many respects (from the famous hollow way which nobody else ever heard of downwards) very much of a dream-battle. Victor does quite as much justice as any one could expect him to do—and, thank heaven, there are still some Englishmen who are perfectly indifferent whether justice is done to them or not in these matters, leaving it to poorer persons in such ways who may be glad of it—to English fighting ; while if he represents Wellington as a mere calculator and Napoleon as a hero, we can murmur politely (like a Roman Catholic bishop, more real in many ways than His Greatness of Digue), " Perhaps so, my dear sir, perhaps so." But what has it all got to do here ? Even when Montalais and her lover sat on the wall and talked for half a volume or so in the *Vicomte de Bragelonne* ; even when His Majesty Louis XIV. and his (one regrets to use the good old English word) pimp, M. le Duc de Saint-Aignan, exhausted the resources of carpentry and the stores of printer's ink to gain access to the apartment of Mlle. de la Vallière, the superabundance, though trivial, was relevant : this is not. When Thénardier tried to rob and was no doubt quite ready to murder, but did, as a matter of fact, help to resuscitate, the gallant French

Republican soldier, who was so glad to receive the title of baron from an emperor who had by abdication resigned any right to give it that he ever possessed, it might have been Malplaquet or Leipsic, Fontenoy or Vittoria, for any relevance the details of the battle possessed to the course of the story.

Now relevance (to make a short paragraph of the kind Hugo himself loved) is a mighty goddess in novelry.

.And so it continues, though, to be absolutely just, the later parts are not exposed to quite the same objections as the earlier. These objections transform themselves, however, into other varieties, and are reinforced by fresh faults. The most inexcusable digressions, on subjects as remote from each other as convents and sewers, insist on poking themselves in. The central, or what ought to be the central, interest itself turns on the ridiculous *émeute* of Saint-Merry, a thing " without a purpose or an aim," a mere caricature of a revolution. The *gamin* Gavroche puts in a strong plea for mercy, and his sister Eponine, if Hugo had chosen to take more trouble with her, might have been a great, and is actually the most interesting, character. But Cosette—the cosseted Cosette—Hugo did not know our word or he would have seen the danger—is merely a pretty and rather selfish little doll, and her precious lover Marius is almost ineffable.

Novel-heroes who are failures throng my mind like ghosts on the other shore of the river whom Charon will not ferry over ; but I can single out none of them who is, without positively evil qualities, so absolutely intolerable as Marius.[1] Others have more such qualities ; but he has no good ones. His very bravery is a sort of moral and intellectual running amuck because he thinks he shall not get Cosette. Having, apparently, for many years thought and cared nothing about his father, he becomes frantically filial on discovering that he has inherited from him, as above, a very doubtful and cer-

---

[1] I am not forgetting or contradicting what was said above (p. 26) of René. But René *does* very little except when he kills the she-beavers ; Marius is always doing something, and doing it offensively.

tainly most un-" citizen "-like title of Baron. Thereupon (taking care, however, to have cards printed with the title on them) he becomes a violent republican.

He then proceeds to be extremely rude to his indulgent but royalist grandfather, retires to a mount of very peculiar sacredness, where he comes in contact with the Thénardier family, discovers a plot against Valjean, appeals to the civil arm to protect the victim, but, for reasons which seem good to him, turns tail, breaks his arranged part, and is very nearly accessory to a murder. At the other end of the story, carrying out his general character of prig-pedant, as selfish as self-righteous, he meets Valjean's rather foolish and fantastic self-sacrifice with illiberal suspicion, and practically kills the poor old creature by separating him from Cosette. When the *éclaircissement* comes, it appears to me—as Mr. Carlyle said of Loyola that he ought to have consented to be damned—that Marius ought to have consented at least to be kicked.

Of course it may be said, " You should not give judgments on things with which you are evidently out of sympathy." But I do not acknowledge any palpable hit. If certain purposes of the opposite kind were obtruded here in the same fashion—if Victor (as he might have done in earlier days) had hymned Royalism instead of Republicanism, or (as perhaps he would never have done) had indulged in praise of severe laws and restricted education,[1] and other things, I should be " in sympathy," but I hope and believe that I should not be " out of " criticism. Unless strictly adjusted to the scale and degree suitable to a novel—as Sir Walter has, I think, restricted his Mariolatry and his Jacobitism, and so forth—I should bar them as I bar these.[2] And it is the fact that they are not so restricted, with the concomi-

---

[1] The " Je ne sais pas lire " argument has more than once suggested to me a certain historical comparison. There have probably never been in all history two more abominable scoundrels for pure cold-blooded cruelty, the worst of all vices, than Eccelino da Romano and the late Mr. Broadhead, patron saint and great exemplar of Trade-Unionism. Broadhead could certainly read. Could Ezzelin ? I do not know. But if he could not, the Hugonic belief in the efficacy of reading is not strongly supported. If he could, it is definitely damaged.

[2] *Vide* what is said below on *Quatre-Vingt-Treize.*

tant faults which, again purely from the point of view of novel-criticism as such, I have ventured to find, that makes me consider *Les Misérables* a failure as a novel. Once again, too, I find few of the really good and great things—which in so vast a book by such a writer are there, and could not fail to be there—to be essentially and specially good and great according to the novel standard. They are, with the rarest exceptions, the stuff of drama or of poetry, not of novel. That there are such exceptions—the treacherous feast of the students to the mistresses they are about to desert ; the escapes of Valjean from the ambushes laid for him by Thénardier and Javert ; some of the Saint-Merry fighting ; the guesting of the children by Gavroche in the elephant ; and others—is true. But they are oases in a desert ; and, save when they would be better done in poetry, they do not after all seem to me to be much better done than they might have been by others—the comparative weakness of Hugo in conversation of the kind suitable for prose fiction making itself felt. That at least is what the present writer's notion of criticism puts into his mouth to say ; and he can say no other.

Les Travailleurs de la Mer, on the other hand, is, according to some persons, among whom that present *Les Travailleurs de la Mer.* writer desires to be included, the summit of Victor Hugo's achievements in prose fiction. It has his " signatures " of absurdity in fair measure. There is the celebrated " Bug-Pipe " which a Highlander of the garrison of Guernsey sold (I am afraid contrary to military law) to the hero, and on which that hero performed the "*melancholy* air " of " Bonny Dundee." [1] There is the equally celebrated " First of the Fourth " (Première de la Quatrième), which is

---

[1] After the lapse of more than half a century some readers may have forgotten, and more may never have heard, the anecdote connected with this. It was rashly and somewhat foolishly pointed out to the poet-romancer himself that the air of " Bonny Dundee " was the very reverse of melancholy, and that he must have mistaken the name. His reply was the most categoric declaration possible of his general attitude, in such cases. " Et moi, je l'appelle ' Bonny Dundee.' " *Victor locutus est : causa finita est* (he liked tags of not recondite Latin himself). And the leading case governs those of the bug-pipe and the (later) wapentake and *justicier-quorum*, and all the other wondrous things of which but a few can be mentioned here.

believed to be Hugonic for the Firth of Forth. There
are some others. There is an elaborate presentation of
a quite impossibly named clergyman, who is, it seems,
an anticipator of " le Puseysme " and an actual high-
churchman, who talks as never high-churchman talked
from Laud to Pusey himself, but rather like the Reverend
Gabriel Kettledrummle (with whom Hugo was probably
acquainted " in translations, Sir ! in translations ").[1]
Gilliatt, the hero, is a not very human prig outside those
extraordinary performances, of which more later, and his
consummate end. Déruchette, the heroine, is, like
Cosette, a pretty nullity.[2] As always, the author *will*
not " get under way "; and short as the book is, and
valuable as is its shortness, it could be cut down to two-
thirds at least with advantage. Clubin and Rantaine,
the villains, are pure melodrama ; Mess Lethierry, the
good old man, is rather an old fool, and not so very good.
The real business of the book—the salvage by Gilliatt
of the steamer wrecked on the Douvres—is, as a schoolboy would say, or would have said, " jolly impossible."
But the book as a whole is, despite or because of its tragic
quality, almost impossibly " jolly."

For here—as he did previously (by the help of the form
that was more his own and of Jersey) in the *Contempla-*
The   *tions*—he had now got in prose, by that of
genius loci. the smaller, more isolated, and less contamin-
ated [3] island, into his own proper country, the dominion

---

[1] I do not know whether any one has ever attempted to estimate his actual debt to
Scott. There are better classes of inquiry, but in the class many worse subjects.

[2] In the opening scene she is something worse. If her writing " Gilliatt " in the
snow had been a sort of rustic challenge of the " malo me petit, et fugit ad salices " kind,
there might have been something (not much) to say for her. But she did not know
Gilliatt ; she did not want to know him ; and the proceeding was either mere silly childishness, or else one of those pieces of bad taste of which her great creator was unluckily
by no means incapable.

[3] I use this adjective in no contumelious sense, and certainly not because I have lived
in Guernsey and only visited Jersey. To the impartial denizen of either, the rivalry of
the two is as amusing as is that of Edinburgh and Glasgow, of Liverpool and Manchester,
or of Bradford and Leeds. But, at any rate at the time of which I am speaking, Jersey
was much more haunted by outsiders (in several senses of that word) than Guernsey.
Residents—whether for the purposes unblushingly avowed by that sometime favourite
of the stage, Mr. Eccles, or for reasons less horrifying to the United Kingdom Alliance—
found themselves more at home in " Caesarea " than in " Sarnia," and the " five-pounder,"
as the summer tripper was despiteously called by natives, liked to go as far as he could
for his money, and found St. Helier's " livelier " than St. Peter Port.

of the Angel of the Visions of the Sea. He has told us in his own grandiloquent way, which so often led him wrong, that when he settled to exile in the Channel Islands, his son François observed, " Je traduirai Shakespeare," and *he* said, " Je contemplerai l'océan." He did ; and good came of it. Students of his biography may know that in the dwelling which he called Hauteville House (a name which, I regret to say, already and properly belonged to another) he slept and mainly lived in a high garret with much glass window, overlooking the strait between Guernsey and Sark. These " gazebos," as they used to be called, are common in St. Peter Port, and I myself enjoyed the possession of a more modest and quite unfamous one for some time. They are worth inhabiting and looking from, be the weather fair or foul. Moreover, he was, I believe, a very good walker, and in both the islands made the best of opportunities which are unmatched elsewhere. Whether he boated much I do not know. The profusion of nautical terms with which he " deaves " us (as the old Scotch word has it) would rather lead me to think *not*. He was in this inferior to Prospero ; but I hope it is not blasphemy to say that, *mutatis mutandis*, he had something of the banished Duke of Milan in him, and that, in the one case as in the other, it was the island that brought it out. And he acknowledged it in his Dedication to " Guernesey— *sevère et douce.*"

Sevère et Douce ! I lived in Guernsey as a Master at Elizabeth College from 1868, two years after Victor Guernsey at Hugo wrote that dedication, to 1874, when the time. he still kept house there, but had not, since the " Année Terrible," occupied it much. I suppose the " severity " must be granted to an island of solid granite and to the rocks and tides and sea-mists that surround it. But in the ordinary life there in my time there was little to " asperate " the *douceur*. Perhaps it does not require so very much to sweeten things in general between the ages of twenty-three and twenty-nine. But the things in general themselves were dulcet enough. The beauty of the place—extraordinarily varied in its triangle of some half-score miles or a little less on each side—was, not then in the least interfered with by the excessive commercial glass-housing which, I believe, has come in since. For what my friend of many days, the late Mr. Reynolds of Brasenose and East Ham, a constant visitor in summer, used to call " necessary luxuries," it was still unique. When I went there you could buy not un-drinkable or poisonous Hollands at four shillings a gallon, and brandy—not, of course, exactly cognac or *fine champagne*, but deserving the same epithets—for six. If you were a luxurious person, you paid half-a-crown a bottle for the genuine produce of the Charente, little or not at all inferior to Martell or Hennessy, and a florin for excellent Scotch or Irish whiskey.[1] Fourpence half-penny gave you a quarter-pound slab of gold-leaf tobacco, than which I never wish to smoke better.

But this easy supplying of the bodily needs of the " horse with wings " and his " heavy rider " was as nothing to other things which strengthened the wings of the spirit and lightened the weight of the burden it bore. I have not been a great traveller outside the kingdom of England : and you may doubtless, in the whole of Europe or of the globe, find more magnificent things than you can possibly find in an island of the dimensions given. But for a miniature and manageable assemblage of amenities I do not think you can easily beat Guernsey. The town of St. Peter Port, and its two castles, Fort George above and Castle Cornet below, looking on the strait above mentioned, with the curiously contrasted islets of Herm and Jethou in its midst ; the wonderful coast, first south- and then westward, set with tiny coves of perfection like Bec-du-Nez, and larger bays, across the mouth of which, after a storm and in calm sunny

---

[1] Really good wines were proportionally cheap ; but the little isle was not quite so good at beer, except some remarkable old ale, which one small brewery had ventured on, and which my friends of the 22nd Regiment discovered and (very wisely) drank up.— It may surprise honest fanatics and annoy others to hear that, despite the cheapness and abundance of their bugbear, there was no serious crime of any kind in Guernsey during the six years I knew it, and no disorder worth speaking of, even among sailors and newly arrived troops.

weather, you see lines of foam stretching from headland to headland, out of the white clots of which the weakest imagination can fancy Aphrodite rising and floating shorewards, to vanish as she touches the beach; the great western promontory of Pleinmont, a scarcely lessened Land's End, with the Hanois rocks beyond; the tamer but still not tame western, northern, and north-eastern coasts, with the Druid-haunted level of L'Ancresse and the minor port of St. Samson—all these furnish, even to the well-girt man, an extraordinary number [1] of walks, ranging from an hour's to a day's and more there and back; while in the valleys of the interior you find scenery which might be as far from the sea as Warwick-shire, or on the heights springs which tell you that they must have come from the neighbourhood of the Mount of Dol or the Forest of Broceliande.

With such colour and form of locality to serve, not merely as inspiration but as actual scene and setting, such genius as Hugo's could hardly fail. The thing is sad and delightful and great. As life, you may say, it could not have happened; as literature it could not but have happened, and has happened, at its best, divinely well. The contrast of the long agony of effort and its triumph on the Douvres, with the swift collapse of any possible reward at St. Samson, is simply a windfall of the Muses to this spoiled and, it must be confessed, often self-spoiling child of theirs. There are, of course, absurdities still, and of a different kind from the bug-pipe. I have always wished to know what the experi-ences of the fortunate and reverend but sheepish Ebenezer had been at Oxford—he must certainly have held a King Charles scholarship in his day—during that full-

---

[1] The shape of the island; the position of its only "residential" town of any size in the middle of one of the coasts, so that the roads spread fan-wise from it; the absence of any large flat space except in the northern parish of "The Vale"; the geological forma-tion which tends, as in Devonshire, to sink the roads into deep and sometimes "water" lanes; lastly, perhaps, the extreme subdivision of property, which multiplies the ways of communication—these things contribute to this *pedestrian*-paradise" character. There are many places where, with plenty of good walking "objectives," you can get to none of them without a disgusting repetition of the same initial grind. In Guernsey except as regards the sea, which never wearies, there is no such even partial monotony'

blooded time of the Regency. The circumstances of the marriage are almost purely Hugonian, though it does Hugo credit that he admires the service which he travesties so remarkably. But the *Dieu* (not *diable*) *au corps* which he now enjoys enables him to change into a beauty (in the wholly natural gabble of Mess Lethierry on the recovery of the *la Durande*) those long speeches which have been already noted as blots. And, beauty or blot, it would not have mattered. All is in the contrast of the mighty but conquered Douvres and the comparatively insignificant rocklet—there are hundreds like it on every granite coast—where Death the Consoler sets on Gilliatt's head the only crown possible for his impossible feat, and where the dislike of the ignorant peasantry, the brute resistance of machinery and material, the violence of the storm, the devilish ambush of the *pieuvre*, and all other evils are terminated and evaded and sanctified by the embrace and the euthanasia of the sea. Perhaps it is poetry rather than novel or even romance—in substance it is too abstract and elemental for either of the less majestical branches of inventive literature. But it is great. "By God! 'tis good," and, to lengthen somewhat Ben's famous challenge, "if you like, you may" put it with, and not so far from, in whatever order you please—the deaths of Cleopatra and of Colonel Newcome.

The book is therefore a success; but that success is an evident *tour de force*, and it is nearly as evident to any student of the subject that such a *tour de force* was not likely to be repeated, and that the thing owed its actual salvage to a rather strict limitation of subject and treatment—a limitation hitherto unknown in the writer and itself unlikely to recur. Also that there were certain things in it—especially the travesties of names and subjects of which the author practically knew nothing— the repetition and extension of which *was* likely to be damaging, if not fatal. In two or three years the " fatality " of which Victor Hugo himself was dangerously fond of talking (the warning of Herodotus in the dawn about things which it is not lawful to mention has been too often neglected) had its revenge.

L'Homme Qui Rit is probably the maddest book in recognised literature; certainly the maddest written by
L'Homme Qui Rit. an author of supreme genius without the faintest notion that he was making himself ridiculous. The genius is still there, and passage on passage shows us the real " prose-poétry," that is to say, the prose which ought to have been written in verse. The scheme of the quartette—Ursus, the misanthrope-Good-Samaritan; Homo, the amiable wolf; Gwynplaine, the tortured and guiltless child and youth; Dea, the adorable maiden—is unexceptionable *per se*, and it could have been worked out in verse or drama perfectly, though the actual termination—Gwynplaine's suicide in the sea after Dea's death—is perhaps too close and too easy a " variation of the same thing " on Gilliatt's parallel self-immolation after Déruchette's marriage.[1] Not a few opening or episodic parts—the picture of the caravan; the struggle of the child Gwynplaine with the elements to save not so much himself as the baby Dea; the revulsions of his temptations and persecutions later; and yet others [2]—show the poet and the master.

But the way in which these things are merged in and spoilt by a torrent of silliness, sciolism, and sheer nonsense is, even after one has known the book for forty years and more, still astounding.

One could laugh almost indulgently over the " bug-pipe " and the " First of the Fourth "; one could, being of those who win, laugh quite indulgently over the little outbursts of spite in *Les Travailleurs* at the institutions and ways of the country which had, despite some rather unpardonable liberties, given its regular and royal asylum

---

[1] It is well known that even among great writers this habit of duplication is often, though very far from always, present. Hugo is specially liable to it. The oddest example I remember is that the approach to the Dutch ship at the end of *L'Homme Qui Rit* reproduces on the Thames almost exactly the details of the iron gate of the sewers on the Seine, where Thénardier treacherously exposes Valjean to the clutches of Javert, in *Les Misérables*, though of course the use made of it is quite different.

[2] It must be remembered that this also belongs to the Channel Islands division: and the Angel of the Sea has still some part in it.

to the exiled republican and almost anarchist author.
Certainly, also, one can laugh over *L'Homme Qui Rit* and
its picture of the English aristocracy. But of such laughter,
as of all carnal pleasures (to steal from Kingsley), cometh
satiety, and the satiety is rather early reached in this same
book.   One of the chief " persons of distinction " in
many ways whom I have ever come across, the late Mr.
G. S. Venables—a lawyer of no mean expertness ; one of
the earliest and one of the greatest of those " gentlemen
of the Press " who at the middle of the nineteenth century
lifted journalism out of the gutter ; a familiar of every
kind of the best society, and a person of infinite though
somewhat saturnine wit—had a phrase of contempt for
absurd utterances by persons who ought to have known
better.   " It was," he said, " like a drunk child."   The
major part of *L'Homme Qui Rit* is like the utterance of a
drunk child who had something of the pseudo-Homeric
Margites in him, who " knew a great many things and
knew them all badly."   I could fill fifty pages here easily
enough, and with a kind of low amusement to myself
and perhaps others, by enumerating the absurdities of
L'Homme Qui Rit.   As far as I remember, when the
book appeared, divers good people (the bad people
merely sneered) took immense pains to discover how and
why this great man of letters made so much greater a
fool of himself.   This was quite lost labour ; and without
attempting the explanation at all, a very small selection of
the facts, being in a manner indispensable, may be given.

The mysterious society of " Comprachicos " (Spanish
for " child-buyers "), on whose malpractices the whole
book is founded ; the entirely false conception of the
English House of Lords, which gives much of the superstructure ; the confusion of English and French times
and seasons, manners and customs, which enables the
writer to muddle up Henri-Trois and Louis-Quinze,
Good Queen Bess and Good Queen Anne : these and
other things of the kind can be passed over.   For things
like some of them occur in much saner novelists than
Hugo ; and Sir Walter himself is notoriously not free

from indisputable anachronisms.[1] But you have barely
reached the fiftieth page when you come to a " Lord
Linnæus Clancharlic, Baron Clancharlie et Hunkerville,
Marquis de Corleone en Sicile," whose English peerage
dates from Edward *the Elder* (the origin of his Sicilian
title is not stated, but it was probably conferred by Hiero
or Dionysius), and whose name " Clancharlie " has
nothing whatever to do with Scotland or Ireland.   This
worthy peer (who, as a Cromwellian, exiled himself after
the Restoration) had, like others of the godly, a bastard
son, enjoying at " *temp.* of tale " the remarkable courtesy
title of " Lord David Dirry-Moir," but called by the
rabble, with whom his sporting tastes make him a great
favourite, " Tom-Jim-Jack."   Most " love-children " of
peers would be contented (if they ever had them) with
courtesy titles ; but Lord David has been further favoured
by Fortune and King James II., who has first induced
the *comprachicos* to trepan and mutilate Clancharlie's real
heir (afterwards Gwynplaine, the eponymous hero of
the book), and has then made Lord David a " *pair substitué* "[2] on condition that he marries one of the king's
natural daughters, the Duchess Josiane, a duchess with
no duchy ever mentioned.   In regard to her Hugo
proceeds to exhibit his etymological powers, ignoring
entirely the agreeable heroine of *Bevis of Hampton*, and
suggesting either an abbreviation of " Josefa y Ana "
(at this time, we are gravely informed, there was a prevalent English fashion of taking Spanish names) or
else a feminine of " Josias."   Moreover, among dozens
of other instances of this Bedlam nomenclature, we have
a " combat of box " between the Irishman " Phelem-ghe-
Madone " (because Irishmen are often Roman Catholics ?)
and the Scotchman " Helmsgail " (there is a place called

---

[1] Those of *Ivanhoe* and *Kenilworth* have enraged pedants and amused the elect for a
century.   But I do not remember much notice being taken of that jump of half a millennium and one year more in *The Talisman*, where Count Henry of Champagne " smiles
like a sparkling goblet of his own wine."   This was in 1192, while the ever-blessed Dom
Pérignon did not make champagne " sparkle " till 1693.   Idolatry may suggest that
" sparkling " is a perpetual epithet of wine ; but I fear this will not do.

[2] *Substitué* means " entailed " in technical French.   But I know no instance of this
kind of " contingent remainder " in England.

Helms*dale* in Scotland, and if " gael " why not " gail " ?),
to the latter of whom a knee is given by " Lord Deser-
tum " (Desart ? Dysart ? what ?).

And so it goes on. There is the immortal scene (or
rather half-volume) in which, Hugo having heard or
read of *peine forte et dure*, we find sheriffs who discharge
the duty of Old Bailey judges, fragments of Law Latin
(it is really a pity that he did not get hold of our inimit-
able Law *French*), and above all, and pervading all, that
most fearful wildfowl the " wapentake," with his " iron
weapon." He, with his satellite the justicier-quorum
(but, one weeps to see, not " custalorum " or " rota-
lorum "), is concerned with the torture of Hardquanonne[1]
—the original malefactor[2] in Gwynplaine's case—and
thereby restores Gwynplaine to his (unsubstituted)
rank in the English peerage, when he himself is antici-
pating similar treatment. There is the presentation by
the librarian of the House of Lords of a " little red book "
which is the passport to the House itself : and the very
unmannerly reception by his brother peers, from which
he is in a manner rescued by the chivalrous Lord David
Dirry-Moir at the price of a box on the ears for depriving
him of his " substitution." There is the misconduct
of the Duchess Josiane, divinely beautiful and diabolically wicked, who covets the monster Gwynplaine as a
lover, and discards him when, on his peerification, he is
commanded to her by Queen Anne as a husband. And
then, after all this tedious insanity and a great deal more,
there is the finale of the despair of Gwynplaine, of his
recovery of the dying Dea in a ship just starting for
Holland, of her own death, and of his suicide in the all-
healing sea — a " reconciliation " not far short of the
greatest things in literature.

Now I am not of those unhappy ones who cannot

---

[1] A compound (as Victor himself might suggest) of " Hardyknut " and " Sine qua non " ? Or " Hardbake " ?

[2] He has been found out through the agency of one " Barkilphedro " (Barkis-Phae-
drus ?), an Irishman of a familiar sept, who is " Decanter of the Bottles of the Sea," and
who finds, in one of his trovers, a derelict gourd of confession thrown overboard by the
Comprachicos when wrecked (in another half-volume earlier) all over the Channel from
Portland to Alderney.

away with the mixture of tragedy and farce. I have not only read too much, but lived too long for that. But then the farce must be in life conceivable and in literature conscious. Shakespeare, and even men much inferior to Shakespeare, have been able to provide for this stipulation munificently.

With Victor Hugo, generally more or less and intensively here, it was unfortunately different. His irony was almost always his weakest point; or rather it was a kind of hit-or-miss weapon, with which he cut himself as often as he cut his inimical objects or persons. The intense absurdity of his personified wapentakes, of his Tom-Jim-Jacks, of his courtesy-title bastards, he deliberately declined (as in the anecdote above given) to see. But these things, done and evidently thought fine by the doer, almost put to rout the most determined and expert sifter of the faults and merits of genius. You cannot enjoy a Garden of Eden when at every other step you plunge into a morass of mire. You cannot drink a draught of nectar, arranged on the plan of certain glasses of liqueur, in superimposed layers of different savour and colour, when every other layer is " stummed " folly or nauseous bad taste. A novel is not like a book of poems, where, as you see that you have hit on a failure, you turn the page and find a success. To which it may be added finally that while erudition of *any* kind is a doubtful set-off to fiction, the presentation of ragbag erudition of this kind is, to speak moderately and in his own words of something else, " a rather hideous thing." [1]

Still, with readers of a certain quality, the good omens may to some extent shame the ill even here. The death of Dea, with its sequel, is very nearly perfect; it only wants the verse of which its author was such an absolute

---

[1] Perhaps there is no more conspicuous instance of irritating futility in this way than the famous ἀνάγκη and ἀναγνεία of *Notre-Dame*. Of course anybody who knows no Greek can see that the first four letters of the two words are the same. But anybody who knows some Greek knows that the similarity is purely *literal*, such as exists between " Chateaubriand " and " Chat Botté," and that the ἀν has a different origin in the two cases. Moreover, ἀναγνεία, " uncleanness," is about the last word one would choose to express the *liaison* of thought—" The dread constraint of physical passion " or " Lust is Fate "—which Hugo wishes to indicate. It is a mere jingle, suggestive of a schoolboy turning over the dictionary.

master, instead of the prose, where he alternately triumphed and bungled, to make it so. And one need not be a common paradoxer to take either side on the question whether on the whole the omen, if not the actuality, of *L'Homme Qui Rit* or that of *Les Travailleurs de la Mer* was the happier. For, while the earlier and better book showed how faults were hardening and might grow worse still, the later showed how these very faults, attaining their utmost possible development, could not entirely stifle the rarer gifts. I do not remember that anybody in 1869 took this apparently aleatory side of the argument. If he did he was justified in 1874.

One enormous advantage of *Quatre-Vingt-Treize* over its immediate predecessor lay on the surface—an advan-

Quatre-Vingt-Treize. tage enormous in all cases, but almost incalculable in this particular one. In *L'Homme Qui Rit* Victor Hugo had been dealing with a subject about which he knew practically nothing, and about which he was prepared to believe, or even practise, anything. Here, though he was still prepared to believe a great deal, he yet knew a very great deal more. A little room for his eccentricities remained, and long after the truth had become a matter of registered history, he could accept the legendary lies about the *Vengeur*; but there was no danger of his giving us French wapentakes brandishing iron-weapons, or calling a French noble by any appellation comparable to Lord Linnæus [1] Clancharlie.

But, it may be said, is not the removal of these annoyances more than compensated, in the bad sense, by things inseparable from such a subject, as treated by such an author?—the glorification of "Quatre-Vingt-Treize" itself, and, in particular, of the Convention—that remarkable assembly which seems to have made up its mind to prove for all time that, in democracies, the scum comes to the top?—that assembly in which Fabre d'Eglantine stood for poetry, Marat for humanitarianism, Robespierre

---

[1] That the only person at all likely to be " name-father " of this name was not born till a considerable time after his name-child's death would perhaps be worth remarking in another writer. In Hugo it hardly counts.

for justice, Hébert and Chaumette for decency, Siéyès and Chabot for different forms of religion, the composers of the Republican Calendar [1] for common sense ? where the only suggestion of a great man was Danton, and the only substitutes for an honest one were the prigs and pedants of the Gironde ?   To which the only critical answer must be, even when the critic does not contest the correctness of this description—" Why, no ! "

It is better, no doubt, that a novelist, and that everybody else, should be a *bien-pensant* ; but, as in the case of the poet, it will not necessarily affect his goodness in his art if he is not.   He had, indeed, best not air his opinions, whatever they are, at too great length ; but *what* they are matters little or nothing.   A Tory critic who cannot admire Shelley or Swinburne, Dickens or Thackeray, because of their politics, is merely an ass, an animal unfortunately to be found in the stables or paddocks of every party.   On the other hand, absurdities and faults of taste matter very much.

Now from these latter, which had nearly ruined *L'Homme Qui Rit*, *Quatre-Vingt-Treize*, if not entirely free, suffers comparatively little.   The early and celebrated incident of the carronade running amuck shows characteristic neglect of burlesque possibilities (and, as I believe some experts have maintained, of actual ones), but it has the qualities of the Hugonian defects. An arm-chair critic may ask, Where was the English fleet in the Channel when a French one was allowed to come out and slowly mob the *Claymore* to destruction, without, as far as one sees, any interference or counter-effort, though the expedition of that remarkable corvette formed part of an elaborate and carefully prepared offensive ? [2]   Undoubtedly, the Convention scenes must

---

[1] Let me do even *them* one justice in this connection. They did not suppose that the only way to make people get up earlier was to make those people's clocks and watches tell lies.

[2] There is a smaller point which might be taken up. Undoubtedly there were many double traitors on both sides in the other Great War. But, like all their kind, they had a knack of being found out. Dumas would, I think, have given us something satisfactory as to the " aristocrat " at Jersey who betrayed the *Claymore* to the Revolutionary authorities.

be allowed—even by sympathisers with the Revolution—to be clumsy stopgaps, unnecessary to the action and possessed of little intrinsic value in themselves. The old fault of verbosity and " watering out " recurs ; and so does the reappearance, with very slight change, of figures and situations. Cimourdain in character is very much of a more respectable Claude Frollo; and in conduct, *mutatis* not so very many *mutandis*, almost as much of a less respectable Javert. The death of Gauvain is far less effective than that of Sydney Carton, which had preceded it ; and the enormous harangue of the Marquis to the nephew who is about to liberate him, though it may be intended to heighten the *peripeteia*, merely gives fresh evidence of Hugo's want of proportion and of his flux of rhetoric.

All this and more is true ; yet *Quatre-Vingt-Treize* is, " in its *fine* wrong way," a great book, and with *Les Travailleurs de la Mer*, completes the pillars, such as they are, which support Hugo's position as a novelist. The rescue of the children by Lantenac is superb, though you may find twenty cavils against it easily : and the whole presentation of the Marquis, except perhaps the speech referred to, is one of the best pictures of the *ancienne noblesse* in literature, one which—to reverse the contrast just made—annihilates Dickens's caricature thereof in *A Tale of Two Cities*. The single-handed defence of La Tourgue by " L'Imanus " has of course a good deal of the hyperbole which began with Quasimodo's similar act in *Notre-Dame* ; but the reader who cannot " let himself go " with it is to be pitied. Nowhere is Hugo's child-worship more agreeably shown than in the three first chapters of the third volume. And, sinking particulars for a more general view, one may say that through the whole book, to an extent surpassing even *Les Travailleurs de la Mer* as such, there is the great Victorian *souffle* and surge, the rush as of mighty winds and mightier waters, which carries the reader resistlessly through and over all obstacles.

Yet although Hugo thus terminated his career as a

novelist, if not in the odour of sanctity, at any rate in a
Final comfortable cloud of incense due to a com-
remarks. parative success ; although he had (it is true
on a much smaller scale) even transcended that success in
Les Travailleurs de la Mer ; although, as a mere novice,
he had proved himself a more than tolerable tale-teller
in *Bug-Jargal,* it is not possible, for any critical historian
of the novel as such, to pronounce him a great artist, or
even a tolerable craftsman, in the kind as a whole. It
has already been several times remarked in detail, and
may now be repeated in general, that the things which
we enjoy in his books of this kind are seldom things which
it is the special business of the novelist to produce, and
practically never those which are his chief business. In
no single instance perhaps, with the doubtful exception
of Gilliatt's battle with brute matter and elemental forces,
is " the tale the thing " purely as tale. Very seldom do
we even want to know what is going to happen—the
childishly simple, but also childishly genuine demand
of the reader of romance as such, if not even of the
novel also. Scarcely once do we—at least do I—take
that interest in the development of character which is
the special subject of appetite of readers of the novel, as
such and by itself. The baits and the rewards are now
splendour of style ; now magnificence of imagery ; sometimes grandeur of idea ; often pathos ; not seldom the
delight of battle in this or that sense. These are all
excellent seasonings of novelry ; but they are not the root
of the matter, the *pièce de résistance* of the feast.

Unfortunately, too, Hugo not merely cannot, or at
any rate does not, give the hungry sheep their proper
food—an interesting story worked out by interesting
characters—but will persist in giving them things as
suitable (granting them to be in the abstract nourishing)
as turnips to the carnivora or legs of mutton to the sheep
which walk on them. It would, of course, not be just
to press too strongly the objections to the novel of purpose, though to the present writer they seem almost
insuperable. But it is not merely purpose in the ordinary

sense which leads Victor astray, or rather (for he was much too wilful a person to be led) which he invents for himself to follow, with his eyes open, and knowing perfectly well what he is doing. His digressions are not *parabases* of the kind which some people object to in Fielding and still more in Thackeray—addresses to the reader on points more or less intimately connected with the subject itself. A certain exception has been made in favour of some of the architectural parts of *Notre-Dame de Paris*, but it has been admitted that this will not cover " Ceci Tuera Cela " nor much else. For the presence of the history of the sewers of Paris in *Les Misérables* and any number of other things ; for not a little of the first volume of *Les Travailleurs* itself ; for about half, if not more, of *L'Homme Qui Rit*, starting from Ursus's Black-book of fancy pleasances, palaces, and estates belonging to the fellow-peers of Lord Linnæus Clancharlie and Hunkerville ; for not a few chapters even of *Quatre-Vingt-Treize*, there is no excuse at all. They are simply repulsive or at least unwelcome " pledgets " of unsucculent matter stuck into the body of fiction, as (but with how different results !) *lardons* or pistachios or truffles are stuck into another kind of composition.

It is partly, but not wholly, due to this deplorable habit of irrelevant divagation that Hugo will never allow his stories to " march " (at least to begin with marching),[1] *Quatre-Vingt-Treize* being here the only exception among the longer romances, for even *Les Travailleurs de la Mer* never gets into stride till nearly the whole of the first volume is passed. But the habit, however great a nuisance it may be to the reader, is of some interest to the student and the historian, for the very reason that it does not seem to be wholly an outcome of the other habit of digression. It would thus be, in part at least, a survival of that odd old " inability to begin " which we noticed

---

[1] It is impossible, with him, not to think of Baudelaire's great line in *L'Albatros* (which some may have read even before *Les Travailleurs*)—

> " Ses ailes de géant l'empêchent de *marcher*,"

though the sense is not absolutely coextensive.

several times in the last volume, aggravated by the
irrepressible wilfulness of the writer, and by his determination not to do like other people, who *had* by this time
mostly got over the difficulty.

If any further " dull moral " is wanted it may be the
obvious lesson that overpowering popularity of a particular form is sometimes a misfortune, as that of allegory
was in the Middle Ages and that of didactics in the
eighteenth century. If it had not been almost incumbent
on any Frenchman who aimed at achieving popularity
in the mid-nineteenth century to attempt the novel, it is
not very likely that Hugo would have attempted it. It
may be doubted whether we should have lost any of the
best things—we should only have had them in the com-
pacter and higher shape of more *Orientales*, more *Chants
du Crépuscule*, more *Légendes*, and so forth. We should
have lost the easily losable laugh over bugpipe and
wapentake—for though Hugo sometimes *thought* sillily
in verse he did not often let silliness touch his expression
in the more majestical harmony—and we should have
been spared an immensely greater body of matter which
now provokes a yawn or a sigh.

This is, it may be said, after all a question of taste.
Perhaps. But it can hardly be denied by any critical
student of fiction that while Hugo's novel-work has
added much splendid matter to literature, it has practically nowhere advanced, nor even satisfactorily exempli-
fied, the art of the novel. It is here as an exception—
marvellous, magnificent, and as such to be fully treated ;
actually an honour to the art of which it discards the
requirements, but an exception merely and one which
proves, inasmuch as it justifies, the cautions it defies.[1]

[1] If I have spoken above " so that the Congregation be thereby offended," let me
point out that there is no other way of dealing with the subject critically, except
perhaps by leaving a page blank save for such words, in the middle of it, as " Victor
Hugo is Victor Hugo; and he is for each reader to take or to leave." *He* would, I
think, have rather liked this ; *I* should not, as a person, dislike it ; but I fear it might
not suit with my duty as a critic and a historian.

CHAPTER IV

BEYLE AND BALZAC

THERE may possibly be some readers who might prefer that the two novelists whose names head this chapter should be treated each in a chapter to himself. But after trying several plans (for I can assure such readers that the arrangement of this History has been the reverse of haphazard) I have thought it best to yoke them. That they have more in common with each other, not merely than either has with Hugo or Dumas, or even George Sand, but than either of these three has with the others, few will deny. And as a *practising* novelist Beyle has hardly substance enough to stand by himself, though as an influence—for a time and that no short one and still existing—scarcely any writer in our whole list has been more efficacious. It is not my purpose, nor, I think, my duty, to say much about their relations to each other ; indeed Beyle delayed his novel-work so long, and Balzac codified his own so carefully and so early, that the examination of the question would need to be meticulous, and might even be a little futile in a general history, though it is an interesting subject for a monograph. It is enough to say that, *generally*, both belong to the analytical rather than to the synthetical branch of novel-writing, and may almost be said between them to have introduced the analytical romance; that they compose their palettes of sombre and neutral rather than of brilliant colours ; that actual " story interest " is not what they, as a rule,[1]

---

[1] Of course there are exceptions, *Le Rouge et le Noir* and *La Peau de Chagrin* being perhaps the chief among long novels ; while some of Balzac's short stories possess the quality in almost the highest degree.

aim at. Finally—though this may be a proposition likely to be disputed with some heat in one case if not in both—their conception of humanity has a certain " other-worldliness " about it, though it is as far as possible from being what is usually understood by the adjective " unworldly " and though the forms thereof in the two only partially coincide.

Of the books of Henri Beyle, otherwise Stendhal,[1] to say that they are not like anything else will only seem banal to those who bring the banality with them. To annoy these further by opposing pedantry to banality, one might say that the aseity is quintessential. There never—to be a man of great power, almost genius, a commanding influence, and something like the founder of a characteristic school of literature—was such a *habitans in sicco* as Beyle ; indeed his substance and his atmosphere are not so much dry as *desiccated*. The dryness is not like that which was attributed in the last volume to Hamilton, which is the dryness of wine : it is almost the dryness of ashes. By bringing some humour of your own [2] you may confection a sort of grim comedy out of parts of his work, but that is all. At the same time, he has an astonishing command of such reality, and even vitality, as will (one cannot say survive but) remain over the process of desiccation.

Beyle—his peculiarity.

That Beyle was not such a passionless person as he gave himself out to be in his published works was of course always suspected, and more than suspected, by readers with any knowledge of human nature. It was finally proved by the autobiographic *Vie de Henri Brulard*, and the other remains which were at last given to the world, nearly half a century after the author's death, by M. Casimir Stryienski. But the great part which he played in producing a new kind of novel is properly

---

[1] He tried several other pseudonyms, but settled on this. Unfortunately he sometimes (not always) made it " *De* Stendhal," without anything before the " De," and, more unfortunately still, in the days of his Napoleonic employment he, if he had not called himself, had allowed himself to be called, " M. *de* Beyle "—an assumption which, though dropped, was not forgotten in the days of his later anti-aristocratism.

[2] Beyle himself recognised the necessity of the reader's collaboration.

concerned with the earlier and larger division of the work, though the posthumous stuff reinforces this.

Some one, I believe, has said—many people may have said—that you never get a much truer notion, though you *Armance.* may afterwards get a clearer and fuller, of a writer than from his earliest work.[1] *Armance*, Beyle's first published novel,[2] though by no means the one which has received most attention, is certainly illuminating. Or rather, perhaps one should say that it poses the puzzle which Beyle himself put briefly in the words quoted by his editor and biographer : " Qu'ai-j'été ? que suis-je ? En vérité je serais bien embarrassé de le dire." To tell equal truth, it is but a dull book in itself, surcharged with a vague political spite, containing no personage whom we are permitted to like (it would be quite possible to like Armance de Zohiloff if we were only told less *about* her and allowed to see and hear more *of* her), and possessing, for a hero, one of the most obnoxious and foolish prigs that I can remember in any novel. Octave de Malivert unites varieties of detestableness in a way which might be interesting if (to speak with only apparent flippancy) it were made so. He is commonplace in his adoration of his mother and his neglect (though his historian calls it " respect ") of his father ; he is constantly a prig, as when he is shocked at people for paying more attention to him when they hear that his parents are going to be indemnified to a large extent for the thefts of their property at the Revolution ; he is such a sneak and such a snob that he is always eavesdropping to hear what people say about him ; such a bounder that he disturbs his neighbours by talking

---

[1] This does not apply to poets so much as to prose-writers : a fact for which reasons could perhaps be given. And it certainly does not apply to Balzac.

[2] He was now forty-four, and had published not a few volumes, mostly small, of other kinds—travel-description (which he did uncommonly well), miscellaneous writing, and criticism, including the famous *Racine et Shakespeare*, an *avant-coureur* of Romanticism which contained, besides matter on its title-subjects, some sound estimate of Scott as a writer and some very unsound abuse of him as a man. This last drew from Byron, who had met Beyle earlier at Milan, a letter of expostulation and vindication which did that noble poet infinite credit, but of which Beyle, by no means to *his* credit, took no notice. He was only too like Hazlitt in more ways than one : though few books with practically the same title can be more different than *De l'Amour* and *Liber Amoris*.

loud at the play; such a brute that he deliberately kills a rather harmless coxcomb of a marquis who rebukes him for making this *tapage*; and such a still greater brute (for in the duel he had himself been wounded) that he throws out of the window an unfortunate lackey who gets in his way at a party where Octave has, as usual, lost his temper. Finally, he is a combination of prig, sneak, cad, brute, and fool when (having picked up and read a forged letter which is not addressed to him, though it has been put by enemies in his way) he believes, without any enquiry, that his unlucky cousin Armance, to whom he is at last engaged, is deceiving him, but marries her all the same, lives with her (she loves him frantically) for a few days, and then, pretending to go to the succour of the Greeks, poisons himself on board ship—rather more, as far as one can make out, in order to annoy her than for any other reason. That there are the elements, and something more than the elements, of a powerful story in this is of course evident; there nearly always are such elements in Beyle, and that is why he has his place here. But, as has been said, the story is almost as dull as it is disagreeable. Unluckily, too, it is, like most of his other books, pervaded by an unpleasant suggestion that the disagreeableness is intimately connected with the author's own nature. As with Julien Sorel (*v. inf.*) so with Octave de Malivert, one feels that, though Beyle would never have behaved exactly like his book-child, that book-child has a great deal too much of the uncanny and semi-diabolical doubles of some occult stories in it—is, in fact, an incarnation of the bad Beyle, the seamy side of Beyle, the creature that Beyle might have been but for the grace of that God in whom he did not believe. Which things, however one may have schooled oneself not to let book and author interfere with each other, are not comfortable.

It ought, however, to be said that *Armance* is an early and remarkable Romantic experiment in several ways, not least in the foreign mottoes, English, Portuguese, Spanish, and German, which are prefixed to the chapters.

Unluckily some of them [1] are obviously retranslated from French versions unverified by the originals, and once there is a most curious blunder. Pope's description of Belinda's neck and cross, not quite in the original words but otherwise exact, is attributed to—Schiller !

I have read, I believe, as much criticism as most men, possibly, indeed, a little more than most, and I ought *La Chartreuse* long ago to have been beyond the reach of *de Parme.* shocking, startling, or any other movement of surprise at any critical utterance whatsoever. But I own that an access of *fou rire* once came upon me when I was told in a printed page that *La Chartreuse de Parme* was a " very lively and very amusing book." A book of great and peculiar power it most undoubtedly is, a book standing out in the formidable genealogy of " psychological " novels as (*salva reverentia*) certain names stand out from the others in the greater list that opens the first chapter of St. Matthew. But " lively " ? and " amusing " ? Wondrous hot indeed is this snow, and more lustrous than any ebony are the clerestories towards the south-north of this structure.

To begin with, there rests on the whole book that oppression of *récit* which has been not unfrequently The Water- dwelt upon in the last volume, and sometimes loo episode. in this. Of the 440 pages, tightly printed, of the usual reprint, I should say that two-thirds at least are solid, or merely broken by one or two paragraphs, which are seldom conversational. This, it may be said, is a purely mechanical objection. But it is not so. Although the action is laid in the time contemporary with the writer and writing, from the fall of Napoleon onwards, and in the country (Italy) that he knew best, the whole cast and scheme are historical, the method is that of a lecturer at a panorama, who describes and points while the panorama itself passes a long way off behind a screen of clear but thick glass. In two or perhaps three mostly minute parts or scenes this description may seem

---

[1] As, for instance, those from Dekker and Massinger; Camoens and Ercilla are allowed their native tongues " neat."

unjust. One, the first, the longest, and the best, is perhaps also the best-known of all Beyle's work : it is the sketch of the *débâcle* after Waterloo. (It is not wonderful that Beyle should know something about retreats, for, though he was not at Waterloo, he had come through the Moscow trial.) This is a really marvellous thing and intensely interesting, though, as is almost always the case with the author, strangely unexciting. The interest is purely intellectual, and is actually increased by comparison with Hugo's imaginative account of the battle itself ; but you do not care the snap of a finger *The subject* whether the hero, Fabrice, gets off or not. *and general* Another patch later, where this same Fabrice *colour.* is attacked by, and after a rough-and-tumble struggle kills, his saltimbanque rival in the affections of a low-class actress, and then has a series of escapes from the Austrian police on the banks of the Po, has a little more of the exciting about it. So perhaps for some—I am not sure that it has for me—may have the final, or provisionally final, escape from the Farnese Tower. And there is, even outside of these passages, a good deal of scattered incident.

But these interesting plums, such as even they are, are stuck in an enormous pudding of presentation of the intrigues and vicissitudes of a petty Italian court,[1] in which, and in the persons who take part in them, I at least find it difficult to take the very slightest interest. Fabrice del Dongo himself,[2] with whom every woman falls in love, and who candidly confesses that he does not know whether he has ever been really in love with any woman—though there is one possible exception precedent, his aunt, the Duchess of Sanseverina, and one subsequent, Clélia Conti, who saves him from prison, as above—is depicted with extraordinary science of human nature. But it is a science which, once more, excludes

---

[1] The actual " Chartreuse " of Parma only makes its appearance on the very last page of the book, when the hero, resigning his archbishopric, retires to it.

[2] He is the younger son of a rich and noble family, but his father disowns and his elder brother denounces him quite early. It is characteristic of Beyle that we hear very little of the father and are practically never even introduced to the brother.

passion, humour, gusto—all the *fluids* of real or fictitious
life. Fabrice is like (only "much more álso") the simul-
acra of humanity that were popular in music-halls a
few years ago. He walks, talks, fights, eats, drinks,
thinks even, and makes love if he does not feel it, exactly
like a human being. Except the " fluids " just mentioned, it is impossible to mention anything human that
he lacks. But he lacks these, and by not having them
lacks everything that moves the reader.

And so it is more or less with all of them : with the
Duchess and Clélia least perhaps, but even with them to
some extent ; with the Duchess's first *cicisbeo* and then
husband, Count Mosca, prime minister of the Duke of
Parma ; with his master, the feebly cruel and feebly
tyrannical Ranuce-Ernest IV.; with the opposition in-
triguers at court; with the Archbishop, to whom Fabrice
is made, by the influence of Count and Duchess, coadjutor
and actual successor ; with Clélia's father and her very
much belated husband—with all of them in short. You
cannot say they are " out " ; on the contrary they do and
say exactly what in the circumstances they would do and
say. Their creator's remarks about them are sometimes
of a marvellous subtlety, expressed in a laconism which
seems to regard Marivaudage or Meredithese with an
aristocratic disdain. But at other times this laconic letter
literally killeth. Perhaps two examples of the two effects
should be given :

*(Fabrice has found favour in the eyes and arms of
the actress Marietta)*

The love of this pretty Marietta gave Fabrice all the charms
of the sweetest friendship. *And this made him think of the happiness
of the same kind which he might have found with the Duchess herself.*

If this is not " piercing to the accepted hells beneath "
with a diamond-pointed plunger, I know not what is.

But much later, quite towards the end of the book,
the author has to tell how Fabrice again and Clélia
" forgot all but love " in one of their stolen meetings
to arrange his escape.

(He has, by the way, told a lie to make her think he is poisoned)

She was so beautiful—half-dressed and in a state of extreme passion as she was—that Fabrice could not resist an almost involuntary movement.   No resistance was opposed.[1]

Now I am not (see *Addenda and Corrigenda* of the last volume) avid of expatiations of the Laclosian kind. But this is really a little too much of the " Spanish-fleet-taken-and-burnt-as-per-margin " order.

Much the same characteristics, but necessarily on a small scale, appear in the short stories usually found *L'Abbesse de* under the title of the first and longest of them, *Castro*, etc. *L'Abbesse de Castro*.   Two of these, *Mina de Wangel* and *Le Philtre*, are *historiettes* of the passion which is absent from *La Chartreuse de Parme*; but each is tainted with the *macabre* touch which Beyle affected or which (for that word is hardly fair) was natural to him.   In one a German girl of high rank and great wealth falls in love with a married man, separates him from his wife by a gross deception, lives with him for a time; and when he leaves her on finding out the fraud, blows her brains out.   In the other a Spanish lady, seduced and maltreated by a creole circus-rider of the worst character, declares to a more honourable lover her incurable passion for the scoundrel and takes the veil. The rest are stories of the Italian Renaissance, grimy and gory as usual.   Vittoria Accoramboni herself figures, but there is no evidence that Beyle (although he had some knowledge of English literature [2]) knew at the time our glorious " White Devil," and his story dwells little on her faults and much on the punishment of her murderers.   *L'Abbesse de Castro* itself, *La Duchesse de Palliano, San Francesco à Ripa, Vanina Vanini* are all of the same type and all full of the gloomier items seen by the Dreamer of Fair Women—

---

[1] These four words somehow make me think of Samuel Newcome's comment on the unfortunate dinner where " Farintosh " did not appear : " Scarcely anything was drank."
[2] See note above.

Scaffolds, still sheets of water, divers woes,
Ranges of glimmering vaults with iron grates,

and blood everywhere. And these unmerry tales are
always recounted *ab extra* ; in fact, many of them are real
or pretended abstracts from chronicles of the very kind
which furnished Browning with the matter of *The Ring
and the Book*. It is, however, more apt and more curious
to compare them with the scenes of Gerard's experiences
with the princess in *The Cloister and the Hearth*, as instances of different handling of the same matter by two
novelists of talent almost, if not quite, reaching genius.

This singular aloofness, this separation of subject
and spectator by a vast and impenetrable though trans-
Le Rouge et lucent wall, as in a museum or a *morgue*, is
le Noir. characteristic of all Beyle's books more or
less. In fact, he somewhere confesses—the confession
having, as always in persons of anything like his stamp,
the nature of a boast — that he cannot write otherwise than in *récit*, that the broken conversational or
dramatic method is impossible to him. But an almost
startling change—or perhaps it would be more accurate
to say reinforcement—of this method appears in what
seems to me by far the most remarkable and epoch-
making of his books, *Le Rouge et le Noir*. That there is
a strong autobiographic element in this, though vigorously and almost violently " transposed," must have been
evident to any critical reader long ago. It became not
merely evident but *evidenced* by the fresh matter published thirty years since.

The book is a long one ; it drags in parts ; and, long
as it is, there is stuff in it for a much longer—indeed
Beyle's   preferably for two or three. It is not only a
masterpiece, *roman passionnel,* as Beyle understood passion,
and why. not only a collection of Parisian and Provincial
scenes, but a romance of secret diplomacy, and one of
Seminarist life, with constant side-excursions of Voltairianism in religion, of the revolutionary element in
politics which Voltaire did not ostensibly favour, however
much he may have been responsible for it, of private

cynicism, and above all and most consistently of all, of that psychological realism, which is perhaps a more different thing from psychological reality than our clever ones for two generations have been willing to admit, or, perhaps, able to perceive.

That—to adopt a division which foolish folk have sneered at directly and indirectly, but which is valuable and almost necessary in the case of second-class literature —it is rather an unpleasant than a pleasant book, must be pretty well apparent from what has been already said of its author and itself. That it is a powerful one follows almost in the same way. But what has to be said, for the first, if not also the last, time in reference to Beyle's fiction, is that it is interesting.

The interest depends almost entirely—I really do not think it would be rash to say entirely—upon the Julien Sorel hero and one of the heroines. The other and Mathilde personages are dramatically and psychologic- de la Mole. ally competent, but Beyle has—perhaps save in one or two cases intentionally—made them something of *comparses* or "supers." There may be two opinions about the other heroine, Madame de Rênal, Julien Sorel's first and last love, his victim in two senses and directly the cause of his death, though he was not directly the cause of hers. She seems to me merely what the French call a *femmelette*, feebly amorous, feebly fond of her children, feebly estranged from and unfaithful to her husband, feebly, though fatally jealous of and a traitress to her lover—feebly everything. Shakespeare or Miss Austen[1] could have made such a character interesting, Beyle could not. Nor do the other " seconds "—Julien's brutal peasant father and brothers, the notables of Verrières, the husband, M. de Rênal (himself a *gentillâtre*, as well as a man of business, a bully, and a blockhead), and the hero's just failure of a father-in-law, the Marquis de la Mole—seem to me to come up to the mark. But, after all, they furnish forth the action, and are necessary in their various ways to set forth the

---

[1] Both would have declined to meddle with her, I think, but for different reasons.

character of that hero and his second love, almost in the mediaeval sense his wife and his widow, Mathilde de la Mole, heiress, great lady, *fille folle de son corps*, and, in a kind of way, Queen Whims.

Julien Sorel, allowance being made for his date, is one of the most remarkable heroes of fiction. He is physically handsome, in fact beautiful,[1] intellectually very clever, and possessed, in especial, of a marvellous memory; also, though not well educated early, capable of learning anything in a very short time—but presented in these favourable lights without any exaggeration. A distinguished Lord Justice was said by his admirers, at the beginning of his manhood, to have obtained more marks in examinations than any youthful person in the United Kingdom: and Julien, with equal opportunities, would probably have done the same in France. Morally, in no limited sense of the word, he does not possess a single good quality, and does possess most bad ones, with the possible exceptions of gluttony and avarice. That, being in each case a family tutor or *employé* under trust, he seduces the wife of his first employer and the daughter of the second, cannot, in the peculiar circumstances, be said to count. This is, as it were, the starting-point, the necessary handicap, in the competition of this kind of novel. It is as he is, and in reference to what he does, after this is put aside, that he has to be considered. He is not a stage villain, though he has the peculiar, and in the circumstances important, if highly-to-be-deprecated habit of carrying pocket-pistols. He is not a Byronic hero with a terrible but misty past. He is not like Valmont of the *Liaisons Dangereuses*,[2] a professional and passionless lady-killer. He is not a swindler nor (though he sometimes comes near to this also) a conspirator like Count Fosco of *The Woman in White*. One might make a long list of such negatives if it were worth

---

[1] Beyle, who had himself no good looks, is particularly lavish of them to his heroes.
[2] Perhaps one of the rare biographical details which, as has been explained, may " force the *consigne* " here, is that Beyle in his youth, and almost up to middle age, was acquainted with an old lady who had the very unenviable reputation of having actually " sat for " Madame de Merteuil.

while. He is only an utterly selfish, arrogant, envious, and generally bad-blooded [1] young man, whom circumstances partly, and his own misdeeds helping them, first corrupt and then destroy. You never sympathise with him for one moment, except in a peculiar fashion to be noted presently ; but at the same time he neither quite bores you nor quite disgusts you. *Homo est*, and it is Beyle's having made him so that makes Beyle a sort of genius and much more than a sort of novelist.

But I am not certain that Mathilde is not even a greater creation, though again it is, except quite towards the end, equally impossible to like her. *Femina est*, though sometimes *furens*, oftener still *furiosa* (in a still wider sense than that in which Mr. Norris has [2] ingeniously " feminated " Orlando *Furioso*), and, in part of her conduct already alluded to, as destitute of any morality as Julien himself. Although there could hardly be (and no doubt had better not be) many like her, she is real and true, and there are not a few redeeming features in her artistically and even personally. She is, as has been said, both rich and noble, the famous lover of the third Valois Marguerite being an (I suppose collateral) ancestor of hers.[3] Her father is not merely a patrician but a Minister at the close of the French Restoration ; she may marry any one she likes ; and has, in fact, a train of admirers whom she alternately cajoles and snubs. Julien is taken into the household as half private secretary, half librarian ; is especially favoured by her father, and treated by her brother (one of Beyle's few thoroughly good fellows) almost on equal terms. But his bad blood and his want of breeding make him stiff and mysterious, and Mathilde takes a perverse fancy to him, the growth of which is skilfully drawn. Although she is nothing so little as a

---

[1] This bad-bloodedness, or κακοήθεια, of Beyle's heroes is really curious. It would have qualified them later to be Temperance fanatics or Trade Union demagogues. The special difference of all three is an intense dislike of somebody else " having something."

[2] In that merry and wise book *Clarissa Furiosa*.

[3] She keeps the anniversary of his execution, and imitates Marguerite in procuring and treasuring, at the end of the story, Julien's severed head. (It may be well to note that Dumas had not yet written *La Reine Margot*.)

Lélia or an Indiana or a Valentine (*vide* next chapter),
she is idiosyncratically romantic, and at last it is a case of
ladders up to the window, "the irreparable," and various
wild performances on her part and her lover's.   But this
is all comparatively banal.   Beyle's touch of genius only
reappears later.   An extraordinary but (when one comes
to think of it) not in the least unnatural series of " ups
and downs " follows.   Julien's bad blood and vulgar
nature make him presume on the advantage he has
obtained ; Mathilde's *morgue* and hot-headedness make
her feel degraded by what she has given.   She neglects
him and he becomes quite frantic about *her* ; he takes
sudden dudgeon and she becomes frantically desirous of
him.   This spiritual or emotional man-and-woman-in-
the-weather-house business continues ; but at last, with
ambages and minor peripeteias impossible to abstract,
it so comes about that the great and proud Marquis de
La Mole, startlingly but not quite improbably, chooses
to recognise this traitor and seducer as a possible by-blow
of nobility, gets him a commission, endows him hand-
somely, and all but gives his consent to a marriage.

Then the final revolution comes.   With again extra-
ordinary but, as it is told, again not inconceivable audacity,
Julien refers for character to his first mistress in both
senses, Madame de Rênal, and she " gives him away."
The marquis breaks off the treaties, and Julien, leaving
his quarters, journeys down to Verrières and shoots
Madame de Rênal (with the pocket-pistols) in church.
She does not die, and is not even very seriously wounded ;
but he is tried, is (according, it would seem, to a state of
French law, which contrasts most remarkably with one's
recent knowledge of it) condemned, and after a time
is executed for a murder which has not been committed.
Mathilde (who is to bear him a child and always considers
herself his wife) and Madame de Rênal both visit him
in prison, the former making immense efforts to save
him.   But Julien, consistently with his character all
through, is now rather bored by Mathilde and exceedingly fond of Madame de Rênal, who dies shortly after

him. What becomes of Mathilde we are not told, except that she devotes herself to her paulo-post-future infant. The mere summary may seem rather pre-posterous ; the book is in a way so. But it is also, in no ordinary sense, once more real and true. It has sometimes been regarded as a childish, but I believe it to be a true, criterion of novels that the reader should feel as if he would like to have had personal dealings with the personages. I should very much like to have shot [1] Julien Sorel, though it would have been rather an honour for him. And I should very much like to have made Mathilde fall in love with me. As for Madame de Rênal, she was only good for suckling fools and telling tales out of school. But I do not find fault with Beyle for drawing her, and she, too, is very human.

In fact the book, pleasant or unpleasant, if we reflect on what the French novel was at the time, deserves a very high place. Compare it with others, and nowhere, except in Balzac, will you find anything like it for firm analysis of character, while I confess that it seems to me to be more strictly human of this world, and at the same time more original,[2] than a good deal of the *Comédie*.

The question, " Would a novelist in altered circumstances have given us more or better novels ? " is some-

The resusci-
tated work—
Lamiel. times treated as *ultra vires* or *nihil ad rem* on the critic's part. I myself have been accused rather of limiting than of extending the province of the literary critic; yet I think this question is, sometimes at least, in place. If so, it can seldom be more in place than with Beyle, first because of the un-usually imperfect character of his actual published work ; and secondly, because of the still more unusual abund-ance of half-done work, or of fragments of self-criticism, which what has been called the " Beyle resurrection " of the close of the last century has furnished. Indeed the unfinished and scarcely more than half-drafted novel of

---

[1] In proper duel, of course ; not as he shot his mistress.

[2] Its great defect is the utter absence of any poetical element. But, as Mérimée (than whom there could hardly be, in this case, a critic more competent or more friendly) said, poetry was, to Beyle, *lettre close*.

Lamiel almost by itself suggests the question and supplies the answer. That answer—except from favourers of the grime - novel which, oddly enough, whether by coincidence or common causation became so popular at about the time of this "resurrection"—can hardly be favourable. *Lamiel* is a very grubby little book. The eponymous heroine is adopted as a child by a parish beadle and his wife, who do not at all maltreat her, except by bringing her up in ways of extreme propriety, which she detests, taking delight in the histories of Mandrin, Cartouche and Co. At early maidenhood she is pitched upon as *lectrice*, and in a way favourite, by the great lady of the neighbourhood, the Duchess of Miossens; and in this position first attracts the attention of a peculiarly diabolical little dwarf doctor, who, bar the comic [1] element, reminds one rather of Quilp. His designs are, however, baulked in a most Beylian manner; for Lamiel (who, by a pleasing chance, was at first called "Amiel"—a delightfully *other* Amiel!) coolly bestows some money upon a peasant to "teach her what love is," and literally asks the Gebirian question about the ocean, "Is this all?" after receiving the lesson. Further, in the more and more unfinished parts of the book, she levants for a time with the young duke, quits him, becomes a professional hetaera in Paris, but never takes any fancy to the business of her avocation till she meets an all-conquering criminal, Valbayre.[2] The scenario tells us that, Valbayre having been caught by justice, she sets fire to the Palace thereof, and her own bones are discovered in the ashes.

This, though Beyle at least meant to season the misanthropy with irony (he might be compared with

---

[1] It seems, curiously enough, that Beyle did mean to make the book *gai*. It is a very odd kind of gaiety!

[2] This attraction of the *forçat* is one of the most curious features in all French Romanticism. It was perhaps partly one of the general results of the Revolutionary insanity earlier, partly a special symptom or sequel of Byronism. But the way it raged not only among folk like Eugène Sue, but among men and women of great talent and sometimes genius—George Sand, Balzac, Dumas, Victor Hugo—the last and greatest carrying it on for nearly two generations—is a real curiosity of literature. (The later and different crime-novel of Gaboriau & Co. will be dealt with in its place.)

Meredith for some slightly cryptic views of " the Comic Spirit "), is rather poor stuff, and certainly shows no improvement or likelihood of improvement on the earlier productions. It is even somewhat lamentable, not so much for the presence of grime as because of the absence of any other attraction. *Le Rouge et le Noir* is not exactly rose-pink, but it derives hardly any, if any, interest from its smirches of mud and blood and blackness. In *Lamiel* there is little else. Moreover, that unchallenge-able " possibility of humanity " which redeems not merely *Le Rouge et le Noir* but the less exciting books, is wanting here. Sansfin, the doctor, is a mere monstrosity in mind as well as in body, and, except perhaps when she ejaculates (as more briefly reported above), " Comment ! ce fameux amour, *ce n'est que ça ?* " Lamiel herself is not made interesting.

The *Vie de Henri Brulard*, of high importance for a History of Novelists, is in strictness outside the subject of a historian of the Novel, though it might be adduced to strengthen the remarks made on Rousseau's *Confessions*.[1] And the rest of the " resurrected " matter is also more autobiographical, or at best illustrative of Beyle's restless and " masterless " habit of pulling his work to pieces—of " never being able to be ready " (as a deservedly unpopular language has it) —than contributory to positive novel-achievement. But the first and by far the most substantive of the *Nouvelles Inédites*, which his amiable but not very strong-minded literary executor, Colomb, published soon after his death, needs a little notice.

The Nouvelles Inédites.

Le Chasseur Vert [2] (which had three other titles, three successive prefaces, and in its finished, or rather unfinished, form is the salvage of five folio volumes of MS., the rest being at best sketched and at worst illegible) contains, in what we have of it,

Le Chasseur Vert.

---

[1] *V. sup.* vol. i. p. 39.

[2] A pseudonymous person has " reconstituted " the story under the title of *Lucien Leewwen* (the hero's name). But some not inconsiderable experience of reconstitutions of this kind determined me to waste no further portion of my waning life on any one of them.

the account of the tribulations of a young sub-lieutenant
of Lancers (with a great deal of money, a cynical but
rather agreeable banker-papa, an adoring mother, and
the record of an expulsion from the Polytechnique for
supposed Republicanism) suddenly pitchforked into
garrison, soon after the Revolution of July, at Nancy.
Here, in the early years of the July monarchy, the whole
of decent society is Legitimist; a very small but not easily
suppressible minority Republican; while officialdom,
civil and military, forms a peculiar *juste milieu*, supporting
itself by espionage and by what Their Majesties of the
present moment, the Trade Unions, call "victimisation,"
but in a constant state of alarm for its position, and "looking over its shoulder" with a sort of threefold squint, at
the white flag, the eagles—and the guillotine.   Nothing
really happens, but it takes 240 pages to bring us to an
actual meeting between Lieutenant Lucien Leeuwen and
his previously at distance adored widow, the Marquise de
Chasteller.

The book is not a *very* good novel, even as a fragment,
and probably nothing would ever have made it so as a
whole.   But there is good novel-stuff in it, and it is
important to a student of the novel and almost indispensable to a student of this novelist.   Of the cynical
papa—who, when his son comes to him in a "high-
falutin" mood, requests him to go to his (the papa's)
opera-box, to replace his sire with some agreeable girl-
officials of that same institution, and to spend at least
200 francs on a supper for them at the Rocher—one
would gladly see more.   Of the barrack (or rather *not*-
barrack) society at Nancy, the sight given, though not
agreeable, is interesting, and to any one who knew
something of our old army, especially before the abolition
of purchase, very curious.   There is no mess-room and
apparently no common life at all, except on duty and at
the "pension" hotel-meals, to which,—rather, it would
seem, at the arbitrary will of the colonel than by "regulation,"—you have to subscribe, though you may, and
indeed must, live in lodgings exactly like a *particulier*.

Of the social-political life of the place we see rather too much, for Beyle, not content with making the politics which he does not like make themselves ridiculous—or perhaps not being able to do so—himself tells us frequently that they *are* ridiculous, which is not equally effective. So also, instead of putting severe or " spiritual " speeches in Lucien's mouth, he tells us that they *were* spiritual or severe, an assurance which, of course, we receive with due politeness, but which does not give us as much personal delectation as might be supplied by the other method.   No doubt this and other things are almost direct results of that preference for *récit* over semi-dramatic evolution of the story by deed and word, which has been noticed.   But they are damaging results all the same : and, after making the fairest allowance for its incomplete condition, the thing may be said to support, even more than *Lamiel* does, the conclusion already based upon the self-published stories (and most of all upon that best of them, *Le Rouge et le Noir*) that Beyle could never have given us a thoroughly hit-off novel.

Still, there is always something unfair in making use of " Remains," and for my part I do not think that, Beyle's place unless they are of extraordinary merit, they in the story. should ever be published.   "Death *should* clear all scores " in this way as in others.   Yet no really critical person will think the worse of Beyle's published work because of these *anecdota*, though they may, as actually before us, be taken as throwing some light on what is not so good in the *publicata*.   There can be no doubt that Beyle occupies a very important position in the history of the novel, and not of the French novel only, as the first, or almost the first, analyst of the ugly for fictitious purposes, and as showing singular power in his analysis.   Unfortunately his synthetic gifts were not equally great.   He had strange difficulty in making his stories *march* ; he only now and then got them to *run* ; and though the real life of his characters has been acknow-ledged, it is after all a sort of " Life-in-Death," a new manifestation of the evil power of that mysterious entity whom Coleridge, if he did not discover, first named and produced in quasi-flesh, though he left us without any indication of more than one tiny and accidental part of her dread kingdom.

He has thus the position of *père de famille*, whether (to repeat the old joke) of a *famille déplorable* in the moral, not the sentimental, sense, must, I suppose, be left matter of opinion. The plentiful crop of monographs about him since M. Stryienski's Pompeian explorations and publications is in a manner—if only in a manner— justified by the numerous followers — not always or perhaps often conscious followers, and so even more important—in his footsteps. Nobody can say that the picaresque novelists, whether in their original country or when the fashion had spread, were given to *berquinades* or fairy-tales. Nobody can say that the tale-writers who preceded and followed them were apostles of virtue or painters of Golden-Age scenes. But, with some exceptions (chiefly Italian) among the latter, they did not, unless their aim were definitely tragical—an epithet which one could show, on irrefragable Aristotelian principles, to be rarely if ever applicable to Beyle and his school— they did not, as the common phrase goes, " take a gloomy view " only. There were cakes and ale; and the cakes did not always give internal pains, nor the ale a bad headache. As even Hazlitt (who has been selected, not without reason, as in many ways like Beyle) said of him- self on his death-bed, rather to some folks' surprise though not to mine, most of the characters " had a happy life," though the happiness might be chequered: and some of them were " good." It is scarcely an exaggera- tion to say that in Beyle's books happiness does not exist, and virtue has hardly a place. There are some characters who may be said to be neutral or " on the line "; they may be not definitely unhappy or definitely bad. But this is about as far as he ever goes in that direction. And accordingly he and his followers have the fault of one-sidedness; they may (he did) see life steadily, but they do not see it whole. There is no need to preach a sermon on the text : in this book there is full need to record the fact.[1]

In dealing with Beyle's greater companion here there are certain things—not exactly difficulties, but circumstances conditioning the treatment — which should be stated. That it is well to know something about your subject has been an accepted doctrine with all save very young persons, idle paradoxers, and (according to Sir Walter Scott) the Scottish Court of Session in former days.[2] That it is also well not to know too much about it has sometimes been maintained, without any idleness in either sense of the word ; the excess being thought likely to cause weariness, " staleness," and absence of interest. If this were necessarily so, it might be better for the writer once more to leave this part of the chapter (since at least the heading of it could not possibly be omitted in the history) a blank or a constellation of asterisks in Sternian fashion.   For it has fallen to his lot to translate one whole novel of Balzac's,[3] to edit a translation of the entire *Comédie*,[4] superintending some of the volumes in narrow detail, and studying each in short, but (intentionally at least) thorough *Introductions*, with a very elaborate preface-study of the whole ; to read all Balzac's rather voluminous miscellanea from the early novel-attempts to posthumous things, including letters ; and, finally, to discuss the subject once more, with the aid or burden of many previous commentaries, in a long *Review* article.[5] Nevertheless, he does not feel that any disgust forbids while a clear duty calls : and he hopes to show that it is not always necessary to weary of quails as in the Biblical,

Balzac— conditions of the present dealing.

---

[1] It may be desirable to glance at Beyle's avowed or obvious " intentions " in most if not all his novels—in the *Chartreuse* to differentiate Italian from French character, in *Le Rouge et le Noir* to embody the Macchiavellian-Napoleonic principle which has been of late so tediously phrased (after the Germans) as " will to " something and the like. These intentions may interest some : for me, I must confess, they definitely get in the way of the interest. For essays, " good " : for novels, " no."

[2] Vide *Guy Mannering* as to the " macers."

[3] *Les Chouans.*

[4] Forty vols. London : 1895-8.

[5] *Quarterly Review* for January 1907.

partridges as in the old *fabliau*, and pigeons in the Dumas *fils* (*v. inf.*) version of the Parable of Satiety.

In no case, however, not even in that of Victor Hugo, is the easement given by the general plan of the book, Limitations of subject. in regard to biographical and other not strictly literary details, more welcome. We shall say nothing on the point whether the author of the *Comédie Humaine* should be called M. de Balzac or M. Balzac or M. Balssa ; nothing about his family, his friends, his enemies, his strangely long-deferred, and, when it came, as strangely ill-fated marriage ; little, though something necessarily, about his tastes, his commercial and other enterprises, and so forth ; and not very much—something here also becoming obligatory—on his manner of producing the immense and wonderful work which he has left us. Those who are curious about such things will find ample satisfaction in the labours of M. Spoelberch de Lovenjoul, of MM. Christophe and Cerfbeer, and of others.[1] Here he is, for us, Honoré de Balzac, author of the *Juvenilia* (saved from, as it is understood, a larger bulk still) in ten ·volumes; of the mighty " Comedy " itself, and, more incidentally, of the considerable epistolary and miscellaneous production referred to above. The manner in which this enormous output was put out has perhaps too much to do with its actual character to be passed over in total silence. It represents thirty years' working time almost entirely spent upon it,[2] the alternatives being the above-mentioned commercial speculations (which were almost invariably unfortunate, and involved him, during the whole of his career, in complicated indebtedness) and a good deal of travel, very frequently connected with these speculations. Of the society which formed so large a part of the life of the time and of which he wrote so often, Balzac saw little. He worked at enormous stretches, and he rewrote his work, in MS., in

[1] I believe I may say, without fatuity, that the general Introduction and the *Quarterly* article, above referred to, contain most things that anybody but a special student will need.

[2] It is, however, important to remember that almost the whole of the first of these three decades was taken up with the tentatives, while the concluding *lustrum* was comparatively infertile. The *Comédie* was, in the main, the crop of fifteen years only.

proof and in temporarily final print, with insatiable and indefatigable industry. To no writer could the commonplace extravagance about burning the candle at both ends be applied so truly as to Balzac. Only, his candle was shaped like a wheel with no felloes, and he burnt it at the end of every spoke and at the nave as well. How he managed to last, even to fifty, is one of the major curiosities of literary biography.

Of the three divisions of this vast but far from chaotic production, the miscellaneous, of course, concerns us *And of Balzac* least. It shows Balzac as a failure of a *himself.* dramatist, a critic of very varying competence,[1] not a particularly effective *writer* merely as such, not possessed of much logical power, but having pretty wide interests and abundantly provided with what we may call the odd tools of the novelist's workshop. As a correspondent his writing has absolutely none of what may be called the " departmental " interest of great letter-writers—of Madame de Sévigné or Lady Mary, of Horace Walpole or Cowper ; its attraction is not epistolary but wholly autobiographic. And it is only fair to say that, despite Balzac's immense and intense self-centredness, it leaves one on the whole with a much better opinion of him as a man than might be derived from his books or from the anecdotes about him. To adapt one of the best known of these, there was, in fact, nothing real to him but Honoré de Balzac, Honoré de Balzac's works and schemes, and, in rare cases (of which Madame Hanska was the chief), Honoré de Balzac's loves. These constituted his subject, his universe of thought and feeling, of action and passion. But at the same time he stands apart from all the other great egotists. He differs from those of whom Byron is the chief in that he does not introduce himself prominently in his fictitious creations. He does not, like those who may take their representative in Goethe, regard everything merely as it relates to his

---

[1] It ought always to be, but has not always been, put as a round sum to his credit in this part of the account that he heartily recognised the value of Scott as a novelist. A hasty thinker might be surprised at this ; not so the wiser mind.

personality. His chief peculiarity, his unique literary character, and, it may be added at once, his greatness and his weakness, all consist in the fact that he evolves a new world out of himself. Now and then he may have taken an actual human model—George Sand, Madame d'Agoult, Madame de Castries, Liszt, Latouche,[1] Rémusat—as many others as anybody likes. But always these had not merely to receive the Balzacian image and superscription, but to be transmuted into creatures of a *Balzacium Sidus.* And it is the humanity of this planet or system, much more than of our world, whereof his *Comédie* is the Comedy—a *Comédie Balzacienne.*

But, it has been said, and the saying has been attributed to no less a critic than M. Faguet, there are no " general Balzac's ideas " in Balzac.[2] One can only reply, "general " Heavens ! Why should there be ? " The ideas." celebrated unreason of " going to a gin-palace for a leg of mutton " (already quoted, and perhaps to be quoted again) is sound and sensible as compared with asking general ideas from a novelist. They are not quite absolutely forbidden to him, though he will have to be very careful lest they get in his way. But they are most emphatically not his business, except as very rare and very doubtful means to a quite different end, means absolutely insufficient by themselves and exceedingly difficult to combine with the other means which—more or fewer of them—are not only sufficient but necessary. The " slice of human life," not necessarily, but preferably ordinary,

---

[1] This remarkable person deserves at least a note here " for one thing that he did "— the novel of *Fragoletta* (1829), which many should know *of*—though they may not know *it*—from Mr. Swinburne's poem, and some perhaps from Balzac's own review. It is one of the followings of *La Religieuse,* and is a disappointing book, not from being too immoral nor from being not immoral enough, but because it does not " come off." There is a certain promise, suggestion, " atmosphere," but the actual characterisation is vague and obscure, and the story is told with no grasp. This habit of " flashing in the pan " is said to have been characteristic of all Latouche's work, which was fairly voluminous and of many different kinds, from journalism to poetry ; and it may have been partly due to, partly the cause of, a cross-grained disposition. He had, however, a high repute for spoken if not for written criticism, had great influence as a trainer or mentor on George Sand, and perhaps not a little on Balzac himself. During the later years of his fairly long life he lived in retirement and produced nothing.

[2] One of the friends who have read my proofs takes a more Alexandrian way with this objection and says " But there *are.*" I do not know that I disagree with him : but as he does not disagree with what follows in itself, both answers shall stand.

presenting probable and interesting characters, connected by sufficient plot, diversified and adorned by descriptive and other devices, and abundantly furnished with the conversation of men and women of this world, the whole forming such a whole as will amuse, thrill, affect, and in other ways, to use the all-important word once more, *interest* the reader,—that is what is wanted. And this definition is as rigid at least as the Aristotelian definition of tragedy and perhaps more exhaustive, as concerns the novel, including, with the necessary modifications, the romance—and the romance, including, with the necessary modifications, the novel. In it "general ideas," unless a very special and not at all usual meaning is attached to the term, can have no right of place. They may be brought in, as almost anything may be brought in if the writer is Samson enough to bring it. But they cannot be demanded of him as facts, images, emotions, style, and a very large number of other things can or may be, not, of course, all at once, but in larger or smaller selection. General ideas may and perhaps should be demanded from the philosopher, the historian, the political student. From the poet and the novelist they cannot be. And that they should be so demanded is one of the chief instances of what seems to the present writer to be the greatest mistake of French novel-, as of other, criticism—its persistent relapse upon the rule-system and its refusal to judge by the result.[1]

It is all the more unreasonable to demand general *ideas* from Balzac himself, because he is so liberal of general *imagery*, and what is more, general *prosopopœia*. Be the Balzacian world real, as some would have it to be, or be it removed from our mundane reality by the subtle "other-planetary" influence which is apparent to others, its complexity, its fullness, its variety, its busy and by no means unsystematic life and motion, cannot be denied. Why on earth cannot people be content with asking Platonism from Plato and Balzacity from Balzac? At any rate, it is Balzacity which will be the subject of the

[1] Cf. Maupassant's just protest against this, to which we shall come.

following pages, and if anybody wants anything else let him go elsewhere.

There is hardly likely to be much grumbling at the absence of such detailed abstract or survey of individual

Abstinence from abstract. books as has been given in cases of what may seem to be much less importance. To begin with, such a survey as is possible[1] exists already from these hands in the Introductions to the translated edition above referred to, and to paraphrase or refashion it here would probably occupy a hundred pages, if not more. Nor would the plan, elsewhere adopted, of analysing afresh one, or two, or more examples, as representative, be satisfactory. Although Balzac is in a sense one of the most intensely individual of all novelists, his individuality, as in a very few others of the greatest cases, cannot be elicited from particular works. Just as *Hamlet* will give you no idea of the probable treatment of *As You Like It*, so *Eugénie Grandet* contains no key to *La Cousine Bette*. Even the groups into which he himself rather empirically, if not quite arbitrarily, separated the *Comédie*, though they lend themselves a little more to specification, do not yield very much to the classifier. The *Comédie*, once more, is a world—a world open to the reader, " all before him." Chronological order may tell him a little about Balzac, but it will not tell him very much about Balzac's work that he cannot gain from the individual books, except in the very earliest stages. There is no doubt that the *Œuvres de Jeunesse*, if not very delightful to the reader (I have myself read them not without pleasure), are very instructive ; the instruction increases, while the pleasure is actually multiplied, when you come to *Les Chouans* and the *Peau de Chagrin*. But it is, after a fashion, only beyond these that the true Balzac begins, and the beginning is, to a large extent, a reaction from previous work in consequence of a discovery that the genius, without

---

[1] An actual reduction of Balzac's books to smaller but still narrative scale is very seldom possible and would be still more rarely satisfactory. The best substitute for it is the already glanced at *Répertoire* of MM. Christophe and Cerfbeer, a curious but very satisfactory Biographical Dictionary of the Comedy's *personae*.

which he had acknowledged that it was all up with him,[1] did not lie that way, and that he had no hope of finding it there. Not that there is no genius in the two books mentioned; on the contrary, it is there first to be found, and in *La Peau* is of the first order. But their ways are not the ways in which he was to find it—and himself—more specially.

As to *Argow le Pirate*[2] and *Jane la Pâle* (I have never ceased lamenting that he did not keep the earlier title, The Œuvres *Wann-Chlore*) and the rest, they have interest of de Jeunesse. various kinds. Some of it has been glanced at already—you cannot fully appreciate Balzac without them. But there is another kind of interest, perhaps not of very general appeal, but not to be neglected by the historian. They are almost the only accessible body, except Pigault-Lebrun's latest and Paul de Kock's earliest, of the popular fiction *before* 1830, of the stuff of which, as previously mentioned, Ducray - Duminil, the lesser Ducange, and many others are representatives, but representatives difficult to get at. This class of fiction, which arose in all parts of Europe during the last years of the eighteenth century and the earlier of the nineteenth, has very similar characteristics, though the examples differ very slightly in different countries. What are known with us as the Terror Novel, the Minerva Press, the Silver Fork school, etc. etc., all have their part in it, and even higher influences, such as Scott's, are not wanting. *Han d'Islande* and *Bug - Jargal* themselves belong to some extent to the class, and I am far from certain that the former is at all better than some of these *juvenilia* of Balzac's. But as a whole they are of course little more than curiosities.

Whether these curiosities are more widely known than they were some five-and-twenty, or thirty, years

---

[1] " Sans génie je suis flambé," as he wrote early to his sister.

[2] This is about the best of the batch, and I agree with those who think that it would not have disfigured the *Comédie*. Indeed the exclusion of these *juvenilia* from the *Édition Définitive* was a great critical blunder. Even if Balzac did once wish it, the " dead hand " is not to be too implicitly given way to, and he was so constantly changing his views that he probably would have altered this also had he lived.

ago, when Mr. Louis Stevenson was the only friend of mine who had read them, and when even special writers on Balzac sometimes unblushingly confessed that they had not, I cannot say. Although printed in the little fifty-five-volume [1] edition which for so many years represented Balzac, they were excluded, as noted above, from the statelier "Définitive," and so may have once more " gone into abscondence." I do not want to read them again, but I no more repent the time once spent on them than I did earlier. In fact I really do not think any one ought to talk about Balzac who has not at least gained some knowledge of them, for many of their defects remained with him when he got rid of the others. These defects are numerous enough and serious enough. The books are nothing if not uncritical, generally extravagant, and sometimes (especially in *Jean Louis*) appallingly dull. Scarf-pins, made of poisoned fish-bones (*Argow le Pirate*), extinction of virgins under copper bells (*Le Centénaire*), attempts at fairy-tales (*La Dernière Fée*) jostle each other. The weaker historical kind figures largely in *L'Excommunié* (one of the least bad), *L'Israëlite*, *L'Héritière de Birague*, *Dom Gigadas*. There is a *Vicaire des Ardennes* (remarkably different from him of Wakefield), which is a kind of introduction to *Argow le Pirate*, and which, again, is not the worst. When I formerly wrote about these curious productions, after reading them, I had not read Pigault-Lebrun, and therefore did not perceive, what I now see to be an undoubted fact, that Balzac was, sometimes at least, trying to follow in Pigault's popular footsteps. But he had not that writer's varied knowledge of actual life or his power of telling a story, and though he for the most part avoided Pigault's *grossièreté*, the chaotic plots, the slovenly writing, and other defects of his model abode with him.

There are not many more surprising things, especially *in pari materia*, to be found in literary history than

---

[1] A certain kind of commentator would probably argue from Mr. Browning's well-known words "*fifty* volumes long " that he *had*, and another that he had *not* read the Œuvres de Jeunesse.

the sun-burst of *Les Chouans* after this darkness-that-can-be-felt of the early melodramas. Not that *Les Chouans* is by any means a perfect novel, or even a great one. Its narrative drags, in some cases, almost intolerably; the grasp of character, though visible, is inchoate; the plot is rather a polyptych of separate scenes than a connected action; you see at once that the author has changed his model to Sir Walter and think how much better Sir Walter would have done the thing. But there is a strange air of " coming alive " in some of the scenes, though they are too much separated, as in the case of the finale and of the execution of the rather hardly used traitor earlier. These possess a character of thrill which may be looked for in vain through all the ten volumes of the *Œuvres de Jeunesse*. Montauran *is* a hero in more than one sense, and Mlle. de Verneuil is still more a heroine. Had Balzac worked her out as he worked out others, who did not deserve it so well, later, she might have been one of the great characters in fiction. Even as it is, the "jour sans lendemain," which in one sense unites, and in another parts, her and her lover for ever, is one of the most really passionate things that the French novel, in its revival, had yet seen. Besides this, there is a sort of extrinsic appeal in the book, giving that curious atmosphere referred to already, and recalling the old prints of the earth yawning in patches and animals rearing themselves from it at the Creation. The names and personages of Hulot and Corentin were to be well known later to readers of the "fifty volumes," and even the ruffianly patriot [1] Marche-à-Terre had his future.

The second [2] blast of the horn with which Balzac challenged admission to the Inner Sanctuaries or strongholds of the novel, *La Peau de Chagrin*, had that character of

---

[1] He would not have liked the name " patriot " because of its corruption, but he was one.

[2] Not a few things, some of them very good, came between—the pleasant *Maison du Chat-qui-Pelote*, several of the wonderful short stories, and the beginning of the *Contes Drôlatiques*. But none of them had the "importance"—in the artistic sense of combined merit and scale—of the *Peau*.

difference which one notices not seldom in the first worthy works of great men of letters—the absence of the mould *La Peau de Chagrin.* and the rut. *Les Chouans* was a Waverley novel Gallicised and Balzacified ; *La Peau de Chagrin* is a cross between the supernatural romance and the novel of psychology. It is one of the greatest of Balzac's books. The idea of the skin—a new " wishing " talisman, which shrinks with every exercise of the power it gives, and so threatens extinction at once of wishing and living—is of course not wholly novel, though refreshed in detail. But then nothing is wholly novel, and if anything could be it would probably be worthless. The endless changes of the eternal substance make the law, the curse, and the blessing of life. In the working out of his theme it may possibly be objected that Balzac has not *interested* the reader quite enough in his personages—that he seems in a way to be thinking more of the play than of the actors or the audience. His " orgie " is certainly not much of a success ; few orgies in print are, except when they are burlesqued. But, on the other hand, the curiosity-shop is splendid. Yet it is not on the details of the book, important as these have been allowed to be throughout Balzac, that attention should be mainly concentrated. The point of it is the way in which the necessary atmosphere of bad dream is kept up throughout, yet with an appropriate contrast of comparatively ordinary life. A competent critic who read *Les Chouans*, knowing nothing about its author or his work, should have said, " Here is more than a promising craftsman " ; reading *La Peau de Chagrin* in the same conditions he should have said, " Here is a great, though by no means a faultless, artist." One who read both ought to have had no doubt as to the coming of something and somebody extraordinary.

Thenceforward Balzac, though hardly ever faultless except in short stories, was almost always great, and *The short stories.* showed what may be called a diffused greatness, to which there are few parallels in the history of the novel. Some of the tales are simply

wonderful. I cannot think of any one else, even Mérimée, who could have done *La Grande Bretèche*—the
story of a lover who, rather than betray his mistress, allows
himself to suffer, without a word, the fate of a nun
who has broken her vows—as Balzac has done it. *La
Recherche de l'Absolu* is one, and *Le Chef-d'œuvre Inconnu* is another, of the greatest known masterpieces in
the world of their kind. *La Fille aux Yeux d'Or* and *Une
Passion dans le Désert* have not the least need of their
" indexable " qualities to validate them. In the most
opposite styles *Jésus Christ en Flandre* and *La Messe
de l'Athée* have their warmest admirers. In fact it is
scarcely too much to say that, in the whole list of nearer
two than one score—as they were published in the old
collection from *Le Bal de Sceaux* to *Maître Cornélius*—
scarcely any are bad or insignificant, few mediocre, and
not a few equal, or hardly inferior, to those specially
pointed out just now. As so often happens, the short
story estopped Balzac from some of his usual delinquencies—over-detail, lingering treatment, etc.,—and
encouraged his virtues—intensity, grandeur, and idiosyncratic tone.

Of his one considerable collection of such stories—
the *Contes Drolatiques*—it is not possible to speak quite
The *Contes* so favourably as a whole; yet the reduction
Drolatiques. of favour need not be much. Of its greatest
thing, *La Succube*, there have hardly been two opinions
among competent and unprejudiced judges. " Pity
and terror " are there well justified of their manipulator.
The sham Old French, if not absolutely " according to
Cocker " (or such substitute for Cocker as may be made
and provided by scholarly authority), is very much more
effective than most such things. Not a few of the stories
are good and amusing in themselves, though of course
the votaries of prunes and prism should keep clear of
them. The book has perhaps only one serious fault,
that of the inevitable and no doubt invited suggestion
of, and comparison with, Rabelais. In some points this
will hold not so badly, for Balzac had narrative power of

the first order when he gave it scope ; the deficiencies
of mere style which sometimes affect his modern French
do not appear so much in this *pastiche,* and he could make
broad jokes well enough. But—and this " but " is
rather a terrible one—the saving and crowning grace of
Pantagruelist humour is not in him, except now and
then in its grimmer and less catholic variety or manifestation. And this absence haunts one in these *Contes
Drolatiques,* though it is to some extent compensated by
the presence of a " sentiment " rare elsewhere in Balzac.

Turning to the longer books, the old double difficulty
of selection and omission comes on one in full force.
Notes on select larger books: *Eugénie Grandet.* There are, I suppose, few Balzacians who have
not special favourites, but probably *Eugénie
Grandet, Le Père Goriot,* and the two divisions
of *Les Parents Pauvres* would unite most
suffrages. If I myself—who am not exactly a Balzacian,
though few can admire him more, and not very many,
I think, have had occasion for knowing his work better—
put *Eugénie Grandet* at the head of all the " scenes " of
ordinary life, it is most certainly not because of its
inoffensiveness. It *is* perhaps partly because, in spite
of that inoffensiveness, it fixes on one a grasp superior
to anything of Beyle's and equal to anything of Flaubert's
or Maupassant's. But the real cause of admiration is
the nature of the grasp itself. Here, and perhaps here
only—certainly here in transcendence—Balzac grapples
with, and vanquishes, the bare, stern, unadorned, unbaited,
ironic facts of life. It is not an intensely interesting
book ; it is certainly not a delightful one ; you do not
want to read it very often. Still, when you have read it
you have come to one of the ultimate things : the *flam-
mantia mœnia* of the world of fiction forbid any one to go
further at this particular point. And when this has been
said of a novel, all has been said of the quality of the
novelist's genius, though not of its quantity or variety.

The other three books selected have greater " interest " and, in the case of the *Parents Pauvres* at least,
much greater variety ; but they do not seem to me to

possess equal consummateness. *Le Père Goriot* is in its own way as pathetic as *Eugénie Grandet*, and Balzac has saved its pathos from being as irri-

Le Père Goriot and *Les Parents Pauvres.* tating as that of the all but idiotic grand-father in *The Old Curiosity Shop*. But the situation still has a share of that fatal helpless ineffectiveness which Mr. Arnold so justly denounced. Of the remaining pair, *La Cousine Bette* is, I suppose, again the favourite ; but I am not a backer. I have in other places expressed my opinion that if Valérie Marneffe is part-model [1] of Becky Sharp, which is not, I believe, absolutely certain, the copy far—indeed infinitely—exceeds the original, and not least in the facts that Becky is attractive while Valérie is not, and that there is any amount of possibility in her. I should not wonder if, some day, a novelist took it into his head to show Becky as she would have been if she had had those thousands a year for which, with their accompanying chances of respectability, she so pathetically sighed. Now Valérie is, and always must have been, a *catin*, and nothing else. Lisbeth, again, though I admit her possibility, is not, to me, made quite probable. Hulot, very possible and probable indeed, does not interest or amuse me, and the angelic Adeline is good but dull. In fact the book, by its very power, throws into disastrous eminence that absence of *delightfulness* which is Balzac's great want, uncompensated by the presence of the magnificence which is his great resource. *La Peau de Chagrin* and some of the smaller things have this relief ; *La Cousine Bette* has not. And therefore I think that, on the whole, *Le Cousin Pons* is the better of the two, though it may seem to some weaker, further " below proof." Everything in it is possible and probable, and though the comedy is rather rueful, it is comedy. It is a play ; its companion is rather too much of a sermon.

The " Scènes de la Vie Privée " (to pass to a rapid general survey of the " Acts " of the Comedy) provide

[1] I mean, of course, as far as books go. We have positive testimony that there was a live Becky, and I would I had known her !

an especially large number of short stories, almost the only ones of length being *Modeste Mignon* and *Béatrix*,

Others—the general "scenic" division.

a strongly contrasted couple. *Modeste Mignon* is perhaps one of the best of Balzac's *second* best; *Béatrix*, a book of more power, appeals chiefly to those who may be interested in the fact (which apparently *is* the fact) that the book contains, almost more than any other, figures taken from real people, such as George Sand—the "Camille" of the novel—and some of those about her. The "Scènes de la Vie de Province" are richer in "magnums." *Eugénie Grandet* is here, with a sort of companion, cheerfuller generally, in *Ursule Mirouet*. The shorter stories are grouped under the titles of *Les Parisiens en Province* (with the first appearance of *Gaudissart*) and *Les Rivalités*. *Le Lys dans la Vallée* (which one is sometimes anxiously begged to distinguish from "the lily *of* the valley," otherwise *muguet*) holds, for some, an almost entirely unique place in Balzac's work, or one shared only in part by *Mémoires de Deux Jeunes Mariées*. I have never, I think, cared much for either. But there is more strength in two pairs of volumes which contain some of the author's masterpieces—*Les Célibataires* with *Pierrette*, *Le Curé de Tours*, and the powerful, if not particularly pleasant, *Un Ménage de Garçon*;[1] and *Illusions Perdues*, running up well with *Un Grand Homme de Province à Paris* and the semi-idyllic *Ève et David*.

But I suppose the "Scenes of Parisian Life" seem to be the citadel to most people. Here are three of the four books specially selected above, *Le Père Goriot* and both the constituents of *Les Parents Pauvres*. Here are the *Splendeurs et Misères des Courtisanes*, which some rank among the very first; not a few short stories in the volumes taking their titles from *La Dernière Incarnation de Vautrin* and *La Maison Nucingen*; with *César Birotteau* (*Balzac on Bankruptcy*, as it has been profanely called) and the celebrated *Histoire des Treize*.

---

[1] Originally and perhaps preferably called *La Rabouilleuse* from the early occupation of its heroine, Flore Brazier, one of Balzac's most notable figures.

This last, I confess frankly, has always bored me, even though the volume contains *La Fille aux Yeux d'Or*. The idea of a secret society in Society itself was not new; it was much more worthy of Sue or Soulié than of Balzac, and it does not seem to me to have been interestingly worked out. But perhaps this is due to my perverse and elsewhere confessed objection to crime and conspiracy novels generally.

Neither have I ever cared much for the group of "Scènes de la Vie Politique," ranging from *Une Ténébreuse Affaire* to *Le Député d'Arcis*, the last being not entirely Balzac's own. The single volume, "Scènes de la Vie Militaire," consisting merely of *Les Chouans* and *Une Passion dans le Désert*, is much better, and the "Scènes de la Vie de Campagne" reach a high level with *Le Médecin de Campagne*, *Le Curé de Village*, and the late, grim, but very noteworthy *Les Paysans*.

None, however, of these sometimes rather arbitrary groups of Balzac's contains such thoroughly satisfactory matter as that which he chose to call "Études Philosophiques." It includes only one full-volume novel, but that is the *Peau de Chagrin* itself.[1] And here are most of the short stories singled out at first, *La Recherche de l'Absolu*, *Jésus Christ en Flandre*, *Le Chef-d'œuvre Inconnu*, with *Melmoth Réconcilié*[2] in the same batch. The two volumes entitled *L'Enfant Maudit* and *Les Marana* contain all but a dozen remarkable tales. Here, too, is the curious treatise *Sur Cathérine de Médicis*, with another, to some people among the most interesting of all, the autobiographic *Louis Lambert*, and also the mystical, and in parts very beautiful, *Séraphita*.

The "Études Analytiques," which complete the original *Comédie* with the two notorious volumes of *Physiologie du Mariage* and *Petites Misères de la Vie Conjugale*, are not novels or tales, and so do not concern

---

[1] It is one of the strangest instances of the limitations of some of the best critics that M. Brunetière declined even to speak of this great book.

[2] The immense influence of Maturin in France, and especially on Balzac, is an old story now, though it was not always so.

us.   They are not the only instance in literature showing
that the sarcasm

The *God* you took from a printed book

extends to other things besides divinity.   The old conventional satires on marriage are merely rehashed with
some extra garlic.   Balzac had no personal experience
of the subject till just before his death, and his singular
claustral habits of life could not give him much opportunity for observation.

    Experience, indeed, and observation (to speak with
only apparent paradox), though they played an im-
"Balzacity": portant, yet played only a subordinate part at
  its con- any time in the great Balzacian achievement.
  stitution. Victor Hugo, in what was in effect a funeral
oration, described that achievement as " un livre qui est
l'Observation et qui est l'Imagination." But no one
familiar with the Victorian rhetoric will mistake the *clou*,
the dominating and decisive word of that sentence.   It
is the conjunction.   Hugo meant to draw attention to
the astonishing *union* of Imagination with Observation—
two things which, except in the highest poetry, are apt
to be rather strangers to each other—and by putting
Imagination last he meant also doubtless that this was
the dominating—the masculine—element in the marriage.
In the immense volume of discussion of Balzac which
the long lifetime succeeding his death has seen, and which
thickened and multiplied towards the close of the last
century and a little later—owing to the conclusion of the
Édition Définitive with its additions and illustrative
matter—this point has perhaps been too frequently lost
sight of.   The great critics who were his contemporaries
and immediate survivors were rather too near.   The
greatest of the later batch, M. Brunetière, was a little
too eager to use Balzac as a stick to beat the Romantics
with for one thing, and to make him out a pioneer of all
succeeding French fiction for another.   But, quite
early, Philarète Chasles hit the white by calling him a
voyant (a word slightly varying in signification from our

" seer "), and recently a critic of less repute than Brunetière, but a good one—M. Le Breton—though perhaps
sometimes not quite fair to Balzac, recognises his Romanticism, his *frénésie*, and so the Imagination of which the
lunatic and the lover are—and of which the devotee of
Romance in verse and prose should be—compact.

Nevertheless it would be of course highly improper,
and in fact absurd, to deny the " observation "—at least
in detail of all kinds. Although—as we have seen and
may see again when we come to Naturalism and look
back—M. Brunetière was quite wrong in thinking that
Balzac *introduced* " interiors " to French, and still more
wrong in thinking that he introduced them to European,
novel-writing, they undoubtedly make a great show in
his work—are, indeed, one of its chief characteristics.
He actually overdoes them sometimes ; the " dragging"
of *Les Chouans* is at least partly due to this, and he
never got complete mastery of his tendency that way.
But undoubtedly this tendency was also a source of
power.

Yet, while this observation of *things* is not to be denied,
Balzac's observation of *persons* is a matter much more
debatable. To listen to some of the more uncritical—
especially among the older and now almost traditional—
estimates of him, an unwary reader who did not correct
these, judging for himself, might think that Balzac was
as much of an " observational " realist in character as
Fielding, as Scott when it served his turn, as Miss
Austen, or as Thackeray. Longer study and further
perspective seem recently to have put more people in the
position which only a few held some years ago. The
astonishing force, completeness, *relative* reality of his
creations is more and more admitted, but it is seen (M.
Le Breton, for instance, admits it in almost the very
words) that the reality is often not *positive*. In fact the
Comédie may remind some of the old nautical laudation
of a ship which cannot only sail close to the wind, but
even a point or two on the other side of it. If even
Frenchmen now confess that Balzac's characters are

very often not *des êtres réels*, no Englishman need be
ashamed of having always thought·so.

The fact is that this giant in novel-writing did actually
succeed in doing what some of his brethren in *Hyperion*
would have liked to do—in setting up a new world for
himself and getting out of the existing universe. His
characters are never *in*human; they never fail to be
human; they are of the same flesh and blood, the
same soul and spirit, as ourselves. But they have,
as it were, colonised the fresh planet—the Balzacium
Sidus—and taken new colour and form from its idiosyncrasies.[1]

It is for this reason that one hesitates to endorse
the opinions quoted above as to the filiation of all or
Its effect on most subsequent French fiction upon Balzac.
successors. Of course he had a great influence on it;
such a genius, in such circumstances, could not but
have. The "interior" business was largely followed
and elaborated; it might be argued—though the contention would have to be strictly limited and freely
provisoed—that Naturalism in general—as the "Rougon-
Macquart" scheme certainly was in particular—was a
sort of bastard of the *Comédie*. Other points of relationship might be urged. But all this would leave the most
characteristic Balzacities untouched. In the most obvious
and superficial quality — pessimistic psychology — the
other novelist dealt with in this chapter—Beyle—is far
more of a real origin than Balzac is. If one takes the most
brilliant of his successors outside the Naturalist school—
Flaubert and Feuillet—very little that is really Balzacian
will be found in either. At least *Madame Bovary* and
M. de Camors—which, I suppose, most people would
choose to represent the greatest genius and the most
flexible talent of the Second Empire in novel-writing—
seem to me to show hardly anything that is like Balzac.
The Goncourts have something of degraded Balzacianism

---

[1] It is possible that some readers may miss a more extended survey, or at least sample,
of these characters. But the plea made above as to abstract of the stories is valid here.
There is simply not room to do justice to, say, Lucien de Rubempré, who pervades a
whole block of novels and stories, or to others from Rastignac to Corentin.

on its lower side in them, and Zola approaches, at least in his "apocalyptic" period, something like a similar though less offensive degradation of the higher. But I can hardly conceive anything less like Balzac's work than Maupassant's.

For the fact is that the real Balzac lies—to and for me —almost entirely in that *aura* of other-worldliness of
And its own which I have spoken. It is in the revelation
character. of this other world, so like ours and yet not the same; in the exploration of its continents; in the frequentation of its inhabitants; that the pleasure which he has to give consists. How he came himself to discover it is as undiscoverable as how his in some sort analogue Dickens, after pottering not unpleasantly with Bozeries, "thought of Mr. Pickwick," and so of the rest of *his* human (and extra-human) comedy. But the facts, in both cases fortunately, remain. And it may be possible to indicate at least some qualities and characteristics of the fashion in which he dealt with this world when he *had* discovered it. In *Les Chouans* he had found out not so much it, as the way to it; in the books between that and *La Peau de Chagrin* he was over the border, and with *La Peau* itself he had " crossed Jordan,"—it was all conquest and extension—as far as permitted—of territory afterwards.

There can, I should suppose, be very little doubt that the fancy for the occult, which played a great part,
The "occult" as far as bulk goes, in the *Juvenilia*, but pro-
element. duced nothing of value there, began to bear fruit at this time. The Supernatural (as was remarked of woman to the indignation of Mr. Snodgrass) is a " rum creetur." It is very difficult to deal with; to the last degree unsatisfactory when of bad quality and badly handled; but possessing almost infinite capabilities of exhibiting excellence, and conveying enjoyment. Of course, during the generation before Balzac's birth and also that between his birth and 1830, the Terror Novel— from the *Castle of Otranto* to Maturin—had circled through Europe, and "Illuminism" of various kinds

had taken particular hold of France just before the Revolution. But Balzac's " Occult," like Balzac's everything, was not the same as anybody else's. Whether you take it in *La Peau de Chagrin* itself, or in *Séraphita*, or anywhere, it consists, again, rather in atmosphere than in " figures." A weaker genius would have attached to the skin of that terrible wild ass—gloomier, but more formidable than even the beast in Job [1]— some attendant evil spirit, genie, or " person " of some sort. A bit of shagreen externally, shrinking—with age—perhaps? with weather?—what not?—a life shrinking in mysterious sympathy—that is what was wanted and what you have, without ekings, or explanations, or other trumpery.

Nor is it only in the ostensibly " occult " or (as he was pleased to call them) " philosophic " studies and *Its action and* stories that you get this atmosphere. It *reaction.* spreads practically everywhere — the very bankruptcies and the sordid details of town and country life are overshadowed and in a certain sense *dis*-realised by it. Indeed that verb which, like most new words, has been condemned by some precisians, but which was much wanted, applies to no prose writer quite so universally as to Balzac. He is a *dis*-realiser, not by style as some are, but in thought—at the very same time that he gives such impressions of realism. Sometimes, but not often, he comes quite close to real mundane reality, sometimes, as in the most " philosophical " of the so-called philosophical works, he hardly attempts a show of it. But as a rule when he is at his very best, as in *La Peau de Chagrin*, in *La Recherche de l'Absolu*, in *Le Chef-d'œuvre Inconnu*, he attains a kind of point of unity between disrealising and realising—he disrealises the common and renders the uncommon real in a fashion actually carrying out what he can never have known— the great Coleridgian definition or description of poetry. In fact, if prose-poetry were not a contradiction in terms,

---

[1] It has sometimes occurred to me that perhaps the skin *was* that of Job's onager.

Balzac would be, except in style,[1] the greatest prose-poet of them all.

On[2] one remarkable characteristic of the *Comédie* very little has usually been said. It has been neglected wholly *Peculiarity* by most critics, though it is of the very first *of the* importance. And that is the astonishingly *conversation.* small use, *in proportion*, which Balzac makes of that great weapon of the novelist, dialogue, and the almost smaller effect which it accordingly has in producing his results (whatever they are) on his readers. With some novelists dialogue is almost all-powerful. Dumas, for instance (as is pointed out elsewhere), does almost everything by it. In his best books especially you may run the eye over dozens, scores, almost hundreds of pages without finding a single one printed " solid." The author seldom makes any reflections at all; and his descriptions, with, of course, some famous exceptions, are little more than longish stage directions. Nor is this by any means merely due to early practice in the drama itself; for something like it is to be found in writers who have had no such practice. In Balzac, after making every allowance for the fact that he often prints his actual conversations without typographical separation of the speeches, the case is just the other way. Moreover, and this is still more noteworthy, it is not by what his characters do say that we remember them. The situation perhaps most of all; the character itself very often; the story sometimes (but of that more presently)—these are the things for and by which we remember Balzac and the vast army of his creations; while sometimes it is not even for any of these things, but for " interiors," " business," and the like. When one thinks of single points in him, it is scarcely ever of such things as the " He has got his discharge, by——— ! "

---

[1] He does try a sort of pseudo-poetical style sometimes; but it is seldom successful, and sometimes mere " fine-writing " of no very fine kind. The close of the *Peau de Chagrin* and *Séraphita* contain about the best passages.

[2] The two next paragraphs are, by the kind permission of the Editor and Publisher of the *Quarterly Review*, reprinted, with some slight alterations, from the article above referred to.

of Dickens; as the "Adsum" of Thackeray; as the
"Trop lourd !" of Porthos' last agony; as the longer
but hardly less quintessenced malediction of Habakkuk
Mucklewrath on Claverhouse.   It is of Eugénie Grandet
shrinking in automatic repulsion from the little bench as
she reads her cousin's letter; of Henri de Marsay's
cigar (his enjoyment of it, that is to say, for his words are
quite commonplace) as he leaves "la Fille aux Yeux
d'Or "; of the lover allowing himself to be built up in
"La Grande Bretèche."   Observe that there is not the
slightest necessity to apportion the excellence implied
in these different kinds of reminiscence; as a matter of
fact, each way of fastening the interest and the appreciation of the reader is indifferently good.[1]   But the distinction remains.

There is another point on which, though no good
critic can miss it, some critics seem to dislike dwelling;
And of the   and this is that, though Balzac's separate
"story"   situations, as has just been said, are arresting
interest.   in the highest degree, it is often distinctly
difficult to read him "for the story."   Even M. Brunetière lets slip an admission that "interest" of the ordinary
kind is not exactly Balzac's forte; while another admirer
of his grants freely that his *affabulation* is weak.   Once
more, we need not and must not make too much of
this; but it is important that it should not be forgotten,
and the extreme Balzacian is sometimes apt to forget it.
That it comes sometimes from Balzac's mania for rehandling and reshaping—that he has actually, like the
hero of what is to some his most unforgettable short
story, daubed the masterpiece into a blur—is certain.
But it probably comes more often, and is much more
interesting as coming, from want of co-ordination between the observing and the imagining faculties which
are (as Hugo meant) the yoked coursers of Balzac's
car.

---

[1] I have known this denied by persons of authority, who would exalt the gift of
conversation even above the pure narrative faculty.   I should admit that the latter was
commoner, but hardly that it was inferior.

The fact is that *exceptis excipiendis*, of which *Eugénie Grandet* is the chief solid example, it is not by the ordinary means, or in the ordinary ways, that Balzac makes any considerable part of his appeal. He is very much more *der Einzige* in novel-writing than Jean Paul was in novel-writing or anything else; for a good deal of Richter's uniqueness depended[1] upon eccentricities of style, etc., from which Balzac is entirely free. And the same may be said, with the proper mutations, of George Meredith. No one ever made less use—despite his "details" and "interiors"—of what may be called intellectual or artistic costume and properties than the author of the *Comédie Humaine*. The most egotistical of men in certain ways, he never thrusts his *ego* upon you. The most personal in his letters, he is almost as impersonal in most of his writings (*Louis Lambert*, etc., being avowedly exceptional) as Shakespeare. Now, though the personal interest may be not illegitimate and sometimes great, the impersonal is certainly greater. Thanks to industrious prying, not always deserving the adjective impertinent, we know a great deal about Balzac; and it is by no means difficult to apply some of the knowledge to aid the study of his creation. But in reading the creation itself you never need this knowledge; it never forces itself on you. The hundreds, and almost thousands, of persons who form the company of the *Comédie*—their frequently recurring parts adjusted with extraordinary, though by no means obtrusive or offensive, consistency to the enormous world of detail and scenery and general "surroundings" in which their parts are played—are never interfered with by the pointing-stick or the prompter. They are *there*; they can't help being there, and you have to make the best or the worst of them as you can. Considering the general complexion of this universe, its inevitableness and apparent αὐτάρκεια may seem, in some moods and to some persons,

---

[1] I believe I may speak without rashness thus, for a copy of the sixteen-volume (was it not?) edition was a cherished possession of mine for years, and I even translated a certain amount for my own amusement—especially *Die unsichtbare Loge*.

a little oppressive ; it is always, perhaps, as has been admitted, productive rather of admiration than of pleasure. Faults of various kinds may be found with it. But it is almost always wonderful ; it is often great, and it is sometimes of the greatest.[1]

[1] I have said nothing here on a point of considerable interest to myself—the question whether Balzac can be said ever (or at least often) to have drawn a gentleman or a lady. It would require too much "justification" by analysis of particular characters. And this would pass into a more general enquiry whether these two species exist in the Balzacium Sidus itself. Which things open long vistas. (*V. inf.* on Charles de Bernard.)

CHAPTER V

GEORGE SAND

THERE is a Scotch proverb (not, I think, among those most generally known), " Never tell your foe when your George Sand foot sleeps " ; and some have held that this —generalities applies specially to the revelation, by an author, about her. of his own weak points. I do not agree with them, having always had a fancy for playing and seeing cards on table — except at cards themselves, where a dummy seems. to me only to spoil the game. Therefore I admit, in coming to George Sand, that this famous novelist has not, *as* a novelist, ever been a favourite of mine—that I have generally experienced some, and occasionally great, difficulty in reading her. Even the " purged considerate mind " (without, I venture to hope, much dulling of the literary palate) which I have brought to the last readings necessary for this book, has but partially removed this difficulty. The causes of it, and their soundness or unsoundness as reasons, must be postponed for a little—till, as usual, sufficient survey and analysis of at least specimens (for here as elsewhere the immense bulk of the total work defies anything more than " sampling ") have supplied due evidence. But it may be said at once that no kind of prejudice or dislike, arising from the pretty notorious history and character of Amantine (Amandine ? Armandine ?) Lucile Aurore Dupin or Dudevant, commonly called George Sand, has anything to do with my want of affection or admiration for her work. I do not recommend her conduct in her earlier days for imitation, and I am bound to say that I do not think it was ever excused by what one may call real love. But she seems to have been an extremely good fellow in her age, and not by any means a very bad fellow in her youth. She was at one time pretty, or at least good-looking;[1] she was at all times clever; and if she did not quite deserve that almost superhuman eulogy awarded in the Devonshire epitaph to

Mary Sexton,
Who pleased many a man and never vexed one,[2]

she did fulfil the primal duty of her sex, and win its greatest triumph, by complying with the first half of the line, while, if she failed as to the second, it was perhaps not entirely her fault.[3] Finally, Balzac's supposed picture of her as Camille in *Béatrix* has the almost unique peculiarity, among its author's sketches of women, of being positively attractive—attractive, that is to say, not merely to the critic as a powerful study and work of art; not perhaps at all to the sentimentalist as a victim or an adorable piece of *candeur*; not to the lover of physical

---

[1] It is attested by the well-known story, more excusable in a man than creditable to a gentleman, of her earliest or earliest known lover, Jules Sandeau (*v. inf.*), seeing a photograph of her in later days, turning to a companion and saying, "Et je l'ai connue belle!"

[2] It is possible that some readers may not know the delightfully unexpected, and not improbably "more-expressive-than-volumes" *third* line—

"Not like the woman who lies under the next stone."

But tradition has, I believe, mercifully omitted to identify this neighbouring antipode.

[3] Details of personal scandal seldom claim notice here. But it may be urged with some show of reason that *this* scandal is too closely connected with the substance and the spirit of the novelist's whole work, from *Indiana* to *Flamarande*, to permit total ignoring of it. *Lucrezia Floriani*, though perhaps more suggestive of Chopin than of Musset, but with "tangency" on both, will be discussed in the text. That most self-accusing of excuses, *Elle et Lui*, with its counterblast Paul de Musset's *Lui et Elle*, and a few remarks on *Un Hiver à Majorque* (conjoined for a purpose, which will be indicated) may be despatched in a note of some length.

The rival novel-*plaidoyers* on the subject of the loves and strifes of George Sand and Alfred de Musset are sufficiently disgusting, and if they be considered as novels, the evil effect of purpose—and particularly of personal purpose—receives from them texts for a whole series of sermons. Reading them with the experience of a life-time, not merely in literary criticism, but (for large parts of that life-time) in study of evidence on historical, political, and even directly legal matters, I cannot help coming to the conclusion that, though there is no doubt a certain amount of *suggestio falsi* in both, the *suppressio veri* is infinitely greater in *Elle et Lui*. If the letters given in Paul de Musset's book were not written by George Sand they were written by Diabolus. And there is one retort made towards the finale by "Edouard de Falconey" (Musset) to "William Caze" (George Sand) which stigmatises like the lash of a whip, if not even like a hot iron, the whole face of the lady's novels.

"Ma chère," lui dit-il, "vous parlez si souvent de chasteté que cela devient indécent. Votre amitié n'est pas plus 'sainte' que celle des autres." [If he had added "maternité"

Note on *Elle et Lui*, etc.,

beauty or passion, but to the reader—" sensible " in the old sense as well as in the new—who feels that here is a woman he should like to have known, even if he feels likewise that his weather-eye would have had to be kept open during the knowledge.

It has been customary—and though these customary things are sometimes delusive and too often mechanical, Phases of there is also occasionally, and, I think, here, her work. something not negligible in them, if they be not applied too rigidly—to divide George Sand's long period (nearly half a century) of novel-production into four sub-periods, corresponding roughly with the four whole decades of the thirties, forties, fifties, and sixties.[1] The first, sometimes called, but, I think, misleadingly,

---

the stigma would have been completer still.] And there is also a startling verisimilitude in the reply assigned to her :

" Mon cher, trouvez bon que je console mes amis selon ma méthode. Vous voyez qu'elle leur plaît assez, puisqu'ils y reviennent."

It was true : they did so, rather to their own discredit and wholly to their discomfort. But she and her " method " must have pleased them enough for them to do it. It is not so pleasing a method for an outsider to contemplate. He sees too much of the game, and has none of the pleasure of playing or the occasional winnings. Since I read Hélisenne de Crenne (v. sup. Vol. I. pp. 150-1) there has seemed to me to be some likeness between the earlier stage of her heroine (if not of herself) and that of George Sand in her " friend-ships." They both display a good deal of mere sensuality, and both seem to me to have been quite ignorant of passion. Hélisenne did not reach the stage of " maternal " affection, and perhaps it was well for her lover and not entirely bad for her readers. But the best face that can be put on the " method " will be seen in Lucrezia Floriani.

The bluntness of taste and the intense concentration on self, which were shown most disagreeably in Elle et Lui, appear on a different side in another book which is not a and on novel at all—not even a novel as far as masque and domino are concerned,— Un Hiver à though indirectly it touches another of George Sand's curious personal Majorque. experiences—that with Chopin. Un Hiver à Majorque is perhaps the most ill-tempered book of travel, except Smollett's too famous production, ever written by a novelist of talent or genius. The Majorcans certainly did not ask George Sand to visit them. They did not advertise the advantages of Majorca, as is the fashion with " health resorts " nowadays. She went there of her own accord ; she found magnificent scenery ; she flouted the sentiments of what she herself describes as the most priest-ridden country in Europe by never going to church, though and while she actually lived in a disestablished and disendowed monastery. To punish them for which (the non sequitur is intentional) she does little but talk of dirt, discomfort, bad food, extortion, foul-smelling oil and garlic, varying the talk only to foul-smelling oil and garlic, extortion, bad food, discomfort, or dirt. The book no doubt yields some of her finest passages of descriptive prose, both as regards landscape, and in the famous record of Chopin's playing ; but otherwise it is hardly worth reading.

[1] She survived into the next decade and worked till the last with no distinct declension, but she did not complete it, dying in 1876. Her famous direction about her grave, Laissez la verdure, is characteristic of her odd mixture of theatricality and true nature. But if any one wishes to come to her work with a comfortable preoccupation in favour of herself, he should begin with her Letters. Those of her old age especially are charming.

"Romantic," is the period of definite and mainly sexual revolt, illustrated by such novels as *Indiana, Valentine, Lélia*, and *Jacques*. The second is that of *illuminé* mysticism and semi-political theorising, to which *Spiridion, Consuelo, La Comtesse de Rudolstadt*, and others belong. The third, one of a certain *apaisement*, when the author had finally settled at her country-house of Nohant in Berry, turns to studies of rural life : *La Petite Fadette, François le Champi, La Mare au Diable*, etc. The last is represented by novels of no one particular, or at least single, scope or bent, *Les Beaux Messieurs de Bois-Doré, Le Marquis de Villemer, Mademoiselle La Quintinie*, etc., reaching to *Flamarande* and its sequel shortly before her death. The thing, as has been hinted already, is one of those first rough sketches of the ground which, if not too closely adhered to, are often useful. As a matter of fact, the divisions often—as one might be sure they would—run cross. There is a lot of occult or semi-occult stuff in *Lélia*, and the "period of appeasement" did not show much reconciliation and forgiveness of injury in *Elle et Lui*, whether we take this as by the injured or as by her who had done the wrong. But if we take the two first novels briefly and *Lélia* itself more fully for Period I. ; *Consuelo* and its sequel (*Spiridion* has been "done and done thoroughly"[1] by Thackeray in the *Paris Sketch-book*) for II. ; the three above-mentioned *berquinades* for the Third, with *Lucrezia Floriani* thrown between as an all-important outsider, and *Les Beaux Messieurs de Bois-Doré* for IV., giving each some detailed criticism, with a few remarks on others, it ought to suffice as a fairly solid groundwork for a general summing-up.

To understand the *furore* with which *Indiana* and *Valentine* were received, one must remember the time and the circumstance with even more care
Indiana. than is usually desirable. They were—if not quite so well written as they seemed even to Thackeray—

---

[1] Cf. Mr. Alfred Lammle on his unpoetical justice to Mr. Fledgeby in *Our Mutual Friend*.

written very well; they expressed the full outburst of the French *Sturm und Drang* movement; there was nothing like them either in French or in any other literature, though Bulwer was beginning similar things with us. Essentially, and when taken *sub specie aeternitatis*, they are very nearly rubbish. The frail (extremely frail) and gentle Indiana, with her terrible husband, whose crimes against her and nature even reach the abominable pitch of declaring himself ready to shoot expected poachers and possible burglars; her creole maid and foster-sister "Noun," who disguises herself in Indiana's garments and occupies her room, receives there a lover who is afterwards her mistress's, but soon commits suicide; the lover himself, a most appalling "tiger," as his own time would have called him; and the enigmatic English cousin, indifferently designated as "Sir Rodolphe Brown," "Sir Ralph," "Sir Brown," and "M. Brown," with whom Indiana makes a third trial of hitherto "incomprised" and unattained happiness—are all inhabitants of a sort of toy doll's-house partaking of the lunatic-asylum. But the author's three prefaces, written at intervals of exactly ten years, passably inconsistent in detail, but all agreeing in contempt of critics and lofty anarchist sentiment, are great fun, and are almost a reward for reading the book.

Valentine has more of the really admirable description of her beloved Berry with which the author so often honeys her drugs; but the novel-part of it

Valentine.

is largely composed of the same sort of violent bosh which almost monopolises *Indiana*. In fact, the peasant-*bourgeois* hero Benedict, whom every woman loves; who is a conceited and ill-mannered mixture of clown and prig; who is angry with his mistress Valentine (Madame de Lansac) for "not knowing how to prefer him to her honour," though one would have said she had given ample proofs of this preference; and who finally appeases the reader by tumbling on the points of a pitchfork placed in his way by an (as it happens) unduly jealous husband, is a more offensive creature than any

one in the earlier book.[1] One is, on the other hand,
a little sorry for Valentine, while one is sorry for nobody
in *Indiana* except perhaps for the husband, who has the
sense to die early.

Lélia, some years younger than these and later than
the Musset tragedy, is a good deal better, or at least
less childish. It is beyond all question an
extra-ordinary book, though it may be well
to keep the hyphen in the adjective to prevent confusion
of sense. It opens, and to a large extent continues, with
a twist of the old epistolary style which, if nothing else,
is ingeniously novel. George Sand was in truth a " well
of ingenuity " as D'Artagnan was a *puits de sagesse*, and
this accounts, to some extent, for her popularity. You
have not only no dates and no places, but no indication
who writes the letters or to whom they are written,
though, unless you are very stupid, you soon find out.
The *personae* are Lélia—a *femme incomprise*, if not incom-
prehensible; Sténio, a young poet, who is, in the pro-
foundest and saddest sense of the adverb, hopelessly in
love with her; and a mysterious personage—a sort of
Solomon-Socrates-Senancour—who bears the Ossian-
esque name of Trenmor, with a later and less pro-
vincially poetical *alias* of " Valmarina." [2] The history
of the *preuves* of Trenmor's novel-nobility are soon
laid before the reader. They are not, in their earlier
stages, engaging to the old-fashioned believer in " good
form."

Trenmor is the sort of exaggeration of Childe Harold
which a lively but rather vulgar mind might conceive.
" He was born great; but they developed the animal in
him." The greatness postponed its appearance, but

Lélia.

---

[1] Valentine has an elder sister who has a son, irregularly existent, but is as much in
love with Benedict as if she were a girl and he were a gentleman; and this son marries
the much older Athenais, a lovely peasant girl who has been the unwilling *fiancée* and
wife of the ingenious pitchforker. You have seldom to go far in George Sand for an
unmarried lady with a child for chastity, and a widow who marries a boy for maternal
affection.

[2] There is also an Irish priest called Magnus, who, like everybody else, is deeply and
(in the proper sense of *sans espoir*) desperately in love with Lélia. He is, on the whole,
quite the maddest—and perhaps the most despicable—of the lot.

the animality did credit to the development. " He used to love to beat his dogs ; before long he beat his prostitutes." This harmless diversion accentuated itself in details, for which, till the acme, the reader must be referred to the original. The climacteric moment came. He had a mistress called " La Mantovana," whom he rather preferred to the others, because she was beautiful and impudent. " In a night of noise and wine " he struck her, and she drew a dagger. This made him love her for a moment ; but unfortunately she made an improper observation ; thereupon he tore off her pearl necklace and trod it under his feet. She wept. This annoyed Trenmor very much. " She had wished revenge for a personal insult, and she cried for a toy ! " Accordingly he had a " crispation of nerves," which obliged him to take a large cut-glass decanter and hit her on the head with it. According to the natural perversity on such occasions of such persons, she died. The brutal justice of mankind—so hateful to Godwin and George Sand and Victor Hugo—sent Trenmor, not, indeed, to the gallows, as it should have done, but to the galleys. Yet the incident made Lélia, who (she must have had a sweet set of friends) somehow knew him, very fond of Trenmor, though she certainly told him that he might as well repent of what he had done, which seems inconsistent.

They let him out after five years (why, Heaven or the other place knows !) and he became a reformed character—the Solomon-Socrates-Senancour above mentioned *plus* a sort of lay " director " to Lélia, with a carbonaro attitude of political revolutionary and free-thinking *illuminé*. Now *corruptio pessimi* is seldom *optima*.

The main interest, however, shifts (with apparitions of Trenmor-Valmarina) to the loves (if they may be called so) of the pitiable Sténio and the intolerable heroine. She is unable to love anybody, and knows it ; she can talk—ye Demons, how she can talk !—but she can never behave like a woman of this world. She alternately

hugs Sténio, so that she nearly squeezes his breath out,
and, when he draws natural conclusions from this process,
pushes him away. But worse and more preposterous
things happen. Lélia has a sister, Pulchérie, who is
very like her (they are of course both impossibly beautiful)
in body, and so far resembles her in mind and soul as to
be unable to behave decently or sensibly. But her want
of decency and sense takes the more commonplace line
of becoming an actual courtesan of the "Imperia"
kind in Italy. By a series of muddles for which Lélia is
—as her plain-spoken sister points out after the catastrophe—herself really responsible, Sténio is induced,
during the excitement of an *al fresco* fête at night in the
grounds of a sort of fairy palace, to take the "coming"
sister for the recalcitrant one, and avail himself of her complaisance, *usque ad finem.* Lélia reproaches him (which
she has not the least right to do), and he devotes himself
entirely to Pulchérie (La Zinzolina is her professional
name) and her group of noble paramours. He gets,
however, generally drunk and behaves with a brutal rudeness, which would, in the Italy of tradition, have finished
things up very soon by a stiletto thrust, and in honest
England by a kicking into the street. There are mysterious plots, cardinals, and anything else you like or don't
like. Lélia becomes an abbess, Sténio a suicide, the
above-mentioned priest, Magnus, being much concerned in this. She admits her unfortunate lover to
burial, and is degraded and imprisoned for it—or for
having saved Trenmor-Valmarina from the law. Everybody else now dies, and the nightmare comes to an
end.

The beauties of style which softened the savage
breast of Thackeray himself in the notice above mentioned, and which, such as they are, appear
even in George Sand's earliest work, will
receive attention when that work comes to
be discussed as a whole. Meanwhile, at the
risk of any charge of Philistinism, I confess that this
part of it seems to me, after fifty years and more of

The moral
of the group
and its tragi-
comedy.

"corrected impression," almost worthless *au fond*. It is, being in prose, and therefore destitute of the easements or at least masquerades which poetry provides for nonsense, the most conspicuous and considerable example —despite the undoubted talent of the writer—of the mischief which Byronism did on the Continent. With us, though it made a great stir, it really did little harm except to some "silly women" (as the apostle, in unkindly and uncourtly, but truly apostolic fashion, had called similar persons of the angelic sex ages before). Counter-jumpers like Thackeray's own Pogson worshipped "the noble poet"; boys of nobler stamp like Tennyson *thought* they worshipped him, but if they were going to become men of affairs forgot all about him; if they were to be poets took to Keats and Shelley as models, not to him. Critics hardly took him seriously, except for non-literary reasons. There was, as I think somebody (perhaps Thackeray himself) says upon something, "too much roast beef about" for us to fill our bellies with this worse than east wind of Sensibility gone rotten. But abroad, for reasons which would be easy but irrelevant to dwell upon, Byron hit the many-winged bird of popular favour on nearly all its pinions. He ran strikingly and delightfully contrary to the accepted *Anglais*, whether of the philosophical or the caricature type; he was noble, but revolutionary; he looked (he never was, except in non-essentials) Romantic; he was new, naughty, nice, all at once. And they went mad over him, and to a large extent and for a long time remained so; indeed, Continental criticism, whether Latin, Teutonic, Scandinavian, or Slav, has never reached "the centre" about Byron. Now George Sand was at no time exactly a silly woman, but she was for a long time a woman off her balance. Byronism was exactly the -ism with which she could execute the wildest feats of half-voluntary and half-involuntary acrobatics, saltimbanquery, and chucking of her bonnet over all conceivable and inconceivable mills. Childe Harold, Manfred, Conrad, Lara, Don Juan, Sardanapalus—the shades of these caught her and waltzed with her and reversed and figured and gesticulated,

With their Sentimentalibus lacrimae rorum, and pathos and bathos delightful to see,

—or perhaps *not* so very delightful ?

But let us pass to the next stage.

Those persons (I think, without tempting Nemesis too much, I might say those fortunate persons) to whom the world of books is almost as real as the *Consuelo.* other two worlds of life and of dream, may or must have observed that the conditions and sensations of the individual in all three are very much the same. In particular, the change from a state of discomfort to one of comfort—or *vice versa* unluckily, but with that we have nothing immediately to do—applies to all. In actual life you are hot, tired, bored, headachy, " spited with fools," what not. A change of atmosphere, a bath, a draught of some not unfermented liquor, the sight of a face, what not again, nay, sometimes a mere shift of clothing, will make you cool, satisfied, at peace. In dreams you have generally to wake, to shake off the " fierce vexation," and to realise that it *is* a dream ; but the relief comes sooner or later. If anybody wants to experience this change from discomfort to comfort in the book-world of a single author, I cannot commend anything better than the perusal, with a short interval— but there should be some—of *Consuelo* after *Lélia*. We may have some things to say against the later novel ; but that does not matter.

It opens with no tricks or *tours de force* ; in no atmo- sphere of darkened footlights and smell of sawdust ; but Much better in frank and free novel-fashion, with a Venetian in parts. church, a famous maestro (Porpora), a choir of mostly Italian girls, and the little Spanish gipsy Consuelo, the poorest, humblest, plainest (as most people think) of all the bevy, but the possessor of the rarest vocal faculties and the most happiness-producing- and-diffusing temper. There is nothing in the least milk-

soppy or prudish about Consuelo, though she is perfectly
" pure " ; nor is there anything tractified about her,
though she is pious and generous. The contrast between
her and her betrothed, the handsome but worthless
Anzoleto, also a singer, is, at first, not overworked ;
and one scene—that in which, when Consuelo has got
over the " scraggy " age and is developing actual beauty,
she and Anzoleto debate, in the most natural manner,
whether she *is* pretty or not—is quite capital, one of the
things that stick in one's memory and stamp the writer's
genius, or, at any rate, consummate talent.

This happy state of affairs continues without much
deterioration, though perhaps with some warnings to
The   the experienced, for some two hundred pages.
degeneration. The situations and the other characters—the
Professor Porpora himself ; Count Zustiniani, *dilettante*,
impresario and of course gallant ; his *prima donna* and
(in the story at least) first mistress, La Corilla ; her
extravagances and seduction of the handsome Anzoleto ;
his irresolution between his still existing affection for
Consuelo, who passes through all these things (and Zustiniani's siege of her) " in maiden meditation, fancy-free "
—all discharge themselves or play their parts quite as
they ought to do. But this comparatively quiet, though
by no means emotionless or unincidented, part of the
story " ends in a blow-up," or rather in a sink-down, for
Anzoleto, on a stolen gondola trip with Clorinda, third
cantatrice and interim mistress of Zustiniani (beautiful,
but stupid, and a bad singer), meets the Count in another
gondola with Corilla herself, and in his fury rams his
rival and the perfidious one. Consuelo, who has at last
had her eyes opened, quits Venice and flees, with a
testimonial from Porpora, to Germany. Even then one
hopes for the best, and acknowledges that at any rate
something not far from the best, something really good,
has been given one for two hundred well-filled pages—
more than the equivalent of the first deck of one of our
old average " three-deckers."

But in the mind of experience such hopes are always

accompanied by fears, and alas ! in this instance "the fears have it." There is on the border of Bohemia a "Castle of the Giants"; and oh ! how one wishes that my Uncle Toby had allowed the sea to execute the ravages he deprecated and sweep that castle into nothingness ! When we get there Byronism is back—nay, its papa and mamma, Lewisism and Radcliffism, are back also— with their cardboard turrets and precipices and grottos; their pine-woods reminding one of the little bristly green things, on round cinnamon-coloured bases, of one's youth; their floods and falls so obviously supplied at so much a thousand gallons by the nearest water company, and their mystery-men and dwarfs and catalepsies and all the rest of the weary old "tremblement." Count Christian of Rudolstadt is indeed a gentleman and an almost too affectionate father; his brother, Baron Frederick, a not disagreeable sportsman and *bon vivant*; their sister, the Canoness, a not too theatrical old maid; and Frederick's daughter, Amélie, though pert and not too good-natured, the most human creature of them all, albeit with the humanities of a soubrette rather than of a great lady. But what shall one say of Albert of Rudolstadt, the heir, the betrothed of Amélie (this fact excusing much in her), and, when Consuelo has joined the circle at Porpora's recommendation as music-mistress and com- panion in the higher kind to Amélie—*her* slave, con- queror, tormentor, and in the long-run husband ? He is perhaps the most intolerable hero [1] ever designed as a gentleman by a novelist who has been classed as great, and who certainly has some qualities necessary to great- ness. In reading about him vague compunctions even come over the mind at having spoken harshly of Sténio and Trenmor. Sténio was always a fool and latterly a cad ; Trenmor first a brute and then a bore. Albert is none of these (except perhaps the last), but he is madder than the Mad Hatter and the March Hare put together, and as depressing as they are delightful. He has hallu-

---

[1] If any one says, "So, then, there are several 'most intolerables,'" let me point out that intolerableness is a more than "twy-peaked" hill or range. Julien Sorel and Marius were not designed to be gentlemen.

cinations which obliterate the sense of time in him ; he
thinks himself one of his ancestors of the days of Ziska ;
he has second sight ; he speaks Spanish to Consuelo and
calls her by her name when he first sees her, though he
has not the faintest *sane* idea who she is or whence she
comes ; and he reduces his family to abject misery by
ensconcing himself for days in a grotto which can be
isolated by means of a torrent turned on and off at pleasure
by a dwarf gipsy called Zdenko, who is almost a greater
nuisance than Albert himself. Consuelo discovers his
retreat at the risk of being drowned ; and various night-
marish scenes occur, resulting in the slight return to
sanity on Albert's part involved in falling in love with
her, and a very considerable advance towards *in*sanity
on hers by falling in love with him. But perhaps this
give-and-take of lovers may seem attractive to some.
And when after a time we get into mere hocus-pocus,
and it seems to Consuelo that Albert's violin " speaks
and utters words as through the mouth of Satan," the
same persons may think it fine. For myself, I believe that
without fatuity I may claim to be, if not a *visionnaire*
(perhaps that also), at least a lover of visions, and of Isaiah
and Ezekiel and the Revelation. Dante, Blake, Shelley,
the best of Lamennais and the best of Hugo excite in
me nothing but a passionate reverence. I can walk
day-long and night-long by Ulai and Chebar and Lethe-
Eunoe and have no thought of sneer or slumber, shrug
or satiety. But when you ask me to be agitated at
Count Albert of Rudolstadt's violin ventriloquising Satan
I really must decline. I do even remember the poor
creature Paul de Kock, and would fain turn to one of
the things he, was writing at this very time.

    Consuelo is a very long book—it fills three of the tightly
printed volumes of the old Michel-Calmann-Lévy
collection, with some three or four hundred
pages in each ; and we have not got, in the
above survey, to more than the middle of the
second. But in its afternoon and evening there
is some light. The creature Anzoleto recurs ; but his

Recovery ; but not main-tained quite to the end.

immediate effect is good,[1] for it starts the heroine on
a fresh elopement of an innocent kind, and we get back
to reality.   The better side of George Sand's Bohemianism revives in Bohemia itself; and she takes Consuelo
to the road, where she adopts male dress (a fancy with her
creatress likewise), and falls in with no less a person
than the composer Haydn in his youth. They meet some
Prussian crimps, and escape them by help of a coxcombical
but not wholly objectionable Austrian Count Hoditz and
the better (Prussian) Trenck. They get to Vienna
(meeting La Corilla in an odd but not badly managed
maternity-scene half-way) and rejoin old Porpora there.
There are interviews with Kaunitz and Maria Theresa :[2]
and a recrudescence of the Venetian musical jealousies.
Consuelo endeavours to reopen communications with the
Rudolstadts, but Porpora—chiefly out of his desire to
retain her on the stage, but partly also from an honest and
not wholly unsound belief that a union between a gipsy
girl and a German noble would itself be madness—plays
false with the letters.   She accepts a professional invitation from Hoditz to his castle in Moravia, meets there
no less a person than Frederic the Second *incognito*, and
by his order (after she has saved his life from the vengeance of the re-crimped deserter rescued with her by
Hoditz and Trenck) is invited to sing at Berlin. The
carrying out of the invitation, which has its Frederici-
ianities [3] (as one may perhaps be allowed to call them),
is, however, interrupted. The mysterious Albert, who
has mysteriously turned up in time to prevent an attempt
of the other and worse (Austrian) Trenck on Consuelo,
is taken with an apparently mortal illness at home, and
Consuelo is implored to return there. She does so,
and a marriage *in articulo mortis* follows, the supposed
dead Zdenko (whom we did not at all want) turning up

---

[1] It is bad for Amélie, who, in a not unnatural revulsion from her *fiancé's* neglects
and eccentricities, lets herself be fooled by the handsome Italian.

[2] George Sand's treatment of the great Empress, Marie Antoinette's mother, is a
curious mixture of half-reluctant admiration and Republican bad-bloodedness.

[3] Porpora is included, but the amiable monarch, who has heard that the old *maestro*
speaks freely of him, gives private orders that he shall be stopped at the frontier.

alive after his master's death. Consuelo, fully if not
cheerfully adopted by the family, is offered all the heirloom
jewels and promised succession to the estates. She
refuses, and the book ends—with fair warning that it
is no ending.

When her history begins again under the title she
has "reneged," the reader may for no short time think
La Comtesse that the curse of the sequel—a curse only
de Rudolstadt. too common, but not universal—is going to
be averted. She is in Berlin alone (see note above);
is successful, but not at all happy—perhaps least of all
happy because the king, partly out of gratitude for
his safety, partly out of something like a more natural
kind of affection than most authors have credited him
with, pays her marked attentions. For a time things are
not unlively ; and even the very dangerous experiment
of a supper—one of those at which Frederic's guests were
supposed to have perfectly " free elbows " and availed
themselves of the supposition at their peril—a supper
with Voltaire, La Mettrie, Algarotti, D'Argens, Pöllnitz,
and " Quintus Icilius " present—comes off not so badly.
One of the reasons of this is that George Sand has the
sense to make Voltaire ill and silent, and puts the bulk
of the " business " on La Mettrie—a person much
cleverer than most people who have only read book-notices
of him may think, but not dangerously brilliant. Then
Consuelo, or " La Porporina," as her stage name is, gets
mixed up—owing to no fault of her own in the first place
at any rate—with the intrigues of the Princess Amélie
of Prussia and her lover, the less bad Trenck. This has
two awkward results—for herself an imprisonment at
Spandau, into which she is cast by Frederic's half
jealous, half purely tyrannical wrath, and for us a revival
of all the *massacrant* illuminism in which the Princess
herself is dabbling. So we have on the scene not only
(as the reader sees at once, though some rather clumsy
efforts are made to hide it) the resuscitated Albert, who
passes as a certain Trismegistus, not only the historical
charlatan Saint-Germain, but another charlatan at this

time not at all historical (seeing that the whole story ends
in 1760, and he never left Palermo till nine years later),
Cagliostro. Even at Spandau Consuelo herself is not
quite uninteresting; but the Illuminati determine to rescue
her, and for the latter part of the first volume and the
whole of the second the entire thing is, once more, Bosh.
The most absurd " double-gangings " take place between
an *inconnu* named Liverani, whom Consuelo cannot help
loving, and Albert himself, who *is* Liverani, as everybody
but herself sees at once, interspersed between endless
tracts of the usual rubbish about underground tribunals,
and judges in red cloaks, and skeletons, and museums
of torture-implements, and all the Weishauptian trumpery
of mixed occultism and revolutionary sentiment. The
author has even the insufferable audacity to fling at us
another resuscitation—that of the Countess Wanda,
Albert's mother, who appears to have transmitted to
him her abominable habit of catalepsy. So ends, un-
satisfactorily enough—unless anybody is satisfied by the
fact that two solid children result from the still mystifying
married life of the pair—the story which had begun so
well in the first volume of *Consuelo*, and which in the
major part of *Consuelo* itself, though not throughout,
maintains the satisfaction fairly.

If any reader, in two ways gentle, has been good
enough to take some interest in the analysis of these books,
The *"making good" of Lucrezia Floriani.* but is also so soft-hearted as to feel slightly
froissé by it, as showing a disqualifying inability
to sympathise with the author, I hope I may
put myself right by what I am going to say of
another. *Lucrezia Floriani* is to me the most
remarkable book that George Sand ever wrote; and the
nearest to a great one, if it be not actually that. I have
read it, with no diminution of interest and no abatement
of esteem, at very different times of my life, and I think
that it is on the whole not only the most perfect revelation
of what at any rate the author would have liked to be her
own temperament, but—a much greater thing—a pre-
sentiment in possible and human form of a real tempera-

ment, and almost of a real character. Further, it is much
the most achieved example of that peculiar style of which
more will be said in a general way presently, and it contains comparatively few blots. One always smiles, of
course, at the picture of Lucrezia swinging in a hammock
in the centre of a large room, the four corners of which
are occupied by four bedsteads containing four children,
in the production of whom not exactly *four* fathers, as
they ought for perfect symmetry, but as a compromise
three, have assisted. One always shudders at her notion
of restoring a patient, suffering under a nervous ailment,
by surrounding his couch with the cherubic countenances
and the balmy breaths of these infants.[1] Prince Karol,
the hero (such as there is), is a poor creature, though not
such a cad as Sténio ; but then, according to Madame
Dudevant, men as a rule *were* poor creatures, unless they
were convicts or conjurors, so the presentation is *ex
hypothesi* or *secundum hypothesin* correct. And the whole
is firmly drawn and well, but neither gaudily nor pitchily,
coloured. It ought to be remembered that, with the
possible exception of Jane Austen, who has no peer or
second among lady novelists, these either confine themselves to representation of manners, external character,
ton, as was said of Fanny Burney, or else, like the other
" George " and Charlotte Brontë, endeavour to represent
themselves as they are or as they would like to be on the
canvas. They never create ; if they " imitate " not in
the degraded modern but the original classical sense,
and do it well, *punctum ferunt—suum* if not *omne*.

Lucrezia Floriani does this higher imitation well—
almost, if not quite, greatly. Had George Sand been
more of a blue-stocking and of an affected
The story. creature than she was, she might have called
the book *Anteros-Nemesis*. The heroine, by her real
name Antonietta Menapace, is the daughter of a fisherman on the Lago d'Iseo, and in her earliest girlhood the
servant-maid of a rich neighbour's wife. As her father,

---

[1] *Cow's* breath has, I believe, been prescribed in such cases by the faculty ; hardly
children's.

a close-fisted peasant, wants her to marry a well-to-do churl of her own rank, she elopes with her employer's son and has two children by him ; but develops a magnificent voice, with no small acting and managing capacity. So she makes a fortune by the time she is thirty, acquiring the two other children by two other lovers, and having so many more who do not leave permanent memorials of their love and necessitate polygonal rooms, that, as she observes, "she cannot count them."[1] At the above-mentioned age, however, she becomes weary of this sort of life, retires to her native district, buys the very house in which she had been a servant, and with the heir of which (now dead) she had eloped, and settles down to be a model mother, a Lady Bountiful, and a sort of recluse. No more "love" for her. In fact, in one of the most remarkable passages of the book she gives a story of her chief attachments, showing that, with brief accesses of physical excitement, it has always been *amour de tête* and never *amour de cœur*.

Things being so, there arrive one evening, at the only inn on the lake, a young German Prince, Karol von Roswald, and his friend the Italian Count Salvator Albani. They are travelling for the Prince's health, he being a sort of spoilt child, pitiably nervous, imperfectly educated, and half paralysed by the recent death of his mother and the earlier one of a *fiancée*. The inn is good to eat in (or rather out of), but for nothing else ; and Salvator, hearing of Lucrezia, whose friend, though not her lover, he has formerly been, determines to ask a hospitality which she very cheerfully gives them. *Cetera quis nescit*, as George Sand herself in other but often-repeated words admits.[2] Karol falls in love at first sight, though he is horrified at his hostess's past. He also falls ill, and she nurses him. Salvator leaves them for a time,

---

[1] She does not make the delicate distinction once drawn by another of her sex : " I can tell you how many people I have kissed, but I cannot tell you how many have kissed *me*."

[2] She is rather fond of taking her readers into confidence in this way. I have no particular objection to it ; but those who object to Thackeray's *parabases* ought to think this a still more objectionable thing.

and though Lucrezia plays quite the reverse of the part of temptress, the inevitable does not fail to happen.

That they were *not* married and that they did *not* live happy ever after, everybody will of course be certain, though it is not Karol's fault that actual marriage does not take place. There is, however, an almost literal, if unsanctified and irregular honeymoon ; but long before Salvator's[1] return, it has " reddened " more than ominously. Karol is insanely jealous, and it may be admitted that a more manly and less childishly selfish creature might be somewhat upset by the arrival of Lucrezia's last lover, the father of her youngest child, though it is quite evident that she has not a spark of love for this one left. But he is also jealous of Salvator ; of an old artist named Beccaferri whom she assists ; of a bagman who calls to sell to her eldest boy a gun ; of the aged peasant whom she had refused to marry, but whose death-bed she visits ; of the *curé* ; of everybody. And his jealousy takes the form not merely of rage, which is bad enough for Lucrezia's desire of peace, but of cold insult, which revolts her never extinguished independence and pride. He has, as noted, begged her to marry him in the time of intoxication, but she has refused, and persists in the refusal. After one or two " scenes " she rows herself over to an olive wood on the other side of the lake, and makes it a kind of " place of sacrifice "——of the sacrifice, that is to say, of all hopes of happiness with him or any one thenceforward. But she neither dismisses nor leaves him ; on the contrary, they live together, unmarried, but with no public scandal, for ten years, his own passion for her in its peculiar kind never ceasing, while hers gradually dies under the stress of the various torments he inflicts, unintentionally if not quite unconsciously, upon her. At last it is too much, and she dies of heart-failure at forty years of age.

---

[1] The Count Albani plays his difficult part of thirdsman very well throughout, though just at first he would make an advance on " auld lang syne " if Lucrezia would let him. But later he is on strict honour, and only quarrels with the Prince for his tyranny.

One might make a few cavils at this. The exact
reason of what has been called the " sacrifice " is not
Its balance made clear, despite Lucrezia's soliloquy in
of power. the olive wood. If it were meant as an
atonement for her ill-spent youth it would be intelligible.
But there is no sign of this, and it would not be in George
Sand's way. Lucrezia merely resolves that she will
try to make everybody happy without trying or expecting
to be happy herself. But she must know more and
more that she is *not* making Karol happy, and that the
cohabitation cannot, even in Italy, but be prejudicial
to her children ; though, to do him the very scanty justice
he deserves, he does not behave ill to them, little as he
likes them.

Again, this long self-martyrdom would need no explanation if she continued to love Karol. But it is very
doubtful whether she had not ceased to do so (she was
admittedly good at " ceasing to love ") when she left
the Wood of Olives, and the cessation admittedly took
place long before the ten years' torture came to an end.
One is therefore, from more than one point of view, left
with a sort of Fakir self-mortification, undertaken and
" dreed " neither to atone for anything, nor to propitiate
any Power, nor really to benefit any man. After all,
however, such a thing is quite humanly possible. And
these *aporiae* hardly touch knots—only very small spots—
in a reed of admirable strength and beauty. We know
that George Sand did *not* sacrifice herself for her lovers—
very much the reverse. But we know also that in her
youth and early middle age she was very much of a
Lucrezia Floriani, something of a genius, if not so great
a one as she made her creature, something of a beauty,
entirely negligent of ordinary sexual morality, but
thoroughly, if somewhat heartlessly, good-natured, and
(not merely at the times mentioned, but to the end of her
life) an affectionate mother, a delightful hostess, and a
very satisfactory friend. No imaginary Sténio or Karol,
no actual Sandeau or Musset or Chopin could have caused
her at any time of her life the misery which the Prince

caused Lucrezia, because she would simply have " sent him walking," as the vigorous French idiom has it. But it pleased her to graft upon her actual nature something else that it lacked, and a life-like and tragical story resulted.

It is not a bad " turn over of the leaf " from this, the strongest, and in the best sense most faultless, of George Sand's novels of analysis, to the " idyllic " group of her later middle and later period—the " prettiest " division, and in another grade of faultlessness the most free from faults, in ordinary estimation, of her entire production.

The most popular of these, the prettiest again, the most of a *bergerie-berquinade-conte-de-fées*, is no doubt The " Idylls " *La Petite Fadette*, the history of two twin-—*La Petite* boys and a little girl—this last, of course, the *Fadette.* heroine. The boys are devoted to each other and as like as two peas in person, but very different in character, one being manly, and the other, if not exactly effeminate, something like it. As for Fadette, she, though never exactly like the other girl of the saying " horrid," but only (and with very considerable excuses) naughty and untidy and rude, becomes " so very, very good when she is good " as to awake slight recalcitrances in those who have acquired the questionable knowledge of good and evil in actual life. But one does not want to cavil. It *is* a pretty book, and when the not exactly wicked but somewhat ill-famed grandmother's stocking yields several thousand francs and facilitates the marriage of Landry, the manly brother, and Fadette, one can be very cheerfully cheerful, and anticipate a real ever-after happiness for both. No doubt, too, the army did knock the girlishness out of the other brother, Sylvinet, and we hope that one of the village gossips was wrong when she said that he would never love any girl but one. For it is hardly necessary to say that his agreement with his twin extends to love for Fadette—love which is quite honourable, and quite kindly extinguished by that agreeable materialisation of one of Titania's lower-class maids-of-honour.

Only one slight piece of *malice* (in the mitigated French sense) may be permitted. We are told that Sylvinet, after the marriage, served for ten years " in the Emperor Napoleon's glorious campaigns." This will hardly admit of a later date for that marriage itself than the breach of the Peace of Amiens. And this, even if Landry was no more than eighteen or nineteen at that time (he could hardly be less), will throw the date of his and his brother's birth well before the Revolution. Now, to insist on chronological exactitude and draw inferences from its absence is—one admits most cheerfully, and more than admits—a mere curmudgeonly pedantry in most cases of great or good fiction, prose or verse. One knows what to think of people who make crimes of these things in Shakespeare or Scott, in Dumas or Thackeray. But when a writer makes a great point of Purpose and sets a high value on Questions, it is not unfair to expect him or her to mind their P's and Q's in other matters. George Sand is never tired, in other books, of insisting on the blessedness of the Revolution itself, on the immense and glorious emancipation from feudal tyranny, etc. But how does it come about that there is not the very slightest sign of that tyranny in the earlier part of the story, or of any general disturbance in the middle and later part ? *Glissons ; n'appuyons pas* on this point, but it may be permitted to put it.

In another book of this group—I think chronologically the earliest, also very popular, and quite " on the side of the angels "—the heroine, another divine little peasant-girl—who, if George Sand had been fond of series-titles, might have caused the book to be named *La Petite Marie*—omits any, however slightly, " horrid " stage altogether. She is, if not " the whole " good—which, as Empedocles said long ago, few can boast to find,—good, and nothing but good, except pretty, and other things which are parts or forms of goodness. The piece really is, in the proper sense which so few people know, or at least use, an idyll, a little picture of Arcadian life. Speaking precisely

La Mare au Diable.

—that is to say in *précis*—it is nothing but the story of
a journey in which the travellers get benighted, and
which ends in a marriage. Speaking analytically, it
consists of a prologue—one of the best examples of
George Sand's style and of her power of description,
dealing with the ploughlands of Berry and the ways of
their population ; of the proposition to a young widower
that he shall undertake re-marriage with a young widow,
well-to-do, of another parish ; of his going a-wooing
with the rather incongruous adjuncts of a pretty young
servant girl, who is going to a " place," and his own
truant elder sonlet ; of the benighting of them as above
by the side of a mere or marsh of evil repute ; of the
insult offered to Marie on the arrival at her new place ;
of the discomfiture of Germain, the hero, at finding
that the young widow keeps a sort of court of pretenders
dangling about her ; of his retirement and vengeance
on Marie's insulter ; and of the proper marriage-bells.
There is also a rather unnecessary appendix, doubtless
dear to the folklorist, of Berrichon wedding customs.

Once more, to cavil at this would be contemptibly easy.
To quote *La Terre* against it would be uncritical, for,
as may be seen later, whatever M. Zola's books are,
they are not evidence that can negative anything. It
would be as sensible to set against the night scene in the
wood by the Devil's Pool the history of the amiable
Dumollard, who, as far as fifty years' memory serves me,
used, some years before George Sand's death, sometimes
to escort and sometimes to lie in wait for servant-girls on
the way to or from places, violate, murder, and rob them,
in another country district of France. Nor would it be
quite critical, though a little more so, to compare George
Sand's own friend, contemporary, and in some sort
counterpart, Balzac's peasant scenes against her. If,
at this time, she viewed all such things *en rose*, Balzac
viewed them, at this and almost all times, *en noir*. Perhaps everybody (except the wicked farmer, who insults
Marie) is a little too good, and it seems rather surprising
that somebody did not say something about Germain

and Marie arriving next morning instead of overnight. But never mind this. The scenery and the writing of the book have real charm. The long conversation by the watch-fire in the wood, where Germain tries to break off his suit to the widow already and transfer himself to Marie, with Marie's cool and (for she has loved him already) self-denying refusal on the most atrociously rational and business-like principles, is first-rate. It may rank, with the above-mentioned discussion about Consuelo's beauty between herself and her lover, as one of the best examples of George Sand's gift for the novel.

The third in the order of mention of what is usually considered her trilogy of idylls, *François le Champi*, if not *François le* the prettiest, is the strongest, and the most *Champi.* varied in interest, of the three. The shadier side of human character lifts itself and says, *Et in Arcadia ego*,[1] much more decidedly than in the childish petulances of *La Petite Fadette* and the merely " Third Murderer " appearance of the unprincipled farmer in *La Mare au Diable*. Even the mostly blameless hero is allowed, towards the close, to exhibit the well-known *rusé* or *madré* characteristics of the French peasant to the extent of more than one not quite white lie ; the husband of the heroine is unfaithful, tyrannical as far as he dare be, and a waster of his family's goods before his fortunately rather early death ; his pretty young sister, Mariette, is a selfish and spiteful minx ; and his paramour (sarcastically named " La Sévère ") is unchaste, malignant, and dishonest all at once—a combination which may be said to exclude any possible goodness in woman.

The only thoroughly white sheep—though the " Champi " or foundling (his cradle being the genial fields and not the steps of stone) has but the grey patches noticed above, and those acquired with the best intentions —is Madeleine Blanchet, his protectress for many years, and finally, after difficulties and her widowhood, his wife. That she is some twelve years older than he is

---

[1] It is very pleasing to see, as I have seen, this famous phrase quoted as if it had reference to the *joys* of Arcadia.

is a detail which need not in itself be of much importance. It lends itself to that combination of maternal and sexual affection of which George Sand is so fond, and of which we may have to speak some harsh words elsewhere. But here it matters little. Arcady is a kind of Saturnian realm, and " mixtures " elsewhere " held a stain " may pass there.

We may make a further *glissade* (to return to some remarks made above), though of a different kind, over Others— a few of the very large number of novels that *Mauprat.* we cannot discuss in detail. But *Mauprat* adds just a little support to the remarks there made. For this (which is a sort of crime-and-detection novel, and therefore appeals to some readers more than to the present historian) turns wholly on the atrocious deeds of a seignorial family of the most melodramatic kind. Yet it is questionable whether the wickedest of them ever did anything worse than the action of their last and renegade member, who actually, when he comes into the property, ruins his ancestral castle because naughty things have been done there. Now, when Milton said, " As well kill a man as kill a good book," though it was no doubt an intentional hyperbole, there was much sound sense in what he said. Still, except in the case of such a book as has been produced only a few times in the world's history, it may be urged that probably something as good might be written by somebody else among the numerous men that were not killed. But, on the same principle, one would be justified in saying, " Better kill a hundred men than ruin a castle with hundreds of years of memories, bad or good." You can never replace *it*, while the hundred men will, at the very moment they are killed, be replaced, just as good on the average, by the ordinary operations of nature. Besides, by partially ruining the castle, you give an opening to the sin of the restorer, for which there is, we know, *no* pardon, here or hereafter.[1]

[1] If any among my congregation be offended by apparent flippancy in this notice of a book which, to my profound astonishment, some people have taken as the author's masterpiece, I apologise. But if I spoke more seriously I should also speak more severely.

La Daniella is a rather long book and a rather dull one. There is a good deal of talkee-talkee of the *Corinne* kind *La Daniella.* in it : the heroine is an angelic Italian soubrette; the hero is one of the coxcombish heroes of French novels, who seem to have set themselves to confirm the most unjust ideas of their nation entertained in foreign climes ; there is a " Miss Medora," who, as the hero informs us, " plays the coquette clumsily, as English girls generally do," etc. *Passons outre*, without inquiring how much George Sand knew about English girls.

One of the best of her books to read, though it has neither the human interest of *Lucrezia Floriani*, nor the *Les Beaux* prettiness of the Idylls, nor the style-colour of *Messieurs de* some other books, is *Les Beaux Messieurs de Bois-Doré.* *Bois-Doré.* It is all the more agreeable that we may even " begin with a little aversion." It suggests itself as a sort of interloper in the great business of Dumas and Co. : it opens, indeed, only a few years before D'Artagnan rode up to the inn on the buttercup-coloured pony. And, in manner, it may look at first as if the writer were following another but much inferior example—our own G. P. R. James ; for there are " two cavaliers," and one tells the other a tale fit to make him fall asleep and off his saddle. But it improves remarkably, and before you have read a hundred pages you are very fairly " enfisted." The figure of the old Marquis de Bois-Doré—an aged dandy with divers absurdities about him,[1] but a gentleman to his by no means yet stiffened or stooping backbone ; a heart of gold, and a wrist with a good core of steel left in it— might easily have been a failure. It is a success. His first guest and then adversary, the wicked Spaniard, Sciarra d'Alvimar or de Villareal, whom the old marquis runs through the body in a moonlight duel for very sufficient reason,[2] may not be thought quite equally

---

[1] He is a frantic devotee of the *Astrée*, and George Sand brings in a good deal about that most agreeable book, without, however, showing very intimate or accurate knowledge of it.

[2] The Spaniard (or rather his servant with his connivance) has murdered and robbed Bois-Doré's brother.

successful. Scoundrel as he is, George Sand has unwisely thrown over him a touch of *guignon*—of shadowing and resistless fate—which creates a certain sympathy ; and she neglects the good old rule that your villain should always be allowed a certain run for his money—a temporary exercise of his villainy. Alvimar, though he does not feel the marquis's rapier till nearly the end of the first half, as it were, of the book, is " marked down " from the start, and never kills anything within those limits except a poor little tame wolf-cub which is going (very sensibly) to fly at him. He is altogether too much in appearance and too little in effectuality of the stage Spaniard—black garments, black upturned moustache, hook-nose, *navaja*, and all the rest of it. But he does not spoil the thing, though he hardly does it much good ; and if he is badly treated he has his revenge on the author.

For the book becomes very dull after his supposed death (he *does* die, but not at once), and only revives when, some way into the second volume, an elaborate attempt to revenge him is made by his servant, Sanche, *âme damnée* and also *damnante* (if one may coin this variant), who is, as it turns out, his irregular father. This again rather stagy character organises a formidable body of wandering *reîtres*, gipsies, and miscellaneous ruffians to attack and sack the marquis's house—a plan which, though ultimately foiled, brings about a very refreshing series of hurly-burlys and hullabaloos for some hundred and fifty pages. The narrative is full of improbable impossibilities, and contrasts singularly with the fashion in which Dumas, throughout all his great books (and not a few of his not so great ones), manages to *escamoter* the difficulty. The boy Mario,[1] orphan of the murdered brother, left unknown for many years, recognised by his uncle, avenger of his father on Sanche, as Bois-Doré himself had been on Alvimar, is altogether too clever and effective for his age ; and the conduct of Bellinde, Bois - Doré's cashiered *gouvernante*, is almost

---

[1] He also is very handsome, and so makes up the plurality of the title.

preposterous throughout. But it is what a schoolboy of the old days would have called a " jolly good scrimmage," and restores the interest of the book for most of the second volume. The end—scarcely, one would think, very interesting to any one—is quite spoilt for some by another example of George Sand's inveterate passion for " maternal " love-making and matches where the lady is nearly double the age of her husband. Others —or the same—may not be propitiated for this by the " horrors " [1] which the author has liberally thrown in. But the larger part of the book, like the larger part of *Consuelo*, is quite good stuff.

It is, indeed, a really lively book. Two duller ones than the first two allotted, at the beginning of this notice, *Le Marquis* to her last period I have seldom read. They *de Villemer.* are both instances (and one at least contains an elaborate vindication) of the " novel of purpose," and they are by themselves almost enough to damn it. M. le Marquis de Villemer is an appalling prig—virtuous, in the Devil-and-his-grandmother style, to the *n*th—who devotes his energies to writing a *History of the Patriciate since the Christian Era*, the object being to reveal the sins of aristocracy. He has a rather nice half-brother spendthrift, Duque d'Aleria (Madame de Villemer the elder has first married a Spaniard), whose debts he virtuously pays, and after a great deal of scandal he marries a poor but noble and noble-minded damsel, Caroline de Saint-Geneix, who has taken the position of companion to his mother in order to help her widowed and four-childed sister. For the virtue of George Sand's virtuous people *is* virtue and no mistake. The lively and amiable duke is fortunately fitted with a lively and amiable duchess, and they show a little light in the darkness of copybook morality and republican principles.

This kindly light is altogether wanting in *Made-*

---

[1] Alvimar lies dying for hours with the infidel Bohemians and roistering Protestant *reîtres* not only disturbing his death-bed, but interfering with the " consolations of religion " ; the worst of the said Bohemians is buried alive (or rather stifled, after he has been *half*-buried alive) by the little gipsy girl, Pilar, whom he has tormented ; and Pilar herself is burnt alive on the last page but one, after she has poisoned Bellinde.

moiselle La Quintinie, where the purpose passes from politics to religion. The book is rather famous,

Mlle. La Quintinie. and was, at the time, much read, because it is not merely a novel of purpose, but an instance of the duello fought, not with sword or pistol, not with quarter-staves or sand-bags, but with *feuilletons* of fiction. It, and Octave Feuillet's *Sibylle*, to which it is the countercheck-quarrelsome, both appeared in the *Revue des Deux Mondes*. It should be seen at a further stage of this volume that I do not think *Sibylle* a masterpiece, either of tale-telling or of argumentation, though it is more on my side than the reply is. But Feuillet, though not a genius, as some people would have George Sand to be, nor yet possessing anything like the talent which no sane criticism can deny her, was a much better craftsman in the art of novel-writing.

For a final notice—dealing also with the last, or almost the last, of all her books—we may take *Flamarande* and its

Flamarande. sequel, *Les Deux Frères*. They give the history of the unfounded jealousy of a husband in regard to his wife—a jealousy which is backed up by an equally unfounded suspicion (supported by the most outrageous proceedings of espionage and something like burglary) on the part of a confidential servant, who, as we are informed at last, has himself had a secret passion for his innocent mistress. It is more like a Feuillet book than a George Sand, and in this respect shows the curious faculty—possessed also by some lady novelists of our own—of adapting itself to the change of novel-fashion. But to me at least it appeals not.

So turn we from particulars (for individual notice of the hundred books is impossible) to generals.

It may be difficult to sum up the characteristics of such a writer as George Sand shortly, but it has to be

Summary and judgment. done. There is to be allowed her—of course and at once—an extraordinary fertility, and a hardly less extraordinary escape from absolute sinking into the trivial. She is preposterous early, somewhat facile and "journalistic" later, but she is never exactly

commonplace. She belongs to the school of immense
and almost mechanical producers who are represented in
English by Anthony Trollope as their "prior" and by
Mrs. Oliphant[1] and Miss Braddon as commandresses of
the order. (I think she runs a good deal below the
Prior but a good deal above the Commandresses.[2]) But,
if she does so belong, it is very mainly due, not to any
pre-eminence of narrative faculty, but to that gift of style
which has been for nearly a hundred years admitted.

Style.   Now I have in this *History* more than once, and
          by no means with tongue in cheek, expressed
a diffidence about giving opinions on this point. I have,
it is true, read French for more than sixty years, and I
have been accustomed to "read for style" in it, and in
divers other languages, for at least fifty. But I see such
extraordinary blunders made by foreigners in regard to this
side of our own literature, that I can never be sure—being
less conceited than the pious originator of the phrase—
that even the Grace of God has prevented me from
going the same way. Still, if I have any right to publish
this book, I must have a little—I will not say "right,"
but *venia* or licence—to say what seems to me to be the
fact of the matter. That fact—or that seeming of fact—
is that George Sand's style is *too* facile to be first-rate.
By this I do not mean that it is too plain. On the contrary, it is sometimes, especially in her early books,
ornate to gorgeousness, and even to gaudiness. And
it was a curious mistake of the late Mr. Pater, in a
quite honorific reference to me, to imply that I preferred
the plain style—a mistake all the more curious that he knew
and acknowledged (and was almost unduly grateful for) my
admiration of his own. I like both forms : but for style
—putting meaning out of the question—I would rather
read Browne than Swift, and Lamennais than Fénelon.

---

[1] Taking her work on the whole. The earlier part of it ran even Trollope hard.
[2] Her points of likeness to her self-naming name-child, "George Eliot," are too
obvious to need discussion. But it is a question whether the main points of *un*likeness—
the facility and extreme fecundity of the French George, as contrasted with the laborious
book-bearing of the English—are not more important than the numerous but superficial
and to a large extent non-literary resemblances.

George Sand has both the plain and the ornate styles (and various shades of " middle " between them) at command. But it seems to me that she has them—to use a financial phrase recently familiar—too much " on tap." You see that the current of agreeable and, so to speak, faultless language is running, and might run volubly for any period of life that might be allotted to her. In fact it did so. Now no doubt there was something of Edmond de Goncourt's bad-blooded fatuity in his claim that his and his brother's epithets were " personal," while Flaubert's were not. Research for more personal " out-of-the-wayness " in style will rarely result in anything but jargon. But, on the other hand, Gautier's great injunction :

Sculpte, lime, cisèle !

is sound. You cannot reach the first class in any art by turning a tap and letting it run.

The one point of what we may call the " furniture " of novels, in which she seems to me to have, occasionally Conversation at least, touched supremacy, is conversation. and It has been observed by those capable of description. making the induction that, close as drama and novel are in some ways, the distinction between dramatic and non-dramatic talk is, though narrow, deeper than the very deepest Alpine crevasse from Dauphiné to Carinthia. Such specimens as those already more than once dwelt on—Consuelo's and Anzoleto's debate about her looks, and that of Germain and Marie in the midnight wood by the Devil's Mere—are first-rate, and there is no more to say. Some of her descriptions, again, such as the opening of the book last quoted (the wide, treeless, communal plain with its various labouring teams), or as some of the Lake touches in *Lucrezia Floriani*, or as the relieving patches in the otherwise monotonous grumble of *Un Hiver à Majorque*, are unsurpassable. Nor is this gift limited to mere *paysage*. The famous account of Chopin's playing already mentioned for praise is only first among many. But whether these things are supported by sufficient strength of character, plot, incident, "thought," and the rest; whether that strange narrative power, so hard to define and so impossible to mistake or to fail to distinguish from these other elements, is present—these are great questions and not easy to answer. I am, as will have been seen throughout, rather inclined to answer them in the unfavourable way.

In fact—impertinent, insolent, anything else as it may seem—I venture to ask the question, " Was George Sand a very great craftswoman in the novel ? " and, what is more, to answer it in the negative. I understand that an ingenious critic of her own sex has recently described her method as " rolling through the book, locked in the embraces of her subject," as distinguished from the aloofness and elaboration of a more recent school. So far, perhaps, so good ; but I could wish to find " the intricacies of Diego and Julia " more interesting to me than as a rule they are. And it must be remembered that she is constantly detaching herself from the forlorn " subject," leaving it *un*embraced and shivering, in order to sermonise it and her readers. I do not make the very facile and somewhat futile criticism that she would have written better if she had written half or a quarter as much as she did. She could not have written little ; it is as natural and suitable for Tweed to " rin wi' speed " as for Till to " rin slaw," though perhaps the result— parallel to but more cheerful than that recorded in the old rhyme—may be that Till has the power not of drowning but of intoxicating two men, where Tweed can only manage one. But this engrained fecundity and facundity of hers inevitably make her work novel-journalism rather than novel-literature in all points but in that of style, which has been discussed already.[1]

[1] I have said little or nothing of the short stories. They are fairly numerous, but I do not think that her *forte* lay in them.

CHAPTER VI

IN arranging this volume I have thought it worth while
to include, in a single chapter and *nominatim* in the
title thereof, five writers of prose novels or tales; all
belonging to " 1830 "; four of them at least ranking
with all but the greatest of that great period; but no one
exclusively or even essentially a novelist as Balzac and
George Sand were in their different ways, and none of
them attempting such imposing bulk-and-plan of novel-
matter as that which makes up the prose fiction of Hugo.
Gautier was an admirable, and Musset and Vigny at their
best were each a consummate, poet; while the first-named
was a " polygraph " of the polygraphs, in every kind of
belles-lettres. Mérimée's novels or tales form a small part
of his whole work. " Gérard " is perhaps only admissible here by courtesy, though more than one or two
readers, I hope, would feel his absence as a dark gap in
the book. Musset, again, not ill at short stories, is far
better at short plays. *One* novel of Vigny's has indeed
enjoyed great fame; but, as will be seen, I am unluckily
unable to admire it very much, and I include him here
—partly because I do not wish to herd so clear a name
with the Sues and the Souliés, even with the Sandeaus
and Bernards—partly because, though his style in prose
is not so marked as that in verse, some of his minor work
in fiction is extremely interesting. But though so much
of their work, and in Musset's and Vigny's cases all their
best work, lies outside our province, and though they

themselves, with the possible exception of Gérard and Gautier, who have strong affinities, are markedly different from one another, there is one point which they all have in common, and this point supplies the general title of this chapter. Style of the more separable and elaborate kind does not often make its appearance very early in literary departments; and there may be (*v. inf.*) some special reasons why it should not do so in prose fiction. With the exception of Marivaux, who had carried his attention to it over the boundary-line of mannerism, few earlier novelists, though some of them were great writers, had made a point of it, the chief exceptions being in the particular line of " wit," such as Hamilton, Crébillon *fils*, and Voltaire. Chateaubriand had been almost the first to attempt a novel-*rhetoric*; and it must be remembered that Chateaubriand was a sort of human *magnus Apollo* throughout the July monarchy. At any rate, it is a conspicuous feature in all these writers, and may serve as a link between them.

Some readers may know (for I, and the others, which I shall probably quote again, have quoted it before Gautier— now) a remark of Émile de Girardin when his burden of Théophile Gautier asked him how people liked "style." a story which " Théo " had prevailed on that experienced editor to insert as a *feuilleton* in the *Presse*: " Mon ami, l'abonné ne s'amuse pas *franchement*. Il est gêné par le style." Girardin, though not exactly a genius, was an exceedingly clever man, and knew the foot of his public—perhaps of " *the* public "—to a hundredth of an inch. But he could hardly have anticipated the extent to which his criticism would reflect the attitude of persons who would have been, and would be, not a little offended at being classed with *l'abonné*. The reproach of " over-styling " has been cast at Gautier by critics of the most different types, and—more curiously at first sight than after a moment's reflection—by some who are themselves style-mad, but whose favourite vanities in that matter are different from his. I can hardly think

of any writer—Herrick as treated by Hazlitt is the chief
exception that occurs to me at the moment—against
whom this cheap and obvious, though, alas! not very
frequently possible, charge of " bright far-shining empti-
ness," of glittering frigidity, of colour without flesh
and blood, of art without matter, etc., etc., has been cast
so violently—or so unjustly. In literature, as in law
and war, the favourite method of offensive defence is to
reserve your *triarii*, your " colophon " of arms or argument, to the last; but there are cases in all three where
it is best to carry an important point at once and hold it.
I think that this is one of these cases; and I do not think
that the operation can be conducted with better chance
of success than by inserting here that outline,[1] with specimens, of *La Morte Amoureuse* which has been already
promised—or threatened—in the Preface. For here
the glamour—if it be only glamour—of the style will
have disappeared; the matter will remain.

You ask me, my brother, if I have ever loved. I answer
" Yes." But it is a wild and terrible story, a memory whose
ashes, with all my sixty-six years, I hardly dare to
disturb. To you I can refuse nothing, but I would
not tell the tale to a less experienced soul. The facts
are so strange that I myself cannot believe in their
actual occurrence. For three years I was the victim
of a diabolical delusion, and every night—God grant it was a dream
—I, a poor country priest, led the life of the lost, the life of the
worldling and the debauchee. A single chance of too great com-
placency went near to destroy my soul; but at last, with God's
aid and my patron saint's, I exorcised the evil spirit which had
gained possession of me. Till then my life was double, and the
counterpart by night was utterly different from the life by day.
By day I was a priest of the Lord, pure, and busied with holy
things. By night, no sooner had I closed my eyes than I became a

Abstract (with transla-tions) of La Morte Amoureuse.

---

[1] Some years after its original appearance Mr. Andrew Lang, in collaboration with
another friend of mine, who adopted the *nom de guerre* of " Paul Sylvester," published a
complete translation under the title of *The Dead Leman*; and I believe that the late Mr.
Lafcadio Hearn more recently executed another. But this last I have never seen.
(The pages which follow to 222, it may not be superfluous to repeat, appeared originally in the *Fortnightly Review* for 1878, and were reprinted in *Essays on French Novelists*,
London, 1891. The Essay itself contains, of course, a wider criticism of Gautier's
work than would be proper here.)

youthful gallant, critical in women, dogs, and horses, prompt with dice and bottle, free of hand and tongue; and when waking-time came at dawn of day, it seemed to me as if I then fell asleep and was a priest only in dreams.   From this sleep-life I have kept the memory of words and things, which recur to me against my will; and though I have never quitted the walls of my parsonage, those who hear me talk would rather think me a man of the world and of many experiences, who has entered the religious life hoping to finish in God's bosom the evening of his stormy day, than a humble seminarist, whose life has been spent in an obscure parish, buried deep in woods, and far removed from the course of the world.

Yes, I have loved—as no one else has loved, with a mad and wild passion so violent that I can hardly understand how it failed to break my heart.

After rapidly sketching the history of the early seminary days of the priest Romuald, his complete seclusion and ignorance almost of the very names of world and woman, the tale goes on to the day of his ordination. He is in the church, almost in a trance of religious fervour; the building itself, the gorgeously robed bishop, the stately ceremonies, seem to him a foretaste of heaven, when suddenly—

By chance I raised my head, which I had hitherto kept bowed, and saw before me, within arm's length as it seemed, but in reality at some distance and beyond the chancel rails, a woman of rare beauty and royally apparelled.   At once, as it were, scales dropped from my eyes.   I was in the case of a blind man whose sight is suddenly restored.   The bishop, but now so dazzling to me, became dim, the tapers in their golden stands paled like the stars at morning, and darkness seemed to pervade the church.   On this background of shade the lovely vision stood out like an angelic appearance, self-illumined, and giving rather than receiving light. I dropped my eyelids, firmly resolving not again to raise them, that so I might escape the distraction of outward things, for I felt the spell more and more, and I hardly knew what I did; but a minute afterwards I again looked up, for I perceived her beauty still shining across my dropped lashes as if with prismatic glory, and encircled by the crimson halo that, to the gazer, surrounds the sun.   How beautiful she was!   Painters, when in their chase of the ideal they have followed it to the skies and carried off therefrom the divine image of Our Lady, never drew near this fabulous reality.

Nor are the poet's words more adequate than the colours of the limner. She was tall and goddess-like in shape and port. Her soft fair hair rolled on either side of her temples in golden streams that crowned her as with a queen's diadem. Her forehead, white and transparent, tinged only by blue vein-stains, stretched in calm amplitude over two dark eyebrows—a contrast enhanced still further by the sea-green lustre of her glittering and unfathomable eyes. Ah, what eyes ! One flash of them was enough to settle the fate of a man. Never had I seen in human eyes such life, such clearness, such ardour, such humid brilliancy ; and there shot from them glances like arrows, which went straight to my heart. Whether the flame which lit them came from hell or heaven I know not, but from one or the other it came, most surely. No daughter of Eve she, but an angel or a fiend, perhaps—who knows ? —something of both. The quarrelets of pearl flashed through her scarlet smile, and as her mouth moved the dimples sank and filled by turns in the blush-rose softness of her exquisite cheek. Over the even smoothness of her half-uncovered shoulders played a floating gloss as of agate, and a river of large pearls, not greatly different in hue from her neck, descended towards her breast. Now and then she raised her head with a peacock-like gesture, and sent a quiver through the ruff which enshrined her like a frame of silver filigree.

The strange vision causes on Romuald strange yet natural effects. His ardent aspiration for the priesthood changes to loathing. He even tries to renounce his vows, to answer " No " to the questions to which he should answer " Yes," and thus to comply with the apparent demand of the stranger's eyes. But he cannot. The awe of the ceremony is yet too strong on his soul, if not on his senses and imagination ; and the fatal words are spoken, the fatal rites gone through, despite the promises of untold bliss which the eyes, evermore caressing and entreating, though sadder, as the completion of the sacrifice approaches, continue to make him.

At last it was over—I was a priest. Never did face of woman wear an expression of such anguish as hers. The girl whose lover drops lifeless at her side, the mother by her dead child's cradle, Eve at the gate of paradise, the miser who finds his buried treasure replaced by a stone, the poet whose greatest work has perished in the flames, have not a more desolate air. The blood left her countenance, and it became as of marble ; her arms fell by her side, as if their muscles had become flaccid; and she leant against a pillar, for her limbs refused to support her. As for me, with a livid face bathed as if in the dews of death, I bent my tottering steps towards the church door. The air seemed to stifle me, the vaulted roof settled on my shoulders, and on my head seemed to rest the whole crushing weight of the dome. As I was on the point of crossing the threshold a hand touched mine suddenly— a woman's hand—a touch how new to me ! It was as cold as the skin of a serpent, yet the contact burnt like the brand of a hot iron. " Unhappy wretch ! What have you done ? " she said to me in a low voice, and then disappeared in the crowd.

On the way to the seminary, whither a comrade has to support him, for his emotion is evident to all, a page, unnoticed, slips into Romuald's hand a tablet with the simple words, " Clarimonde. At the Concini Palace." He passes some days in a state almost of delirium, now forming wild plans of escape, now shocked at his sinful desires, but always regretting the world he has renounced, and still more Clarimonde.

I do not know how long I remained in this condition, but, as in one of my furious writhings I turned on my bed, I saw the Father Serapion standing in the middle of the cell gazing steadily at me. Shame seized me, and I hid my face with my hands. " Romuald," said he, at the end of a few minutes, " something extraordinary has come on you. Your conduct is inexplicable. You, so pious, so gentle, you pace your cell like a caged beast. Take heed, my brother, of the suggestions of the Evil One, for he is wroth that you have given yourself to the Lord, and lurks round you like a ravening wolf, if haply a last effort may make you his."

Then, bidding him redouble his pious exercises, and telling him that he has been presented by the bishop to a country cure, and must be ready to start on the morrow, Serapion leaves him. Romuald is in despair at quitting the neighbourhood of Clarimonde. But his seminarist inexperience makes him feel, more than ever, the impossibility even of discovering her, and the hints of Serapion have in a manner reawakened his conscience. He departs on the morrow without protest. They quit the city, and begin to climb the hills which surround it.

At the top I turned round once more to give a last look to the place where dwelt Clarimonde. The city lay wholly in the shadow of a cloud; its blue and red roofs were blended in one general half-tint, above which here and there white flakes of the smoke of morning fires hovered. By some optical accident a single edifice stood out gilded by a ray of light, and more lofty than the mass of surrounding buildings. Though more than a league off, it seemed close to us. The smallest details were visible—the turrets, the terraces, the windows, and even the swallow-tailed vanes. "What is that sunlit palace yonder?" I asked of Serapion. He shaded his eyes with his hand, and after looking he answered, "It is the palace which Prince Concini gave to the courtesan Clarimonde. Terrible things are done there." As he spoke, whether it were fact or fancy I know not, it seemed to me that I saw a slender white form glide out on the terrace, glitter there for a second, and then disappear. It was Clarimonde! Could she have known that at that moment, from the rugged heights of the hill which separated me from her, and which I was never more to descend, I was bending a restless and burning gaze on the palace of her abode, brought near me by a mocking play of light, as if to invite me to enter? Ah yes! she knew it doubtless, for her soul was bound to mine too nearly not to feel its least movements; and this it must have been which urged her to climb the terrace in the cold morning dews, wrapped only in her snowy nightgear.

But the die is cast, and the journey continues. They reach the modest parsonage where Romuald is to pass the rest of his days, and he is installed in his cure, Serapion returning to the city. Romuald attacks his work desperately, hoping to find peace there, but he very partially succeeds. The words of Clarimonde and the touch of her hand haunt him constantly, and sometimes even stranger things happen. He sees the flash of the sea-green eyes across his garden hedges; he seems to find the imprint of feet, which are assuredly not those of any inhabitant of the village, on the gravel walks. At last one night he is summoned late to the bedside of a dying person, by a messenger of gorgeous dress and outlandish aspect. The journey is made in the darkness on fiery steeds, through strange scenery, and in an unknown direction. A splendid palace is at length reached—too late, for the priest is met by the news that his penitent has already expired. But he is entreated, and consents, at least to watch and pray by the body during the night. He is led into the chamber of death, and finds that the corpse is Clarimonde. At first he mechanically turns to prayer, but other thoughts inevitably occur. His eyes wander to the appearance and furniture of the boudoir suddenly put to so different use : the gorgeous hangings of crimson damask contrasting with the white shroud, the faded rose by the bedside, the scattered signs of revelry, distract and disturb him. Strange fancies come thick. The air seems other than that to which he is accustomed in such chambers of the dead. The corpse appears from time to time to make slight movements ; even sighs seem to echo his own. At last he lifts the veil which covers her, and contemplates the exquisite features he had last seen at the fatal moment of his sacrifice. He cannot believe that she is dead. The faint blush-rose tints are hardly dulled, the hand is not colder than he recollects it.

The night was now far spent. I felt that the moment of eternal separation was at hand, and I could not refuse myself the last sad pleasure of giving one kiss to the dead lips of her, who, living, had had all my love. Oh, wonder ! A faint breath mingled with mine, the eyes opened and became once more brilliant. She sighed, and uncrossing her arms she clasped them round my neck with an air of ineffable contentment. "Ah !" she said, with a voice as faint and as sweet as the last dying vibrations of a harp, "is it you, Romuald ? I have waited for you so long that now I am dead. But we are betrothed to one another from this moment, and I can see you and visit you henceforward. Romuald, I loved you ! Farewell ; this is all I have to say ; and thus I restore the life you gave me for a minute with your kiss. We shall soon meet again." Her head fell back, but she still held me encircled. A furious gust of wind forced in the window and swept into the room : the last leaflet of the white rose quivered for a minute on its stalk and then fell, and floated through the open casement, bearing with it the soul of Clarimonde. The lamp went out, and I sank in a swoon.

He wakes in his own room, and hears from his ancient *gouvernante* that the same strange escort which carried him off has brought him back. Soon afterwards his friend Serapion comes to visit him, not altogether to his delight, for he rightly suspects the father of some knowledge of his secret. Serapion announces to him, as a matter of general news, that the courtesan Clarimonde is dead, and mentions that strange rumours have been current respecting her—some declaring her to be a species of vampire, and her lovers to have all perished mysteriously. As he says this he watches Romuald, who cannot altogether conceal his thoughts. Thereat Serapion—

"My son," said he, "it is my duty to warn you that your feet are on the brink of an abyss; take heed of falling. Satan's hands reach far, and the grave is not always a faithful gaoler. Clarimonde's tombstone should be sealed with a triple seal, for it is not, say they, the first time she has died. May God watch over you." Saying this, Serapion slowly went out, and I saw him no more. I soon recovered completely, and returned to my usual occupations; and though I never forgot the memory of Clarimonde and the words of the father, nothing extraordinary for a time occurred to confirm in any way his ill-omened forebodings, so that I began to believe that his apprehensions and my own terror were unfounded. But one night I had a dream. Scarcely had I fallen asleep when I heard my bed-curtains drawn, the rings grating sharply on the rods. I raised myself abruptly on my elbow and saw before me the shadowy figure of a woman. At once I recognised Clarimonde. She carried in her hand a small lamp of the shape of those which are placed in tombs, and the light of it gave to her tapering fingers a rosy transparency which, with gradually fainter tints, prolonged itself till it was lost in the milky whiteness of her naked arm. The only garment she had on was the linen shroud which covered her on her death-bed, and she tried to hold up its folds on her breast as if shame-stricken at her scanty clothing. But her little hand was not equal to the task; and so white was she that the lamplight failed to make distinction between the colour of the drapery and the hue of the flesh. Wrapped in this fine tissue, she was more like an antique marble statue of a bather than a live woman. Dead or alive, woman or statue, shadow or body, her beauty was unchangeable, but the green flash of her eyes was somewhat dulled, and her mouth, so red of old, was now tinted only with a faint rose-tint like that of her cheeks. The blue flowerets in her hair were withered and had lost almost all their petals; yet she was still all charming— so charming that, despite the strangeness of the adventure and the unexplained fashion of her entrance, no thought of fear occurred to me. She placed the lamp on the table and seated herself on the foot of my bed; then, bending towards me, she spoke in the soft and silvery voice that I have heard from none but her. " I have kept you waiting long, dear Romuald, and you must have thought that I had forgotten you. But I come from very far—from a place whence no traveller has yet returned. There is neither sun nor moon, nor aught but space and shadow; no road is there, nor pathway to guide the foot, nor air to uphold the wing; and yet here am I, for love is stronger than death, and is his master at the last. Ah! what sad faces, what sights of terror, I have met! With what pains has my soul, regaining this world by force of will, found again my body and reinstalled itself! With what effort have I lifted the heavy slab they laid upon me, even to the bruising of my poor feeble hands! Kiss them, dear love, and they will be cured." She placed one by one the cold palms of her little hands against my mouth, and I kissed them again and again, while she watched me with her smile of ineffable content. I at once forgot Serapion's advice, I forgot my sacred office; I succumbed without resistance at the first summons, I did not even attempt to repulse the tempter.

She tells him how she had dreamed of him long before she saw him; how she had striven to prevent his sacrifice; how she was jealous of God, whom he preferred to her; and how, though she had forced the gates of the tomb to come to him, though he had given life back to her with a kiss, though her recovery of it has no other end than to make him happy, she herself is still miserable because she has only half his heart. In his delirium he tells her, to console her, that he loves her " as much as God."

" Instantly the glitter as of chrysoprase flashed once more from her eyes. ' Is that true ?—as much as God ?' cried she, winding her arms round me. ' If 'tis so you can come with me ; you can follow me whither I will.' " And fixing the next night for the rendezvous, she vanishes. He wakes, and, considering it merely a dream, resumes his pious exercises. But the next night Clarimonde, faithful to her word, reappears—no longer in ghostly attire, but radiant and splendidly dressed. She brings her lover the full costume of a cavalier, and when he has donned it they sally forth, taking first the fiery steeds of his earlier nocturnal adventure, then a carriage, in which he and Clarimonde, heart to heart, head on shoulder, hand in hand, journey through the night.

Never had I been so happy. For the moment I had forgotten everything, and thought no more of my priesthood than of some previous state of life. From that night forward my existence was as it were doubled, and there were in me two men, strangers each to the other's existence. Sometimes I thought myself a priest who dreamt that he was a gallant, sometimes a gallant who dreamt that he was a priest. . . . . I could not distinguish the reality from the illusion, and knew not which were my waking and which my sleeping moments. Two spirals, entangled without touching, form the nearest representation of this life. The young cavalier, the coxcomb, the debauchee, mocked the priest; the priest held the dissipations of the gallant in horror. Notwithstanding the strangeness of the situation, I do not think my reason was for a moment affected. The perceptions of my two existences were always firm and clear, and there was only one anomaly which I could not explain, and this was that the same unbroken sentiment of identity subsisted in two beings so different. Of this I could give myself no explanation, whether I thought myself to be really the vicar of a poor country village, or else Il Signor Romualdo, lover in possession of Clarimonde.

The place, real or apparent, of Il Signor Romualdo's sojourn with his beloved is Venice, where they inhabit a gorgeous palace, and where Romuald enters into all the follies and dissipations of the place. He is unalterably faithful to Clarimonde, and she to him ; and the time passes in a perpetual delirium. But every night —as it now seems to him—he finds himself once more a poor country priest, horrified at the misdeeds of his other personality, and seeking to atone for them by prayer and fasting and good works. Even in his Venetian moments he sometimes thinks of Serapion's words, and at length he has especial reason to remember them.

For some time Clarimonde's health had not been very good ; her complexion faded from day to day. The doctors who were called in could not discover the disease, and after useless prescriptions gave up the case. Day by day she grew paler and colder, till she was nearly as white and as corpse-like as on the famous night at the mysterious castle. I was in despair at this wasting away, but she, though touched by my sorrow, only smiled at me sweetly and sadly with the fatal smile of those who feel their death approaching. One morning I was sitting by her. In slicing some fruit it happened that I cut my finger somewhat deeply. The blood flowed in crimson streamlets, and some of it spurted on Clarimonde. Her eyes brightened at once, and over her face there passed a look of fierce joy which I had never before seen in her. She sprang from the bed with catlike activity and pounced on the wound, which she began to suck with an air of indescribable delight, swallowing the blood in sips, slowly and carefully, as an epicure tastes a costly vintage. Her eyelids were half closed, and the pupils of her sea-green eyes flattened and became oblong instead of round. . . . From time to time she interrupted herself to kiss my hand; then she began again to squeeze the edges of the wound with her lips in order to draw from it a few more crimson drops. When she saw that the blood ran no longer, she rose with bright and humid eyes, rosier than a May morning, her cheeks full, her hands warm, yet no longer parched, fairer in short than ever, and in perfect health. " I shall not die ! I shall not die ! " she said, clasping my neck in a frenzy of joy. " I can live long and love you. My life is in yours, my very existence comes from you. A few drops of your generous blood, more precious and sovereign than all the elixirs of the world, have given me back to life."

This scene gave me matter for much reflection, and put into my head some strange thoughts as to Clarimonde. That very evening, when sleep had transported me to my parsonage, I found there Father Serapion, graver and more careworn than ever. He looked at me attentively and said, " Not content with destroying your soul, are you bent also on destroying your body ? Unhappy youth, into what snares have you fallen ! " The tone in which he said this struck me much at the time ; but, lively as the impression was, other thoughts soon drove it from my mind. However, one evening, with the aid of a glass, on whose tell-tale position Clarimonde had not counted, I saw her pouring a powder into the cup of spiced wine which she was wont to prepare after supper. I took the cup, and, putting it to my lips, I set it down, as if intending to finish it at leisure. But in reality I availed myself of a minute when her back was turned to empty it away, and I soon after went to bed, determined to remain awake and see what would happen. I had not long to wait. Clarimonde entered as soon as she had convinced herself that I slept. She uncovered my arm and drew from her hair a little gold pin ; then she murmured under her breath, " Only one drop, one little crimson drop, one ruby just to tip the bodkin ! As you love me still I must not die. Ah, poor love ! I am going to drink his blood, his beautiful blood, so bright and so purple. Sleep, my only treasure ; sleep, my darling, my deity ; I will do you no harm ; I will only take so much of your life as I need to save my own. Did I not love you so much I might resolve to have other lovers, whose veins I could drain ; but since I have known you I hate all others. Ah, dear arm, how round it is, and how white ! How shall I ever dare to pierce the sweet blue veins ! " And while she spoke she wept, so that I felt her tears rain on the arm she held. At last she summoned courage ; she pricked me slightly with the bodkin and began to suck out the blood. But she drank only a few drops, as if she feared to exhaust me, and then carefully bound up my arm after anointing it with an unguent which closed the wound at once. I could now doubt no longer : Serapion was right. Yet, in spite of this certainty, I could not help loving Clarimonde, and I would willingly have given her all the blood whereof she had need, to sustain her artificial life. Besides, I had not much to fear ; the woman was my warrant against the vampire ; and what I had heard and seen completely reassured me. I had then well-nourished veins, which were not to be soon drawn dry, nor had I reason to grudge and count their drops. I would have pierced my arm myself and bid her drink. I was careful to make not the slightest allusion to the narcotic she had given me, or to the scene that followed, and we lived in un-broken harmony. But my priestly scruples tormented me more than ever, and I knew not what new penance to invent to blunt my passion and mortify my flesh. Though my visions were wholly involuntary and my will had nothing to do with them, I shrank from touching the host with hands thus sullied and spirit defiled by debauchery, whether in act or in dream. To avoid falling into these harassing hallucinations, I tried to prevent myself sleeping ; I held my eyelids open, and remained in a standing posture, striving with all my force against sleep. But soon the waves of slumber drowned my eyes, and seeing that the struggle was hopeless, I let my hands drop in weariness, and was once more carried to the shores of delusion. . . . Serapion exhorted me most fervently, and never ceased reproaching me with my weakness and my lack of zeal. One day, when I had been more agitated than usual, he said to me, " There is only one way to relieve you from this haunting plague, and, though it be extreme, we must try it. Great evils need heroic remedies. I know where Clarimonde was buried ; we must disinter her, and you shall see the real state of your lady-love. You will hardly be tempted to risk your soul for a vile body, the prey of worms and ready to turn to dust. That, if anything, will restore you to yourself." For my part, I was so weary of this double life that I closed with his offer. I longed to know once for all, which—priest or gallant—was the dupe of a delusion, and I was resolved to sacrifice one of my two lives for the good of the other—yea, if it were necessary, to sacrifice both, for such an existence as I was leading could not last. . . . Father Serapion procured a mattock, a crowbar, and a lantern, and at midnight we set out for the cemetery, whose plan and arrangements he knew well. After directing the rays of the dark lantern on the inscriptions of several graves, we came at last to a stone half buried under tall grass, and covered with moss and lichen, whereon we deciphered this epitaph, "Here lies Clarimonde, who in her lifetime was the fairest in the world." " 'Tis here," said Serapion; and, placing his lantern on the ground, he slipped the crowbar into the chinks of the slab and essayed to lift it. The stone yielded, and he set to work with the spade. As for me, stiller and more gloomy than the night itself, I watched him at work, while he, bending over his ill-omened task, sweated and panted, his forced and heavy breath sounding like the gasps of the dying. The sight was strange, and lookers-on would rather have taken us for tomb-breakers and robbers of the dead than for God's priests. The zeal of Serapion was of so harsh and savage a cast, that it gave him a look more of the demon than of the apostle or the angel, and his face, with its severe features deeply marked by the glimmer of the lantern, was hardly reassuring. A cold sweat gathered on my limbs and my hair stood on end. In my heart I held Serapion's deed to be an abominable sacrilege, and I could have wished that a flash of lightning might issue from the womb of the heavy clouds, which rolled low above our heads, and burn him to ashes. The owls perched about the cypress trees, and, disturbed by the lantern, came and flapped its panes heavily with their dusty wings, the foxes barked in the distance, and a thousand sinister echoes troubled the silence. At length Serapion's spade struck the coffin with the terrible hollow sound that nothingness returns to those who intrude on it. He lifted the lid, and I saw Clarimonde, as pale as marble, and with her hands joined; there was no fold in her snow-white shroud from head to foot; at the corner of her blanched lips there shone one little rosy drop. At the sight Serapion broke into fury. "Ah! fiend, foul harlot, drinker of gold and blood, we have found you!" said he, and he scattered holy water over corpse and coffin, tracing the sign of the cross with his brush. No sooner had the blessed shower touched my Clarimonde than her fair body crumbled into dust, and became nought but a hideous mixture of ashes and half-burnt bones. "There, Signor Romuald," said the inexorable priest, pointing to the remains, "there is your mistress. Are you still tempted to escort her to the Lido or to Fusina?" I bowed my head; a mighty ruin had taken place within me. I returned to my parsonage, and Il Signor Romualdo, the lover of Clarimonde, said farewell for ever to the poor priest whose strange companion he had been so long. Only the next night I again saw Clarimonde. She said to me, as at first in the church porch, "Poor wretch, what have you done ? Why did you listen to that frantic priest ? Were you not happy ? And what harm had I done you that you should violate my grave, and shamefully expose the misery of my nothingness ? Henceforward all communication between us, soul and body, is broken. Farewell, you will regret me." She vanished in the air like a vapour, and I saw her no more.

Alas ! she spoke too truly. I have regretted her again and again. I regret her still. The repose of my soul has indeed been dearly bought, and the love of God itself has not been too much to replace the gap left by hers. This, my brother, is the history of my youth. Never look at woman, and let your eyes as you walk be fixed upon the ground ; for, pure and calm as you may be, a single moment is sufficient to make you lose your eternal peace.

Now, though to see a thing in translation be always to see it "as in a glass darkly" ; and though in this *Criticism thereof.* case the glass may be unduly flawed and clouded, my own critical faculties must not only now be unusually [1] enfeebled by age, but must always have been crippled by some strange affection, if certain things are not visible here to any intelligent and impartial reader. The story, of course, is not pure invention ; several versions of parts, if not the whole, of it will occur to any one who has some knowledge of literature ; and I have recently read a variant of great beauty and "eeriness" from the Japanese.[2] But the merit of a story depends, not on its originality as matter, but on the manner in which it is told. It surely cannot be denied that this is told excellently. That the part of Serapion (though somebody or something of the kind is almost necessary) is open to some criticism, may be granted. He seems to know too much and yet not enough : and if he was to interfere at all, one does not see why he did not do it earlier. But this is the merest

---

[1] For, as a rule, the critical faculty is like wine—it steadily improves with age. But of course anybody is at liberty to say, " Only, in both cases, when it is good to begin with."

[2] I suppose this was what attracted Mr. Hearn ; but, as I have said, I do not know his book itself.

hole-picking, and the biggest hole it can make will not catch the foot or the little finger of any worthy reader. As to the beauty of the phrasing, even in another language, and as rendered by no consummate artist, there can be little question about that.   Indeed there we have consent about Gautier, though, as has been seen, the consent has not always been thoroughly complimentary to him.   To go a step further, the way in which the diction and imagery are made to provide frame and shade and colour for the narrative leaves very little room for cavil.   Without any undue or excessive " prose poetry," the descriptions are like those of the best imaginative-pictorial verse itself.   The first appearance of Clarimonde ; the scene at her death-bed and that of her dream-resurrection, have, I dare affirm it, never been surpassed in verse or prose for their special qualities : while the backward view of the city and the recital of what we may call Serapion's soul-murder of the enchantress come little behind them.

But, it may be said, " You are still kicking at open doors. The degree of your estimate is, we think, extravagant, but that it is deserved to some extent nobody denies. In mere point of expression, and even to some extent, again, in conception of beauty, Gautier's manner, though too much of one kind, and that too old-fashioned, is admitted ; it is his matter which is questioned or denied."

Here also, I think, the counter-attack can be completely barred or broken to the satisfaction of all but A parallel those who cannot or will not see.   In the from painting. first place one must make a distinction, which ought not to be regarded as over-subtilising, but which certainly seems to be ignored by many people. There are in all arts, and more especially in the art of literature, two stages or sets of stages in the discharge of that duty of every artist—the creation of beauty. The one is satisfied by the achievement of the beautiful in the presentation itself ; the other gives you, in your own interior collection or museum, the thing presented. This is not the common distinction between form and matter, between style and substance, between subject and treatment; it is something more intimate and "metaphysical." To illustrate it, let me take a pair of instances, not from letters, but from painting as produced by two dead masters of our own, Rossetti and Albert Moore. I used to think the last-named painter disgracefully undervalued both by the public and by critics. One could look at those primrose-tinted ladies of his, with their gossamer films of raiment and their flowerage always suggestive of the asphodel mead, for hours: and if one's soul had had a substantial Palace of Art of her own, there would have been a corridor wholly Albert Moorish—a corridor, for his things never looked well with other people's and they could not, by themselves, have filled a hall.

But their beauty, as has been untruly said of Gautier's representation in the other art, *was* "their sole duty." You never wanted to kiss even the most beautiful of them, or to talk to her, or even to sit at her feet, except for purposes of looking at her, for which that position has its own special advantages. And although by no means mere pastiches or replicas of each other, they had little of the qualities which constitute personality. They were almost literally "dreams that waved before the half-shut eye," and dreams which you knew to be dreams at the time; less even than dreams—shadows, and less even than shadows, for shadows imply substance, and these did not. If you loved them you loved them always, and could not be divorced from them. But it was an entirely contemplative love; and if divorce was unthinkable it was because there was no *thorus* and no *mensa* at which they could possibly have figured.[1] They were the Eves of a Paradise of *two* dimensions only.

Now with Rossetti it was entirely different. His drawing may have been as faulty as people said it was, and he may have been as fond as they also said of bestow-

---

[1] I do not know how many of the users of the catch-word "purely decorative," as applied to Moore, knew what they meant by it; but if they meant what I have just said, I have no quarrel with them.

ing upon all his subjects exaggerated and almost ungainly features, which possibly belonged to the Blessed Damozel, but were not the most indisputable part of her blessedness. But they were, despite their similarity of type, all personal and individual, and all suggestive to the mind and the emotions of real women, and of the things which real women are and do and suffer. And they were all differently suggestive. Proserpine and Beata Beatrix; the devotional figures in their quietude or their ecstasy, and the forlorn leaguer-lasses of that little masterpiece of the novitiate, "Hesterna Rosa"; the Damozel herself and a Corsican lady whose portrait, unpublished and unexhibited, has been familiar to me for six-and-thirty years;—all these and all the others would behave to you, and you would behave to them, if they could be vivified, in ways different individually but real and live.

Now it is beauty of reality as well as of presentation that I at least find in *La Morte Amoureuse*. Clarimonde The reality. alive is very much more than a "shadow on glass"; Clarimonde dead is more alive than many live women.

But the audacity of infatuation need not stop here. I should claim for *La Morte Amoureuse*, and for Gautier And the passion of it. as the author of it, more than this. It appears to me to be one of the very few expressions in French prose of really passionate love. It is, with *Manon Lescaut* and *Julie*, the most consummate utterance that I at least know, in that division of literature, of the union of sensual with transcendental enamourment. Why this is so rare in French is a question fitter for treatment in a *History of the French Temperament* than in one of the French Novel. That it is so I believe to be a simple fact, and simple facts require little talking about. No prose literature has so much love-making in it as French, and none so much about different species of love: *amour de tête* and *amour des sens* especially, but also not unfrequently *amour de cœur*, and even *amour d'âme*. But of the combination that *we* call "passionate love"—that fills our own late sixteenth,

early seventeenth, and whole nineteenth century literature, and that requires love of the heart and the head,
the soul and the senses, together—it has (outside poetry
of course)[1] only the three books just mentioned
and a few passages such as Atala's dying speech,
Adolphe's, alas ! too soon obliterated reflections on his
first success with Ellénore, perhaps one or two more
before *La Morte Amoureuse*, and even since its day
not many. Maupassant (*v. inf.*) *could* manage the combination, but too often confined himself to exhibitions
of the separate and imperfect divisions, whereof, no
doubt, the number is endless.

That Gautier always or often maintained himself at
this pitch, either of what we may call power of projecting
live personages or of exhibition of great passions, it would
be idle and uncritical to contend ; that he did so here,
and thereby put himself at once and for ever on the
higher, nay, highest level of literature, I do, after fifty
years' study of the thing and of endless other things,
impenitently and impavidly affirm.

What is more, in his shorter productions he was
often not far below it, save in respect of intensity. If I
Other short do not admire *Fortunio* quite so much as some
stories. people do, it is not so much because of its
comparative heartlessness—a thing rare in Gautier—as
because for once, and I think once only in pieces of its
scale, the malt of the description *does* get above the meal
of the personal interest, though that personal interest
exists. But *Jettatura*, with its combination of romantic
and tragical appeal ; *Avatar*, with its extraordinary
mixture of romance, again, with humour, its " exciting-
ness," and its delicacy of taste ; the equally extraordinary
felicity of the dealings with that too often unmanageable
implement the " classical dictionary " in *Arria Marcella*,
Une Nuit de Cléopâtre, and perhaps especially *Le Roi
Candaule* ; the tiny sketches — half-*nouvelle* and half-
" middle " article—of *Le Pied de la Momie*, *La Pipe
d'Opium*, and *Le Club des Haschischins*,—what marvellous

[1] Yet even inside poetry not so very much before 1830.

consummateness in the various specifications and conditions do these afford us !

Sometimes, however, I have thought that just as *La Morte Amoureuse* is almost or quite sufficient text for vindicating the greatness or greaterness of "Théo," so his earliest book of prose fiction, *Les Jeune-France*, will serve the same purpose for another side of him, lesser if anybody likes, but exceptionally "complementary." In particular it possesses a quality which up to his time was very rare in France, has not been extraordinarily common there even since, and is still, even in its ancestral home with ourselves, sometimes inconceivably blundered about —the quality of Humour.[1]

For wit, France can, of course, challenge the world ; nay, she can do more, she can say to the world, " I have ₍Gautier's₎ taught you this ; and you are no match for your humour—*Les* teacher." But in Humour the case is notori-*Jeune-France.* ously altered. None of the Latin nations, except Spain, the least purely Latin of them, has ever achieved it, as the original or unoriginal Latins themselves never did, with the exception of the lighter forms of it in Catullus, of the grimmer in Lucretius—those greatest and most un-Roman of Roman poets.[2] In all the wide and splendid literature of French before the nineteenth century only Rabelais and Molière[3] can lay claim to it. Romanticism brings humour in its train, as Classicism brings wit ; but it is curious how slow was the Romanticisation of French in this respect, with one exception. There is no real humour in Hugo, Vigny, George Sand, Balzac, scarcely even in Musset.

---

[1] Of course I know what a dangerous word this is ; how often people who have not a glimmering of it themselves deny it to others ; and how it is sometimes seen in mere horse-play, often confounded with " wit " itself, and generally " taken in vain." But one must sometimes be content with φωνήεντα or φωνᾶντα (the choice is open, but I prefer the latter) συνετοῖσι, and take the consequences of them with the ἀσύνετοι.

[2] Some would allow it to Plautus, but I doubt ; and even Martial did not draw as much of it from Spanish soil as must have been latent there—unless the Goths absolutely imported it. Perhaps the nearest approach in him is the sudden turn when the obliging Phyllis, just as he is meditating with what choice and costly gifts he shall reward her varied kindnesses, anticipates him by modestly asking, with the sweetest preliminary blandishments, for a jar of wine (xii. 65).

[3] La Fontaine may be desiderated. His is certainly one of the most *humouresque* of wits ; but whether he has pure humour I am not sure.

Dumas, though showing decidedly good gifts of possibility in his novels, does not usually require it there ; the absence of it in his dramas need hardly be dwelt on. Mérimée, one cannot but think, might have had it if he had chosen ; but Mérimée did not choose to have so many things ! If Gérard de Nerval's failure of a great genius had failed in the comic instead of the romantic-tragical direction, he would have had some too—in fact he had it in the embryonic and unachieved fashion in which the author of *Gaspard de la Nuit*, and Baudelaire, and Paul Verlaine have had it since in verse and prose. But Gautier has it plump and plain, and without any help from the strange counterfeiting fantasy of verse which sometimes confers it. He has it always ; at all times of his life ; in the hack-work which made abortion of so much greater literature, and in his actually great literature, poems, novels, travels—what not. But he never has it more strongly, vividly, and originally than in *Les Jeune-France*, a coming-of-age book almost as old as *mil-huit-cent-trente*, written in part no doubt in the immortal *gilet rouge* itself, if only as kept for study wear like Diderot's old dressing-gown.

There are two dangers lying in wait for the reader of the book. One is the ordinary and quite respectable putting-out-of-the-lip at its juvenile improprieties ; the other, a little more subtle, is the notion that the things, improper or not (and some of them are quite *not*), are mere *juvenilia*—clever undergraduate work. The first requires no special counterblast ; the old monition, " Don't like it for its impropriety, but also don't let its impropriety hide its merits from you if it has any," will suffice. The other is, as has been said, more insidious. I can only say that I have read much undergraduate or but slightly post-graduate literature of many generations —before the day of *Les Jeune-France*, about its date, between that day and my own season of passing through those " sweet hours and the fleetest of time," and since that season till the present moment. But many equals of this book I have not read.

It is of course necessary to remember that it is expressly subtitled " Romans Goguenards," thereby preparing the reader for the reverse of seriousness. That reverse, especially in young hands, is a difficult thing to manage. " Guffaw " and " yawn " are two words which have actually two letters in common ; *y* and *g* are notoriously interchangeable in some dialects and circumstances, while *n* and *u* are the despair of the copyist or the student of copies. There remain only " ff "—the lightest of literals. We need not cite *nominatim* (indeed it might be rash) the endless examples in French and English where the guffaw of the writer excites the yawn of the reader. But this is hardly ever the case, at least as I find it, with Gautier.

The *Preface*, in which the author presents himself in his unregenerate and un-" young-France " condition, is really a triumph ; I wish I could give the whole of it here. And what is more, it is a sort of epitome by anticipation of the entire Gautier, though without, of course, the mastery of artistry he attained in years of laborious prose and verse. For that quality of humour which his younger friend Taine was to define happily, though by no means to his own comfort or approval, in the phrase devoted to one of our English masters of it, " Il se moque de ses émotions à l'instant même où il s'y livre," you must go to Fielding or to Thackeray to beat it.

He (the supposed author) *was* the most ordinary and insignificant creature in the world. He had never either killed a policeman nor committed suicide ; he possessed neither pipe, nor dagger, *ni quoi que ce soit qui ait du caractère*. He *did* like cats (which taste fortunately remained with Gautier himself throughout his life), and his reflections on politics had arrived at a final result of zero (another abiding feature, by the way, with " Théo "). He never could learn to play at cards. He thought artists were merely mountebanks, etc., etc. But some kind friends took him in hand and made him an accomplished Jeune-France. He took to himself a very long *nom de guerre*, a very short moustache, a middle parting to his hair (the history of the middle parting would be worth writing), and a " delirious " waistcoat. He learnt to smoke, and to get " Byronically " drunk. He bought an Italian stiletto (by great luck he had a sallow complexion naturally); a silk rope-ladder (" which is of the first importance "); several reams of paper for love-letters, and a supply of rose-coloured and avanturine wax.[1] He is going to be, if he is not as yet, " fatal," " vague," " fallen-angelical," " volcanic." There is only one desirable quality which unkind fate has put beyond his reach. He is not, and cannot make himself, an illegitimate child ! Now, I am sorry for any one who, having read this, cannot lean back in his chair and follow it up for himself by a series of fancy pictures of Jeunes-something from 1830 to 1918.[2]

Of the actual stories " Daniel Jovard " takes up the cue of the *Preface* directly, and describes the genesis of a *romantique à tous crins*. " Onuphrius " honestly subtitles itself " Les Vexations Fantastiques d'un admirateur d'Hoffmann," and has, I think, sometimes been dismissed as a Hoffmannesque *pastiche*. Far be it from me to hint the slightest denigration of the author of the *Phantasie-stücke* and the *Nacht-stücke*, of the *Serapion's-brüder* and the *Kater Murr*—not the least pleasing features on the right side of the half-glorious, half-ghastly contrast between the Germany of a hundred years ago and the Germany of to-day. But " Onuphrius " is Hoffmann Gautierised, German " Franciolated," a *Walpurgis-nacht* softened by Morgane la Fée. " Elias Wildmanstadius," one of the earliest, remains one of the

---

[1] This is an exception to the rule of *tout passe*, if not of *tout casse*. You can still buy avanturine wax ; only, like all waxes, except red and black, it seals very badly, and makes " kisses " in a most untidy fashion. Avanturine should be left to the original stone—to peat-water running over pebbles with the sun on it—and to eyes.

[2] I once knew an incident which might have figured in these scenes, and which would, I think, have pleased Théo. But it happened just after his own death, in the dawn of the aesthetic movement. A man, whom we may call A, visited a friend, say B, who was doing his utmost to be in the mode. A had for some time been away from the centre ; and B showed him, with hopes to impress, the blue china, the Japanese mats and fans, the rush-bottomed chairs, the Morris paper and curtains, the peacock feathers, etc. But A looked coldly on them and said, " Where is your brass tray ? " And B was saddened and could only plead, " It is coming directly ; but you know too much."

most agreeable, pictures of a fanatic of the mediaeval.
The overture and the finale, both pieces in which the
great motto " Trinq ! " is perhaps a very little abused,
nevertheless contain a considerable amount of wisdom,
and the last not a little wit.[1] But the central story
Celle-ci et Celle-là, which fills nearly half the book, is
no doubt the article on which one must—as far as this
essay-piece is concerned—judge Gautier's tale-telling
gifts. It is "improper" in part ; indeed, the thing,
which is largely dialogic, may be thought to have been a
young romantic's challenge to Crébillon. The points
of the contest would require a very careful judge to reckon
them out. Although Gautier was no democrat, and
certainly no misogynist, his lady of quality, Madame
de M., is terribly below the Crébillonesque Marquises
and Célies in every respect, except the beauty, which
we have to take on trust ; while, if she is not quite such
a fiend as Laclos's heroine, she is also unlike her
in being stupid. The hero, Rodolphe, though by no
means a cad and possessed of much more heart than
M. de Clerval or Clitandre, has neither their manners
nor their wit. But Mariette, the *servante-maîtresse*, though
much less moral, is much more attractive than Pamela ;
the whole of the story is hit off with a pleasant mixture
of humour, narrative faculty, bright phrase,[2] and good
nature, of which the first is simply absent in Crébillon
and the last rather dubiously present.

We may return very shortly to the later, longer, and,
I suppose, more accomplished stories before relinquishing
Gautier.

I have known very good people who liked *Fortunio* ;
I care for it less than for any other of its author's tales.
Return to The fabulously rich and entirely heartless hero
Fortunio. has not merely the extravagance but (which
is very rare with Gautier) the vulgarity of Byronism ;

---

[1] They are both connected with the " orgie "-mania, and the last is a deliberate
burlesque of the originals of P. L. Jacob, Janin, Eugène Sue, and Balzac himself.

[2] It is here that the famous return of a kiss *revu, corrigé et considérablement augmenté*
is recorded.

the opening orgie, by an oversight so strange that it
may almost seem to be no oversight at all, reminds one
only too forcibly of the ironic treatment accorded to
that institution in *Les Jeune-France*, and suffers from the
reminder; the blending of East and West and the
Arabian Night harems in Paris, "unbeknown" to
everybody,[1] almost attain that *plusquam*-Aristotelian
state of reprobation, the impossible which is also improbable; and the courtesan heroines—at least two of
them, Musidora and Arabelle—are even more faulty
in this respect. No doubt

$$\pi o\lambda\lambda a\grave{\iota} \ \mu o\rho\phi a\grave{\iota} \ \tau\hat{\omega}\nu \ o\grave{\upsilon}\rho a\nu\acute{\iota}\omega\nu,$$

and the forms of the Pandemic as well as of the Uranian
Aphrodite are numerous likewise. But among them
one finds no probability or possibility of Gautier's Musidora of eighteen, who might be a young duchess gone
to the bad. Neither is the end of the girl, suicide, in
consequence of the disappearance of her lover, though
quite possible and even probable, at all suitable to
Gautier's own fashion of thinking and writing.
Mérimée could have done it perfectly well. Of almost
no others of the delectable contents of the two volumes
of *Nouvelles* and of *Romans et Contes* has one to speak
in this fashion, while some of them come very nearly
up to their companion *La Morte Amoureuse* itself.

How Gautier managed to keep all this comparatively
serious, if not quite so, in treatment, is perhaps less
difficult to make out than why he took the trouble to do
so. But it is the entire absences of irony on the one side
and on the other of the dream-quality—the pure imagina-

---

[1] He (it is some excuse for him that this suggested a better thing in certain *New
Arabian Nights*) buys, furnishes, and subsequently deserts an empty house to give a ball in,
and put his friends on no scent of his own abode; but he makes this "own abode" a
sort of Crystal Palace in the centre of a whole ring-fence of streets, with the old fronts
of the houses kept to avert suspicion of the Seraglio of Eastern beauties, the menagerie
and beast-fights, and the slaves whom (it is rather suggested than definitely stated)
he occasionally murders. He performs circus-rider feats when he meets a lady (or at
least a woman) in the Bois de Boulogne; he sets her house on fire when it occurs to him
that she has received other lovers there; and we are given to understand that he blows
up his own palace when he returns to the East. In fact, he is a pure anticipated cognition
of a Ouidesque super-hero as parodied by Sir Francis Burnand (and independently by
divers schoolboys and undergraduates) some fifty years ago.

tion which makes the impossibilities of *La Morte* and of
Arria Marcella, and even of the trifle *Omphale,* so delightful—that deprives *Fortunio* of attraction in my eyes.
Such faint glimmerings of it as there are are confined
to two very minor characters :—one of the courtesans,
Cinthia, a beautiful statuesque Roman, who has simplified
the costume-problem by wearing nothing—literally
nothing—except one of two dresses, one black velvet
and the other white watered silk ; and the " Count
George " (we are never told his surname), who gives the
overture-orgie.   One might, as the lady said to Professor
Wilson in regard to the *Noctes,* say to him, " I really
think you eat too many oysters, and drink too much [not
indeed in his case] whisky," and I can find no excuse for
his deliberately upsetting an enormous bowl of flaming
arrack punch on a floor swept by women's dresses.   But
he is quite human, and he makes the best speech and
scene in the book when he remonstrates with Musidora
for secluding herself because she cannot discover the
elusive marquis-rajah tiger-keeper,—and, I fear I must
add, " tiger " himself,—from whom the thing takes its
title.[1]

It is, however, almost worth while to go through the
freak-splendours and transformation-scene excitements

And   of *Fortunio* to prepare the palate [2] to enjoy
others. *La Toison d'Or* which follows.   Here is once
more the true Gautieresque humour, good humour,
marvellous word-painting, and romance, agreeably—
indeed charmingly—twisted together.   There is no
fairy-story transposed into a modern and probable key
which surpasses this of the painter Tiburce ; and the
disorderly curios of his rooms ; and his sudden and
heroic determination to fall desperately in love with a
blonde ; and his setting off to Flanders to find one ;
and the fruitlessness of his search and his bewitchment
with the Magdalen in the " Descent from the Cross "

---

[1] I have seen an admirable criticism of this " thing " in one word, " Cold ! "
[2] On the cayenne-and-claret principle which Haydon (one hopes libellously, in point
of degree) attributed to Keats. (It was probably a devilled-biscuit, and so quite allowable.)

at Antwerp (ah ! what has become of it ?) ; and his casual discovery and courtship of a girl like that celestial convertite ; and her sorrow when she finds that she is only a substitute; and her victory by persuading her lover to paint her *as* the Magdalen and so work off the witchery.[1] Of course some one may shrug shoulders and murmur, "Always the *berquinade?*" But I do not think *La Morte Amoureuse* was a *berquinade*.

Of Gautier's longer books it is not necessary to say much, because, with perhaps one exception, they are admittedly not his forte.[2] Of the longest, *Le Capitaine Fracasse*, I am myself very fond. Its opening and first published division, *Le Château de la Misère*, is one of the finest

Longer books,
Le Capitaine
Fracasse and
others.

pieces of description in the whole range of the French novel ; and there are many interesting scenes, especially the great duel of the hero Sigognac with the bravo Lampourde. But some make it a reproach, not, I think, of very damaging validity, that so much of the book is little more than a "study off" the *Roman Comique*;[3] and it is, though not exactly a reproach, a great misfortune that in time, kind, and almost everything else it enters into competition with Dumas, whose gifts as a manager of such things were as much above Gautier's as his powers as a writer were below Théo's. *Le Roman de la Momie*, though possessing the abiding talisman of style, suffers in the first place from being mere Egyptology novelised, and in the second from the same thing having been done, on a scale much better suited to the author, in *Le* Pied *de la Momie*. Nor are *Spirite* and *Militona* free from parallel charges : while *La Belle Jenny* —that single and unfortunate appeal to the *abonné* noted above—really may fail to amuse those who are not "irked by the style."

---

[1] "Théo" has no repute as a psychologist ; but I have known such repute attained by far less subtle touches than this.

[2] For more on them, with a pretty full abstract of *Le Capitaine Fracasse*, see the Essay more than once mentioned.

[3] *V. sup.* Vol. I. p. 279-286. Of course the duplication, *as literature*, is positively interesting and welcome.

There remains the most notorious and the most
abused of all Gautier's work, *Mademoiselle de Maupin.*
Mlle. de Perhaps here also, as in the case of *La Morte*
Maupin. *Amoureuse,* I cannot do better than simply
reprint, with very slight addition, what I said of the book
nearly forty years ago. For the case is a peculiar one,
and I have made no change in my own estimate, though
I think the inclusion of the *Preface*—not because I agree
with it any less—more dubious than I did then. In
this *Preface* the doctrine of "art for art's sake" and
of its consequent independence of any *licet* or *non-licet*
from morality is put with great ability and no little
cogency, but in a fashion essentially juvenile, from its
want of measure and its evident wish to provoke as much
as to prove.[1] Without it the book would probably have
excited far less odium and opprobrium than it has actually
done; it would, if separate, be an excellent critical essay
on the general subject; while in its actual position
it almost subjects the text to the curse of purpose, from
which nothing which claims to be art ought (according
to the doctrine of both preface and book) to be more free.

With the novel itself it is difficult to deal in the way
of abstract and occasional excerpt, not merely because of
its breaches of the proprieties, but on account of the plan
on which it is written. A mixture of letters and narrative,[2] dealing almost entirely with emotions, and scarcely
at all with incidents, it defies narrative analysis such as
that which was given to its elder sister in naughtiness,
La Religieuse. It would seem that Goethe, who in many
ways influenced Gautier, is responsible to some extent
for its form, and perhaps for the fact that *As You Like
It* plays an even more important part in it than *Hamlet*
plays in *Wilhelm Meister.* No one who has read it can
fail thenceforward to associate a new charm with the image

---

[1] I—some fifty years since—knew a man who, with even greater juvenility, put pretty
much the same doctrine in a Fellowship Essay. He did not obtain that Fellowship.

[2] It might possibly have been shortened with advantage in concentration of effect.
But the story (pleasantly invented, if not true) of Gautier's mother locking him up in
his room that he might not neglect his work (of the nature of which she was blissfully
ignorant) nearly excuses him. A prisoner will naturally be copious rather than terse.

of Rosalind, even though she be one of Shakespeare's most gracious creations; and this I know is a bold word. But, in truth, it is in more ways than one an unspeakable book. Those who like may point to a couple of pages of loose description at the end, a dialogue in the style of a polite *Jacques le Fataliste* in the middle, a dozen phrases of a hazardous character scattered here and there. Diderot himself—no strait-laced judge, indeed *particeps ejusdem criminis*—remarked long ago, and truly enough, that errors of this sort punish themselves by restricting the circulation, and diminishing the chance of life of the book, or other work, that contains them. But it is not these things that the admirers of *Mademoiselle de Maupin* admire. It is the wonderful and final expression, repeated, but subtly shaded and differenced, in the three characters of Albert, Rosette, and Madeleine herself, of the aspiration which, as I have said, colours Gautier's whole work. If he, as has been justly remarked, was the priest of beauty, *Mademoiselle de Maupin* is certainly one of the sacred books of the cult. The apostle to whom it was revealed was young, and perhaps he has mingled words of clay with words of gold. It would be difficult to find a Bowdler for this Madeleine, and impossible to adapt her to the use of families. But those who understand as they read, and can reject the evil and hold fast the good, who desire sometimes to retire from the meditation of the weary ways of ordinary life to the land of clear colours and stories, where there is none of this weariness, who are not to be scared by the poet's harmless puppets or tempted by his guileless baits—they at least will take her as she is and be thankful.[1]

Still, as has been said, the book might have been made still better by being cut down a little; not, indeed, to the dimensions of a very short story, but to something like those of *Fortunio* or of *Jettatura*. For undoubtedly,

[1] It may amuse some readers to know that I saw the rather famous lithograph (of a lady and gentleman kissing each other at full speed on horseback), which owes its subject to the book, in no more romantic a place than a very small public-house in " Scarlet town," to which I had gone, not to quench my thirst or for any other licentious purpose, but to make an appointment with—a chimney-sweep.

while Gautier had an all but unsurpassed command of
the short story proper, a really long one was apt to de-
velop some things in him which, if they were not essentially faults, were not likely to improve a full-sized novel.
He would too much abound in description; the want
of *evolution* of character—his character is not bad in
itself, but it is, to use modern slang, rather static than
dynamic—naturally shows itself more; and readers who
want an elaborate plot look for it longer and are more
angry at not being fed. But for the short, shorter, and
shortest kind—the story which may run from ten to a
hundred pages with no meticulous limitations on either
side—it seems to me that in the French nineteenth century there are only three other persons who can be in
any way classed with him. One of these, his early
contemporary, Charles de Bernard, and another, who only
became known after his death, Guy de Maupassant, are
to be treated in other chapters here. Moreover, Bernard
was slighter, though not so slight as he has sometimes
been thought; and Maupassant, though very far from
slight, had a *lésion* (as his own school would say) which
interfered with universality. The third competitor, not
yet named, who was Gautier's almost exact contemporary,
though he began a very little earlier and left off a little
earlier too, carried metal infinitely heavier than the
pleasant author of *Le Paratonnerre*, and though not free
from partly disabling prejudices, had more balance [1]
than Maupassant. He had more head and less heart,
more prose logic and less poetical fancy, more actuality
and less dream than " Théo." But I at least can find no
critical abacus on which, by totting up the values of
both, I can make one greatly outvalue the other. And
to the understanding I must have already spoken the
name of Prosper Mérimée. [2]

All the world knows *Carmen*, though it may be feared
that the knowledge has been conveyed to more people

---

[1] Some might even say he had too much.
[2] For reference to previous dealings of mine with Mérimée see *Preface*.

by the mixed and inferior medium of the stage and music than by the pure literature of the original tale.

Mérimée. Yet it may be generously granted that the lower introduction may have induced some to go on, or back, to the higher. Of the unfaulty faultlessness of that original there has never been any denial worth listening to; the gainsayers having been persons who succumbed either to non-literary prejudice[1] of one kind or another or to the peculiarly childish habit of going against established opinion. For combined interest of matter and perfection of form I should put it among the dozen best short stories of the world so far as I am acquainted with them. The appendix about the gipsies is indeed a superfluity, induced, it would seem, partly by Mérimée's wish to have a gibe at Borrow for being a missionary, and partly by a touch of inspectorial-professorial[2] habit in him which is frequently apparent and decidedly curious. But it is an appendix of the most appendicious, and can be cut away without the slightest Manx-cat effect. From the story itself not a word could be abstracted without loss nor one added to it without danger. The way in which the narrator— it is impossible to tell the number of the authors who have wrecked themselves over the narrator when he has to take part in the action—and the guide are put and kept in their places, as well as the whole part of José Navarro, are *impayables*. If the Hispanolatry of French Romanticism had nothing but Gastibelza and L'Andalouse in verse and José Navarro in prose to show, it would stand justified and crowned among all the literary manias in history.

About Carmen herself there has been more—and may justly be a little more—question. Is her *diablúra*

Carmen. slightly exaggerated? Or, to put the complaint in a more accurately critical form, has Mérimée attended a little too much to the task of throwing on the

---

[1] It is sad, but necessary, to include M. Brunetière among the latter class.

[2] He was never a professor, but he was an inspector; and, though I may be biassed, I think the inspector is usually the more " donnish " animal of the two.

canvas a typical Rommany *chi* or *callee*, and a little too little to that of bodying forth a probable and individual human girl? As an advocate I think I could take a brief on either side of the question without scandalising the, on this point, almost neurotic conscience of the late Mr. Anthony Trollope. But, as a juryman, my verdict on either indictment would be "Not guilty, and *please* do it again."

But I had much rather decline both functions and all litigious proceedings, and go from the courts of law to the cathedral of literature and thank the Lord thereof for this wonderful triumph of letters. And, in the same way, if any quarrelsome person says, "But only a few pages back you were in parallel ecstasies about *La Morte Amoureuse*," I decline the daggers. Each is supreme in its kind, though the kinds are different. Of each it may be said, "It cannot be better done," but there may be—in fact there is nearly sure to be—something in the individual taste of each reader which will make the appeal of one to his heart, if not to his head, more intimate and welcome. That has nothing to do with their general literary value, which in each case is consummate. And happy are those who can appreciate both.

Consummateness, in the various kinds, is, indeed, the mark of Mérimée's stories. The variety is greater than in those of Gautier, because, just as "Théo" had the advantage of Prosper in point of poetry, he had a certain disadvantage in point of range of intellect, or, to prevent mistake, let us say interest—which perhaps is only another *tropos* (as the Greeks would have said and as the chemists in a very limited sense do say after them) of the same thing. Beauty was Gautier's only idol; Mérimée had more of a pantheon.

As to *Colomba* compared with *Carmen*, there is, I believe, a sort of sectarianism among Prosperites. I

Colomba. hope I am, as always, catholic. I do not know that, in the terms of classical scholarship, it is "castigated" to the same extent as its rival in point of superfluities. Not that I wish anything away from it;

but I think a few things might be away without loss—
which is not the case with *Carmen*. Yet, on the other
hand, the danger of the type seems to me more completely avoided.[1] At any rate, my admiration for the
book is not in any way bribed by that Rossetti portrait
of a Corsican lady to which I have referred above. For
though she certainly *is* Colomba, I never saw the face
till years—almost decades—after I knew the story.

But of the smaller tales which usually accompany
her, who shall exaggerate the praise? *Mateo Falcone*,
that modern Roman father (by the way, there
is said to be more Roman blood in Corsica
than in any part of the mainland of Italy, and
the portrait above mentioned is almost pure
Faustina), is another of those things which are *à prendre
ou à laisser*. It could not, again, be better done; and
if any one will compare it with the somewhat similar
anecdote of lynch-law in Balzac's *Les Chouans*, he ought
to recognise the fact—good as that also is. *Les Âmes
du Purgatoire* is also " first choice." Of what may be
called the satellites of the great *Don Juan* story—satellites
with a nebula instead of a planet for their centre—it is
quite the greatest. But of this group *La Vénus d'Ille*
is my favourite, perhaps for a rather illegitimate reason.
That reason is the possibility of comparing it with Mr.
Morris's *Ring given to Venus*—a handling of the same
subject in poetry instead of in prose, with a happy ending
instead of an unhappy one, and pure Romantic in every
respect instead of, as *La Vénus d'Ille* is, late classical,
with a strong Romantic *nisus*.[2]

For, though it might be improper here to argue out
the matter, these last words can be fitted to Mérimée's
ethos from the days of " Clara Gazul " and " Hyacinthe
Maglanovich " to those when he wrote *Lokis* and

Its smaller companions —Mateo Falcone, etc.

---

[1] And perhaps in actual life, if not in literature, I should prefer a young woman who
might possibly have me murdered if she discovered a blood-feud between my ancestors
and hers, to one in whose company it would certainly be necessary to keep a very sharp
look-out on my watch. The two risks are not equally " the game."

[2] Many a reader, I hope, has been reminded, by one or the other, or both, of the
Anatomy of Melancholy, which also contains the story: and has gone to it with the usual
consequence of reading nothing else for some time.

La Chambre Bleue. A deserter from Romanticism he was never; a Romantic free-lance (after being an actual Romantic pioneer) with a strong Classical element in him he was always.

The almost unavoidable temptation of taking *Colomba* and *Carmen* together has drawn us away from the companions, as they are usually given, of the Spanish story among Mérimée's earlier works. More than two-thirds of the volume, as most people have seen it, consist of translations from the Russian of Poushkin and Gogol, which need no notice here. But *Arsène Guillot* and *L'Abbé Aubain,* the two pieces which immediately follow *Carmen,* can by no means be passed over. If (as one may fairly suppose, without being quite certain) the selection of these for juxtaposition was authentic and deliberate, it was certainly judicious. They might have been written as a trilogy, not of sequence, but of contrast—a demonstration of power in essentially different forms of subject. *Arsène Guillot,* like *Carmen,* is tragedy; but it is *tragédie bourgeoise* or *sentimentale.* There are no daggers or musquetoons, and though (since the heroine throws herself out of a window) there is some blood, she dies of consumption, not of her wounds. She is only a *grisette* who has lost her looks, the one lover she ever cared for, and her health; while the other characters of importance (Mérimée has taken from the stock-cupboard one of the cynical, rough-mannered, but really good-natured doctors common in French and not unknown in English literature) are the lover or gallant himself, Max de Saligny (quite a good fellow and perfectly willing, though he had tired of Arsène, to have succoured her had he known her distress), and the Lady Bountiful, Madame de Piennes. How a "triangle" is established nobody versed in novels needs to be told, though everybody, however well versed, should be glad to read. Arsène of course must die; what the others who lived did with their lives is left untold. The thing is quite unexciting, but is done with the author's miraculous skill; nor perhaps is there

Those of Carmen; Arsène Guillot.

any piece that better shows his faculty of writing like the " gentleman," [1] which, according to a famous contrast, he was, on a subject almost equally liable to more or less vulgar Paul-de-Kockery, to sloppy sentimentalism, and to cheap cynical journalese.

As for *L'Abbé Aubain*, it is slight but purely comic, of the very best comedy, telling how a great lady, obliged **And L'Abbé** by pecuniary misfortunes to retire with her **Aubain.** husband to a remote country house, takes a fancy to, and imagines she has possibly excited fatal passion in, the local priest; attributes to him a sentimental past; but half good-naturedly, half virtuously obtains for him a comfortable town-cure in order to remove him, and perhaps herself, from temptation. This moving tale of self-denial and of averted sorrow, sin, and perhaps tragedy, is told in letters to another lady. Then follows a single epistle from the Abbé himself to his old Professor of Theology, telling, with the utmost brevity and matter-of-factness, how glad he is to make the exchange, what a benevolent nuisance the patroness has been, and how he looks forward to meeting the Professor in his new parsonage, with a plump chicken and a bottle of old bordeaux between them. There is hardly anywhere a better bit of irony of the lighter kind. It is rather like Charles de Bernard, with the higher temper and brighter flash of Mérimée's style.

All the stories just noticed, except *Carmen* itself (which is of 1847), appeared originally in the decade **La Prise de** 1830–40, as well as others of less note, and **la Redoute.** one wonderful little masterpiece, which deserves notice by itself. This is *La Prise de la Redoute*, a very short thing — little more than an anecdote—of one of the " furious five minutes," or hours, not unknown in all great wars, and seldom better known than in that of these recent years, despite the changes of armament and tactics. It is almost sufficient to say of it that no one who has the slightest critical

---

[1] " Mérimée était gentilhomme : Sainte-Beuve ne l'était pas." I forget who said this, but it was certainly said, and I think it was true.

faculty can fail to see its consummateness, and that any
one who does not see or will not acknowledge that
consummateness may make up his mind to one thing—
that he is not, and—but by some marvellous exertion of
the grace of God—never will be, a critic. He may
have in him the elements of a capital convict or a faithful
father of a family; he may be a poet—poets, though
sometimes very good, have sometimes been very bad
critics—or a painter, or a philosopher, as distinguished
as any of those whose names the Bertram girls learnt; or
an elect candlestick-maker, fit to be an elder of any Little
Bethel. But of criticism he can have no jot or tittle, no
trace or germ. The question is, for once, not one of
anything that can be called merely or mainly " taste."
A man who is not a hopelessly bad critic, though he may
not have in him the *catholicon* of critical goodness, may
fail to appreciate *La Morte Amoureuse* because of its
dreaminess and supernaturality and all-for-loveness;
Carmen because Carmen shocks him; *La Venus d'Ille*
because of its *macabre* tone; *Les Jeune-France* because
of their *goguenarderie* or *goguenardise*. But the case of
the *Redoute* is one of those rare instances where the intellect and the aesthetic sense approach closest—almost
merge into each other,—as, indeed, they did in Mérimée himself. The principles as well as the practice of
narrative are here at once reduced to their lowest and
exalted to their highest terms. The thing is not merely
fermented but distilled ; not so much a fact as a formula,
with a formula's precision but without its dryness. If
we take the familiar trichotomy of body, soul, and spirit
and apply it to subject, style, and narrative power in a
story, we shall find them all perfectly achieved and perfectly wedded here.[1]

About the same time as that at which *Carmen* was
published (indeed a year earlier) Mérimée wrote a shorter,
but not very short story, *Il Viccolo di Madama Lucrezia,*

---

[1] This is not merely a waste of explosives. I have actually seen the story dismissed
as a " merely faithful record of the facts " or something of that sort. One was at least
obliged to the man for reminding one of Partridge on Garrick.

which for some reason only appeared, at least in book form, long after, with the *Dernières Nouvelles* and post-humously. It is, I think, his one attempt in the explained [1] supernatural—a kind for which I have myself no very great affection. But it is extremely well done, and if there are some suggestions of impropriety in it, Hymen, to use Paul de Kock's phrase (it is really pleasant to think of Paul and Prosper—the farthest opposites of French contemporary novel-craft—together), covers up the more recent of them with his mantle.

The
*Dernières
Nouvelles;
Il Viccolo di
Madama
Lucrezia.*

But some at least of the other contents of the same volume are worthy of greater praise. One, *Le Coup de Pistolet*, is a translation from Poushkin; another, *Federigo*, an agreeable version of an Italian folk-tale—one of the numerous legends in which a 'cute and not unkindly sinner escapes not only perdition, but Purgatory, and takes Paradise by storm of wit.[2] A third piece, *Les Sorcières Espagnoles*, is folklorish in a way likewise, but inferior.

Yet another trio remains, and its constituents, *Lokis*, *La Chambre Bleue*, and *Djoumane*, are among Mérimée's greatest triumphs. *Djoumane* is not dated; the other two date from the very last years of his life and of the Second Empire; and, unless I mistake, were written directly to amuse that Imperial Majesty who lives yet, and who, as all good men must hope, may live to see the *revanche*, if not of the dynasty, at any rate of the country, which she did so much to adorn.

Of the three, *Djoumane*—the account of a riding dream during a campaign in Algeria—is the slightest, no doubt, and to a certain extent a "trick" story. But it has the usual Mériméan consummate-ness in its own way; and I can give it one testimonial which, like all testimonials, no doubt depends on the

Djoumane.

---

[1] A very "gentle" reader may perceive something *not* quite explained, and I should be happy to allow it.

[2] And perhaps—though Mérimée does not allege this—by doing good to his neighbours likewise; for he rescues twelve companions of his own naughtiness from the infernal regions. The mixture of pagan and Christian eschatology, if not borrowed, is exceedingly well and suitably " found."

importance of the giver, but which, to that extent, is solid. I have read dozens, scores, almost hundreds of dream-stories. I cannot remember a single one, except this, which " took me in " almost to the very awaking.

There is no trick in either of the others, though in one of them there is the supernatural—*not* explained. But they are examples—closely and no doubt intentionally juxtaposed—in two different kinds, both of them exceptionally difficult and dangerous : the story of more or less ordinary life, with only a few suggestions of anything else, which resolves itself into horrible tragedy; and the story, again of ordinary life, with a tragic suggestion in the middle, which unknits itself into pure comedy at the end.

Lokis is a story of lycanthropy, or rather *arct*anthropy. A Lithuanian Count's mother has been carried off, soon after her marriage, by a bear, and just rescued with a lucky shot at the monster. She goes, as is not very wonderful, quite mad, does not recover when her child is born, and is under restraint in her own house, as wife and widow, for the term of her life. Her son, however, shows no overt symptoms of anything wrong except fits of melancholy and seclusion, being in other respects a gentleman of most excellent " havings "— handsome, brave, sportsmanlike, familiar with the best European society, and even something of a scholar. He entertains a German minister and professor, whose special forte is Lithuanian, in order that the pundit may study some rare books and MSS. in his library ; and his guest, being a great traveller, a good rider, and, though simple in his ways, not at all unlike a man of this world, makes a friend of him. It so happens, too, that they have a common acquaintance—a neighbour, and, as is soon seen, an idol of the Count's, Mademoiselle Julie Ivinska, very pretty, very merry, and, if not very wise, clever enough to take in the scholar, on his own ground, with a vernacular ("jmoude ") version of one of Mickiewitz's poems. All goes well in a way, except for occasional apparitions of the poor mad Countess; but there is a rather threatening episode of a ride into a

Lokis.

great forest, which is popularly supposed to contain a
" sanctuary of the beasts," impenetrable by any hunter,
and in which they actually meet a local sorceress, with
a basket of poisonous mushrooms and a tame snake in it.
Another episode gives us odd comments, and a sort of
nightmare afterwards, of the Count, when his guest
happens to mention the blood-drinking habits of the
South American gauchos, in which the professor himself
has been forced to take part.

But these things and other " lights ": of the catastrophe
are very artistically kept down, and you are never nudged
or winked at in the offensive " please note " manner.
The guest goes away, but, not much to anybody's surprise, is very soon asked to return and celebrate the
wedding of the Count and Mlle. Ivinska, who are both
Lutherans. He goes, and finds a great semi-pagan
feast of the local peasantry (which does not much please
him) and one or two bad omens, including an appearance
of the mad old Countess with evil words, which please
him still less. But the feast ends at last and the newly
married couple retire, there being, of course, no " going
away." Early in the morning the pastor is waked by the
sound of a heavy body (a sound which he had noticed
before but never interpreted) clambering down a tree
just outside his window. A little later, as the bridal
pair do not appear, their door is broken open, and the
new Countess is found alone, dead, drenched in blood,
and her throat, not cut, but *bitten* through.

The whole story is told by the minister himself to
an otherwise unidentified Theodore and Adelaide (who
may be anybody, but who adroitly soften the conclusion),
and with that consummate management of the difficult
part of actor-narrator which has been noted. In every
respect but the purely sentimental one it seems to me
beyond reproach and almost beyond praise.[1]

---

[1] He had at one time introduced a smirch of grime by which nothing was gained and
a good deal lost—the abduction being not at once cut short, and the bear being suggested
as the Count's actual sire (see Burton again). But he had the taste as well as the sense
to cut this out. The management of the outsiders mentioned above contrasts remarkably in point of art with the similar things which, as noted (*v. sup.* pp. 93-4), do *not*
improve *Inès de las Sierras.*

There could not, as has been said, be a greater contrast than *La Chambre Bleue* in everything but crafts-
La Chambre manship. Two lovers (being French they
Bleue.   have to be unlawful lovers, but the story would
be neither injured nor improved, as a story, if the relation
were taken quite out of the reach of the Divorce and
Admiralty division, as it could be by a very little ingenuity) meet, in slight disguise,[1] at a railway station to
spend " a day and a night and a morrow " together at
a country hotel—not a great way from Paris, but outside
the widest *banlieue*. They meet and start all right ;
but Fortune begins, almost at once, to play them tricks.
They are not, as of course they wish to be, alone in the
carriage. A third traveller (one knows the wretch)
gets in at the last moment, and when, not to waste too
much time, they begin to make love in English, he very
properly tells them that he is an Englishman, assuring
them, however, that he is probably going to sleep, and
in any case will not attend to anything they say. Then
he takes a Greek book from his bag, and devotes himself
first to it and then to slumber. When their journey
comes to an end, so does his, and he goes to the same
hotel, but not before he has had an angry interview
on the platform with some one who calls him " uncle."
However, at the moment this does not matter much.
Still, the *guignon* is on them ; their *chambre bleue* is
between two other rooms, and—as is the common habit
of French hotels and the not uncommon one of English—
has doors to both, which, though they can be fastened,
by no means exclude sound. One of the next rooms
is the Englishman's ; the other, unfortunately, is a large
upper chamber, in which the officers of a departing
regiment are entertaining their successors. They are
very noisy, very late, and somewhat impertinent when
asked not to disturb their neighbours ; but they break
up at last, and the lovers have, as the poet says, " moonlight [actually] and sleep [possibly] for repayment."
But with the morning a worse thing happens. The

---

[1] He blue-spectacled, she black-veiled.

lover, waking, sees at the foot of the bed, flowing slug-
gishly from the crack under the Englishman's door, a
dark brownish-red fluid. It is blood, certainly blood !
and what on earth is to be done ? Apparently the Englishman (they have heard a heavy bump in the night)
has either committed suicide or been murdered, perhaps
by the nephew; the matter will be enquired into; in
the circumstances they themselves cannot escape examination, and the escapade will come out (blue spectacles
and black veils being alike useless against Commissaries
of Police and Judges of Instruction). The only hope
is an early Paris train, if they can get their bill, obtain
some sort of breakfast, and catch it. But, just as they
have determined to do so, the facts next door are discovered. The Englishman, who has ordered two bottles
of *porto*, has fallen asleep over the second, knocked it
down while still half-full, followed it himself to the floor,
and reclined there peacefully, while the fluid from the
broken bottle trickled over the boards,[1] under the door,
and into the agapemone beyond. Once more (but
for one horrible[2] piece of libel), the thing could hardly
be better.

Mérimée's largest and most ambitious attempt at
pure prose fiction—the *Chronique de Charles IX*—has
been rather variously judged. That the present writer once translated the whole of it
may, from different points of view, be regarded
as a qualification and a disqualification for judging it
afresh. For a mere amateur (and there are unfortunately[3] only too many amateur translators) it might be

The Chronique de Charles IX.

---

[1] Uncarpeted and polished, French fashion, of course.

[2] Mérimée represents his Englishman (and an Englishman who could read Greek,
too !) as satisfied with, and ordering a second bottle of, an extemporised " port " made of
ratafia, " quinze sous " *ordinaire*, and brandy ! This could deceive few Englishmen ;
and (till very recent years) absolutely no Englishman who could read Greek at a fairly
advanced period of life. From most of the French novelists of the time it would not
surprise us ; but from Mérimée, who was constantly visiting England and had numerous
English friends, it is a little odd. It may have been done *lectoris gratia* (but hardly
lectricis), to suit what even the other novelists just mentioned occasionally speak of as
the *Anglais de vaudeville*.

[3] I use this adverb from no trade-jealousy : for I have made as many translations
myself as I have ever wished to do, and have always been adequately paid for them. But

one or the other, according as the executant had been pleased or bored by his occupation. But to a person used to the manner, something of an expert in literary criticism, and brought by the writing of many books to an even keel between *engouement* and disgust, it certainly should not be a *dis*qualification. I do not think that the *Chronique*, as a romance of the Dumas kind, though written long before Dumas so fortunately deserted the drama for the kind itself, is entirely a success. It has excellent characters, if not in the actual hero, in his two Dalilahs—the camp-follower girl, who is a sort of earlier Carmen, and the great lady—and in his fear-neither-God-nor-Devil brother ; good scenes in the massacre and in other passages also. But as a whole—as a modernised *roman d'aventures*—it does not exactly *run* : the reader does not devour the story as he should. He may be—I am—delighted with the way in which the teller tells ; but the things which he tells are of much less interest. One cannot exactly say with that acute critic (if rather uncritical acceptor of the accomplished facts of life and death and matrimony), Queen Gertrude of Denmark, " More matter with less art," for there is plenty of matter as well as amply sufficient and yet not over-lavish art. But one is not made to take sufficient interest in the particular matter supplied.

The other considerable and early attempt in historical romance, *La Jacquerie*, is not in pure novel form, but The semi-dramatic stories. *La Jacquerie*. it may fitly introduce some notice of its actual method, in which Mérimée frequently, Gautier more than once, and a third eminent man of letters to be noticed presently most of all, distinguished themselves. This was what, in Old French, would have been called the story *par personnages*—the manner in which the whole matter is conveyed, not by *récit*, not by the usual form of mixed narrative and conversation, but

---

there is no doubt that the competition of amateur translation too often, on the one hand, reduces fees to sweating point, and on the other affects the standard of competence rather disastrously. I once had to review a version of *Das Kalte Herz*, in which the wicked husband persecuted his wife with a "*pitcher*," *Peitsche* being so translated by the light of nature, or the darkness of no dictionary.

by dramatic or semi-dramatic dialogue only, with action and stage direction, but no connecting language of the author to the reader. The early French mysteries and miracles—still more the farces—were not altogether unlike this ; we saw that some of the curious intermediate work of the late sixteenth and early seventeenth centuries took it, and that both of Crébillon's most felicitous, if not most edifying exercises are in dialogue form. The admiration of the French Romantics for the "accidented" and "matterful" English, Spanish, and German drama naturally encouraged experiment in this kind. Gautier has not very much of it, though there is some in *Les Jeune-France*, and his charming ballets might be counted in. But Mérimée was particularly addicted thereto. *La Jacquerie* is injured to some tastes by excessive indulgence in the grime and horror which the subject no doubt invited. We do not all rejoice in the notion of a Good Friday service, "extra-illustrated" by a real crucifixion alive of a generous Jacques who has surrendered himself ; or in violence offered (it is true, with the object of securing marriage) to a French heiress by an English captain of Free Companions. Even some of those who may not dislike these touches of *haut goût*, may, from the coolest point of view of strict criticism, say that the composition is too *décousu*, and that, as in the *Chronique*, there is little actual interest of story. But the phantasmagoria of gloom and blood and fire is powerfully presented. The earlier *Théâtre de Clara Gazul*,[1] one of the boldest and most successful of all literary mystifications, belongs more or less to the same class, which Mérimée never entirely deserted.

The best of all these is, to my thinking, undoubtedly the *Carrosse du Saint-Sacrement*. It is also, I believe,

---

[1] Professed renderings of Spanish plays which never existed. *La Guzla*—a companion volume with an audacious anagrammatising of "Gazul," etc., etc.—is a collection of pure ballads similarly attributed to a non-existent Slav poet, Hyacinthe Maglanovich. Both, in their influence on the Romantic movement, were only second to the work of actual English, German, and Spanish predecessors, and may rank with that of Nodier.

the only one that ever was tried on the actual stage—it
is said without success—though surely this cannot have
Le Carrosse du Saint-Sacrement, etc. been the form that it took in *La Périchole*,
not the least amusing of those levities of Offen-
bach's which did so disgust the Pharisees of
academic music and so arride the guileless public. *Le
Carrosse* itself is a charming thing—very, very merry
and by no means unwise—without a drop of bad blood
in it, and, if no better than, very nearly as good as it should
be from the moral point of view. *La Famille Carvajal*
has the same fault of gruesomeness as *La Jacquerie*,
with less variety, and *Une Femme est un Diable*, a fresh
handling of something like the theme of *Le Diable
Amoureux* and *The Monk*, if better than Lewis, is not so
good as Cazotte. But *L'Occasion* is almost great, and
I think *Le Ciel et l'Enfer* absolutely deserves that too
much lavished ticket. Indeed Doña Urraca in this,
like La Périchole in *Le Carrosse*, seems to me to put
Mérimée among the greatest masters of feminine character in the nineteenth century, and far above some others
who have been held to have reached that perilous position.

At the same time, this hybrid form between *nouvelle*
and *drame* has some illegitimate advantages. You can,
some one has said, " insinuate character," whereas in a
regular story you have to delineate it ; and though in
some modern instances critics have seemed disposed to
put a higher price on the insinuation than on the delineation, not merely in this particular form, I cannot
quite agree with them. All the same, Mérimée's accomplishments in this mixed kind are a great addition to his
achievements in the story proper, and, as has been confessed before, I should be slow to deny him the place
of the greatest " little master " in fiction all round, though
I may like some little masterpieces of others better than
any of his.

By an interesting but not at all inexplicable contrast
the only writer of prose fiction (except those to whom
separate chapters have been allotted and one other who

follows him here) to be in any way classed with Mérimée and Gautier as a man of letters generally—Alfred de

Musset: charm of his dramatised stories; his pure narration unsuccessful. Musset—displays the contrast of values in his work of narrative and dramatic form in exactly the opposite way to (at least) Méri-mée's.   Musset's *Proverbes*, though, I believe, not quite successful at first, have ever since been the delight of all but vulgar stage-goers: they have, from the very first, been the delight of all but vulgar readers for their pure story interest.   Even some poems, not given as intended dramas at all, possess the most admirable narrative quality and story-turn.

As for the *Comédies-Proverbes*, it is impossible for the abandoned reader of plays who reads them either as poems or as stories, or as both, to go wrong there, which-ever of the delightful bunch he takes up. To play upon some of their own titles—you are never so safe in swearing as when you swear that they are charming; when the door of the library that contains them is opened you may think yourself happy, and when it is shut upon you reading them you may know yourself to be happier. But in pure prose narratives this exquisite poet, delightful playwright, and unquestionable though too much wasted genius, never seems quite at home.   For though they sometimes have a poignant appeal, it is almost always the illegitimate or at any rate extrinsic one of revelation of the author's personal feeling; or else that of formulation of the general effects of passion, not that of embodiment of its working.

Thus, for instance, there are few more pathetic stories in substance, or in occasional expression of a half-aphor-

Frédéric et Bernerette. istic kind, than *Frédéric et Bernerette*. The grisette heroine has shed all the vulgarity of Paul de Kock's at his worst, and has in part acquired more poignancy than that of Murger at his best. Her final letter to her lover, just before her second and successful attempt at suicide, is almost consummate. But, somehow or other, it strikes one rather as a marvellous single study —a sort of modernised and transcended *Spectator* paper—

a " Farewell of a Deserted Damsel "—than as part, or even as *dénouement*, of a story. When the author says, " Je ne sais pas lequel est le plus cruel, de perdre tout à coup la femme qu'on aime par son inconstance, ou par sa mort," he says one of the final things finally. But it would be as final and as impressive if it were an isolated *pensée*. The whole story is not well told ; Frédéric, though not at all a bad fellow, and an only too natural one, is a thing of shreds and patches, not gathered together and grasped as they should be in the hand of the tale-teller ; the narrative " backs and fills " instead of sweeping straight onwards.

So, again, the first story,[1] *Les Deux Maîtresses*, with its inspiring challenge-overture, " Croyez-vous, madame, *Les Deux* qu'il soit possible d'être amoureux de deux *Maîtresses,* personnes à la fois ? " is in parts interesting. *Le Fils du* But one reader at least cannot help being *Titien, etc.* haunted as he reads by the notion how much better Mérimée would have told it. *Le Fils du Titien*— the story of the great master's lazy son, on whom even love and entire self-sacrifice—life-long too—on the part of a great lady, cannot prevail to do more in his father's craft than one exquisite picture of herself, inscribed with a sonnet renouncing the pencil thenceforth—is the best told story in the book. But Gautier would certainly have done it even better. *Margot*, in the same fatal way and, I fear, in the same degree, suggests the country tales of Musset's own faithless love.

But the most crucial example of the " something wrong " which pursues Musset in pure prose narrative *Emmeline.* is *Emmeline*. It is quite free from those unlucky, and possibly unfair, comparisons with contemporaries which have been affixed to its companions. A maniac of parallels might indeed call it something of a modernised *Princesse de Clèves* ; but this would be quite idle. The resemblance is simply in situation ; that is to say, in the *publica materies* which every artist has a right to make his own by private treatment. Emme-

[1] Of the collection definitely called *Nouvelles*.

line Duval is a girl of great wealth and rather eccentric character, who chooses to marry (he has saved her life, or at any rate saved her from possible death and certain damage) a person of rank but no means, M. de Marsan. There is real love between the two, and it continues on his side altogether unimpaired, on hers untroubled, for years. A conventional lady-killer tries her virtue, but is sent about his business. But then there turns up one Gilbert, to whom she yields—exactly how far is not clearly indicated. M. de Marsan finds it out and takes an unusual line. He will not make any scandal, and will not even call the lover out. He will simply separate and leave her whole fortune to his wife. She throws her marriage contract into the fire (one does not presume to enquire how far this would be effective), dismisses Gilbert through the medium of her sister, and—we don't know what happened afterwards.

Now the absence of *finale* may bribe critics of the present day; for my part, as I have ventured to say more than once before, it seems that if you accept this principle you had much better carry it through, have no middle or beginning, and even no title, but issue, in as many copies as you please, a nice quire or ream of blank paper with your name on it. The purchasers could cut the name out, and use it for original composition in a hundred forms, from washing bills to tragedies.

But I take what Musset has given me, and, having an intense admiration for the author of *A Saint Blaise* and *L'Andalouse* and the *Chanson de Fortunio*, a lively gratitude to the author of *Il ne faut jurer de rien* and *Il faut qu'une porte soit ouverte ou fermée*, call *Emmeline* a very badly told and uninteresting story. The almost over-elaborate description of the heroine at the beginning does not fit in with her subsequent conduct; Gilbert is a nonentity; the husband, though noble in conduct, is pale in character, and the sister had much better have been left out.[1] So the rest may be silence.

[1] I have left the shortest story in the volume, *Croisilles*, to a note. It has, I believe, been rather a favourite with some, but it seems to me that almost anybody could have

I have been accused (quite good-naturedly) of putting Rabelais in this history because I liked him, though Gérard de Nerval—his peculiar position. he was not a novelist. My conscience is easy there; and I think I have refuted the charge beforehand. But I might have a little more difficulty (though I should still lose neither heart nor hope) in the case of the ill-fated but well-beloved writer whom gods and men call Gérard de Nerval, or simply Gérard, though librarians and bibliographers sometimes insist on his legal surname, Labrunie. It certainly would be difficult, from the same point of view of strict legality, to call anything of his exactly a novel. He was a poet, a dramatist, a voyage-and-travel writer, a bibliographer (strange trade, which associates the driest with the most " nectaweous " of men !) even sometimes a tale-teller by name, but even then hardly a novelist. Yet he managed to throw over the most unlikely material a novelish or at least a romantic character, which is sometimes—nay, very often—utterly wanting in professed and admitted masters of the business ; and he combines with this faculty—or rather he exalts and transports it into—a strange and exquisite charm, which nobody else in French, except Nodier [1] (who very possibly taught Gérard something), possesses, and which, though it is rather commoner in English and in the best and now almost prehistoric German, is rare anywhere, and, in Gérard's peculiar brand of it, almost entirely unknown.

For this " Anodos "—the most unquestionably entitled to that title of all men in letters ; this wayless wanderer on the earth and above the earth ; this inhabit-

---

written it, as far as anything but the mere writing goes. Nor shall I criticise *Mimi Pinson* and other things at length. I cannot go so far as a late friend of mine, who maintained that you must always praise the work of a writer you like. But I think one has the option of silence—partial at any rate.

[1] If anybody pleads for Louis Bertrand of *Gaspard de la Nuit* as a thirdsman, I should accept him gladly, though he is even farther from the novel-norm than Gérard himself. I once had the pleasure of bringing him to the knowledge of the late Lord Houghton, who, the next time I met him, ejaculated, " I've got him, and covered him all over with moons and stars as he deserves." I hope Lord Crewe has the copy. (For Baudelaire's still less novelish following of *Gaspard*, see below. As far as style goes, both would enter this chapter " by acclamation.")

ant of mad-houses; this victim, finally, either of his own despair and sorrow or of some devilry on the part of others,[1] unites, in the strange spell which he casts over all fit readers, what, but for him, one might have called the idiosyncrasies in strangeness of authors quite different from each other and—except at the special points of contact—from him. He is like Borrow or De Quincey (though he goes even beyond both) in the singular knack of endowing or investing known places and commonplace actions with a weird second essence and second intention. He is like Charles Lamb in his power of dropping from quaintness and almost burlesque into the most touching sentiment and emotion. Mr. Lang, in his Introduction to Poe, has noticed how Gérard resembles America's one " poet of the first order " in fashioning lines " on the further side of the border between verse and music "—a remark which applies to his prose as well.[2] He has himself admitted a kind of *sorites* of indebtedness to Diderot, Sterne, Swift, Rabelais, Folengo, Lucian, and Petronius. But this is merely on the comic and purely intellectual side of him, while it is further confined, or nearly so, to the trick of deliberate " promiscuousness." On the emotional-romantic if not even tragic score he may write off all imputed indebtedness— save once more in some degree, to Nodier. And the consequence is that those who delight in him derive their delight from sources of the most extraordinarily various character, probably never represented by an exactly similar group in the case of any two individual lovers, but quite inexhaustible. To represent him to those who do not know him is not easy ; to represent him to those who do is sure, for this very reason, to arouse mild or

---

[1] This has been already referred to above. After one of the abscondences or disappearances brought about by his madness, he was found dead—hanging to a balcony, or outside stair, or lamp-post, or what not, in one of those purlieus of Old Paris which were afterwards swept away, but which Hugo and Méryon have preserved for us in different forms of " black and white." Suicide, as always in such cases, is the orthodox word in this, and may be correct. But some of his friends were inclined to think that he had been the victim of pure murderous sport on the part of the gangs of *voyous*, ancestors of the later " apaches," who infested the capital.

[2] The quality will not be sought in vain by those who read Mr. Lang's own poems —there are several—on and from Gérard.

not mild complaints of inadequacy. And it must be clear, from what has been already said, that some critic may very likely exclaim, in reference to any selected piece, " Why, this is neither a novel nor a romance, nor even in any legitimate sense a tale ! " The inestimable rejoinder already quoted,[1]—episcopal, and dignifying even that order though it was made only by a bishop *in partibus* —is the only one here.

The difficulty of discussing or illustrating, in short space and due proportion, the novel or *roman* element in such a writer must be sufficiently obvious. *La Bohême Galante, Les Filles du Feu, and Le Rêve et la Vie.* His longer travels in Germany and the East are steeped in this element ; and the shorter compositions which bear names of novel-character are often "little travels" in his native province, the Isle of France, and that larger *banlieue* of Paris, towards Picardy and Flanders, which our Seventy Thousand saved, by dying, the other day. But it is impossible—and might even, if possible, be superfluous—to touch the first group. Of the second there are three subdivisions, which, however, are represented with not inconsiderable variation in different issues.[2] Their titles are *La Bohême Galante, Les Filles du Feu,* and *Le Rêve et la Vie,* the last of which contains only one section, *Aurélia,* never, if I do not mistake, revised by Gérard himself, and only published after his most tragic death. Its *supra*-title really describes the most characteristic part or feature of all the three and of Gérard's whole work.

To one who always lived, as Paul de Saint-Victor put it in one of the best of those curious exercises of his mastery over words, "in the fringes[3] of the actual world,"

---

[1] " Perhaps not, my dear ; perhaps not."

[2] What, I suppose, is the "standard" edition—that of the so-called *Œuvres Complètes*—contains them all, but with some additions and more omissions to and from the earlier issues. And the individual pieces, especially *Sylvie,* which is to be more fully dealt with here than any other, are subjected to a good deal of rehandling.

[3] I may be taken to task for rendering *lisière* " fringes," but the actual English equivalent " list " is not only ambiguous, not only too homely in its specific connotation, but wrong in rhythm. And " selvage," escaping the first and last objections, may be thought to incur the middle one. Moreover, while both words signify a well-defined edge, *lisière* has a sense—special enough to be noted in dictionaries—of the looser-planted border of trees and shrubs which almost literally " fringes " a regular forest.

this confusion of place and no place, this inextricable blending of fact and dream, imagination and reality, Their general was natural enough; and no one but a character. Philistine will find fault with the sometimes apparently mechanical and Sternian transitions which form part of its expression. There was, indeed, an inevitable *mixedness* in that strange nature of his; and he will pass from almost "true Dickens" (he actually admits inspiration from him) in accounts of the Paris *Halles*, or of country towns, to De Quinceyish passages, free from that slight touch of *apparatus* which is undeniable now and then in the Opium Eater. Here are longish excursions of pure family history; there, patches of criticism in art or drama; once at least an elaborate and—for the time—very well informed as well as enthusiastic sketch of French seventeenth-century poetry. It may annoy the captious to find another kind of confusion, for which one is not sure that Gérard himself was responsible, though it is consistent enough with his peculiarities. Passages are redistributed among different books and pieces in a rather bewildering manner; and you occasionally rub your eyes at coming across—in a very different context, or simply shorn of its old one—something that you have met before. To others this, if not exactly an added charm, will at any rate be admitted to "grace of congruity." It would be less like Gérard if it were otherwise.

In fact it is in these mixed pieces that Gérard's great attraction lies. His regular stories, professedly of a Particular Hoffmannesque kind, such as *La Main En-*examples. *chantée* and *Le Monstre Vert*, are good, but not extraordinarily good, and classable with many other things of many other people. I, at least, know nothing quite like *Aurélia* and *Sylvie*, though the dream-pieces of Landor and De Quincey have a certain likeness, and Nodier's *La Fée aux Miettes* a closer one.

Aurélia (which, whether complete in itself or not, was pretty clearly intended to be followed by other things under the general title of *Le Rêve et la Vie*) has, as

might be expected, more dream than life in it.   Or rather
it is like one of those actual dreams which themselves mix
Aurélia. up life—a dream in the composition.   Aurélia
is the book-name of a lady, loved (actually,
it seems) and in some degree responsible for her lover's
aberrations of mind.   He thinks he loves another, but
finds he does not.   The two objects of his passion meet,
and the second generously brings about a sort of reconciliation with the first.   But he has to go to Paris on
business, and there he becomes a mere John-a-Dreams,
if not, in a mild way, a mere Tom of Bedlam.   The
chief drops into reality, indeed, are mentions of his actual
visits to *maisons de santé*.   But the thing is impossible
to abstract or analyse, too long to translate as a whole,
and too much woven in one piece to cut up.   It must
be read as it stands, and any person of tolerable intelligence will know in a page or two whether Gérard is the
man for him or not.   But when he was writing it
he was already over even the fringe of ordinary sane
life, and near the close of life itself.   In *Sylvie* he had
not drifted so far; and it is perhaps his best diploma-
piece.[1]

For *Sylvie*, with its sub-title, " Souvenirs du Valois,"
surely exhibits Gérard, outside the pure travel-books,
And
especially
Sylvie. at his very best, as far as concerns that mixture
of *rêve* and *réalité*—the far-off goal of Gautier's [2]
Chimère—which has been spoken of.   The
author comes out of a theatre where he has only seen
Her, having never, though a constant worshipper,
troubled himself to ask, much less to seek out, what She
might be off the stage.   And here we may give an actual
piece of him.

[1] *Angélique*, which used to head *Les Filles du Feu*, in front of *Sylvie*, but was afterwards cut away by the editors of the *Œuvres Complètes* for reasons given under the head
of *Les Faux Saulniers* (vol. iv. of that edition), is a specially Sternian piece, mixing up
the chase for a rare book, and some other matters, with the adventures of a seventeenth-
century ancestress of this book's author, who eloped with a servant, zigzagged as much
as possible.   It is quite good reading, but a little *mechanical*.   Perhaps it is not too
officious to remark that *Filles du Feu* is to be interpreted here in the sense of our " *Faces
in the fire.*"

[2] Gérard was a slightly older man than Théo, but they were, as they could not but
be, close friends.

We were living then in a strange kind of time,[1] one of those which are wont to come after revolutions, or the decadences of great reigns. There was no longer any gallantry of the heroic kind, as in the time of the Fronde; no vice, elegant and in full dress, as in that of the Regency; no " Directory " scepticism and foolish orgies. It was a mixture of activity, hesitation, and idleness—of brilliant utopias; of religious or philosophical aspiration; of vague enthusiasms mingled with certain instincts of a sort of Renaissance. Men were weary of past discords; of uncertain hopes, much as in the time of Petronius or Peregrinus. The materialist part of us hungered for the bouquet of roses which in the hands of Isis was to regenerate it—the Goddess, eternally young and pure, appeared to us at night and made us ashamed of the hours we had lost in the day. We were not at the age of ambition, and the greedy hunt for place and honours kept us out of possible spheres of work. Only the poet's Ivory Tower remained for us, and we climbed it ever higher and higher to be clear of the mob. At the heights whither our masters guided us we breathed at last the pure air of solitude; we drank in the golden cup of legend; we were intoxicated with poetry and with love. But, alas ! it was only love of vague forms; of tints roseal and azure; of metaphysical phantoms. The real woman, seen close, revolted our ingenuousness : we would have had her a queen or a goddess, and to draw near her was fatal.

But he went from the play to his club, and there somebody asked him for what person (in such cases one regrets *laquelle*) he went so constantly to the same house ; and, on the actress being named, kindly pointed out to him a third member of this club as the lady's lover-in-title. The peculiar etiquette of the institution demanded, it seems, that the fortunate gallant should escort the beloved home, but then go to the *cercle* and play (they were wise enough to play whist then) for great part of the night before exercising the remainder of his rights and privileges. In the interval, apparently, other cats might be grey. And, as it happened, Gérard saw in a paper that some shares of his, long rubbish, had become of value. He would be better off; he might aspire to

---

[1] Even those who care little for mere beauty of style—or who cannot stand the loss of it in translation—may find here a vivid picture, by a hand of the most qualified, of the mental condition which produced the masterpieces of 1825–1850. And the contrast with the " discouraged generation " which immediately followed is as striking.

a portion of the lady's spare hours. But this notion, it is not surprising to hear, did not appeal to our Gérard. He sees in the same paper that a *fête* is going to take place in his old country of the Valois; and when at last he goes home two "faces in the fire" rise for him, those of the little peasant girl Sylvie and of the châtelaine Adrienne—beautiful, triumphant, but destined to be a nun. Unable to sleep, he gets up at one in the morning, and manages to find himself at Loisy, the scene of the *fête*, in time.

One would fain go on, but duty forbids a larger allotment of space; and, after all, the thing itself may be read by any one in half an hour or so, and will not, at least ought not, to be forgotten for half a lifetime—or a whole one. The finding of Sylvie, no longer a *little* girl, but still a girl, still not married, though, as turns out, about to be so, is chequered with all sorts of things— sketches of landscape; touches of literature; black- and-white renderings of the *Voyage à Cythère*; verses to Adrienne; to the actress Aurélie (to become later the dream-Aurélia); and, lastly—in the earlier forms of the piece at any rate—snatches of folk-song, including that really noble ballad:

> Quand Jean Renaud de la guerre revint,

which falls very little, if at all, short of the greatest specimens of English, German, Danish, or Spanish.

And over and through it all, and in other pieces as well, there is the faint, quaint, music—prose, when not verse—which reminds one [1] somehow of Browning's famous Toccata-piece. Only the "dear dead women" are dear dead fairies; and the whole might be sung at that "Fairy's Funeral" which Christopher North imagined so well, though he did not carry it out quite impeccably.

The felicity of being enabled to know the causes of things, a recognised and respectable form of happiness,

---

[1] Especially, it may be, if one has heard Galuppi's own music played by a friend who is himself now dead.

is also one which I have recently enjoyed in respect of
Alfred de Vigny's *Cinq-Mars*. For Vigny as a poet my
admiration has always been profound. He appears to me to have completed, with Agrippa
d'Aubigné, Corneille, and Victor Hugo, the
quatuor of French poets who have the secret of magnificence;[1] and, scanty as the amount of his poetical
work is, *Eloa, Dolorida, Le Cor*, and the finest passages
in *Les Destinées* have a definite variety of excellence and
essence which it would not be easy to surpass in kind,
though it might be in number, with the very greatest
masters of poetry. But I have never been able, frankly
and fully, to enjoy his novels, especially *Cinq-Mars*. In
my last reading of the chief of them I came upon an
edition which contains what I had never seen before—
the somewhat triumphant and strongly defiant tract,
Réflexions sur la Vérité dans l'Art, which the author
prefixed to his book after its success. This tractate is
indeed not quite consistent with itself, for it ends in
confession that truth in art is truth in observation of
human nature, not mere authenticity of fact, and that
such authenticity is of merely secondary importance at
best. But in the opening he had taken lines—or at
any rate had said things—which, if not absolutely inconsistent with, certainly do not lead to, this sound
conclusion. In writing historical novels (he tells us) he
thought it better not to imitate the foreigners (it is clear
that this is a polite way of indicating Scott), who in their
pictures put the historical dominators of them in the
background; he has himself made such persons principal
actors. And though he admits that "a treatise on the
decline and fall of feudalism in France; on the internal
conditions and external relations of that country; on
the question of military alliances with foreigners; on
justice as administered by parliaments, and by secret
commissions on charges of sorcery," might not have

Alfred de Vigny: Cinq-Mars.

[1] Some would make it a quintet with Leconte de Lisle, but I think "the King
should consider of it" as to this. He is grand *sometimes*: but so are the Père Le Moyne
and others. It is hit or miss with them; the Four can make sure of it.

been read while the novel *was*; the sentence suggests, with hardly a possibility of rebuttal, that a treatise of this kind was pretty constantly in his own mind while he was writing the novel itself. And the earlier sentence about putting the more important historical characters in the foreground remains " firm," without any necessity for argument or suggestion.

Now I have more than once in this very book, and often elsewhere, contended, rightly or wrongly, that The faults in this " practice of the foreigners," in *not* making its general dominant historical characters their own domin-scheme. ant personages, is *the* secret of success in historical novel-writing, and the very feather (and something more) in the cap of Scott himself which shows his chieftainship. And, again rightly or wrongly, I have also contended that the hand of purpose deadens and mummifies story. Vigny's own remarks, despite subsequent—if not recantation—qualification of them, show that the lie of his land, the tendency of his exertion, *was* in these two, as I think, wrong directions. And I own that this explained to me what I had chiefly before noticed as merely a fact, without enquiring into it, that *Cinq-Mars*, admirably written as it is ; possessing as it does, with a hero who might have been made interesting, a great person like Richelieu to make due and not undue use of ; plenty of thrilling incident at hand, and some actually brought in ; love interest *ad libitum* and fighting hardly less so ; a tragic finish from history, and opportunity for plenty of lighter contrast from Tallemant and the Memoirs—that, I say, *Cinq-Mars*, with all this and the greatness of its author in other work, has always been to me not a live book, and hardly one which I can even praise as statuesque.[1]

It is no doubt a misfortune for the book with its later readers—the earlier for nearly twenty years were free from this—that it comes into closest comparison with

---

[1] It does, of course, deserve, and in this place specially should receive, the credit of being the first French historical novel of the modern kind which possessed great literary merit.

Dumas' best work. Its action, indeed, takes place in the very " Vingt Ans " during which we know (except from slight retrospect) nothing of what D'Artagnan and the Three were doing. But more than one or two of the same historical characters figure, and in the chapters dealing with the obscure *émeute* which preceded the actual conspiracy, as well as in the scenes touching Anne of Austria's private apartments, the parallel is very close indeed.·

Now of course Dumas could not write like Vigny; and though, as is pointed out elsewhere, to regard him And in its as a vulgar fellow is the grossest of blunders details. as well as a great injustice, Vigny, in thought and taste and *dianoia* generally, was as far above him as in style.[1] But that is not the question. I have said[2] that I do not quite *know* D'Artagnan, though I think I know Athos, as a man ; but as a novel-hero the Gascon seems to me to " fill all numbers." Cinq-Mars may be a succession or chain of type-personages— generous but headlong youth, spoilt favourite, conspirator and something like traitor, finally victim ; but these are the " flat " characters (if one may so speak) of the treatise, not the " round " ones of the novel. And I cannot *unite* them. His love-affair with Marie de Gonzague leaves me cold. His friend, the younger De Thou, is hardly more than " an excellent person." The persecution of Urbain Grandier and the sufferings of the Ursuline Abbess seem to me—to use the old schoolboy word—to be hopelessly " muffed " ; and if any one will compare the accounts of the taking of the " Spanish bastion " at Perpignan with the exploit at that other bastion—Saint-Gervais at Rochelle—he will see what I mean as well as in any single instance. The second part, where we come to the actual conspiracy, is rather better than the first, if not much ; and I think Vigny's presentment of Richelieu has been too much censured.·

---

[1] Alexander, though he actually wrote histories of a kind, was also far below Alfred in political judgment.
[2] *Vide infra* on Dumas himself.

Armand Duplessis was a very great man ; but unless you accept the older Machiavellian and the more modern German doctrines as to what a great man may do, he must also be pronounced a most unscrupulous one; while there is little doubt (unless you go back to Louis XI.) that Vigny was right in regarding him as the original begetter of the French Revolution. But he is not here made by any means wholly inhuman, and Vigny makes it justly clear that, if he had not killed Cinq-Mars, Cinq-Mars would have killed him. In such cases of course the person who begins may be regarded as the assassin ; but it is doubtful whether this is distributive justice of the highest order. And I do not see much salvation for France in Henry d'Effiat.

This, however, is a digression from our proper subject, but one justifying itself after a fashion, inasmuch as it results from Vigny's own faulty handling of the subject itself and is appropriate to his line of argument in his *Examen*. He has written the novel not as he ought and as he ought not. The political and historical interests overshadow, confuse, and hamper the purely " fictional " (as people say now), and when he has got hold of a scene which *is* either purely " fictional," or historical with fictitious possibilities, he does not seem (to me) to know how to deal with it. There is one—of the extremest melodramatic character and opportunities— where, in a hut perched on the side of a Pyrenean gorge or cañon, Richelieu's villainous tool, the magistrate Laubardemont; his mad niece, the former Ursuline Abbess, who has helped to ruin Urbain Grandier ; his outcast son Jacques, who has turned Spanish officer and general bravo ; and a smuggler who has also figured in the Grandier business, forgather ; where the mad Abbess dies in terror, and Jacques de Laubardemont by falling through the flimsy hut-boards into the gorge, his father taking from him, by a false pretence before his death, the treaty between the Cinq-Mars conspirators and Spain. All this is sufficiently " horrid," as the girls in *Northanger Abbey* would say, and divers French con-

temporaries of Vigny's from Hugo to Soulié would have
made good horrors of it. In his hands it seems (to me)
to miss fire. So, again, he has a well-conceived interview, in which Richelieu, for almost the last time, shows
"the power of a strong mind over a weak one," and
brings the King to abject submission and the surrender of
Cinq-Mars, by the simple process of leaving his Majesty
to settle by himself the problems that drop in from
France, England, and where or whence not, during the
time of the Cardinal's absence. It is less of a failure
than the other, being more in Vigny's own line; but
it is impossible not to remember several scenes—not one
only—in *Quentin Durward*, and think how much better
Scott would have done it; several in the Musketeer-
trilogy, if not also in the Margot-Chicot series, and make
a parallel reflection. And as a final parry by anticipation
to the objection that such comparison is "rascally," let
it be said that nothing of the kind ever created any
prejudice against the book in my case. I failed to get
on with it long before I took the least trouble to discover
critical reasons that might excuse that failure.

But if any one be of taste sufficiently like mine to find
disappointment of the unpleasant kind in *Cinq-Mars*,
I think I can promise him an agreeable, if
somewhat chequered, surprise when, remembering *Cinq-Mars* and basing his expectations
upon it, he turns to *Stello*. It is true that the
book is, as a whole, even less "precisely a
novel" than Sainte-Beuve's *Volupté*. But for that very
reason it escapes the display of the disabilities which
Cinq-Mars, being, or incurring obligation to be, precisely a novel, suffers. It is true also that it exhibits
that fancy for putting historical persons in the first "plan"
which he had avowed, and over which heads have been
shaken. The bulk of it, indeed, consists of romanticised
histoires or historiettes (the narrator calls them "anecdotes") of the sad and famous fates of two French
poets, Gilbert and André Chénier, and of our English
Chatterton. But, then, no one of these can be called

Stello less of
a novel,
but contain-
ing better
novel-stuff.

" a dominant historical personage," and the known facts permit themselves to be, and are, " romanticised " effectively enough. So the flower is in each case plucked from the nettle. And there is another flower of more positive and less compensatory kind which blooms here, which is particularly welcome to some readers, and which, from *Cinq-Mars* alone, they could hardly have expected to find in any garden of Alfred de Vigny's. For this springs from a root of ironic wit which almost approaches humour, which, though never merry, is not seldom merciful, and is very seldom actually savage, though often sad. Now irony is, to those who love it, the saving grace of everything that possesses it, almost equal in charm, and still more nearly equal in power, to the sheer beauty, which can dispense with it, but which sometimes, and not so very rarely, is found in its company.

The substance, or rather the framework, of *Stello, ou Les Diables Bleus*, requires very little amplification of its double title to explain it. Putting that title in charade form, one might say that its first is a young poet who suffers from its second —like many other young persons, poetical and unpoetical, of times Romantic and un-Romantic. Having an excessively bad fit of his complaint, he sends for a certain *docteur noir* to treat the case. This " Black Doctor " is not a trout-fly, nor the sort of person who might be expected in a story of *diablerie*. It is even suggested that he derived the name, by which he was known to society, from the not specially individual habit of wearing black clothes. But there must have been something not quite ordinarily human about him, inasmuch as, having been resident in London at the time of Chatterton's death in 1770, he was—apparently without any signs of Old Parr-like age—a fashionable doctor at Paris in the year 1832. His visit ends, as usual, in a prescription, but a prescription of a very unusual kind. The bulk of it consists of the " anecdotes "—again perhaps not a very uncommon feature of a doctor's visit, but told at such length on the three subjects above mentioned that, with " links " and conclusion,[1] they run to nearly four hundred pages.

It is possible that some one may say " *Connu !* " both to the stories themselves and to the moral of real suffering, as opposed to mere megrim, which is so obviously deducible from them. But Stello was quite as clever as the objectors, and knew these things quite as well—perhaps, as far as the case of Gilbert is concerned, rather better than most Englishmen. It is in the manner of the Black Doctor's telling and handling that the charm lies.

Even for those gluttons of matter who do not care much for manner there is a good deal in the three stories. The death The first avails itself—as Vigny had unwisely of Gilbert. *not* availed himself in *Cinq-Mars*, though he was well acquainted with Shakespeare and lesser English masters—of the mixture of comic and tragic. The suffering[2] of the unfortunate youth who was partly a French Chatterton and partly a French Clare, his strange visit to the benevolent but rather ineffectual Archbishop of Paris, and the scene at his deathbed, exhibit, at nearly its best, the tragic power which Vigny possessed in a very high, though not always well exercised, degree. And the passage of the poet's death is of such *macabre* power that one must risk a translation :

(*The doctor has been summoned, has found the patient in his garret, bare of all furniture save a bed with tattered clothes and an old trunk.*)

His face was very noble and very beautiful ; he looked at me with fixed eyes, and between them and the nose, above the cheeks, he showed that nervous contraction which no ordinary convulsion can imitate, which no illness gives, but which says to the physician, " Go your ways ! " and is, as it were, a standard which Death plants on his conquests. He clutched in one hand his pen, his poor last pen, inky and ragged, in the other a crust of his last piece of bread. His legs knocked together, so as to make the crazy bed crackle. I listened carefully to his hard breathing ; I heard the

---

[1] About Plato and Homer, who are very welcome, and " Le Mensonge Social," which is, perhaps, a little less so.
[2] But see note 2 on next page.

rattle with its hollow husk; and I recognised Death in the room as a practised sailor recognises the tempest in the whistle of the wind that precedes it.

"Always the same, to all thou comest," I said to Death, he himself speaking low enough for my lips to make, in dying ears, only an indistinct murmur. "I know thee always by thine own hollow voice, lent to youth and age alike. How well I know thee and thy terrors, which are no longer such to me![1] I feel the dust that thy wings scatter in the air as thou comest; I breathe the sickly odour of it; I see its pale ashes fly, invisible as they may be to other men's sight. O! thou Inevitable One, thou art here, verily thou comest to save this man from his misery. Take him in thine arms like a child; carry him off; save him; I give him to thee. Save him only from the devouring sorrow that accompanies us ever on the earth till we come to rest in thee, O Benefactor and Friend!"

I had not deceived myself, for Death it was. The sick man ceased to suffer, and began suddenly to enjoy the divine moment of repose which precedes the eternal immobility of the body. His eyes grew larger, and were charged with amazement; his mouth relaxed and smiled; his tongue twice passed over his lips as if to taste once more, from some unseen cup, a last drop of the balm of Life. And then he said with that hoarse voice of the dying which comes from the inwards and seems to come from the very feet:

ERRATUM.

Page 269, *Note* 2.—By a slip of the pen which I only noticed on the eve of publication, I have made Louis XV. die of scarlet fever instead of smallpox. The blunder is all the sadder in that the actual fact not only is one of the best known in anecdotic history, but has supplied the subject of two of the most famous passages of Carlyle and Thackeray.

A History of the French Novel, Vol. II. G. S.

---

[1] One wonders if the Black Doctor was so sure of this on his own death-bed.

[2] The first line of Gilbert's swan-song—the only song of his that is remembered. It sets Stello himself on the track which the "Black Doctor" has concealed up to the point. As the original rhythm could not be kept without altering the substance, I have substituted another—not so unconnected as it may seem.—By the way, Vigny has taken as much liberty with French dates in this story as with English facts in the Chatterton one. Gilbert died in 1780, and Louis XV. had passed from the arms of his last mistress, Searlatina Maligna, six years before, to be actually made the subject of a funeral panegyric by the poet. In fact, the sufferings of the latter have been argued to be pure legend. But this of course affects *literature* hardly at all; and Vigny had a perfect right to use the accepted version.

justify the description, assigned earlier to one of her official predecessors in a former reign, of being "belle comme un ange, et bête comme un panier."[1] At first the lovers (if we are to call them so) are lying, most beautifully dressed and quite decorously, on different sofas, both of them with books in their hands, but one asleep and the other yawning. Suddenly the lady springs up shrieking, and the polite and amiable monarch (apart from his Solomonic or Sultanic weaknesses, and the perhaps graver indifference with which he knowingly allowed France to go to the devil, Louis le Bien-Aimé was really *le meilleur fils du monde*) does his best to console his beloved and find out the reason of her woes. It appears at last that she thinks she has been bitten by a flea, and as the summer is very hot, and there has been much talk of mad dogs, she is convinced that the flea was a mad flea, and that she shall die of hydrophobia. (As it happens, the flea is not a flea at all, but a grain of snuff.) However, the Black Doctor is sent for, and finds the King as affable as usual, but Mlle. de Coulanges coiled up on a sofa—like something between a cat and a naughty child afraid of being scolded—and hiding her face. On being coaxed with the proper medical manner, she at last bursts out laughing, and finally they all laugh together, till his Majesty spills his coffee on his gold waistcoat, and then pulls the doctor down on a sofa to talk Paris gossip. And now the Black One clears himself from any connection with the serpent as far as wisdom is concerned, though he has plenty of a better kind. Fresh from Gilbert's appeal to the Archbishop, he tries to interest this so amiable Royalty in the subject. But the result is altogether unfortunate. The lady is merely contemptuous and bored. The King gets angry, and displays that indifference to anybody else's suffering which moralists (whether to an exaggerated extent or not, is another question) are wont to connect with exces-

---

[1] Why should a " basket " be specially silly ? The answer is that the original comparison was to a " panier *percé*," a basket which won't hold anything. But the phrase got shortened.

sive attention to a man's own sensual enjoyments. After some by no means stupid but decidedly acid remarks on Voltaire, Rousseau, and others, he takes (quite good-naturedly in appearance) the doctor's arm, walks with him to the end of the long apartment, opens the door, quotes certain satiric verses on literary and scientific " gents," and—shuts it on his medical adviser and guest.

I know few things of the kind more neatly done, or better adjusted to heighten the tragic purpose.

To an Englishman the next episode may be less satisfactory, though it was very popular in France under
The Chatterton part.
its original form, and still more so when Vigny dramatised it in his famous *Chatterton*. It is not that there is any (or at any rate much) of the usual caricature which was (let us be absolutely equitable and say) exchanged between the two countries for so long a time. Vigny married an English wife, knew something of England, and a good deal of English literature. But, regardless of his own historical *penchants* and of the moral of this very book—that Sentiment must be kept under the control of Reason—he was pleased to transmogrify Chatterton's compassionate Holborn landlady into a certain Kitty Bell—a pastry-shop keeper close to the Houses of Parliament, who is very beautiful except that she has the inevitable " large feet " (let us hope that M. le Comte de Vigny, who was a gentleman, took only the first *signalement* from Madame la Comtesse), extraordinarily sentimental, and desperately though (let us hope again, for she has a husband and two children) quite virtuously in love with the boy from Bristol. He entirely transforms Lord Mayor Beckford's part in the matter;[1] changes, for his own purposes, the arsenic into opium (a point of more importance than it may seem), and in one blunt word does

---

[1] He not only, in the face of generally known and public history, makes the man who was positively insolent to George III. a flunky of royalty, but assigns, as the immediate cause of the poet's suicide, the offer to him of a lucrative but menial office in the Mansion House ! Now, if not history, biography tells us that Beckford's own death, and the consequent loss of hope from him, were at least among the causes, if not the sole cause, of the *subsequent* catastrophe.

all he can to spoil the story. It is too common an experience when foreigners treat such things, and I say this with the fullest awareness of the danger of *De te fabula*.

These two stories, however, fill scarcely more than a third of the book, and the other two-thirds, subtracting the moral at the end, deal with a matter which Vigny, once more, understood thoroughly. The fate of André Chénier is " fictionised " in nearly the best manner, though with the author's usual fault of inability to " round out " character. We do not sufficiently realise the poet himself. But his brother, Marie-Joseph, requiring slighter presentment, has it; and so, on a still smaller scale, has the well-meaning but fatuous father, who, hopelessly misunderstanding the signs of the times, actually precipitates his elder son's fate by applying, in spite of remonstrance, to the tiger-pole-cat Robespierre for mercy. The scene where this happens—and where the " sea-green incorruptible " himself, Saint-Just (prototype of so many Republican enthusiasts, ever since and to-day), Marie-Joseph, and the Black Doctor figure—is singularly good. Hardly less so are the picture—often painted by others but seldom better—of the ghastly though in a way heroic merriment of the lost souls in Saint-Lazare, between their doom and its execution, and the finale. In this the doctor's soldier-servant Blaireau ("Badger"), still a gunner on active service (partly, one fancies, from former touches,[1] by concealed good intention, partly from mere whim and from disgust at the drunken hectorings of General Henriot), refuses to turn his guns on the Thermidorists, and thus saves France from at least the lowest depths of the Revolutionary Inferno.[2] Perhaps there is here, as with Vigny's fiction throughout, a certain amateurishness, and a very distinct inability to keep apart

The tragedy of André Chénier.

---

[1] He has contrived, with the help of the gaoler's daughter Rose, to suppress an earlier inclusion of Chénier's name in the tumbril-list ; and thus might have saved him altogether, but for the father's insane reminder to Robespierre.

[2] But she had to go backwards through the circles between Thermidor and Brumaire, and can hardly be said to have " seen the stars " even then. Vigny has, as we shall see, touched on the less enormous and flagrant—but as individual things scarcely less atrocious—crimes of the Directory in the first story of his next book.

things that had better not be mixed. But there is also evidence of power throughout, and there is actually some performance.

His third and last work, of anything like the kind, *Servitude et Grandeur Militaires*, is no more of a regular *Servitude et* novel than *Stello*; but, though perhaps in *Grandeur* an inferior degree, it shares the superiority *Militaires.* of *Stello* itself over *Cinq-Mars* in power of telling a story. Like *Stello*, too, it is a frame of short tales, not a continuous narrative; and like that, and even to a greater degree, it exhibits the intense melancholy (almost unique in its particular shade, though I suppose it comes nearer to Leopardi's than to that of any other great man of letters) which characterises Alfred de Vigny. His own experience of soldiering had not been fortunate. He had begun, as a mere boy, by accompanying Louis XVIII. in his flight before the Hundred Days; he had seen, for another fourteen or fifteen years during the Restoration,

> No wars where triumphs on the victors wait,

but only the dreary garrison life (see on Beyle, *sup.* p. 149) of French peace time, and, in the way of active service, only what all soldiers hate, the thankless and inglorious police-work which comes on them through civil disturbance. Whether he was exactly the kind of man to have enjoyed the livelier side of martialism may be the subject of considerable doubt. But at any rate he had no chance of it, and his framework here is little more than a tissue of transcendental " grousing."

The first story illustrating " Servitude " is sufficiently horrible, and has a certain element of paradox in it. The first The author, actually on his very disagreeable story. introduction to a military career by flight, meets with an old officer who tells him his history. He has been at one time a merchant sailor; and then in the service of the Directory, by whom he was commissioned to carry convicts to Cayenne. The most noteworthy of these, a young man of letters, who had libelled one of the tyrants, and his still younger wife, are very charming people ; and the captain, who makes them his guests, becomes so fond of them that he even proposes to give up his profession and farm with them in the colony. He has, however, sealed orders, to be opened only in mid-Atlantic; and when he does open them, he finds, to his unspeakable horror, a simple command to shoot the poet at once. He obeys ; and the " frightfulness " is doubled by the fact that a rather clumsy device of his to spare the wife the sight of the husband's death is defeated by the still greater clumsiness of a subordinate. She goes mad ; and, as expiation, he takes charge of her, shifts from navy to army, and carries her with him on all his campaigns, being actually engaged in escorting her on a little mule-cart when Vigny meets him. They part; and ten years afterwards Vigny hears that the officer was killed at Waterloo—his victim-charge following him a few days later. The story is well told, and not, as actual things go, impossible. But there are some questions which it suggests. " Is it, *as literature*, a whole ? " " Is it worth telling ? " and " Why on earth did the captain obey such an order from a self-constituted authority of scoundrels to whom no ' sacrament ' could ever be binding, if it could even exist ? "[1]

The second is also tragical, but less so ; and is again very well told. It is concerned with the explosion of a powder-magazine—fortunately not the main one—at Vincennes, brought about by the over-zeal of a good old adjutant, the happiness of whose domestic interior just before his fate (with some other things) forms one of Vigny's favourite contrasts.

The second

But, as in *Stello*, he has kept the best wine to the last. The single illustration of *Grandeur* must have, for some people, though it may not have for all, the very rare interest of a story which would rather gain than lose if it were true. It opens in the

and third.

---

[1] There might of course have been spy-subordinates (cf. the case of D'Artagnan and Belleisle), with secret commissions to meet and render futile his disobedience ; but nothing of the sort is even hinted.

thick of the July Revolution, when the veteran French army—half-hearted and gaining no new heart from the half-dead hands which ought to have guided it—was subjected, on a larger scale, to the same sort of treatment which the fresh-recruited Sherwood Foresters (fortunately *not* half-hearted) experienced in Dublin at Easter 1916. The author, having, luckily for himself, resigned his commission a year or two before, meets an old friend—a certain Captain Renaud—who, though a *vieux de la vieille*, has reached no higher position, but is adored by his men, and generally known as " Canne de Jonc," because he always carries that not very lethal weapon, and has been known to take it into action instead of a sword.

In the " sullen interval " of the crisis the two talk; and Renaud is led into telling the chief experiences of his life. He had known little of his father—a soldier before him—but had been taken by that father on Bonaparte's Egyptian expedition till, at Malta, he was stopped by Bonaparte himself, who would have no boy on it save Casabianca's (pity he did not stop him too !). But he only sends Renaud back to the Military Academy, and afterwards makes him his page. The father is blown up in the *Orient*, but saved, and, though made prisoner by us, is well treated, and, as being of great age and broken health, allowed, by Collingwood's interest, to go to Sicily. He dies on the way ; but is able to send a letter to his son, which is one of the finest examples of Vigny's peculiar melancholy irony. In this he recants his worship of the (now) Emperor. It has, however, no immediate effect on the son. But before long, by an accident, he is an unwilling and at first unperceived witness of the famous historical or half-historical interview at Fontainebleau between Napoleon and the Pope, where the bullied Holy Father enrages, but vanquishes, the conqueror by successively ejaculating the two words *Commediante!* and *Tragediante!* (This scene is again admirable.) The page's absence from his ordinary duty excites suspicion, and the Emperor, *more suo*, exiles him to the farce-tragedy of the Boulogne flotilla, where the clumsy flat-bottoms are sunk at pleasure as they exercise [1] by English frigates. The father's experience is repeated with the son, for he also is captured and also falls into the beneficent power of Collingwood, whom Vigny almost literally beatifies.[2] The Admiral keeps the young man on parole with him four years at sea, and when he has—" so as by water " if not fire—overcome the temptation of breaking his word, effects exchange for him. But, as is well known (the very words occur here, though I do not know whether for the first time or not), Napoleon's motto in such cases was : " Je n'aime pas les prisonniers. On se fait tuer." He goes back to his duty, but avoids recognition as much as possible, and receives no, or hardly any, promotion. Once, just after Montmirail, he and the Emperor meet, whether with full knowledge on the latter's part is skilfully veiled. But they touch hands. Still Captain Renaud's *guignon* pursues him in strange fashion ; and during a night attack on a Russian post near Reims he kills, in a mere blind mellay, a boy officer of barely fourteen, and is haunted by remorse ever afterwards.

A few days after telling the story he is shot by a *gamin* whom older men have made half-drunk and furnished with a pistol with directions to do what he does. And all this is preserved from being merely sentimental (" Riccobonish," as I think Vigny himself—but it may be somebody else—has it) by the touch of true melancholy on the one hand and of all-saving irony on the other.

So also these two curious books save Vigny himself to some extent from the condemnation, or at any rate *The moral* the exceedingly faint praise, which his principal *of the three.* novel may bring upon him as a novelist. But they do so to some extent only. It is clear even from

[1] Vigny, with perfect probability, but whether with complete historical accuracy or not I do not know, represents this useless exposure as wanton bravado on Napoleon's part.

[2] There may perhaps have been some private reasons for his enthusiasm. At any rate it is pleasant to compare it with the offensive manner in which this " heroic sailor-soul " and admirably good man has sometimes been treated by the more pedantic kind of naval historian.

them, though not so clear as it is from their more famous companion, that he was not to the manner born. The riddles of the painful earth were far too much with him to permit him to be an unembarrassed master or creator of pastime—not necessarily horse-collar pastime by any means, but pastime pure and simple. His preoccupations with philosophy, politics, world-sorrow, and other things were constantly cropping up and getting in the way of his narrative faculty. I do not know that, even of the scenes that I have praised, any one except the expurgated Crébillonade of the King and the Lady and the Doctor goes off with complete " currency," and this is an episode rather than a whole tale, though it gives itself the half-title of *Histoire d'une Puce Enragée*. He could never, I think, have done anything but short stories; and even as a short-story teller he ranks with the other Alfred, Musset, rather than with Mérimée or Gautier. But, like Musset, he presents us, as neither of the other two did (for Mérimée was not a poet, and Gautier was hardly a dramatist), with a writer, of mark all but the greatest, in verse and prose and drama; while in prose and verse at least he shows that quality of melancholy magnificence which has been noted, as hardly any one else does in all three forms, except Hugo himself.

Note on Fromentin's *Dominique*

I have found it rather difficult to determine the place most proper for noticing the *Dominique* of Eugène Fromentin—one of the most remarkable " single-speech " novels in any literature. It was not published till the Second Empire was more than half-way through, but it seems to have been written considerably earlier; and as it is equally remarkable for *lexis* and for *dianoia*, it may, on the double ground, be best attached to this chapter, though Fromentin was younger than any one else here dealt with, and belonged, in fact, to the generation of our later, though not latest, constituents. But, in fact, it is a book like no other, and it is for this reason, and by no means as confessing omission or after-thought, that I have made the notice of it a note. In an

[marginal note: Note on Fromentin's *Dominique* : its altogether exceptional character.*]*

outside way, indeed, it may be said to belong to the school of *René*, but the resemblance is very partial.

The author was a painter—perhaps the only painter-novelist of merit, though there are bright examples of painter-poets. His other literary work consists of a good book on his Netherlandish brethren in art, and of two still better ones, descriptive of Algeria. And *Dominique* itself has unsurpassed passages of description at length, as well as numerous tiny touches like actual *remarques* on the margin of the page. Only once does his painter's eye seem to have failed him as to situation. The hero, when he has thrown himself on his knees before his beloved, and she (who is married and " honest ") has started back in terror, " drags himself after her." Now I believe it to be impossible for any one to exe- cute this manœuvre without producing a ludicrous effect. For which reason the wise have laid it down that the kneeling posture should never be resorted to unless the object of worship is likely to remain fairly still. But this is, I think, the only slip in the book. It is exceedingly interesting to compare Fromentin's descriptions with those of Gautier on the one hand before him, and with those of Fabre and Theuriet on the other later. I should like to point out the differences, but it is probably better merely to suggest the comparison. His actual work in design and colour I never saw, but I think (from attacks on it that I *have* seen) I should like it.

But his descriptions, though they would always have given the book distinction, would not—or would not by themselves—have given it its special appeal. Neither does that appeal lie in such story as there is—which, in fact, is very little. A French squire (he is more nearly that than most French landlords have cared to be, or indeed have been able to be, since the Revolution and the Code Napoléon) is orphaned early, brought up at his remote country house by an aunt, privately tutored for a time, not by an abbé, but by a young schoolmaster and literary aspirant ; then sent for three or four years to the nearest " collége," where he is bored but triumphant; and at last, about his *vingt ans*, let loose in Paris. But—except once, and with the result, usual for him, of finding the thing a failure—he does not make the stock use of liberty at that age and in that place. He has, at school, made friends with another youth of good family in the same province, who has an uncle and cousins living in the town where the college is. The eldest she-cousin of Olivier d'Orsel, Madeleine, is a year older than Dominique de Bray, and of course he falls in love with her. But though she, in a way, knows his passion, and, as one finds out afterwards, shares or might have been made to share it, the love is " never told," and she marries another. The destined victims

of the *un*smooth course, however, meet in Paris, where Dominique
and Olivier, though they do not share chambers, live in the same
house and flat; and the story of just overcome temptation is broken
off at last in a passionate scene like that of " Love and Duty "—
which noble and strangely undervalued poem might serve as a
long motto or verse-prelude to the book. It is rather questionable
whether it would not be better without the thin frame of actual
proem and conclusion, which does actually enclose the body of the
novel as a sort of *récit*, provoked partly by the suicide, or attempted
suicide, of Olivier after a life of fastidiousness and frivolity.
The proem gives us Dominique as—after his passion-years, and
his as yet unmentioned failure to achieve more than mediocrity
in letters—a quiet if not cheerful married man with a charming
wife, pretty children, a good estate, and some peasants not in
the least like those of *La Terre*; while in the epilogue the tutor
Augustin, who has made his way at last and has also married
happily, drives up to the door, and the book ends abruptly. It is
perhaps naughty, but one does not want the wife, or the children,
or the good peasants, or the tutor Augustin, while the suicide of
Olivier appears rather copy-booky. It is especially annoying thus
to have what one does not want to know, and not what one,
however childishly, does want to know—that is to say, the after-
history of Madeleine.

Yet even in the preliminary forty or fifty pages few readers
can fail to perceive that they have got hold of a most uncommon
book. Its uncommonness, as was partly said above, does not consist merely in the excellence of its description; nor in the acuteness
of the occasional *mots*; nor in the passion of the two main characters;
nor in the representation of the mood of that " discouraged
generation of 1850 " of which it is, in prose and French, the other
Testament corresponding to Matthew Arnold's in verse and
English. Nor does it even consist in all these added together; but
in the way in which they are fused; in which they permeate
each other and make, not a group, but a whole. It might even,
like Sainte-Beuve's *Volupté* (*v. inf.*), be called " not precisely a
novel " at all, and even more than Fabre's *Abbé Tigrane* (*v. inf.*
again), rather a study than a story. And it is partly from this
point of view that one regrets the prologue and epilogue. No
doubt—and the plea is a recurring one—in life these storms and
stresses, these failures and disappointments, do often subside into
something parallel to Dominique's second existence as squire,
sportsman, husband, father, and farmer. No doubt they

Pulveris exigui jactu compacta quiescunt,

whether the dust is of the actual grave and its ashes, or the more symbolical one of the end of love. But on the whole, for art's sake, this somewhat prosaic *versöhnung* is better left behind the scenes. Yet this may be a private—it may be an erroneous—criticism. The positive part of what has been said in favour of *Dominique* is, I think, something more. There are few novels like it; none exactly like, and perhaps one does not want many or any more. But by itself it stands—and stands crowned.

CHAPTER VII

THE MINORS OF 1830

THERE is always a risk (as any one who remembers a somewhat ludicrous outburst of indignation, twenty or thirty years ago, among certain English versemen will acknowledge) in using the term "minor." But it is too useful to be given up ; and in this particular case, if the very greatest novelists are not of the company, there are those whose greatness in other ways, and whose more than mediocrity in this, should appease the admirers of their companions. We shall deal here with the novel work of Sainte-Beuve, the greatest critic of France ; of Eugène Sue, whose mere popularity exceeded that of any other writer discussed in this half of the volume except Dumas ; of men like Sandeau, Charles de Bernard, and Murger, whose actual work in prose fiction is not much less than consummate in its own particular key and sub-divisions ; of one of the best political satirists in French fiction, Louis Reybaud ; and of others still, like Soulié, Méry, Achard, Féval, Ourliac, Roger de Beauvoir, Alphonse Karr, Émile Souvestre, who, to no small extent individually and to a very great extent when taken in battalion, helped to conquer that supreme reputation for amusingness, for pastime, which the French novel has so long enjoyed throughout Europe. And these will supply not a little material for the survey of the general accomplishment of that novel in the first half of the century, which will form the subject of a " halt " or Inter-chapter, when Dumas himself—the one "major" left, and left purposely—has been discussed.

When Sainte-Beuve, thirty years after the book first appeared, subjoined a most curious Appendix to his only novel, *Volupté*, he included a letter of his own, in which he confesses that it is "not in the precise sense a novel at all." It is certainly in some respects an outlier, even of the outlying group to which it belongs—the group of *René* and *Adolphe* and their followers.

Sainte-Beuve. —*Volupté.*

I do not remember anything, even in a wide sense, quite like this Appendix—at least in the work of an author *majorum gentium*. It consists of a series of extracts, connected by remarks of Sainte-Beuve's own, from the "puff"-letters which distinguished people had sent him, in recompense for the copies of the book which he had sent *them*. Most people who write have had such letters, and "every fellow likes a hand." The persons who enjoy being biographied expect them, I suppose, to be published after their deaths; and I have known, I think, some writers of "Reminiscences" who did it themselves in their lifetimes. But it certainly is funny to find the acknowledged "first critic" in the Europe or the world of his day paralleling from private sources the collections which are (quite excusably) added as advertisements from published criticisms to later editions of a book. Intrinsically the things, no doubt, have interest. Chateaubriand, whose *René* is effusively praised in the novel, opens with an equally effusive but rather brief letter of thanks, not destitute of the apparent artificiality which, for all his genius, distinguished that "noble *Why*count," and perhaps, for all its "butter," partly responsible for the *aigre-doux* fashion in which the prais*ee* subsequently treated the prais*er*. Michelet, Villemain, and Nisard are equally favourable, and perhaps a little more sincere, though Nisard (of course) is in trouble about Sainte-Beuve's divagations from the style of the seventeenth and eighteenth centuries. Brizeux applauds in prose *and* verse. Madame de Castries (Balzac's "Duchesse de Langeais"), afterwards an intimate personal friend of

Its "puff-book."

the critic's, acknowledges, in an anonymous letter, her
"profound emotion." Lesser, but not least, people
like Magnin join. Eugénie de Guérin bribes her future
eulogist. Madame Desbordes-Valmore, *the* French
poetess of the day, is enthusiastic as to the book: and
George Sand herself writes a good half-dozen small-
printed and exuberant pages, in which the only (but
repeated) complaint is that Sainte-Beuve actually makes
his hero find comfort in Christianity. Neither Lamartine (as we might have expected) nor Lamennais (whose
disciple Sainte-Beuve had tried to be) liked it; but
Lacordaire did not disapprove.

Before saying anything more about it, let us give a
brief argument of it—a thing which it requires more
Itself. (for reasons to be given later) than most
books, whether "precisely" novels or not.
It is the autobiographic history of a certain "Amaury"
(whose surname, I think, we never hear), addressed as
a caution to a younger friend, no name of whom we ever
hear at all. The friend is too much addicted to the
pleasures of sense, and Amaury gives him his own
experience of a similar tendency. Despite the subject
and the title, there is nothing in the least "scabrous"
in it. Lacordaire himself, it seems, gave it a "vu et
approuvé" as being something that a seminarist or
even a priest (which Amaury finishes, to the great annoyance of George Sand, as being) might have composed
for edifying purposes. But the whole is written to show
the truth of a quatrain of the Judicious Poet:

> The wise have held that joys of sense,
> The more their pleasure is intense,
> More certainly demand again
> Usurious interest of pain ;

though the moral is enforced in rather a curious manner.
Amaury is the only, and orphan, representative of a good
Norman or Breton family, who has been brought up by
an uncle, and arrives at adolescence just at the time of
the Peace of Amiens or thereabouts. He has escaped
the heathendom which reigned over France a decade

previously, and is also a good Royalist, but very much
"left to himself" in other ways. Inevitably, he falls
in love, though at first half-ignorant of what he is doing
or what is being done to him. The first object is a
girl, Amélie de Liniers, in every way desirable in herself,
but unluckily not enough desired by him. He is
insensibly divided from her by acquaintance with the
chief royalist family of the district, the Marquis and
Marquise de Couaën, with the latter of whom he falls
again in much deeper love, though never to any guilty
extent. She, who is represented as the real " Elle,"
is again superseded, at least partially, by a " Madame
R.," who is a much less immaculate person, though the
precise extent of the indulgence of their affections is
left veiled. But, meanwhile, Amaury's tendency towards
" Volupté " has, after his first visit to Paris, led him to
indulge in the worship of Venus Pandemos, *parallèlement*
with his more exalted passions. No individual object
or incident is mentioned in any detail ; and the passages
relating to this side of the matter are so obscurely phrased
that a very innocent person might—without stupidity
quite equal to the innocence—be rather uncertain what
is meant. But the twin ravages—of more or less pure
passion unsatisfied and wholly impure satisfied appetite—
ruin the patient's peace of mind. Alongside of this
conflict there is a certain political interest. The Marquis
de Couaën is a fervent Royalist, and so willing to be a
conspirator that he actually gets arrested. But he is an
ineffectual kind of person, though in no sense a coward
or a fool. Amaury meets with a much greater example
of " Thorough " in Georges Cadoudal, and only just
escapes being entangled in the plot which resulted in
the execution [1] of Cadoudal himself ; the possible suicide
but probable murder [1] of Pichegru, if not of others ; the
kidnapping and unquestionable murder [1] of the Duc

---

[1] It will be observed that I use the words referred to in this note with more dis-
crimination than is always the case with some excellent folk. I sympathise with Cadoudal most of the three, but I quite recognise that Bonaparte had a kind of right to try,
and to execute him. So, if Pichegru had been tried, he might have been executed.
The Enghien business was pure murder. In some more recent instances these distinc-
tions have not, I think, been correctly observed by public speakers and writers.

d'Enghien, and the collapse of the career of Moreau. Some other real persons are brought in, though in an indirect fashion. Finally, the conflict of flesh and spirit and the general tumult of feeling are too much for Amaury, and he takes refuge, through the seminary, in the priesthood. The last event of the book is the death and burial of Madame de Couaën, her husband and Amaury somewhat melodramatically—and perhaps with a slight suggestion both of awkward allegory and possible burlesque—hammering literal nails into her coffin, one on each side.

In addition to the element of passion (both " passion-*ate* " in the English and " passion*nel* " in the French sense) and that of politics, there is a good deal of more abstract theology and philosophy, chiefly of the mixed kind, as represented in various authors from Pascal—indeed from the Fathers—to Saint-Martin.[1]

Now the book (which is undoubtedly a very remarkable one, whether it does or does not deserve that other Its character epithet which I have seen denied to it, of in various " interesting ") may be regarded in two ways. aspects. The first—as a document in regard to its author—is one which we have seldom taken in this *History*, and which the present historian avoids taking as often as he can. Here, however, it may be contended (and discussion under the next head will strengthen the contention) that it is almost impossible to do the book justice, and not very easy even to understand it, without some consideration of the sort. When Sainte-Beuve published it, he had run up, or down, a rather curious gamut of creeds and crazes. He had been a fervent Romantic. He had (for whatever mixture of reasons need not be entered into here) exchanged this first faith, wholly or partially, for that singular *un*faith of Saint-Simonianism, which, if we had not seen other things like it since and at the present day, would seem

---

[1] This *philosophe inconnu* (as his ticket-name goes in French) is, I fancy, even more unknown in England. I have not read much of him ; but I think, if it had come in my way, I should have read more.

incredible as even a hallucination of good wits. He had left this again to endeavour to be a disciple of Lamennais, and had, not surprisingly, failed. He was now to set himself to the strange Herculean task of his *Port-Royal*, which had effects upon him, perhaps stranger at first sight than on reflection. It left him, after these vicissitudes and pretty certainly some accompanying experiences adumbrated in *Volupté* itself, " L'oncle Beuve " of his later associates—a free-thinker, though not a violent one, in religion ; a critic, never perhaps purely literary, but, as concerns literature and life combined, of extraordinary range, sanity, and insight ; yet sometimes singularly stunted and limited in respect of the greatest things, and—one has to say it, though there is no need to stir the mud as it has been stirred [1]—something of a " porker of Epicurus."

Now, with such additional light as this sketch may furnish, let us return to the book itself. I have said that it has been pronounced " uninteresting," and it must be confessed that, in some ways, the author has done all he could to make it so. In the first place it is much too long ; he has neglected the examples of *René* and *Adolphe*, and given nearly four hundred solid and closely packed pages to a story with very little incident, very little description, only one solidly presented character, and practically no conversation. There is hardly a novel known to me from which the disadvantages of some more or less mechanical fault of presentation— often noticed in this *History*—could be better illustrated than from *Volupté*. I have called the pages " solid," and they are so in more than the general, more even than the technical printer's sense. One might imagine that

---

[1] Without doing this, it may be suggested that the contrast elsewhere quoted, " Mérimée était gentilhomme ; Sainte-Beuve ne l'était pas," was likely to make its unfavourable side especially felt in this connection. He seems to have disgusted even the Princess Mathilde, one of the staunchest of friends and certainly not the most squeamish or prudish of women. Nor, in another matter, can I approve his favourite mixture of rum and curaçao as a liqueur. I gave it a patient trial once, thinking it might be critically inspiring. But the rum muddles the curaçao, and the curaçao does not really improve the rum. It is a pity he did not know the excellent Cape liqueur called Vanderhum, which is not a mixture but a true hybrid of the two.

the author had laid a wager that he would use the smallest number of paragraph-breaks possible. There are none at all till page 6 (the fourth of the actual book); blocks of the same kind occur constantly afterwards, and more than one, or at most two, "new pars" are very rare indeed on a page. Even such conversation as there is is not extracted from the matrix of narrative, and the whole is unbroken *récit*.

It may seem that there is, and has been elsewhere, too much stress laid upon this point. But if I, who am something of a *helluo librorum*, and very seldom find anything that resists my devouring faculty, feel this difficulty, how much more must persons who require to be tempted and baited on by mechanical and formal allurements ?

Still, some strong-minded person may say: "These are 'shallows and miseries'—base mechanical considerations. Tell me *why* the book, as matter, has been found uninteresting." In this instance there will be no difficulty in complying with the request. Let me at once say that I do not consider it uninteresting myself; that, in fact (and stronger testimony is hardly possible), after reading great part of it without appetite and " against the grain," I began to take a very considerable interest in it. But this did not prevent my having a pretty clear notion of what seem to me faults of treatment, and even of conception, quite independent of those already mentioned.

The main one is somewhat " tickle of the sere " to handle. It has been said that, despite its alarming title, there is nothing in the book that even prudery, unless it were of the most irritable and morbid kind, could object to. There is no dwelling on what Defoe ingeniously calls " the vicious part " of the matter ; there is no description of it closer than, if as close as, some passages of the Book of Proverbs (which are actually quoted), and, above all, there is no hint of any satisfaction whatever being derived from the sins by the sinner. His course in this respect might have been a succession of fits of vertigo or epilepsy as far as pleasure goes. There is even a rather fine piece of real psychology as to his state of mind after his first succumbing to temptation. But all this abstinence and reticence, however laudable in a sense it may be, necessarily deprives the passages of anything but purely psychological interest, and leaves most of them not much of that. Luxury *in vacuo* may, no doubt, be perilous to the culprit; but it has, for others, nearly as much of the unreal and chimerical as Gluttony confined to " Second intentions."

Yet there is another objection to *Volupté* which is even more closely " psychological," and which has been indicated in the word " parallèlement," suggested by, though largely transposed from, Verlaine's use thereof in a title. There is no connection established—there is even, it may seem, a great gulf fixed between Amaury's actual " loves " for Amélie de Liniers, for Lucy de Couaën, and even for the more questionable Madame R., and those " sippings of the lower draught " which are so industriously veiled. If Amaury had " disdamaged " himself, for his inability to possess any of his real and superior loves, by lower indulgences, it would have been discreditable but human. But there is certainly no expression—there is, unless I mistake, hardly any suggestion—of anything of the kind. The currents of spiritual and animal passion seem to have run independently of each other, like canals at different heights on the slope of a hill. I do not know that this is less discreditable; but it seems to me infinitely less human. And, while carefully abstaining from any attempt to connect the peculiarity with the above-mentioned scandals about Sainte-Beuve's life and conversation in detail, one may suggest that it offers some explanation of the unquestioned facts about this; also (and this is of infinitely more importance) of that absence of ability to love literature in anything like a passionate way, which, with a certain other inability to love literature for itself, prevents him from attaining the absolutely highest level in criticism, though his command of ranges just below the highest is wider and firmer than that of any other critic on record.

We may next take, to some extent together, two writers of the novel who made their reputation in the Jules Sandeau July Monarchy, though one of them long and Charles outlived it; who, though this one inclined to de Bernard. a sort of domestic tragedy and the other to pure comedy, resembled each other not a little in clinging to ordinary life, and my estimate of whom is considerably higher than that recently (or, I think, at present) entertained by French critics or by those English critics who think it right to be guided by their French *confrères*. This estimate, however, has been given at length in another place,[1] and I quite admit that the subjects, though I have not in the least lowered my opinion of them, can hardly be said (like Gautier, Mérimée, Balzac, and Dumas, in the present part of this volume, or others later) to demand, in a general History, very large space in dealing with them. I shall therefore endeavour to summarise my corrected impressions more briefly than in those other cases. This shortening may, I think, be justified doubly : in the first place, because any one who is enough of a student to want more can go to the other handling ; and, in the second, because the only excellent way, of reading the books themselves, may be adopted with very unusual absence of any danger of disappointment. I hardly know any work of either Jules Sandeau or of Charles de Bernard which is not worth reading by persons of fairly catholic tastes in novel pastime.

The first-named—the younger by some half-dozen years, but the first to publish by more than as many— concerns those who take a merely or mainly anecdotic interest in literature by his well-known *liaison* with George Sand—to whom he gave *dimidium nominis*, and perhaps for a time at least *dimidium cordis*, though he

---

[1] In articles written for the *Fortnightly Review* during a large part of the year 1878, and reprinted in the volume of *Essays on French Novelists* frequently referred to.

probably did not get it back so much "in a worse estate"[1] as was the case with Musset and Chopin. Sandeau's collaboration with her in novel-writing was long afterwards succeeded by another in dramaturgy with Émile Augier, which resulted in at least one of the most famous French plays of the nineteenth century, *Le Gendre de M. Poirier*, based on Sandeau's *Sacs et Parchemins*. But we need busy ourselves only with the novels themselves.

Sandeau was barely twenty when he wrote *Rose et Blanche*, during the time of, and with his partner in,

Sandeau's work. that most dangerous of all possible *liaisons*. But he was nearly thirty when he produced his own first work of note, *Marianna*. In this, in *Fernand*, and in *Valcreuse*, all books above the average in merit, there is what may be called, from no mere Grundyite point of view, the drawback that they are all studies of "the triangle." They are quite decently, and in fact morally, though not goodily, handled. But it certainly may be objected that trigonometry[2] of this kind occupies an exorbitant place in French literature, and one may be a little sorry to see a neophyte of talent taking to it. However, though Sandeau in these books showed his ability, his way did not really lie *in*, though it might lie *through*, them. He had, indeed, as a novelist should have, good change of strings to his bow, if not even more than one or two bows to shoot in.

No Frenchman has written a better boy's book than

---

[1] *Vide* the wonderful poem—one of Mr. Anon's pearls, but Donne's for more than a ducat—"Thou sent'st to me a heart was crowned," etc. However, the bitter remark quoted elsewhere (*v. inf.*) looks like a lasting wound.

[2] I can conceive a modernist rising up and saying, "And your mawkish ante-nuptial wooings? Haven't *we* had enough of *them*?" To which I should reply, "Impossible." The sages of old have rightly said that 'The way of a man with a maid' is a mystery always, and the proofs thereof are well seen in literature as in life. But the way of an extra-man with another person's wife can, as illustrated, if not demonstrated, by the myriads of treatises thereon in French and the thousands of imitations in other languages (reinforced, if the Stoic scavenger-researcher so pleases, by the annals of the Divorce Court and its predecessors), be almost scientifically reduced to two classes. (1) Is the lady *adulteraturient*? In that case results can be attained anyhow. (2) Is she not? In that case results can be attained nohow. Which considerably minishes the interest of this situation. The interest of the other is the interest of "the world's going round" in quality, and almost infinitely various in detail. But when something has once happened the variety ceases, or is immensely reduced.

La Roche aux Mouettes, deservedly well known to English readers in translation: and whether he did or did not enter into designed competition with his *quondam* companion on the theme of Pastoral *berquinade*, I do not myself think that *Catherine* is much below *La Petite Fadette* or *La Mare au Diable*. He was a very considerable master of the short story; you cannot have much better things of the kind than *Le Jour sans Lendemain* and *Un Début dans la Magistrature*. But his special gift lay in treating two situations which sometimes met, or crossed, or even substantially coincided. The one was the contrast of new and old, whether from the side of actual " money-bags and archives " or from others. The second and higher development of, or alternative to, this was the working out of the subdued tragical, in which, short of the very great masters, he had few superiors, while the quietness of his tones and values even, enhances to some tastes the poignancy of the general effect. *Mlle. de La Seiglière* is, I suppose, the best representative of the first class as a novel, for *Sacs et Parchemins*, as has been said, waited for dramatisation to bring out its merits. The pearls or pinks of the other are *Mlle. de Kérouare* and *La Maison de Penarvan*, the latter the general favourite, the former mine. Both have admirably managed *peripeteia*s, the shorter story (*Mlle. de Kérouare*) having, in particular, a memorable setting of that inexorable irony of Fate against which not only is there no armour, but not even the chance and consolement of fighting armourless. When Marie de Kérouare accepts, at her father's wish, a suitor suitable in every way, but somewhat undemonstrative; when she falls in love (or thinks she does) with a handsome young cousin; when the other aspirant loses or risks all his fortune as a Royalist, and she will not accept what she might have, his retirement, thereby eliciting from her father a *mot* like the best of Corneille's; [1] when, having written to the cousin excusing herself, she gets

---

[1] " *Bien! mon sang.*" I suppose " democratic " sentiment is quite insensible to this, Which seems to be a pity.

a mocking letter telling her that *he* is married already; when the remorseless turn of Fortune's wheel loses her the real lover whom she at last really does love—then it is not mere sentimental - Romantic twaddle; it is a slice of life, soaked in the wine of Romantic tragedy.[1]

In Charles de Bernard (or, if anybody is unable to read novels published under a pseudonym with sufficient comfort, Charles Bernard du Grail de la Villette[2]) one need not look for high passions and great actions of this kind. He does try tragedy sometimes,[3] but, as has been already admitted, it is not his trade. Occasionally, as in *Gerfaut*, he takes the "triangle" rather seriously *à la* George-Sand-and-the-rest-of-them. The satirists have said that, though not invariably (our present author contains cautions on that point) yet as a rule, if you take yourself with sufficient seriousness, mankind will follow suit. It is certainly very risky to appear to take yourself not seriously. *Gerfaut*, I believe, is generally held to be Bernard's masterpiece. I remember that even my friend Mr. Andrew Lang, who seldom differed with me on points of pure literature, almost gravely remonstrated with me for not thinking enough of it. There are admirable things in *Gerfaut*; but they are, as it seems to me, *separately* admirable, and so are more like grouped short stories than like a whole long novel. He wrote other books of substance, two of them, *Un Beau-père* and *Le Gentilhomme Campagnard*, each extending to a brace of well-filled volumes. But these, as well as the single-volume but still substantial *Un Homme Sérieux* and *Les Ailes d'Icare*, like *Gerfaut* itself, could all, I think, be split up into shorter stories without difficulty

Bernard's.

---

[1] I think it should be added to Sandeau's credit that (as it appears to me at least) he had a strong influence on the reaction against Naturalism at the end of the century.

[2] Most of his contemporaries would have envied him this admirably *moyen-âge* and sonorous designation. But it is certainly cumbrous for a title-page, and its owner—a modest man with a sense of humour—may perhaps have thought that it *might* be rather more ridiculous than sublime there.

[3] As is usual and natural with men of his time, La Vendée mostly supplies it; but that glorious failure did not inspire him quite so well as it did Sandeau or even (*v. inf.*) Édouard Ourliac, However, he was a sound Royalist, for which peace be to his soul!

and with advantage. It is of course very likely that the comparative slighting which the author has received from M. Brunetière and other French critics of the more theoretic kind is due to this. The strict rule-system no doubt disapproves of the mere concatenation of scenes—still more of the mere accumulation of them.

We, on the other hand, *quibus est nihil negatum*, or who at any rate deny nothing to our favourite authors so long as they amuse or interest us, ought to be—and some of the best as well as the not-best of us have been—very fond of Charles de Bernard. How frankly and freely Thackeray praised, translated, and adapted him ought to be known to everybody; and indeed there was a great similarity between the two. The Frenchman had nothing of Thackeray's strength—of his power of creating character; of his intensity when he cared to be intense; of his satiric sweep and "stoop"; of his spacious view and masterly grasp of life. But in some ways he was a kind of Thackeray several degrees under-proof—a small-beer Thackeray that was a very excellent creature. In his grasp of a pure and simple comic situation; in his faculty of carrying this out decently to its appropriate end; and, above all, in the admirable quality of his conversation, he was really a not so very minor edition of his great English contemporary. Almost the only non-technical fault that can be found with him— and it has been found by French as well as English critics, so there is no room for dismissing the charge as due to a merely insular cult of "good form"—is the extreme unscrupulousness of some of his heroes, who appear to have no sense of honour at all. Yet, in other ways, no French novelist of the century has obtained or deserved more credit for drawing ladies and gentlemen. It has been hinted that the inability to do this has been brought as a charge against even the mighty Honoré,[1] and that, here at any rate, it has been found impossible to deny it absolutely. But if the company of the Human

---

[1] Who, by the way, was a good friend and a good appreciator of Bernard.

Comedy falls short in this respect, it is not because some of its members do " shady " things. It is because the indefinable, but to those who can perceive it unmistakable, *aura* of " gentility "—in the true and not the debased sense—is, at best, questionably present. This is not the case with Bernard.

It is particularly difficult, in such a book as this, to deal with so large a collection of what may be most appropriately called " Scenes and Characters " as that which constitutes his most valuable if not all his valuable work. In the older handling referred to, I selected, for pretty full abstract and some translation, *Un Homme Sérieux* among longer books, and *Le Gendre* among the short stories ; and I still think them the best, except *Le Pied d'Argile*, which, from Thackeray's incomparable adaptation [1] of it in *The Bedford Row Conspiracy*, remains as a standing possibility of acquaintance with Charles de Bernard's way for those who do not read French, or do not care to " research " for the original. Thackeray also gave a good deal of *Les Ailes d'Icare* in abstract and translation, and he borrowed something more from it in *A Shabby Genteel Story*. *La Peau du Lion* and *La Chasse aux Amants* have some slight resemblance to *Le Gendre*, in that the gist of all three is concerned with the defeat of unscrupulous lovers, and neither is much inferior to it. I never knew anybody who had read *La Femme de Quarante Ans* and its history of sentimental star-gazing *à deux* without huge enjoyment ; and *L'Arbre de la Science*, as well as the shorter *Un Acte de Vertu*, deserve special mention.

But, in fact, take the volumes entitled *L'Écueil*, *Le Nœud Gordien*, *Le Paravent*, and *Le Paratonnerre* ; open any of them where you like, and it will go hard but, in the comic stories at any rate, you will find yourself well off. The finest of the tragic ones is, I think, *L'Anneau*

---

[1] For any one who cares for the minor " arts and crafts " of literature this is *the* example of Adaptation itself. The story is not translated ; it is not imitated ; it is not parodied. It is simply *transfused* from one body of a national literature into another, and I defy the acutest and most experienced critic to find in the English, if he did not previously know the facts, any trace of a French original.

d'Argent, which in utilising the sad inefficacy of the Legitimist endeavours to upset the July Monarchy, comes close to the already-mentioned things of Sandeau and Ourliac.

That a critic like M. Brunetière should dismiss Bernard as " commonplace " (I forget the exact French word, but the meaning was either this or " mediocre "), extending something the same condemnation, or damningly faint praise, to Sandeau, may seem strange at first sight, but explains itself pretty quickly to those who have the requisite knowledge. Neither could, by any reasonable person, be accused of that *grossièreté* which offended the censor so much, and to no small extent so rightly. Neither was extravagantly unacademic or in other ways unorthodox. But both might be called *vulgaire* from the same point of view which made Madame de Staël so call her greatest contemporary as a she-novelist—one, too, so much greater than herself.[1] That is to say, they did deal with strictly ordinary life, and neither attempted that close psychological analysis and ambitious *schematism* which (we have been told) is the pride of the French novel, and which, certainly, some French critics have supposed to be of its essence. These points of view I have left undiscussed for the most part, but have consistently in practice declined to take, in the first volume, while they are definitely opposed and combated in more than one passage of this.[2] I admit that Sandeau, save in the one situation where I think he comes near to the first class—that of subdued resignation to calamity—is not passionate ; I admit that Bernard has a certain superficiality, and that, as has been confessed already, his " form " sometimes leaves to desire. But they both seem to me to have, in whatever measure and degree, what, with me, is the article of standing or falling in novels—humanity. And they seem—also to me, and

[1] Corinne made a great blunder : but admirers of Miss Austen have sometimes taken it as being greater than it was. " Vulgaire" and "vulgar" are by no means exact synonyms : in fact the French word is probably used much oftener in a more or less inoffensive sense than otherwise.

[2] Especially in the next chapter but one.

speaking under correction—to *write*, if not consummately, far more than moderately well, and to *tell* in a fashion for which consummate is not too strong a word. While for pure gaiety, unsmirched by coarseness and unspoilt by ill-nature, you will not find much better pastime anywhere than in the work of the author of *L'Écueil* and *Le Paratonnerre*.

Indeed these two—though the *berquinade* tendency, considerably *masculated*, prevails in one, and the *esprit gaulois*, decorously draped, in the other—seem to me to run together better than any two other novelists of our company. They do not attempt elaborate analysis ; they do not grapple with thorny or grimy problems ; they are not purveyors of the indecent, or dealers in the supernatural and fantastic, or poignant satirists of society at large or individuals in particular. But they can both, in their different ways, tell a plain tale uncommonly well, and season it with wit or pathos when either is suitable. Their men and women are real men and women, and the stages on which they move are not *mere* stages, but pieces of real earth.

As regards one formerly almost famous and still well-known novelist, Eugène Sue, I am afraid I shall

Sue, Soulié, and the novel of melo- drama— *Le Juif Errant*, etc. be an unprofitable servant to such masters in the guise of readers as desire to hear about him. For he is one more of those—I do not think I have had or shall have to confess to many—whom I have found it almost impossible to read. I acknowledge, indeed, that though at the first reading (I do not know how many years ago) of his most famous work, *Le Juif Errant*, I found no merit in it at all, at a second, though I do not think that even then I quite got through it, I had to allow a certain grandiosity. *The Mysteries of Paris* has always defeated me, and I am now content to enjoy Thackeray's very admirable *précis* of part of it. Out of pure goodness and sheer equity I endeavoured, for the present volume, to make myself acquainted with one of his later books—

the immense *Sept Péchés Capitaux*, which is said to be
a Fourierist novel, and explains how the vices may be
induced, in a sort of Mandeville-made-amiable fashion,
to promote the good of society. I found it what Mrs.
Browning has made somebody pronounce Fourier himself
in *Aurora Leigh*, " Naught ! " [1] except that I left them
at the end actually committing an Eighth deadly sin by
drinking *iced* Constantia ! [2]   Sue, who had been an
army surgeon and had served during the Napoleonic
war, both on land and at sea, wrote, before he took to his
great melodramas, some rather extravagant naval novels,
which are simply rubbish compared with Marryat, but
in themselves not quite, I think, so difficult to read as
his better known work. I remember one in particular,
but I am not certain whether it was *La Coucaratcha* or
La Vigie de Koatven. They are both very nice titles,
and I am so much afraid of disillusionment that I have
thought it better to look neither up for this occasion. [3]

The fact is, as it seems to me, that the proper place
for melodrama is not the study but the stage. I fear
Melodramatic I have uttered some heresies about the theatre
fiction   in this book, and I should not be sorry if I
generally.   never passed through its doors again. If I
must, I had rather the entertainment were melodrama
than anything else. The better the play is as literature,
the more I wish that I might be left to read it in comfort
and see it acted with my mind's eye only. But I can
rejoice in the valiant curate when (with the aid of an
avalanche, if I remember rightly) he triumphs over the
wicked baronet, who is treading on the fingers of the

---

[1] Or was it Comte that was " naught " and Fourier that was " void " ? I am sure
the third person, namely, Cabet, was " puerile " ; but I do not think I could read
Aurora Leigh again, even to make sure of the distribution of the other epithets.

[2] The real *old* Constantia has, I believe, ceased to exist. It was a delicious *vin de
liqueur*, but you might as well ice Madeira or a brown sherry.

[3] Thackeray pays Sue the very high compliment of having " tried almost always
[to attain], and in *Mathilde* very nearly succeeded in attaining, a tone of *bonne compagnie*."
I found the particular book difficult to get hold of. Apropos of French naval novels,
will somebody tell me who wrote *Le Roi des Gabiers*, an immense *feuilleton*-romance,
which I remember reading a vast number of years ago ? I think he had (or took) a
Breton name, and wrote others. But the navy, even with Jean Bart and Surcouf and the
Bailli, has never attracted any of the *great* French novelists.

heroine as she hangs over the precipice. I can laugh and applaud when the heroic mother slashes her daughter's surreptitious portrait in full Academy. The object of melodrama is to make men rejoice and laugh; but it seems to me to require the stage to do it on, or at any rate to receive an immense assistance from theatrical presentation. So given, it escapes the curse of *segnius irritant*, because it attacks both ear and eye; being entirely independent of style (which *is* in such cases actually *gênant*), it does not need the quiet and solitary devotion which enjoyment of style demands; and it is immensely improved by dresses and *décor*, scenery and music, and " spectacle " generally—all things which, again, interfere with pure literary enjoyment. I shall hope to have demonstrated, or at any rate done something to show, how Dumas, when at his best, and even not quite at his best, escapes the actual melodramatic. Perhaps this was because he had purged himself of the stagy element in his abundant theatric exercise earlier. Sue, of course, dramatised or got dramatised a considerable part of his many inventions; but I think one can see that they were not originally stage-stuff.

If, however, any one must have melodrama, but at the same time does not want it in stage form, I should myself recommend to him Frédéric Soulié in preference to Eugène Sue. Soulié is, indeed, a sort of blend of Dumas and Sue, but more melodramatic than the former, and less full of grime and purpose and other " nonnaturals " of the novel than the latter. It is evident that he has taken what we may call his schedules pretty directly from Scott himself; but he has filled them up with more melodramatic material. It is very noteworthy, too, that Soulié, like Dumas, turned *his* stagy tastes and powers on to actual stage-work, and so kept the two currents duly separate. And it seems to be admitted that he had actual literary power, if he did not achieve much actual literary performance.

For myself, I think that *Le Château des Pyrénées* is a thing, that in De Quincey's famous phrase, you *can* recommend to a friend whose appetite in fiction is melodramatic. Here is, if not exactly " *God's* plenty," *Le Château des Pyrénées.* at any rate plenty of a kind—plenty whose horn is inexhaustible and the reverse of monotonous. You never, though you have read novels as the waves of the sea or the sands of the shore in number, know exactly what is going to happen, and when you think you know what is happening, it turns out to be something else. Persons who wear, as to the manner born, the jackets of lackeys turn out to be bishops ; and bishops prove to be coiners. An important *jeune premier* or *quasi-premier*, having just got off what seems to be imminent danger, is stabbed in the throat, is left for dead, and then carries out a series of risky operations and conversations for several hours. A castle, more than Udolphian in site, size, incidents, and opportunities, is burnt at a moment's notice, as if it were a wigwam. Everybody's sons and daughters are somebody else's daughters and sons—a state of things not a little facilitated by the other fact that everybody's wife is somebody else's mistress. Everybody knows something mysterious and exceedingly damaging about everybody else ; and the whole company would be cleared off the stage in the first few chapters if something did not always happen to make them drop the daggers in a continual stalemate. Dukes who are governors of provinces and peers of France are also heads (or think they are) of secret societies—the orthodox members of which chiefly do the coining, but are quite ignorant that a large number of other members are Huguenots (it is not long after the " Revocation ") and are, in the same castle, storing arms for an insurrection. Spanish counts who are supposed to have been murdered fifteen years ago turn up quite uninjured, and ready for the story to go on sixteen years longer. When you have got an ivory casket supposed to be full of all sorts of compromising documents, somebody produces another, exactly like it, but containing documents more compromising still. There is a counsellor of the Parliament of Toulouse—supposed to be not merely a severe magistrate, but a man of spotless virtue, and one who actually submits fearlessly to great danger in doing his duty, but who turns out to be an atrocious criminal. And in the centre of all the turmoil there is a wondrous figure, a sorcerer-shepherd, who is really an Italian prince, who pulls all the strings, makes all cups slip at all lips, sets up and upsets all the puppets, and is finally poniarded by the wicked counsellor, both of them having been caught at last, and the counsellor going mad after commission of his final crime.

Now, if anybody wants more than this—there is, in fact, a great deal more in the compass of two volumes,[1] containing between them less than six hundred pages— all I can say is that he is vexatious and unreasonable, and that I have no sympathy whatever with him. Of course the book is of its own kind, and not of another. Some people may like that kind less than others ; some may not like it at all. But in that case nobody obliges them to have anything to do with it.

Soulié wrote nearly two score novels or works of fiction, ranging from *Contes pour les Enfants* to *Mémoires du Diable*. I do not pretend to have read all or even very many of them, for, as I have confessed, they are not my special kind. In novels of action there should be a great deal of fighting and a great deal of love-making, and it does not seem to me that either [2] was Soulié's forte. But as the *Mémoires* are sometimes quoted as his masterpiece, something should, I suppose, be said about them.

One thing about the book is certain—that it is much more ambitiously planned than the *Château*; and I do

Les Mémoires not think it uncritical to say that the ambition
du Diable. is, to a certain extent, successful. One credit, at any rate, can hardly be denied it. Considering the immense variety in circumstances of the bargains with

---

[1] I ought perhaps to say that the second volume does not seem to me to be quite equal to the first. The " sixteen years allowed for refreshment " do not justify themselves.
[2] In *La Lionne* (which is not to be confused with *Le Lion Amoureux*, a " psychological " diploma-piece praised by some) there are chapters and chapters of love-making " of a sort." But it is not the right sort.

the Devil which are made in actual life, it may seem
strange that the literary treatment of the subject should
be so comparatively monotonous as it is. Soulié, I
think, has been at least as original as anybody else, though
it was of course almost impossible for him to avoid
suggestions, if not of Marlowe, of Lesage, Goethe,
Maturin (whose wide popularity in France at this time
must never be forgotten), and others. At the very
beginning there is one touch which, if not absolutely
invented, is newish in the connection. The Château of
Ronquerolles, again in the Pyrenean district (besides the
advantages of a mountainous country, Soulié himself
was born at Foix), has a range of mysterious windows,
each of which has for many generations emerged, with
the room appertaining, from wall and corridor without
anybody remembering it before.[1] As a matter of fact
these chambers have been the scenes of successive
bargains between the Lords of Ronquerolles and the
Prince of Darkness ; and a fresh one is opened whenever
the last inheritor of an ancestral curse (details of which
are explained later) has gone to close his account. The
new Count de Luizzi knows what he has to do, which is
to summon Satan by a certain little silver bell at the not
most usual but sufficiently witching hour of *two* A.M.,
saying at the same time, " Come ! " After a slightly
trivial farce-overture of apparitions in various banal forms,
Luizzi compels the fallen archangel to show himself in
his proper shape ; and the bargain is concluded after
some chaffering. It again is not quite the usual form ;
there being, as in Melmoth's case, a redemption clause,
though a different one. If the man can say and show,
after ten years, that he has been happy he will escape.
The " consideration " is also uncommon. Luizzi does
not want wealth, which, indeed, he possesses ; nor,
directly, pleasure, etc., which he thinks he can procure

---

[1] The famous or legendary chamber at Glamis—and perhaps another not so generally
known story of a mansion farther north still, where you see from the courtyard a window
the room belonging to which cannot be found from the inside—will occur. But Soulié,
though he might have heard of the former, is very unlikely to have known the latter,
which comes nearer to his arrangement.

for himself. He wants (God help him !) to know all about other people, their past lives, their temptations, etc.—a thing which a person of sense and taste would do anything, short of selling himself to the Devil, *not* to know. There are, however, some apparently liberal, if discreditable, concessions—that Luizzi may reveal, print, and in any other way avail himself of the diabolic information. But, almost immediately, the metaphorical cloven foot and false dice appear. For it seems that in certain circumstances Luizzi can only rid himself of his ally when unwelcome, and perform other acts, at the price of forfeiting a month of his life—a thing likely to abridge and qualify the ten years very considerably, and the " happiness " more considerably still.[1] And this foul play, or at any rate sharp practice, continues, as might be expected, throughout. The evil actions which Luizzi commits are not, as usual, committed with impunity as to ordinary worldly consequences, while he is constantly enlarging the debt against his soul. He is also always getting into trouble by mixing up his supernatural knowledge with his ordinary life, and he even commits murder without intending or indeed knowing it. This is all rather cleverly managed ; though the end—the usual sudden " foreclosure " by Diabolus, despite the effort of no less than three Gretchens who go upwards, and of a sort of inchoate repentance on Luizzi's own part before he goes downwards—might be better.

The bulk, however, of the book, which is a very long one—three volumes and nearly a thousand closely printed pages—consists of the *histoires* or " memoirs " (whence the title) of other people which the Devil tells Luizzi, sometimes by actual *récit*, sometimes otherwise. Naturally they are most of them grimy ; though there is nothing of the Laclos or even of the Paul de Kock kind. I find them, however, a little tedious.

The fact, indeed, is that this kind of novel—as has been hinted sometimes, and sometimes frankly asserted—

---

[1] The contact *here* with the *Peau de Chagrin* need hardly be dwelt upon.

has its own peculiar appeals ; and that these appeals, as is always the case when they are peculiar, leave Later writers some ears deaf. There is no intention here and writings to intimate any superfine scorn of it. It has of the class. another and a purely literary, or at least literary-scientific, interest as descending from the Terror Novel of the end of the eighteenth century. It shows no sign of ceasing to exist or to appeal to those to whom it is fitted to appeal, and who are fitted to be appealed to by it. Towards the close of the period at which I ceased to see French novels generally, I remember meeting with many examples of it. There was one which, with engaging candour, called itself *L'Hôtellerie Sanglante*, and in which persons, after drinking wine which was, as Rogue Riderhood says, "fur from a 'ealthy wine," retired to a rest which knew no or only a very brief and painful waking, under the guardianship of a young person, who, to any one in any other condition, would have seemed equally " fur " from an attractive young person. There was another, the title of which I forget, in which the intended victim of a plunge into a water-logged *souterrain* connected with the Seine made his way out and saw dreadful things in the house above. There is really no great interval or discrepancy (except in details of manners and morals) between these and the novels of detective, gentleman-thief, and other impolite life which delight many persons indubitably respectable and presumably intelligent in England to-day.[1] To sneer at these would be ridiculous.

Henry Murger is not the least of the witnesses to the truth of a remark—which I owe to one of the critics Murger. of my earlier volume—that in England people (he was kind enough to except me) are too apt to accept the contemporary French estimates of French contemporary literature and the traditional French estimates of earlier authors. Murger had, I believe, a hardly earned and too brief popularity in his

---

[1] A little more on this subject may be given later to Gaboriau and Ponson du Terrail.

own country; and though it was a little before my time, I can believe that this overflowed into England. But the posthumous and accepted judgments of him altered *there* to a sort of slighting patronage; and I remember that when, nearly twenty years after his death, I wrote on him in the *Fortnightly Review*,[1] some surprise at my loftier estimate was expressed *here*. The reasons for this depreciation are not hard to give, and as they form a base for, and indeed really a part of, my critical estimate they may be stated shortly. The " Bohemia "[2] of which Murger was the laureate, both in prose and verse, is a country whose charms have been admitted by some of the greatest, but which no wise person has ever regarded, much less recommended, as providing any city to dwell in; and which has certainly been the scene if not the occasion, not merely of much mischief, which does not particularly concern us, but of much foolishness and bad taste, which partly does. It was almost—not quite— the only theme of Murger's songs and words. And— last and perhaps most dangerous of all—there was the fact that, if not in definite Bohemianism, there was in other respects a good deal in him of a far minor Musset, and both in Bohemianism and other things still more of an inferior Gérard de Nerval. I believe the case *against* has been fairly stated here.

The case *for* I have put in the essay referred to with the full, though, I think, not more than the fair emphasis

The *Vie de* allowed to even a critical advocate when he has
Bohème. to demolish charges. The historian passes from bar to bench; and neither ought to speak, nor in this instance is inclined to speak, quite so enthusiastically. I admitted there that I did not think Murger's comparatively early death lost us much; and I admit even more frankly here, that in what he has left there is no great variety of excellence, and that while there are

[1] Reprinted in *Essays on French Novelists*.

[2] A somewhat fuller discussion of this heretical *bona patria* of literature may be found in the original Essay. I had at one time thought of reprinting it—in text or appendix— here. But perhaps it would be superfluous. I ought, however, to add that I have seen, in French writers, later again than those referred to in the text, some touches of revived interest in Murger.

numerous good things in the work, there is little that
can be called actually great. But after these admissions
no small amount remains to his credit as a writer who
can manage both comedy and pathos ; who, if he has
no wide range or variety of subject, can vary his treatment
quite efficiently, and who has a certain freshness rarely
surviving the first years of journalism of all work. His
faintly but truly charming verse is outside our bounds,
and even prose poetry like " The Loves of a Cricket
and a Spark of Flame " [1] are on the line, though this
particular thing is not far below Gérard himself. The
longer novels, *Adeline Protat* and *Le Sabot Rouge*, are
competent in execution and pleasant enough to read ;
yet they are not above good circulating-library strength.
But the *Vie de Bohême*, in its various sections, and a
great number of shorter tales and sketches, are thoroughly
agreeable if not even delightful. Murger has completely shaken off the vulgarity which almost spoilt
Pigault, and damaged Paul de Kock not a little. If any
one who has not yet reached age, or has not let it make
him " crabbed," cannot enjoy Schaunard and the tame
lobster ; the philosophic humours of Gustave (afterwards
His Excellency Gustave) Colline ; the great journal
Le Castor,[2] which combined the service of the hat-trade
with the promotion of high thinking and great writing ;
and the rest of the comedy of *La Vie de Bohême* proper,
I am sorry for him. He must have been, somehow,
born wrong.

The serious Bohemia of the *Buveurs d'Eau* (the
devotees of High Art who carry their devotion to the
point of contemning all " commission " work
whatsoever) may require more effort, or more
special predestination, to get into full sympathy
with it. The thing is noble ; but it is nobility *party
per* a very thin *pale* with and from silliness ; and the
Devil's Advocate has no very hard task in suggesting

*Les Buveurs
d'Eau and the
Miscellanies.*

---

[1] Translated at length in the Essay.

[2] I have always been a little curious to know whether that remarkable periodical,
Cope's *Tobacco Plant*, which gave us not a little of James Thomson the Second's work,
was really, as it might have been, conceived as a follower of *Le Castor*.

that it is not even nobility at all, but a compound of idleness and affectation.[1] With rare exceptions, the greatest men of art and letters have never disdained, though they might not love, what one of them called " honest journey-work in default of better " ; and when those exceptions come to be examined—as in the leading English cases of Milton [2] and Wordsworth—you generally find that the persons concerned never really felt the pinch of necessity. However, Murger makes the best of his Lazare and the rest of them ; and his power over pathos, which is certainly not small, assists him as much here as it does *more* than assist him—as it practically carries him through—in other stories such as *Le Manchon de Francine* and *La Biographie d'un Inconnu*. And, moreover, he can use all these means and more in handfuls of little things—some mere *bleuettes* (as the French call them)—*Comment on Devient Coloriste, Le Victime du Bonheur, La Fleur Bretonne, Le Fauteuil Enchanté, Les Premières Amours du Jeune Bleuet*.

With such high praise still allotted to an author, it may seem unfair not to give him more room; and I should certainly have done so if I had not had the other treatment to refer to. Since that existed, as in the similar cases of Sandeau, Bernard, and perhaps one or two more, it seemed to me that space, becoming more and more valuable, might be economised, especially as, in his case and theirs, there is nothing extraordinary to interest, nothing difficult to discuss. *Tolle, lege* is the suitable word for all three, and no fit person who obeys will regret his obedience.

Any one who attempts to rival Thackeray's abstract (" *with* translations, Sir ! ") of the first part of Louis Reybaud's *Jérôme Paturot* must have a better conceit of himself than that with which the present writer has been gifted, by the Divinity or any other power. The

---

[1] Murger knows this and allows it.
[2] Who, moreover, *did* work, and that pretty hard, in his Secretaryship, and by no means disdained pay for it—purely " patriotic " as (in his view) it was.

essay[1] in which this appears contains some of the rather rash and random judgments to which its great author Reybaud— was too much addicted ; he had not, for *Jérôme* instance, come to his later and saner estimate *Paturot*, and Thackeray of Dumas,[2] and still ranks him with Sue and on its earlier Soulié. But the Paturot part itself is simply part. delightful, and must have sent many who were not fortunate enough to know (or fortunate enough *not* to know) it already to the book. This well deserved and deserves to be known. Jérôme's own earlier career as a romantic and unread poet is not so brilliantly done as similar things in Gautier's *Les Jeune-France* and other books ; but the Saint-Simonian sequel, in which so many *mil-huit-cent-trentiers* besides Jérôme himself and (so surprisingly) Sainte-Beuve indulged, is most capitally hit off. The hero's further experiences in company-meddling (with not dissimilar results to those experienced by Thackeray's own Samuel Titmarsh, and probably or certainly by Thackeray himself) ; and as the editor of a journal enticing the *abonné* with a *bonus*, which may be either a pair of boots, a greatcoat, or a *gigot* at choice ; the side-hits at law and medicine ; the relapse into trade and National Guardism ; the visit to the Tuileries ; the sad bankruptcy and the subsequent retirement to a little place in the prefecture of a remote department—all these things are treated in the best Gallic fashion, and with a certain weight of metal not always achievable by " Gigadibs, the literary man," whether Gallic or Anglo-Saxon. Reybaud himself was a serious historian, a student of social philosophy, who has the melancholy honour of having popularised, if he did not invent, the word " Socialist " and the cheerfuller one of having faithfully dealt with the thing Socialism. And Jérôme is well set off by his still more " Jeune-France " friend Oscar, a painter, not exactly a bad fellow, but a *poseur*,

---

[1] *Jérôme Paturot, with Considerations on Novels in General*, originally appeared in *Fraser* for September 1843. Not reprinted in the author's lifetime, or till the supplementary collection of 1885–86. May be found, with some remarks by the present writer, in the " Oxford " Thackeray, vol. vi. pp. 318–342.

[2] It is fair to say that some of the best Alexandriana were still to come.

a dauber (he would have been a great Futurist or Cubist to-day), a very Bragadochio in words and flourish, and, alas ! as he turns out presently, a Bragadochio also in deeds and courage.

But the gem of the book perhaps, as far as good novel-matter is concerned (for Jérôme himself is not much The windfall more than a stalking - horse for satire), is of Malvina. Malvina, his first left-handed and then "regularised" spouse, and very much his better half. Malvina is Paul de Kock's grisette (like all good daughters, she is very fond of her literary father) raised to a higher power, dealt with in a satiric fashion unknown to her parent, but in perfectly kindly temper. She is, though just a little imperious, a thoroughly "good sort," and, with occasional blunders, really a guardian angel to her good-hearted, not uncourageous, but visionary and unpractical lover and husband. She has the sharpest of tongues ; the most housewifely and motherly of attitudes ; the flamingest of bonnets. It is she who suggests Saint-Simonianism (as a resource, not as a creed), and actually herself becomes a priestess of the first class—till the funds give out. She, being an untiring and unabashed canvasser, gets Jérôme his various places ; she reconciles his nightcap-making uncle to him ; she, when the pair go to the Palace and he is basely occupied with supper, carries him off in dudgeon because none of the princes (and in fact nobody at all) has asked her to dance. And when at last he subsides upon his shelf at the country prefecture, she becomes delightfully domesticated—and keeps canaries.

The book (at least its first two parts) appeared in 1843, when the July Monarchy was still in days of such palminess as it ever possessed, and Thackeray reviewed it soon after. At the close of his article he expressed a hope that M. Reybaud "had more of it, in brain or portfolio, for the benefit of the lazy, novel-reading, unscientific world." Whether, at that time, the hope was in course of gratification I do not know ; but years later, when February had killed July, Thackeray's wish was granted. It cannot be said that, as too often happens with wishes, the result was entirely disappointing; but it certainly justified the famous description of a still larger number of them, in that only half was granted and the rest " whistled down the wind."

Jérôme Paturot à la recherche de la meilleure des Républiques almost dooms itself, by its title, to be a very much less merry book than *Jérôme Paturot à la recherche d'une position sociale.* The " sparkle " which Thackeray had justly seen in the first part is far rarer in the second; in fact, were it not for Oscar to some extent and Malvina to a much greater, there would hardly be any sparkle at all. The Republic has been proclaimed; a new " Commissary " (" Prefect " is an altogether unrepublican word) is appointed; he is shortly after stirred up to vigorous action (usually in the way of cashiering officials), and Jérôme is a victim of this *mot d'ordre.* He goes to Paris to solicit; after a certain interval (of course of failure) Malvina comes to look after him, and to exercise the charms of her *chapeau grénat* once more. But even she fails to find the birds which (such as they were) she had caught in the earlier years' nests, until after the bloodshed of the barricades, where Oscar unfortunately fails to show himself a hero, while Jérôme does useful work as a fighter on the side of comparative Order, and Malvina herself shines as a nurse. At last Paturot is appointed " Inspector-General of Arab Civilisation in North Africa," and the pair set out for this promised, if not promising, land. He, like Gigadibs, provides himself with " instruments of labour "; Malvina, agreeable to the last, provides *herself* with several new dress-patterns of the latest fashion, and a complete collection of the *Journal des Modes.*

This not very elaborate scenario, as worked out, fills nearly a thousand pages; but it is very much to be feared that the " lazy novel-reader " will get through but a few of them, and will readily return the book to his own or other library shelves. It is, in fact, a bitterly satiric but perfectly serious study—almost history—of

The difference of the Second Part.

the actual events of the earlier part of the interregnum between Louis Philippe and Napoleon the Third, of the latter of whom Reybaud (writing, it would seem, before he was even President), gives a very unflattering, though unnamed, description. Certainly more than half, perhaps more than three-quarters, of the book can claim no novel character at all.[1]

It would be possible to extract (if one had space and it were proportionately worth while) passages from the remaining portion of very fair novel interest— Not much of a novel. the visit of the "Super-Commissary" to the Commissary; the history of the way in which, under the *régime* of that *atelier national* which some wiseacres want now with us, a large body of citizens was detailed to carry trees of liberty from a nursery garden in the suburbs of Paris to the *boulevards*; how these were uprooted without any regard to their arboreal welfare; how the national working-men got mainly drunk and wholly skylarky on the way, and how the unfortunate vegetables were good for nothing but firewood by the time they reached their destination; the humours of the open-air feast of the Republic; the storming of the Assembly by the clubs; the oratory of Malvina (a very delectable morsel) in one of the said clubs devoted to the Rights of Women;[2] the scene where Oscar, coming by his own account from the barricades "with his hands and his feet and his raiment all red," manifests a decided disinclination to return thither—all these are admirable. But they would have to be dug out of a mass of history and philosophy which the "lazy novel-reader" would, it is to be feared, refuse with by no means lazy indignation and disgust.

Yet one may venture, at the risk of the charge of

---

[1] The retort courteous, if not even the countercheck quarrelsome, "Then why do you notice it?" is pretty obvious. Taking it as the former, it may be answered, "The political novel, if not the most strictly legitimate species of the kind, is numerous and not unimportant. It may therefore be allowed a specimen, and an examination of that specimen."

[2] Malvina, as one might expect, is by this time an "Anti-" of the most stalwart kind; though, in the Saint-Simonian salad days, she had (as naturally) taken the other side.

stepping out of one's proper sphere, to recommend the perusal of the book, very strongly, to all who care either
But an invaluable document. to understand its "moment" or to prepare themselves for other moments which are at least announced as certain to come. The French revolutionary period of 1848 and the following years was perhaps the most perfect example in all history of a thing being allowed to show itself, in all its natural and therefore ineluctable developments, without disturbing influences of any kind. It was (if one may use patristic if not classical Latin in the first word of the phrase) *Revolutio sibi permissa*. There was, of course, a good deal of somewhat similar trouble elsewhere in Europe at the time ; but there was no European war of much importance, and no other power threatened or was in a position to threaten interference with French affairs—for the excellent reason that all were too much occupied with their own. There was no internal tyranny or trouble such as had undoubtedly caused—and as has been held by some to justify—the outburst of sixty years earlier, nor was there even any serious, though perhaps there was some minor, maladministration. But there had been, for twenty years, a weak, amorphous, discreditable, and discredited government ; and there was a great deal of revolutionary spirit, old and new, about. So France determined — in a word unacademic but tempting—to " revolute," and she " revoluted " at discretion, or indiscretion, to the top of her bent. This part of *Jérôme Paturot* gives a minute and (having had a good deal to do with the study both of history and of politics in my time), I think I may say boldly, a faithful account of *how* she did it. And I think, further, that, if at least some of the innocent folk who the other day hailed the dawn of the Russian revolution had been acquainted with the book, they might have been less jubilant ; while acquaintance would have helped others to anticipate the actual consequences. And I wish that some one would, in some form or other, bring its contents before those who, without being actual

scoundrels, utter fanatics, or hopeless fools, want to bring revolution nearer home. Reybaud brings out, too verbosely and heavily perhaps, but with absolute truth and justice, the waste, the folly, the absolute illogicality of the popular cries, movements, everything. "Labour" was, happily, not then organised in France as it is in England to-day. But if any one would extract, and translate in a pamphlet form, the dying speech of the misguided tool Comtois in reference to his misleader, the typical "shop-steward" Percheron, he would do a mighty good deed.

Still, of course this is a parenthesis; and the parenthesis is a thing hateful, I am told, perhaps not to gods but to some men.

Students of literature, even in a single language, much more in wider range, are well acquainted with a class of writers, largely increased since the introduction of printing, and more largely still since that of "periodicals," who enjoy a considerable—sometimes almost a great—reputation in their own time, and then are not so much discredited or disapproved as simply forgotten. They disappear, and their habitation is hardly even the dust-bin; it is the *oubliette*; and their places are taken by others whose fates are *not* other. In fact, they are, in the famous phrase, "Priests who slay the slayer," etc.

Of these, in French, I myself hardly know a more remarkable example than Joseph Méry, who, born two years before the end of the eighteenth century, lived for just two-thirds of the nineteenth, wrote, from a very early age till his death, in prose and in verse and in drama; epics, satires, criticisms, novels, travels, Heaven knows what; who had the reputation of being one of the most brilliant talkers of his day; who collaborated [1] with Gautier and Gérard de Nerval and Sandeau and Mme. de Girardin, and other people much greater than himself; from whose pen the beloved

Méry.

---

[1] Probably more people know *La Croix de Berny*, which he wrote with Sandeau, Gautier, and Madame de Girardin, than anything exclusively his.

old " Collection Michel Lévy " contained at least thirty volumes at the date of his death—the wreckage of perhaps a possible three hundred—and of whom, though I have several times in the half-century since dived into his work, I do not think I can find a single story of first, second, or even third-rate quality.[1]

As it happens, one volume of his, *Les Nuits Anglaises*, contains examples of his various manners, some of *Les Nuits* which may be noticed. Not all of them are *Anglaises.* stories, but it is fair to throw in a non-story because it is so very much better than the others. This is a " physionomie " of Manchester, written, it would · seem, just at the beginning of the reign of Queen Victoria ; and it shows that Méry, as a writer of those middle articles or transformed *Spectator* essays, which have played so large a part in the literature of the last century and a quarter, was not quite a negligible person. Moreover, the sort of thing, though not essential to the novelist's art, is a valuable tool at his disposal.

But here the author, who was a considerable traveller and not a bad judge of art, was to a large extent under The minor the grip of fact : when he got into fiction he stories. exhibited a sad want of discipline. One must allow something, no doubt, for the fact that the *goguenard* element is avowedly strong in him. The second English Night, with its Oxfordshire election (he has actually got the name of " Parker " right, though Woodstock wobbles from the proper form to " Woo-stock," " Wostoog," etc.) and its experiences of an Indian gentleman who is exposed at Ellora (near Madras) to the influence of the upas tree, by a wicked emissary of the Royal Society, Sir Wales, as a scientific experiment ; and the last, where two Frenchmen, liberated from the hulks at the close of the Napoleonic War, make a fortune by threatening to blow up the city of Dublin ; may sue out their writ of ease under the statute of Goguenarderie. A third half-Eastern, half-English story (Méry was

---

[1] Others may have been more fortunate. In any case, what follows, whatever its intrinsic merit, is typical of a great mass of similar French fiction, and therefore may claim attention here.

fond of the East), *Anglais et Chinois*, telling quite delicately the surprising adventures of a mate of H.M.S. *Jamesina*[1] in a sort of Chinese harem, has some positive merit, though it is too long. The longest and most ambitious tale, *Histoire d'une Colline*, if not " wholly serious " (as a famous phrase has it), seems to aim at a good deal of seriousness. Yet it is, as a matter of fact, rather more absurd than the pure extravaganzas.

Sir John Lively—who appears neither to have inherited the title (seeing that his sainted father, a victim of English *Histoire d'une* tyranny, was named Arthur O'Tooley, perhaps *Colline.* one of the tailors of that ilk) nor to have paid M. Méry five or ten thousand pounds for it—is an Irishman of the purest virtue and the noblest sentiments, who possesses a cottage on a hill not far from the village and castle of Stafford. From this interesting height there are two views : one over the beautiful plains of Lancashire, another towards the brumous mountains of Oxfordshire. Lively always looks this latter way, because in coming from London he has seen, at the other village of Bucks, a divine creature who dispenses soda-water and some stronger liquors to the thirsty. She, like the ninepenny kettle of the song, " is Irish *tu*," and belongs to the well-known sept of the O'Killinghams. They are both fervent Roman Catholics (Méry is astoundingly severe on our " apostate " church, with its " insulted " Saint Paul's and Saint Martin's). She is also persecuted by an abominable English landlord, Mr. Igoghlein. The two meet at mass in " *the* Catholic Church of the City," to which, " as in the time of Diocletian " (slightly altered to 1830–40), " a few faithful ones furtively glide, and

---

[1] It would be interesting to know where Méry got this hideous, cacophonous, hopelessly anti-analogical and anti-etymological but, alas ! actually existing name. I never heard of a ship called by it, but I once knew a poor lady on whom it had been inflicted at her baptism. Why any one with Jemima (not, of course, originally a feminine of " Jem," but adopted as such), which, though a little comic, is not intolerable, Jacqueline and Jaquetta (which are exceedingly pretty), and Jacobina (which, though with unfortunate historical associations, is not itself ugly) to choose from, should have invented this horrible solecism, I never could make out. It is, I believe, confined to Scotland, and the only comfort connected with it is the negative one that, in two considerable residences there, I never heard of a " *Charles*ina." I suppose " Caroline " and " Charlotte " sufficed ; or, perhaps, while Whigs disliked the name (at least before that curious purifier of it, Fox); Tories shrank from profanation thereof.

seem to be in fear." To get money, Lively gambles,
and (this is the sanest part of the book, for the reason
that things went on in much the same way at Paris and
at London) is cheated. But the cottage, and the hill
with such commanding views, are discovered to be in
the way of a new line and to conceal coal. He sells
them to a Mr. Copperas ; marries the beautiful O'Killingham ; the bells of Dublin ring head over heels, " and
Ireland hopes." Let it also be mentioned that in the
course of the story we are more than once told of the
double file of Mauresque, Spanish, Gothic, and Italian
colonnades which line the marvellous High Street of
Oxford ; and that Mr. Copperas visited that seat of
learning to consult an expert in railways [1] and see his
three largest shareholders. (Oh, these bloated dons !)
That three members of " the society of *ti*total abstinence "
drank, at the beautiful O'Killingham's cottage, twenty
pints of porter (White-bread), two flagons of whisky,
and three of claret, may meet with less incredulity, though
the assortment of liquor is barbarous and the quantity
is certainly large. But let us turn from this nonsense
to the remarkable Manchester article.

It was not for some thirty years later than Méry's
visit that I myself knew, and for some time lived in, the
The "Man- new-made " city," as it became, to the horror
chester" of Mr. Bright, just before Méry saw it. But
article. though there must have been many changes
in those thirty years, they were nothing to those which
have taken place in the fifty that have passed subsequently.
And I can recognise the Manchester I knew in Méry's
sketch. This may seem to be at first an exceedingly
moderate compliment—in fact something close to an
insult. But it is nothing of the kind. It is true that
there is considerable *naïveté* in a sentence of his own :
" En général les nationaux sont fort ignorants sur les
phénomènes de leur pays ; il faut s'adresser aux étran-
gers pour en obtenir la solution." And it is also true

---

[1] Was it Mr. Augustus Dunshunner ? It was just about the time of the Glen-
mutchkin Railway, and most of " Maga's " men were Oxonians.

that our " nationals," at that time and since, have been excessively ignorant of phenomena which the French tourists of Louis Philippe's reign discovered here, and surprised, not to say diverted, at the solutions thereof preferred by these obliging strangers. That Méry had something of the Michiels [1] in him, what has been said above should show. But in some strange way Manchester—foggiest and rainiest of all our industrial hells,[2] except Sheffield—seems to have made his brain clear and his sight dry, even in drawing a sort of half-Rembrandt, half-Callot picture. He takes, it is true, some time in freeing himself from that obsession by one of our *not*-prettiest institutions, " street-walking," which has always beset the French.[3] But he does get clear, and makes a striking picture of the great thoroughfares of Market Street and Piccadilly ; of the view—a wonderful one certainly, and then not interfered with by railway viaducts—from and of the Cathedral ; and of the extraordinary utilisation of the scanty " naval " capabilities of Irk and Irwell and Medlock. But, as has been said, such things are at best but accidents of the novel.

If not much is found here about Alphonse Karr, it is certainly not because the present writer undervalues his general literary position. As a journalist and miscellanist, Karr had few superiors in a century of miscellaneous journalism ; and as a maker of telling and at the same time solid phrase, he was Voltaire's equal in the first respect and his superior in the second. The immortal " Que MM. les assassins commencent," already referred to, is perhaps the best example in all literature of the terse *argumentum joculare* which is not more sparkling as a joke than it is crushing as an argument ; " Plus ça change plus c'est la

Karr.

---

[1] See in vol. v. of the Oxford edition of Thackeray (for the thing, though never acknowledged, is certainly his) an exemplary " justification " of this very impudent offender.

[2] I have no quarrel with Manchester—quite the reverse—in consequence of divers sojourns, longer and shorter, in the place, and of much kindness shown me by the not at all barbarous people. But neither the climate nor the general " conditions " of the city can be called paradisaical.

[3] They were as much shocked at it as we were at their " Houses of Tolerance " and at the institution of the *grisette*.

même chose"[1] is nearly as good; and if one were writing a history, not of the novel, but of journalism or essay-writing of the lighter kind, Karr would have high place and large room. But as a novelist he does not seem to me to be of much importance, nor even as a tale-teller, except of the anecdotic kind. He can hardly be dull, and you seldom read him long without coming to something[2] refreshing in his own line; but his tales, as tales, are rarely first-rate, and I do not think that even *Sous les Tilleuls*, his best-known and perhaps best production, needs much delay over it.

Roger de Beauvoir (whose *de* was genuine, but who embellished "Bully," his actual surname, into the one

Roger de Beauvoir— Les Cabaret des Morts.

by which he was generally known) also had, like Bernard and Reybaud, the honour of being noticed, translated, and to some extent commented on by Thackeray.[3] I have, in old times, read more of his novels than I distinctly remember; and they are not very easy to procure in England now. Moreover, though he was of the right third or fourth *cru* of *mil-huit-cent-trente*, there was something wanting in his execution. I have before me a volume of short stories, excellently entitled (from the first of them) *Le Cabaret des Morts*. One imagines at once what Poe or Gautier, what even Bulwer or Washington Irving, would have made of this. Roger (one may call him this without undue familiarity, because it is the true factor in both his names) has a good idea—the muster of defunct painters in an ancient Antwerp pot-house at ghost-time, and their story-telling. The contrast of them with the beautiful *living* barmaid might have been—but is not—

---

[1] Not the worst perhaps of the myriad attempts to do something of the same kind in English was made recently: " If a man conscientiously objects to be shot *for* his country, he may be conscientiously shot *by* it."

[2] Here is one from " Un Diamant " (*Contes et Nouvelles*), which, though destitute of the charms of poetry, rivals and perhaps indeed suggested our own

> And even an Eastern Counties' train
> Comes in at last.

" Quelque loin qu'on aille, on finit par arriver ; *on arrive bien à Saint-Maur—trois lieues à faire—en coucou.*"

[3] In the same article in which he dealt with Charles de Bernard.

made extremely effective. In fact the fatal improbability —in the Aristotelian, not the Barbauldian sense— broods over the whole. And the Cabaret des Morts itself ceases, not in a suitable way, but because the Burgomaster shuts it up ! ! ! All the other stories—one of Marie Antoinette's Trianon dairy; another of an anonymous pamphlet; yet another of an Italian noble and his use of malaria for vengeance; as well as the last, told by a Sister of Mercy while watching a patient—miss fire in one way or another, though all have good subjects and are all in a way well told. It is curious, and might be made rather instructive by an intelligent Professor of the Art of Story-telling, who should analyse the causes of failure. But it is somewhat out of the way of the mere historian.[1]

Édouard Ourliac, one of the minor and also one of the shorter-lived men of 1830, seems to have been *Ourliac—* pleasant in his life—at least all the personal *Contes du* references to him that I remember to have seen, *Bocage.* in a long course of years, were amiable; and he is still pleasant in literature. He managed, though he only reached the middle of the road, to accumulate work enough for twelve volumes of collection, while probably more was uncollected. Of what I have read of his, the *Contes* and *Nouveaux Contes du Bocage*—tales of La Vendée, with a brief and almost brilliant, certainly vivid, sketch of the actual history of that glorious though ill-fated struggle—deserve most notice. Two of the *Nouveaux Contes*, *Le Carton D.* (a story of the rescue of her husband by a courageous woman, with the help of the more amiable weaknesses of the only amiable Jacobin leader, Danton) and *Le Chemin de Keroulaz* (one of treachery only half-defeated on the Breton coast), may rank with all but the very best of their kind. In another, *Belle-Fontaine*, people who cannot be content with a story unless it instructs their minds on points of history,

---

[1] I know that many people do not agree with me here; but Blake did: " Tell me the facts, O historian, and leave me to reason on them as I please; away with your reasoning and your rubbish. . . . Tell me the What: I do not want you to tell me the Why and the How. I can find that out for myself."

morality, cosmogony, organo-therapy, and everything
quod exit in y, except jollity and sympathy, may find a
section on the youth of 1830—really interesting to compare
with the much less enthusiastic account by Gérard de
Nerval, which is given above.   And those who like
to argue about cases of conscience may be glad to discuss
whether Jean Reveillère, in the story which bears his
name, *ought* to have spared, as he actually did, the accursed
conventionnel, who, after receiving shelter and care from
women of Jean's family, had caused them to be massacred
by the *bleus*, and then again fell into the Vendéan's hands.

But, with one or two more notices, we must close
this chapter.

Although Dumas, by an odd anticipatory reversal
of what was to be his son's way, spent a great deal of
time on more or less trashy[1] plays before he took to
his true line of romance, and so gave opportunity to
others to get a start of him in the following of Scott,
it was inevitable that his own immense success should
stir emulation in this kind afresh.   In a way, even, Sue
and Soulié may be said to belong to the class of his
unequal competitors, and others may be noticed briefly
in this place or that.   But there is one author who, for
one book at least, belonging to the successors rather
than the *avant-coureurs*, but decidedly of the pre-Empire
kind, must have a more detailed mention.

Many years ago somebody was passing the small
tavern which, dating for aught I know to the times of

Achard.   Henry Esmond, and still, or very lately, surviving, sustained the old fashion of a thorough-
fare, fallen, but still fair, and fondly loved of some—
Kensington High Street, just opposite the entrance to the
Palace.   The passer-by heard one loiterer in front of it say
to his companion in a tone of emotion, and almost of awe:

[1] If my friend Mr. Henley were alive (and I would he were) I should have to " look
out for squalls."   It was, as ought to be well known, his idea that *Henri Trois et Sa
Cour* was much more the rallying trumpet of 1830 than *Hernani*, and I believe a large
part of his dislike for Thackeray was due to the cruel fun which *The Paris Sketch-book*
makes of *Kean*.   But I speak as I think and find, after long re-thinking and researching.

" There was beef, and beer, and bread, and greens, and
everything you can imagine." This *pheme* occurred to me
when, after more than half a century, I read again Amédée
Achard's *Belle-Rose*. I had taken it up with some qualms
lest crabbed age should not confirm the judgment of
ardent youth ; and for a short space the extreme
nobility of its sentiments did provoke the giggle of
degeneracy. But forty of the little pages of its four
original volumes had not been turned when it reassured
me as to the presence of " beef, and beer, and bread,
and greens, and everything you can imagine " in its
particular style of romance. The hero, who begins as a
falconer's son and ends as a rich enough colonel in the
army and a Viscount by special grace of the Roi Soleil,
is a *sapeur*, but far indeed from being one of those grace-
less comrades of his to whom nothing is sacred. At one
time he does indeed succumb to the sorceries of a certain
Geneviève de Châteaufort, a duchess *aux narines frémis-
santes*. But who could resist this combination ? even if
there were a marquise of the most beautiful and virtuous
kind, only waiting to be a widow in order to be lawfully his.
Besides, the Lady of the Quivering Nostrils becomes an
abbess, her rather odd abbey somehow accommodating
not merely her own irregularly arrived child (*not* Belle-
Rose's), but Belle-Rose himself and his marchioness after
their marriage ; and she is poisoned at the end in the
most admirably retributive fashion. There are actually
two villains—a pomp and prodigality (for your villain is
a more difficult person than your hero) very unusual—
one of whom is despatched at the end of the second volume
and the other at the actual curtain. There is the proper
persecuting minister—Louvois in this case. There are
valiant and comic non-commissioned officers. There
is a brave, witty, and generous Count ; a lover of the
" fatal " and ill-fated kind ; his bluff and soldierly
brother ; and more of the " affair of the poisons " than
even that mentioned above. You have the Passage
of the Rhine, fire-raisings, duels, battles, skirmishes,
ambuscades, treachery, chivalry—in fact, what you will

comes in. And you must be a very ill-conditioned or feeble-minded person if you *don't* will. Every now and then one might, no doubt, " smoke " a little reminiscence ; more frequently slight improbabilities ; everywhere, of course, an absence of any fine character-drawing. But these things are the usual spots, and very pardonable ones, of the particular sun. I do not remember any French book of the type, outside the Alexandrian realm, that is as good as *Belle-Rose* ;[1] and I am bound to say that it strikes me as better than anything of its kind with us, from James and Ainsworth to the excellent lady[2] who wrote *Whitehall*, and *Whitefriars*, and *Owen Tudor*.

It must, however, be evident that of this way in making books, and of speaking of them, there is no end.[3]

Souvestre, Féval, etc. Fain would I dwell a little on Émile Souvestre, in whom the " moral heresy," of which he was supposed to be a sectary, certainly did not corrupt the pure milk of the tale-telling gift in such charming things as *Les Derniers Bretons*, *Le Foyer Breton*, and the rather different *Un Philosophe sous les Toits* ; also on the better work of Paul Féval, who as certainly did not invariably do suit and service to morality, but Sue'd and Soulié'd it in many books with promising titles ;[4] and who, once at least, was inspired (again by the witchery of the country between the Baie des Trépassés and the Rock of Dol) to write *La Fée des Grèves*, a most agreeable thing of its kind. Auguste Maquet (or Augustus MacKeat) will come better in the next chapter, for reasons obvious to some readers no doubt already, but to be made so to others there. And so—for this division or

[1] I have made some further excursions in the work of Achard, but they did not incline me to continue them, and I do not propose to say anything of the results here. I learn from the books that there were some other Achards, one of whom " improved the production of beet-root sugar." I would much rather have written *Belle-Rose*.

[2] Emma Robinson. I used, I think, to prefer her to either of her more famous companions in the list. But I never read her *Caesar Borgia*. It sounds appetising.

[3] Some may say, " There might have been an end much sooner with some of the foregoing." Perhaps so—once more. I do not claim to be *hujus orbis Papa* and infallible. But I sample to the best of my knowledge and judgment.

[4] *Beau Démon, Cœur d'Acier, La Tache Rouge*, etc. Féval began a little later than most of the others in this chapter, but he is of their class.

subdivision—an end, with one word more on Pétrus Borel's *Champavert*.

Borel, whose real Christian name, it is almost unnecessary to say, was Pierre, and who was a sort of incarnation *Borel's* of a "Jeune-France" (beginning as a *bousingot* *Champavert.* —not ill translated by the contemporary English "bang-up" for an extreme variety of the kind—and ending as a *sous-préfet*), wrote other things, including a longer and rather tedious novel, *Madame Putiphar*. But the tales of *Champavert*,[1] which had the doubly-"speaking" sub-title of *Contes Immoraux*, are capital examples of the more literary kind of "rotting." They are admirably written ; they show considerable power. But though one would not be much surprised at reading any day in the newspaper a case in which a boatman, plying for hire, had taken a beautiful girl for "fare," violated her on the way, and thrown her into the river, the subject is not one for art.

[1] Thackeray, when very young and wasting his time and money in editing the *National Standard*, wrote a short and very savage review of this which may be found in the Oxford Edition of his works (vol. i., as arranged by the present writer). It is virtuously indignant (and no wonder, seeing that the writer takes it quite seriously), but, as Thackeray was almost to the last when in that mood, quite bull-in-a-china-shoppy. You *might* take it seriously, and yet critically in another way, as a "degeneracy" of the Terror-Novel. But the "rotting" view is better.

CHAPTER VIII

DUMAS THE ELDER

With Dumas [1] *père* the same difficulties (or nearly the same) of general and particular nature present themselves The case of as those which occurred with Balzac. There Dumas. is, again, the task—not so arduous and by no means so hopeless as some may think, but still not of the easiest—of writing pretty fully without repetition on subjects on which you have written fully already. There is the enormous bulk, far greater than in the other case, of the work: which makes any complete survey of its individual components impossible. And there is the wide if not universal knowledge of this or that—if not of this *and* that—part of it; which makes such survey unnecessary and probably unwelcome. But here, as there, in whatever contrast of degree and kind, there is the importance in relation to the general subject, which needs pretty abundant notice, and the particular character of that importance, which demands special examination.

There are probably not quite so many readers as there might have been a generation ago who would express indignation at the idea that the two novelists can be

---

[1] The postponement of him, to this last chapter of the first division of the book, was determined on chiefly because his *novels* were not begun at all till years after the other greater novelists, already dealt with, had made their reputation, while the greatest of them—the " Mousquetaire " and " Henri Trois " cycles—did not appear till the very last *lustrum* of the half-century. But another—it may seem to some a childish—consideration had some weight with me. I wished to range father and son on either side of the dividing summary; for though the elder wrote long after 1850 and the younger some time before it, in hardly any pair is the opposition of the earlier and later times more clearly exposed ; and the identity of name emphasises the difference of nature.

· held in any degree [1] comparable. Between the two periods a pretty strong and almost concerted effort was made by persons of no small literary position, such as Mr. Lang, Mr. Stevenson, and Mr. Henley, who are dead, and others, some of whom are alive, to follow the lead of Thackeray many years earlier still. They denounced, supporting the denunciation with all the literary skill and vigour of which they were capable, the notion, common in France as well as in England, that Dumas was a mere *amuseur*, whether they did or did not extend their battery to the other notion (common then in England, if not in France) that he was an amuser whose amusements were pernicious. These efforts were perhaps not entirely ineffectual; let us hope that actual reading, by not unintelligent or prejudiced readers, had more effect still.

But let us also go back a little and, adding one, repeat what the charges against Dumas are. There is the Charge and moral charge just mentioned; there is the discharge. not yet mentioned charge of plagiarism and "devilling"; and there is the again already mentioned complaint that he is a mere "pastimer"; that he has no literary quality; that he deserves at best to take his chance with the novelists from Sue to Gaboriau who have been or will be dismissed with rather short shrift elsewhere. Let us, as best seems to suit history, treat these in order, though with very unequal degrees of attention.

The moral part of the matter needs but a few lines. The objection here was one of the still fewer things Morality. that did to some extent justify and "*sensify*" the nonsense and injustice since talked about Victorian criticism. In fact this nonsense may (there

---

[1] In using this phrase I remembered the very neat "score" made off the great Alexander himself by a French judge, in some case at Rouen where Dumas was a witness. Asked as usual his occupation, he replied somewhat grandiloquently: "Monsieur, si je n'étais pas dans la ville de Corneille, je dirais ' Auteur dramatique.'" "Mais, Monsieur," replied the official with the sweetest indulgence, "il y a des degrés." (This story is told, like most such, with variants; and sometimes, as in the particular case was sure to happen, not of Alexander the father, but of Alexander the son. But I tell it, as I read or heard it, long years ago.)

is always, or nearly always, some use to be made even of nonsense) be used against its earlier brother. It is customary to objurgate Thackeray as too moral. Thackeray never hints the slightest objection on this score against these novels, whatever he may do as to the plays. For myself, I do not pretend to have read everything that Dumas published. There may be among the crowd something indefensible, though it is rather odd that if there is, I should not merely never have read it but never have heard of it. If, on the other hand, any one brings forward Mrs. Grundy's opinion on the Ketty and Milady passages in the *Mousquetaires*; on the story of the origin of the Vicomte de Bragelonne ; on the way in which the divine Margot was consoled for her almost tragic abandonment in a few hours by lover and husband—I must own that as Judge on the present occasion I shall not call on any counsel of Alexander's to reply. "Bah ! it is bosh," as the greatest of Dumas' admirers remarks of another matter.

The plagiarism (or rather devilling + plagiarism) article of the indictment, tedious as it may be, requires a little Plagiarism longer notice. The facts, though perhaps and devilling. never to be completely established, are sufficiently clear as far as history needs, on the face of them. Dumas' works, as published in complete edition, run to rather over three hundred volumes. (I have counted them often on the end-papers of the beloved tomes, and though they have rather a knack, like the windows of other enchanted houses, of " coming out " different, this is near enough.) Excluding theatre (twenty-five volumes), travels, memoirs, and so-called history, they must run to about two hundred and fifty. Most if not all of these volumes are of some three hundred pages each, very closely printed, even allowing for the abundantly "spaced" conversation. I should say, without pretending to an accurate " cast-off," that any *three* of these volumes would be longer even than the great " part "-published works of Dickens, Thackeray, or Trollope ; that any *two* would exceed in length our own

old average " three-decker "; and that any *one* contains
at least twice the contents of the average six-shilling
masterpiece of the present day.

Now it stands to reason that a man who spent only
the later part of his working life in novel-production,
who travelled a great deal, and who, according to his
enemies, devoted a great deal of time to relaxation,[1]
is not likely to have written all this enormous bulk
himself, even if it were physically possible for him to
have done so. One may go farther, and say that pure
internal evidence shows that the whole was *not* written
by the same person.

As for the actual collaborators—the "young men,"
as Thackeray obligingly called them, who carried out
the works in a less funereal sense than that in
which the other " young men " carried out
Ananias and Sapphira—that is a question on which I
do not feel called upon to enter at any length. Anybody
who cannot resist curiosity on the point may consult
Alphonse Karr (who really might have found something
fitter on which to expend his energies); Quérard, an
ill-tempered bibliographer, for whom there is the excuse
that, except ill-temper, idleness, with a particularly
malevolent Satan to find work for its hands to do, or
mere hunger, hardly anything would make a man a
bibliographer of his sort ; and the person whom the law
called Jacquot, and he himself by the handsomer title
of Eugène de Mirecourt. Whether Octave Feuillet
exercised himself in this other kind before he took to his
true line of novels of society ; whether that ingenious
journalist M. Fiorentino also played a part, are matters
which who so lists may investigate. The most dangerous
competitor seems to be Auguste Maquet—the " Augustus
MacKeat " of the Romantic dawn—to whom some have

The colla-
borators ?

---

[1] You may possibly do as an English novelist of the privileged sex is said to have
done, and write novels while people are calling on you and you are talking to them (though
I should myself consider it bad manners, and the novels would certainly bear traces of
the exploit). But you can hardly do it while, as a famous caricature represents the scene,
persons of that same sex, in various dress or undress, are frolicking about your chair
and bestowing on you their obliging caresses. Nor are corricolos and speronares, though
they may be good things to write on in one sense, good in another to write in.

even assigned the *Mousquetaires* [1] bodily, as far as the
novel adds to the Courtils de Sandras "memoirs." But
even with him, and still more with the others, the good old
battle-horse, which never fails one in this kind of *chevau-
chée*, will be found to be effective in carrying the banner
of Alexander the Greatest safe through. How does it
happen that in the independent work of none of these,
nor of any others, do the *special* marks and merits of
Dumas appear ? How does it happen that these marks
and merits appear constantly and brilliantly in all the
best work assigned to Dumas, and more fitfully in almost
all its vast extent ? There may be a good deal of apple
in some plum-jam and perhaps some vegetable-marrow.
But plumminess is plumminess still, and it is the plumminess of "Dumasity" which we are here to talk of, and that
only—the quality, not the man. And whether Dumas
or Diabolus conceived and brought it about matters, in
the view of the present historian, not a *centime*. By
"Dumas" is here and elsewhere—throughout this
chapter and throughout this book—meant Dumasity,
which is something by itself, and different from all other
"-nesses and -tudes and -ties."

We can therefore, if we choose, betake ourselves with
a joyful and quiet mind to the real things—the actual
The positive characteristics of that Dumasity, Diabolicity,
value as or *Dieu-sait-quoi*, which distinguishes (in
fiction and as measures and degrees varying, perhaps essenti-
literature of ally, certainly according to the differing castes ·
the books: of readers) the great Mousquetaire trilogy ;
the less
worthy works. the hardly less great collection of *La Reine
Margot* and its continuations ; the long eighteenth-
century set which, in a general way, may be said to be
two-centred, having now Richelieu (the Duke, not the
Cardinal) and now Cagliostro for pivot ; and *Monte
Cristo*—with power to add to their number. In what
will be said, attention will chiefly be paid to the books
just mentioned, and perhaps a few more, such as *La*

---

[1] As far as I know Maquet, his line seems to me to have been drama rather than
fiction.

Tulipe Noire ; nor is even this list so closed that anybody
may not consider any special favourites of his own
admissible as subjects for the almost wholly unmitigated
appreciation which will follow. I do not think that
Dumas was ever at his best before the late sixteenth
century or after the not quite latest eighteenth. *Isabel
de Bavière* and the *Bâtard de Mauléon*, with others, are
indeed more readable than most minor historical novels ;
but their wheels drive somewhat heavily. As for the
revolutionary set, after the *Cagliostro* interest is disposed
of, some people, I believe, rate *Le Chevalier de Maison
Rouge* higher than I do. It is certainly better than *Les
Blancs et les Bleus* or *Les Louves de Machecoul*, in the latter
of which Dumas has calmly " lifted " (or allowed a lazy
" young man " to lift) the whole adventure of Rob Roy
at the Fords of Frew, pretty nearly if not quite *verbatim*.[1]
Of more avowed translations such as *Ivanhoe* and *Jacques
Ortis* (the latter about as much out of his way as anything
could be), it were obviously superfluous to take detailed
notice. In others the very titles, such as, for instance,
Les Mohicans de Paris, show at once that he is merely
imitating popular styles. Yet others, such as *Madame
de Chamblay*[2] (in which I cannot help thinking that the
" young man " was Octave Feuillet not yet come to his
prime), have something of the ordinary nineteenth-century
novel—not of the best kind.

But in all these and many more it is simply a case of
" Not here ! " though in the historical examples, before
Saint Bartholomew and after Sainte-Guillotine, the sentence may be mitigated to " Not here *consummately*."
And it may be just, though only just, necessary to say
that this examination of Dumas' qualities should itself,
with very little application or moral, settle the question

---

[1] I seem to remember somebody (I rather think it was Henley, and it was very
likely to be) attempting a defence of this. But, except *pour rire*, such a thing is
hopeless.

[2] I think (but it is a long time since I read the book) that it is the heroine of this
who, supposed to be dead, escapes from " that grewsome thing, premature interment "
(as Sandy Mackay justly calls it), because of the remarkable odour of *violettes de Parme*
which her unspotted flesh evolves from the actual grave.

whether he is a mere circulating-library caterer or a producer of real literature.

To give brief specifications of books and passages in the novels mentioned above, in groups or individually, The worthier may seem open to the objections often made —treatment to a mere catalogue of likes and dislikes. of them not But, after all, in the estimation of aesthetic so much individually matters, it *is* likes and dislikes that count. as under Nowhere, and perhaps in this case less than heads. anywhere else, can the critic or the historian pretend to dispense his readers from actual perusal; it is sufficient, but it is at the same time necessary, that he should prepare those who have not read and remind those who have. For champion specimen-pieces, satisfying, not merely in parts but as wholes, the claim that Dumas shall be regarded as an absolute master in his own craft and in his own particular division of it, the present writer must still select, after fifty years' reading and re-reading, *Vingt Ans Après* and *La Reine Margot.* Parts of *Les Trois Mousquetaires* are unsurpassed and unsurpassable; but the Bonacieux love - affair is inadequate and intruded, and I have never thought Milady's seduction of Felton quite " brought off." In *Le Vicomte de Bragelonne* this inequality becomes much more manifest. Nothing, again, can surpass the single-handed achievement of D'Artagnan at the beginning in his kidnapping of General Monk, and few things his failure at the end to save Porthos, with the death of the latter—a thing which has hardly a superior throughout the whole range of the novel in whatever language (so far as I know) it has been written. But the " young men " were allowed their heads, by far too frequently and for too long periods, in the middle;[1] and these heads were by no means always equal to the occasion. There is no such declension in the immediate followers of *La Reine Margot, La Dame de Monsoreau,* and *Les Quarante-Cinq.*

[1] I do not mind Montalais, but I object to Malicozne both in himself and as her lover. Mlle. de la Vallière and the plots against her virtue give us " pious Selinda " at unconscionable length, and, but that it would have annoyed Athos, I rather wish M. le Vicomte de Bragelonne himself had come to an end sooner.

Chicot is supreme, but the personal interest is less distributed than in the first book and in the *Mousquetaire* trilogy.

This lack of distribution, and the inequalities of the actual adventures, are, naturally enough, more noticeable still in the longer and later series dealing with the eighteenth century, while, almost of necessity, the purely " romantic" interest is at a lower strength. I can, however, find very little fault with *Le Chevalier d'Harmental*—an excellent blend of lightness and excitement. *Olympe de Clèves* has had very important partisans; [1] but though I like Olympe herself almost better than any other of Dumas' heroines, except Marguerite, she does not seem to me altogether well " backed up"; and there is here, as there had been in the *Vicomte de Bragelonne*, and was to be in others, too much insignificant court-intrigue. The Cagliostro cycle again appeals very strongly to some good critics, and I own that in reading it a second time I liked it better than I had done before. But I doubt whether the supernatural of any kind was a circle in which Dumas could walk with perfect freedom and complete command of his own magic. There remains, as among the novels selected as pieces, not of conviction, but of diploma, *Monte Cristo*, perhaps the most popular of all, certainly one of the most famous, and still holding its popularity with good wits. Here, again, I have to confess a certain " correction of impression." As to the *Château d'If*, which is practically an independent book, there can hardly be two opinions among competent and unprejudiced persons. But I used to find the rest—the voluminous rest—rather heavy reading. Recently I got on better with them; but I can hardly say that they even now stand, with me, that supreme test of a novel, " Do you want to read it again?" I once, as an experiment, read " Wandering Willie's

---

[1] My friend Mr. Henley, I believe, ranked it very high, and so did a common friend of his and mine, the late universally regretted Mr. George Wyndham. It so happened that, by accident, I never read the book till a few years ago; and Mr. Wyndham saw it, fresh from the bookseller's and uncut (or technically, " unopened "), in my study. I told him the circumstances, and he said, in his enthusiastic way, " I *do* envy you !"

Tale " through, every night for a week, having read it
I don't know how many times before ; and I found it
no more staled at the seventh enjoyment than I should
have found the charm of Helen or of Cleopatra herself.
I do not know how many times I have read Scott's longer
novels (with one or two exceptions), or Dickens', or
Thackeray's, or not a few others in French and English,
including Dumas himself. And I hope to read them
all once, twice, or as many times more as those other
Times which are in Some One's hand will let me. But
I do not want to read *Monte Cristo* again.

It will be clear from these remarks that, whether
rightly or wrongly, I think Dumas happiest in his dealings
with historical or quasi-historical matters, these dealings
being subject to the general law, given more than once
elsewhere, that the historical personages shall not, in
their historically registered and detailed character, occupy
the chief positions in the story. In other words, he seems
to me to have preferred an historical canvas and a few
prominent figures outlined thereon—in which respect
he does not greatly differ from other historical novelists
so far as they are historical novelists merely. But
Dumas, as a novelist of French history, had at his disposal
sources and resources, for filling up his pictures, which
were lacking elsewhere, and which, in particular, English
novelists possessed hardly at all, as regards anything
earlier than the eighteenth century. I dare say it has
often occurred to other people, as it has to me, how
vastly different *Peveril of the Peak*—one of the least
satisfactory of Scott's novels—would have been if Pepys's
Diary had been published twenty years earlier instead of
two years later. Evelyn was available, but far less
suitable to the purpose, and was only published when
Scott had begun to write rather than to read.[1] For almost
every year, certainly for every decade and every notable
person's life with which and with whom he wished to
deal, Dumas had " Memoirs " on to which, if he did not
care to take the trouble himself, he had only to turn one

---

[1] I do not need to be reminded of the conditions of health that also affected *Peveril.*

of the "young men" to get facts, touches, ornaments, suggestions enough for twenty times his own huge production. Of course other people had these same stores open to them, and that other people did not make the same use thereof[1] is one of the chief glories of Alexander the Great in fiction. But in any real critical-historical estimate of him, the fact has to take its place, and its very great place.

But there is the other fact, or collection of facts, of greater importance still, implied in the question, " What did he do with these stores ? " and " How did he, as it seems to Alexandrians at least, do so much better than those other people, to whom they were open quite as freely ? "

It is, however, before answering these questions at large, perhaps once more necessary to touch on what may be called the historical-*accuracy* objection. If anybody says, " The man represents Charles I. as having been taken, after he had been sold by the Scotch, direct from Newcastle to London, tried at once, and executed in a day or two. This was not the way things happened " —you are bound to acknowledge his profound and recondite historical learning. But if he goes on to say that he cannot enjoy *Vingt Ans Après* as a novel because of this, you are equally bound to pity his still more profound aesthetic ignorance and impotence. The facts, in regard to the criticism of historical novels as such, illustrate the wisdom of Scott in keeping his historical characters for the most part in the background, and the *un*wisdom of Vigny in preferring the opposite course. But they do nothing more. If Dumas had chosen, he might have separated the dramatic meeting of the Four at Newcastle itself—and the intenser tale of their effort to save Charles, with its sequel of their own narrow escape from the *Éclair* felucca—by chapters, or a book, of adventures in France. But he did not choose ; and the liberty of juxtaposition which he took is more appar-

---

[1] I need not repeat, but merely refer to, what I have said of *Cinq-Mars* and of *Notre-Dame de Paris.*

ently than really different from that which Shakespeare
takes, when he jumps ten years in *Antony and Cleopatra*.
What Dumas *really* borrows from history—the tragic
interest of the King's fate—is in each case historically
true, though it is eked and adapted and manipulated
to suit the fictitious interest of the Quadrilateral. You
certainly could not, then or now, *ride* from Windsor to
London in twenty minutes, though you could now motor
the distance in the time, at the risk of considerable fines.
And an Englishman, jealous of his country's honour,
might urge that, while the "Vin *de Porto*" itself came in
rather later, there were few places in the England of the
seventeenth century where that "Vin *d'Espagne*," so
dear to Athos, was not more common than it was in
France, though one would not venture to deny that the
shortly-to-become Baron de Bracieux *had* some genuine
Xérès (as we are told) in his cellar. But these things
are—no more and no less than the greater ones—utter
trifles as far as the actual novel interest is concerned.
They are, indeed, less than trifles : they can hardly be
said to exist.

The "four wheels of the novel" have been sometimes,
and perhaps rightly, said to be Plot, Character, Descrip-
His attitude tion, and Dialogue—Style [1] being a sort of
to Plot.   fifth. Of the first there is some difficulty in
speaking, because the word "plot" is by no means used,
as the text-books say, "univocally," and its synonyms
or quasi-synonyms, in the different usages, are themselves
things "kittle" to deal with. "Action" is sometimes
taken as one of these synonyms—certainly in some senses
of action no novelist has ever had more ; very few have
had so much. But of concerted, planned, or strictly
co-ordinated action, of more than episode character, he

---

[1] On the very day on which I was going over the rough draft of this passage I saw,
in a newspaper of repute, some words which perhaps throw light on the objection to
Dumas as having no literary merit. In them "incident, coherence, humour, and
dramatic power" were all excluded from this merit, "style" alone remaining. Now
I have been almost as often reproved for attaching too much value to style in others as
for attending too little to it myself. But I certainly could not give it such a right to
"reign alone." It will indeed "do" almost by itself ; but other things can "do"
almost without it.

can hardly be said to have been anything like a master. His best novels are chronicle-plays undramatised—large numbers of his scenes could be cut out with as little real loss as foolish "classical" critics used to think to be the case with Shakespeare; and his connections, when he takes the trouble to make any, are often his very weakest points. Take, for instance, the things that bring about D'Artagnan's great quest for the diamonds—one of the most excellent episodes in this department of fiction, and something more than an episode in itself. The author actually cannot think of any better way than to make Constance Bonacieux—who is represented as a rather unusually intelligent woman, well acquainted with her husband's character, and certainly not likely to overestimate him through any superabundance of wifely affection or admiration—propose that he, a middle-aged mercer of sedentary and *bourgeois* habits, shall undertake an expedition which, on the face of it, requires youth, strength, audacity, presence of mind, and other exceptional qualities in no ordinary measure, and which, if betrayed to an ever vigilant, extremely powerful, and quite unscrupulous enemy, is almost certain to be frustrated.

Still the "chronicle"-action dispenses a man, to a large extent, in the eyes of some readers at any rate, from even attempting exact and tight *liaisons* of scene in this fashion, though of course if he does attempt them he submits himself to the perils of his attempt just as his heroes submit themselves to theirs. But other readers—and perhaps all those predestined to be Alexandrians—do not care to exact the penalties for such a failure. They are quite content to find themselves launched on the next reach of the stream, without asking too narrowly whether they have been ushered decorously through a lock or have tumbled somehow over a lasher. Such troubles never drown or damage *them*. And indeed there are some of them sufficiently depraved by nature, and hardened by indulgence in sin, to disregard *general* action altogether, and to look mainly if not wholly to

the way in which the individual stories are told, not at
that in which they come to have to be told. Of Dumas'
power of telling a story there surely can be no two
opinions. The very reproach of *amuseur* confesses it.
Of the means—or some of them—by which he does
and does not exercise this power, more may be said
under the heads which follow. We are here chiefly
concerned with the power as it has been achieved and
stands—in, for instance, such a thing, already glanced
at, as the " Vin de Porto " episode or division of *Vingt
Ans Après*, which, though there are scores of others
nearly as good, seems to me on the whole the very finest
thing Dumas ever did in his own peculiar kind. There
are just two dozen pages of it—pages very well filled—
from the moment when Blaisois and Mousqueton express
their ideas on the subject of the unsuitableness of beer,
as a fortifier against sea-sickness, to that when the corpse
of Mordaunt, after floating in the moonlight with the
gold-hilted dagger flashing from its breast, sinks for the
last time. The interest grows constantly ; it is never,
as it sometimes is elsewhere, watered out by too much
talk, though there is enough of this to carry out the
author's usual system (*v. inf.*). Nothing happens sufficiently extravagant or improbable to excite disgust or
laughter, though what does happen is sufficiently " palpi-
tating." If this is melodrama, it is melodrama free from
most of the objections made elsewhere to the kind. And
also if it is melodrama, it seems to me to be melodrama
infinitely superior, not merely in degree, but in kind, to
that of Sue and Soulié.

It is in this " enfisting " power of narrative, constantly
renewed if not always logically sustained and connected,
To Character. that Dumas' excellence, if not his actual
supremacy, lies ; and the fact may dispense
us from saying any more about his plots. As to Character, we must still keep the offensive-defensive line.
Dumas' most formidable enemies—persons like the late
M. Brunetière—would probably say that he has no
character at all. Some of his champions would content

themselves with ejaculating the two names "D'Artagnan !" and "Chicot !" shrugging their shoulders, and abstaining from further argument as likely to be useless, there being no common ground to argue upon. In actual life this might not be the most irrational manner of proceeding ; but it could hardly suffice here. As is usually, if not invariably, the case, the difference of estimate *is* traceable, in the long run, to the fact that the disputants or adversaries are not using words in the same sense—working in conjunction with the other fact that they do not like and want the same things. Almost all words are ambiguous, owing to the length of time during which they have been used and the variety of parts they have been made to play. But there are probably few which—without being absolutely equivocal like "box" and our other "foreigners' horrors"—require the use of the *distinguo* more than "character." As applied to novels, it may mean (1) a human personality more or less deeply analysed ; (2) one vividly distinguished from others ; (3) one which is made essentially *alive* and almost recognised as a real person ; (4) a "personage" ticketed with some marks of distinction and furnished with a dramatic "part" ; (5) an eccentric. The fourth and fifth may be neglected here. It is in relation to the other three that we have to consider Dumas as a character-monger.

In the competition for representation of character which depends upon analysis, "psychology," "problem-projection," Dumas is of course nowhere, though, to the disgust of some and the amusement of others, *Jacques Ortis* figures in the list of his works. *René, Adolphe,* the works of Madame de Staël (if they are to be admitted) and those of Beyle (which no doubt must be) found nothing corresponding in his nature ; and there was not the slightest reason why they should. The cellar of the novel contains even more than the "thousand dozen of wine" enshrined by that of Crotchet Castle, but no intelligent possessor of it, any more than Mr. Crotchet himself, would dream of restricting it to one kind of vintage. Nor, probably, would any really intelligent possessor arrange his largest bins for this kind, which at its best is a very exquisite *vin de liqueur*, but which few people wish to drink constantly ; and which at its worst, or even in mediocre condition, is very poor tipple— " shilpit," as Peter Peebles most unjustly characterises sherry in *Redgauntlet*. Skipping (2) for the moment, I do not know that under head (3) one can make much fight for Alexander. D'Artagnan and Chicot are doubt- less great, and many others fall not far short of them. I am always glad to meet these two in literature, and should be glad to meet them in real life, particularly if they were on my side, though their being on the other would add considerably to the excitement of one's exist- ence—so long as it continued. But I am not sure that I *know* them as I know Marianne and Des Grieux, Tom Jones and My Uncle Toby, the Baron of Bradwardine and Elizabeth Bennet. Athos I know or should know if I met him, which I am sorry to say I have not yet done ; and La Reine Margot, and possibly Olympe de Clèves ; but there is more guess-work about the knowledge with her than in the other cases. Porthos (or somebody very like him) I did know, and he was most agreeable ; but he died too soon to go into the army, as he ought to have done, after leaving Oxford. And though I never met a complete Aramis, I think I have met him in parts. There are not many more of this class. On the other hand, there is almost an entire absence in Dumas of those mere lay-figures which are so common in other novelists. There is great plenty of something more than toy-theatre characters cut out well and brightly painted, fit to push across the stage and justify their " words " and vanish ; but that is a different thing.

And this leads us partly back and partly up to the second head, the provision of characters sufficiently distinguished from others, and so capable of playing their parts effectually and interestingly. It is in this that he is so good, and it is this which distinguishes himself from all his fellows but the very greatest.

D'Artagnan and Chicot are again the best; but how good, at least in the better books, are almost all the others! D'Artagnan would be a frightful loss, but suppose he were not there and you knew nothing about him, would you not think Planchet something of a prize? Without Chicot there would be a blank horrible to think of. But do we not still "share"? Have we not Dom Gorenflot?

It is in this provision of vivid and sufficiently, if not absolutely, vivified characters and personages—"company" for his narrative dramas—that Dumas is so admirable under this particular head. If they are rarely detachable or independent, they work out the business consummately. Lackeys and ladies' maids, inn-keepers and casual guests at inns, courtiers and lawyers, noblemen and "lower classes," they all do what they ought to do; they all "answer the ends of their being created,"—which is to carry out and on, through two or three or half a dozen volumes, a blissful suspension from the base realities of existence. And if anybody asks of them more than this, it is his own fault, and a very great fault too.[1]

Of Description, as of the "fifth wheel" style, there is little to say about Dumas, though the littleness is in neither To Descrip- respect damaging. They are both adequate to tion (and the situation and the composition. Can you "style"). say much more of him or of anybody? If it were worth while to go into detail at all, this adequacy could be made out, I think, a good deal more than sufficiently. Take one of his greatest things, the "Bastion Saint-Gervais" in the *Mousquetaires*. If he has not made you see the heroic hopeless town, and the French leaguer and the shattered redoubt between, and the forlorn hope of the Four foolhardy yet forethoughtful and for ever delightful heroes, with their not so cheerful

[1] To be absolutely candid, Dumas himself did sometimes ask more of them than they could do; and then he failed. There can, I think, be little doubt that this is the secret of the inadequacy (as at least it seems to me) of the Felton episode. As a friend (whose thousand merits strive to cover his one crime of not admiring Dumas quite enough), not knowing that I had yet written a line of this chapter, but as it happened just as I had reached the present point, wrote to me : "Think what Sir Walter would have made of Felton ! "

followers, eating, drinking, firing, consulting, and flaunting the immortal napkin-pennant in the enemy's face—
you would not be made to see it, though the authors of
Inès de las Sierras or of *Le Château de la Misère* had
given you a cast of their office. And, what is more, the
method of *Inès de las Sierras* and of *Le Château de la
Misère* would have been actually out of place. It would
have got in the way of the business, the engrossing
business, of the manual fight against the Rochellois,
and the spiritual fight against Richelieu and Rochefort
and Milady. So, again—so almost tautologically—
with "style" in the more complicated and elaborate
sense of the word. One may here once more thank
Émile de Girardin for the phrase that he used of Gautier's
own style in *feuilleton* attempts. It *would* be *gênant pour
l'abonné*—even for an *abonné* who was not the first comer.
It is not the beautiful phrase, over which you can linger,
that is required, but the straightforward competent
word-vehicle that carries you on through the business,
that you want in such work. The essence of Dumas'
quality is to find or make his readers thirsty, and to
supply their thirst. You can't quench thirst with
liqueurs; if you are not a Philistine you will not quench
it with vintage port or claret, with Château Yquem, or
even with fifteen-year-old Clicquot. A "long" whisky
and potash, a bottle of sound Medoc, or, best of all,
a pewter quart of not too small or too strong beer—
these are the modest but sufficient quenchers that suit
the case. And Dumas gives you just the equivalents
of these.

But it may seem that, for the last head or two, the
defence has been a little "let down"—the pass, if not
To Conver- "sold," somewhat weakly held.[1] No such
sation. half-heartedness shall be chargeable on what
is going to be said under the last category, which, in a
way, allies itself to the first. It is, to a very large extent,

---

[1] I could myself be perfectly content to adapt George III. on a certain *Apology*, and
substitute for all this a simple "I do not think Dumas needs any defence." But where
there has been so much obloquy, there should, perhaps, be some refutation.

by his marvellous use of conversation that Dumas attains his actual mastery of story-telling ; and so this characteristic of his is of double importance and requires a Benjamin's allowance of treatment. The name just used is indeed specially appropriate, because Conversation is actually the youngest of the novelist's family or staff of work-fellows. We have seen, throughout or nearly throughout the last volume, how very long it was before its powers and advantages were properly appreciated ; how mere *récit* dominated fiction ; and how, when the personages were allowed to speak, they were for the most part furnished only or mainly with harangues— like those with which the "unmixed" historian used to endow his characters. That conversation is not merely a grand set-off to a story, but that it is an actual means of telling the story itself, seems to have been unconscionably and almost unintelligibly slow in occurring to men's minds; though in the actual story-telling of ordinary life by word of mouth it is, and always must have been, frequent enough.[1] It is not impossible that the derivation of prose from verse fiction may have had something to do with this, for gossippy talk and epic or romance in verse do not go well together. Nor is it probable that the old, the respectable, but the too often mischievous disinclination to "mix kinds" may have had its way, telling men that talk was the dramatist's not the novelist's business. But whatever was the cause, there can be no dispute about the fact.

It was, it should be hardly necessary to say, Scott who first discovered the secret[2] to an effectual extent, though he was not always true to his own discovery. And it is not superfluous to note that it was a specially valuable and important discovery in regard to the novel of historical adventure. It had, of course, and almost necessarily, forced itself, in regard to the novel of ordinary life, upon our own great explorers in that line earlier.

[1] " And then he says, says he. . . ."
[2] In modern novels, of course. You have some good talk in Homer and also in the Sagas, but I am not thinking or speaking of them.

Richardson has it abundantly. But when you are borrowing the *subjects* of the historian, what can be more natural than to succumb to the *methods* of the historian—the long continuous narrative and the intercalated harangue ? It must be done sometimes ; there is a danger of its being done too often. Before he had found out the true secret, Scott blunted the opening of *Waverley* with *récit* ; after he had discovered it he relapsed in divers places, of which the opening of *The Monastery* may suffice for mention here. Dumas himself (and it will be at once evident that this is a main danger of " turning on your young man ") has done it often—to take once more a single example, there is too much of it in the account of the great *émeute*, by which Gondy started the Fronde. But it is the facility which he has of dispensing with it— of making the story speak itself, with only barely necessary additions of the pointer and reciter at the side of the stage—which constitutes his power. Instances can hardly be required, for any one who knows him knows them, and every one who goes to him, not knowing, will find them. Just to touch the *apices* once more, the two scenes following the actual overtures of the *Mousquetaires* and of *La Reine Margot*—that where the impossible triple duel of D'Artagnan against the Three is turned into triumphant battle with the Cardinalists, blood-cementing the friendship of the Four ; and that where Margot, after losing both husband and lover, is supplied with a substitute for both ; adding the later passage where La Mole is saved from the noose at the door— may suffice.

Of course this device of conversation, like the other best things—the beauty of woman, the strength of wine, the sharpness of steel, and red ink—is " open to abuse." [1] It has been admitted that even the fervency of the present writer's Alexandrianism cools at the " wall-game " of Montalais and Malicorne. There may be some who are

---

[1] " Red ink for ornament and black for use—
  The best of things are open to abuse."
        (*The Good Clerk* as vouched for by Charles Lamb.)

not even prepared to like it in places where I do. They are like Porthos, in the great initial interchange of compliments, and "would still be *doing*." But surely they cannot complain of any lack of incident in this latest and not least *Alexandreid* ?

It may seem that the length of this chapter is not proportionate to the magnitude of the claims advanced for Dumas. But, as in other cases, I think it may not be impertinent to put in a reference to what I have previously written elsewhere. Moreover, as, but much more than, in the cases of Sandeau, Bernard, and Murger, there is an argument, paradoxical in appearance merely, for the absence of prolixity.

His claim to greatness consists, perhaps primarily, in the simplicity, straightforwardness, and general human interest of his appeal. He wants no commentaries, no introductions, no keys, no dismal Transactions of Dumas Societies and the like. Every one that thirsteth may come to his fountain and drink, without mysteries of initiation, or formalities of licence, or concomitant nuisances of superintendence and regulation. In the *Camp of Refuge* of Charles Macfarlane (who has recently, in an odd way, been recalled to passing knowledge)—a full and gallant private in the corps of which Dumas himself was then colonel *vice* Sir Walter deceased—there is a sentence which applies admirably to Dumas himself. After a success over the other half of our ancestors, and during a supper on the conquered provant, one of the Anglo-Saxon-half observes, " Let us leave off talking, and be jolly." Nothing could please me better than that some reader should be instigated to leave off my book at this point, and take up *Les Trois Mousquetaires* or *Les Quarante-Cinq*, or if he prefers it, *Olympe de Clèves* —" and be jolly " [1]

---

[1] Yet, being nothing if not critical, I can hardly agree with those who talk of Dumas' " *wild* imagination " ! As the great Mr. Wordsworth was more often made to mourn by the gratitude of men than by its opposite, so I, in my humbler sphere, am more cast down sometimes by inapposite praise than by ignorant blame.

CHAPTER IX

THE FRENCH NOVEL IN 1850

IT was not found necessary, in the last volume, to suspend the current of narrative or survey for the purpose of The drawing interim conclusions in special "Inter-peculiarity of chapters."[1] But the subjects of this present the moment. are so much more bulky and varied, in proportion to the space available and the time considered; while the fortunes of the novel itself altered so prodigiously during that time, that something of the kind seemed to be desirable, if not absolutely necessary. Moreover, the actual centre of the century in France, or rather what may be called its precinct, the political interregnum of 1848–1852, is more than a *mere* political and chronological date. To take it as an absolute apex or culmination would be absurd; and even to take it as a definite turning-point might be excessive. Not a few of the greatest novelists then living and working—Hugo, whose most popular and bulkiest work in novel was yet to come; George Sand, Mérimee, Gautier—were still to write for the best part of a quarter of a century, if not more; and the most definite fresh start of the second period, the rise of Naturalism, was not to take place till a little later. But already Chateaubriand, Beyle, Charles de Bernard, and, above all, Balzac, were dead or soon to die: and it cannot be said that any of the survivors developed new characters of work, for even Hugo's was

---

[1] I have not called this so, because the division into " Books," with which the *raison d'être* of " Interchapters " is almost inseparably connected, has not been adopted in this *History*.

343

(*v. sup.*) only the earlier "writ large" and modernised in non-essentials. On the other hand, it was only after this time that Dumas *fils*, the earliest of what may be called the new school, produced his most remarkable work.

But the justification of such an "Interchapter" as this practically is depends, not on what is to come after, but on what has come before; and in this respect we shall find little difficulty in vindicating the position and arrangement assigned to the remarks which are to follow, though some of these may look forward as well as backward.[1]

I should imagine that few Frenchmen—despite the almost infinite and sometimes very startling variety of selection which the *laudator temporis acti* exhibits —look back upon the reign of Louis Philippe as a golden age in any respect but one. Regarding it from the point of view of general politics, the ridiculous change[2] from "King of France" to "King of the French" stamped it at once, finally and hopelessly, as the worst kind of compromise—as a sort of spiritual imitation of the methods of the Triumvirate, where everybody gives up, not exactly his father or his uncle or his brother, but his dearest and most respectable convictions, together with the historical, logical, and sentimental supports of them. The king himself—though certainly no fool, and though hardly to be called an unmitigated knave— was one of those unfortunate persons whose merits do not in the least interest and whose defects do very strongly disgust. Domestically, the reign was a reign, in the other sense, of silly minor revolutions, which, till the end, came to nothing, and then came to something only less absurd than the Russian revolution of the other day, though fortunately less disastrous;[3] of bureaucracy

A political nadir.

---

[1] This fact, as well, perhaps, as others, should be taken into account by any one who may be at first sight surprised, and perhaps in the Biblical sense "offended," at finding two-thirds of the volume allotted to half of the time.

[2] To vary a good epigram of the *Rolliad* crew on Pitt:

"'The French' for 'France' can't please the *Blanc*,
The *Bleu* detests the 'King.'"

[3] *V. sup.* on Reybaud.

of the corrupt and shabby character which seemed to cling to the whole *régime*; and of remarkable vying between two distinguished men of letters, Guizot and Thiers, as to which should do most to confirm the saying of the wicked that men of letters had much better have nothing to do with politics.[1]   Abroad (with the exception of the acquisition of Algeria, which had begun earlier, and which conferred no great honour, though some profit, and a little snatching up of a few loose trifles such as the Society Islands, which we had, according to our custom, carelessly or benevolently left to gleaners), French arms, despite a great deal of brag and swagger, obtained little glory, while French diplomacy let itself wallow in one of the foulest sloughs in history, the matter of the Spanish marriages.

But this unsatisfactory state of things was made up— and more than made up—for posterity if not for con- temporaries—by the extraordinary development of literature and the arts—especially literature and most especially of all the *belles-lettres*. If (which would be rather impossible) one were to evaluate the relative excellence of poetry and of prose fiction in the time itself, a great deal could be said on both sides. But if one took the larger historic view, it would certainly have to be admitted that, while the excellence of French poetry was a magnificent Renaissance after a long period of something like sterility, the excellence of the novel was something more—an achievement of things never yet achieved; an acquisition and settlement of territory which had never previously been even explored.

And almost a literary zenith.

I venture to hope that no great injustice has been done to the previous accomplishments of France in this depart- ment as they were surveyed in the last volume. She had been, if not the inventress of Romance, the αἰδοίη ταμίη—the revered distributress—of it to all nations; she had made the short story her own to such an extent

---

[1] This is of course quite a different thing from saying that politicians had better have nothing to do with letters, or that men of letters may not *discuss* politics.   It is when they become Ministers that they too often disgust men and amuse angels.

that, in almost all its forms, she had reached and kept
mastery of it; and in various isolated instances she had
done very important, if not now universally acceptable,
work in the practice of the " Heroic." With Rabelais,
Lesage, almost Marivaux, certainly, in his one diploma-
piece, Prévost, she had contributed persons and things
of more or less consummateness to the novel-staff and
the novel treasury. But she had never quite reached,
as England for two full generations had reached before
1800, the consummate expression of the *pure* novel—
the story which, not neglecting incident, but as a rule
confining itself to the incidents of ordinary life; advan-
cing character to a position at least equal with plot;
presenting the manners of its own day, but charging
them with essence of humanity in all days; re-creates,
for the delectation of readers, a new world of probable,
indeed of actual, life through the medium of literature.
And she had rarely—except in the fairy-tale and a very
few masterpieces like *Manon Lescaut* again and *La
Nouvelle Héloïse*[1]—achieved what may be called the
Romantic or passionate novel; while, except in such
very imperfect admixtures of the historic element as *La
Princesse de Clèves*, she had never attempted, and even in
these had never attained, the historical novel proper.

Now, in 1850, she had done all this, and more.

As has been seen, the doing was, if not solely effected
between 1830 and 1848, mainly and almost wholly
carried out in the second quarter of the century.
In the first, only three persons possessing
anything like genius—Benjamin Constant,
Madame de Staël, and Chateaubriand—had
busied themselves with the novel, and they were all
strongly charged with eighteenth-century spirit. Indeed,
Constant, as we saw in the last volume, though he left
pattern and stimulus for the nineteenth and the future
generally, really represented the last dying words of that
" Sensibility " school which was essentially of the past,
though it was undoubtedly necessary to the future.

*The per-
formance of
the time in
novel.*

---

[1] *Adolphe* actually belongs to the nineteenth century.

Likewise in Madame de Staël, and still more in Chateaubriand, there was model, stimulus, germ. But they also were, on the whole, of the eve rather than of the morrow. I have indeed sometimes wondered what would have happened if Chateaubriand had gone on writing novels, and had devoted to fiction the talent which he wasted on the *mesquin*[1] politics of the France of his later days and on the interesting but restricted and egotistic *Mémoires d'Outre-Tombe*. It is no doubt true that, though old men have often written great poetry and excellent serious prose, nobody, so far as I remember, has written a great novel after seventy. For *Quatre-Vingt-Treize*, if it be great, is a romance rather than a novel, and a romance which had much better have been poetry. But this is an excursion into the Forbidden Country of the Might-Have-Been. We are concerned with what was.

The accomplishment of these twenty or five-and-twenty years is so extraordinary—when bulk, variety, novelty, and greatness of achievement are considered together—that there is hardly anything like it elsewhere. The single work of Balzac would mark and make an epoch; and this is wholly the property of the period. And though there is still, and is likely always to be, controversy as to whether the Balzacian men and women are exactly men and women of *this* world, there can, as may have been shown, be no rational denial of the fact that they represent *a* world—not of pure romance, not of fairy-tale, not of convention or fashion or coterie, but a world human and synthetically possible in its kind.

But while the possession of Balzac alone would have sufficed, by itself, to give the time front rank among The *personnel.* the periods of the novel, it is not in the least extravagant to add that if Balzac had been blotted out of its record it could still prove title-deeds enough, and more than enough, to such a place. Fault

[1] As I write this I remember how my friend the late M. Beljame, who and whose "tribe" have done so nobly for English literature in France for forty years past, was shocked long ago at my writing "Mazarin Library," and refused to be consoled by my assurance that I should never dream of writing anything but "Bibliothèque Mazarine." But I had, and have, no doubt on the principle.

has here been found—perhaps not a few readers may
think to an excessive, certainly to a considerable extent—
with the novel-work of Hugo and with that of George
Sand. But the fault-finder has not dreamed of denying
that, as literature in novel-form, *Les Misérables* and
L'Homme Qui Rit and *Quatre-Vingt-Treize* are great,
and that *Les Travailleurs de la Mer* is of the greatest.[1]
And on the other hand, while strong exceptions have
been taken from several sides to the work of George
Sand, the fact remains—and no attempt has been made
to obscure or to shake it—that George Sand gave novel
delectation, in no vulgar fashion, and to no small extent
in the form of the pure novel itself, probably to as large
a number of readers as any novelist except Scott and
Dumas, and perhaps Dickens, has ever given. Of the
miraculous production of Dumas himself almost enough
should have been said before, though a little more may
come after; and whatever controversy there may be
about its purely literary value, there can—with reasonable
people who are prepared to give and take—be little
anxiety to deny that each of these three, like Balzac,
might have taken the burden of the period on his or her
own shoulders, while as a matter of fact they have
but to take each a corner. Nor, even when thus divided,
is the burden left wholly to them. The utmost perfection, at least in the short story, is reached by Mérimée
and Gautier, little less than such perfection by others.
For suggestions of new kinds and new treatments, if
for no single performance, few periods, if any, have a
superior to Beyle.

But, once more, just as the time need not rely on any
single champion of its greatest to maintain its position,
so, if all the greater names just mentioned were struck
out, it would still be able to " make good " by dint of
the number, the talent, the variety, the novelty of its
second- and third-rate representatives. Even those who

---

[1] I *hope*, but do not trust, that no descendant of the persons who told Charles Lamb
that Burns could not at the time be present because he was dead, will say, " But all these
were subsequent to 1850."

may think that I have taken Paul de Kock too seriously
cannot deny—for it is a simple fact—the vigorous
impulse that he gave to the *popularity* of the novel as a
form of the printed book, if not of literature; while I can
hardly imagine any one who takes the trouble to examine
this fact refusing to admit that it is largely due to an
advance in reality of a kind—though they may think
this kind itself but a shady and sordid one. On the
other hand, I think less of Eugène Sue than at one time
"men of good" used to think ; but I, in my turn, should
not dream of denying his popularity, or the advance
which he too effected in procuring for the novel its share,
and a vast share, in the attention of the general reader.
Jules Sandeau and Charles de Bernard, Soulié and Féval
and Achard, and not a few others mentioned or not
mentioned in the text, come up to support their priors,
while, as I have endeavoured to point out, two others
still, Charles Nodier and Gérard de Nerval, though it
may seem absurd to claim primacy for them, contribute
that idiosyncrasy without which, whether it be sufficient
to establish primacy or not, nothing can ever claim to
possess that quality.

But while it is not necessary to repeat the favourable
estimates already given of individuals, it is almost super-
The kinds— fluous to rest the claims of the period to import-
the historical ance in novel history upon them. Elsewhere [1]
novel.   I have laid some emphatic and reiterated stress
on the mischief which has sometimes arisen from too
exclusive critical attention to "kinds," classes, and the
like in literature—to the oblivion or obscuring of individual men and works of letters. But as there has
been, and I hope will be, no ignoring of individuals
here, and as this whole book endeavours to be a history
of a kind, remarks on subdivisions of that kind as such
can hardly be regarded as inopportune or inconsistent.

Now it is impossible that anybody who is at all
inclined or accustomed to think about the characteristics
of the pleasure he receives from literature, should not

[1] In my *History of Criticism, passim.*

have noticed in this period the fact—beside and outside of the other fact of a provision of delectable novelists—

Appearance of new classes—the historical. of a great splitting up and (as scientific slang would put it) fissiparous generation of the classes of novel. It is, indeed, open to the advocates of generic or specific criticism—though I think they cannot possibly maintain their position as to poetry—to urge that a great deal of harm was done to the novel, or at least that its development was unnecessarily retarded, by the absence of this division earlier. And in particular they might lay stress on the fortunes and misfortunes of the historical element. That element had at least helped to start—and had largely provided the material of—the earlier verse-romances and stories generally; but the entire absence of criticism at the time had merged it, almost or altogether, in mere fiction. It had played, as we saw, a great part in the novels of the seventeenth century; but it had for the most part merely " got in the way " of its companion ingredients and in its own. I have admitted that there are diversities of opinion as to its value in the *Astrée*; but I hold strongly to my own that it would be much better away there. I can hardly think that any one, uninfluenced by the sillier, not the nobler, estimate of the classics, can think that the " heroic " novels gain anything, though they may possibly not lose very much, by the presence in them of Cyrus and Clelia, Arminius and Candace, Roxana and Scipio. But perhaps the most fruitful example for consideration is *La Princesse de Clèves*. Here, small as is the total space, there is a great deal of history and a crowd, if for the most part mute, of historical persons. But not one of these has the very slightest importance in the story; and the Prince and the Princess and the Duke—we may add the Vidame—who are the only figures that *have* importance, might be the Prince and Princess of Kennaquhair, the Duke of Chose, and the Vidame of Gonesse, in any time or no time since the creation of the world, while retaining their fullest power of situation and appeal.

But this side of the matter is of far less consequence than another. This historical element of the *historia mixta* [1] was not merely rather a nuisance and quite a superfluity as regarded the whole of the stories in which it appeared; but its presence there and the tricks that had to be played with it prevented the development of the historical novel proper—that, as it has been ticketed, "bodiless childful of life," which waited two thousand years in the ante-natal gloom before it could get itself born. Here, indeed, one may claim—and I suppose no sensible Frenchmen would for a moment hesitate to admit it—that even more than in the case of Richardson's influence nearly a century earlier, help came to their Troy from a Greek city. To France as to England, and to all the world, Scott unlocked the hoard of this delightful variety of fictitious literature, though it was not quite at once that she took advantage of the treasury.

But when she did, the way in which she turned over the borrowed capital was certainly amazing, and for a long time she quite distanced the followers of Scott himself in England. James, Ainsworth, and even Bulwer cannot possibly challenge comparison with the author of *Notre Dame de Paris* as writers, or with Dumas as story-tellers; and it was not till the second half of the century was well advanced, and when Dumas' own best days were very nearly over, that England, with Thackeray's *Esmond* and Kingsley's *Westward Ho!* and Charles Reade's *The Cloister and the Hearth*, re-formed the kind afresh into something which France has never yet been able to rival.

In order, however, to obviate any possible charge of insular unfairness, it may be well to note that Chateaubriand, though he had never reached (or in all probability attempted to reach) anything of the true Scott kind, had made a great advance in something the same direction, and had indeed to some extent sketched a different variety of historical novel from Scott's own; while, before Scott's death, Victor Hugo imbued the Scott

[1] *V. sup.* Vol. I., on the "heroic" romance.

romance itself with intenser doses of passion, of the subsidiary interests of art, etc., and of what may be in a way called "theory," than Scott had cared for. In fact, the Hugonic romance is a sort of blending of Scott and Byron, with a good deal of the author's country, and still more of himself, added. The connection again between Scott and Dumas is simpler and less blended with other influences; the chief differences should have been already pointed out. But the important thing to notice is that, with a few actual gaps, and several patches which have been more fully worked over and occupied than others, practically the whole of French history from the fourteenth century to, and including, the Revolution was "novelised" by the wand of this second magician.[1]

That the danger of the historical variety was entirely avoided by these its French practitioners cannot indeed be said. Even Scott had not wholly got the better of it in his less perfect pieces, such, for instance, as those already glanced-at parts of *The Monastery*, where historical *récit* now and then supplies the place of vigorous novel-action and talk. Dumas' co-operative habits (which are as little to be denied as they are to be exaggerated) lent themselves to it much more freely. But, notwithstanding this, the total accession of pleasure to the novel-reader was immense, and the further possibility of such accession practically unlimited. And accordingly the kind, though sometimes belittled by foolish criticism, and sometimes going out of favour by the vicissitudes of mere fashion, has constantly renewed itself, and is likely to do so. Its special advantages and its special warnings are of some interest to discuss briefly. Among the first may be ranked something which the foolish belittlers above mentioned entirely fail to appreciate, and indeed positively dislike. The danger of the novel of ordinary and contemporary life (which accompanied this and which is to be considered shortly as

[1] It seems unnecessary to repeat what has been said on Vigny and Mérimée; but it is important to keep constantly in mind that they came before Dumas. As for the still earlier *Solitaire*, I must repeat that M. d'Arlincourt's utter failure as an individual ought not completely to obscure his importance as a pioneer in kind.

such) is that there may be so much *mere* ordinariness
and contemporariness that the result may be distasteful,
if not sickening, to future ages. This has (to take one
example out of many) happened with the novels of so
clever a person as Theodore Hook in England, even
with comparatively elect judges ; with the vulgar it is
said to have happened even with such consummate things
as those of Miss Austen. With a large number of another
sort of vulgar it is said to happen with " Victorian "
novels generally, while even the elect sometimes find it difficult to prevent its happening with Edwardian and Fifth
Georgian. Now the historical novelist has before him
the entire range of the most interesting fashions, manners,
incidents, characters, literary styles of recorded time.
He has but to select from this inexhaustible store of
general material, and to charge it with sufficient power
of humanity of all time, and the thing is done.[1] Under
no circumstances can the best historical novels ever lose
their attraction with the best readers ; and as for the
others in each kind, who cares what happens to *them* ?

There are, moreover, some interesting general rules
about the historical novel which are well worth a moment's
notice, even if this partake to some extent of the nature
of repetition. The chief of them, which at least ought
to be well known, is that it is never safe to make a prominent historical character, and seldom safe to make a
prominent historical event, the central subject of your
story. The reason is of course obvious. The generally
known facts cramp and hamper the writer ; he is constantly knocking against them, and finding them in the
way of the natural development of his tale. No doubt
there is, and has been, a good deal of otiose and even
rather silly criticism of details in historical novels which
do not satisfy the strict historian. The fuss which some
people used to make about Scott's anachronisms in
Ivanhoe and *Kenilworth* ; the shakings of heads which
ought to know better, over Thackeray's dealings with

---

[1] " Suppose you go and do it ? " as Thackeray says of another matter, no doubt.
But I am Crites, not Poietes.

the Old Chevalier and his scandals about Miss Oglethorpe in *Esmond*, can be laughed or wondered at merely. But then these are matters of no importance to the main story. It is Ivanhoe and Rebecca, Henry Esmond and Beatrix,[1] all of them persons absolutely unknown to history, in whom we are really interested ; and in the other case mentioned, Amy Robsart is such a creature or "daughter," if not " of dreams " " of debate," that you may do almost what you like with her ; and the book does not sin by presentation of a Leicester so very different from the historical.[2] But, on the other hand, the introduction of historical persons, skilfully used, seasons, enforces, and vivifies the interest of a book mightily ; and the action of great historical scenes supports that of the general plot in a still more remarkable manner. On the whole, we may perhaps say that Dumas depends more on the latter, Scott on the former, and that the difference is perhaps connected with their respective bulk and position as dramatists. Dumas has made of no historical magnate anything like what Scott has made of Richard and of Mary and of Elizabeth ; but Scott has not laid actual historical scenes under contribution to anything like the same extent as that by which Dumas has in a fashion achieved a running panorama-companion to the history of France from the fourteenth century to the Revolution and, more intensively, from the Massacre of Saint Bartholomew to the establishment of Louis XIV.'s autocracy.

In fact, the advantages, both to the novelist and to his readers, of the historical kind can hardly be exaggerated. The great danger of invented prose narrative— of *all* invented narrative, indeed, prose or verse—has always been, and has always from the first shown itself as being, that of running into moulds. In the old epics (the Classical, not the *Chansons*) this danger was accentu-

---

[1] Pedantius may urge, " But ' James III.' is made to affect the fortunes of Esmond and Beatrix very powerfully." True ; but he himself is by no means a *very* " prominent historical character," and the exact circumstances of the agony of Queen Anne, and the *coup d'état* of Shrewsbury and Argyle, have still enough of the unexplained in or about them to permit somewhat free dealing.

[2] If any one says "*Leicester's Commonwealth ?* " I say " *The Faerie Queene ?* "

ated by the rise of rule-criticism ; but the facts had
induced, if they did not justify, that rule-system itself.
The monotony of the mediaeval romance, whether
Chanson or *Roman*, has been declared more than once
in this book to be exaggerated, but it certainly exists.
The " heroic " succumbs to a similar fate rather fatally,
though the heroic element itself comes slightly to the
rescue ; and even the picaresque by no means escapes.
To descend, or rather to look, into the gutter for a moment,
the sameness of the deliberately obscene novel is a by-
word to those who, in pursuit of knowledge, have in-
curred the necessity of " washing themselves in water
and being unclean until the evening " ; and we saw that
even such a light and lively talent as Crébillon's, keeping
above the very lowest gutter-depths, could not escape
the same danger wholly.   In the upper air the fairy-tale
flies too often in prescribed gyres ; and the most modern
kinds of all—the novel of analysis, the problem-novel,
and all the rest of them — strive in vain to avoid the
curse of—as Rabelais put something not dissimilar long
ago—" fatras *à la douzaine.*"   " All the stories are told,"
saith the New, even as the Old, Preacher ; all but the
highest genius is apt to show ruts, brain-marks, common
orientations of route and specifications of design.   Only
the novel of creative—not merely synthetised—character
in the most expert hands escapes—for human character
undoubtedly partakes of the Infinite ; but few are they
who can command the days and ways of creation.

  Yet though history has its unaltering laws ; though
human nature in general is always the same ; though
that which hath been shall be, and the dreams of new
worlds and new societies are the most fatuous of vain
imaginations—the details of historical incident vary as
much as those of individual character or feature, and
the whole of recorded time offers them, more than half
ready for use, in something like the same condition as
those patterns of work which ladies buy, fill up, and
regard as their own.   To make an historical novel of
the very highest class, such as the best of Scott and

Thackeray, requires of course very much more than this—
to make one of all but the highest class, such as *Les
Trois Mousquetaires*, requires much more. But that "tolerable pastime," which it is the business of the average
novelist to supply at the demand of the average reader,
can perhaps be attained more easily, more abundantly,
and with better prospect of average satisfaction in the
historical way than in any other.

It would, however, of course be an intolerable absurdity
to rest the claims of the French novel of 1825 to 1850
Other kinds wholly—it would be somewhat absurd to rest
and classes. them mainly—on its performances in this
single kind. It found out, continued, or improved many
others; and perhaps most of its greatest achievements were
in these others. In fact "others" is an incorrect or at
least an inexact term; for the historic novel itself is only
The a subdivision or offshoot of the great literary
Novel of revolution which we call Romanticism. Indeed
Romanticism the entire novel of the nineteenth century,
generally. misapprehend the fact as people may, is in fact
Romantic, from the first novel of Chateaubriand to the
last of Zola, though the Romanticism is chequered and
to a certain extent warped by that invincible French
determination towards "Rule" which has vindicated
itself so often, and on which shortly we may have to make
something almost like an excursus. But this very fact,
if nothing else, would make a discussion of the Romantic
novel as such out of place *here*; it will have to come,
to some extent at any rate, in the Conclusion itself. Only
for the present need it be said, without quite the same
danger of meeting with scornful or indignant protest,
that all the books hitherto discussed from *René* to *Dominique*, from *Le Solitaire* to *Monte Cristo*—even the work
of Mérimée and Sainte-Beuve, those celebrated
" apostates " as some would have them to be—is really
Romantic. It may follow the more poetical romanticism
of Nodier and Hugo, of Gautier and Gérard; the historical romanticism of Vigny and Mérimée; the individualism and analysis of Beyle and his disciples; the super-

naturalism of George Sand and Nodier again ; the adventurous incident of Sue and Soulié and Dumas and the Dumasians generally; it may content itself with that modified form of the great Revolt which admits " low " or " middle " subjects and discards the classical theories that a hero ought to be dignified. But always there is something of the general Romantic colour about—something over which M. Nisard has shaken or would have shaken his respectable *perruque*.[1]

So turn we to the other larger group—the largest group of all that come under our survey—the New Ordinary Novel, that which concerns itself with the last shade of his colour just described.

We had seen, before the beginning of this volume, how Pigault-Lebrun, in vulgar ways and with restricted talent, had nevertheless made distinct advances in this direction ; and we saw in the beginning of this how Paul de Kock—with something of the same limitations but with the advantage of a predecessor in Pigault and of further changes in society towards the normal—improved upon the earlier progression. But Pigault and Paul were thrown into the shade by those writers, younger contemporaries of both, who brought to their task greater genius, better taste, and if not knowledge of better society, at any rate better knowledge how to use their knowledge. Whether Balzac's books can be ticketed *sans phrase*, as " novels of *ordinary* life," has been, or should have been, duly discussed already. It is certain that, as a rule, they intend to be so. So it is with at least the majority of George Sand's ; so with all those of her first lover and half name-father Sandeau ; so with Charles de Bernard ; so with some at least of Mérimée's best short stories and Musset's, if not exactly of Gautier's ; so with others who have had places, and a good many more for whom no place could be found.

The "ordinary."

[1] I intend nothing offensive in thus mentioning his attitude. In my *History of Criticism* I have aimed at justice both to his short stage of going with, or at least not definitely against, the Romantic vein, and his much longer one of reaction. He was always vigorous in argument and dignified in manner ; but his nature, when he found it, was essentially neo-classic.

France, indeed, may be said to have caught up and passed England in this kind, between the time when Miss Austen died and that when Thackeray at last did justice to himself with *Vanity Fair*.   And this novel of ordinary life has continued, and shows no signs of ceasing, to be the kind most in demand, according to the usual law of " Like to Like."   We shall see further developments of it and shall have to exercise careful critical discretion in deciding whether the apparent improvement only means nearer approximation to our own standard of ordinariness, or to a more abstract one.   But that it was in these twenty or five and twenty years that something like a norm of ordinariness was first reached, hardly admits of any question.   Still, very much question may arise, and must be faced, on the point whether this novel of ordinary life has not redeveloped a *non*-ordinary subdivision, or many such, in the " problem " novel, the novel of analysis, of abnormal individualism, of theory, naturalist and other, etc.   To this we must turn ; for at least part of this new question is a very important one, though it may require something of a digression to deal with it properly.

I have in these volumes, rather sedulously—some readers no doubt may think too sedulously—avoided "fighting prizes" on general points of the criticism of novel-theory.   Not that I have the slightest objection to fighting "for my own hand " or to seeing or reading about a good fight between others—very much the contrary. I never thought it the worst compliment paid to Englishmen—the Indian opinion of us, as reported by the late M. Darmesteter—that we cared for nothing but fighting, sport, and making love.   But the question now to be discussed is so germane to our subject, both general and special ; and the discussion of it once for all (with *renvois* thereto elsewhere) will save so much space, trouble, and inconvenience, that it may as well be handled at full length.

Discussion on a point of general novel criticism.

There was hinted—in a review[1] of the first volume
of this work otherwise so complimentary that it must
have satisfied the Archbishop of Granada himself—a
doubt whether I had given sufficient weight to something
which I shall let the reviewer express in his own words;[2]
and whether my admission of Rabelais (of which admission, except on principle, he was himself very glad);
my relegation of Laclos to the Condemned Corps; and
my comparative toleration of Pigault-Lebrun, did not
indicate heresy. Now I feel pretty certain that such a
well-wisher would hardly suspect me of doing any of
these things by inadvertence; and as I must have gone,
and shall still go, much further from what is the right
line in his (and no doubt others') opinion, I may as well
state my point of view here. It should supply a sort of
justificatory comment not merely on the chapters and
passages just referred to, and others in the last volume,
but on a much larger number in this—in fact, after a
fashion, to the whole of this. Any difference of it
from the normal French view will even help to explain my attitude in those parts of this book (*e.g.* the
remarks on Dumas *père*) to which it does not directly
apply, as well as those (*e.g.* on Dumas *fils*) to which it
does.

The whole question seems to me to turn on the
curiously different estimates which different people make
of what constitutes "humanity." To cite another
dictum of my friend the enemy, he, while, as I have said,
speaking with extraordinary kindness of my chapter on
Rabelais in itself, disallows it in a *History of the Novel*
because, among other reasons, Panurge is not, or is very
slightly, human. I should have said that Panurge was
as human as Hamlet, though certainly not so *gentle-*

---

[1] In the *Times Literary Supplement* for Thursday, Nov. 1, 1917.

[2] " It is vain to ask, as is the modern custom, whether the leap from the word ' copy '
to the word ' recreate ' (*v. sup.* Vol. I. p. 471) does not cover a difference in kind. . . .
One feels that Prof. S. is rather unsympathetic to that which traditional French criticism
regards as essential . . . close psychological analysis of motive," etc. And so he even
questions whether what I have given, much as he likes and praises it, *is* " A History of
the French Novel." But did I ever undertake to give this *from the French point of view*,
or to write a *History of French Novel-Criticism* ? Or need I do so ?

human.[1] I never met either; but I might do so, and I am sure I should recognise both as men and brothers. Still, the comparison here is of course somewhat rhetorical. Let us take Panurge with Laclos' Valmont, whom, I think, my critic *does* consider human; whom I am sure I never have met and never shall meet, even if I should be so unfortunate as to go to the place which (but, of course, for the consolations of the Church) would have been his, *if* he had been human; and whom I never could in the most impossible event or *milieu* recognise as anything but a synthetised specification. One may perhaps dwell on this, for it is of immense importance to the general question. Panurge and Valmont, comparatively considered, have beyond doubt points in common. Both are extremely immoral, and both are—though the one only sometimes, the other always—ill-natured. Neither is a fool, though the one does, or is going to do, at least one very foolish thing with his eyes open; while nothing that the other does—even his provocation of Madame de Merteuil—can be said to be exactly "foolish." Both are attempts to do what Thackeray said he attempted to do in most of the characters of *Vanity Fair*—to draw people "living without God in the world." Yet I can tolerate Panurge, and recognise him as human even when he indirectly murders Dindenault, even when (which is worse) he behaves so atrociously to the Lady of Paris; and I cannot tolerate or validate Valmont even when he excogitates and puts in practice that very ingenious and picturesque idea of a writing-desk, or when he seeks the consolations and fortifications of the Church after Danceny has done on him the first part of the judgment of God. And I think I can give reasons, both for my intolerance and for my toleration, "rightly and in mine own division."

The reason why I think that Panurge is rightly and Valmont wrongly " copied or re-created " is that Panurge

[1] It might, however, be a not uninteresting matter of debate whether Panurge's conduct to the Lady of Paris was *really* so very much worse than part of Hamlet's to Ophelia.

is made at the hazard of the artist, Valmont according
to prescription. There might be—there have been—
fifty or a hundred Valmonts, the prescription being
followed, and slightly—still remaining a prescription—
altered. There is and can be only one Panurge. This
difference reminds me of, and may be illustrated by, a
fact which, in one form or another, must be familiar to
many people. I was once talking to a lady who had
just come over from China, and who wore a dress of soft
figured silk of the most perfect love-in-a-mist colour-
shade which I had ever seen, even in turning over the
wonder-drawers at Liberty's. I asked her if (for she
then intended to go back almost at once) she could get
me any like it. "No," she said, "at least not exactly.
They never make two pieces of just the same shade, and
in fact they couldn't if they tried. They take handfuls
of different dyes, measured and mixed, as it seems, at
random." Now that is the way God and, in a lesser
degree, the great artists work, and the result is living
creatures, according to the limitations of artistic and the
no-limitations of natural life. The others weigh out a
dram of lust, a scruple of cleverness, an ounce of malice,
half an ounce of superficial good manners, etc., and say,
"Here is a character for you. Type No. 12345."
And it is not a living creature at all. But, having been
made by regular synthesis,[1] it can be regularly analysed,
and people say, "Oh, how clever he is." The first
product, having grown rather than been made, defies
analysis, and they say, "How commonplace!"

One can perhaps lay out the ropes of the ring of
combat most satisfactorily and fairly by using the distinction of the reviewer (if I do not misunderstand him),
that I have neglected the interval between "to copy"
and "to re-create." I accept this dependence, which

---

[1] By one of those odd coincidences which diversify and relieve literary work, I read,
for the first time in my life, and a few hours *after* writing the above words, these in Dumas
fils' Thérèse: "Il procède par synthése." They do not there apply to authorship, but
to the motives and conduct of one of the writer's questionable quasi-heroes. But the
whole context, and the usual methods of Dumas *fils* himself, are saturated with synthesis
by rule. (Of course the other process is, as also according to the strict meaning of the
word, "synthetic," but *not* "by rule.")

may perhaps be illustrated further from that (in itself) foolish and vulgar boast of Edmond de Goncourt's that his and his brother's epithets were " personal " while Flaubert's were only " admirably good specimens of the epithets of *tout le monde*."

To translate : Should the novelist aim, by *mimesis*— it is a misfortune which I have lamented over and over again in print that " Imitation " and " Copying " are such misleading versions of this—of actual characters, to evolve a personality which will be recognised by all competent observers as somebody whom he has actually met or might have met ? Or should he, trusting to his own personal powers of putting together qualities and traits, but more or less neglecting the patterns which the Almighty has put before him in *tout le monde*—sometimes also regarding conventional types and " academies "—either (for this is important) to follow or violently *not* to follow them— produce something that owes *its* personality to himself only ? The former has been the aim of the great English novelists since Fielding, if not since Richardson [1] or even Defoe. It was the aim of Lesage : he has told us so in so many words. It is by no means alien from that of Marivaux, though he did not pursue it with a single eye ; and the same may be said even of Crébillon. Whether Prévost aimed at it or not, he hit the white in *Manon* as certainly and unmistakably as he lost his arrows elsewhere. Rousseau both did it and meant it in the first part of *Julie*. Pigault, in a clumsy, botcherly fashion, made " outers " not infrequently. But Laclos seems to me to have (as his in some sense follower Dumas *fils* has it in the passage noted above) " proceeded by syn- thesis "—to have said, " Let us make a mischievous Marquise and a vile Viscount. Let us deprive them of every amiable quality and of every one that can be called in any sense ' good,' except a certain kind of intellectual ability, and, in the Viscount's case, an ingenious fancy in the matter of extemporising writing-desks." And he

---

[1] I own I see a little less of it and a little more of the other in him ; whence a certain lukewarmness with which I have sometimes been reproached.

did it; and then the people who think that because
(to adopt the language of George de Barnwell) " the True
is not always the Beautiful " the Ugly must always be
the True, hail him as a master.[1]

That this half-digression, half-dilemma, is prospective
as well as retrospective will hardly form a subject of
objection for any one but a mere fault-finder. From
the top of a watershed you necessarily survey both slopes.
The tendency which we have been discussing is certainly
more prevalent in the second half of the century than in
the first half. It is prominent in Dumas *fils*, with whom
we shall be dealing shortly ; it increases as time goes on ;
and it becomes almost paramount in the practice of and
the discussions about the Naturalist School. In the
time on which we look back it is certainly important in
Beyle and Balzac. But I cannot admit that it is pre-
dominant elsewhere, and I am prepared to deny utterly
that, until the time of the Sensibility and *Philosophe*
novels, it is even a notable characteristic of French fiction.
Many hard things have been said of criticism ; but,
acknowledging the badness of a bird who even admits
any foulness in his own nest—far more in one who causes
it—I am bound to say that I think the state of the department of literature now under discussion was happier
before we meddled with it. Offence must come ; it
would even be sometimes rather a pity if it didn't
come : but perhaps the old saying is true in the case of
those by whom some kinds of it come. If criticism
and creation could be kept as separate as some creators
pridefully pretend, it would not matter. And the best
critics never attempt to show how things should be done,
but merely to point out how they have been done—well
or badly. But when men begin to write according to
criticism, they generally begin to write badly, just as
when women begin to dress themselves according to
fashion-mongers they usually begin (or would but for the
grace of God) to look ugly. And there are some mistakes

---

[1] My very amiable reviewer thinks that eighteenth-century French society *did*
behave *à la Laclos*. I don't, though I think it did *à la Crébillon*.

which appear to be absolutely incorrigible. When I
was a Professor of Literature I used to say every year
in so many words, as I had previously written for more
than as many years, when I was only a critic of it, " I
do not wish to teach you how to write. I wish to teach
you how to read, and to tell you what there is to read."
The same is my wish in regard to the French Novel.
What has been done in it—not what these, even the
practitioners themselves, have said of it—is the burden
of my possibly unmusical song.

The excuse, indeed, for this long digression may be,
I think, made without impropriety or " forcing " to
coincide with the natural sequel and correlation of this
chapter. The development of the novel of ordinary
life in the second half of the century *was* extraordinary ;
but it was to a very large extent marked by the peculiarities—some of them near to corruptions—which have
been just discussed. With the possible exception of
Beyle, there was little more theory, or attempt at synthesis
in accordance therewith, in the " ordinary " than in the
" historical " division of this earlier time. We have
seen how the absence of " general ideas "—another way
of putting it—has been actually brought as a charge
against Balzac. George Sand had, especially at first,
something of it ; and this something seems, to me at
least, by no means to have improved her work. In none
or hardly any of the rest is there any evidence of " school,"
" system," " pattern," " problem," or the like. Yet
they give us an immense amount of pastime, and I do
not think their or their readers' state was any the less
gracious for what they did *not* give us.

CHAPTER X

DUMAS THE YOUNGER

No one who has not had some experience in writing literary history knows the difficulties—or perhaps I Division of future subjects. should say the "unsatisfactorinesses"—which attend the shepherding of examples into separate chronological folds. But every one who has had that experience knows that mere neglect to attempt this shepherding has serious drawbacks. In such cases there is nothing for it but a famous phrase, "We will do what we can." An endeavour has been made in the last chapter to show that, about the middle of the nineteenth century, a noteworthy change *did* pass over French novel-literature. In a similar retrospect, at the end of the volume and the *History*, we may be able, *si Dieu nous prête vie*, to show that this change was not actually succeeded by any other of equal importance as far as our own subject goes. But the stage had, like all such things, sub-stages; and there must be corresponding breaks, if only mechanical ones, in the narrative, to avoid the distasteful "blockiness" resulting from their absence. After several changes of plan I have thought it best to divide what remains of the subject into five chapters (to which a separate Conclusion may be added). The first of these will be allotted, for reasons to be given, to Alexandre Dumas *fils* ; the second to Gustave Flaubert, greatest by far, if not most representative, of all dealt with in this latter part of the volume ; the third to others specially of the Second Empire, but not specially of the Naturalist School ; the fourth to that School itself; and the fifth to those now defunct novelists of the Third Republic, up to the close of the century, who may not have been dealt with before.

There should not, I think, be much doubt that we ought to begin with Alexandre Dumas, the son, who —though he launched his most famous novel five years before Napoleon the Third made himself come to the throne, had been writing for about as many earlier still, and lived till long after the Terrible Year, and almost to the end of our own tether—is yet almost more essenti-ally *the* novelist of the Second Empire than any one else, not merely because before its end he practically gave up Novel for Drama, but for other reasons which we may hope to set forth presently.

Before sitting down comfortably to deal with him in my critical jacket, I have to put on, for ceremonial pur-poses, something of a white sheet, and to hold
A confession. a candle of repentance in my hand. I have never said very much about the younger Dumas anywhere, and I am not conscious of any positive injustice in what I *have* said;[1] but I do suspect a certain imperfection of justice. This arose, as nearly all positive and com-parative injustices do, from insufficient knowledge and study. What it was exactly in him that "put me off" of old I could not now say; but I think it was because I did come across some of his numerous and famous fisticuffs of Preface and Dissertation and controversy. I thought then, and I still think, that the artist has something better to do than to "fight prizes": he has to do things worthy of the prize. "They say. What say they? Let them say" should be his motto. And later, when I might have condoned this (in the proper sense of that appallingly misused word) in virtue of his positive achievements, he had left off novel-writing and had taken to drama, for which, in its modern forms, I have never cared. But I fear I must

---

[1] As, for instance, in *A Short History of French Literature* (Oxford, 7th ed., 1917), pp. 550-552.

make a further confession. The extravagant praise
which was lavished on him by other critics, even though
they were, in some cases at least, φίλοι ἄνδρες, once
more proved a stumbling-block.[1] I have endeavoured
to set matters right here by serious study of his novel
work and some reference to the rest; so I hope that I
may discard the sheet, and give the rest of the candle
to the poor, now much requiring it.

One thing about him is clear from his first famous,
though not his first, book[2]—a book which, as has been
His general said, actually preceded the Second Empire,
character. but which has been thought to cast something
of a prophetic shadow over that period of revel and
rottenness—that is to say, from *La Dame aux Camélias*
—that he was even then a very clever man.[3]

" The Lady with the Camellias " is not now the widely
known book that once it was; and the causes of its loss
La Dame aux of vogue might serve as a text for some " Medi-
Camélias. tations among the Tombs," though in respect
of rather different cemeteries from those which Addison
or Hervey frequented. As a mere audacity it has long
faded before the flowers, themselves " over " now, of
that Naturalism which it helped to bring about; and the

---

[1] At the same time, and admitting (see below) that it is wrong to meet overpraise
with overblame, I think that it may be met with silence, for the time at any rate.

[2] I have, for reasons unnecessary to particularise, not observed strict chronological
order in noticing his work or that of some others; but a sufficient " control " will, I
hope, be supplied by the Appendix of dated books under their authors' names as treated
in this volume.

[3] I observe with amusement (which may or may not be shared by " the friends of
Mr. Peter Magnus ") that I have repeated in the case of Dumas *fils* what I said on
Crébillon *fils*. The contrast-parallel is indeed rather striking. Partly it is a case of
reversal, for Crébillon *père* was a most respectable man, most serious, and an academician;
the son, though not personally disreputable, was the very reverse of serious, and academic
neither by nature nor by status. In Dumas' case the father was extremely lively, and
the Academy shuddered or sneered at him; the son was very serious indeed, and duly
academised. Some surprise was, I remember, occasioned at the time by this promotion.
There are several explanations of it; mine is Alexander the son's fondness for the correct
subjunctive. George Sand, in a note to one of her books (I forget which), rebelliously
says that the speaker in the text *ought* to have said, " aimasse," not " aimais," but that
he didn't, and she will not make him do it. On the other hand, I find " aimasse,"
" haïsse," and " revisse " in just three lines of *La Dame aux Camélias*. And everybody
ought to know the story of the Immortal who, upon finding a man " where nae mon
should be," and upon that " mon " showing the baseness derived from Adam by turning
on his accomplice and saying, " Quand je vous disais qu'il était temps que je m'en aille ! "
neglected *crim. con.* for *crim. gram.* and cried in horror, " Que je m'en allasse, Monsieur ! "
But this preciseness did not extend to the younger Alexander's choice of subjects.

once world-popular composer who founded almost, if
not quite, his most popular opera on it, has become for
many years an abomination and a hissing to the very
same kind of person who, sixty years since, would have
gone out of his way to extol *La Traviata*, and have found
in *Il Trovatore* something worth not merely all Rossini [1]
and Bellini and Donizetti put together, but *Don Giovanni*,
the *Zauberflöte*, and *Fidelio* thrown in ; while if (as he
might) he had known *Tannhäuser* and *Lohengrin* he would
have lifted up his hoof against them. It is the nature of
the fool of all times to overblame what the fools of other
times have overpraised. But the fact that these changes
have happened, and that other accidents of time have
edulcorated that general ferocity which made even men of
worth in England refuse to lament the death of the Prince
Imperial in our service, should on the whole be rather
favourable to a quiet consideration of this remarkable book.
Indeed, I daresay some, if not many, of the "warm young
men" to whom the very word "tune" is anathema might
read the words, "Veux-tu que nous quittions Paris ?"
without having their pure and tender minds and ears
sullied and lacerated by the remembrance of "Parigi, O
cara, noi lasceremo"—simply because they never heard it.

A very remarkable book it is. Camellias have gone
out of fashion, which is a great pity, for a more beautiful
flower in itself does not exist: and those who have seen,
in the Channel Islands, a camellia tree, as big as a good-
sized summer-house, clothed with snow, and the red
blossoms and green leaf-pairs unconcernedly slashing
the white garment, have seen one of the prettiest sights
in the world. But I should not dream of transferring
the epithets "beautiful" or even "pretty." from the
flower to the book. It *is* remarkable, and it is clever in
no derogatory sense. For it has pathos without mere
sentiment, and truth, throwing a light on humanity, which
is not wholly or even mainly like that of

> The blackguard boy
> That runs his link full in your face.

---

[1] To whose "music" also our young friends,
As they tell us, have "lost the key."

The story of it is, briefly, as follows. Marguerite Gautier, its heroine, is one of the most beautiful and popular *demi-mondaines* of Paris, also a *poitrinaire*,[1] and as this, if not as the other, the pet and protégée, in a *quasi*-honourable fashion, of an old duke, whose daughter, closely resembling Marguerite, has actually died of consumption. But she does not give up her profession; and the duke in a manner, though not willingly, winks at it. One evening at the theatre a young man, Armand Duval, who, though by no means innocent, is shy and *gauche*, is introduced to her, and she laughs at him. But he falls frantically in love with her, and after some interval meets her again. The passion becomes mutual, and for some time she gives herself up wholly to him. But the duke cannot stand this open *affiche*, and withdraws his allowances. Duval is on the point of ruining himself (he is a man of small means, partly derived from his father) for her, while she intends to sell all she has, pay her debts, and, as we may say, plunge into mutual ruin with him. Then appears the father, who at last makes a direct and effective appeal to her. She returns to business, enraging her lover, who departs abroad. Before he comes back, her health, and with it her professional capacity, breaks down, and she dies in agony, leaving pathetic explanations of what has driven him away from her. A few points in this bare summary may be enlarged on presently. Even from it a certain resemblance, partly of a topsy-turvy kind, may be perceived by a reader of not less than ordinary acuteness to *Manon Lescaut*. The suggestion, such as it is, is quite frankly admitted, and an actual copy of Prévost's masterpiece figures not unimportantly in the tale.[2] Of the difference between the two, again presently.

The later editions of *La Dame aux Camélias* open with an "Introduction" by Jules Janin, dealing with a

[1] Dumas, like other mid-nineteenth century novelists in France and England both, is perhaps too fond of this complaint. But, after all, it *does* " stage " more prettily than appendicitis or typhoid.

[2] Nor is this the only place where *Manon* figures in the work of Alexander the younger. Especially in the early books direct references, more or less obvious, are frequent ; and, as will be seen, the inspiration reappears in his best and almost last novel.

certain Marie Duplessis—the recently living original, as we are told, of Marguerite Gautier. A good deal has been said, not by any means always approvingly, of this system of "introductions," especially to novels. In the present instance I should say that the proceeding was dangerous but effective—perhaps not entirely in the way in which it wâs intended to be so. "Honest Janin," [1] as Thackeray (who had deservedly rapped his knuckles earlier for a certain mixture of ignorance and impudence) called him later, was in his degree almost as "clever" a man as young Dumas; but his kind was different, and it did involve the derogatory connotation of cleverness. It is enough to say of the present subject that it displays, in almost the highest strength, the insincerity and superficiality of matter and thought which accompanied Janin's bright and almost brilliant facility of expression and style. His Marie Duplessis is one of those remarkable young persons who, to alter Dr. Johnson very slightly, unite "the manners of a *duchess* with the morals of" the other object of the doctor's comparison unaltered; superadding to both the amiability of an angel, the beauty of Helen, and the taste in art of all the great collectors rolled into one. The thing is pleasantly written bosh; and, except to those readers who are concerned to know that they are going to read about "a real person," can be no commendation, and might even cause a little disgust, not at all from the moral but from the purely critical side.

A lover of paradox might almost suggest that "honest Janin" had been playing the ingenious but dangerous finesse of intentionally setting up a foil to his text. He has

---

[1] It may perhaps seem to some readers that Janin's own novel-work should have been noticed earlier. I had at one time thought of doing this. But his most famous book of the sort, *L'Âne Mort et la Femme Guillotinée*, is a foolish *fatrasie* of extravagant, undigested, unaffecting horrors, from the devouring by dogs of the *live* donkey, at the beginning, to the "resurrectioning" of the guillotined woman, at the end. Sterne has played tricks with many clumsy imitators, but with none to more destructive effect than in this case. I read it first in the flush of my early enthusiasm for 1830, and was miserably disappointed; I tried to read it again the other day, and simply broke down. *Barnave* is interesting only as referred to by Gautier; and so on. The fact is that "J. J." was "J. J. 𝒴."—a journalist merely—with a not unpleasant frothy ginger-beery style, but with nothing whatever within it or beyond it.

certainly, to some tastes, done this.   There is hardly any
false prettiness, any sham Dresden china (a thing, by
the way, that has become almost a proverbial phrase in
French for *demi-monde* splendour), about *La Dame
aux Camélias* itself.   Nor, on the other hand, is there
to be found in it—even in such anticipated " natural-
isms " as the exhumation of Marguerite's *two*-months'-old
corpse,[1] and one or two other somewhat more veiled but
equally or more audacious touches of realism—anything
resembling the exaggerated horrors of such efforts o
1830 itself as Janin's own *Âne Mort* and part of Borel's
Champavert.   In her splendour as in her misery, in her
frivolity as in her devotion and self-sacrifice, repulsive as
this contrast may conventionally be, Marguerite is never
impossible or unnatural.   Her chief companion of her
own sex, Prudence Duvernoy, though, as might be
expected, a good deal of a *proxénète*, and by no means
disinterested in other ways, is also very well drawn, and
assists the general effect more than may at first be seen.
    The " problem " of the book, at least to English
readers, lies in the person whom it is impossible to call
the hero—Armand Duval.   It would be very sanguine
to say that he is unnatural ; but the things that he does
are rather appalling.   That he listens at doors, opens
letters not addressed to him, and so on, is sufficiently
fatal ; but a very generous extension of lovers' privileges
may perhaps just be stretched over these things.[2]   No
such licence will run to other actions of his.   In his
early days of chequered possession he writes, anony-
mously, an insulting letter to his mistress, which she
forgives ; but he has at least the grace to repent of this
almost immediately.   His conduct, however, when he
returns to Paris, after staying in the country with his
family, and finds that she has returned to her old ways,
is the real crime.   A violent scene might, again, be

---

[1] And, with dim-fretted foreheads all,
  On corpses *three* months old at noon she came.
                    (*The Palace of Art.*)

[2] If anybody cannot tolerate the stretching he had better abstain from Alexander the
younger's work, for " they all do it " there.   The fact may have conciliated some of
our own contemners of " good form."

excusable, for he does not know what his father has done. But for weeks this young gentleman of France devotes all his ingenuity and energies to tormenting and insulting the object of his former adoration. He ostentatiously " keeps " a beautiful but worthless friend of hers in her own class, and takes every opportunity of flaunting the connection in Marguerite's face. He permits himself and this creature to insult her in every way, apparently descending once more to anonymous letters. And when her inexhaustible forgiveness has induced a temporary but passionate reconciliation, he takes fresh umbrage, and sends money to her for her complaisance with another letter of more abominable insult than ever. Now it is bad to insult any one of whom you have been fond ; worse to insult any woman ; but to insult a prostitute, faugh ! [1]

However, I may be reading too much English taste into French ways here,[2] and it is impossible to deny that a man, whether French or English, *might* behave in this ineffable manner. In other words, the irresistible *humanum est* clears this as it clears Marguerite's own good behaviour, so conventionally inconsistent with her bad. The book, of course, cannot possibly be put on a level with its pattern and inspiration, *Manon Lescaut* : it is on a much lower level of literature, life, thought, passion—everything. But it has literature ; it has life and thought and passion ; and so it shall have no black mark here.

Few things could be more different from each other than *Tristan le Roux*—another early book of Dumas *fils*—

Tristan le is from *La Dame aux Camélias*. Indeed it is
Roux. a good, if not an absolutely certain, sign that so young a man should have tried styles in novel-writing

---

[1] Every one is entitled to write this word once in his life, I believe ; so I have selected my occasion at last. Of course some one may say : " You have admitted that he did not know Marguerite's pact with his father." True ; and this might excuse the wrath, but not the way of showing it.

[2] As I write this I remember a comic experience of fifty years ago. I was trying to find out the ruins of a certain castle in Brittany, and appealed, in my very best bad French, to an old road-mender. He scowled at me, as if it had been in the days of the *Combat des Trente*, and answered, " *Mais c'est de l'Anglais que vous me parlez là !* "

so far apart from each other. *Tristan* is a fifteenth-century story of the later part of the Hundred Years' War, and of Gilles de Retz, and of Joan of Arc, and of *diablerie*, and so forth. I first heard approval of it from a person whose name may be unexpected by some readers—the late Professor Robertson Smith. But the sometime editor of the *Encyclopædia Britannica* was exceptionally well qualified for the literary side of his office, and could talk about French quite as knowledgeably as he could about Arabic and Hebrew.[1] He was rather enthusiastic about the book, an enthusiasm which, when I myself came to read it, for a considerable time puzzled me a little. It opens pretty well, but already with a good deal of the " possible-improbable " about it ; for when some twenty wolves have once pulled a horse down and a man off it, his chance of escaping (especially without revolvers) seems small, even though two rescuers come up, one of whom has a knack of shooting these creatures [2] and the other of throttling them. It is on these rescuers that the central interest of the story turns. Olivier de Karnak and Tristan le Roux are, though they do not at the time know it, brothers by the same mother, the guiltless Countess of Karnak having been drugged, violated, and made a mother by Gilles de Retz's father. They are also rivals for the love of their cousin Alix, and as she prefers Olivier, this sends Tristan literally " to the Devil." The compact is effected by means of a Breton sorceress, who has been concerned in the earlier crime, and is an accomplice of Gilles himself. That eminent patriot performs,[3] for Tristan's benefit or ruin, one of his black masses, with a murdered child's blood for wine. Further *diablerie* opens a great tomb near Poitiers, where, seven hundred years earlier, in Charles Martel's

---

[1] Another trait of his may not displease readers, though it be not strictly relevant. I once, perhaps with some faint mischievous intent, asked him about the competence of Dr. Pusey and of M. Renan in the sacred tongue. " Pusey," he said, " knew pretty well everything about Hebrew that there was to be known in his day." He was not quite so complimentary about Renan ; though, as he put his judgment less pointedly, I do not remember the exact words.

[2] With a bow and arrows, remember ; not a Browning pistol.

[3] The indebtedness to Michelet is pretty obvious.

victory, an ancestor of the Karnaks has been buried alive,
with the Saracen Emir he had just slain, by the latter's
followers ; and where the two have beguiled the time by
continuous ghostly fighting. The Saracen, when the
tomb is opened, evades, seen by no one but Tristan,
and becomes the apostate's by no means guardian devil.
Then we have the introduction of the Maid (whom
Tristan is specially set by his master to catch), the
siege of Orleans and the rest of it, to the tragedy of
Rouen.

Up to this point—that is to say, for some seven-
eighths of the book—I confess that I did not, and do
not, think much of it. I am very fond of fighting in
novels ; and of *diablerie* even "more than reason";
and of the Middle Ages ; and of many other things
connected with the work. But it does not seem to me
well managed or well told. One never can make out
whether the "Sarrazin" is, as he is actually sometimes
called, Satan himself, or not. If he is not, why call him
so ? If he is, why was there so little evidence of his
being constantly employed in fighting with M. de
Karnak between the Battle of Poitiers (not ours, but the
other) and the Siege of Orleans ? I love my Dark and
Middle Ages ; but I should say that there was considerable diabolic activity in them, outside tombs. Or was
the Princedom of the Air "in commission" all that
time ? Minor improbabilities constantly jar, and there
are numerous small blunders of fact [1] of the unintentional

---

[1] It may be well to illustrate this, lest it be said that having been more than just to
the father (*v. sup.*) I am still less than just to the son. Merlin is made to visit Morgane
la Fée in the *eleventh* century. It is quite true that people generally began to hear about
Merlin and Morgane at that time. But he had then been for about half a millennium
in the sweet prison of the Lady of the Lake—over whom even Morgane had no power.
The English child-King, for whom Bedford was regent, is repeatedly called Henry *IV*.
There would have been quite other fish for Joan to fry, and other thread for her to retwist,
if she had had to do with Henry of Bolingbroke instead of Henry of Windsor. Tristan's
Mauthe Doog—not a bad kind of hound, though—bears the "Celtic" name of Thor.
Of course all these things are trifles, but they are annoying and useless. When the father
abridged Charles the First's captivity from years to days, he did it for the good of his
story. The son had no such justification. He is also very careless about minute join-
ings of the flats at a most important point of the conclusion (*v. inf.*). Tristan has
no sword, begs one of the *bourreau*, and is refused. He goes straight to church, and
immediately afterwards we find him sword in hand. Where did he get it ? By an
unmentioned miracle ?

kind, which irritate more than intentional ones of some importance.

But at the end the book improves quite astonishingly. Tristan, as has been said, has been specially commissioned by the fiend to effect the ruin of Joan. He has induced his half-brother, Gilles de Retz—not, indeed, to take the English side, for patriotism, as is well known, was the one redeeming point of that extremely loathsome person, but—to join the seigneurs who were malcontent with her, and if possible drug her and violate her, a process, as we have seen, quite congenial, hereditarily as well as otherwise, to M. de Laval. He is foiled, of course, and pardoned. But Tristan himself openly takes the English side, inflicts great damage on his countrymen, and after our defeat at the bastilles or bastides round Orleans, resumes his machinations against Joan, helps to effect her capture, and does his utmost to torment and insult her, and if possible resume Gilles's attempt, in her imprisonment; while, on the contrary, his brother Olivier (they are both disguised as monks) works on her side, nearly saves her,[1] and attends her on the scaffold. It is somewhat earlier than this that the author, as has been said, "wakes up" and wakes *us* up. When Tristan, admitted to Joan's cell, designs the same outrage to which he had counselled his brother, it is the Maid's assumption of her armour to protect herself from him that (in this point for once historically) seals her fate. But at the very last his hatred is changed, *not* at all impossibly or improbably, to violent love as she smiles on him from the fire; and he sees the legendary dove mount to heaven, after he himself has flung to her, at her dying cry, an improvised crucifix, or at least cross. And then a choice miracle happens, told with almost all the vigour of the "Vin de Porto" itself. Tristan seeks absolution, but is, though not harshly, refused, before penitence and penance. He begs his brother Olivier's pardon, and is again refused—this time with vituperation—but

---

[1] Tristan defeats an effort of Xaintrailles to rescue her, in a way vaguely resembling the defeat, in the greater Alexander's work, of the rescue of King Charles by the Four.

bears it calmly. He takes, meekly, more insult from the very executioner. At last he makes the sign of the compact and summons the "Saracen" fiend. And then, after a very good conversation, in which the Devil uses all his powers of sarcasm to show his victim that, as usual, he has sold his soul for naught, Tristan draws his sword, calls on the Trinity, Our Lady, and Joan, and one of the strangest though not of the worst fights in fiction begins.

The Red Bastard is himself almost a giant; but the Saracen is a fiend, and though it seems that in this case the Devil *can* be dead, he can, it seems also, only be killed at Poitiers in his original tomb. So

> They wrestle up, they wrestle down,
> They wrestle still and sore,

for two whole years, the Demon constantly giving ground and misleading his enemy as much as he can. But Tristan, in the strength of repentance and with Joan's unseen help, lives, fights, and forces the fiend back over half France and half the world. By a good touch, after long combat, the Devil tries to tempt his adversary on the side of chivalry, asking to be allowed to drink at a stream on a burning day, to warm himself at a fire they pass in a snow-storm, to rest a moment. But Tristan has the single word " Non ! " for any further pact with or concession to the Evil One ; the two years' battle wears away his sin ; and at last he finds himself pressing his fainting foe towards the very tomb in the fields of Poitou. It opens, and the combatants entering, find themselves by the actual graves. They drop their swords and now literally wrestle. Tristan wins, throws the Saracen into his own tomb, and runs him through the body, once more inflicting on him such death as he may undergo.[1]

---

[1] Unluckily, with a young man's misjudgment, Dumas would not let it be the actual end, though that is not a couple of pages off. After the fight Tristan goes out of the tomb to rest himself ; and meets the herald Bretagne, whom he had saved from the wolves in the overture. Bretagne tells him what has happened since the Maid's death, including the fate of his half-brother on the father's side, Gilles de Retz, who, like himself, has repented in time to save his soul, if not his life. Having also seen afar off a cavalcade in

There is a grandiose extravagance about it which is really Oriental ; [1] and perhaps it was this which conciliated Robertson Smith, as it certainly reconciled me.

A third " book of the beginning," *Antonine*, is far inferior to these.   It is, in fact, little more than a decentish
Antonine.   Paul-de-Kockery, with a would-be philosophical conclusion.   Two young men, Gustave Daunont and Edmond de Péreux, saunter after breakfast looking for young ladies' ankles, and Edmond sees a pair so beautiful that he follows the possessor and her unobservant father home.   Having then ascertained that the father is a doctor, he adopts the surprisingly brilliant expedient of going to consult him, and so engineering an entry.   *He* thinks there is nothing the matter with him ; but the doctor (it was apparently " at temp. of tale "—1834, while the port was getting ready,— the practice of French physicians, to receive their patients in dressing-gowns) discovers that he is in an advanced stage of Dumas *fils*' favourite *poitrine*.   He says, however, nothing about it (which seems odd) to his patient, merely prescribing roast-meat and Bordeaux ; but (which seems odder) he *does* mention it to his daughter Antonine, the Lady with the Ankles.   For the moment nothing happens.   But Gustave the friend has for mistress an adorable *grisette*—amiability, in the widest sense, *nez retroussé*, garret, and millinery all complete—whom Madame de Péreux, Edmond's mother—a *sainte*, but without prejudices—tolerates, and in fact patronises.   It is arranged that Nichette shall call on Antonine to ask, as a milliner, for her custom.   Quite unexpected explanations follow in a not uningenious manner, and the explosion is completed by Edmond's opening (not at all treacherously) a letter addressed to Gustave and containing the news of his own danger.   The rest of the story need not be told at length.   A miraculous cure effected

---

which are Olivier and Alix, now married and rapturous, Tristan retires into the tomb, which closes over him. His horse " Baal " and his dogs, the " Celtically " (in the latter case we may say *Piratically*) named Thor and Brinda, are petrified round its entrance.
[1] Crusading times, and Jôf or Edessa for Rouen and Poitiers as places, might seem preferable. But the fifteenth century did a lot of *diablerie* in the West.

by M. Devaux, Antonine's father ; marriage of the pair ; pensioning off of Nichette, and marriage of Gustave to another adorable girl (ankles not here specified) ; establishment of Nichette at Tours in partnership with a respectable friend, etc., etc., can easily be supplied by any novel-reader.

But here the young author's nascent seriousness, and his still existing Buskbody superstition, combine to spoil the book, not merely, as in the *Tristan* case, to top-hamper it. Having given us eight pages of rather cheap sermonising about the poetry of youth not lasting ; having requested us to imagine Manon and Des Grieux "decrepit and catarrhous," Paul and Virginie shrivelled and toothless, Werther and Charlotte united but wrinkled,[1] he proceeds to tell us how, though Gustave and his Laurence are as happy as they can be, though Nichette has forgotten her woes but kept her income and is married to a bookseller, things are not well with the other pair. Antonine loves her husband frantically, but he has become quite indifferent to her—says, indeed, that he really does not know whether he ever *did* love her. Later still we take leave of him, his " poetry " having ended in a prefecture, and his passion in a *liaison*, commonplace to the *n*th, with a provincial lawyer's wife. *La moralité de cette comédie* (to quote, probably not for the first time, or I hope the last, words of Musset which I particularly like) would appear to be—first, that to secure lasting happiness in matrimony it is desirable, if not necessary, to have lived for eighteen months antenuptially with a charming *grisette*—amiability, *nez retroussé*, garret, and millinery all complete—or to have yourself been this grisette ; while, on the other hand, it is an extremely dangerous thing to recover a man of his consumption. Which last result the folklorists would doubtless assimilate to the well-known superstition of the shore as to the rescue of the drowning.

[1] A curious variant of this fancy of his will be noticed later. What is more curious still need, perhaps, hardly be indicated for any intelligent reader—the " sicklying over " of Paul-de-Kockery with a " cast of thought "—" pale," or " dry," or up to " Old Brown " in strength and character as it may seem to different people.

Two other early books of this author promise the
Pauline influence in their titles and do not belie it in their
La Vie à contents, though in varying way and degree.
Vingt Ans. Indeed, the first story of *La Vie à Vingt Ans*—
that of a schoolboy who breaks his bounds and " sells
his dictionaries " to go to the Bal de l'Opéra ; receives,
half in joy, half in terror, an assignation from a masked
débardeur, and discovers her to be an aged married
woman with a drunken husband (the pair knowing from
his card that his uncle is a Deputy, and having determined to get a *débit de. tabac* out of him)—made me laugh
as heartily as the great Paul himself can ever have made
Major Pendennis.   The rest—they are all stories of the
various amatory experiences of a certain Emmanuel de
Trois Étoiles, and have a virtuous epilogue extolling
pure affection and honest matrimony—are inferior, the
least so being that of the caprice-love of a certain Augustine, Emmanuel's neighbour on his staircase, who admits
only one other lover and finally marries *him*, but conceives a frantic though passing affection for her *voisin*.
Unluckily there is in this book a sort of duplicate but,
I think, earlier sketch of the atrocious conduct of Duval
to the Dame aux Camélias ; and there are some of the
author's curious " holes where you can put your hand "
(as a Jacobean poet says of the prosodic licences in
nomenclature and construction of his fellows).

The other, much longer, and much more ambitious
and elaborate book, *Aventures de Quatre Femmes et d'un
Aventures de Perroquet*, seems to me on the whole worse
Quatre than any just mentioned, though it at least
Femmes. attempts to fly higher than *Antonine*. It
begins by one of those *goguenardises* which 1830 itself
had loved, but it is not a good specimen.   Two men
who have determined on suicide—one by shooting, one
by hanging—meet at the same tree in the Bois de Boulogne and wrangle about possession of the spot, till the
aspirant to suspension *per coll.* recounts his history from
the branch on which he is perched.   After which an
unlucky thirdsman, interfering, gets shot, and buried

as one of the others—"which is witty, let us 'ope," as the poetical historian of the quarrel between Mr. Swinburne and Mr. Buchanan observes of something else.[1] As the book begins with two attempted and disappointed suicides, so it ends with two accomplished ones. A great part, and not the least readable, is occupied by a certain English Countess of Lindsay (for Dumas the younger, like Crébillon the younger, commits these *scandala magnatum* with actual titles). The hero is rather a fool, and not much less of a knave than he should be. His somewhat better wife is an innocent bigamist, thinking him dead; and one of the end-suicides is that of her second husband, who, finding himself *de trop*, benevolently makes way. As for the parrot, he nearly spoils the story at the beginning by "*singing*" (which I never heard a parrot do), and atones at the end by getting poisoned without deserving it. I am afraid I must call it a rather silly book.

It does not, however, lack the cleverness with which silliness, especially in the young *and* the old, is often associated, and so does not break the assignment of that quality to its author. All these five books were produced (with others) in a very few years, by a man who was scarcely over twenty when he began and was not thirty when he wrote the last of them. Now people sometimes write wonderful poetry when they are very young, because, after all, a poet is not much more than a mouthpiece of the Divine, whose spirit bloweth where it listeth. But it is not often that they write thoroughly good novels till, like other personages who have to wait for their "overseership" up to thirty, they have had time and opportunity roughly to scan and sample life. There is, in this work of Alexander the younger, plenty of imitation, of convention, of that would-be knowingness which is the most amusing form of ignorance, etc., etc. But

---

[1] As I have received complaints, mild and other, of the frequency of my unexplained allusions, I may here refer explicitly to Mr. Traill's *Recaptured Rhymes*; and if anybody, after looking up the book, is not grateful to me, I am sorry for him. For the commoner practice here I can only plead that I follow the Golden Rule. Nothing pleases *me* so much as an allusion that I understand—except one that I don't and have to hunt up.

there is a good deal more: and especially there is plenty of the famous *diable au corps*, of *verve*, of " go," of refusal to be content with one rut and one model. And all this came once, even at this period, in *La Dame aux Camélias*, to something which I shall not call a masterpiece, but which certainly is a powerful thesis for the attainment of the master's degree.

Perhaps there is no better example of the curious mixture of *verve*, variety, and vigorous hitting-off which *Trois Hommes* characterised the youth of Dumas *fils* than *Forts.* *Trois Hommes Forts*—a book of the exact middle of the century, which begins with an idyll, passing into a tragedy; continues with a lively ship-and-yellow-fever scene; plunges into a villainous conspiracy against virtue and innocence diversified with a bull-throwing; and winds up with another killing, which, this time, *is* no murder; a trial, after which and an acquittal the accused and the Crown Prosecutor embrace before (and amidst the chalorous applause of) the whole Court; not forgetting a final *panache* of happy marriage between innocence, a very little damaged, and the bull-thrower-avenger-*ouvrier*, Robert. It is of course pure melodrama —*Minnigrey* and the Porte-Saint-Martin pleasantly accommodated. But it is not too long; it never drags; and it knocks about in the cheerfullest " pit-box-and-gallery " fashion from first to last. When the wicked " Joseph le Mendiant," *alias* M. Valéry, *alias* Frédéric Comte de La Marche [1]—who has stabbed a priest with one hand and throttled an old woman with the other; then made a fortune in Madagascar; then nearly died of yellow-fever on board ship, but recovered (something after the fashion of one of Marryat's heroes) by drinking a bottle of Madeira; then gone home and bought an estate and given himself the above title; then seduced the innocent sister of the person who heard his confession; then tried to marry a high-born maiden; [2] then threat-

---

[1] *Rather* too big a title for an adventurer to meddle with, surely ?

[2] He has found out a secret about her. When she learns his crimes and his fate, she puts an end to herself in a way which I fear Octave Feuillet borrowed, rather unceremoniously, though he certainly improved it, in *Julia de Trécœur* (*v. inf.*). I did not read

ened to betray the sister's shame if her brother " tells "—
when this villain has his skull broken by Robert, all
right-minded persons will clap their hands sore. But
remembrance of one passage at the beginning may
" leave a savour of sorrow." Could you, even in
Meridional France, to-day procure a breakfast consisting
of truffled pigs' feet, truffled thrush, tomato omelette (I
should bar the tomatoes), and strawberries in summer,
or " quatre - mendiants " (figs, nuts, and almonds and
raisins) in winter, *with* a bottle of sound Roussillon or
something like it, for three francs ? Alas ! one fears
not.

Diane de Lys, a little later than most of the books
just mentioned, and one, I think, of the first to be dramatised, so announcing the author's change of
" kind," acquired a certain fame by being
made (in which form I am not certain, but probably as
a play) the subject of one of those odd " condemnations "
by which the Second Empire occasionally endeavoured
to show itself the defender of morality and the prop of
family and social life. I do not think that Flaubert and
Baudelaire had much reason to pride themselves on their
predecessor in this particular pillory. Alexander the
younger is not here even a coppersmith ; his metal is,
to me, not attractive at all. The Marquise de Lys is
one of those beauties, half Greek, half Madonnish, and
wholly regular-scholastic, to whom it has been the habit
of modern novelists and poets to assign what our Elizabethan ancestors would have called " cold hearts and
hot livers." Dumas *fils'* theory—for he must, Heaven
help him ! always have one [1]—is that it all depends on
ennui. I know not. At any rate, Diane is not a heroine
that I should recommend, for personal acquaintance, to
myself or my friends. With one of those rather silly
excuses which chequer his cleverness equally, whether
they are made honestly or with tongue in cheek, our

Diane de Lys.

Trois Hommes Forts till many years after I had read and praised Feuillet's work. Also,
is it absolutely blasphemous to suggest that the beginning of the book has a faint likeness
to that of *Les Misérables* much later ?

[1] *V. sup.* last chapter, *passim.*

author says : " On va sans doute nous dire que nous
présentons un caractère impossible, que nous faisons de
l'immoralité " (which the compositors of the stereotyped
edition pleasantly misprint "immor*a*lité "), etc. Far be
it from me to say that any woman is impossible. I
would only observe that when Diane, neglected by and
neglecting her husband for some two years, determines
to take a lover, being vexed at the idea of reaching the
age of thirty without having one ; when she takes him
without any particular preference, as one might call a
cab from a longish rank, and then has a fancy to make a
scientific comparison of forgotten joys with her husband,
deciding finally that there is nothing like alternation—
when, I say, she does this, I think she is not quite nice.[1]
Nor does her school-friend Marceline Delaunay—who,
being herself a married woman irreproachably faithful
to her own husband, makes herself a go-between, at
least of letters, for Diane—seem very nice either. It
is fair to say that Mme. Delaunay gets punished in the
latter part of the story, which any one may read who
likes. It is, if not white, a sort of—what shall we say ?
—French grey, compared with the opening.

That standard edition of *Diane de Lys* which has
enabled us to pick up such a pleasant *coquille d'imprimerie*
Shorter   contains three shorter stories (*Diane* itself is
stories—Une not very long). Two of them are not worth
Loge à   much : *Ce qu'on ne sait pas* is a pathetic
Camille.   grisetterie, something of the class of Musset's
Frédéric et Bernerette ; *Grangette* deals with the very true
but very common admonition that in being " on with "
two loves at once there is always danger, particularly
when, as M. le Baron Francis de Maucroix does here,
you write them letters (to save time) in exactly the same
phraseology. Neither love, Adeline the countess or the
Gris-Grang-ette, is disagreeable ; indeed Francis himself
is a not detestable idiot, and there is a comfortable conversation as he sits at Adeline's feet in proper morning-

---

[1] One remembers, as so often, Dr. Johnson to Boswell : " This lady of yours, Sir,
is very fit for," etc.

call costume, with his hat and stick on a chair. (Even kneeling would surely be less dangerous, from the point of view of recovering a more usual attitude when another caller comes.) But the whole thing is slight. The third and last, however, *Une Loge à Camille*, is the only thing in the whole volume that is thoroughly recommendable. It begins with an obviously " felt " and " lived " complaint of the woes which dramatic authors perhaps most of all, but others more or less, experience from that extraordinary inconsecutiveness (to put it mildly) of their acquaintances which makes people—who, to do them justice, would hardly ask for five, ten, or fifty shillings except as a loan, with at least pretence of repayment—demand almost, or quite, as a right, a box at the theatre or a copy of a book. This finished, an example is given in which the hapless playwright, having rashly obliged a friend, becomes (very much in the same way in which Mr. Nicodemus Easy killed several persons on the coast of Sicily) responsible for the breach, not merely of a left-handed yet comparatively harmless *liaison*, but of a formal marriage, the knitting of a costly and disreputable amour, a duel, an imprisonment for debt, and—for himself—the abiding reputation of having corrupted, half ruined, and driven into enlistment for Africa a guileless scientific student. It is good and clean fun throughout.[1]

Some others must have shorter shrift. One volume of the standard edition contains two stories, *Le Docteur Servans* and *Un Cas de Rupture*. The latter is short and not very happy, beginning with a rather feeble following of Xavier de Maistre,[2] continuing with stock *liaison*-matter, and ending rather vulgarly. Let us, however, give thanks to Alexander the younger in that he nobly defends the sacred persons of our English

Le Docteur Servans.

---

[1] This is, I think, the best of his short stories. *Thérèse* is rather a sermon on the somewhat unsavoury text of morbid appetite in the other sex, than a real story. The little *Histoires Vraies*, which he wrote with a friend for the *Moniteur* in 1864, are fairly good. For the formally entitled *Contes et Nouvelles* and the collection headed by *Ilka, v. inf.*

[2] He represents himself as suffering forty-eight hours of very easy imprisonment for not mounting guard as a " National," and writing the story to pass the time.

ladies against the venerable Gallic calumny of large feet, though he unhappily shows imperfect knowledge of the idioms of our language by using " Lady " as if it were like " Milady ": "Reprit Lady," " Lady vit," etc. *Le Docteur Servans* is more substantial, though itself not very long.   It is a rather well-engineered story (illustrative of a fact to be noticed presently in regard to much of its author's work) about a benevolent doctor who, at first as a method of kindness and then as a method of testing character, " makes believe," and makes others believe, that he has the secret of Resurrection.[1]   On *Le Roman d'une Femme.* the other hand, I have only read *Le Roman d'une Femme* in the beloved little old Belgian edition which gave one one's first knowledge of so many pleasant things, and the light - weighting and large print of which are specially suitable to fiction. Putting one thing aside, it is not one of its author's greatest triumphs.   It begins with a good deal of that rather nauseous gush about the adorable candour of young persons which, in a French novel, too often means that the " blanche colombe " will become a very dingy dunghill hen before long—as duly happens here.   There is, however, a chance for the novel reader of comparing the departure of two of these white doves [2] from their school-dovecot with that of Becky and Amelia from Miss Pinkerton's.   And I must admit that, after a middle of commonplace grime, the author works up an end of complicated and by no means unreal tragedy.

The point referred to about the two principal books just noticed, and indeed about Alexander the Younger's The habit of books generally, is the remarkable faculty— quickening and not merely faculty but actual habit—which up at the end. he displays, of turning an uninteresting beginning into an interesting end.   I cannot remember any other novelist, in any of the literatures with which I am

---

[1] The author has shown his skill by inducing at least one very old hand to wonder, for a time at least, whether Dr. Servans is a quack, or a lunatic, or Hoffmannishly uncanny, when he is, in fact, something quite different from any of these.

[2] The other, Clémentine (who is not very unlike a more modern Claire d'Orbe), being not nearly so " candid " as her comrade Marie, continues honest.

acquainted, who possesses, or at least uses, this odd gift
to anything like the same degree. On the contrary,
some of the greatest—far greater than he is—give results
exactly contrary. Lady Louisa Stuart's reproach to
Scott for "huddling up" his conclusions is well known
and by no means ill-justified, while Sir Walter is far from
being a solitary sinner. I must leave it to those who
have given more study than I have to drama, especially
modern drama, to decide whether this had anything to
do with the fact that Dumas turned to the other kind.
The main fact itself admits, as far as my experience and
opinion go, of absolutely no dispute. Again and again,
not merely in *Le Docteur Servans* and *Le Roman d'une
Femme*, but in *La Dame aux Camélias* itself, in *Tristan le
Roux*, in *Les Aventures de Quatre Femmes*, and in others
still, I have been, at first reading, on the point of
dropping the book. But, owing to the mere "triarian"
habit of never giving up an appointed post, I have been
able to turn my defeat (and his, as it seemed to me) into
a victory, which no doubt I owe to him, but which has
something of my own in it too. His heroes very
frequently disgust and his heroines do not often delight
me ; I have "seen many others" than his baits of voluptuousness ; he does not amuse me like Crébillon ; nor
thrill me like Prévost in the unique moment ; nor interest
me like his closest successor, Feuillet. I cannot place
his work, despite the excellence of his mere writing, high
as great literature. He is altogether on a lower level
than Flaubert or Maupassant ; and one could not think
of evening him with Hugo in one way, with Balzac in
another, with his own father in a third, with Gautier
or Mérimée in a fourth. But he does, somehow or other,
manage that, in the evening time, there shall be such
light as he can give ; and I am bound to acknowledge
this as a triumph of craft, if not of actual art. That
while a gift and a remarkable one, it is rather a dangerous
gift for a novelist to rely on, needs little argument.

The formally titled *Contes et Nouvelles* do not contain
very much of the first interest. In the opening one

there is a lady who, not perhaps in the context quite taste-
fully, remarks that " Nous avons toutes notre calvaire,"
Contes et her own Golgotha consisting of the duty of
Nouvelles. adjusting "the extremest devotion" to her
husband with "remembrance" (there was a good deal
to remember) of her lover "to her last heart-beat." To
help her to perform this self-immolation, she bids the
lover leave her, refuses him, and that repeatedly, permission to return, till, believing himself utterly cast off, he
makes up his mind to love a very nice girl whom his
parents want him to marry. *Then* the self-Calvarised lady
promptly discovers that she wants him again ; and as
he, acknowledging her claim, does not disguise his actual
state of feeling, she, though going off in a huff, tells him
that she had never meant him either to leave her at first
or to accept her command not to return. All this, no
doubt, is not unfeminine in the abstract ; but the concrete
telling of it required more interesting personages. *Le
Prix de Pigeons* is a good-humoured absurdity about an
English scientific society, which offers a prize of £2000
to anybody who can eat a pigeon every day for a month ;
Le Pendu de la Piroche, a fifteenth-century anecdote,
which may be a sort of *brouillon* for *Tristan* ; *Césarine*,
a fortune-telling tale. But *La Boîte d'Argent*, the story
of a man who got rid of his heart and found himself
none the better for getting it back again (the circumstances in each case being quite different from those of
Das kalte Herz), and *Ce que l'on voit tous les jours*, a
sketch of "scenes" between keeper and mistress, but
of much wider application, go far above the rest of the
book. The first (which is of considerable length and very
cleverly managed in the change from ordinary to extraordinary) only wants "that" to be first-rate. The
second shows in the novelist the command of dialogue-
situation and of dialogue itself which was afterwards to
stand the playwright in such good stead.

Some forty years afterwards—indeed I think post-
humously—another collection appeared, with, for main
title, that of its first story, *Ilka*. Subject to the caution,

several times already given, of the inadequacy of a foreigner's judgment, I should say that it shows a great improvement in mere style, but somewhat of a falling off in originality and *verve*. The most interesting thing, perhaps, is an anecdote of the author's youth, when, having in the midst of a revolution extracted the mighty sum of two hundred francs in one bank-note from a publisher for a bad novel (he does not tell us which), he gives it to a porter to change, and the messenger being delayed, entertains the direst suspicions (which turn out to be quite unjust) of the poor fellow's honesty. The sketch of mood is capitally done, and is set off by a most pleasant introduction of Dumas *père*. More ambitious but less successful, except as mere descriptive *ecphrases*,[1] are the title-story of a beautiful model posing, and *Le Songe d'une Nuit d'Été*, with a companion picture of two lovers bathing at night; *Pile ou Face* (a girl who is so divided between two lovers that a friend advises her to toss up, with the pessimist-satiric addition that no doubt, between tossing and marriage, she will be sorry she did not take the other, but afterwards will forget all about him) is slighter; and *Au Docteur J.P.* looks like a kind of study for a longer novel or at least a more elaborate novel-hero.[2]

And so, at last, we may come to the book which curiously carries out, with a slight deflection, but an almost equivalent intensification, of meaning, what has been observed before of others—the singular habit which Dumas *fils* has of quickening up

Ilka.

Affaire Clémenceau.

---

[1] *V. sup.* Vol. I. p. 204.

[2] Two early and slight books (one of them, perhaps, the " bad " one referred to above) may find place in a note. *Revenants* is a fantasy, in which the three most famous pairs of lovers of the later eighteenth century, Des Grieux and Manon, Paul and Virginie, Werther and Charlotte, are revived and brought together (*v. sup.* p. 378). This sort of thing, not seldom tried, has very seldom been a success ; and *Revenants* can hardly be said to be one of the lucky exceptions. *Sophie Printemps* is the history of a good girl, who, out of her goodness, deliberately marries an epileptic. It has little merit, except for a large episode or parenthesis of some forty or fifty pages (nearly a sixth of the book), telling the prowess of a peremptory but agreeable baron, who first foils a dishonest banker, and then defends this very banker against an adventurer more rascally than himself, whom the baron kills in a duel. This is good enough to deserve extraction from the book, and separate publication as a short story.

Revenants.

Sophie Printemps.

for the run-in. This book was, I believe, in all important respects actually his run-in for the novel-prize ; and what he had hitherto shown in the conduct of individual books he now showed in regard to his whole novel-list, betaking himself thenceforward, though he had nearly a third of a century to live, to the theatre, to pamphlets, etc. Against *Affaire Clémenceau* [1] there are some things to be said, and in criticism, not necessarily hostile, a great many about it. But nobody who knows strength when he sees it can deny that this is a strong book from start to finish. I can very well remember the hubbub it caused when it first appeared, and the debates about " Tue-la ! " but I did not then read it, having, as I have confessed, a sort of prejudice—not then or at any time common with me—against the author—a prejudice strengthened rather than weakened by reviews of the book. What did I care (I am bound to say that I might add, " What *do* I care ? ") about discussions whether if somebody breaks the Seventh Commandment to your discomfort you may break the Sixth to theirs ? Did I want diatribes on the non-moral character of women, or anything of that sort ? I wanted an interesting story ; an attractive (no matter in what fashion) heroine ; a hero who is a gentleman, if possible, a man anyhow ; and I did not think I should find them here. *Now*, I can " dichotomise " to some extent ; and I can get an interesting story, striking moments, if not exactly an attractive heroine or hero, at any rate such as take their part in the interest, though I may have crows to pluck with them. It is, once more, a strong book : it is nearly—though I do not think quite—a great book. And to all sportsmanlike lovers of letters it is, despite its discomfortable matter, a comfortable book, because it shows us a considerable man of letters who has never yet, save perhaps in *La Dame aux Camélias*, quite " come

---

[1] It is constantly called (and I fear I have myself sinned in this respect) *L'Affaire Clémenceau*. But this is not the proper title, and does not really fit. It is the heading of a client's instruction—a sort of irregular " brief "—to the advocate who (*resp. fin.*) is to defend him ; and is thus an autobiographic narrative (diversified by a few " put-in " letters) throughout. The title is the label of the brief.

off," coming off beyond all fair doubt or reasonable question.

Probably a good many people know the story of it, but certainly some do not. It can be told pretty shortly. Pierre Clémenceau, the *fils naturel* (for this *vulnus* is *eternum*) of a linen-draperess, is made, partly on account of his birth, unhappy at school, being especially tormented by an American-Italian boy, André Minati, whom, however, he thrashes, and who dies—but not of the thrashing. The father of another and *not* hostile school-fellow, Constantin Ritz, is a sculptor, and accident helps him to discover the same vocation in young Clémenceau, who is taken into his protector's household as well as his studio, and makes great progress in his art—the one thing he cares for. He goes, however, a very little into society, and one evening meets a remarkable Russian-Polish Countess, whose train (for it is a kind of fancy ball) is borne by her thirteen-year-old daughter Iza, dressed as a page. The girl is extraordinarily beautiful, and Clémenceau, whose heart is practically virgin, falls in love with her, child as she is ; improving the acquaintance by making a drawing of her when asleep, as well as later a bust from actual sittings, *gratis*. After a time, however, the Countess, who has some actual and more sham " claims " in Poland and Russia, returns thither. Years pass, during which, however, Pierre hears now and then from Iza in a mixed strain of love and friendship, till at last he is stung doubly, by news that she is to marry a young Russian noble named Serge, and by a commission for the trousseau to be supplied by his mother,[1] who has retired from business. The correspondence changes to sharp reproach on his part and apparently surprised resentment on hers. But before long she appears in person (the Serge marriage having fallen through), and, to speak vernacularly, throws herself straight at Pierre's head, even offering to

---

[1] This is probably meant as the first " light " on the shady side of Iza's character ; not that, in this instance, she means to insult or hurt, but that the probability of hurting and insulting does not occur to her, or leaves her indifferent.

be his mistress if she cannot be his wife.[1] They are
married, however, and spend not merely a honey-moon,
but nearly a honey-year in what is, in *Hereward the Wake*,
graciously called "sweet madness," the madness, however, being purely physical, though so far genuine, on
her side, spiritual as well as physical on his. The
central scene of the book (very well done) gives a picture
of Iza insisting on bathing in a stream running through
the park (private, but practically open to the public)
of the house lent to them. When her husband has
brought her warm milk in a chased-silver cup of their
host's, she casts it, empty, on the ground, and on the
husband's exclamation, "Take care!" replies coolly,
"What does it matter? It isn't *mine*."

This may be said to be the third warning-bell; but
though it shocks even the "ensorceressed" Pierre for
the moment, his infatuation continues. At last he begins
to have an idea that people look askance at him; trains of
suspicion are laid; after one or two clever evasions of Iza's,
the usual "epistolary communication" forces the matter,
and Constantin Ritz at last tells the unhappy husband
that not merely has "Serge" reappeared, but there are
nearly half-a-dozen "others," and that doubts have even
been suggested as to connivance on Pierre's part—doubts
strengthened by Iza's treacherous complaints as to her
husband having employed her as a model. A violent
scene follows, Iza brazening it out, and calmly demanding
separation. Clémenceau goes to Rome after forcing
a duel on Serge and wounding him; but the blow has
weakened, if not destroyed, his powers in art. Fresh
scandals follow, and the irresistible Iza seduces Constantin
himself, characteristically communicating the fact in an
anonymous letter to her miserable husband. He returns
(for the second time), takes no vengeance on his friend, but
sees his wife. The interview provides an audaciously
devised but finely executed curtain. She calmly proposes
—how shall we say it?—to "put herself in commission."
She loves nobody but him, she says, and knows he has

[1] Second "light," and now not dubious, for it is made a point of later.

loved, loves, and will love nobody but her. He ought, originally, to have taken her offer of being his mistress, and then no harm would have happened. She would really like to go back with him to Saint-Assise (the honeymoon place). Suppose they do? As for *living* with him and being "faithful" to him—that is impossible. But she will come to him, at his whistle, whenever he likes, and be absolutely his for a day and a night and a morrow. In fact he may begin at once if he likes: and she puts her arms round his neck and her mouth to his. He takes her at her word; but when the night is half passed and she is asleep, he gently rises, goes into the next room, fetches a stiletto paper-knife with which he has seen her playing, half wakes her, asks her if she loves him, to which, still barely conscious, she answers "Yes!" with a half-formed kiss on her lips. Then he stabs her dead with a single blow, leaving the house quietly, and giving himself up to the police at dawn.

If anybody asks me, "Is this well done?" expecting me to enter on the discussion of the *lex non scripta*, I shall reply that this is not my trade. But if the question refers to the merits of the handling, I can reply as confidently as the dying Charmian, "It is well done, and fitting for a novelist." In no book, as it seems to me, has the author obtained such a complete command of his <small>Criticism of</small> subject or reeled out his story with such steady <small>it and of its</small> confidence and fluency. No doubt he some- <small>author's work</small> times preaches too much.[1] The elder Ritz's <small>generally.</small> advice against suicide, for instance, if sound is superfluous. But this is not a very serious evil, and the steady *crescendo* of interest which prevails throughout the story carries it off. There are also numerous separate passages of real distinction, the fateful bathing-scene being, as it should be, the best, except the finale; but others, such as the history of Pierre's first modelling from the life, being excellent. The satire on the literary

---

[1] It has sometimes amused me to remember that some of the warmest admirers of Dumas *fils* have been among the most violent decriers of Thackeray—*for* preaching. I suppose they preferred the Frenchman's texts.

coteries of the Restoration is about the best thing of the kind that the author has done ; and many of the " interiors "—always a strong point with him—are admirable. It is on the point of character that the chief questions may arise ; but here also there seems to me to be only one of these—it is true it is the most important of all— on which there should be much debate.   The succumbing of Constantin seems perhaps a little more justifiable by its importance to the story than by its intrinsic probability.[1]   Clémenceau seems to me " constant to himself," or in the " good childlikeness " of his character, throughout ; and to ask whether it was necessary to make him smash the bust that he finds in Serge's possession seems to be equivalent to asking whether it was necessary to put the Vice-Consul of Tetuan in petticoats.[2] It is only about Iza herself that there can be much dispute. Has that process synthetic which is spoken of elsewhere been carried too far with her ?   Have doses of childlikeness, beauty, charm, ill-nature, sensual appetite, etc., been taken too " boldly " (in technical doctors' sense) and mixed too crudely to measure ?   A word or two may be permissible on this.

I do not think that Iza is an impossible personage ; nor do I think that she is even an improbable one to such an extent as to bar her out, possible or impossible.   But I am not sure that she is not rather arbitrarily synthetised instead of being re-created, or that she, though possible and not quite improbable, is not singly abnormal[3] to the verge of monstrosity.   It must be evident to any reader of tolerable acuteness that the obsession of *Manon Lescaut* has not left Dumas *fils*.   Although the total effect of Manon and of Iza is very different, and although they are differently " staged," their resemblances in detail

---

[1] Neither morality, nor friendship, nor anything like sense of " good form " could be likely to hold him back.   But he is represented as nothing if not *un homme fort* in character and temperament, who knows his woman thoroughly, and must perceive that he is letting himself be beaten by her in the very act of possessing her.

[2] Vide *Mr. Midshipman Easy*.

[3] This phrase may require just a word of explanation.   I admitted (Vol. I. p. 409) the abnormality in *La Religieuse* as not disqualifying.   But this was not an abnormality of the *individual*.   Iza's is.

are very great; and, to speak paradoxically, the differences are almost more resembling still. Iza offers herself as mistress if there are any difficulties in the way of her being a wife; would, in fact, as she admits long afterwards, have preferred the less honourable, but also less fettering, estate. On the other hand, be it remembered, it was something of an accident that Manon and Des Grieux were *not* actually married. The two women are alike in their absolute insistence on luxury and pleasure before anything else; but they differ in that Iza does—as we said Manon did *not*, or did not specially —want "what Messalina wanted." On the other hand, Iza is ill-natured and Manon is not. In these respects we may say that the Manon-formula has passed through that of Madame de Merteuil, and bears unpleasant signs of the passage. Manon repents, which Iza never could do. But they agree in the courtesan essence—the readiness to exchange for other things that commodity of theirs which should be given only for love. I never wish to supply my readers with problem-tabloids; but I think that in this paragraph I have supplied them with materials for working out the double question, "Is Iza less human than Manon? and if so, why?" for themselves, as well as, if by any chance they should care to do so, of guessing my own answers to it.[1]

---

[1] Perhaps I may add another subject for those who like it. "Both Manon and Iza do *prefer*, and so to speak only *love*, the one lover. Does this in Iza's case aggravate, or does it partially redeem, her general behaviour?" A less disputable addition, for the reason given above, may be a fairly long note on the author's work outside of fiction.

With the drama which has received such extraordinary encomia (the great name of Molière having even been brought in for comparison) I have no exhaustive acquaintance; but I have read enough not to wish to read any more. If the huge prose tirades of *L'Étrangère* bore me (as they do) in the study, what would they do on the stage, where long speeches, not in great poetry, are always intolerable? (I have always thought it one of the greatest triumphs of Madame Sarah Bernhardt that, at the very beginning of her career, she made the heroine of this piece—*if* she did so—interesting.) Over the *Fils Naturel* I confess that even I, who have struggled with and mastered my thousands, if not my tens of thousands, of books, broke down hopelessly. *Francillon* is livelier, and might, in the earlier days, have made an amusing novel. But discounting, judicially and not prejudicially, the excessive laudation, one sees that even here he did what he meant to do, and though there is higher praise than that, it is praise only too seldom deserved. As for his Prefaces and Pamphlets, I think nearly as much must be granted; and I need not repeat what has been said above on the other side. The charity "puff" of *Les Madeleines Repenties* is an admirable piece of rhetoric not seldom reaching eloquence; and it has the not unliterary side-interest of suggesting the question whether its ironic treatment of the general estimate

(marginal note: Note on Dumas fils' drama, etc.)

It is more germane to custom and purpose here to add a few general remarks on the story, and more, but still few, on its author's general position.

Reflections.

Affaire Clémenceau is certainly, as has been said before, his strongest book, and, especially if taken together with *La Dame aux Camélias* (which, if less free from faults, contains some different merits), it constitutes a strong thesis or diploma-piece for all but the highest degree as a novelist. Taking in the others which have been surveyed, we must also acknowledge in the author an unusually wide range and a great display of faculty—even of faculties—almost all over that range, though perhaps in no other case than the two selected has he thoroughly mastered and firmly held the ground which he has attempted to win. If he has not—if *Tristan le Roux* is, on the whole, only a second- or third-rate historical romance ; *Trois Hommes Forts* a fair and competent, but not thrilling melodrama, and so on, and so on—it is no doubt partly, to speak with the sometimes useful as well as engaging irrationality of childhood, " because he couldn't." But I think it is also because of something that can be explained. It was because he was far too prone to theorise about men and women and to make his books attempted demonstrations, or at least illustrations, of his theories. Now, to theorise about men is seldom very satisfactory ; but to theorise about women is to weigh gossamer and measure moonbeams. The very wisest thing ever said about them is said in the old English couplet :

> Some be lewd, and some be shrewd,
>   *But all they be not so,*

<hr>

of the author as Historiographer Royal to the venal Venus is genuine irony, or a mere mask for annoyance. The Preface to the dreary *Fils Naturel* (it must be remembered that Alexander the Younger himself was originally illegitimate and only later legitimated), though rhetorical again, is not dreary at all. It contains a very agreeable address to his father—he was always agreeable, though with a suspicion of rather amusing patronage-upside-down, on this subject—and a good deal else which one would have been sorry to lose. In fact, I can see, even in the dramas, even in the prose pamphleteering, whether the matter gives me positive delight or not, evidence of that *competence*, that not so seldom mastery, of treatment which entitles a man to be considered not the first comer by a long way.

and I think that our fifteenth- or early sixteenth-century *vates* showed his wisdom most in sticking to the strict negative in his exculpatory second line, here italicised.

Now if Alexander the Younger does not absolutely insist that " all they *be* so," he goes very near to it, excepting only characters of insignificant domesticity. When he does give you an " honnête femme " who is not merely this, such as the Clémentine of the *Roman d'une Femme* or the Marceline of *Diane de Lys*, he gives them some queer touches. His " *shady* Magdalenes " (with apologies to one of the best of parodies for spoiling its double rhyme) and his even more shady, because more inexcusable, *marquises*; his adorable innocents, who let their innocence vanish " in the heat of the moment " (as the late Mr. Samuel Morley said when he forgot that Mr. Bradlaugh was an atheist), because the husbands pay too much attention to politics; and his affectionate wives, like the Lady in *Thérèse*,[1] who supply their missing husbands' place just for once, and forget all about it—these *might* be individually creatures of fact, but as a class they *are* creatures of theory. And theory never made a good novel yet : it is lucky if it has sometimes, but too rarely, failed to make a good into a bad one. But it has been urged—and with some truth as regards at least the later forms of the French novel—that it is almost founded on theory, and certainly Dumas *fils* can be cited in support—perhaps, indeed, he is the first important and thoroughgoing supporter. And this of itself justifies the place and the kind of treatment allotted to him here, the justification being strengthened by the fact that he, after Beyle, and when Beyle's influence was still little felt, was a leader of a new class of novelist, that he is the first novelist definitely of the Second Empire.

---

[1] The obliging gentleman who on this occasion plays the part of " substitute " in a cricket-match, is the most elaborate and confessed example of Dumas' " theorised " *men*. He is what the seedsmen call an " improved Valmont," with more of lion in him than to meddle with virgins, but absolutely destructive to duchesses and always ready to suggest substitution to distressed grass-widows.

CHAPTER XI

GUSTAVE FLAUBERT

I N doing, as may at least be hoped, justice to M. Alexandre Dumas *fils* in the last chapter, one point was excepted— The contrast that though I could rank him higher than I of Flaubert ever expected to do as a novelist, I could not and Dumas exactly rank his work in the highest range of *fils.* literature. When you compare him—not merely with those greatest in novel-work already discussed, but with Musset or Vigny, with Nodier, or with Gérard de Nerval, not to mention others, there is something which is at once " weird and wanting," as the admirable Captain Mayne Reid says at the beginning of *The Headless Horseman,* though one cannot say here, as there, " By Heavens ! it is ' the head ! ' " There is head enough of a kind—a not at all unkempt or uncomely headpiece, very well filled with brains. But it has no aureole, as the other preferred persons cited in the last sentence and earlier have. This aureole may be larger or smaller, brighter or less bright—a full circlet of unbroken or hardly broken splendour, or a sort of will-o'-the-wisp cluster of gleam and darkness. But wherever it is found there is, in differing degrees, *literature* of the highest class ; of the major prose *gentes* ; literature that can show itself with poetry, under its own conditions and with its own possibilities, and fear no disqualification. Of this I am bound to say I do not find very much in this second division of our volume, and I find none in Dumas *fils.* But I find a great deal more than in any one else in Gustave Flaubert.

As I have said this, the reader may expect, magisterially, dreadingly, or perhaps in some very "gentle"
Some former dealings with him. cases hopefully, a full chapter on Flaubert. He shall have it. But the same cause, or group of causes, which has been at work before prevents this from being a very long one, and from containing very full accounts of his novels. One of the longest and most careful of those detailed surveys of forty years ago, to which I have perhaps too often referred, was devoted to Flaubert, and was slightly supplemented after his death. The earlier form had, though I did not know it for a considerable time, not displeased himself— a fortunate result not too common between author and critic [1]—and there are, consequently, special reasons for leaving it unaltered and unrehashed. I shall, therefore, as with Balzac and Dumas, attempt a shorter but more general judgment, which—his work being so much less voluminous than theirs—may be perhaps even less extensive than in the other cases,[2] but which should leave no doubt as to the writer's opinion of his "place in the story."

No small part of that high claim to purely literary rank which has been made for him rests, of course, upon his mere style—that famous and much debated
His style. "chase of the single word" which, especially since Mr. Pater took up the discussion of it, has been a "topic" of the most usitate in England as well as in France. When I left my chair and my library at Edinburgh I burnt more lecture-notes on the subject than would have furnished material for an entire chapter here, and I have no intention of raking my memory for their ashes. The battle on the one side with the anti-Unitarians who regard "monology" as a fond thing vainly

---

[1] He *might* have said—to make a Thackerayan translation of what was actually said later of an offering of roses rashly made to some French men of letters at their hotel in London: "Who the devil is this ? Let them flank him his vegetables to the gate !" But what he did say, I believe, though he did not know or mention my name, was that "a blonde son of Albion" had ventured something *gigantesque* on him. And *gigantesque* had, if I do not again fondly err, sometimes if not always its "milder shade" of meaning in Flaubert's energetic mouth.

[2] As in those cases, and perhaps even more than in most, I have taken pains to make the new criticism as little of a replica of the old as possible.

invented, and on the other with Edmond de Goncourt's foolish and bumptious boast that Flaubert's epithets were not so "personal" as his own and his brother's, would be for a different division of literary history. But there is something—a very important, though not a very long something—which must be said on the subject here. I have never found myself in the very slightest degree *gêné*—as the *abonné* was by Gautier's and as others are by the styles of Mr. George Meredith and Mr. Henry James—by Flaubert's style. It has never put the very smallest impediment, effected the most infinitesimal delay, in my comprehension of his meaning, or my enjoyment of his art and of his story.[1] What is more, though it has intensified that enjoyment, it has never—as may perhaps have been the case with some other great "stylists"—*diverted*, a little illegitimately, my attention and fruition from the story itself. Stylecraft and story-craft have married each other so perfectly that they are one flesh for the lover of literature to rejoice in. And if there be higher praise than this to be bestowed in the cases and circumstances, I do not know what it is. It seems to belong in perfection—I do not deny it to others in lesser degree—to three writers only in this volume—Gautier, Mérimée, and Flaubert—though if any one pleads hard for the addition of Maupassant, it will be seen when we come to him that I am not bound to a rigid *non possumus*; and though there is still one living writer with whom, if he were not happily disqualified by the fact of his living, I should not refuse to complete the Pentad. But let this suffice for the mere point of style in its purer and therefore more controversial aspect. There may be a little more to say incidentally as we take the general survey under the old heads of plot, etc. But before doing this we must—the books being so few and so individually remarkable—say a little about each of them, though only a very little about one.

Flaubert, after fairly early promise, the fulfilment of which was postponed, began late, and was a man of

---

[1] Possibly this is exactly what M. de Goncourt meant.

eight and thirty when his first complete book, *Madame Bovary*, appeared in 1859—a year, with its predecessor

The books —Madame Bovary. 1858, among the great years of literature, as judged by the books they produced. An absurd prosecution was got up against it by the authorities of that most moral of *régimes*, the Second Empire, with the even more absurd result of a " not guilty, but please don't do anything of the kind again " judgment. This, however, belongs mostly — not (*v. inf.*) entirely—to the biographical part of the matter, with which we have little or nothing to do.[1] The book itself is, beyond all question, a great novel—if it had a greater subject[2] it would have been one of the greatest of novels. The immense influence of *Manon Lescaut* appears once more in it ; but Emma Bovary, with far more than all the bad points of Manon, has none of her good ones. Nor has she the half-redeeming greatness in evil of her somewhat younger sister Iza in *Affaire Clémenceau*. Except her physical beauty (of which we do not hear much), there is not one attractive point in her. She sins, not out of passion, but because she thinks a married woman ought to have lovers. She ruins her husband, not for any intrinsic and genuine love of splendour, luxury, or beauty, but because other women have things and she ought to have them. She has a taste *for* men, but none *in* them. Yet her creator has made her absolutely " real," and, scum of womanhood as she is, has actually evolved something very like tragedy out of her worthlessness, and has saved her from being detestable, because she is such a very woman. He has, indeed, subjected her to a *kenosis*, an evisceration, exantlation—or, in plain English, " emptying out "—of everything positively good (she has the negative but necessary salve of not being absolutely ill-natured) that can be

---

[1] There is some scandal and infinite gossip about Flaubert, with all of which I was once obliged to be acquainted, but which I have done the best that a rather strong memory will allow me to forget. I shall only say that his early friend and quasi-biographer, Maxime du Camp, seems to me to have had nearly as hard measure dealt out to him as Mr. Froude in the matter of Mr. Carlyle. Both were indiscreet ; I do not think either was malevolent or treacherous.

[2] For in novels, to a greater degree than in poems, greatness *does* depend on the subject.

added to an abstract pretty girl; and no more. I have
paid a little attention to the heroines of the greater
fiction; but she is the only one of all the *mille e tre* I
know whom the author has managed to present as acceptable, without its being in the least possible to fall in love
with her, and at the same time without its being necessary
to detest her.

This defiant and victorious naturalness—not " naturalism "—pervades the book: from the other main
characters—the luckless, brainless, tasteless, harmless
husband; the vulgar Don Juans of lovers; the apothe-
cary Homais [1]—one of the most original and firmly drawn
characters in fiction—from all, down to the merest
" supers." It floods the scene-painting (admirable in
itself) with a light of common day—not too cheerful,
but absolutely real. It animates the conversation, though
Flaubert is not exactly prodigal of this; [2] and it presides
over the weaving of the story as such in a fashion very
little, if at all, inferior to that which prevails in the very
greatest masters of pure story-telling.

Hardly any one, speaking critically, could, I suppose,
also speak thus positively about Flaubert's second book,
Salammbô. *Salammbô*—a romance of Carthaginian history
at the time of the Mutiny of the Mercenaries.
Even Sainte-Beuve—no weak-stomached reader—was
put off by its blotches of blood and grime, and by the sort
of ghastly gorgeousness which, if it does not " relieve "
these, forms a kind of background to throw them up. It
was violently attacked by clever carpers like M. de Pont-
martin, by eccentrics of half-genius and whole prejudice
like M. Barbey d'Aurevilly, and by dull pedants like
M. Saint-René Taillandier; while it may be questioned

[1] Somebody has, I believe, suggested that if Emma had married Homais, all would
have been well. If this means that he would have promptly and comfortably poisoned
her, for which he had professional facilities, there might be something in it. Otherwise,
hardly.

[2] His forte is in single utterances, such as the unmatched " J'ai un amant ! " to which
Emma gives vent after her first lapse (and which " speaks " her, and her fate, and the
book in ten letters, two spaces, and an apostrophe), or as the " par ce qu'elle avait touché
au manteau de Tanit " of *Salammbô*; and the " Ainsi tout leur a craqué dans la main "
of the unfinished summary of *Bouvard et Pécuchet*.

whether, to the present day, its friends have not mostly belonged to that "Save-me-from-them" class which simply extols the "unpleasant" because other people find it unpleasant.[1] For my own part, I did not enjoy it much at the very first; but I felt its power at once, and, as always happens in such cases when admiration does not come from the tainted source just glanced at, the enjoyment increased, and the sense of power increased with it, the "unpleasantness," as a known thing, becoming merely "discountable" and disinfected. The book can, of course, never rank with *Madame Bovary*, because it is a *tour de force* of abnormality—a thing incompatible with that highest art which consists in the transformation and transcendentalising of the ordinary. The leprosies, and the crucifixions, and the sorceries, and the rest of it are ugly; but then Carthage *was* ugly, as far as we know anything about it.[2] Salammbô herself is shadowy; but how could a Carthaginian girl be anything else? The point to consider is the way in which all this unfamiliar, uncanny, unpleasant stuff is *fused* by sheer power of art into something which has at least the reality of a bad dream—which, as most people know, is a very real thing indeed while it lasts, and for a little time after. It increases the wonder—though to me it does not increase the interest—to know that Flaubert took the most gigantic pains to make his task as difficult as possible by acquiring and piecing together the available knowledge on his subject. This process—the ostensible *sine qua non* of "Realism" and "Naturalism"—will require further treatment. It is almost enough for the present to say that, though not a novelty, it had been, and for the matter of that has been, rarely a success. It has, as was pointed out before, spoilt most classical novels, reaching its acme of boredom in the German work of

[1] It is known that Flaubert, perhaps out of rather boyish pique (there was much boyishness in him), had originally made its offence ranker still. One of the most curious literary absurdities I have ever seen—the absurd almost drowning the disgusting in it—was an American attempt in verse to fill up Flaubert's *lacuna* and "go one better."

[2] The old foreign comparison with London was merely rhetorical; but there really would seem to have been some resemblance between Carthage and modern Berlin, even in those very points which Flaubert (taking advice) left out.

Ebers and Dahn ; and it has scarcely ever been very successful, even in the hands of Charles Reade, who used it " with a difference." But it can hardly be said to have done *Salammbô* much harm, because the " fusing " process which is above referred to, and to which the imported elements are often so rebellious, is here perfectly carried out. You may not like the colour and shape of the ingot or cast ; but there is nothing in it which has not duly felt and obeyed the fire of art.

That there was no danger of Flaubert's merely palming off, in his novel work, replicas with a few superficial dif-*L'Éducation* ferences, had now been shown. It was further *Sentimentale.* established by his third and longest book, *L'Éducation Sentimentale.* This was not only, as the others had been, violently attacked, but was comparatively little read—indeed it is the only one of his books, with the usual exception of *Bouvard et Pécuchet*, which has been called, by any rational creature, dull. I do not find it so ; but I confess that I find its intrinsic interest, which to me is great, largely enhanced by its unpopularity— which supplies a most remarkable pendant to that of *Jonathan Wild*, and is by no means devoid of value as further illustrating the cause of the very limited popularity of Thackeray, and even of the rarity of whole-hearted enthusiasm for Swift. Satire is allowed to be a con- siderable, and sometimes held to be an attractive, branch of literature. But when you come to analyse the actual sources of the attraction, it is to be feared that you will generally find them to lie outside of the pure exposure of general human weaknesses. A very large proportion of satire is personal, and personality is always popular. Satire is very often " naughty," and " naughtiness " is to a good many, *qua* naughtiness, " nice." It lends itself well to rhetoric ; and there is no doubt, whatever superior persons may say of it, that rhetoric *does* " persuade " a large portion of the human race. It is constantly associated with directly comic treatment, sometimes with something not unlike tragedy ; and while the first, if of any merit, is sure, the second has a fair though more restricted chance, of favourable reception. Try Aristophanes, Horace, Juvenal, Lucian, Martial; try the modern satirists of all kinds, and you will always find these secondary sources of enjoyment present.

There is hardly one of them—if one—to be found in *L'Éducation Sentimentale*. It is simply a panorama of human folly, frailty, feebleness, and failure—never permitted to rise to any great heights or to sink to any infernal depths, but always maintained at a probable human level. We start with Frédéric Moreau as he leaves school at the correct age of eighteen. I am not sure at what actual age we leave him, though it is at some point or other of middle life, the most active part of the book filling about a decade. But " vanity is the end Of all his ways," and vanity has been the beginning and middle of them—a perfectly quiet and everyday kind of vanity, but vain from centre to circumference and entire surface. He (one cannot exactly say " tries," but) is brought into the possibility of trying love of various kinds—illegitimate-romantic, legitimate-not-un-romantic, illegitimate-professional but not disagreeable, illegitimate-conventional. Nothing ever " comes off " in a really satisfactory fashion. He is " exposed " (in the photographic-plate sense) to all, or nearly all, the influences of a young man's life in Paris—law, literature, art, insufficient means, quite sufficient means, society, politics—including the Revolution of 1848—enchant-ments, disenchantments—*tout ce qu'il faut pour vivre*—to alter a little that stock expression for " writing materials " which is so common in French. But he never can get any real " life " out of any of these things. He is neither a fool, nor a cad, nor anything discreditable or disagreeable. He is " only an or'nary person," to reach the rhythm of the original by adopting a slang form in not quite the slang sense. And perhaps it is not unnatural that other ordinary persons should find him too faithful to their type to be welcome. In this respect at least I may claim not to be ordinary. One goes down so many empty wells, or wells with mere rubbish at the bottom of them, that to find Truth at last is to be happy with her (without prejudice to the convenience of another well or two here and there, with an agreeable Falsehood waiting for one). I do not know that *L'Éducation Sentimentale* is a book to be read very often ; one has the substance in one's own experience, and in the contemplation of other people's, too readily at hand for that to be necessary or perhaps desirable. But a great work of art which is also a great record of nature is not too common —and this is what it is.

Yet, as has been remarked before, nothing shows Flaubert's greatness better than his absolute freedom *La Tentation* from the " rut." Even in carrying out the *de Saint-* general " Vanity " idea he has no monotony. *Antoine.* The book which followed *L'Éducation* had been preluded, twenty years earlier, by some fragments in *L'Artiste*, a periodical edited by Gautier. But *La Tentation de Saint-Antoine*, when it finally appeared, far surpassed the promise of these specimens. It is my own favourite among its author's books ; and it is one of those which you can read merely for enjoyment or take as a subject of study, just as you please—if you are wise you will give " five in five score " of your attentions to the latter occupation and the other ninety-five to the former. The people who had made up their minds to take Flaubert as a sort of Devil's Gigadibs—a " Swiss, not of Heaven," but of the other place, hiring himself out to war on all things good—called it " an attack on the idea of God " ! As it, like its smaller and later counterpart *Saint Julien l'Hospitalier*, ends in a manifestation of Christ, which would do honour to the most orthodox of Saints' Lives, the " attack " seems to be a curious kind of offensive operation.

As a matter of fact, the book takes its vaguely familiar subject, and *embroiders* that subject with a fresh collection of details from untiring research. The nearest approach to an actual person, besides the tormented Saint himself, is the Evil One, not at first *in propria persona*, but under the form of the Saint's disciple Hilarion, who at first acts

as usher to the various elements of the Temptation-
Pageant, and at last reveals himself by treacherous
suggestions of unbelief. The pageant itself is of wonderful variety. After a vividly drawn sketch of the hermitage
in the Thebaid, the drama starts with the more vulgar
and direct incitements to the coarser Deadly Sins and
others—Gluttony, Avarice, Ambition, Luxury. Then
Hilarion appears and starts theological discussion, whence
arises a new series of actual visions—the excesses of the
heretics, the degradation of martyrdom itself, the Eastern
theosophies, the monstrous cults of Paganism. After
this, Hilarion tries a sort of Modernism, contrasting
the contradictions and absurdities of actual religions
with a more and more atheistic Pantheism. This
failing, the Temptation reverts to the moral forms,
Death and Vice contending for Anthony and bidding
against each other. The next shift of the kaleidoscope
is to semi-philosophical fantasies—the Sphinx, the
Chimaera, basilisks, unicorns, microscopic mysteries.
The Saint is nearly bewildered into blasphemy; but at
last the night wanes, the sun rises, and the face of Christ
beams from it. The Temptation is ended.[1]

The magnificence of the style, in which the sweep of
this dream-procession over the stage is conveyed to the
reader, is probably the first thing that will strike him;
and certainly it never palls. But, if not at once, pretty
soon, any really critical mind must perceive something
different from, and much rarer than, mere style. It is
the extraordinary power—the exactness, finish, and
freedom from any excess or waste labour, of the narrative,
in reproducing dream-quality. A very large proportion
—and there is nothing surprising in the fact—of the
best pieces of ornate prose in French, as well as in English,
are busied with dreams; but the writers have not invariably remembered one of the most singular—and
even, when considered from some points of view, dis-
quieting—features of a dream,—that you are never,
while dreaming, in the least surprised at what happens.

---

[1] There is a recent and exceptionally good translation of the book.

Flaubert makes no mistake as to this matter. The real realism which had enabled him to re-create the most sordid details of *Madame Bovary*, the half-historic grime and gorgeousness mixed of *Salammbô*, and the quint-essentially ordinary life of *L'Éducation*, came mightily to his assistance in this his Vision of the Desert. You see and hear its external details as Anthony saw and heard them : you almost feel its internal influence as if Hilarion had been—as if he *was*—at your side.

The *Trois Contes* which followed, and which practically completed (except for letters) Flaubert's finished work

Trois Contes. in literature,[1] have one of those half-extrinsic interests which, once more, it is the duty of the historian to mention. They show that although, as has been said, Flaubert suffered from no monotony of faculty, the range of his faculty—or rather the range of the subjects to which he chose to apply it—was not extremely wide. Of the twin stories, *Un Cœur Simple* is, though so unlike in particular, alike in general *ordinariness* to *Madame Bovary* and *L'Éducation Sentimentale*. The unlikeness in particular is very striking, and shows that peculiar *victoriousness* in accomplishing what he attempted which is so characteristic of Flaubert. It is the history-no-history of a Norman peasant woman, large if simple of heart, simple and not large of brain, a born drudge and prey to unscrupulous people who come in contact with her, and almost in her single person uniting the Beatitudes of the Sermon on the Mount. I admire it now, without even the touch of rather youthful impatience which used, when I read it first, to temper my admiration. It is not a *berquinade*, because a *berquinade* is never quite real. *Un Cœur Simple* shares Flaubert's Realism as marvellously as any equal number of pages of either of the books to which I have compared it. But there *is*, perhaps, something provocative—something almost placidly insolent—about the way in which the author says, "Now, I will give you nothing

---

[1] The Letters are almost, if not quite, of first-rate quality. The play, *Le Candidat*, is of no merit.

of the ordinary baits for admiration, and yet, were you
the Devil himself, you shall admire me." And one
does—in youth rather reluctantly—not so in age.

Herodias groups itself in the same general fashion,
but even more definitely in particulars, with *Salammbô*—
of which, indeed, it is a sort of miniature replica cunningly
differentiated. Anybody can see how easily the story
of the human witchcraft of Salome, and the decollation
of the Saint, and the mixture of terror and gorgeousness
in the desert fortress, parallel the Carthaginian story.
But I do not know whether it was deliberate or unconscious repetition that made Flaubert give us something
like a duplicate of the suffete Hanno in Vitellius. , There
is no lack of the old power, and the shortness of the story
is at least partly an advantage. But perhaps the Devil's
Advocate, borrowing from, but reversing, Hugo on
Baudelaire, might say, " Ce frisson *n'est pas* nouveau."

The third story, *Saint Julien l'Hospitalier*, has always
seemed to me as near perfection in its own kind as anything I know in literature, and one of the best examples,
if not the very best example, of that adaptableness of
the *Acta Sanctorum* to modern rehandling of the right
kind, which was noticed at the beginning of this *History*.[1]
The excessive devotion of the not yet sainted Julian to
sport; the crime and the dooms that follow it; the double
parricide which he commits under the false impression
that his wife has been unfaithful to him; his self-
imposed penance of ferrying, somewhat like Saint
Christopher, and the trial—a harder one than that good
giant bore, for Julian has, not merely to carry over
but, to welcome, at board *and* bed, a leper—and the
Transfiguration and Assumption that conclude the story,
give some of the best subjects—though there are endless
others nearly or quite as good—in Hagiology. And
Flaubert has risen to them in the miraculous manner in
which he could rise, retaining the strangeness, infusing
the reality, and investing the whole with the beauty,
deserved and required. There is not a weak place in the

[1] Vol. I. p. 4.

whole story; but the strongest places are, as they should be, the massacre of hart, hind, and fawn which brings on the curse; the ghastly procession of the beasts Julian has slain or *not* slain (for he has met with singular ill-luck); the final "Translation."[1] Nowhere is Flaubert's power of description greater; nowhere, too, is that other power noticed —the removal of all temptation to say "Very pretty, but rather *added* ornament"—more triumphantly displayed.

Little need be said of the posthumous torso and failure,[2] *Bouvard et Pécuchet*. Nothing ever showed the wisdom of the proverb about half-done work, children and fools, better; and, alas! there is something of the child in all of us, and something of the fool in too many. It was to be a sort of extended and varied *Éducation*, not *Sentimentale*. Two men of retired leisure and sufficient income resolve to spend the rest of their lives "in books and work and healthful play," and almost as many other recreative occupations (including "teaching the young idea how to shoot") as they or you can think of. But the work generally fails, the books bore and disappoint them, the young ideas shoot in the most "divers and disgusting" ways, and the play turns out to be by no means healthful. Part of it is in scenario merely; and Flaubert was wont to alter so much, that one cannot be sure even of the other and more finished part. Perhaps it was too large and too dreary a theme, unsupported by any real novel quality, to acquire even that interest which *L'Éducation Sentimentale* has for some. But the more excellent way is to atone for the mistake of his literary executors, in not burning all of it except the monumental phrase quoted above,

Ainsi tout leur a craqué dans la main,

---

[1] All these will be found Englished in the Essay referred to.

[2] Too much must not be read into the word "failure": indeed the next sentence should guard against this. I know excellent critics who, declining altogether to consider the book as a novel, regard it as a sort of satire and *satura*, Aristophanic, Jonsonian or other, in gist and form, and by no means a failure as such. But as such it would have no, or very small, place here. I think myself that it is, from that point of view, nearer to Burton than to any one else: and I think further that it might have been made into a success of this kind or even of the novel sort itself. But *as it stands with the sketch of a completion*, I do not think that Flaubert's alchemy had yet achieved or approached projection.

by simply remembering this—which is the initial and conclusion of the whole matter—and letting the rest pass.

There is one slight danger in the estimate of Flaubert to which, though I actually pointed it out, I think I may have succumbed a little when I first wrote about him. He is so great a master of literature that one may be led to concentrate attention on this ; and if not to neglect, to regard somewhat inadequately, his greatness as a novelist. Here at any rate such failure would be petty, if not even high, treason.

One may look at his performance in the novel from two points of view—that of "judging by the result" General con-simply and in the fashion of a summing-up ; siderations. and that of bringing him under certain ticket-qualifications, and enquiring whether they are justly applicable to him or not. I need hardly tell any one who has done me the honour to read either this or any other critical work of mine, which of these two I think the more excellent way ; but the less excellent in this particular instance, may demand a little following.

Was Flaubert a Romantic ? Was he a Realist ? Was he a Naturalist ? This is how the enquiries come in chronological order. But for convenience of discussion the first should be postponed to the others.

"Realist," like a good many other tickets, is printed on both sides, and the answer to our question will be by no means the same whichever side be looked at. That Flaubert was a Realist "in the best sense of the term" has been again and again affirmed in the brief reviews of his novels given above. He cannot be unreal—the "convincingness" of his most sordid as of his most splendid passages ; of his most fantastic *diableries* as of his most everyday studies of society ; is unsurpassed. It is, in fact, his chief characteristic. But this very fact that it *pervades*—that it is as conspicuous in the *Tentation* and in *Saint Julien l'Hospitalier* as in *Madame Bovary* and the *Éducation*—at once throws up a formidable, I think an impregnable, line of defence against those who would claim him for "Realism" of the other kind—

the cult of the ugly, because, being ugly, it is more real than the beautiful. He has no fear of ugliness, but he cultivates the ugly because it is the real, not the real because it is the ugly. Being to a great extent a satirist and (despite his personal boyishness) saturnine rather than jovial in temperament, there is a good deal in him that is *not* beautiful. But he can escape into beauty whenever he chooses, and in these escapes he is always at his best.

This fact, while leaving him a Realist of the nobler type, at once shuts him off from community with his friends Zola and the Goncourts, and saves him from any stain of the "sable streams." But besides this— or rather looking at the same thing from a slightly different point of view—there is something which not only permits but demands the most emphatic of "Noes!" to the question, "Was Flaubert a Naturalist?"

This something is itself the equally emphatic "Yes!" which must be returned to the third and postponed question, "Was he a Romantic?" There are many strange things in the History of Literature: its strangeness, as in other cases, is one of its greatest charms. But there have been few stranger than the obstinacy and almost passion with which the Romanticism of Heine, of Thackeray, and of Flaubert has been denied. Again and again it has been pointed out that "to laugh at what you love" is not only permissible, but a sign of the love itself. Moreover, Flaubert does not even laugh as the great Jew and the great Englishman did. He only represents the failures and the disappointments and the false dawns of Love itself, while in other respects he is *romantique à tous crins*. Compare *Le Rêve* with *La Tentation* or *Saint-Julien l'Hospitalier*; compare *Madame Bovary* with *Germinie Lacerteux*; even compare *L'Éducation Sentimentale*, that voyage to the Cythera of Romance which never reaches its goal, with *Sapho* and *L'Évangéliste*, and you will see the difference. It is of course to a certain extent "Le Coucher du Soleil Romantique" which lights up Flaubert's work, but the *crapauds imprévus* and the *froids limaçons* of Baudelaire's epitaph have not yet appeared, and the hues of the sunset itself are still gorgeous in parts of the sky.

Of Flaubert's famous doctrine of " the single word " perhaps a little more should, after all, be said. The results are so good, and the processes by which they are attained get in the way of the reader so little, that it is difficult to quarrel with the doctrine itself. But it was perhaps, after all, something of a superstition, and the almost " fabulous torments " which it occasioned to its upholder and practitioner seem to have been somewhat Fakirish. We need not grudge the five years spent over *Salammbô* ; the seven over *L'Éducation* ; the earlier and, I think, less definitely known gestation of *Madame Bovary* ; and that portion of the twenty which, producing these also, filled out those fragments of *La Tentation* that the July Monarchy had actually seen. Perhaps with *Bouvard et Pécuchet* he got into a blind alley, out of which such labour was never like to get him, and in which it was rather likely to confine him. But if the excess of the preparation had been devoted to the completion of, say, only half a dozen of such *Contes* as those we actually have, it would have been joyful.

Yet this is idle pining, and the goods which the gods provided in this instance are such as ought rather to make us truly thankful. Flaubert was, as has been said, a Romantic, but he was born late enough to avoid the extravagances and the childishnesses of *mil-huit-cent-trente* while retaining its inspiration, its *diable au corps*, its priceless recovery of inheritances from history. Nor, though he subjected all these to a severe criticism of a certain kind, did he ever let this make him (as something of the same sort made his pretty near contemporary, Matthew Arnold, in England) inclined to blaspheme.[1] He did not, like his other contemporary and peer in greatness of their particular country and generation, Baudelaire, play unwise tricks with his powers and his

---

[1] I have sometimes wished that Mr. Arnold had written a novel. But perhaps *Volupté* frightened him.

life.[1] He was fortunately relieved from the necessity of journey-work—marvellously performed, but still journey-work—which had beset Gautier and never let go of him.[2]

And he utilised these gifts and advantages as few others have done in the service of the novel. One thing may be brought against him—I think one only. You read—at least I read—his books with intense interest and enjoyment, but though you may recognise the truth and humanity of the characters; though you may appreciate the skill with which they are set to work; though you may even, to a certain extent, sympathise with them, you never—at least I never—feel that intense interest in them, as persons, which one feels in those of most of the greatest novelists. You can even feel yourself in them—a rare and great thing—you can *be* Saint Anthony, and feel an unpleasant suspicion as if you had sometimes been Frédéric Moreau. But this is a different thing (though it is a great triumph for the author) from the construction for you of loves, friends, enemies even—in addition to those who surround you in the actual world.

Except this defect—which is in the proper, not the vulgar sense a defect—that is to say, not something bad which is present, but only something good which is absent—I hardly know anything wrong in Flaubert. He is to my mind almost [3] incomparably the greatest novelist of France specially belonging to the second half of the nineteenth century, and I do not think that Europe at large has ever had a greater since the death of Thackeray.

[1] There is controversy on this point, and Baudelaire's indulgence in artificial and perilous Paradises may have been exaggerated. That it existed to some extent is, I think, hardly doubtful.

[2] I know few things of the kind more pathetic than Théo's quiet lament over the "artistic completeness" of his ill-luck in the collapse of the Second Empire just when, with Sainte-Beuve dead and Mérimée dying, he was its only man of letters of the first rank left, and might have had some relief from collar-work. But it must be remembered that though he had ground at the mill with slaves, he had never been one of them, and perhaps this would always have prevented his promotion.

[3] Reserving Maupassant under the "almost."

CHAPTER XII

IF any excuse is needed for the oddity of the title of this chapter, it will not be to readers of Burton's *Anatomy*. The way in which the phrase "Those six non-natural things" occurs and recurs there; the inextinguishable tendency—in view of the eccentricity of its application—to forget that the six include things as "natural" (in a non-technical[1] sense) as Diet, to forget also what it really means and expect something uncanny—these are matters familiar to all Burtonians. And they may excuse the borrowing of that phrase as a general label for those novelists, other than Flaubert and Dumas *fils*, who, if their work was not limited to 1850–70, began in (but not "with") that period, and worked chiefly in it, while they were at once *not* "Naturalists" and yet more or less as "natural" as any of Burton's six. One of the two least "minor," Alphonse Daudet, was among Naturalists but scarcely of them. The other, Octave Feuillet, was anti-Naturalist to the core.

This latter, the elder of the two, though not so much the elder as used to be thought,[2] was at one time one of Feuillet. the most popular of French novelists both at home and abroad; but, latterly in particular, there were in his own country divers "dead sets" at him. He had been an Imperialist, and this excited one kind of

---

[1] The technical-scholastic being "things born *with* a man."

[2] By some curious mistake his birth used for a long time to be ante-dated ten years from 1822 to 1812. At the risk of annoying my readers by repeating such references, I should perhaps mention that there is an essay on Feuillet in the book already cited.

prejudice against him; he was, in his way, orthodox
in religion, and this aroused another; while, as has been
already said, though his subjects, and even his treatment
of them, would have sent our English Mrs. Grundy
of earlier days into "screeching asterisks," the peculiar
grime of Naturalism nowhere smirches his pages. For
my own part I have always held him high, though there
is a smatch about his morality which I would rather not
have there. He seems to me to be—with the no doubt
numerous transformations necessary—something of a
French Anthony Trollope, though he has a tragic power
which Trollope never showed; and, on the other side of
the account, considerably less comic variety.

As a "thirdsman" to Flaubert and Dumas *fils*, he
shows some interesting differences. Merely as a maker
His novels of literature, he cannot touch the former,
generally. and has absolutely nothing of his poetic
imagination, while his grasp of character is somewhat
thinner and less firm. But it is more varied in itself and
in the plots and scenery which give it play and setting—
a difference not necessary but fortunate, considering
his very much larger "output." Contrasted with Dumas
fils, he affords a more important difference still, indeed
one which is very striking. I pointed out in the appropriate place—not at the moment thinking of Feuillet at
all—the strange fashion in which Alexander the Younger
constantly "makes good" an at first unattractive story;
and, even in his most generally successful work, increases
the appeal as he goes on. With Feuillet the order of
things is quite curiously reversed. Almost (though,
as will be seen, not quite) invariably, from the early days
of *Bellah* and *Onestà* to *La Morte*, he "lays out" his
plan in a masterly manner, and accumulates a great deal
of excellent material, as it were by the roadside, for use
as the story goes on. But, except when he is at his very
best, he flags, and is too apt to keep up his curtain for a
fifth act when it had much better have fallen for good at
the end of the fourth. As has been noted already, his
characters are not deeply cut, though they are faithfully

enough sketched. That he is not strong enough to carry through a purpose-novel is not much to his discredit, for hardly anybody ever has been. But the *Histoire de Sibylle*—his swashing blow in the George Sand duel (*v. sup.* p. 204)—though much less dull than the *riposte* in *Mlle. la Quintaine*, would hardly induce "the angels," in Mr. Disraeli's famous phrase, to engage him further as a Hal-o'-the-Wynd on their side.

But Feuillet's most vulnerable point is the peculiar sentimental morality-in-immorality which has been more than once glanced at. It was frankly found fault with by French critics—themselves by no means strait-laced—and the criticisms were well summed up (I remember the wording but not the writer of it) thus : " An honest woman does not feel the temptations " to which the novelist exposes his heroines. That there *is* a certain morbid sentimentality about Feuillet's attitude not merely to the "triangle" but even to simple " exchange of fantasies " between man and woman in general, can hardly be denied. He has a most curious and (one might almost say) Judaic idea as to woman as a temptress, in fashions ranging from the almost innocent seduction of Eve through the more questionable [1] one of Delilah, down to the sheer attitude of Zuleika - Phraxanor, and the street-corner woman in the Proverbs. And this necessitates a correspondingly unheroic presentation of his heroes. They are always being led into serious mischief (" in a red-rose chain " or a ribbon one), as Marmontel's sham philosopher [2] was into comic confusion by that ingenious Présidente. Yet, allowing all this, there remains to Feuillet's credit such a full and brilliant series of novels, hardly one of which is an actual failure, as very few novelists can show. Although he lived long and wrote to the end of his life,

---

[1] I give Delilah (for whom Milton's excessive rudeness naturally inspires a sort of partisanship) the benefit of a notion that her action was, partly if not mainly, due to unbearable curiosity. How many women are there who could resist the double temptation of seeing whether the secret *did* lie in the hair, and if so, of possessing complete mistress-ship of their lovers ? Some perhaps : but many?

[2] *V. sup.* Vol. I. pp. 420-1.

he left no " dotages "; hardly could the youngest and strongest of any other school in France—Guy de Maupassant himself—have beaten *La Morte*, though it is not faultless, in power.

I suppose few novels, succeeding not by scandal, have ever been much more popular than the *Roman d'un jeune homme pauvre*, the title of which good English folk have been known slightly to alter in meaning by putting the *pauvre* before the *jeune*. It had got into its third hundred of editions before the present century had reached the end of its own first lustrum, and it must have been translated (probably more than once) into every European language. It is perfectly harmless; it is admirably written; and the vicissitudes of the loves of the *marquis déchu* and the headstrong creole girl are conducted with excellent skill, no serious improbability, and an absence of that tendency to " tail off " which has been admitted in some of the author's books. It was, I suppose, Feuillet's diploma-piece in almost the strictest technical sense of that phrase, for he was elected of the Academy not long afterwards. It has plenty of merits and no important faults, but it is not my favourite.

Brief notes on some—*Le Roman d'un jeune homme pauvre.*

Neither is the novel which, in old days, the proud and haughty scorners of this *Roman*, as a *berquinade*, used to prefer—*M. de Camors*.[1] Here there is plenty of naughtiness, attempts at strong character, and certainly a good deal of interest of story, with some striking incident. But it is spoilt, for me, by the failure of the principal personage. I think it not quite impossible that Feuillet intended M. de Camors as a sort of modernised, improved, and extended Lovelace, or even Valmont—superior to scruple, destined and able to get the better of man or woman as he chooses. Unfortunately he has also endeavoured to make him a gentleman; and the compound, as the chemists say, is not " stable." The coxcombry of Lovelace and the

M. de Camors.

---

[1] It may be worth while to remind the reader that Maupassant included this in his selection of remarkable novels of all modern times and languages.

priggishness, reversed (though in a less detestable form), of Valmont, are the elements that chiefly remain in evidence, unsupported by the vigorous will of either. I have myself always thought *La Petite Comtesse* and *Julia de Trécœur* among the earlier novels, *Honneur d'Artiste* and *La Morte* among the later, to be Feuillet's masterpieces, or at least nearest approaches to a masterpiece.

Other books. *Un Mariage dans le Monde* (one of the rare instances in which the "honest woman" does get the better of her "temptations") is indeed rather interesting, in the almost fatal cross-misunderstanding of husband and wife, and the almost fabulous ingenuity and good offices of the "friend of the family," M. de Kevern, who prevents both from making irreparable fools of themselves. *Les Amours de Philippe* is more commonplace—a prodigal's progress in love, rewarded at last, very undeservedly, with something better than a fatted calf—a formerly slighted but angelic cousin. But to notice all his work, more especially if one took in half- or quarter-dramatic things (his pure drama does not of course concern us) of the "Scène" and "Proverbe" kind, where he comes next to Musset, would be here impossible. The two pairs, early and late respectively, and already selected, must suffice.

They are all tragic, though there is comedy in them as well. Perhaps *La Petite Comtesse*, a very short *La Petite* novel and its author's first thing of great *Comtesse.* distinction, might by some be called pathetic rather than tragic; but the line between the two is a "leaden" barrier (if indeed it is a barrier at all) and "gives" freely. Perhaps the Gigadibs in any man of letters may be conciliated by one of his fellows being granted some of the fascinations of the "clerk" in the old Phyllis-and-Flora *débats* of mediaeval times; but the fact that *this* clerk is also represented as a fool of the most disastrous, though not the most contemptible kind, should be held as a set-off to the bribery. It is a "story of three"—though not at all the usual three—graced (or not) by a really brilliant picture of the society of the

early Second Empire. One of the leaders of this—a
young countess and a member of the " Rantipole "[1] set
of the time, but exempt from its vulgarity—meets in
the country, and falls in love with, a middle-aged *savant*,
who is doing archaeological work for Government in
the neighbourhood. He despises her as a frivolous
feather-brain at first, but soon falls under the spell.
Yet what has been called " the fear of the ' Had-I-wist ' "
and the special notion—more common perhaps with
men than is generally thought—that she cannot *really*
love him, makes him resist her advances. By rebound,
she falls victim for a time to a commonplace Lovelace ;
but finds no satisfaction, languishes and dies, while the
lover, who would not take the goods the gods provided,
tries to play a sort of altered part of Colonel Morden
in *Clarissa*, and the gods take their revenge for
" sinned mercies." In abstract (it has been observed
elsewhere that Feuillet seldom abstracts well, his work
being too much built up of delicate touches) there may
seem to be something of the preposterous in this ; but it
must be a somewhat coarse form of testing which discovers any real preposterousness in the actual story.

It may, however, as has been said, seem to some to
belong to the pathetic-sentimental rather than to the
actually tragic ; I at least could not allow
any such judging of *Julia de Trécœur*, though
there are more actual faults in it than in *La Petite Comtesse*, and though, as has been mentioned elsewhere, the
rather repulsive catastrophe may have been more or less
borrowed. The *donnée* is one of the great old simple
cross-purposes of Fate—not a mere " conflict," as the
silly modern jargon has it. Julia de Trécœur is a wilful
and wayward girl, as are many others of Feuillet's heroines.
Her mother is widowed early, but consoles herself ;
and Julia—as such a girl pretty certainly would do—
resents the proceeding, and refuses to live at home or

Julia de Trécœur.

---

[1] How sad it is to think that a specific reference to that all-but-masterpiece, as a
picture of earlier *fin-de-siècle* society, Miss Edgeworth's *Belinda*, may perhaps be necessary
to escape the damning charge of unexplained allusion !

to see her stepfather. He, however, is a friend of his wife's own cousin, and this cousin, conceiving a passion for Julia, offers to marry her. Her consent, in an English girl, would require some handling, but offers no difficulties in a French one. As a result, but after a time, she agrees to meet her mother and that mother's new husband. And then the tragedy begins. She likes at once, and very soon loves, her stepfather—he succumbs, more slowly, to Moira and Até. But he is horrified at the notion of a quasi-incestuous love, and Julia perceives his horror. She forces her horse, like the Duchess May, but over the cliffs of the Cotentin, not over a castle wall; and her husband and her step-father himself see the act without being able—indeed without trying—to prevent it. The actual place had nearly been the scene of a joint suicide by the unhappy lovers before.

Once more, the thing comes badly out of analysis—perhaps by the analyst's fault, perhaps not. But in its own presentation, with some faults hardly necessary to point out, it is both poignant and *empoignant*, and it gives a special blend of pity and terror, the two feelings being aroused by no means merely through the catastrophe, but by the rise and progress of the fatal passion which leads to it. I know very few, if any, things of the same kind, in a French novel, superior, or indeed equal to, the management of this, and to the fashion in which the particular characters, or wants of character, of Julia's mother and Julia's husband (excellent persons both) are made to hurry on the calamity[1] to which she was fated.

This tragic undercurrent, surging up to a more tragic catastrophe, reappears in the two best of the later issues, *Honneur d'Artiste.* when Feuillet was making better head against the burst sewers[2] of Naturalism. *Honneur d'Artiste* is the less powerful of the two; but what of failure

---

[1] " Where'er I came
I brought *calamity*."

When I read the foolish things that foolish people still write about Tennyson, I like to repeat to myself that " lonely word " in its immediate context.

[2] If you can " take arms against a sea " you can, I suppose, make head against a sewer.

there is in it is rather less glaring. Beatrice de Sardonne, the heroine, is a sort of "Petite Comtesse" transformed—very cleverly, but perhaps not quite successfully. *Her* "triangle" consists of herself, a somewhat New-Yorkised young French lady of society (but too good for the worst part of her); and her two lovers, the Marquis de Pierrepont, a much better Lovelace, in fact hardly a Lovelace at all, whom she is engineered into refusing for honourable love—with a fatal relapse into dishonourable; and the "Artiste" Jacques Fabrice. He adores her, but she, alas! does not know whether she loves him or not till too late; and, after the irreparable, he falls by the hazard of the lot in that toss-up for suicide, the pros and cons of which (as in a former instance) I should like to see treated by a philosophical historian of the duello.

In *La Morte*, on the other hand, the power is even greater—in fact it is the most powerful book of its author, and one of the most powerful of the later nineteenth century. But there is in it a reversion to the "purpose" heresy; and while it is an infinitely finer novel than the *Histoire de Sibylle*, it is injured, though not quite fatally, by the weapon it wields. One of the heroines, Sabine, niece and pupil of an Agnostic *savant*, deliberately poisons the other, Aliette, that she may marry Aliette's husband. But the Agnostic teaching extends itself soon from the Sixth Commandment to the Seventh, and M. de Vaudricourt, who, though not ceasing to love Aliette, and having no idea of the murder, has been ensnared into second marriage by Sabine, discovers, at almost the same time, that his wife is a murderess and a strumpet. She is also (one was going to say) something worse, a daughter of the horse-leech for wealth and pleasure and position. Now you *may* be an Agnostic and a murderess and a strumpet and a female snob all at once: but no anti-Agnostic, who is a critic likewise, will say that the second, third, and fourth characteristics necessarily, and all together, follow from Agnosticism. It may remove some bars in their way; but I can frankly admit that I do not think it need definitely superinduce

La Morte.

them, or that it is altogether fair to accumulate the *post hocs* with their inevitable suggestion of *propter*.

However, " Purpose " here is simply at its old tricks, and I have known it do worse things than caution people against Agnostics' nieces.

On the other hand, the vigour, the variety, and (where the purpose does not get too much the upper hand) the satiric skill are very nearly first-rate. And, with the cautions and admissions just given, there is not a little in the purpose itself, with which one may be permitted to sympathise. After all " misters the assassins " were being allowed very generous " law," and it was time for other people to " begin." As for Feuillet's opposition to the " modern spirit," which was early denounced, it is not necessary—even for any one who knows that this modern spirit is only an old enemy with a new face, or who, when he sees the statement that " Nothing is ever going anywhere to be the same," chuckles, and, remembering all history to the present minute, mutters, " Everything always has been, is, and always will be the same "—to call in these knowledges of his to the rescue of Feuillet's position as a novelist. That position is made sure, and would have been made sure if he had been as much of a Naturalist as he was the reverse, by his power of constructing interesting stories ; of drawing, if not absolutely perfect, passable and probable characters ; of throwing in novel-accessories with judgment ; and of giving, by dint of manners and talk and other things necessary, vivid and true portrayals of the society and life of his time.

Misters the assassins.

Perhaps there is no novelist in French literature— or, indeed, in any other—who, during his life-time, occupied such a curiously " mixed " position as Alphonse Daudet.[1] No contemporary of his obtained wider general popularity, without a touch of irregular bait

---

[1] His brother Ernest was a novelist of merit sufficient to make it not unnatural that he should—as, unless my memory plays me tricks, he did—resent being whelmed in the fraternal reputation. But he does not require much notice here.

or of appeal to popular silliness in it, than he did with
Le Petit Chose, with the charming bundle of pieces called
Alphonse *Lettres de Mon Moulin*, and later with the world-
Daudet and delighting burlesque of *Tartarin de Tarascon*.
his curious *Jack* and *Fromont Jeune et Risler Aîné* con-
position. tained more serious advances, which were,
however, acknowledged as effective by a very large
number of readers. But he became more and more
personally associated with the Naturalist group of Zola
and Edmond de Goncourt; and though he never was
actually " grimy," he had, from a quite early period,
when he was secretary or clerk to the Duc de Morny,
adopted, and more and more strenuously persisted in,
a kind of " personal " novel-writing, which might be
regarded as tainted with the general Naturalist principle
that nothing is *tacendum*—that private individuality may
be made public use of, to almost any extent. Of course
a certain licence in this respect has always been allowed
to novelists. In the eighteenth century English writers
His "per- of fiction had very little scruple in using and
sonality." abusing that licence, and French, though with
the fear of the arbitrary justice or injustice of their time
and country before them, had almost less. As the nineteenth went on, the practice by no means disappeared
on either side of the Channel. With us Mr. Disraeli
indulged in it largely, and even Thackeray, though he
condemned it in others, and was furious when it was
exercised on himself, in journalism if not in fiction, pretty
notoriously fell into it now and then. As to Dickens,
one need not go beyond the too notorious instance of
Skimpole. Quite a considerable proportion of Balzac's
company are known to have been Balzacified from the
life ; of George Sand's practice it is unnecessary to say
more.

But none of these is so saturated with personality
as Daudet ; and while some of his " gentle " readers
seem not to care much about this, even if they do not
share the partiality of the vulgar herd for it, it disgusts
others not a little. Morny was not an estimable public

or private character, though if he had been a " people's man " not much fault would probably have been found with him. I daresay Daudet, when in his service, was not overpaid, or treated with any particular private confidence. But still I doubt whether any gentleman could have written *Le Nabab.* The last Bourbon King of Naples was not hedged with much divinity; but it is hardly a question, with some, that his *déchéance*, not less than that of his nobler spouse, should have protected them from the catch-penny vulgarity of *Les Rois en Exil.* Gambetta was not the worst of demagogues; there was something in him of Danton, and one might find more recent analogies without confining the researches to France. But even if his weaknesses gave a handle,

His books from this point of view and others. which his merits could not save from the grasp of the vulgariser, *Numa Roumestan* bore the style of a vulture who stoops upon recent corpses, not that of a dispassionate investigator of an interesting character made accessible by length of time. *L'Évangéliste* had at least the excuse that the Salvation Army was fair game; and that, if there was personal satire, it was not necessarily obvious—a palliation which (not to mention another for a moment) extends to *Sapho.* But *L'Immortel* revived—unfortunately, as a sort of last word—the ugliness of this besetting sin of Daudet's. Even the saner members of Academies would probably scout the idea of their being sacrosanct and immune from criticism. But *L'Immortel*, despite its author's cleverness, is once more an essentially vulgar book, and a vulturine or ghoulish one—fixing on the wounds and the bruises and the putrefying sores of its subject—dragging out of his grave, for posthumous crucifixion, a harmless enough pedant of not very old time; and throwing dirty missiles at living magnates. It is one of the books—unfortunately not its author's only contribution to the list—which leave a bad taste in the mouth, a " flavour of poisonous brass and metal sick."

Of another charge brought against Daudet I should

make much shorter work; and, without absolutely clearing him of it, dismiss it as, though not unfounded, comparatively unimportant. It is that of His "plagiarisms." plagiarism—plagiarism not from any French writer, but from Dickens and Thackeray. As to the last, one scene in *Fromont Jeune et Risler Aîné* simply *must* be " lifted " from the famous culmination of *Vanity Fair*, when Rawdon Crawley returns from prison and catches Lord Steyne with his wife. But, beyond registering the fact, I do not know that we need do much more with it. In regard to Dickens, the resemblance is more pervading, but more problematical. " Boz " had been earlier, and has been always, popular in France. *L'excentricité anglaise* warranted, if it did not quite make intelligible, his extravaganza; his semi-republican sentimentalism suited one side of the French temperament, etc. etc. Moreover, Daudet had actually, in his own youth, passed through experiences not entirely unlike those of David Copperfield and Charles Dickens himself, while perhaps the records of the elder novelist were not unknown to the younger. In judging men of letters as shown in their works, however, a sort of " *cadi*-justice " —a counter-valuation of merits and faults—is allowable. I cannot forgive Daudet his inveterate personality : I can bid him sit down quickly and write off his plagiarism—or most of it—without feeling the withers of my judicial conscience in the very least wrung. For if he did not, as others have done, make what he stole entirely his own, he had, *of* his own, very considerable property in rather unusually various kinds.

The charm of his short Tales, whether in the *Lettres de Mon Moulin* or in collections assuming the definite His merits. title, is undeniable. The satiric-pathetic— a not very common and very difficult kind— has few better representatives than *La Chèvre de M. Séguin*, and the purely comic stories are thoroughly " rejoicing." *Tartarin*, in his original appearances, " touches the spot," " carries off all the point " in a manner suggestive at once of Horace and Homocea;

and though, as was almost inevitable, its sequels are less effective, one would have been very glad indeed of them if they had had no forerunner. In almost all the books— *Robert Helmont*, by the way, though not yet mentioned, has some strong partisans—the grip of actual modern society, which is the boast of the later, as opposed to the earlier, nineteenth-century novel, cannot be missed. Even those who are most disgusted by the personalities cannot deny the power of the satiric presentation from *Le Nabab* to *Numa Roumestan*. *Fromont Jeune et Risler Aîné* is, quite independently of the definite borrowing from us, more like an English novel, in some respects, than almost any other French one known to me up to its date ; and I have found persons, not in the least sentimentalists and very widely read in novels both English and French, who were absolutely enthusiastic about *Jack*.

L'Évangéliste is perhaps the nearest approach to a failure, the atmosphere being too alien from anything French to be favourable to the development of a good story, and perhaps the very subject being unsuited to anything, either English or French, but an episode. In more congenial matter, as in the remark in *Numa Roumestan* as to the peculiar kind of unholy pleasure which a man may enjoy when he sees his wife and his mistress kissing each other, Daudet sometimes showed cynic acumen nearer to La Rochefoucauld than to Laclos, and worthy of Beyle at his very best. And I have no shame in avowing real admiration for *Sapho*. It does not by any means confound itself with the numerous studies of the infatuation of strange women which French fiction contains ; and it is almost a sufficient tribute to its power to say that it does not, as almost all the rest do, at once serve itself heir to, and enter into hopeless competition with, *Manon Lescaut*. Nor is the heroine in the least like either Marguerite Gautier or Iza Clémenceau, while the comparison with Nana, whose class she also shares, vindicates her individuality most importantly of all these trials. She seems to me Daudet's

best single figure : though the book is of too specialised
a kind to be called exactly his best book.

He never had strong health, and broke down early,
so that his total production is decidedly smaller than that
of most of his fellows.[1]   Nor has he, I think, any pretensions to be considered a novelist of the very first
class, even putting bulk out of the question. But he
can be both extremely amusing and really pathetic ;
he is never unnatural ; and if there is less to be said about
him than about some others, it is certainly not because
he is less good to read. On the contrary, he is so easy
and so good to read, and he has been read so much,
that elaborate discussion of him is specially superfluous.
It is almost a pity that he was not born ten or fifteen years
earlier, so that he might have had more chance of hitting
a strictly distinct style. As it is, with all his pathos and
all his fun, you feel that he is of the *Epigoni* a successor
of more than one or two Alexanders, that he has a whole
library of modern fiction behind—and, in more than one
sense of the word, before—him.

There was a time when Englishmen of worth and
Englishwomen of grace thought a good deal of Edmond
About : *Le* About.   Possibly this was because he was one
Roi des of the pillars of the *Revue des Deux Mondes*.
Montagnes. Far be it from me to speak with the slightest
disrespect of that famous periodical, to which I have
myself divers indebtednesses, and which has, in the last
hundred years or thereabouts, harboured and fostered
many of the greatest writers of France and much of
her best literary work. But persons of some age and
some memory must remember a time in England when
it used to be " mentioned with *hor* " as Policeman X
mentioned something or somebody else about the same
date or a little earlier. Even Matthew Arnold, in whose
comely head the bump of Veneration was not the most
remarkable protuberance, used to point to it—as some-

---

[1] I do not call Flaubert " his fellow," or the fellow of any one noticed in this chapter,
for which reason I kept him out of it.

thing far above *us*—to be regarded with reverence and striven towards with might and main. What justification there might be for this in general we need not now consider; but at any rate About has never seemed to the present historian very much of a pillar of anything. His chief generally accepted titles to the position in novel-writing are, I suppose, *Le Roi des Montagnes* and *Tolla*, each of which, and perhaps one other, we may examine in some detail, grouping the rest (with one further exception) more summarily. They are the better suited for our purpose in that one is comedy if not farce, and the other a gradually threatening and at last accomplished tragedy.

Of course it would be a very dull or a very curmudgeonly person who should fail to see or refuse to acknowledge "fun" in the history of Hadji or Hadgi Stavros. The mixture of sense, science, stupidity, and unconscious humour[1] in the German narrator; the satire on the toleration of brigandage by government in Greece (it must be confessed that, of all the reductions to the absurd of parliamentary and constitutional arrangements in countries unsuited for them, wherein the last hundred years have been so prolific, Greece has provided the most constant and reversed-sublime examples, as Russia has the most tragic); the contrast of amiability and atrocity in the brigands themselves—all these provide excellent opportunities, by no means always missed, for the display of a sort of anticipated and Gallicised Gilbertianism. Nor need the addition of stage Englishness in Mrs. Simons and her brother and Mary Ann, of stage Americanism in Captain John Harris and his nephew Lobster, spoil the broth.

But, to the possibly erroneous taste[2] of the present taster, it does not seem to be a consummated *consommé*. To begin with, there is too much of it; it is watered out

---

[1] It must be remembered that it was long before even 1870. I suppose some one, in the mass of war-literature, must have dealt with "The Ideal German in European Literature between 1815 and 1864." If nobody has, an excellent subject has been neglected.

[2] And, according to one reviewer, the deficient sense of humour.

to over three hundred pages when it might have been "reduced" with great advantage to one hundred. Nor is this a mere easy general complaint ; it would be perfectly possible to point out where reductions should take place in detail. No one skilled in the use of the blue pencil could be at a loss where to apply it in the preliminary matter ; in the journey ; in the Hadgi's gravely burlesqued correspondence ; in the escape of the ladies ; in Hermann's too prolonged yet absurdly ineffective tortures ; in the civil war between the King and his subjects ; in the rather transpontine victory of the two Americans and the Maltese over both ; and, above all, in the Royal Ball, where English etiquette requires that the rescuer must be duly introduced to those he has rescued. Less matter (or rather less talking about matter) with more art might have made it a capital thing, especially if certain traces of vulgarity, too common in About, were removed together with the mere superfluities. At any rate, this is how it strikes, and always has struck, a younger but now old contemporary.

The same fault of *longueurs* makes itself felt in *Tolla* : and indeed the author seems to have been conscious of

Tolla.   it, and confesses it in an apologetic *Preface* to the editions after the first. But this does not form the chief ground of accusation against it. Nor, certainly, do the facts, as summarised in a note, justify any serious charge of plagiarism,[1] though the celebrated Buloz seems for once to have been an unwise editor, in objecting to a fuller acknowledgment of indebtedness on the part of his contributor. A story of this tragical kind will bear much fuller handling than a comic tale of scarcely more than one situation, recounted with a perpetual "tongue-in-cheek" accompaniment.

But, from another point of view, the book does justify

---

[1] They *might* serve to exemplify About's often doubtful taste. The central story and main figures of *Tolla* were taken from a collection of the poor girl's letters published by her family a few years before ; and the original of "Lello" was still alive. *His* relations tried to buy up the book, and nearly succeeded. In the MS. About had, while slightly altering the names, referred pretty fully to this document. The whole thing has, however, rather a much-ado-about-nothing air, and, save as connected with a periodical of such undoubted "seriousness," might suggest a trick.

the drawing of a general literary moral, that true *données* are very far from being certain blessings—that they are, in fact, *dona Danaorum*—to the novelist; that he should not hug the shore of fact, but launch out into the ocean of invention. About, in a fashion rather cheerfully recalling the boasts of poor Shadwell, who could "truly say that he had made it[1] into a play" and that "four of the humours were entirely new," assures us that he has invented everything but the main situation, and written everything out of his own head except a few of the letters of Tolla. Some of these added things are good, though one of the author's besetting sins may be illustrated by the fact that he gives nearly half a score pages to a retrospective review of the history of a Russian General's widow and her daughter, when as many lines— or, better still, a line or two of explanation here and there—would be all that the story requires.[2] But the "given" situation itself is a difficult one to handle interestingly: and, in some estimates at any rate, the difficulty has not been overcome here. The son—a younger, but still amply endowed son—of one of the greatest Roman families, compact of Princes and Cardinals, with reminiscences of Venetian dogedom, falls in love, after a half-hearted fashion, with the daughter of another house of somewhat less, but still old repute, and of fair, though much lesser wealth. By a good deal of "shepherding" on the part of her family and friends, and (one is bound to say) some rather "downright Dunstable" on her own, he is made to propose; but *her* family accepts the demand that the thing shall, for a time, be kept secret from *his*. Of course no such secrecy is long possible; and his people, especially a certain wicked cavaliere-colonel, with the aid of a French Monseigneur and the Russians above mentioned, plot to break the thing off, and finally succeed. "Lello" (Manuel) Coromila finds out the plot too late. Tolla dies of a broken heart.

---

[1] "It" was *Timon of Athens*.

[2] It may please the historically given reader to regard this as an actual survival of the Scudéry *histoire—Histoire de Madame Fratieff et de sa fille Nadine*. Only it would, as such, have occupied a score or two of pages for each one.

It seems to me—speaking with the humility which I do not merely affect, but really feel on the particular point—that this might make a good subject for a play : that in the hands of Shakespeare or Shelley it might make a very great one in two different kinds. But— now speaking with very much less diffidence—I do not think it a promising one for a novel ; and, speaking with hardly any at all, I think that it has certainly not made a good one here. Shut up into the narrow action of the stage ; divested of the intervals which make its improbabilities more palpable ; and with the presentation of Lello as a weaker and baser Hamlet, of Tolla as a betrayed Juliet—with all this brought out and made urgent by a clever actor and actress, the thing might be made very effective. Dawdled over in a novel again of three hundred pages, it loses appeal to the sympathy and constantly starts fresh difficulties for the understanding.

That a very delightful girl[1] may fall in love with a nincompoop who is also notoriously a light-of-love, is quite possible : and, no doubt, is fortunate for the nincompoops, and, after a fashion, good for the continuation of the human race. But, in a novel, you must make the process interesting, and that is not, *me judice*, done here. The nincompoop, too, is such an utter nincompoop (he is not a villain, nor even a rascal) that, no comic use being made of his nincompoopery, he is of no use at all. And though an old and haughty Italian family like the Feraldis *might* no doubt in real life—there is nothing that may not happen in real life—consent to clandestine engagements of the kind described, it certainly is one of the possible-improbables which are fatal, or nearly so, to art. Two or three subordinate characters—the good-natured and good-witted Marquis Filippo Trasimeni, the faithful peasant Menico, Tolla's foster-brother, and even the bad chambermaid Amarella—have some merit. But twenty of them could not save the book, which, after dawdling till close upon its end, huddles itself up in a few pages, chiefly of *récit*, in a singularly inartistic fashion.

[1] 'Tolla is not so *very* delightful : but she is meant to be.

Germaine, which has been (speaking under correction) a much less popular book than either *Le Roi des Montagnes* or *Tolla*, is perhaps better than either. *Germaine.* Except for a very few pages, it does not attempt the somewhat cackling irony of the Greek book; and though it ends with one failure of a murder, one accomplished ditto, and two more deaths of no ordinary kind, it does not even attempt, as the Italian one does, real tragedy. But it has a fairly well-knit plot, some attempt at character, sufficient change of incident and scene, and hardly any *longueurs*. Even the hinge of the whole, though it presents certain improbabilities, is not of the brittle and creaking kind reprobated in that of *Tolla*.

A Neapolitan-Spanish Count of Villanera, whose second title is " Marquis of the Mounts of Iron," possessed also not only of the bluest of blood, but of mountains of gold, has fallen in love, after an honour-in-dishonour fashion, with the grass-widow of a French naval captain, Honorine Chermidy, and has had a child by her. She is really a worse Becky Sharp, or a rather cleverer Valérie Marneffe (who perhaps was her model[1]), and she forms a cunning plan by which the child may be legitimated and she herself, apparently renouncing, will really secure a chance of, the countdom, the marquisate, and the mountains of iron and gold. (Of the latter she has got a good share out of her lover already.) The plan is that Villanera shall marry some girl (of noble birth but feeble health and no fortune), which will, according to French law, effect or at least permit the legitimation of the little Marques de las Montes de Hierro—certain further possibilities being left ostensibly to Providence, but, in Madame Chermidy's private intentions, to the care of quite another Power. The Dowager Countess de Villanera—rather improbably, but not quite impossibly—accepts this, being, though proud, willing to derogate a little to make sure of an heir to the House of Villanera

---

[1] About has a gird or two at Balzac, but evidently imitates him. In this very book, when the old duke (*v. inf.*) comes under Madame Chermidy's influence, he suggests Baron Hulot ; and *Madelon* (*v. inf. ib.*) is almost throughout imitation-Balzacian.

with at any rate a portion (the sceptical would say a rather doubtful portion [1]) of its own blood.

Villanera himself, though in most ways the soul of honour, accepts this shady scheme chiefly through blind devotion to his mistress; and it only remains to find a family whose poverty, if not their will, consents to sell their daughter. Through the agency of that stock and pet French novel-character, a doctor who is very clever, very benevolent, very sceptical, and not over-scrupulous, the exact material for the mischief is found. There is an old Duc de la Tour-D'Embleuse, who, half-ruined by the original Revolution, has been almost completely so by that of 1830, has thrown away what remained, and has become an amiable and adored but utterly selfish burden on his angelic wife and daughter, the latter of whom, like so many of the heroines of the 'fifties, especially in France, is an all but "given-up" *poitrinaire*. The price of the bargain—an "inscription" of fifty thousand francs a year in Rentes—is offered on the very day when the family has come to its last *sou*; accepted, after short and sham refusal, by the duke; acquiesced in unselfishly by the mother, who despairs of saving her husband and daughter from starvation in any other way; and submitted to by the daughter herself in a spirit of martyrdom, strengthened by the certainty that it is but for a little while. How the situation works out to an end of liberal but not excessive poetical justice, the reader may discover for himself: the book being, though not a masterpiece, nor even very high in the second rank, quite worth reading. One or two things may be noticed. The first is a really clever sketch, the best thing perhaps in About's novel-work, of the peculiar "naughty-childishness" [2] which belongs to lovely woman, which does not materially affect her

---

[1] For Honorine, though managing to retain some public reputation, has long been practically "unclassed"; and it is not only her husband's profession which has made him leave her.

[2] Germaine, quite naturally and properly, starts with a strong dislike to her husband. When he takes her to Italy, and devotes himself to the care of her health, this changes to affection. And the more it changes, the more disagreeable she makes herself to him.

charm or even her usefulness in some ways, but makes her as politically impossible in one way as does that "incapacity for taking more than one side of a question" which Lord Halsbury has pointed out, in another.[1] The second is the picture, in the later half of the book, of those Ionian Islands, then still English, the abandonment of which was the first of the many blessings conferred by Mr. Gladstone[2] on his country, and the possession of which, during the late or any war, would have enabled us almost to pique, repique, and capot the attempts of our enemies in the adjacent Mediterranean regions.

All these books, and perhaps one or two others, are about the same length—an equality possibly due (as we have seen in English examples on a different scale) to periodical publication. But once, in *Madelon*, About attempted something of much "longer breath," as his countrymen say. Here we have nearly six hundred pages instead of three hundred, and each page (which is a large one) contains at least half as much again as a page of the others. The book is a handsome one, with a title in red ink; and the author says he took three years to write the novel—of course as an avocation from his vocation in journalism. It is difficult to repress, though probably needless to utter, the most obvious remark on this; but it is not hard to give it another turn. Diderot said (and though some people believe him not, I do) that Rousseau originally intended, in the Dijon prize essay which made his fate and fame, to argue that science and letters had *improved* morality, etc.; and that he, Diderot, had told Jean Jacques that this was *le pont aux ânes*, and determined him to take the paradoxical side instead. The "Asses' bridge" (*not* in the Euclidic sense, nor as meaning that all who took it were asses) of the mid-nineteenth century French novelist was the biography of the *demi-monde*. Balzac had been the first and greatest engineer of these *ponts*

Madelon.

[1] This also has, in matters not political, the "charming and useful" side. It would be very unpleasant if she always saw all sides of all questions.

[2] I am quite aware that the giving up of the islands was not the *immediate* result of his mission.

et chaussées; Dumas *fils* had shown that they might
lead to no mean success; so all the others followed in a
fashion certainly rather ovine and occasionally asinine.
Madelon is a young woman, attractive rather than beautiful, who begins as a somewhat mysterious favourite of
men of fashion in Paris; establishes herself for a time
as a married woman in an Alsatian town; ruins nearly,
mais non tout, a country baron; and ends, as far as the
book goes, by being a sort of inferior Lola Montès to a
German princeling. It has cost considerable effort to
justify even this short summary. I have found few
French novels harder to read. But there is at least one
smart remark—of the "publicist" rather than the
novelist kind—towards the end:

> C'est un besoin inné chez les peuplades germaniques; il faut,
> bon gré mal gré, qu'ils adorent quelqu'un.

They did not dislike puns and verbal jingles, either in
France or in England in the mid-nineteenth century,
as much as their ancestors and their descendants in both
countries have done before and since. A survivor to-day
might annotate " Et quel quelqu'un quelquefois ! "

In fact, to put the matter brutally, but honestly, as
far as the present writer's knowledge extends, Edmond

*Maître
Pierre*, etc.

Summing up.

About was not a novelist at all " in his heart."
He was a journalist (he himself admits the
impeachment so far), and he was a journalist
in a country where novel- or at least tale-writing had
long established itself as part of the journalist's business.
Also he was really a good *raconteur*—a gift which, though
perhaps few people have been good novelists without it,
does not by itself make a good novelist. As a publicist,
too, he was of no small mark: his *Question Romaine*
could not be left out of any sufficient political library of
the nineteenth century. Some of his shorter tales, such
as *Le Nez d'un Notaire* and *L'Homme à l'Oreille Cassée*,
have had a great vogue with those who like comic situations described with lively, if not very refined, wit. He
was also a good topographer; indeed this element enters

largely into most of his so-called novels already noticed, and constitutes nearly all the interest of a very pleasant book called *Maître Pierre*. This is a description of the *Landes* between Bordeaux and Arcachon, and something like a " puff " of the methods used to reclaim them, diversified by an agreeable enough romance. The hero is a local " king," a foundling-hunter-agriculturist who uses his kingdom, not like Hadji Stavros, to pillage and torment, but to benefit his subjects. The heroine is his protégée Marinette, a sort of minor Isopel Berners, with a happier end.[1] The throwing into actual tale-form of curious and decidedly costly local fashions of courtship is clever ; but the whole thing is a sort of glorified advertisement. Other books, *Les Mariages de Paris* and *Les Mariages de Province*, almost tell their tales, and something more,[2] in their titles.

One cannot but be sorry if this seems an unfair or shabby account of a pleasant and popular writer, but the right and duty of historical criticism is not to be surrendered. One of the main objects of literary history is to separate what is quotidian from what is not. To neglect the quotidian altogether is—whatever some people may say—to fall short of the historian's duty ; to put it in its proper place *is* that duty.

What ought to be said and done about Ponson du Terrail and Gaboriau—the younger Sue and Soulié ; Ponson du Terrail and Gaboriau. the protagonists of the melodramatic and criminal *feuilleton* during the later middle of the century—has been rather a problem with me. Clearly they cannot be altogether neglected. Deep would answer to deep, Rocambole to M. Lecoq, in protesting against such an omission of their manufacturers. I do not know, indeed, that any English writer of distinction has done for M. le Vicomte Ponson du Terrail

---

[1] That is to say, supposing that Isopel ever could have been happy with a lover

So *laggard* in love, *though* so dauntless in war

as George Borrow.

[2] As well as the Balzacian following, *haud passibus aequis*, above referred to.

what Mr. Lang did, "under the species of eternity" which verse confers, for "(Miss Braddon and) Gaboriau." I have known those who preferred that *other* Viscount, "Richard O'Monroy"—who shared with "Gyp" and Armand Silvestre the cheerful office of cheering the cheerable during the 'eighties and later—to the more canonical possessor of the title before him. But du Terrail was what I believe is called, in Scottish "kirk" language, a "supply"—a person who could undertake the duty of filling gaps—of enormous efficacy in his day. That is a claim on this history which cannot be neglected, though the people who would fain have Martin Tupper blotted out of the history of English poetry, might like to drop Ponson du Terrail in that of the French novel down an oubliette, like one of his own heroes, and *not* give him the file mercifully furnished to that robustious marquis. Gaboriau claims, in the same way, even more "clamantly."

The worst of it is (to play cards on table with the strictness which is the only virtue of this book, save perhaps an occasional absence of ignorance) that neither of them appeals to me. I have no doubt that this recalcitrance to the crime-novel is a *culpa*, if not a *culpa maxima*. I suppose it was born in me. It is certainly not merely due to the fact that, in my journalist days, perhaps because I was a kind of abortion of a barrister, I had to write endless articles on crimes.

> Penge murders knew
> The pencil blue

as regards my "copy," and a colleague once upbraided me for arguing in favour of Mrs. Maybrick. But I had read crime-novels before those days, and they never amused me. Yet perhaps it may be possible to show cause—other than my personal likings—for not ranking these high.

I have somewhere seen it said that Ponson du Terrail, before he took to driving *feuilletons* five-in-hand, showed some power of less coarse fiction-writing on a smaller scale. But I have not seen any of these essays, and real success in them on his part would surprise me. For

The first— his general character. it is exactly in the qualities necessary to such a success that he seems to me to come short. He *did* possess what, though it may seem almost profane to call it imagination, is really a cheap and drossy lower kind thereof. He could frame and accumulate, even to some extent connect, melodramatic situations, not so very badly, and not in very glaring imitation of anybody else. But, perhaps for that very reason, the difference between him and the others strikes one all the more painfully. *Les Orphelins de la Saint-Barthélemy* awakes the saddest sighs for Dumas or Mérimée. *La Femme Immortelle*, with its *diablerie* explained and then *dis*-explained and then clumsily solved with a laugh, makes one wish for an hour or two even of Soulié. And when one comes to the nineteenth century and *Les Gandins* and a fiendish *docteur rouge*[1] (who is in every conceivable way inferior to Vigny's *docteur noir*), and a wicked count who undergoes a spotty transcorporation, it is worse. If any one says, " This is possible, but you yourself have said that excellence in some one else ought not to affect the estimate of the actual subject," I reply, " Granted ; but Ponson du Terrail bores me." I have dropped every book of his that I have taken up, and only at a second—even a third—struggle have been able to get knowledge enough of it to speak without critical treason. Moreover, his style (always under caution given) seems to me flat, savourless, and commonplace ; his thought childish, his etceteras (if I may so say) absurd. The very printing is an irritation. Who can read such stuff as this ?

Tout à coup une sonnette se fit entendre.
Nana se leva.
Cette sonnette état celle qui avertissait la soubrette que sa maîtresse réclamait son office.
La jolie fille prit un flambeau et quitta la cuisine.

---

[1] I do not know whether any other novelists continued the series of diversely coloured " doctors," as the fly-makers have done.

Here you have four separate paragraphs, five lines, and thirty-five words to express, in almost idiotic verbiage, the following :

"Here her mistress's bell rang, and she left the kitchen."

One might conduct not merely five, but five and twenty novels abreast at this rate.

Not thus would it be proper to write of Gaboriau. With him, except incidentally, and when he is diverging *The second.* from his proper line,[1] one finds no mere "piffle." He has a business and he does that. Moreover, it is a business which, if not intrinsically, is historically important. Of course there had been crime-novels and crime-tales before : there always has been everything before. But Gaboriau undoubtedly refashioned and restarted them, and has been ever since the parent or master of a family, or whole school, of novelists and tale-tellers who have sometimes seemed, at any rate to themselves, to be pillars, and to be entitled to talk about politics and religion and morals, and the other things which, as Chesterfield so delightfully remarked, need no troublesome preparation in the talker. His place here, therefore, is secured. If it is not a large place, that is not entirely due to the mere fact that, as has been frankly acknowledged, the present writer takes little pleasure in the crime-novel. It is because the kind, plentiful for those who like it to read, can be conveniently knocked off in specimen for others. For the latter purpose it would not matter very much whether *L'Affaire Lerouge,* or *Le Crime d'Orcival,* or *M. Lecoq* itself, or perhaps even others, were taken. The first named, which was, I think, one of the first, if not the actual overture of the series, and which happens to be best known to the historian, will perhaps suffice.

No one who takes it up, having some little critical

---

[1] He *could* "piffle" when he went out of it. The would-be satirical characterisation of two aristocrats, Madame d'Arlange and M. de Commarin, in the book shortly to be noticed, is the thinnest and most conventional of things, except, perhaps, the companion trap-to-catch-the-French-Philistine of anti-clericalism which also shows itself sometimes.

aptitude and experience, will fail to see, very shortly,
L'Affaire that it does mean business and does do it.
Lerouge. The murder of Claudine Lerouge is well
plunged into ; the arrangements for its detection—professional and amateur—are "gnostically" laid out ;
and the plot thickens and presents various sides of
itself, like a craftsmanly made and tossed pancake. If
you read it at all, you will not skip much ; first, because
the interest, such as it is, is continuous ; and, secondly,
for one of those reasons which keep would-be sinners in
other paths of rectitude—that, *if* you skip, you will almost
certainly find you have lost your way when you come
down from skipping. Some oddities—partly, but not
entirely, connected with the strange and well-known
differences between French and English criminal pro-
cedure—will, of course, strike an Englishman—the
collaboration of professional *juge d'instruction* and amateur
detective being perhaps the most remarkable. The
love-affair, in which the Judge himself and the plotted-
against Albert de Commarin are rivals, though a useful
poker to stir the fire, is not quite a well-managed one :
and the long harangue of Madame Gerdy, between her
resurrection from brain-fever and her death, seems a
little to strain probability. But no one of these things,
nor all together, need be fatal to the enjoyment of the
book on the part of, as was once said, "them as likes"
the kind.[1]

Short notice may again serve for another novelist
enormously popular in his day ; very characteristic of
Feydeau— the Second Empire ; a favourite[2] for a time
Sylvie. (rather inexplicably) of Sainte-Beuve ; but not
much of a rose, and very much of many days before

---

[1] Two people, thinking of moving house in London, went once to inspect an advertised abode in the Kensington district. They did not much like the street ; they still less liked a very grim female who opened the door and showed them over the house ; and there was nothing to reconcile them in the house itself. But, wishing to be polite, the lady of the couple, as they were leaving, addressed to the grim guardian some feeble compliment on something or other as being "nice." "P'raps," was the reply, "for them as likes the —— Road." It is unnecessary to say that the visitors went down the steps in a fashion for which we have no exact English term, but which is admirably expressed by the French verb *dégringoler*.

[2] The favouritism declined, and the history of its decline was anecdotised in a fashion

yesterday—Ernest Feydeau. He did one thing, *Sylvie*, as different as possible from Gérard's book of the same name, but still, as it seems to me, good enough, though it never enjoyed a tenth part of the popularity of his more " scabrous " things, though itself is very far from prudish, and though it makes no appearance in some lists and collections of his work. Feydeau (it is a redeeming point) was one of " those about " Gautier, and *Sylvie* is by no means unlike a pretty free and fairly original transfer from *Les Jeune-France*. The hero is a gentleman, decadent by anticipation and romantic by survival to the very *n*th. He abides in a vast chamber, divanned, and hung with Oriental curtains : he smokes endless tchibouks, and lives chiefly upon preserved ginger. To him enters Sylvie, a sort of guardian angel, with a rather Mahometan angelism, who devotes herself to him, and succeeds, by this means and that, in converting him to a somewhat more rational system of life and " tonvelsasens," as Swift would say. It is slight enough, but very far from contemptible.

As has been said or hinted, however, this was not at all the sort of thing that brought or, so long as he did *Fanny.* keep it, kept Feydeau's vogue. *Fanny*, with which he " broke out " considerably more than " ten thousand strong," as far as sale of copies went, is certainly not a book of the " first-you-meet " kind. There is some real passion in its handling of the everlasting triangle. But it is passion of the most morbid and least " infinite " kind possible. Whenever Feydeau's heroes are sincere they have a peculiar kind of sentimental immorality—a sort of greasy gush—which is curiously nauseous. His Aphrodite, if the goddess will pardon the profanation of her name, is neither laughter-loving, nor tragic (as Aphrodite can be), nor Uranian in the sense, not of being superior to physical passion,

---

somewhat *gaulois*, but quite harmless. " Uncle Beuve," to the astonishment of literary mankind, put the portrait of this " nephew " of his in his *salon*. After *Daniel* (I think) it was moved to the dining-room, and thence to his bedroom. Later it was missed even there, and was, or was said to be, relegated to *un lieu plus intime encore*. The *trovatore* of this probably remembered his Rabelais.

but of transcending it. She is not exactly Pandemic, for Feydeau, like Malvolio, does talk, or tries to talk, of ladies ; but she is something like the patroness of the old Sensibility novel " gone to the bad."

Madame de Chalis, according to a memory of many years which I have not thought it worth while to freshen,

Others—
Daniel. has a weaker draught of this rancid and mawkish sentimentality. But having in those days missed (or failed over) *Daniel*, I thought it incumbent on me to gird myself up to its eight hundred pages. A more dismal book, even to skim, I have seldom taken up. The hero—a prig of the first water—marries one of those apparently only half-flesh-and-blood wives who, novelistically, never fail to go wrong. He cannot, in the then state of French law, divorce her, but he is able to return her on her mother's hands. Going to Trouville (about which, then a quite new-fashioned resort, there is a great deal in the book), he meets a beautiful girl, Louise de Grandmont, and the pair fall—not merely hopelessly, which is, in the circumstances, a matter of course, but, it would seem, innocently—in love with each other. But in such a case scandal must needs come ; and it is engineered by revenge of the discarded wife and the mother-in-law, by the treachery of some of Daniel's friends and the folly of others, as well as, it must be added, by his own weak violence, thoughtless conduct, and general imbecility. All this is developed at enormous length, and it ends in a general massacre, Louise's uncle being killed in a duel which Daniel ought to have fought (he is no coward, but a hopeless blunderer), the girl herself dying of aneurism, and Daniel putting an end to himself in her grave, much more messily and to quite infinitely less tragic effect than Romeo. There is one scene in which he is represented as gathering all his enemies together (including a lawyer, who is half-rogue, half-dupe) and putting them all to confusion by his oratory. The worst of it is that one does not in the least see *why* they were confused, except in one case, where the foe is literally kicked downstairs—an effective method, and one rare enough in French novels up to this date to be worth notice.[1]

It was, for all contemporary readers of the French novel, except those of the gravest and most precise kind, a day to be marked, not with vanishing forms in chalk, but with alabaster or Parian, when " Marcellin " of the *Vie Parisienne*—one of those remarkable editors who, without ever writing themselves, seem to have the knack of attracting and almost creating writers, enlisted one " Z," the actual final letter of the name of Gustave Droz, and published the first article of those to be later collected as *Monsieur, Madame et Bébé* and *Entre Nous*. Although the contents of these books only added a fresh sprout to the age-old tree that, for more than half a millennium, had borne *fabliau* and *nouvelle* and *conte* and *histoire*, and so forth, they had a remarkable, if not easily definable, differentia of their own, and have influenced fiction-writing of the same kind for a good half-century since. The later-working " Gyp " and others owed a good deal to them ; and I am bound to say that—reading the two books recently after a long interval—I found my old favourites just as amusing as I found them the very first time, shortly after they came out.

Of course—and only those who have made much study of criticism know how seldom critics recognise this " of course "—you must take the things in, and not out of, their own class. They are not bread, or meat, or milk of literature. They are, to take one order of

---

[1] The labour of reading the book has been repaid by a few useful specimens of Feydeau's want of anything like distinction of thought or style. He makes his hero (whom he does not in the least mean for a fool, though he is one) express surprise at the fact that when he was *in statu pupillari* he liked *fredaines*, but when he became his own master did not care about them ! Again : " Were I to possess the power and infinite charm of HIM [*sic*] who invented the stars I could never exactly paint the delightful creature who stood before me." Comment on either of these should be quite needless. Again : " Her nose, by a happy and bold curve, joined itself to the lobes, lightly expanded, of her diaphanous nostrils." Did it never occur to the man that a nose, separately considered from its curve and its nostrils, is terribly like that of La Camarde herself ? I wasted some time over the tedious trilogy of *Un Début à L'Opera, M. de Saint Bertrand, Le Mari de la Danseuse*. Nobody—not even anybody *qui* Laclos *non odit*—need follow me.

gastronomic preference and taste, devilled biscuits; to take another, chocolate with whipped cream on it. And the devilling and the creaming are sometimes better than the chocolate and the biscuit.

It is not very easy to say—and perhaps not very important to know—whether the mixture of naughtiness *Mr., Mme.* and sentimentality which characterises these *et Bébé* and books [1] was what Mr. Carlyle, I think, was *Entre Nous.* the first to call an " insurance " or only a spontaneous and in no way ". dodgy " or " hedgy " expression of the two sides of the French character. For everybody ought to know that the complaint of Dickens's " Mr. the Englishman " as to the French being " so d—d sentimental " is at least as well justified as Mr. Arnold's disapproval of their " worship of Lubricity." I suppose there are some people who would prefer the sentiment and are others who would choose the " tum-te-dy," while yet a third set might find each a disagreeable alternative to the other. For myself, without considering so curiously, I can very frankly enjoy the best of both. The opening story of the earlier and, I think, more popular book, " Mon Premier Reveillon," is not characteristic. It might have been written by almost anybody, and is in substance a softened and genteel version of the story of Miss Jemima Ivins, and her luckless (but there virtuous) suitor, in the " Boz " *Sketches*. " L'Âme en Peine," which follows, strikes the peculiar Drozian note for the first time; and very pleasant is the painting of the struggles of a pious youth— pious and pudibund to a quite miraculous extent for a French *collégien* of good family—with the temptations of a beautiful Marquise and cousin who, arrayed in an ultra-Second-Empire bathing-costume, insists on his bathing with her. " Tout le Reste de Madame de K." may a little remind an English reader of the venerable chestnut about the Bishop and the housemaid's knee; but the application is different. There is nothing wicked

---

[1] Their author wrote others—*Babolin, Autour d'une Source*, etc. But the wise who can understand words will perhaps confine themselves to *Mr., Mme. et Bébé* and its sequel.

in it, but it contains some of the touches of varying estimate of " good form " in different countries which make the comparative reading of English and French novels so interesting. " Souvenirs de Carême " is (or rather are, for the piece is subdivided) the longest of several bits of Voltairianism, sometimes very funny and seldom offensive. But, alas ! one cannot go through them all. The most remarkable exercise in the curious combination or contrast noticed above is afforded by *Une Nuit de Noce* and *Le Cahier Bleu* (tricks of ingeniously " passed-off " naughtiness which need not shock anybody), combined with the charming and pathetic " Omelette " which opens the second book, and which gives the happy progress and the sad termination of the union so merrily begun. All are drawn with equal skill and with no real bad taste. In one or two articles of both books the *gauloiserie* broadens and coarsens, while in the more purely " Bébé " sections of the first the sentimentality may seem a little watered out. But you cannot expect acrobatics on wine-glasses of this kind always to " come off " without some slips and breakages.

On the whole, I think *Entre Nous* contains the very best things, and most good ones. The pathos of the first (which is itself by no means mere *pleurnicherie*) is balanced at the other end by the audacity of " Le Sentiment à l'Épreuve," a most agreeable " washing white " of the main idea of Wycherley's *Country Wife ;* and between the two, few in the whole score are inferior. " Nocturne," " Oscar," " Causerie," and " Le Maillot de Madame " were once marked for special commendation by a critic who certainly deserved the epithet of competent, in addition to those of fair and gentle. It is, however, in this volume that what seems to me Droz's one absolute failure occurs. It is neither comic nor tragic, neither naughty nor nice, and one really wonders how it came to be put in. It is entitled " Les de Saint-Paon," and is a commonplace, hackneyed, quite unhumorous, and rather ill-tempered satire on certain dubious aristocrats and anti-modernists. Nothing could be cheaper or less pointed. And the insertion of it is all the stranger because, elsewhere, there is something very similar, in subject and tendency, but of half the length and ten times the wit, in " Le Petit Lever," a conversation between a certain Count and his valet.

The plain critical fact is that the non-pathetic serious was in no way Droz's trade. His satire on matters ecclesiastical is sometimes delightful when it is mere *persiflage* : an Archbishop might relax over the conversation in Paradise between two great ladies, one of whom has charitably stirred up the efforts of her director in favour of her own coachman to such effect, that she actually finds that menial promoted to a much higher sphere Above than that which she herself occupies. But here, also, the more gravity the less goodness.

Yet, as was hinted at the beginning of this notice, we ought not to quarrel with him for this, and to do so would be again to fall into the old " gin-shop and leg-of-mutton " unreasonableness. It was M. Droz's mission to start a new form of Crébillonade—*panaché* (to use an excellent term of French cookery), here and there, with another new form of Sensibility. He did it quite admirably, and he taught the simpler device—the compound one hardly—to pupils, some of whom still divert, or at least distract, the world. I am not at all ashamed to say that I think the best of his and their work capital stuff, continuing worthily one of the oldest and most characteristic strains of French literature ; displaying no contemptible artistry ; and contributing very considerably to that work of pleasure-giving which has been acknowledged as supplying the main subject of this book.

Few more striking contrasts—though we have been able to supply a fair number of such things—could be found than by passing from Gustave Droz Cherbuliez. to Victor Cherbuliez. Scion of a Genevese family already distinguished in letters, M. Cherbuliez became one of the *Deux-Mondains*, a " publicist " as well as a novelist of great ability, and finally an Academician ; but his novels, clever as they are, were never quite " frankly " liked in France—at least by the critics. This may have been partly due to the curious latent grudge with which French writers—to the country as well as to the language and manners born—have always regarded their Swiss comrades or competitors—the attitude as to a kind of poacher or interloper.[1] But to leave the matter there would be not only to miss thoroughness in the individual case, but also to overlook a point of very considerable importance to the history of the French novel generally. There is undoubtedly something in M. Cherbuliez's numerous, vigorous, and excellently readable novels which reminds one more of English than of French fiction. We have noticed a certain resemblance in Feuillet to Trollope : it is stronger still in Cherbuliez. Not, of course, that the Swiss novelist denies himself—though he uses them more sparingly—the usual latitudes of the French as contrasted with the English novelist during nine-tenths of the nineteenth century. But he does use them more sparingly, and he is apt to make his heroines out of unmarried girls, to an extent which might at that time seem, to the conventional French eye, simply indecent.

His general character-istics. He is much more prodigal of " interest " —that is to say, of incident, accident, occurrence—than most French novelists who do not affect somewhat melodramatic romance. On the other hand, his character-drawing, though always efficient, is seldom if ever masterly; and that " schematisation," on which, as is pointed out in various places of this book, French critics are apt to insist so much, is not always present. Of actual passion he has little, and his books are somewhat open to the charge—which has been brought against those of so many of our own second-best novelists—that they are somewhat machine-made, or, if that word be too unkind, are rather works of craft than of art. Yet the work of a sound craftsman, using good materials, is a great help in life ; and a person who wants

[1] Cf. *inf.* on M. Rod.

good story-pastime for a certain number of nights, without possessing a Scheherazade of his own, will find plenty of it in the thirty years' novel turn-out of Victor Cherbuliez.

He did not find his way at once, beginning with " mixed " novels of a Germanish kind—art-fiction in Short survey *Un Cheval de Phidias* ; psychological-literary of his books. matter (Tasso's madness) in *Le Prince Vitale* ; politico-social subjects in *Le Grand-œuvre*. But these things, which have not often been successes, certainly were not so in M. Cherbuliez's hands. He broke fresh ground and " grew " a real novel in *Le Comte Kostia*, and he continued to till this plot, with good results, for the rest of his life. The " scenes and characters " are sufficiently varied, those in the book just mentioned being Russian and those in *Ladislas Bolski* Polish—neither particularly complimentary to the nationalities concerned, and the latter decidedly melodramatic. *Le Comte Kostia* is sometimes considered his best novel ; but I should put above it both *Le Roman d'une Honnête Femme* (his principal attempt in purely French society and on Feuilletesque lines, with a tighter morality) and *Meta Holdenis*, a story of a Swiss girl—not beautiful, but " *vurry* attractive," and not actually " no better than she should be," but quite ready to be so if it suited her. *Miss Rovel* with another girl-heroine—eccentric, but not in the lines of the usual French-English caricatures— is a great favourite with some. *La Revanche de Joseph Noirel* is again melodramatic ; and *Prosper Randoce* is not good for much. But *Paule Méré*, one of its author's best character-books, is very much better—it is a study of ill-starred love, as is *Le Fiancé de Mlle. Saint-Maur*, a book not so good, but not bad. *Samuel Brohl et Cie* is a very clever story of a rascal. I do not know that any of his subsequent novels, *L'Idée de Jean Téterol*, *Noirs et Rouges*, *La Ferme du Choquard*, *Olivier Maugant*, *La Vocation du Comte Ghislain*, *La Bête*, *Une Gageure*, which closes the list of my acquaintance with them, will disappoint the reader who does not raise his expectation too high. *Olivier Maugant* is perhaps the strongest. But the expression just used must not be taken as belittling. In both France and England such novel-writing had become almost a trade—certainly a profession: and the turning out of workmanlike and fairly satisfying articles for daily consumption is, if not a noble ambition, a quite respectable aim. M. Cherbuliez did something more than this : there are numerous scenes and situations in his work which do not merely interest, but excite, if they never exactly transport. And the provision of interest itself is, as has been allowed, remarkably bounteous. I should not despise, though I should be a little sorry for, a reader—especially an English reader—who found more of it in Cherbuliez than even in Feuillet, and much more than in Flaubert or Maupassant. The causes of such preference require no extensive indication, and I need not say, after or before what is said elsewhere, that this order of estimate is not mine. But it is to some extent a " fact in the case." [1]

Before finishing this chapter we ought, perhaps, to consider three odd persons, two of them much extolled Three by some — Jules Barbey d'Aurevilly, Léon eccentrics. Cladel, and " Champfleury " of *Les Excentriques*. The two first were themselves emphatically " eccentrics "—one an apostle of dandyism (he actually wrote a book about Brummel, whom he had met early), a disdainful critic of rather untrustworthy vigour, and a stalwart reactionary to Catholicism and Royalism ; the other a devotee of the exact opposite of dandyism, as the title of his best-known book, *Les Va-nu-pieds*, shows, and a Republican to the point of admiring the Commune. The opposition has at least the advantage of disproving prejudice, in any unfavourable remarks that may be made about either. To Barbey d'Aurevilly's criticism I have endeavoured to do justice in a more

[1] There is a paper on Cherbuliez in *Essays on French Novelists*, where fuller account of individual works, and very full notice, with translations, of *Le Roman d'une Honnête Femme* and *Meta Holdenis* will be found.

appropriate place than this.[1] His fiction occupied a much smaller, but not a small, proportion of his very voluminous work. *Les Diaboliques* and *L'Ensorcelée*, as well as *Les Va-nu-pieds*, are titles which entitle a reader to form certain more or less definite expectations about the books they label ; and an author, by choosing them, deprives himself, to some extent, of the right justly claimed for him in Victor Hugo's well-known manifesto, to be judged *merely* according to his own scheme, and the goodness or badness of its carrying out. If Hugo himself had made *Les Orientales* studies of Montmartre and the Palais Royal, he could not have made out his right to the privilege he asserted. The objection applies to Barbey d'Aurevilly even more than to Cladel, but as the work of the latter is the less important, we may take it first.

At more times in my life than one I have striven to like—or at any rate to take an interest in—*Les Va-nu-*

Léon Cladel *pieds*. Long ago it had for me the passport of
—Les Va-nu- the admiration of Baudelaire,[2] to whom and to
pieds, etc. Victor Hugo (this latter circumstance an im-
portant *visa* to the former) Cladel announced himself a pupil. But an absolute, if perhaps unfortunate, inability to follow anything but my own genuine opinion prevented me from enjoying it. And I cannot enjoy it now. It is not a commonplace book, nor is anything else of its author's ; but the price paid for the absence of commonplaceness is excessive. A person possessing genius, and sure of it, does not tell you that he has been rewriting his book (not for correction of fact, but for improvement of style) for ten years, and that now he doesn't care anything for critics, and endorses it NE VARIETUR (*sic*).[3] The style itself is a mosaic of preciousness, literary jargon, and positive *argot*—not quite contemptible, but, like some actual mosaic, unattractive ; and the matter

---

[1] *History of Criticism*, vol. iii. See also below.
[2] The author of the *Fleurs du Mal* himself might have been distinguished in prose fiction. The *Petits Poëmes en Prose* indeed abstain from story-interest even more strictly than their avowed pattern, *Gaspard de la Nuit*. But *La Fanfarlo* is capitally told.
[3] Hugo might do this ; hardly a Hugonicule.

does not attract me, though it may attract people who like tiger-taming scenes, crimes, grimes, etc. The address of the dedication, " Mienne," and nothing more, is rather nice, and some of the local scenes (Cladel was passionately patriotic towards his remote province of Quercy-Rouergue) are worth reading. But this devotion is better shown in the short single book (*Les Va-nu-pieds* is a collection) called *Crête-Rouge*—the regimental nickname of the heroine (an Amazon), who actually serves in the war of the Terrible Year, and comes off much better, when her sex is discovered by the Prussians, than she would have done forty and odd years later. The end-scenes of this book, with her Druid-stone marriage to a comrade, are really good. Of *Le Bouscassié*, *Titi-Froissac IV*, and *La Fête Votive de Saint-Bartholomée Porte-Glaive* I shall not say much. The "province," which is strong in them, saves them sometimes. But Cladel's hopeless lack of self-criticism shows itself in the fact of his actually reprinting in full an article of Veuillot's (by no means uncomplimentary) on himself, as a prelude in the book last mentioned, and adding a long reply. The proceeding was honest, but rather suicidal. One may not wholly admire the famous editor of the *Univers*.[1] But nothing could better throw up his clear, vigorous, classical French and trenchant logic, than the verbose and ambaginous preciousness, and the cabbage-stick cudgel-play, of Cladel.[2]

Jules Barbey d'Aurevilly, also a favourite of Baudelaire's, is a writer of an altogether greater clan—indeed one of those who come short but a little, and one does not quite know how, of individual greatness. Something has been said of his criticism, but a volume of it which was not within my reach when I wrote what is there quoted, *Le*

Barbey d'Aurevilly— his criticism of novels.

---

[1] There used to be a fancy for writing books about groups of characters. Somebody might do worse in book-making than " Great Editors," and Veuillot should certainly be one of them.

[2] The inadvertences which characterise him could hardly be better instanced than in his calling the eminent O'Donovan Rossa "*le député-martyr* de Tipperary." In English, if not in French, a " deputy-martyr " is a delightful person.

Roman Contemporain, is a closer introduction to a notice of him as a novelist. As of all his work it may be said of this, that anybody who does not know the subjects will probably go away with a wrong idea of them, but that anybody who does know them will receive some very valuable cross-lights. The book consists [1] of a belittlement, slightly redressed at the end, of Feuillet as a feeble person and an impertinent patroniser of religion ; of a rather " magpie " survey of the Goncourts ; of a violent and quite blind attack on Flaubert (the worst criticism of Barbey's that I have ever read) ; of a somewhat unexpectedly appreciative notice of Daudet ; of an almost obligatory panegyric of Fabre ; of another *éreintement,* at great length, of Zola ; and of shorter articles, again " magpied " of praise and blame, on MM. Richepin, Catulle Mendès, and Huysmans.[2]

All this is interesting, but I fear it confirms a variation of the title of a famous Elizabethan play—

His novels themselves— *Les Diaboliques* and others.

" Novelists beware novelists." Poets have a worse reputation in this way, of course ; but, I think, unjustly. Perhaps the reason is that the quality of poetry is more *definite,* if not more definable, than that of prose fiction, or else that poets are more really sure of themselves. Barbey d'Aurevilly [3] had an apparently undoubting mind, but perhaps there were unacknowledged doubts, which transformed themselves into jealousies, in his heart of hearts. For myself, I sympathise with his political and religious (if not exactly with his ecclesiastical) views pretty decidedly ; I think (speaking as usual with the due hesitation of a foreigner) that he writes excellent French ; and I am sure—a point of some consequence with me, and not too commonly met—that he generally writes (when he does not get *too* angry) like a gentleman. He sometimes has phrases which please me very much,

---

[1] Its articles are made up—rather dangerously, but very skilfully—of shorter reviews of individual books published sometimes at long intervals.

[2] Who replied explosively.

[3] There used to be something of a controversy whether it should be thus or Aurévilly. But the modern editions, at least, never have the accent.

as when he describes two lovers embracing so long that they " must have drunk a whole bottle of kisses," or when he speaks of the voice of a preacher " *tombant* de la chaire dans cette église où *pleuvaient* les ténèbres du soir," where the opposition-combination of " tombant " and " pleuvaient," and the image it arouses, seem to me of a most absolute fancy.   He can write scenes—the finale of his best book, *L'Ensorcelée*; the overture of *Un Prêtre Marié*; and nearly the whole of the last and best *Diabolique*, " Une Vengeance de Femme "—which very closely approach the first class. And, whether he meant me to do so or not, I like him when in " Un Dîner d'Athées " he makes one of them " swig off " (*lamper*) a bumper of Picardan, the one wine in all my experience which I should consider fit *only* for an atheist.[1]   But a good novelist I cannot hold him.

His merits.

The inability does not come from any mere " un-pleasantness " in his subjects, though few pleasant ones seem to have lain in his way, and he certainly did not go out of that way to find them.   But *L'Ensorcelée* can only be objected to on this score by an absurdly fastidious person, and I do not myself want any more rose-pink and sky-blue in *Un Prêtre Marié*;[2] while the last *Diabolique*, already mentioned, is a capital example of grime made more than tolerable.[3]   Indeed, nothing of the sort can be more unmistakable than the sincerity of Barbey's " horrors."   They mark, in that respect, nearly the apex of the triangle, the almost disappearing lower angles of which may be said to be represented by the crude and clumsy vulgarities of Janin's *Âne Mort*, and the more craftsmanlike, indeed in a way almost artistic, but unconvinced and unconvincing atrocities of Borel's *Champavert*.

---

[1] Very little above it I should put the not wholly dissimilar liquor obtained, at great expense and trouble, by a late nobleman of high character and great ability from (it was said) an old monkish vineyard in the Isle of Britain.   The monks must have exhausted the goodness of that *clos*; or else have taken the wine as a penance.

[2] Huysmans on this is very funny.

[3] A Spanish duchess of doubly and trebly " azured " blood revenges herself on her husband, who has massacred her lover before her eyes and given his heart to dogs, by becoming a public prostitute in Paris, and dying in the Salpêtrière.   It is almost, if not quite, a masterpiece.

The objection, and the defect which occasions the objection, are quite different. Barbey d'Aurevilly has many gifts and some excellencies. But his work in novel constantly reminds me of the old and doubtless well-known story of a marriage which was almost ideally perfect in all respects but one—that the girl "couldna bide her man." He can do many things, but he cannot or will not tell a story, save in such fragments and flashes as those noted above. His *longueurs* are exasperating and sometimes nearly maddening, though perhaps many readers would save themselves by simply discontinuing perusal. The first *Diabolique* has metal attractive enough of its kind. A young officer boards with a provincial family, where the beautiful but at first silent, abstracted, and, as the Pléiade would have said, *marbrine* daughter suddenly, though secretly, develops frantic affection for him, and shows it by constant indulgence in the practice which that abominable cad in Ophelia's song put forward as an excuse for not "wedding." But, on one of these occasions, she translates trivial metaphor into ghastly fact by literally dying in his arms. Better stuff—again of its kind—for a twenty-page story, or a little more, could hardly be found. But Barbey gives us *ninety*, not indeed large, but, in the usual editions, of exceptionally close and small print, watering out the tale intolerably almost throughout, and giving it a blunt and maimed conclusion. *Le Bonheur dans le Crime,*[1] *Le Dessous de Cartes*, and the above-mentioned *Dîner d'Athées*, which fill a quarter of a thousand of such pages, invite slashing with a hook desperate enough to cut each down to a quarter of a hundred. *Un Prêtre Marié*, which perhaps comes next to *L'Ensorcelée* in merit, would be enormously improved by being in one volume instead of two. Of *Une Vieille Maîtresse* I think I could spare both, except a vigorously told variant (the suggestion is acknowledged, for Barbey

And defects.

---

[1] Barbey's dislike of Feuillet was, evidently and half-confessedly, increased by his notion that *M. de Camors* had "lifted" something from *L'Ensorcelée*. There is also perhaps a touch of *Le Bonheur dans le Crime* in *La Morte*.

d'Aurevilly was much too proud to steal) of Buckingham's duel[1] and the Countess (not "Duchess," by the way) of Shrewsbury. *Une Histoire sans Nom*, a substantial though not a very long book, is only a short story spun

Especially as shown in *L'Ensorcelée*.

out. Even in *L'Ensorcelée* itself the author, as a critic, might, and probably would, have found serious fault, had it been the work of another novelist. There is less surplusage and more continuous power, so that one is carried through from the fine opening on the desolate moor (a *little* suggested, perhaps, by the meeting of Harry Bertram and Dandie Dinmont, but quite independently worked out) to the vigorous close above referred to. But the story is quite unnecessarily muddled by information that part of it was supplied by the Norman Mr. Dinmont, and part by an ancient countess. We never get any clear idea *why* Jeanne le Hardouey was bewitched, and *why* the Chevalier-Abbé de la Croix-Jugan suffered and diffused so gruesome a fate.[2] Yet the fate itself is enough to make one close, with the sweet mouth, remarks on this very singular failure of a genius. Few things of the sort in fiction are finer than the picture of the terrible unfinished mass (heralded over the desolate moor at uncertain times by uncanny bell-ringing), which the reprobate priest (who has been shot at the altar-steps before he could accomplish the Sacrifice of Reconciliation [3]) endeavours after his death to complete, being always baffled before the consecrating moment.

Cladel had a considerable, and Barbey d'Aurevilly an almost exclusive, fancy for the tragical. On the other hand, Champfleury (who, no doubt partly for a biblio-

---

[1] He knew a good deal (quite independently of Byron and Brummel) about English literature. One is surprised to find somewhere a reference to Walpole's story of Fielding and his dinner-companions.

[2] Observe that this is no demand for the explanation of the supernatural. Let the supernatural remain as it is, by all means. But curses should have causes. Até and Weird are terrible goddesses, but they are not unreasonable ones. They might be less *terrible* if they were.

[3] He has for two years been ordered to be present, but forbidden to celebrate; in punishment for his having, uncanonically, fought as a Chouan—if not also for attempted suicide. But we hear of no amorousness, and the husband Le Hardouey's jealousy, though prompted by his wife's apparent self-destruction, is definitely stated to have no foundation in actual guilt with the priest. On the contrary, she declares that he cared nothing for her.

graphical memory,[1] prefixed the Champ- to his actual surname) occupies, as has been said, a curious, but in part far from unsatisfactory, position in regard to our subject, and one blessed by the Comic Spirit. His confessed fictions are, indeed, not very successful. To take one volume only, *Madame Eugénio*, the title-story, *not* the first in order, but the longest, is most unfortunately, but far too accurately, characterised by a phrase towards its end, " ce *triste* récit," the adjective, like our " poor," being capable of two different meanings. *Histoire du Lieutenant Valentin*, on the other hand—a story of a young soldier, who, leaving Saint-Cyr in cholera-time, has to go to hospital, and, convalescing pleasantly while shelling peas and making rose-gays for the Sisters, is naïvely surprised at one of them being at first very kind and then very cold to him—is a miss of a masterpiece, but still a miss, partly owing to too great length. And so with others.

Champfleury.

But in his much earlier *Les Excentriques* (not unnaturally but wrongly called " *Contes* Excentriques " by some), handling what profess to be true stories, he shows a most excellent narrative faculty. Whether they are true or not (they rather resemble, and were perhaps inspired by, some things of Gautier and Gérard) matters little—they are quite good enough to be false. They are, necessarily, not quite equal, and there may be for some tastes, not for all, too much of the Fourierism and other queernesses of the mid-nineteenth century. Indeed, the book is of 1852, and its subjects are almost all of the decade preceding. But some are exceedingly refreshing, the dedication, of some length, to the great caricaturist Daumier being not the least so. Yet it is not so unwise as to disappoint the reader by being better than the text. " Lucas," the circle-squarer, who explains how, when he was in a room with a lady and her two daughters, he perceived that " this was all that was necessary for him to attain the cubation of two

Les Excentriques.

---

[1] Of Geoffroy Tory's book which (*v. sup.* Vol. I. p. 124) helped to give us the Limousin student.

pyramids," is very choice. "Cambriel"—who not only attained the philosopher's stone and the universal medicine, but ascertained that God is six feet six high, of flame-coloured complexion, and with particularly perfect ankles—runs him hard. And so does Rose Marius Sardat, who sent a copy of his *Loi d'Union*, a large and nicely printed octavo, to every Parisian newspaper-office, informing the editors that they might reprint it in *feuilletons* for nothing, but that he should not write the second volume unless the first were a success. Some of us ought to be particularly obliged to Rose Marius for holding that persons over seventy are indispensable, and that, if there are not enough in France, they must be imported. The difference of this from the callous short-sightedness which talks about "fixed periods" is most gratifying. But perhaps the crown and flower of the book is the vegetarian Jupille, who wrote pamphlets addressed :

AUX GOURMANDS DE CHAIR !

decided that meat is of itself atheistical, though he admitted a "siren" quality about it; and held that the fact of onions making human beings weep attests their own "touching sensibility for us" (albeit he had to admit again that garlic was demoniac). M. Jupille (who was a practical man, and cooked cabbage and cauliflower so that his meat-eating visitor could not but acknowledge their charm) explained St. Peter's net of animal food with ease as a diabolic deception, but was floored by crocodiles' teeth. And not the worst thing in the book is the last, where a waxwork-keeper—a much less respectable person than Mrs. Jarley, and of the other sex—falls in love with one of his specimens, waltzes with her, and unwittingly presents a sort of third companion to one of the less saintly kings of the early Graal legends, and to yet another character of Dickens's, much less well known than Mrs. Jarley, the hairdresser in *Master Humphrey's Clock*, who, to the disgust of his female acquaintances, "worshipped a hidle" in the shape of the turning bust of a beautiful creature in his own shop-window. The book is a book to put a man in a good temper—and to keep him in one—for which reason it affords an excellent colophon to a chapter.[1]

---

[1] It is possible that some readers may say, "Where are Erckmann-Chatrian ?" The fact is that I have never been able to find, in those twin-brethren, either literature or that not quite literary interest which some others have found. But I do not wish to abuse them, and they have given much pleasure to these others. So I let them alone.

CHAPTER XIII

NATURALISM—THE GONCOURTS, ZOLA, AND MAUPASSANT

IF I were writing this *History* on the lines which some
of my critics (of whom, let it be observed, I do not make
the least complaint) seem to prefer, or at least
to miss their absence, a very large part of
this chapter would give me the least possible difficulty.
I should simply take M. Zola's *Le Roman Expérimental*
and M. Brunetière's *Le Roman Naturaliste* and " combine
my information." The process—easy to any one of
some practice in letters—could be easier to no one than
to me. For I read and reviewed both books very carefully
at their first appearance; I had them on my shelves
for many years; and the turning of either over for a
quarter of an hour, or half at the most, would put its
contents once more at my fingers' ends. But, as I have
more than once pointed out, elaborate boiling down of
them would not accord with my scheme and plan.
Inasmuch as the episode or passage [1] is perhaps, of all
those which make up our story, the most remarkable
instance of a deliberate " school "—of a body of work
planned and executed under more or less definite
schedules—something if not much more of the critical

*The be-
ginnings.*

---

[1] For the early divisions of verse and prose story were all Topsies, and simply
" growed "; although the smaller romances of the late sixteenth and early seventeenth
century, and the larger of the latter date, were undoubtedly influenced by the Greek, it
was more a case of general imitation than specific endeavour; the Sensibility school
was very limited and chiefly attended to tricks of manner; and the " Romantic vague "
was never vaguer than in the vast and rather formless, though magnificent and delightful,
novel-work started by Nodier, Mérimée, Vigny, and Hugo. The Naturalists, on the
other hand, had a deliberate idea of revolutionising the novel—of abolishing old things
and creating new. They could not, and did not, succeed: but their scheme, as well as
its results, may claim consideration.

kind than usual may be given, either here or in the Conclusion.[1] But we shall, I think, learn far better things as to M. Zola and those about him by considering what they—at least what he, his would-be teachers, and his greatest disciple—actually did, than by inquiring what they meant, or thought they meant, to do, or what other people thought about them and their doings.

Let us therefore, in the first place and as usual, stick to the history, though even this may require more than one mode and division of dealing.

The body of Naturalist or Experimental novels which, beginning in the 'sixties of the century, extended "Les deux to, and a little over, its close, has long been, Goncourt." and will probably always continue to be, associated with the name of Émile Zola. But the honour or dishonour of the invention and pioneering of the thing was claimed by another, for himself and a third writer, that is to say, by Edmond de Goncourt for himself and his brother Jules. The elder of the Goncourts—the younger died in early middle age, and knowledge of him is in a way indirect, though we have some letters—might be said to have, like Restif, a *manie de paternité*, though his children were of a different class. He thought he invented Naturalism ; he thought he introduced into France what some unkind contemporaries called " Japoniaiserie";[2] he certainly had a good deal to do with reviving the fancy for eighteenth-century art, artists, *bric-à-brac* generally, and in a way letters ; and he ended by fathering and endowing an opposition Academy. It was with art that " Les deux Goncourt "[3] (who were inseparable in their lives, and whom Edmond—to do him

---

[1] To which a brief consideration of the curious fancy of some French critics that there is something " classical " about Naturalism may be specially relegated.

[2] Mérimée, though after his fashion making no fuss about it, was also an early virtuoso in this kind ; and one of his letters contains an excellent example of the quiet cynicism in which he excelled. Some ladies had asked to see his collection, and he had very properly warned them that the " curios " of that ingenious and valiant nation were sometimes " curious " in a special sense, and had offered to " select." " Elles ont tout vu," he adds simply, and one hopes his correspondent (I forget whether it was one of the *Inconnues* or Madame de Montijo) appreciated the Mount-Everest-like Laconism.

[3] The banal phrase has been framed in the amber of " Théo's " verse, and so debanalised.

the justice which in his case can rarely be done pleasantly
—did his best to keep undivided after Jules's death) began
their dealings with eighteenth-century and other artists[1]
—perhaps the most valuable of all their work.   But it
was not till the Second Empire was nearly half-way
through, till Jules was thirty and Edmond thirty-eight,
that they tried fiction (drama also, but always unsuccess-
fully), and brought out, always together and before 1870
(when Jules died), a series of some half-dozen novels :
Charles Demailly (afterwards re-titled) (1860), *Sœur
Philomène* (next year), *Renée Mauperin* (1864), *Germinie
Lacerteux* (next year), *Manette Salomon* (1867), and
Madame Gervaisais (1869).

It is desirable to add that, besides the work already
mentioned and published before 1870, the two had given
Their work. a book called *Idées et Sensations*, setting forth
their literary psychology ; and that, after the
cataclysm, Edmond published a description of their house
and its collections, his brother's letters, and an immense
Journal des Goncourt in some half-score of volumes, which
was, naturally enough, one of the most read books of its
time.   Naturally, for it appealed to all sorts of tastes,
reputable and disreputable, literary-artistic and Philistine,
with pairs enough of antithetic or complementary epithets
enough to fill this page.   Here you could read about
Sainte-Beuve and Gautier, about Taine and Renan, about
Tourguénieff and Flaubert, as well as about Daudet and
Zola, and a score of other more or less interesting people.
Here you could read how Edmond as a boy made irrup-
tions into a newly-married cousin's bedroom, and about
the interesting sight he saw there ; how an English
virtuoso had his books bound in human skin ; how people
dined during the siege of Paris, and a million other things ;
the whole being saturated, larded, or whatever word
of the kind be preferred, with observations on the taste,
intellect, and general greatness of the MM. de Goncourt,

---

[1] The first book of theirs, or rather of Edmond's, though it bore both names, that I
read, and the second French book I ever reviewed, was the mainly artistic *Gavarni* of
1873.   One has a human weakness in such cases, but I think one might not have been
wholly well disposed to the author from it.

and on the lamentable inferiority of other people, etc.,
etc. If it could be purged of its bad blood, the book
would really deserve to rank, for substance, with Pepys'
diary or with Walpole's letters.[1] As it is, when it has
become a little forgotten, the quarterly reviewers, or
their representatives, of the twenty-first century will be
able to make endless *réchauffés* of it. And though not
titularly or directly of our subject, it belongs thereto,
because it shows the process of accumulation or incuba-
tion, and the temper of the accumulators and incubators
in regard to the subjects of the novels themselves.

To analyse all these novels, or even one of them, at
length, would be a process as unnecessary as it would be
disagreeable. The "chronicles of wasted
The novels. *grime*" may be left to themselves, not out of
any mere finical or fastidious superiority, but simply
because their own postulates and axioms make such
analysis (if the word unfairness can be used in such a
connection) unfair to them. For they claimed—and
the justice, if not the value, of the claim must be allowed—
to have rested their fashion of novel-writing upon two
bases. The substance was to be provided by an elaborate observation and reproduction of the facts of actual
life, not in the least transcendentalised, inspirited, or in
any other way brought near Romance, but considered
largely from the points of view which their friend Taine,
writing earlier, used for his philosophical and historical
work—that of the *milieu* or "environment," that of
heredity, though they did not lay so much stress on this
as Zola did—and the like. The treatment, on the other
hand, was to be effected by the use of an intensely " personal " style, a new Marivaudage, compared to which,
as we remarked above, Flaubert's doctrine of the single
word was merely rudimentary. After Jules's death
Edmond wrote, alone, *La Fille Elisa*, which was very
popular, *La Faustin*, and *Chérie*, the last of which, with

---

[1] Pepys had nothing that could be called *bad* blood. Horace perhaps had a little,
but it was sweet and childlike compared to the "acrid-quack" fluid of Edmond de
Goncourt's veins and heart. Probably several people have seen in M. de Goncourt the
suggestion of an *un*-Puritan Malvolio.

Germinie Lacerteux, may form the basis of a short critical examination.   Those who merely wish to see if they can like or tolerate the Goncourtian novel had perhaps better begin with *Renée Mauperin* or *Madame Gervaisais.* Both have been very highly praised,[1] and the first named of them has the proud distinction of putting "le mot de Cambronne" in the mouth of a colonel who has been mortally wounded in a duel.

To return to our selected examples, *Germinie Lacerteux* is the story of an actual *bonne* of the brothers, whose story, *Germinie* without "trimmings," is told in the *Journal Lacerteux* and itself.[2]   The poor creature is as different as *Chérie* taken possible, not merely from the usual heroine, but as specimens. from the *grisette* of the first half of the century and from the *demi-mondaine* of Dumas *fils,* and Daudet, and even Zola.   She is not pretty ; she is not fascinating in any way ;   she is neither good- nor ill-natured in any special fashion ;   she is not even ambitious of " bettering " herself or of having much pleasure, wealth, etc.   If she goes to the bad it is in the most commonplace way and with the most unseductive seducer possible.   Her progress and her end are, to borrow a later phrase and title metaphorically, merely a tale of the meanest streets ; untouched and unconfirmed by the very slightest art ; as destitute of any aesthetic attraction, or any evidence of artistic power, as the log-books of a common lodging-house and a hospital ward could be.   In *Chérie* there is nothing exactly improper ;   it is merely an elaborate study of a spoilt—at least petted—and unhealthy girl in the upper stages of society, who has at last the kindness— to herself, her relations, and the reader—to die.   If M. de Goncourt had had the slightest particle of humour, of which there is no trace in any of his works, one might have taken this, like other things perhaps, as a slightly

---

[1] Not, however, in the second case, by Sainte-Beuve, whose lukewarmness Edmond— a " Sensitive Plant " in this way if hardly in others—never forgave.

[2] She served them for a very long period without giving them any apparent cause for complaint.   They only found out her delinquencies after her death, or in her last illness —I forget which.   Probably nothing could better show " the nature of the animals " than this *post-mortem* grubbing belowstairs for a " subject," and washing your own household dirty linen in public—for profit.

cryptic parody—of the *poitrinaire*-heroine mania of times a little earlier; but there is no hope of this. The subject was, in the sense attached to the word by these writers, " real " ; it could be made useful for combined physiological and psychological detail ; and, most important of all, it was more or less repulsive.[1]

For this is what it really comes to in the Goncourts, in Zola, and in the rest, till Guy de Maupassant, not

The impression produced by them.

seldom dealing with the same material, sublimes it, and so robs it of its repulsiveness, by the force of true comic, tragic, or romantic art. Of course it is open to any one to say, " It may repel *you*, but it does not repel *me*." But this is very cheap sophistry. We do not require to be told, in the words which shocked Lord Chesterfield but do not annoy a humble admirer of his, that " One man's meat is another man's poison." Carrion is not repulsive to a vulture. Immediately before writing these words I was reading the confession of an unfortunate American that he or she found *The Roundabout Papers* " depressing." For my part, I have never given up the doctrine that *any* subject *may* be deprived of its repulsiveness by the treatment of it. But when you find a writer, or a set of writers, deliberately and habitually selecting subjects which are generally held to be repellent, and deliberately and habitually refusing or failing to pass them through the alembic in the manner suggested—then I think you are justified, not merely in condemning their taste, but in thinking not at all highly of their art. A cook who cannot make his meat savoury unless it is " high " is not a good cook, and if he cannot do without pepper and garlic[2] he is not much better.

Dismissing, however, for a moment the question of mere taste, it should be evident that the doctrine of

---

[1] It may be well to smash, in a passing note, a silly catchword popular with some rather belated English admirers of the Naturalist school a few years ago. They praised its "frankness." You might as well praise the "straightforwardness" of a man who goes out of his way to explore laystalls and, having picked up ordure, holds it up to public view.

[2] Both excellent things in their way, of course. Perhaps it would be better to say asafœtida.

rigid " observation," " document," " experience," and the like is bad in art.   Like so many — some opti- *The rotten-* mists would say like all—bad things, it is, of *ness of their* course, a corruption, by excess and defect *theory.* both, of something good or at least true.   It cannot be necessary here, after scores of expressions of opinion on the subject throughout this book, to admit or urge the importance of observation of actual life to the novelist.   The most ethereal of fairy-tales and the wildest of extravaganzas would be flimsy rubbish if not corroborated by and contrasted with it : it can be strengthened, increased, varied almost at discretion in the novel proper.   I hold it, as may be argued perhaps in the Conclusion, to be the principle and the justification of Romance itself.   But, independently of the law just mentioned, that you must not confine your observation to Ugliness and exclude Beauty—it will not do to pull out the pin of your cart, and tilt a collection of observed facts on the hapless pavement of the reader's mind. You are not a reporter ; not a compiler of *dossiers* ; not a photographer.   You are an artist, and you must do something with your materials, add something of yourself to them, present something not vamped from parts of actual life itself, but reinforcing those parts with aesthetic re-creation and with the sense of " the whole."   I find this—to confine ourselves strictly to the famous society so often mentioned in the *Journal*—eminently in Flaubert, and as far as one can judge from translations, in Tourguénieff ; I find it, to a less extent, in Daudet ; I find it sometimes even in Zola, especially, but not merely, in his shorter stories ; I find it again, and abundantly, in Maupassant.   But I never find it in the Goncourts : and when I find it in the others it is because they have either never bowed the knee to, or have for the nonce discarded, the cult of the Naturalist, experimental, documentary idol, in itself and for itself.

" But," some one may say, " you have neglected one very important point to which you have yourself referred, and as to which you have just recommitted yourself.

Did not *les deux* 'add something,' a very considerable something, ' of their own ' ? How about their style ? "

Certainly they prided themselves on this, and certainly they took a great deal of trouble about it. If any one

And the likes the result, let him like it. It appears
unattractive- to me only to prove that an unsound principle
ness of their is not a certain means to secure sound practice.
style. Possibly, as Edmond boasted, this style is not the style *de tout le monde.* And *tout le monde* may congratulate itself on the fact. One can see that it *must* have given them a good deal of trouble—perhaps as much as, say, Paul de Saint-Victor's gave him. But then his excites a cheerful glow of satisfaction, whereas theirs only creates, as Saint-Victor himself (to one's regret) says of Swift, *un morne étonnement.*

The tone which has been adopted[1] in speaking of the Goncourts (or rather of Edmond de Goncourt, for Jules

Émile Zola seems to have been the better fellow pretty
to be treated certainly, as well as probably the more genuine
differently. talent, of the two) would be grossly unfair
in dealing with Émile Zola. One may think his principle demonstrably wrong, and his practice for the most part a calamitous mistake. One may, while, if indeed it concerned us, clearing him of the charge of doing any moral harm—such harm would be as likely to be done by records of Bedlam, or the Lock Hospital, or a dipsomaniacs' home—put on the wrong side of his account a quantity of dull and dirty trash,[2] which, without his precept and example, would never have been written, or, if written, read. But the great, if mostly wasted, power

[1] It is perhaps only fair to warn readers who may not know the fact, that some very good and (in the French as well as the English sense) respectable judges think much better of the work, and even of the men or man, than I do. *Renée Maupérin* especially (as indeed I have admitted) has a considerable body of suffrage ; the general style pleases some, and it has been urged for Edmond that good men liked him. But these good men had not read his diary. There is, however, no doubt that it is an exceptionally strong case of " rubbing the [right or the] wrong way." Books and men and style all rub me the wrong way ; and, though I have some knack at using the brushes and *fixatures* of pure criticism, I can't get myself smoothed down.

[2] See note at close of chapter. One of the most comic things in the whole Naturalist episode was the rising up of some of these disciples to rebuke their master, in a round robin, for " right-hand and left-hand defections " from the pure gospel of the sect.

displayed in his work is quite undeniable by any real
critic ; he did some things—and more parts of things—
absolutely good ; and if, as has been admitted, he did
literary evil, he upset in a curious fashion the usual
dictum that the evil that men do lives after them. At
least it was not his fault if such was the case. He
undoubtedly, whether he actually invented it or not,
established, communicated, spread the error of Naturalism. But he lived long enough and wrote hard enough
to " work it out " in a singular fashion—to illustrate the
rottenness of the tree by the canker of the fruit to such an
extent, and in such variety of application and example, that
nobody for a long time has had any excuse for grafting
the one or eating the other. Personally—in those points
of personality which touch literature really, and out of
the range of mere gossip—he had many good qualities.
He was transparently honest, his honesty being tested
and attested by a defect which will be noticed presently.
He appears to have had no bad blood in him. His
fidelity and devotion to what he thought art were as
unflinching as Flaubert's own.

Nor was he deficient in good qualities which were
still more purely literary. We shall speak later of the
Some points excellence of his short stories ; if he had never
in his person- written anything else there would be hardly
ality—literary anything but praise for him. When he does
and other. not lose himself in the wilderness of particulars,
he sometimes manages to rise from it to wonderful
Pisgah-sights of description. He has a really vast,
though never an absolute or consummate, and always a
morbid, hold on what may be called the second range of
character, and a drastic, if rather mechanical, faculty of
combining scenes and incidents. The mass of the
Rougon-Macquart books is very much more coherent
than the *Comédie Humaine.* He has real pathos. But
perhaps his greatest quality, shown at intervals throughout
but never fully developed till the chaotic and sometimes
almost Blake-like Apocalypses of his last stage, was a
grandiosity of fancy—nearly reaching imagination, and

not incapable of dressing itself in suitable language—
which, though one traces some indebtedness to Lamennais and Michelet and Hugo, has sufficient individuality,
and, except in these four, is very rarely found in French
literature later than the sixteenth or early seventeenth
century. To set against these merits—still leaving the
main fault alone—there are some strange defects. Probably worst of all, for it has its usual appalling pervasive-
ness, is his almost absolute want of humour. Humour
and Naturalism, indeed, could not possibly keep house
together ; as we shall see in Maupassant, the attempt
has happier results than in the case of " Long John Brown
and Little Mary Bell," for the fairy expels the Devil at
times wholly. The minor and particular absurdities
which result from this want of humour crop up constantly in the books ; and it is said to have been taken
advantage of by Maupassant himself in one instance,
the disciple " bamming " the master into recording the
existences of peculiarly specialised places of entertainment,
which the fertile fancy of the author of *Boule de Suif*
had created.

The Naturalist Novel, as practised by Zola, rests on
three principal supports, or rather draws its materials

The Pillars of Naturalism. from, and guides its treatment by, three
several processes or doctrines. The general
observational-experimental theory of the Goncourts is very widely, in fact almost infinitely extended,
" documents " being found or made in or out of the
literal farrago of all occupations and states of life. But,
as concerns the definitely " human " part of the matter,
immense stress is laid on the Darwinian or Spencerian
doctrines of heredity, environment, evolution, and the
like. While, last of all in order, if the influence be
taken as converging towards the reason of the failure,
comes the " medico-legal " notion of a " lesion "—of
some flaw or vicious and cancerous element—a sort of
modernised πρώταρχος ἄτη in the family, which develops itself variously in individuals.

Now, before pointing out the faulty results of this

as shown generally in the various books, let us, reversing the order in which the influences or elements have been stated, set out the main lines of error in the elements themselves.

In the first place, it must surely be obvious that insistence on the "lesion," even if the other points of the theory were unassailable, is grossly excessive, if not wholly illegitimate. If you are to take observation and experience for your sole magazine of subjects, you must take *all* experience and *all* observation. Not the veriest pessimist who retains sense and senses can say that their results are *always* evil, ugly, and sordid. If you are to go by heredity you must attend to :

> Fortes creantur fortibus et bonis,

as well as to :

> Aetas parentum pejor avis tulit, etc.

Remounting the stairs, it must be evident that Heredity, Natural Selection, Evolution, Environment, etc., are things which, at the very best, can be allowed an exceedingly small part in artistic re-creation. Not only do they come under the general ban of Purpose, but their purpose-character is of the most thankless and unsucculent kind. I do not know that any one has ever attempted a mathematical novel, though the great Mr. Higgins of St. Mary Axe, as we all know, wrote a beautiful mathematical poem, of which the extant fragments are, alas ! too few. If he had only lived a generation later, how charming would have been the fytte or canto on Quaternions ! But, really, such a thing would not be more than a "farthest" on a road on which heredity-and-selection novels travel far. It is no use to say, "Oh ! but human beings exemplifying those things can be made interesting." If they are it will not be because they are dealt with *sub specie hereditatis*, and confined in the circle of *milieu*.

Yet the master error lies, farther back still, in the strictly "Naturalist" idea itself—the theory of Experiment, the observation-document-"note," all for their own sake. Something has been said of this in relation to the Goncourts, but M. Zola's own exemplification of the doctrine was so far "larger" in every sense than theirs, and reinforced with so much greater literary power, that it cannot be left merely to the treatment which was sufficient for them. Once more, it is a case of "corruption of the best." It is perfectly true that all novel-writing—even in a fashion all romance-writing too—ought to be based on experience [1] in practical life, and that infinite documents are procurable, infinite notes may be made, from that life. It is utterly *untrue* that *any* observation, *any* experiment, *any* document is good novel or romance stuff.

A very few remarks may perhaps be made on approaches to Zolaism—not in the sense of scabrousness—before Zola.

A writer of one of those theses *à la mode Germanorum*, of which, at different times and in different occupations, it is the hard lot of the professional man of letters to read so many, would probably begin with the Catalogue of Ships, or construct an inventory of the "beds and basons" which Barzillai brought to David. Quite a typical "program" might be made of the lists of birds, beasts, trees, etc., so well known in mediaeval literature, and best known to the ordinary English reader from Chaucer, and from Spenser's following of him. We may, however, pass to the Deluge of the Renaissance and the special emergence therefrom of French fiction. It would not be an absolute proof of the "monographitis" just glanced at if any one were to instance the curious discussions on the propriety of introducing technical terms into heroic poetry—which is, of course, very close to heroic romance, and so to prose fiction generally.

"Document" and "detail" before Naturalism.

---

[1] The word is used, designedly but not fraudulently, as combining "observation" and "experiment" *to the extent proper to art*. Deliberate and after-thought "experiments" in actual life are (except in trivial matters) very risky things ; and the *Summa Rerum* itself is apt to resent them, as, for instance, Mr. Thomas Day and Mr. Felix Graham found in the matter of wife-culture.

But, for practical purposes, Furetière and the *Roman Bourgeois* (*vide* Vol. I.) give the starting-point. And here the Second Part, of which we formerly said little, acquires special importance, though the first is not without it. *All* the details of *bourgeois* life and middle-class society belong to the department which was afterwards preferred—and degraded—by the Naturalists; and the legal ins and outs of the Second Part are Zola in a good deal more than the making. Indeed the luckless " Charroselles " himself had, as we pointed out, anticipated Furetière in not a few points, such as that most interesting reference to *bisque*.[1] Scarron himself has a good deal of it; in fact there is so much in the Spanish picaresque novel that it could not be absent from the followings thereof. For which same reason there is not a very little of it in Lesage, while, for an opposite one, there is less in Marivaux, and hardly any at all in Crébillon or Prévost. The *philosophes*, except Diderot—who was busy with other things and used his acquaintance with miscellaneous " documents " in another way—would have disdained it, and the Sentimentalists still more so. But it is a sign of the shortcomings of Pigault-Lebrun—especially considering the evident discipleship to Smollett, in whom there is no small amount of such detail—that, while in general he made a distinct advance in " ordinary " treatment, he did not reinforce this advance with circumstantial accounts of " beds and basons."

But with the immense and multifarious new birth of the novel at the beginning of the nineteenth century, this development also received, in the most curiously diverse ways, reinforcement and extension. The Terror novel itself had earlier given a hand, for you had to describe, more or less minutely, the furniture of your haunted rooms, the number and volume of your drops

General stages traced. (margin note)

---

[1] *V. sup.* Vol. I. p. 278. I was much pleased to find that the quotation considerably " put out " one of my few unfavourable critics. " The Importance of Gastronomy in Novels " is a beautiful subject—still, I think, virgin, though Thackeray has touched on it in others once or twice, and illustrated it magnificently himself.

of blood, the anatomical characteristics of your skeletons,
and the values of your palette of coloured fires. The
Historical novel lugged document in too often by head
and shoulders, introducing it on happier occasions as
the main and distinguishing ornament of its kind.
Romanticism generally, with its tendency to antiquarian
detail, its liking for *couleur locale*, its insistence on the
" streaks of the tulip " and the rest, prompted the use
and at least suggested the abuse.

Nor did the great individual French novelists—for
we need not specify any others—of the earlier part of
the century, while they themselves kept to
the pleasant slopes above the abyss, fail to
point the way to it. Chateaubriand with his
flowery descriptions of East and West, and
Madame de Staël with her deliberate guide-
bookery, encouraged the document-hunter and detail-
devotee. Balzac, especially in the directions of finance
and commerce, actually set him an example. George
Sand, especially in pure country stories, was prodigal
of local and technical matters and manners. The
gorgeous scenery of Gautier, and the soberer but
important " settings " of Mérimée, might be claimed as
models. And others might be added.

Some individual pioneers— especially Hugo.

But from one point of view, as an authority above all
earlier authorities, and from another as a sinner beyond
all earlier sinners, might be quoted Victor Hugo, even
putting his *juvenilia* aside. He had flung a whole
glossary of architecture, not to mention other things of
similar kind, into *Notre Dame de Paris*; and when after
a long interval he resumed prose fiction, he had ransacked
the encyclopaedia for *Les Misérables*. *Les Travailleurs
de la Mer* is half a great poem and half a *real-lexikon*
of mechanics, weather-lore, seafaring, ichthyology, and
God knows what else ! If *L'Homme Qui Rit* had been
written a very little later, parts of it might have been
taken as a deliberate burlesque, by a French Sir Francis
Burnand, of Naturalist method. Now, as the most acute
literary historians have always seen, Naturalism was

practically nothing but a degeneration of Romanticism : [1] and degeneracy always shows itself in exaggeration. Naturalism exaggerated detail, streak of tulip, local colour, and all the rest, of which Romanticism had made such good use at its best. But what it exaggerated most of all was the Romantic neglect of classical *decorum*, in the wider as well as the narrower sense of that word. Classicism had said, " Keep everything indecorous out." Naturalism seemed sometimes to say, " Let nothing that is not indecorous come in." [2]

It was, however, by no means at first that M. Zola took to the " document " or elaborated the enormous Survey of scheme of the Rougon-Macquart cycle: though books—the whether the excogitation of this was or was not short stories. due to the frequentation, exhortation, and imitation of MM. de Goncourt is not a point that we need discuss. He began, after melodramatic and negligible *juvenilia*, in 1864 with a volume of delightful short stories,[3] *Contes à Ninon*, in which kind he long afterwards showed undiminished powers. And he continued this practice at intervals for a great number of years, with results collected, after the first set, in *Nouveaux Contes à Ninon*, and in volumes taking their general titles from special tales—*Le Capitaine Burle* and *Naïs Micoulin*. In 1880 he gave the first story, *L'Attaque du Moulin*, to that most remarkable Naturalist " symposium," *Les Soirées de Médan*, which, if nothing of it survived but that story itself and Maupassant's *Boule de Suif*, and if this represented the sole extant work of the

---

[1] For something on the opposite view, that Naturalism is " classical," see Conclusion.

[2] That Flaubert escaped their error only so as by fire has been allowed. One might indeed say so as by death. For *Bouvard et Pécuchet* as it stands, and as outlined further, is very near Naturalism. Earlier he had carried the principle far in *Salammbô*, and would have carried it farther if he had not listened to good advice for once. But he had fire enough in his interior to burn the rubbish and smelt the ore in his better books, and skill enough to run off the metal from the dross, into proper shape. The others had not.

[3] I learn from the lucubrations of some Americans—who, having been, rather late and with some difficulty, induced to perceive that Edgar Poe was their chief literary glory, have taken vehemently to his favourite kind, and written voluminously in and on it— that it ought to be called a " brief-narrative," the hyphen being apparently essential. This is very interesting : and throws much light on the subject. However, having read a great deal on it, I do not find myself much advanced beyond a position which I think I occupied some fifty years ago—to wit, that a short story is not merely a long one cut down, nor a long story a short one spun out.

School, would certainly induce the fortieth century to think that School one of the very best in fiction, and to utter the most pathetic wails over the loss of the rest of its production. Of *Boule de Suif*—in more senses than one the feminine of the pair—more presently. But *L'Attaque* itself is a splendid and masculine success—the best thing by far, in respect of flawlessness, that its author ever did, and not far below Mérimée's *Prise de la Redoute*.

Unfortunately it was not in these breaches that M. Zola chose to abide. After the war, having no doubt laid his plans long before, he undertook the vast Rougon-Macquart scheme with its score of volumes; and when this was finished, carried on two others, smaller in bulk but hardly less ambitious in scope, " Les Trois Villes "—*Lourdes, Paris, Rome*; and " Les Quatre Évangiles "—*Fécondité, Travail,* and *Vérité*, the fourth of which was never written, while the third, *Vérité*, appeared with a black line round its cover, denoting posthumous issue.

In all these books the Experimental and Documentary idea is worked out, with an important development in the "Les Rougon-Macquart." other directions above glanced at. The whole of the Rougon-Macquart series was intended to picture the varying careers of the branches, legitimate and illegitimate, of two families, under the control of heredity, and the evolution of the cerebral lesion into various kinds of disease, fault, vice, crime, etc. But further scope was found for the use of the document, human and other, by allotment of the various books, both in this and in the later groups, to the special illustration of particular places, trades, professions, habits of life, and *quicquid agunt homines* generally. The *super*-title of the first and largest series, " Les Rougon-Macquart : Histoire naturelle et sociale d'une famille sous le Second Empire," can hardly need comment or amplification to any intellect that is not hopelessly enslaved to the custom of having its meat not only killed, dressed, cooked, and dished, but cut up, salted, peppered, and put into its mouth with assiduous spoonings. *La*

Fortune des Rougon, in the very year when Europe invited
a *polemos aspondos* by acquiescing in the seizure of Alsace-
Lorraine, laid the foundation of the whole. *La Curée*
and *Son Excellence Eugène Rougon* show how the more
fortunate members of the clan prospered in the somewhat
ignoble *tripotage* of their time. Anybody could see the
" power " of which the thing was " effect " (to borrow one
half of a celebrated aphorism of Hobbes's) ; but it must
have been a curious taste to which (borrowing the other)
the books were " a cause of pleasure." *La Faute de
l'Abbé Mouret* rose to a much higher level. To regard
it as merely an attack on clerical celibacy is to take a very
obvious and limited view of it. It is so, of course, but it
is much more. The picture of the struggle between
conscience and passion is, for once, absolutely true and
human. There is no mistake in the psychology ; there
is no resort to " sculduddery " ; there is no exaggeration
of any kind, or, if there is any, it is in a horticultural
extravagance—a piece of fairy Bower-of-Bliss scene-
painting, in part of the book, which is in itself almost if
not quite beautiful—a Garden of Eden provided for a
different form of temptation.[1] There is no poetry in
La Conquête de Plassans or in *Le Ventre de Paris* ; but
the one is a digression, not yet scavenging, into country
life, and the other empties one of M. Zola's note-books
on a theme devoted to the Paris Markets—the famous
" Halles " which Gérard had done so lightly and differently long before.[2] The key of this latter is pretty well
kept in one of the most famous books of the whole
series, *L'Assommoir,* where the beastlier side of pot-house
sotting receives hundreds of pages to do what William
Langland had done better five centuries earlier in a few
score lines. *Pot-Bouille*—ascending a little in the social
but not in the spiritual scale—deals with lower middle-
class life, and *Au Bonheur des Dames* with the enormous
" stores " which, beginning in America, had already

---

[1] Barbey d'Aurevilly's (*v. sup.*) attack on the book is one of the most remarkable
instances of the irresponsibility of his criticism.
[2] *V. sup.* p. 258.

spread through Paris to London. *Une Page d'Amour*
recovers something of the nobler tone of *L'Abbé Mouret* ;
and *La Joie de Vivre*—a title, as will readily be guessed,
ironical in intention—still keeps out of the gutter. *Nana*
may be said, combining decency with exactitude, to stand
in the same relation to the service of Venus as *L'Assommoir* does to that of Bacchus, though one apologises to
both divinities for so using their names. It was supposed, like other books of the kind, to be founded on
fact—the history of a certain young person known as
Blanche d'Antigny—and charitable critics have pleaded
for it as a healthy corrective or corrosive to the morbid
tone of sentimentality-books like *La Dame aux Camélias*.
I never could find much amusement in the book, except
when Nana, provoked at the tedious prolongation of
a professional engagement, exclaims, " Ça ne finissait
pas ! " or " Ça ne voulait pas finir." [1] The strange
up-and-down of the whole scheme reappears in *L'Œuvre*
—chiefly devoted to art, but partly to literature—where
the opening is extraordinarily good, and there are fine
passages later, interspersed with tedious grime of the
commoner kind. *La Terre* and *Germinal* are, I suppose, generally regarded as, even beyond *L'Assommoir*
and *Nana*, the "farthest" of this griminess. Whether
the filth-stored broom of the former really does blot out
George Sand's and other pictures of a modified Arcadia
in the French provinces, nothing but experience, which
I cannot boast, could tell us ; and the same may be said
of *Germinal*, as to the mining districts which have since
received so awful a purification by fire. That more and
more important person the railway-man takes his turn
in *La Bête Humaine*, and the book supplies perhaps
the most striking instance of the radically inartistic
character of the plan of flooding fiction with technical
details. But there is, in the vision of the driver and his
engine as it were going mad together, one of the earliest
and not the least effective of those nightmare-pieces in

---

[1] One ought perhaps to verify ; but it would be hard lines to have to read *Nana*
twice !

which Zola, evidently inspired by Hugo, indulged more and more latterly. Then came what was intended, apparently, for the light star of this dark group, *Le Rêve*. Although always strongly anti-clerical, and at the last, as we shall see, a " Deicide " of the most uncompromising fanaticism, M. Zola here devoted himself to cathedral services and church ritual generally, and, as a climax, the administration of extreme unction to his innocent heroine. But, as too often happens in such cases, the saints were not grateful and the sinners were bored. *L'Argent* was at least in concatenation accordingly, seeing that the great financial swindle and " crash "[1] it took for subject had had strong clerical support ; but purely financial matters, stock-exchange dealings, and some exceedingly scabrous " trimmings " occupied the greater part of it. Of the penultimate novel, *La Débâcle*, a history of the terrible birth-year of the series itself, few fair critics, I think, could speak other than highly ; of the actual ultimatum, *Le Docteur Pascal*, opinions have varied much. It is very unequal, but I thought when it came out that it contained some of its author's very best things, and I am not disposed to change my opinion.

Before giving any general comment on this mass of fiction, it will probably be best to continue the process of brief survey, with the two remaining groups. "Les Trois Villes." It is, I believe, generally admitted that in " Les Trois Villes " purpose, and the document, got altogether the better of any true novel-intention. The anti-religiosity which has been already remarked upon seems not only to have increased, but for the moment to have simply flooded our author's ship of thought and art, and to have stopped the working of that part of its engine-room which did the novel-business. The miracles at, and the pilgrimages to, Lourdes filled the newspapers at one time, and Zola could think of nothing else ; the transition to Rome was almost inevitable in any such case ; and the return upon Paris quite inevitable in a Frenchman.

---

[1] That of the *Union Générale*.

With the final and incomplete series—coinciding in its latter part with the novelist's passionate interference, "Les Quatre at no small inconvenience to himself, in that Évangiles." inconceivable modern replica of the Hermocopidae business, the Dreyfus case, and cut short by his unfortunate death—things are different. I have known people far less "prejudiced," as the word goes, against the ideas of these books than I am myself, who plumply declare that they cannot read *Fécondité*, *Travail*, or (most especially) *Vérité*: while of course there are others who declare them to be not "Gospels" at all, but what Mr. Carlyle used to call "Ba'spels"—not Evangels but Cacodaemonics. I read every word of them carefully some years since, and I should not mind reading *Fécondité* or *Travail* again, though I have no special desire to do so.[1]

Both are "novels of purpose," with the purpose developing into mania. *Fécondité* is only in part—and in that part mainly as regards France—revolutionary. It is a passionate gospel of "Cultivate *both* gardens ! Produce every ounce of food that can be raised to eat, and every child that can be got to eat it:" an anti-Malthusian and Cobbettist Apocalypse, smeared with Zolaesque grime and lighted up with flashes, or rather flares, of more than Zolaesque brilliancy. The scene where the hero (so far as there is one) looks back on Paris at night, and his tottering virtue sees in it one enormous theatre of Lubricity, has something of Flaubert and something of Hugo.

Travail is revolutionary or nothing, revolutionary "in the most approved style," as a certain apologist of robbery and murder put it not long ago as to Bolshevism, amid the "laughter and cheers" of English aspirants thereto. It takes for scene a quite openly

---

[1] *Vérité*, though a remarkable "human document" itself, and an indispensable *historical* document for any student of the particular popular madness with which it deals, need surely be inflicted a second time on no mortal. It is a transposition into the regions of the unmentionable, of the Dreyfus case itself. But nobody save a failure of something like a novelist of genius, with this failure pushed near the confines of madness, could have written it.

borrowed representation of the famous forges of Creusot, and attacks Capital, the *bourgeois*, and everything established, quite in the purest Bolshevist fashion. Both books, and *Vérité*, display throughout a singular delusion, aggravating the anti-theism rather than atheism above mentioned, my own formulation of which, in another book some decade ago, I may as well, in a note,[1] borrow, instead of merely paraphrasing it. The milder idiosyncrasy referred to therein will certainly not adjust itself, whatever it might do to the not ungenial ideals of *Fécondité*, to those of *Travail*. This ends in a sort of Paradise of Man, where electricity takes every kind of labour (except that of cultivating the gardens ?) off men's hands, and the Coquecigrues have come again, and the pigs run about ready roasted, and a millennium or mill*iard*ennium of Cocaigne begins. Yet there are fine passages in *Travail*, and the author reflects, powerfully enough, the grime and glare and scorch of the furnaces ; the thirst and lust and struggles of their slaves ; the baser side of the life of their owners and officials—and of the wives of these. There is nothing in the book quite equal to the Vision of the City of Lubricity in *Fécondité*, but there are one or two things not much below it. And the whole is once more Blake-like, with a degraded or defiled Blakishness. In fact, *Fécondité* and *Travail*, illustrated in the spirit of the Prophetic Books, are quite imaginable possessions ; and, though a nervous person might not like to go to sleep in the same room with them, not uncovetable ones.[2]

The everlasting irony of things has seldom, in literature (though, as we have seen, it reigns there if anywhere), secured for itself a more striking opportunity of exemplification than this ending, in a pseudo-apocalyptic paroxysm, of the *Roman Expérimental* ; perhaps one may add that never has Romanticism, or indeed any school of letters,

---

[1] " M. Zola [is] apparently persuaded that, if you can only kill God, the Devil will die—an idea which seems to leave out of consideration the idiosyncrasy of a third personage, Man " (*The Later Nineteenth Century*, Edinburgh and London, 1907, pp. 93, 94).
[2] Only it would have to be real Blake, not imitation, which latter is one of the furthest examples of dreary futility known to the present writer.

scored such a triumphant victory over its decriers. It
has been contended here, and for many years in other
places by the present writer, that Naturalism was itself
only a "lesion," a *sarcoma*, a morbidly allotropic form
of Romance. At this point the degeneration turned
into a sort of parody of the attitude of Ezekiel or Hosea ;
the business-like observer, in counting-house and workshop, in church and stock-exchange, in tavern and
brothel, in field and town generally, became himself a
voyant, beholding all things in nightmare. Yet, in doing
so, he effected a strange semi-reconciliation with some
who had been, if not exactly his enemies, the exceedingly
frank critics and unsparing denouncers of his system.
Not much more than half sane, and almost more than
half disgusting, as are *Fécondité* and *Travail*, they connect
themselves, as wholes, not with *L'Assommoir* or *Nana*,
not with *La Terre* or *Germinal*, but with *La Faute de
l'Abbé Mouret*, with *Une Page d'Amour*, and *La Joie de
Vivre*, with the best things in *L'Œuvre*, *La Débâcle*, and
Le Docteur Pascal. Students of English literature will
remember how the doctrine of *Furor poeticus* was once
applied to Ben Jonson by a commentator who, addressing
him, pointed out that he was very mad in his primer
works, not so mad in his dotages. There was always a
good deal of *furor prosaicus* smouldering in Zola, and it
broke out with an opposite result on these occasions, the
flames, alas ! being rather devastating, but affording
spectacles at least grandiose. *He* kept sane and sordid
to his loss earlier, and went mad later—partially at least
to his advantage.

Passing to those more general considerations which
have been promised—and which seem to be to some
General con- readers a Promised Land indeed, as compared
siderations. with the wilderness of *compte-rendu* and book-
appreciation—let us endeavour briefly to answer the
question, "What is the general lesson of Zola's work ?"
I think we may say, borrowing that true and final judgment
of Wordsworth which doth so enrage Wordsworthians,
that whenever Zola does well he either violates or neglects

his principles, and that the more carefully he carries these out the worse, as a rule, his work is. The similarity, of course, is the more quaint because of the dissimilarity of the personages and their productions ; but it has not been insisted on from any mere spirit of mischief, or desire to make a paradoxical parallel. On the contrary, this parallel has been made in order to support, at least *obiter*, a more general dictum still, that principles are much more often fatal than useful to the artist. The successful miniatures of the short stories hardly prove more thoroughly than the smoky flaming Blakish-Turneresque cartoons of the latest " Gospels," though they may do so more satisfactorily, that Émile Zola had the root of the Art of Fiction in him. But he chose to subject the bulk of the growths from this root to something much worse than the *ars topiaria*, to twist and maim and distort them like Hugo's Comprachicos ; to load their boughs, forbidding them to bear natural fruit, with clumsy crops of dull and foul detail, like a bedevilled Christmas-tree. One dares say quite unblushingly, that in no single instance [1] has this abuse of the encyclopaedia added charm, or value, or even force to Zola's work. A man with far less ability than he possessed could have given the necessary touch of specialism when it *was* necessary, without dumping and deluging loads and floods of technicalities on the unhappy reader.

Little more need be said about the disastrous *ugliness* which, with still rarer exception, pervades the whole work. There are those who like the ugly, and those— perhaps more numerous—who think they *ought* to like it. With neither is it worth while to argue. As for me and my house, we will serve Beauty, giving that blessed word the widest possible extension, of course, but never going beyond or against it.

A point where there is no such precedent inaccessibility of common ground concerns Zola's grasp of character. It seems to me to have been, if not exactly weak, curiously

---

[1] The horticulture of *L'Abbé Mouret* is nearest to an exception ; but even that is overdone.

limited.   I do not know that his people are ever
unhuman ; in fact, by his time the merely wooden
Especially in character had ceased to be " stocked " (as an
regard to unpleasant modern phrase has it) by the
character. novelist.   The "divers and disgusting things "
that they do are never incredible.   The unspeakable
villain-hero of *Vérité* itself is a not impossible person.
But the defect, again as it seems to me, of all the personages may best be illustrated by quoting one of those
strange flashes of consummate critical acuteness which
diversify the frequent critical lapses of Thackeray.   As
early as *The Paris Sketch-book*, in the article entitled
" Caricatures and Lithography," Mr. Titmarsh wrote,
in respect of Fielding's people, " Is not every one of them
a real substantial *have been* personage now ? . . . We
will not take upon ourselves to say that they do not exist
somewhere else, that the actions attributed to them have
not really taken place."

There, put by a rather raw critic of some seven and
twenty, who was not himself to give a perfect creative
exemplification of what he wrote for nearly a decade, is
the crux of the matter.   Observe, not " *might* have
been " merely, but " have been now."   The phrase
might have holes picked in it by a composition-master
or -monger.[1]   Thackeray is often liable to this process.
But it states an eternal verity, and so marks an essential
differentia.

This differentia is what the present writer has, in many
various forms, endeavoured to make good in respect of
the novels and the novelists with which and whom he has
dealt in this book, and in many books and articles for
the last forty years and more.   There are the characters
who never might or could have been—the characters
who, by limp and flaccid drawing ; by the lumping
together of "incompossibilities " ; by slavish following

---

[1] Who might even say, " Is not this a slip of pen or press ?   Has not ' might '
dropped out ? "   I should doubt it, even if a copy of the original edition had the missing
word, for it might easily have been put in by a dull but conscientious " reader."   The
plural, in Thackeray's careless way, comes from his *thinking* as he wrote " Are they not
all . . . personages. . . ."   The context confirms this.

of popular models ; by equally slavish, though rather
less ignoble, carrying out of supposed rules ; by this,
that, and the other want or fault, have deprived themselves
of the fictitious right to live, or to have lived, though
they occupy the most ghastly of all limbos and the most
crowded shelves of all circulating libraries.   At the other
end of the scale are the real men and women of fiction—
those whom more or less (for there are degrees here as
everywhere) you *know*, whose life is as your life, except
that you live by the grace of God and they by that of
God's artists.   These exist in all great drama, poetry,
fiction ; and it never would cause you the least surprise
or feeling of unfamiliarity if they passed from one sphere
to the other, and you met them—to live with, to love or
to hate, to dance or to dine with, to murder (for you
would occasionally like to kill them) or to marry.[1]   But
between the two—and perhaps the largest crowd of the
three, at least since novel-writing came to be a business—
is a vast multitude of figures occupying a middle position,
sometimes with little real vitality but with a certain stage-
competence ; sometimes quite reaching the " might-
have-been," but never the full substance of " has been "
for us.   To these last, I think, though to a high division
of them, do Zola's characters belong.

Of plot I never care to say very much, because it is
not with me a wedding-garment, though I know an ugly
or ill-fitting one when I see it, and can say, " Well tailored
or dress-made ! " in the more satisfactory circumstances.
Moreover, Zola hardly enters himself for much competition here.   There is none in the first two Apocalypses;
Vérité has what it has, supplied by the " case " and merely
adjusted with fair skill ; the *Trois Villes* lie quite outside
plot ; and the huge synoptic scheme of the Rougon-
Macquart series deals little with it in individual books.
Of conversation one might say very much what has been
said of character.   The books have the conversation

---

[1] There are, of course, comparatively few of these ; but the fewness is not positive,
even keeping to prose-fiction.   Poetry and drama—under their less onerous conditions
for this special task—would enlarge the list in goodly fashion.

which they require, and sometimes (in examples generally even more difficult to quote than that of Nana's given above) a little more. But in Description, the Naturalist leader rises when he does not fall. It is obviously here that the boredom and the beastliness of the details offend most. But it is also by means of description that almost all the books well spoken of before, from the too earthly Paradise of *L'Abbé Mouret* to the Inferno of *Travail*, produce some of their greatest effects.

So let this suffice as banning for what is bad in him, and as blessing for what is good, in regard to Émile Zola : a great talent—at least a failure of a genius—in literature ; a marvellous worker in literary craft. As for his life, it can be honestly avowed that the close of it, in something like martyrdom, had little or nothing to do with the fact that the writer's estimate of his work changed, from very unfavourable, to the parti-coloured one given above. Until about 1880 I did not read his books regularly as they came out, and the first " nervous impression " of what I did read required time and elaboration to check and correct, to fill in and to balance it. I have never varied my opinion that his methods and principles— with everything of that sort—were wrong. But I have been more and more convinced that his practice some- times came astonishingly near being right.

My introduction to the greatest of M. Zola's associ- ates was more fortunate, for it was impossible to mistake the quality of the new planet.[1] One day in 1880 the editor of a London paper put into my hands a copy of a just-issued volume of French verse, which had been specially sent to him by his Paris correspondent in a fit of moral indignation. It was entitled *Des Vers*, and the author of it was a certain Guy de Maupassant, of whom I then knew nothing. The correspondent had seen in

---

[1] Shortly after Maupassant's death, I contributed an article on him to the *Fortnightly Review*. It has never been reprinted, but, by the kindness of the Editor of that *Review*, I have been permitted to use it as a basis for this notice. I have, however, altered, omitted, and added to a much greater extent than in the few other rehandlings acknow- edged in this History. The account of the actual books is wholly new.

it a good opportunity for a denunciation of French
wickedness ; and my editor handed it over to me to see
what was to be done with it. I saw no exceptional
wickedness, and a very great deal of power ; indeed,
though I was tolerably familiar with French verse and
prose of the day, it seemed to me that I had not seen so
much promise in any new writer since Baudelaire's
death ;[1] and I informed my editor that, though I had
not the slightest objection to blessing Maupassant, I
certainly would not curse him. He thought the blessing
not likely to please his public, while it would annoy
his correspondent, and on my representation declined
to have anything to do with the cursing. So *nous passasmes
oultre*, except that, like Mr. Bludyer, I "impounded"
the book ; but, unlike him, did not either sell it, dine
off it, or abuse the author.

Shortly afterwards, I think, the *Soirées de Médan* reached
me, and this very remarkable person appeared likewise,
but in a new character. Certainly no one can ever
have shown to better advantage in company than M. de
Maupassant did on this occasion. *L'Attaque du Moulin*,
which opened the volume, has already been spoken of
as part of the best of all M. Zola's voluminous work.
But as for the works of the young men, other than M.
de Maupassant, they had the Naturalist faults in fullest
measure, unredeemed by their master's massive vigour
and his desperate intensity. The contribution of M.
Huysmans, in particular (*v. inf.*) has always appeared
to me one of those voluntary or involuntary caricatures,
of the writer's own style and school, which are well
known at all times, and have never been more frequent
than recently. But *Boule de Suif*? Among the others
that pleasant and pathetic person was not a *boule* ; she
was a pyramid, a Colossus, a spire of Cologne Cathedral.
Putting the unconventionality of its subject aside, there
is absolutely no fault to be found with the story. It is
as round and smooth as "Boule de Suif" herself.

---

[1] I had known Verlaine since his appearance in the *Parnasse Contemporain* years
earlier, but not yet in his most characteristic work.

Maupassant's work is of very substantial bulk. Of the verse enough for our purpose has been or will be said, though I should like to repeat that I put it much higher than do most of Maupassant's admirers. The volumes of travel-sketches do not appear to me particularly successful, despite the almost unsurpassed faculty of their writer for sober yet vivid description. They have the air of being written to order, and they do not seem, as a rule, to arrive at artistic completeness either objectively or subjectively. Of the criticism, which concerns us more nearly, by far the most remarkable piece is the famous Preface to *Pierre et Jean* (to be mentioned again below), which contains the author's literary creed, refined and castigated by years of practice from the cruder form which he had already promulgated in the Preface to Flaubert's *Correspondence with George Sand*. It extols the " objective " as against the psychological method of novel-writing, but directs itself most strongly against the older romance of plot, and places the excellence of the novelist in the complete and vivid projection of that novelist's own particular " illusion " of the world, yet so as to present events and characters in the most actual manner. But, as promised, we shall return to it.

To run through the actual " turn-out " in novel[1] and tale as far as is possible here, *Bel-Ami* started, in
Bel-Ami. England at least, with the most favouring gales possible. It was just when the decree had gone forth, issued by the younger Later Victorians, that all the world should be made naughty ; that the insipid whiteness of their Early and Middle elders should be washed black and scarlet, and especially " blue " ; and that if possible, by this and other processes, something like real literature might be made to take the place of the drivellings and botcheries of Tennyson and Browning ; of Dickens and Thackeray ; of Ruskin and Carlyle. To these persons *Bel-Ami* was a sweet content, a really

---

[1] The following summary, to p. 505, formed no part of the original article and is based on fresh and continuous reading. It is purposely rather more minute than anything else in these later chapters, and was not the easiest part of the book to do, owing to the large number of Maupassant's short stories.

" *shady* boon." The hero never does a decent thing and never says a good one ; but he has good looks and insinuating manners of the kind that please some women, whence his name, originally given to him by an innocent little girl, and taken up by her by no means innocent mamma and other quasi-ladies.[1] He starts as a soldier who has served his time in Algeria, but has found nothing better to do than a subordinate post in a railway office. He meets a former comrade who is high up in Paris journalism, and who very amiably introduces Georges Duroy to that bad resting-place but promising passage-way. Duroy succeeds, not so much (though he is not a fool) by any brains as by impudence ; by a faculty of making use of others ; by one of the farce-duels in which combatants are put half a mile off each other to fire *once*, etc.; but most of all by his belamyship (for the word is good old English in a better sense). The women of the book are what is familiarly called "a caution." They revive the old Hélisenne de Crenne[2] "sensual appetite" for the handsome bounder ; and though of course jealous of his infidelities, are quite ready to welcome the truant when he returns. They also get drunk at restaurant dinners, and then call their lovers—quite correctly, but not agreeably—" Cochon ! " " Sale bête," etc. This of course is what our *fin-de-siècle* critics *could* " recommend to a friend."

But if the reader thinks that this summary is a prelude to anything like the "slate" that I thought it proper to bestow upon *Les Liaisons Dangereuses*, or even to such remarks as those made on the Goncourts, he is quite mistaken. Laclos had, as it seemed to me, a disgusting subject and no real compensation of treatment. In *Bel-Ami* the merits of the treatment are very great. The scenes pass before you ; the characters play their

---

[1] Maupassant *could* draw gentlemen and ladies, but he often did not do so. His pretty young countesses (*not* the same persons as those referred to in text), who get drunk together *tête-à-tête*, and discourse on the best way of making more effectual Josephs out of their footmen, are not pleasing, though they are right in holding that no perfume, save Eau de Cologne, doth become a *man*.

[2] Vol. I. pp. 150-1.

part in the scenes—if not in an engaging manner, in a completely life-like one. There is none of the *psychologie de commande*, which I object to in Laclos, but a true adumbration of life. The music-hall opening; the first dinner-party; the journalist scenes; the death of Forestier and the proposal of re-marriage over his corpse;[1] the honeymoon journey to Normandy—a dozen other things—could not be better done in their way, though this way may not be the best. It did not fall to me to review *Bel-Ami* when it came out, but I do not think I should have made any mistake about it if it had. There are weak points technically; for instance, the character of Madeleine Forestier, afterwards Duroy—still later caught in flagrant delict and divorced—is left rather enigmatic. But the general technique (with the reservations elsewhere made) is masterly, and two passages— a Vigny-like[2] descant on Death by the old poet Norbert de Varenne and the death-scene of Forestier itself—give us Maupassant in that mood of *macabre* sentiment— almost Romance — which chequers and purifies his Naturalism.

But the main objection which I should take to the book is neither technical nor goody. The late Mr. Locker, in, I think, that most fascinating " New Omniana " *Patchwork*,[3] tells how, in the Travellers' Club one day, a haughty member thereof expressed surprise that he should see Mr. Locker going to the corner-house next door. The amiable author of *London Lyrics* was good enough to explain that some not uninteresting people also used the humbler establishment—bishops, authors, painters, cabinet-ministers, etc. " Ah ! " said the Traverser of Perilous Ways, " that would be all very well if one *wanted* to meet that sort of people. But, you see,

---

[1] The usual gutter-Naturalist certainly would—and even M. Zola, I fear, might— have done the " Ephesian matron " business thoroughly : Maupassant, as so often, knew other and better things.

[2] It may suggest Leconte de Lisle to others and may even have been meant for him, but I think it worthy of the earlier and greater poet.

[3] It went, I fear, by mistake with the rest of my books ; so I quote from memory. But Southey and Locker have had their duet pleasantly changed into a trio since by Mr. Austin Dobson's *Bookman's Budget*.

one *doesn't* want to meet them." Now, I do not want to
meet anybody in *Bel-Ami*; in fact, I would much rather
not.

    Une Vie is, in this respect and others, a curious
pendant to *Bel-Ami*. It illustrates another side of
   Une Vie.   Maupassant's pessimism—the overtly, but for
           the most part quietly, tragic. It might almost
(borrowing a second title from the *Index*) call itself
" Jeanne ; ou Les Malheurs de la Vertu." The heroine
is perfectly innocent, though both a *femmelette* and a
fool. She never does any harm, nor, except through
weakness and folly, deserves that any should be done to
her. But she has an unwise and not blameless though
affectionate and generous father, with a mother who is
an invalid, and whom, after her death, the daughter
discovers to have been, in early days, no better than she
should be. Both of them are, if not exactly spend-
thrifts, " wasters," very mainly through careless and
excessive generosity. She marries the first young man
of decent family, looks, and manners that she comes
across ; and he turns out to be stingy, unfaithful in the
most offensive way, with her own maid and others, and
unkind. She loses him, by the vengeance of a husband
whom he has wronged, and her second child is born dead
in consequence of this shock. Her first she spoils for some
twenty years, till he goes off with a concubine and nearly
ruins his mother. We leave her consoling herself, in a
half-imbecile fashion, with a grandchild. Her only
earthly providence is her *bonne* Rosalie, the same who had
been her husband's mistress, but a very " good sort "
otherwise. The book is charged with grime of all kinds.
It certainly cannot be said of M. de Maupassant, to alter
the pronoun in Mr. Kipling's line, that " [*He*] never
talked obstetrics when the little stranger came," for
Une Vie contains two of these delectable scenes ; and in
other respects we are treated with the utmost " candour."
But the book is again saved by some wonderful passages
—specially those giving Jeanne's first night at the seaside *château* which is to be her own, and her last visit

to it a quarter of a century after, when it has passed to strangers—and generally by the true tragedy which pervades it. When Maupassant took Sorrow into cohabitation and collaboration, there was no danger of the result.

Mont-Oriol, though not, save in one respect, the most " arresting " of Maupassant's books, has rather more varied and at the same time coherent interest than some others. It is also that one which most directly illustrates —on the great scale—the general principles of the Naturalist school. Not, indeed, in specially grimy fashion, though there is the usual adultery (*not* behind the scenes) and the (for Maupassant) not unusual *accouchement*. (His fondness for this most unattractive episode of human life is astonishing: if he were a more pious person and a political feminist, one might think that he was trying to make us modern Adams share the curse of Eve, at least to the extent of the disgust caused by reading about its details.) The main extra-amatory theme throughout is the " physiologie " of an inland watering-place, its extension by the discovery of new springs, the financing of them, the jealousies of the doctors, the megrims of the patients, etc. All these are treated quite on the Zolaesque scheme, but with a lightness and beauty not often reached by the master, though common enough in the pupil.[1] The description of Christiane Andermatt's first bath, and the sensations of mild bliss that it gave her, is as true as it is pretty; and others of scenery have that vividness without over-elaboration which marks their author's work. Nor are his ironic-human touches wanting. Almost at its birth he satirises, in his own quiet Swiftian way, an absurd tendency which has grown mightily since, and flourishes now : " 'Très *moderne* ' — entre ses lèvres, était le comble de l'admiration." As for the love-affair itself, one's feelings towards it are mixed. A good deal of it shows that unusual grasp of the proper ways of the game

---

[1] It may be just, and only just necessary to observe (what I know perfectly well) that Maupassant was, in the direct sense, Flaubert's pupil and not Zola's.

with which Maupassant is fully credited here. Personally, I should not, after quoting Baudelaire to a lady (so far so good), inform her that I was a donkey for expecting her to enjoy anything so subtle. But perhaps Paul Brétigny, though neglectful of the Seventh Commandment, was an honester man than I am. And it is quite true that Christiane was *not* subtle. Her hot lover's [1] cooling partly dated from the time when she expected him to show palpable interest in the fact that she was likely to have a child by him. And though her cry (on the question what name this infant, of course accepted as his own by the unfortunate Andermatt, should bear) that as for *her* name, " Cela promet trop de souffrances de porter le nom du Crucifié," could not be better as a general sentiment, the particular circumstances in which it is uttered show a slight want of grace of congruity. Still, the minor characters are not only more in number, but more interesting than is always the case ; and the book, if you skip the obstetrics, is readable throughout. Yet it is, to use wine-language, not above " Maupassant *premier bourgeois*," except in some of the earlier love-scenes.

In *Fort comme la Mort* the author rises far above these two books, powerful as they are in parts. The basis is indeed the invariable and unsatisfactory " triangle." But the structure built on it might almost have been lifted to another, and stands foursquare in nearly all respects of treatment. The chief technical objection that can be brought against it is that there is a certain want of air and space ; the important characters are too few, the situations too uniform ; so that a kind of oppression results. Olivier Bertin, one of the most popular of Parisian painters though no longer young, a great man of society, etc., has, for many years, been the lover of the Countess de Guilleroy, and, of course, the dear friend of her husband. We are introduced to them just at the time when a sort

Fort comme la Mort.

---

[1] He was, says his historian well, " de la race des amants et non point de la race des pères."

of disgust of middle age is coming over him, as well as a certain feeling that the springs of his genius are running low. He is not tired of the Countess, who is passionately devoted to him ; and, except that they do not live together, their relations are rather conjugal than anything else. Just at this moment her daughter Annette comes home from a country life with her grand-mother, and proves to be the very double of what her mother was in her own youth. Bertin, without ceasing to love the mother, conceives a frantic passion for the daughter ; and the vicissitudes of this take up the book. At last the explosives of the situation are " fused," as one may say, by one of the newspaper attacks of youth on age. Annette's approaching marriage, and this *Figaro* critique of his own " old-fashioned " art, put Bertin beside himself. Either hurrying heedlessly along, or deliberately exposing himself, he is run over by an omnibus, is mortally hurt, and dies with the Countess sitting beside him and receiving his last selfishness—a request that she will bring the girl to see him before he dies.

The story, though perhaps, as has been said, too much concentrated as a whole, is brilliantly illuminated by sketches of society on the greater and smaller scale : of Parisian club-life ; of picture-shows ; of the diversions of the country, etc. : but its effect, though certainly helped by, is not derived from, these. As always with Maupassant, it is out of the bitter that comes the sweet. Hardly anywhere outside of *Ecclesiastes*, Thackeray,[1] and Flaubert is the irony of life more consummately handled in one peculiar fashion ; while the actual *passion* of love is nowhere better treated by this author,[2] or perhaps by

---

[1] The resemblances between Thackeray and Maupassant are very numerous and most remarkable. That they have both been accused of cynicism *and* sentimentality is only, as it were, the index-finger to the relationship.

[2] At the risk, however, of wearying the reader and "forcing open doors," one may exemplify, from this book also, the artificial character of this obligatory adultery. Anne de Guilleroy has all the qualifications of an almost perfect mistress (in the honourable sense) and wife. She is charming ; a flirt to the right point and not beyond it ; passion-ate ditto ; affectionate ; not capricious ; inviolably faithful (in her unfaithfulness, of course) ; jealous to her own pain, but with no result of malice to others. Yet in order to show all this she has to be an adulteress first—in obedience to this mysterious

any other French novelist of the later century, except
Fromentin.

The line of ascent was continued in *Pierre et Jean*.
It is not a long book—a fact which perhaps has some
Pierre et significance—and no small part of it is taken
Jean. up by a Preface on " Le Roman " generally
(*v. sup.*), which is the author's most remarkable piece of
criticism ; one of the most noteworthy from a man who
was not specially a critic ; and one of the few but precious
examples of an artist dealing, at once judicially and
masterfully, with his own art.[1]   In fact, recognising the
truth of the " poetic moment," he would extend it to
the moments of all literature ; and lays it down that the
business of the novelist is, first to realise his own illusion
of the world and then to make others realise it too.

Pierre et Jean itself has no weakness except that
narrowing of interest which has been already noted in
Maupassant, and which is rather a limitation than a
positive fault.   There is practically one situation throughout ; and though there are several characters, their interest
depends almost wholly on their relations with the central
personage.   This is Pierre Roland, a full-fledged physician of thirty, but not yet successful, and still living with,
and on, his parents.   His father is a retired Paris trades-
man, who has come to live at Havre to indulge a mania
for sea-fishing ; he has a mother who is rather above her
husband in some ways ; and a brother, Jean, who, though
considerably younger, is also ready to start in his own
profession—that of the law.   A " friend of the family,"
Mme. Rosémilly—a young, pretty, and rather well-

---

modernisation and topsy-turvification of ancient Babylonian custom, and the *jus primae
noctis*, and the proverb as to second thoughts being best, and Heaven or the other place
knows what else.   Here also, as elsewhere, Maupassant—satirist of women as he is—
makes her lover a very inferior creature to herself.   For Bertin is a selfish coxcomb,
and *does*, at least half, allow himself to be " snuffed out by an article."

[1] Any one who chooses may compare it with the utterances of the late Mr. Henry
James.   Maupassant's own selection of novels, to illustrate the impossibility of defining
a novel, is of the first interest.   They are : *Manon Lescaut, Paul et Virginie, Don
Quichotte, Les Liaisons Dangereuses, Werther, Les Affinités Électives, Clarissa* [he adds
Harlowe, an unauthentic addition, pardonable in a Frenchman, though not in one of us],
*Émile, Candide, Cinq-Mars, René, Les Trois Mousquetaires, Mauprat, Le Père Goriot,
La Cousine Bette, Colomba, Le Rouge et Le Noir, Mademoiselle de Maupin, Notre Dame
de Paris, Salammbô, Madame Bovary, Adolphe, M. de Camors. L'Assommoir*, and *Sapho*.

to-do widow—completes the company, with one or two
"supers." Just as the story opens, a large legacy to
Jean by an older friend of the family—this time a man—
is announced, to the surprise of almost everybody, but
at first only causing a little natural jealousy in Pierre.
Charitable remarks of outsiders, however, suggest to
him the truth—that Jean is the fruit of his mother's
adultery with the testator—and this "works like poison
in his brain," till—Jean, having gained another piece of
luck in Mme. Rosémilly's hand, and having, though
enlightened by Pierre and by his mother's confession,
very common-sensibly decided that he will not resign
the legacy, smirched as it is—Pierre accepts a surgeon-
ship on a Transatlantic steamer, and the story ends.

On its own scheme and showing there is scarcely a
fault in it. The mere settings—the fishing and prawn-
catching; the scenery of port and cliff; the "interiors";
the final sailing of the great ship—are perfect. The
minor characters—the good-tempered, thick-headed *bourgeois* husband and father; the wife and mother, with
her bland acceptance of the transferred wages of shame,
and (after discovery only) her breaking down with the
banal blasphemy of "marriage before God" and the
rest of it; the younger brother—not exactly a bad
fellow, but thoroughly convinced of the truth of *non
olet*; the widow playing her part and no more,—all are
artistically just what they should be. And so, always
remembering scale and scheme, is Pierre. One neither
likes him (for he is not exactly a likeable person) nor
dislikes him (for he is quite excusable) very much; one
is only partially sorry for him. But one knows that he
is—he has that actual and indubitable existence which
is the test and quality alike of creator and creation.
His first vague envy of his brother's positive luck in
money and probable luck in love—for both have had
floating fancies for the pretty widow; the again perfectly
natural spleen when this lucky brother, by an accident,
secures the particular set of rooms in which Pierre had
hoped to improve his position as a doctor; the crushing

blow of finding out his mother's shame; the process
(the truest thing in the whole book, though it is all true)
by which he tortures both her and himself in constant
oblique references to her fault; the explosion when he
directly informs his brother; and all the rest, could
hardly be improved. It is not a novel on the great scale,
but rather what may be called a long short story. It
does not quite attain to the position of some books on a
small scale in different kinds—*Manon Lescaut* itself,
Adolphe, *La Tentation de Saint-Antoine*. But the author
has done what he meant to do, and has done it in such a
fashion that it could not, on its own lines, be done
better.

Maupassant's last novel of some magnitude, *Notre
Cœur*, was written when the shadow was near enveloping
him; and it cannot be said to have the perfection of
Pierre et Jean. But it still rises higher in certain very
important ways—it is perhaps the book that one likes
him best for, outside of pure comedy; and there is
none which impresses one more with the sense of his
loss to French literature.

The story, like all Maupassant's stories, is of the
simplest. André Mariolle, a well-to-do young Parisian

Notre Cœur. bachelor of no profession, is a member of a
set of mostly literary and artistic people,
almost all of whom have, as a main rendezvous, the
house of a beautiful, wealthy, and variously gifted young
widow, Mme. de Burne. She lives chaperoned in a manner
by her father; indisposed to a second marriage by the
fact that she has had a tyrannical husband; accepting
homage from all her familiars and being very gracious
in differing degrees to all of them; but having no " lover
in title " and not even being suspected of having (in the
French novel-sense [1]) any " lover " at all. For a long
time Mariolle has, from whim, refused introduction to
her, but at last he consents to be taken to the house by
his friend the musician Massival, and of course falls a

---

[1] " Amant " as accurately distinguished by M. Jean Richepin in *Césarine* (for the
benefit of an innocent Hungarian) from " amoureux."

victim. It cannot be said that she is a Circe,[1] nor that, as perhaps might be expected, she revenges herself for his holding aloof by snaring and throwing him away. Quite the contrary. She shows him special favour : when she has to go to stay with friends at Avranches she privately asks him to follow her ; and finally, when the party pass the night at Mont Saint-Michel, she comes— uninvited, though of course much longed for—to his room, and (as they used to say with elaborate decency) " crowns his flame." Nor does she turn on him—as again might be expected—even then. On the contrary, she comes constantly to a secret Eden which he has pre- pared for her in Paris, and though, after long practice of this, she is sometimes rather late, and once or twice actually puts off her assignation, it is " no more than reason,"[2] and she by no means jilts or threatens jilting, though she tells him frankly that his way of loving (which *is* more than reason) is not hers. At last he cannot endure seeing her surrounded with admirers, and flies to Fontainebleau, where he is partly—only partly— consoled by a pretty and devoted *bonne*. Yet he sends a despairing cry to Mme. de Burne ; and she, gracious as ever, actually comes to see him, and induces him to return to Paris. He does so, but takes the *bonne* Elisa- beth with him ; and the book ends abruptly, leaving the

---

[1] Not that I wish to blaspheme Circe, who always seems to me to have adjusted her- self to a disconcertingly changed situation with more than demi-goddesslike dexterity and good humour. It may perhaps be not irrelevant, to discussion of novels in general, to mention something which I have never yet seen put in Homeric discussion, though the bare idea of anything new there being possible may seem preposterous. The argu- ments of the splitters-up are, naturally enough, seldom if ever literary, belonging as they do to the class of Biblical, that is to say, *un*literary, criticism. But strictly literary considerations, furnishing argument of the strongest kind for unity, might be brought by comparing the behaviour of Circe, at the moment referred to, and that of Helen when Paris returned from his defeat. These situations are, of course, in initial circumstance as opposite as possible, though they *arrivent à pareille fin*. But behind their very opposi- tion there is a conception of the eternal feminine—partly human, partly divine—which it would be very surprising to find in two different persons, and which might, if any one cared to do it, be interestingly worked out from divers other Homeric characters of women or goddesses, from Hera and Aphrodite in the one poem to Nausicaa and Calypso in the other. " How great a *novelist* was in *Homer* lost " is a theme too much neglected.

[2] For do not fixed hours always become a bore—except in respect of meals ? To have to love, or to lecture, or to do anything but eat, at *x* A. or P.M. precisely, on such and such days in the week, is a weariness to the spirit and the flesh alike.

reader to imagine what is the outcome of this " double arrangement "—or failure to arrange.

But, as always with Maupassant's longer stories and not quite never with his shorter ones, the " fable is the least part." The " atmosphere " ; the projection of character and passion ; the setting ; the situations ; the phrase—these are the thing. And, except for the enigmatic and " stump-ended " conclusion, and for a certain overdose of words (which rather grew on him), they make a very fine thing. It is here that, on one side at least, the author's conception of love—which at some times might appear little more than animal, at others conventional-capricious in a fashion which makes that of Crébillon universal and sincere—has sublimed itself, as it had begun to do in *Fort comme la Mort* (*Pierre et Jean* is in this respect something of a divagation), into very nearly the true form of the Canticles and Shakespeare, of Donne and Shelley and Heine, of Hugo and Musset and Browning. But it is curious, in the first place, that he whom his friends fondly called a *fier mâle*, who has sometimes pushed masculinity near to brutality, and who is always cynical more or less, has made his André Mariolle, though a very good lover, a distinct weakling in love. He is a " too quick despairer," and his despair is more illogical than even a lover's has a right to be. And this is very interesting, because, evidently without the author's knowledge (though perhaps, if things had gone more happily, he might have come to that knowledge later), it shows the rottenness of the foundation, and the flimsiness of the superstructure, on and in which the Covenant of Adultery—even that of Free Love—is built. Michelle de Burne gives André Mariolle everything with one exception, if even with that, that the greediest lover can want. She "distinguishes" him at once ; she shows keen desire for his company ; she makes the last (or first) surrender like a goddess answering a hopeless and unspoken prayer ; she is strangely generous in continuing the *don d'amoureux merci* ; she never really wearies of or jilts him, though he is a most exacting lover ;

and when he has flung away from her she allows him, in the most gracious manner, to whistle himself back. But there is one thing, or rather two which are one, that she will not, or perhaps cannot, give him. It is the idealised passion which nature has denied to her, though not to him, and the absolute faithfulness and " forsaking of all others " proper to what ?—to a perfect wife. So here, in the realms of spouse-breach, marriage is once more king, or rather the throne is felt to be empty—the kingdom an anarchy—without it !

The lighter side of the matter reminds one of two celebrated utterances. The first is Paul de Florac's criticism on the Lady Clara-Barnes-Highgate triangle, " Do not adopt our institutions à demi." Here the situation is topsy-turvied in the most curious fashion, for it is the character of marriage that is desiderated in the absence thereof, and in a country where that character itself is scoffed at. Further, it reminds one still more of Sydney Smith's excellent jest when Lady Holland, having previously asked him to stay at Holland House, sent him a formal invitation to dinner, for a day within the period of the larger hospitality. This, said Sydney, was " an attempt to combine the stimulus of gallantry with the security of connubial relations." That was precisely the moon that Mariolle sighed for, and that his not exactly Artemis would not—indeed could not be expected to—give him.

Of Michelle de Burne herself there is less to be said. The curious misogyny which chequered Maupassant's gynomania seems to have tried hard to express itself in her portrait. It is less certain that it does. The other characters are quite subordinate, except the *bonne* Elisabeth (who, promising as she is, merely makes her *début*) and a novelist, Gaston de Lamarthe, who may sometimes be taken as the author's mouthpiece, but who does not do him justice. The book on the whole does much to confirm, and hardly anything to invalidate, the position that its writer had far more to say than he ever said.

The ordinary list of Maupassant's "Romans," as distinct from "Nouvelles" and "Contes," ends with *Les Dimanches d'un Bourgeois de Paris.* This, however, is merely a series of tales (some of them actually rehandled from earlier ones), with a single figure for centre, to wit, a certain M. Patissot, a bachelor government-official, who is a sort of mixture of Leech's Mr. Briggs and of Jérôme Paturot, with other predecessors who get into scrapes and "fixtures." It is not unamusing, but scarcely first-class, the two political skits at the end being about the best part of it.

Les Dimanches, etc.

On the other hand, *Yvette,* which is only allowed the eponymship of a volume of short stories, though it fills to itself some hundred and seventy pages, is one of Maupassant's most carefully written things and one of his best—till the not fully explained, but in any case unsatisfactory, end.[1] Its heroine is the daughter of a sham Marquise and real courtesan, who has attained wealth, who can afford herself lovers " for love "[2] and not for money, when she chooses, and who keeps up a sort of demi-monde society, in which most of the men are adventurers and all the women adventuresses, but which maintains outward decencies. In consequence of this Yvette herself—in a fashion a little impossible, but artistically made not improbable—though she allows herself the extreme "tricks and manners" of faster society, calls half the men by nicknames, wanders about alone with them, etc., preserves not merely her personal purity but even her ignorance of unclean things in general, and especially of her mother's real character and conduct. Her relations with a clever and not ungentlemanly *roué,* one M. de Servigny; his difficulties (these are very curiously and cleverly told) in making love to a girl not of the lower class (at least apparently) and not vicious; his attempt to brusque the matter; her horror at it and at the coincident discovery of her mother's ways; her

Yvette.

---

[1] "The Novelists Who Cannot End " is one of the title-subjects which, "reponing my senescent art," I relinquish to others.

[2] In the card sense.

attempt to poison herself; and her salvage by Servigny's coolness and devotion—are capitally done. Out of many passages, one, where Madame la Marquise Obardi, otherwise Octavie Bardin, formerly domestic servant, drops her mask, opens her mouth, and uses the crude language of a procuress-mother to her daughter, is masterly. But the end is not from any point of view satisfactory. Apparently (for it is not made quite clear) Yvette retracts her refusal to be a kept mistress. In that case certainly, and in the almost impossible one of marriage probably, it may be feared that the catastrophe is only postponed. Now Yvette has been made too good (I do not mean goody) to be allowed to pine or poison herself, as a soon-to-be-neglected concubine or a not-much-longer-to-be-loved wife.

That the very large multitude [1] of his short stories (or, one begs pardon, brief-narratives) is composed of Short stories units very different in merit is not wonderful. —the various It was as certain that the covers of the author of collections. *Boule de Suif* [2] would be drawn for the kind of thing frequently, as that these would sometimes be drawn either blank, or with the result of a very indifferent run. To an eye of some expertness, indeed, a good many of these pieces are, at best, the sort of thing that a clever contributor would turn off to editorial order, when he looked into a newspaper office between three and five, or ten and midnight. I confess that I once burst out laughing when, having thought to myself on reading one, "This is not much above a better written Paul-de-Kockery," I found at the end something like a frank

---

[1] They run well into, if not over, the second hundred, and it is proper to warn readers (and still more buyers) that different editions vary the contents of individual volumes; so that, without some care, and even with it, duplication is nearly certain. This bad habit, not quite unknown in England, is rather common in France.

[2] If any one is fortunate, or unfortunate, enough not to know this admirable story, it may be well to say that the title is the nickname of a young person, more pleasing than proper, who forms part of a convoy or cartel of non-combatants passing through the Prussian lines in 1871. The Prussian officer, imitating more mildly (and without the additional villainy) the conduct of Colonel Kirke, refuses passage to the whole party, unless she will give him a cast of her office. The story is told as inoffensively as possible, and the crowning irony of the shocked attitude of her respectable companions at her liberating them, though they have been frantically anxious she should do so, is sublime.

acknowledgment of the fact, *with the name*. In fact, Maupassant was not good at the pure *grivoiserie*; his contemporary M. Armand Silvestre (*v. inf.*) did it much better. Touches of tragedy, as has been said, save the situation sometimes, and at others the supernatural element of dread (which was to culminate in *Le Horla*, and finally to overpower the author himself) gives help; but the zigzags of the line of artistic success are sharp and far too numerous. For a short story proper and a "proper" short story, *L'Épave*, where an inspector of marine insurance visits a wreck far out on the sands of the Isle of Rhé, and, finding an Englishman and his daughter there, most unprofessionally forgets that the tides come up rapidly in such places, is nearly perfect. On the other hand, *Le Rosier de Mme. Husson*, one of the longest, is almost worthless.

At one time I had designed—and to no small extent written—a running survey of a large number of these stories as they turn up in the volumes, most of which—the *Contes de la Bécasse* is the chief exception—have no unity, and are merely "scoopings" of pieces enough to fill three hundred pages or so. But it would have occupied far too much space for its importance and interest. As a matter of fact, they are to some extent classifiable, and so may be dealt with on a representative system. There is the division of "La Revanche," which might have saved some of our fools at home from mistaking the Prussian for anything but a Prussian. *Boule de Suif* heads this, of course; but *Mlle. Fifi*, which is a sort of tragic *Boule de Suif*—the tragedy being, one is glad to say, at the invaders' expense—is not far below it. *Deux Amis*, one of the best, records how two harmless Parisian anglers, pursuing their beloved sport too far, were shot for refusing to betray the password back; and *La Mère Sauvage*, the finest of all, how a French mother, hearing of her son's death, burnt her own house with some Germans billeted in it, and was, on her frank confession, shot. But *Un Duel*, though a Prussian officer (*vile*

Classes— stories of 1870–71.

damnum) pays for his brutality with his life, restores the comic element, partly at the expense of the two English seconds.[1]

Connected with the war of 1870 too, though not military, is the capital *Coup d'État*, in which a Monarchist French squire checkmates, for the moment at least, a blatant Republican village doctor.

Very much larger than any other group is, naturally enough, that on Norman subjects. Maupassant does **Norman** not flatter his fellow-subjects of the great **stories.** Duchy, but he loves them, and knows them, and delights to talk of them—talking always well and often at his best. There must be, in all, several volumes-full of these, though they are actually scattered over a dozen: and it is not easy to go wrong with them. Perhaps a new "Farce du Cuvier," quite different from those known to readers of Boccaccio and the Fabliaux (a very drunk peasant sells his wife [2] by weight or measure to another, and scientifically ascertains the exact sum to be paid by making her fill a butt with water and putting her into it—the displacement giving the required result) is the merriest. The story of the schoolboy who negotiates a marriage between his Latin tutor and a young person is excellent; and that of "Boitelle," a poor fellow who is prevented (through that singular abuse of *patria potestas* so long allowed by French law) from marrying an agreeable negress, is the most pathetic. But I myself am rather fond of the *Légende du Mont Saint-Michel.* At first one is a little shocked at finding "the great vision of the guarded mount"[3] yoked to the old Scandinavian

---

[1] Maupassant does not caricature us (at least our men) very extravagantly. But he, like the rest of them, always makes us say, "Aoh." I have frequently endeavoured to produce, otherwise than as a diphthong, this mysterious word (a descendant, perhaps, of the equally mysterious *Aoi* of the *Chanson de Roland* ?). But I cannot make it like the way in which I say, or in which any well-educated Englishman says, "Oh!" American it may be, and it is not unlike the "Ow" of some dialects, but pure English it is not. It may be, for aught I know, phonetic: and has been explained as representing an affected sneer. The curious thing is that "Oh-*a*" actually is a not unfrequent, though slovenly, pronunciation.

[2] Evidently, therefore, the practice with which we have been so often reproached is of French—at least Norman—origin.

[3] The *other* one, of course, but here one must admit the superiority of the foreign "strength." And the "story" has French antecedents.

troll-and-farmer story of the fraudulent bargain as to alternate upper- and under-ground crops. But the magnificent opening description of "the fairy castle planted in the sea "[1] excuses, and is thrown up by, the sequel. Mont-Saint-Michel is not like Naples. When you have seen it, it is not your business to die, but to live and remember the sight of it ; and, if you are lucky, your remembrance will have anticipated Maupassant's words, and be freshened by them.

Algiers and the Riviera were also fruitful in quantity, rather less so in quality. But on the former two stories, Algerian *Allouma* and *Au Soir*, may be found together, and Sporting. the whole of the first of which, and the beginning of the second, are first-rate. The above mentioned *Contes de la Bécasse* are almost all good, though by no means all sporting.

For pure comedy one might put as the first three— with the caution that Mrs. Grundy had better keep Purely away from them— *Les Sœurs Rondoli*,[2] for comic. which I feel certain that, when Maupassant reached the Elysian Fields, Aristophanes and Rabelais jointly requested the pleasure of introducing him to the company, and crowned him with the choicest laurels ; *Mouche*, which is really touching as well as tickling at the end, though the grave and precise must be doubly warned off this ; and *Enragée*—which is a sort of blend of an old smoking-room story of the perils of the honeymoon when new, and that curious tale[3] of Vigny's which has been given above.

For pure, or almost pure, tragedy and pathos, again,

[1] This is an actual translation of the Norman poet's words. It makes no bad blank-verse line.

[2] Its companions, in the volume to which it gives title, are mostly inferior specimens of the same class. But some, especially *Le Pain Maudit*, are very amusing, and *Lui ?* is a curious and melancholy anticipation of *Le Horla*. *La Maison Tellier*, which opens and titles another volume of no very different kind, has never seemed to me quite worthy of its fame. It is not unamusing in itself, and very amusing when one thinks of its greatly-daring imitators, but rather schoolboyish or even monkeyish in its determination to shock. (It doesn't shock *me*.) Another "shocker," but tragic, not comic, *La Femme de Paul*, which closes the book, is more powerful. (It is on the theme of *Mlle. Giraud ma Femme* (*v. inf.*) ; only the male person, instead of drowning his she-rival, far less wisely drowns himself.) But most of its contents suffer, not merely from Naturalist grime, but from Naturalist *meticulousness*.   [3] *V. sup.* p. 269 *sq.*

Monsieur Parent stands first—the history of the late vengeance of a deceived husband and friend. *Miss*

Tragic. *Harriet* gives us something more than a stage Englishwoman with large feet, projecting teeth, tartan skirts, and tracts, though it gives us this too. *Madame Baptiste*—the very short tale of a hapless woman who, having been the victim of crime in her youth, is pursued by the scandal thereof to suicide, in spite of her having found a worthy husband—is one of Maupassant's intensest.

As examples, bending sometimes to the comic, sometimes to the pathetic side of studies in the irony of

Tales of life, one may recommend *A Cheval* (a holiday Life's Irony. taken by a poor but well-born family, which saddles them with an unconscionable " run-over " Old-*W*oman-of-the-*Land*) ; *La Parure* and *Les Bijous* (the first a variant of *A Cheval*, the second a discovery by a husband, after his wife's death, of her shame) ; and perhaps best of all, *Regret*, in which a gentleman of sixty, reflecting on his wasted life, remembers a picnic, decades earlier, where the wife of his lifelong friend—both of them still friends and neighbours—behaved rather oddly. He hurries across to ask her (whom he finds jam-making) what she would have done if he had " failed in respect," and receives the cool answer, " J'aurais cédé." It is good ; but fancy not being able to take a walk, and observe the primroses by the river's brim, without being bound in honour to observe likewise whether the lady by your side was ready to " cede " or not ! It seems to me that in such circumstances one would, to quote a French critic on an entirely different author and matter, " lose all the grace and liberty of the composition."

Some oddments[1] may deserve addition. *Fini*, which might have been mentioned in the last group, is a very

Oddments. perfect thing. A well-preserved dandy in middle age meets, after many years, an old love, and sees, mirrored in *her* decay, his own so long ignored. Nobody save a master could have done this

---

[1] For the " Terror " group see below.

as it is done. *Julie Romain* is a quaint half-dream based on some points in George Sand's life, and attractive. The *title* of *L'Inutile Beauté* has also always been so to me (the *story* is worth little). It would be, I think, a fair test of any man's taste in style, whether he did or did not see any difference between it and *La Beauté Inutile*. In *Adieu*, I think, Maupassant has been guilty of a fearful heresy in speaking of part of a lady's face as " ce *sot* organe qu'on appelle le nez." Now that a nose, both in man and woman, can be foolish, nobody will deny. But that foolishness is an organic characteristic of it—in the sense of inexpressiveness, want of character, want of charm—is flatly a falsehood.[1] Neither mouth nor eyes can beat it in that respect ; and if it has less variety individually, it gives perhaps more general character to the face than either. However, he is, if I mistake not, obliged to retract partially in the very story.

I have notes of many others—some of which may be special favourites with readers of mine—but room for no more. Yet for me at least among all these, despite the glaring inequality, despite the presence of some things utterly ephemeral and not in the least worth giving a new day to ; despite the " *saleté* bête "[2] and the monotonous and obligatory adultery,[3] there abides, as in the large books,

---

[1] Curiously enough, a few days *after* writing the above I came across, in the last *Diabolique* of that curious flawed genius, Barbey d'Aurevilly (*v. sup.* p. 453), words which redress, by long anticipation, the wrong done by his fellow Norman : " Les ailes du nez, aussi *expressives que des yeux*."

[2] In a novel by a contemporary of his, otherwise not worth notice, Sir Walter Scott was accused of " *pruderie* bête " ; I am sure the adjective and substantive are much better mated in my text.

[3] I remember, in a book which I have not seen for about two-thirds of a century, Miss Martineau's *Crofton Boys*, an agreeable anecdote (for the good Harriet, when not under the influence of Radicalism, the dismal science, Anti-Christianity, or Mr. Atkinson, could tell a story very well) of a little English girl. It occurred to her one morning that she should have to wash and dress, do her hair, etc., *every day for her whole life*, and she sat down and wept bitterly. Now, if I were a little girl or boy in the French novel-world, when as I remembered that I should have, as the one, never to marry, or to commit adultery with every one who asked me ; that, as the other, I must not be left five minutes alone with a married woman, without offering her the means of carrying out her and her husband's destiny ; I really think I should imitate Miss Martineau's child, if I did not even go and hang myself. " Fay ce que voudras " may be rather a wide commandment. " Fay ce que dois " may require a little enlarging. But " Do what you ought not, not because you wish to do it, but because it is the proper thing to do " is not only " the limit," but beyond it. I think if I were a Frenchman of the novel-type I should hate the sight of a married woman. Stone walls would not

and from circumstances now and then with gathered intensity, that quality of above-the-commonness which has obliged me to speak of Maupassant as I have spoken.

The vividness and actuality of his power of presentation are unquestioned, and there has been complaint rather General con- of the character of his "illusions" (*v. sup.*) than siderations. of his failure to convey them to others. It is not merely that nature, helped by the discipline of practice under the severest of masters, had endowed him with a style of the most extraordinary sobriety and accuracy—the style of a more scholarly, reticent, and tightly-girt Defoe. It is not merely that his vision, and his capacity of reproducing that vision, were unsurpassed and rarely equalled for sharpness of outline and perfection of disengagement. He had something else which it is much less easy to put into words—the power of treating an incident or a character (character, it is true, less often and less fully than incident) as if it were a phrase or a landscape, of separating it, carving it out (so to speak), and presenting it isolated and framed for survey. His performances in these tracks are so numerous that it is difficult to single out any. But I do not know that finer examples (besides those noticed above in *Une Vie*) of his power of thus isolating and projecting a scene are to be found than two of the passages in *Pierre et Jean*, the prawn-catching party and Pierre's meditation at the jetty-head. Of his similar but greater faculty of treating incident *and* character *Monsieur Parent* is perhaps the very finest example (for *Boule de Suif* is something greater than a mere slice), though *Promenade*, *Les Sœurs Rondoli*, *Boitelle*, *Deux Amis*, and others are almost as good. But this very excellence of our author's carries with it a danger which most of his readers must have recognised. His definition and vignetting of separate scenes, incidents, and characters is so sharp and complete that he finds a difficulty in combining them. The

---

a prison make nor iron bars a cage—so odious as this unrelieved tyranny of *concupiscentia carnis*—to order! Perhaps Wilberforce's Agathos had a tedious time of it in being always ready to resist the Dragon; but how much more wearisome would it be to be always on the *qui vive*, lest you should miss a chance of *not* resisting him!

attempt to disdain and depreciate plot which the above-mentioned Preface contains is, I suspect (though I am, as often confessed, no plot-worshipper), as our disdains and depreciations so often are, itself a confession. At any rate, it is allowed that the longer books, with the exception of *Pierre et Jean* (which was for that very reason, and perhaps for others, disdained by the youngest and most impressionist school of critics), are deficient in beginning, middle, and end. *Une Vie* and *Bel-Ami* are surveys or chronicles, not dramas or histories. *Mont-Oriol*, open enough to objection in some ways, is rather better in this point. *Fort Comme la Mort* relapses under the old curse of the situation of teasing unhappiness from which there is no outlet, and in which there is little action. *Notre Cœur* should perhaps escape criticism on this head, as the shadow of the author's fate was already heavy on him. In fact, as observed above, it is little more than a torso. Even *Pierre et Jean*, by far the greatest of all, if scale and artistic perfection be taken together, falls short in the latter respect of *Boule de Suif*, which, small as it is, is a complete tragi-comedy in little, furnished with beginning, middle, and end, complying fully with those older exigences which its author affected to despise, and really as great as anything of Mérimée's— greater it could not be.

There is no doubt that the theory which Maupassant says he learnt from Flaubert (in whose own hands it was always subordinated to an effort at larger completeness) does lead to the composition of a series or flock of isolated vignettes or scenes rather than to that of a great picture or drama. For it comes perilously close—though perhaps in Maupassant's own case it never actually reached—the barest and boldest (or baldest) individual-ising of impressions, and leaving them as they are, without an attempt at architectonic. For instance, once upon a time[1] I was walking down the Euston Road. There

---

[1] The "time" was five and twenty years ago. But this passage, trifling as it may seem to some readers, appeared to me worth preserving, because my recent very careful reperusal of Maupassant, as a whole, made its appositeness constantly recur to me.

passed me a fellow dragging a truck, on which truck there were three barrels with the heads knocked out, so that each barrel ensheathed, to a certain extent, the one in front of it. Astride of the centre barrel, his arms folded and a pipe in his mouth, there sat a man in a sort of sailor-costume—trousers, guernsey, and night-cap—surveying the world, and his fellow who dragged him, with an air of placid *goguenarderie*. It was really a striking impression, and absorbed me, I should think, for five or six seconds. I can conceive its coming into a story very well. But Maupassant's theories would have led to his making a whole story out of it, and his followers have already done things quite as bad, while he has himself come near to it more than once.[1] In other words, the method tends to the presentations of scraps, orts, fragments, instead of complete wholes. And Art should always seek the whole.

As for the character of Maupassant's "illusions," there could never be much doubt about some of them. *Boule de Suif* itself pretty clearly indicated, and *La Maison Tellier* shortly after showed, at the very opening of his literary career, the scenes, the society, and the solaces which he most affected : while it was impossible to read even two or three of his stories without discovering that, to M. de Maupassant, the world was most emphatically *not* the best of all possible worlds. This was by no means principally shown in the stories of supernatural terror to which, with an inconsistency by no means uncommon in declared materialists, and, had it not been for his unhappy end, very amusing, he was so much given. The chief of these, *Le Horla*, has not been much of a favourite with the lovers of "ghost-stories" in general. I think they are rather unjust to it. But if it has a fault, that fault lies (and, to avoid the charge of being wise after the event, I may observe that I thought so at the time) in too much conviction. The darkness is darkness which has been felt, and felt so much

---

[1] Nearest, perhaps, in the story called "En Famille," to be found in the *Maison Tellier* volume.

by the artist that he has lost his artistic grasp and command.   There was, perhaps, in his own actual state,
too much reason for this.   In earlier things of the kind
it is less perceptible.   *Fou ?* is rather splendid.   *Auprès
d'un Mort*—an anecdote of the death-bed of Schopen-
hauer, whom Maupassant naturally admired as the
greatest of *saccageurs de rêves*, though there are some
who, admiring the first master of thoroughly good
German prose style and one of the best of German critics,
have kept the fort of their dreams safe from all he could
do — has merits.   *Lettre trouvée sur un noyé* is good ;
L'Horrible not quite so good ; *Le Loup* (a sort of fancy
from the " bête du Gévaudan " story) better ; *Apparition*
of the best, with *La Morte* to pair it, and *Un Cas de
Divorce* and *Qui sait ?* to make up the quartette.·   Perhaps the best of all (I do not specify its title in order that
those who do not know it may read till they find it out)
is that where the visionary sees the skeletons of the dead
rising and transforming their lying epitaphs into confessions—the last tomb now bearing the true cause of
his own mistress's death.   But the double-titled *La
Nuit—Cauchemar* runs it hard.

Yet it is not in these stories of doubt and dread, or
in the ostensible and rather shallow philosophisings of
the travel-books, that Maupassant's pessimism is most
obvious.   His preference for the unhappy ending
amounts almost to a *tic*, and would amount wholly to a
bore—for *toujours* unhappy-ending is just as bad as
toujours marriage-bells—if it were not relieved and lightened by a real presence of humour.   With this sovereign
preservative for self, and more sovereign charm for
others, Guy de Maupassant was more richly provided
than any of his French contemporaries, and more than
any but a very few of his countrymen at any time.   And
as humour without tenderness is an impossibility, so,
too, he could be and was tender.   Yet it was seldom and
malgré lui, while he allowed the mere exercise of his
humour itself too scantily for his own safety and his
readers' pleasure.   That there was any more *fanfaron-*

nade either of vice or of misanthropy about him, I do not believe. An unfortunate conformity of innate temperament and acquired theory made such a *fan-faronnade* as unnecessary as it would have been repugnant to him. But illusion, in such cases, is more dangerous, if less disgusting, than imposture. And so it happened that, in despite of the rare and vast faculties just allowed him, he was constantly found applying them to subjects distasteful if not disgraceful, and allowing the results to be sicklied over with a persistent " soot-wash " of pessimism which was always rather monotonous, and not always very impressive.

It was, of course, inevitable that, on this side of the Channel at least, strictures should be passed —and appealed against—on a writer of this kind. The impropriety of M. de Maupassant's subjects, the " cruelty," the " brutality," the " pessimism," and what not, of his handling, were sure to be denounced or defended, as the case may be. Although the merely " shoking " tone (as the spelling dear to Frenchmen has it) has waned persistently ever since his day, expressions in it have not been wanting ; while, on the other hand, newer-fashioned and probably younger censors have scornfully waved aside the very consideration of this part of the subject. Further, no less a critic than my friend Mr. Traill entered, long ago, a protest against the admission of Maupassant's pessimism as a drawback. " He did not," says Mr. Traill (I quote from memory), "*pose* as a pessimist ; he was perfectly sincere, and an artist's sincere life-philosophy, whatever it is, is not to be urged against the products of his art."

I think that these questions require a little discussion, even in a general *History*.

With reference to the impropriety matter, I have myself, after a lifetime of fighting against the *hérésie de l'enseignement*, not the very slightest intention of deserting to or transacting with it. I do most heartily agree and affirm that the subject of a work of art is not, as such, the better or the worse, the more or the less legitimate, because of its tastefulness or distastefulness on moral considerations. But there is a perpetual danger, when we are clearing our minds of one cant, of allowing them to be invaded by another; and I think I have seen cases where the determination not to be moral of malice prepense has been so great that it has toppled over into a determination to be immoral of malice prepense. Now, the question is, whether Maupassant and some of Maupassant's admirers are not somewhat in this case? It is surely impossible for any impartial critic to contend that the unlucky novelist's devotion to the class of subjects referred to, and his manner of handling them, did not amount to what has been pedantically, but accurately, termed an "obsession of the *lupanar*." Now, it seems to me that all obsession, no matter of what class or kind, is fatal, or, at least, injurious, to the artist. It is almost impossible that he should keep his judgment and his taste cool and clear under it; it is almost impossible that his poring shall not turn into preaching. And I think it not much less hard to defend Maupassant from the charge of having become a kind of preacher in this way, and so a heretic of instruction, just as much as if he had taken to theology, dogmatic or undogmatic. Perpetual representation amounts to in-culcation.[1]

So, again, in reference to the apologies for Mau-passant's pessimism. I cannot see how it can be con-tended that the perpetual obtrusion of a life-philosophy of any special kind is other than a fault in art. I have no particular objection to pessimism as such; I suppose most people who have thought and felt a good deal are nearer to it than to its opposite; and, though both opposites bore me when they are obtruded, I think rose-pink and sky-blue bore me rather more than the various shades of grey and brown and black. I admit further that, but for the pessimist *diathesis*, we might

---

[1] Remarks already made on the particular novels and stories from this point of view need only be referred to, not repeated. But it is fair to say that some good judges plead for "warning off" instead of "inculcation."

not have had that peculiar tragedy in which he has been admitted to excel. But it seems to me that the creative artist, as such, and as distinguished from the critical, has no more business to display—to *arborer*—a life-philosophy, than he has to display a philosophy of any other kind. Signs of it may escape him at times ; but they should be escapes, not deliberate exhibitions. He is to see life whole as far as he can ; and it is impossible that he should see it whole if he is under the domination of any 'ism to the extent that Maupassant was under the domination of this. In the one supreme artist (I am talking, of course, throughout of the art of letters only) whom we know, there is, perhaps, no more distinctive peculiarity than his elusion of all attempts to class him as " Thissist " or " Thattist." And in those who come nearest to him, though they may have strong beliefs and strong pro- clivities, we always see the capacity of taking the other side. The fervent theologian of the *Paradiso* treats hardly any of his victims with more consideration than the inhabitants of the City of Dis : the prophet and poet of his own Uranian love for Beatrice swoons at the sight of Francesca's punishment, and feels " so that boiling glass were coolness," the very penalty of the Seventh Circle of Purgatory. But Maupassant's materialism and his pessimism combined shut out from him vast parts and regions of life and thought and feeling, as it were with the blank wall of his very earliest poem. The fantastic shadows of his peculiar imagination play on that wall fascinatingly enough ; and the region of passion and of gloom within is not without a charm, if a somewhat unholy and unhealthy one. But beyond the wall there is a whole universe which Maupassant does not merely neglect, but of which he seems to be blankly ignorant and unconscious, except in flashes of ignorant disdain. That the infinite province of religious emotion and reflection is shut out is a matter of course ; but most of the other regions, in which those who decline religion take refuge, are equally closed. I can remember in Maupassant only the slightest signs of interest in general literature (except so far as it bears upon his own special craft), in the illimitable ranges of history, in politics, in the higher philosophy.[1] It cannot be said of him, as of his master's dismal heroes, that *tout lui a craqué dans la main*. There is no sign of trial on his part ; he starts where Bouvard and Pécuchet end, and takes for granted a failure which he has not given himself the trouble to experience.

But, it may be said, " What does it matter what he does not do, know, feel, care for, if he treats what he does do, know, feel, and care for, well ? " The objection is ingenious, and, as Petruchio would say, " 'a might have a little galled me " if its ingenuity had not been the ingenuity of fallacy. For the question is whether this insensibility to large parts of life has not injured Maupassant's treatment of the parts in which he did feel an interest. I think it has. There were too many things in emotion and in thought of which he was ignorant. Mrs. Piozzi, in her *Anecdotes of Johnson*, observes that the Doctor, despite his freedom from gush and his dislike to religious verse, could never repeat the stanza of *Dies Irae* which ends "Tantus labor non sit cassus" without bursting into tears. I know a person very different from Johnson who, though he had not read the *Anecdotes* till an advanced period of his life, had never failed to experience something like the same result at the same line. And, for a third point, it is well known that actual agnostics have often confessed to like affections in similar cases. The numerous and complicated causes of this weakness, or, if any one prefers to call them so, the numerous and complicated causes of this enjoyment, had no hold whatever on Maupassant.

But this hemiplegia of the intellect and the imagination —this sterilising of one-half, or more than one-half, of the sources of intellectual and imaginative experience and delight—did not prevent him from leaving durable and perdurable results of the vigour of his mind and his sense, in the regions which were open to him. He

---

[1] There are some, but they are very few.

wrote—as almost every popular writer in these days who does not shut himself up in a *tour d'ivoire* and neglect popularity must write—too much ; and, in the special circumstances and limitations of his interests and his genius, this was specially unfortunate. He repeated himself too often ; and he too frequently failed to come up to himself in the repetition. The better part of him, as with Flaubert before, transcended—even openly contemned—the 'isms of his day: but he too often let himself be subservient to them, if he was never exactly their Helot.

Yet in recompense—a recompense largely if not wholly due to the strong Romantic [1] element which countervails the Naturalist—he was certainly the greatest novelist who was specially of the last quarter of the nineteenth century in France. In verse he showed the dawn, and in prose the noon-day, of a combination of veracity and vigour, of succinctness and strength, which no Frenchman who made his *début* since 1870 could surpass. The limitations of his art have been sufficiently dealt with ; the excellences of it within those limitations are unmistakable. He had no tricks—the worst curse of art at all times, and the commonest in these days of what pretends to be art. He had no splash of so-called " style " ; no acrobatic contortions of thought or what does duty for thought ; no pottering and peddling of the psychological kind, which would fain make up for a faulty product by ostentatiously parading the processes of production. Had he once got free—as more than once it seemed that he might—from the fatal conventionalities of his unconventionalism, from the trammels of his obtrusive negations, there is hardly a height in prose fiction which he might not have attained. As it is, he gave us in verse *Au bord de l'eau*, which is nearly

---

[1] See Conclusion. After the above notice of Maupassant was, in its reconstituted form, entirely completed, there came into my hands a long and careful paper on the novelist's Romanticism, published by Mr. Oliver H. Moore in the Transactions of the American Modern Language Association for March 1918. Those who are curious as to French opinion of him, and especially as to the strange superstition of his " classicism " (see Conclusion again), will find large extracts and references on this subject given by Mr. Moore, who promises further discussion.

the " farthest possible " in a certain expression, of a
certain mood of youth, and not of youth only ; in prose
Boule de Suif, Monsieur Parent, Pierre et Jean, which are
all in their way masterpieces, and a hundred things hardly
inferior.   And so he put himself in the company of
" Les Phares "—a light-giver at once and a warner of
danger, as well as a part of

cet ardent sanglot qui roule d'âge en âge,
Et vient mourir au bord de *notre* éternité.[1]

The Naturalist rank and file are so far below Zola
and Maupassant that they cannot now, whatever they
might have done twenty years ago, claim much

Huysmans.

notice in such a history as this.   The most
remarkable of them was probably J. K. Huysmans.   It
has been charitably suggested or admitted above that
his contribution to the *Soirées de Médan*—a deeply felt
story, showing the extreme disadvantage, when, as Mr.
De la Pluche delicately put it, " your midlands are out
of order," of wandering quarters and vicissitudes in the
country, and the intense relief experienced on return to
your own comfortable chambers in town,—that this *may*
have been written in the spirit of a *farceur*, reducing the
Goncourtian and Zolaesque principle to the lowest
terms of the absurd.   But I am by no means sure that
it was so, though this suspicion of parody pursues the
earlier work of Huysmans to such an extent that a certain
class of critic might take his later developments as
evidence of design in it.   *Les Sœurs Vatard* is a sort of
apodiabolosis of the Goncourts and Zola—a history of
entirely uninteresting persons (the " sisters " are work-
girls in a printing-house, and their companions suit
them) doing entirely uninteresting things, in an atmosphere of foul smells, on a scene littered with garbage,
cheered by wine which is red ink, and brandy which is

---

[1] One never knows what is necessary or not in the way of explanation.   But perhaps
it is wiser to say that I am quite aware that, besides writing *votre*, not " notre,"
Baudelaire had originally written " ce long hurlement " before the immense improvement in the text, and that the original " Light-houses " were painters.

vitriol. *À Rebours*, not really a novel at all, is the history of a certain M. Des Esseintes, who is a sort of transposed "Bouvard et Pécuchet" in one—trying all arts and sensations ; his experiences being made by his historian a vehicle of mostly virulent and almost always worthless criticism on contemporaries. Perhaps the most intolerable thing is the *affiche* of idolatry for Baudelaire. One remembers the glorious lines :

> Et Charles Baudelaire
> Dédaigneux du salaire.

He certainly might have been disdainful of the salary of the admiration of one of the *farceurs* of his own " Coucher du Soleil Romantique."   But on the whole there is a better way of taking leave of this first Naturalist, and then mystic, and always *blagueur*.   " Almost thou persuadest me to be a Philistine."   Which perhaps was his cryptic and circuitous intention.   Later M. Huysmans took to Black Arts ; and at the last he turned devout—a sort of sequence not by any means uncommon, and one of the innumerable illustrations of the irony of things. Gautier and others had anticipated and satirised all these stages in the Romantic dawn ; they reappeared, serious and dreary, in the twilight of the dusk.

Adolphe Belot was not, strictly speaking, a Naturalist, for he was a dozen years older than Zola, and ran up a huge list of novels ranging in character between Naturalism and melodrama.   His most famous book, *Mlle. Giraud ma Femme*, was the most popular of a large number of attempts, about the last third of the century, in the school of *La Religieuse*, but with more or less deliberately pornographic effect.   There is, however, some power in this book, and the " curtain "—the foiled husband, after Mlle. Giraud's death, seeing his she-rival swimming, swims out after and drowns her—is quite refreshing.   But I have always liked M. Belot best for a thoughtful and delightful remark in *La Femme de Feu*. " Heureuse elle-même, elle trouva naturel de faire les autres heureux," which, translated into plain English,

Belot and others.

means that she was so happy with her husband that she couldn't help making her lover happy. M. Belot did not work out this modification of the Golden Rule—he was not a philosophic novelist. But it is very humorous in itself, and the extensions and applications of it are illimitable and vertiginous.[1]

Below him it is unnecessary to go.

[1] One slight alteration may seem almost to justify Belot's criticism of life : " Uncomfortable herself, she thought it natural to make others uncomfortable." There is certainly no want of psychological observation *there*.

CHAPTER XIV

THE remaining novelists of the Third Republic, apart
from the survivors of the Second Empire and the Natural-
The last ist School, need not occupy us very long,
stage. but must have some space. There would be
no difficulty on my part in writing a volume on them,
for during half the time I had to produce an article on
new French books, including novels, every month,[1] and
during no small part of the rest, I did similar work on a
smaller and less regular scale, reading also a great deal
for my own purposes. But acknowledging, as I have
elsewhere done, the difficulty of equating judgment of
contemporary and non-contemporary work exactly, I
think I shall hardly be doing the new writers of this time
injustice if I say that no one, except some excluded by
our specifications as living, could put in any pretensions to be rated on level with the greater novelists
from Lesage to Maupassant. There are those, of course,
who would protest in favour of M. Ferdinand Fabre,
and yet others would " throw for " M. André Theuriet,
both of whom shall have due honour. I cannot wholly
agree with them. But both of them, as well as, for very
opposite reasons, MM. Ohnet and Rod, may at least
require notice of some length.

---

[1] It was in connection with this, at some time in the 'eighties, that I came across a
curious survival of the old prejudice against novels—deserving perhaps, with better claim
than as a mere personal anecdote, record in this history. One French publisher, who
held himself above the " three-fifty," and produced dainty books of art and letters, once
sent a pathetic remonstrance against his wares being reviewed " sometimes unkindly,
and always with the novels."

L'Abbé Tigrane, by Ferdinand Fabre, may be described
as one of not the least remarkable, and as certainly one

Ferdinand
Fabre:
L'Abbé
Tigrane.

of the most remarked, novels of the later nineteenth century.   It never, I think, had a very
large sale; for though at the time of its author's
death, over thirty years and more after its appearance, it had reached its sixteenth thousand, that is not
much for a *popular* French novel.   Books of such different
appeal as Zola's and Feuillet's (not to mention for the
present a capital example to be noted below) boasted ten
times the number.   But it dared an extremely non-popular
subject, and treated that subject with an audacious disregard of anything like claptrap.   There is no love in it
and hardly a woman; there is no—at least no military—
fighting;   no adventure of any ordinary sort.   It is
neither a *berquinade,* nor a crime-story, nor (except in
a very peculiar way) a novel of analysis.   It relies on no
preciousness of style, and has not very much description,
though its author was a great hand at this when and
where he chose.   It is simply the history of an ambitious,
strong-willed, strong-minded, and violent-tempered priest
in an out-of-the-way diocese, who strives for and attains
the episcopate, and after it the archiepiscopate, and is
left aspiring to the Papacy—which, considering the
characters of the actual successors of Pius IX., the Abbé
Capdepont[1] cannot have reached, in the fifty years (or
nearly so) since the book was published.

Now, in the first place, it is generations since a
clerical novel was likely to please the French novel-
reading public.   In this very book there is an amusing
scene where the *abbé,* then a private tutor, induces his
employer, a deputy, to invite clerics of distinction to
a party, whereat the other guests melt away in disgust.
And this was a long time before a certain French minister
boasted that his countrymen " had taken God out of
Heaven."   Moreover, while there are two obvious ways
of reconciling extremists to the subject, M. Fabre rejected

---

[1] " Tigrane " is a nickname, early accounted for and perhaps suggesting its own
explanation.

both. His book is neither a panegyric on clericalism
nor a libel on it. His hero is as far as possible from
being a saint, but he is perfectly free from all the vulgar
vices. The rest of the characters—all, with insignificant
exceptions, clerics—are quite human, and in no case—
not even in that of Capdepont's not too scrupulous
aide-de-camp the Abbé Mical—offensive. But at the
beginning the bishop, between whom and the hero there
is truceless war, is, though privately an amiable and
charitable gentleman (Capdepont is a Pyrenean peasant
by origin), rather undignified, and even a little tyrannical ;
while a cardinal towards the end makes a distinction—
between the impossibility of the Church lying and the
positive duty of Churchmen, in certain circumstances,
to lie—which would have been a godsend to Kingsley
in that unequal conflict of his with a colleague of his
Eminence's.[1]

Yet critics of almost all shades agreed, I think, in
recognising the merits of M. Fabre's book ; and it
established him in a special position among French
novelists, which he sustained not unworthily with nearly
a score of novels in a score and a half of years. It is
undoubtedly a book of no small power, which is by no
means confined to the petty matters of chapter-and-
seminary wrangling and intrigue. On the contrary, the
scene where, owing to Capdepont's spite, the bishop's
coffin is kept, in a frightful storm, waiting for admission
to its inmate's own cathedral, is a very fine thing indeed—
almost, if not quite, in the grand style—according to
some, if not according to Mr. Arnold. The figure of
the arch-priest Clamousse, both in connection with this
scene[2] and others—old, timid, self-indulgent, but not
an absolutely bad fellow—is of first-rate subordinate

---

[1] At the extreme end there is an interesting reminder of that curious moment when it
was thought on the cards that Pius IX. might accept an English asylum at Malta, and
that, as a part-consequence, not of course Newman but Manning might be his successor.
The probable results of this, to " those who knew " at the time, are still matter of interesting, if unpractical, speculation.

[2] He is playing whist comfortably with the cathedral keys in his pocket, and has
nearly made a slam (Fr. *chelem*), while the pelting of the pitiless storm is on the dead
bishop's bier and its faithful guardians.

quality. Whether Capdepont himself has not a little too much of that synthetic character which I have discussed elsewhere—whether he is quite a real man, and not something of a composition of the bad qualities of the peasant type, the intriguing ecclesiastic type, the ambitious man, the angry man, and so on—must, I suppose, be left to individual tastes and judgments. If I am not so enthusiastic about the book as some have been, it is perhaps because it seems to me rather a study than a story.[1]

This criticism—it is not intended for a reproach—does not extend to other, perhaps not so powerful, but _Norine, etc._ more _pastimeous_ books, though M. Fabre seldom entirely excluded the clerical atmosphere of his youth.[2] A very pleasant volume-full is _Norine_, the title-piece of which is full at once of Cevenol scenery and Parisian contrast, of love, and, at least, preparations for feasting; of sketches of that " Institute " life which comes nearest to our collegiate one ; and of pleasant bird-worship. But M. Fabre should have told us whether the bishop actually received and appreciated [3] the dinner of Truscas trout and Faugères wine (alas ! this is a blank in my fairly extensive wine-list), and the miscellaneous _maigre_ cookery of the excellent Prudence, and the splendid casket of _liqueurs_ borrowed from a brother _curé_. _Cathinelle_ (an unusual and pretty diminutive of Catherine) is an admirably told pendant to it ; and I venture to think the " idyllic " quality of both at least equal, if not superior, to the best of George Sand. _Le R. P. Colomban_ is, according to M. Fabre's habit, a sort of double-edged affair—a severe but just

---

[1] There is something Browningesque about it, a something by no means confined to the use of the history—actually referred to in the text, but likely to be anticipated long before by readers—of Popes Formosus and Stephen. That it did not satisfy Ultramontanes is not surprising ; _v. inf._ on one of the smaller pieces in _Norine_.

[2] He had actually been intended for the Church.

[3] One thing, for the credit of the Gallican Church, we may trust that he did _not_ do. An Anglican prelate, like this his brother on a Confirmation tour, is alleged to have pointed to a decanter on his host's sideboard and said, " I hope, on my next visit, I shall not see _that_." I do not know what the rector answered : I do know what _I_ should have said, despite my reverence for the episcopate : " My Lord, you will not have the opportunity."

rebuke of the " popular preacher," and a good-humoured
touch at the rebuker, Monseigneur Ônésime de la
Boissière, Evêque de Saint-Pons, who incidentally proposes to submit *L'Abbé Tigrane* to the Holy Congregation
of the Index.   Finally, the book closes with a delightful
panegyric of Alexandre Dumas *père*, and an anecdote
avowedly autobiographic (as, indeed, the whole book
gives itself out to be, though receivable with divers pinches
of salt) of that best-natured of men franking a bevy
of impecunious students at a *première* of one of his
plays.

   To read *Le Marquis de Pierrerue* after these two
books—one the piece with which Fabre established his
Le Marquis reputation, and the other a product of his
de Pierrerue. proved mastery—is interesting to the critic.
Whether it would be so to the general reader may
be more doubtful.   It is the longest of its author's
novels ; in fact its two volumes have separate sub-titles ;[1]
but there is no real break, either of time, place, or action,
between them.   It is a queer book, quite evidently of
the novitiate, and suggesting now Paul de Kock (the
properer but not *quite* proper Paul), now Daudet (to
whom it is actually dedicated), now Feuillet, now Murger,
now Sandeau, now one of the melodramatic story-tellers.
Very possibly all these had a share in its inspiration.
It is redolent of the medical studies which the author
actually pursued, between his abandonment of preparation
for the Church and his settling down as a man of letters.
Its art is palpably imperfect—blocks of *récit*, wedges of
not very novel or acute reflection, a continual reluctance
or inability to " get forrard."   Of the two heroes, Claude
Abrial, Marquis de Pierrerue—a fervent Royalist and
Catholic, who lavishes his own money, and everybody
else's that he can get hold of, on a sort of private Literary
Fund,[2] allows himself to be swindled by a scoundrelly
man of business, immures his daughter, against her
wish, as a Carmelite nun, and dies a pauper—is a quite

[1] *La Rue du Puits qui Parle* and *Le Carmel de Vaugirard.*
[2] The *Société des Secours Intellectuels.*

possible but not quite " brought off " figure. Théven
Falgouët, the Breton *buveur d'eau*,[1] who is introduced
to us at actual point of starvation, and who dies, self-
transfixed on the sharp spikes of the Carmelite *grille*,
is perhaps not *im*possible, and occasionally pathetic.
But the author seems, in his immaturity as a craftsman,
never to have made up his mind whether he is producing
an "alienist" study, or giving us a fairly ordinary *étudiant*
and aspirant in letters.   Of the two heroines, the noble
damsel Claire de Pierrerue—object of Falgouët's love
at first sight, a love ill-fated and more insane than even
love beseems—is quite nice in her way ; and Rose
Keller—last of grisettes, but a grisette of the Upper House,
an artist grisette, and, as some one calls her, the " sœur
de charité de la galanterie "[2]—is quite nice in hers.
But Rose's action—in burning, to the extent of several
hundred thousand francs' worth, notes and bonds,
the wicked gains of one of her lovers (Grippon, the
Marquis's fraudulent intendant), and promptly expiring
—may pair off with Falgouët's repeating on himself the
Spanish torture-death of the *guanches*,[3] as pure melodrama.   In fact the whole thing is undigested, and
shows, in a high degree, that initial difficulty in getting
on with the story which has not quite disappeared in
L'Abbé Tigrane, but which has been completely conquered [4] in *Norine* and *Cathinelle*.

This mixed quality makes itself felt in others of
Fabre's books.   Perhaps there is none of them, except
Mon Oncle *L'Abbé Tigrane* itself, which has been a greater
Célestin. favourite with his partisans than *Mon Oncle
Célestin.*   Here we have something of the same easy
autobiographic quality, with the same general scene and
the same relations of the narrator and the principal
characters, as in other books ; but " Mr. the nephew "

---

[1] See on Murger.
[2] Whenever she hears that any of her numerous lovers has fallen ill, she promptly
" plants there " the man in possession, and tends and, as far as she can, supports the
afflicted.
[3] *Vide* the frontispiece of Settle's *Empress of Morocco.*
[4] It would be curmudgeonly to say, " evaded by shortness of space."

(the agreeable and continuous title by which the faithful
parishioners address their beloved pastor's boy relative)
has a different uncle and a different *gouvernante*, at least
in name, from those in *Norine* and *Cathinelle*. The
Abbé Célestin, threatened with consumption, exchanges
the living in which he has worked for many years, and
little good comes of it. He is persecuted, actually to
the death, by his rural dean, a sort of duplicate of the
hero of *L'Abbé Tigrane*; but the circumstances are not
purely ecclesiastical. He has, in his new parish, taken
for goat-girl a certain Marie Galtier, daughter of his
beadle, but, unluckily, also step-daughter of a most
abominable step-mother. Marie, as innocently as
possible, " gets into trouble," and dies of it, accusations
being brought against her guiltless and guileless master
in consequence. There are many good passages ; the
opening is (as nearly always with M. Fabre) excellent ;
but both the parts and the whole are, once more, too long
—the mere " flitting " from one parish to another seems
never to be coming to an end. Still, the book should be
read ; and it has one very curious class of personages,
the " hermits " of the Cevennes—probably the latest
(the date is 1846) of their kind in literature. The general
characteristics of that kind do not seem to have been
exactly saintly ;[1] and the best of them, Adon Laborie,
after being " good " throughout, and always intending
to be so, brings about the catastrophe by calmly sup-
pressing, in the notion that he will save the Abbé trouble,
three successive citations from the Diocesan Council,
thereby getting him " interdicted." The shock, when
the judgment in contumacy is announced by the brutal
dean, proves fatal.

In *Lucifer* M. Fabre is still nearer, though with no
repetition, to the *Tigrane* motive. The book justifies
Lucifer. its title by being the most ambitious of all the
novels, and justifies the ambition itself by
showing a great deal of power—most perhaps again, of

---

[1] They are, however, orthodox after a fashion ; and I do not think that M. Fabre,
in the books that I have read, ever introduces descendants of the Camisards, though
dealing with their country.

all; though whether that power is used to the satisfaction
of the reader must depend, even more than is usual, on
individual tastes. Bernard Jourfier, at the beginning
of the book and of the Second Empire, is a young *vicaire*,
known to be of great talents and, in especial, of unusual
preaching faculty, but of a violent temper, ill at ease
about his own vocation, and suspected—at least by
Ultramontanes—of very doubtful orthodoxy and not
at all doubtful Gallicanism. He is, moreover, the
grandson of a *conventionnel* who voted for the King's
death, and the son of a deputy of extreme Liberal views.
So the Jesuits, after trying to catch him for themselves,
make a dead set at him, and secure his appointment to
out-of-the-way country parishes only, and even in these
his constant removal, so that he may acquire as little
influence as possible anywhere. At last, in a very striking
interview with his bishop, he succeeds in clearing his
character, and enters on the way of promotion. The
cabals continue; but later, on the overthrow of Bona-
partism, he is actually raised to the episcopate. His
violent temper, however, is always giving handles to
the enemy, and he finally determines that life is intolerable.
After trying to starve himself, he makes use of the
picturesque but dangerous situation of his palace, and
is crushed by falling, in apparent accident, through a
breach in the garden wall with a precipice beneath
—"falling like Lucifer," as his lifelong enemy and rival
whispers to a confederate at the end. For the appellation
has been an Ultramontane nickname for him long before,
and has been not altogether undeserved by his pride
at least. It has been said that the book is powerful;
but it is almost unrelievedly gloomy throughout, and
suffers from the extremely narrow range of its interest.

Those who are not tired of the Cevenol atmosphere—
which, it must be admitted, is quite a refreshing one—
Sylviane and will find a lighter example in *Sylviane*, once
Taillevent. more recounted by "Mr. the nephew," but
with his movable uncle and *gouvernante* shifted back
to "M. Fulcran" and "Prudence"; and in *Taillevent*,

a much longer book, which is independent of uncle and nephew both. *Sylviane* has agreeable things in it, but perhaps might have been better if its form had been different. It is a long *récit* told by a gamekeeper, with frequent interruptions[1] and a very thin "frame." *Taillevent* ends with two murders, the second a quite excusable lynch-punishment for the first, and the marriage of the avenger just afterwards to the daughter of the original victim, a combination of "the murders *and* the marriages" deserving Osric's encomia on sword furniture. So vigorous a conclusion had need have a well-stuffed course of narrative to lead up to it, and this is not wanting. There is a wicked—a *very* wicked— Spaniard for the lynched-murderer part; an exceedingly good dog-, bear-, and man-fight in the middle; an extensive and well-utilised wolf-trap in the woods; bankruptcies; floods; all sorts of things; with a course of "idyllic" true love running through the whole. There *is* a *curé*—a rather foolish one; but the ecclesiastical interest in itself is almost absent from the book. The weakest part of it lies in the characters of what may be called the hero and heroine of the beginning and middle —Frédéric Servières and Madeleine his wife. That the former should fall into the most frantic love before marriage, and almost neglect his wife as soon as she has borne him a child, may be said to be common enough in books, and, unluckily, by no means uncommon in life. But there may be more question about the repetition of the inconsistency in other parts of the character— extreme business aptitude and fatal neglect of business, extreme energy and fatal depression over quite small things, etc. The general combination is not impossible; it is not even improbable; but it is not quite "made so." And something is the same with Madeleine, who is, moreover, left "in the air" in so curious a fashion that one begins to wonder whether the Mrs. Martha Buskbody attitude, so often jibed at, does not possess some excuse.

---

[1] M. Fabre is so fond of these interrupted *récits* that one is sometimes reminded of *Jacques le Fataliste* and its landlady. But, to do him justice, he "does it more natural."

A pleasant contrast in this respect, though the end here is tragic in a way, may be found in *Toussaint Galabru*, *Toussaint* the last, perhaps, of M. Fabre's books for *Galabru.* which we can find special room here, though no doubt some favourites of particular readers may have been omitted. The novel is divided into two pretty equal halves, with an interval first of ten years between them and, almost immediately, of sixteen more. The first half is occupied by an adventure of " Mr. the nephew's," though he is not here " Mr. the nephew," but " Mr. the son," living with his father and mother at Bédarieux, M. Fabre's actual birthplace. He plays truant from Church on Advent Sunday to join a shooting expedition with his school-fellow Baptistin and that school-fellow's not too pious father, who is actually a church *suisse*, but has received an exeat from the *curé* to catch a famous hare for that *curé* to eat. The vicissitudes of the chase are numerous, and the whole is narrated with extraordinary skill as from the boy's point of view, his entire innocence, when he is brought into contact with very shady incidents, being—and this is a most difficult thing to do—hit off marvellously well. It is only towards the end of this part (he has been heard of before) that Toussaint Galabru, sorcerer and Lothario, makes his appearance—as clever as he is handsome, and as vicious as he is clever. When he does appear he has his way—with the game shot by others, and with a certain *métayer's* wife—after the same hand-gallop fashion in which the personage in Blake's lines enjoyed both the peach and the lady.

The earlier and shorter, but not short, interval, mentioned above, passes to 1852, and does little more than bring the now " Parisian " narrator into fresh contact with his old school-fellow Baptistin, now a full-grown priest, but, though very pious, in some difficulties from his persistent love of sport. Sixteen years later, again, in 1868, reappears, " coming to his death," [1] Galabru

---

[1] " Come to thy death,
Victor *Galbraith*."—Longfellow.

himself. The part is chiefly occupied by a *récit* of intervening history (including a sadly unsuccessful attempt,
both at spiritual and physical combat, by Baptistin) and
by a much-interrupted journey in snow.[1]   But it gives
occasion for another agreeable "idyll" between Vincinet,
Galabru's son, and the Abbé Baptistin's god-child Lalie ;
and it ends with a striking procession to carry, hardly in
time, the *viaticum* to the dying wizard, whereby, if not
his own weal in the other world, that of the lovers in this
is happily brought about.

Not very many generalities are required on M.
Ferdinand Fabre. How completely his way lies out of
most of the ruts in which the wain of the French novel
usually travels must have been shown ; and it may be
hoped that enough has been said also to show that there
are plenty of minor originalities about him.   No novelist[2]
in any language known to me (unless you call Richard
Jefferies a novelist) has such an extraordinary command
of "the country"—bird-nature and rock scenery being
his favourite but by no means his only subjects.   For
"Scenes of Clerical Life" he stands admittedly alone
in France, and has naturally been dealt with most often
from this point of view.   Of that intense provincialism,
in the good sense, which is characteristic of French
literature, there have been few better representatives.
Wordsworth himself is scarcely more the poet of our
Lake and Hill country than Fabre is the novelist of the
Cevennes. Peasant life and child life of the country
(he meddles little, and not so happily, with towns of any
size) find in him admirably "vatical" properties and
combinations ; and if he does not run any risk of Feste's
rebuke by talking much of "ladies," he knows as much
about women as a man well may.   His comedy is never
coarse or trivial, and the tragedy never goes off through
the touch-hole.   Of one situation—very easy to spoil by
rendering it mawkish—the early but not "calf"-love
of rustic man and maid, beginning in childhood, he was

[1] See note above on M. Fabre's weakness for this style of narrative.
[2] The next to be mentioned runs him hard perhaps.

curiously master. George Sand herself[1] has nothing to
beat (if she has anything to equal) the pairs of Taillevent
and Riquette (in the novel named from the lover), and of
Vincinet and Lalie (in *Toussaint Galabru*). As for his
pictures of clerical cabals and clerical weaknesses, they
may be too much of a good thing for some tastes ; but
that they are a good thing, both as an exercise in craftsmanship and as an alternative to the common run of
French novel subjects, can hardly be denied. In this
respect, and not in this respect only, M. Fabre has his
own place, and that no low one.

In coming to M. André Theuriet I felt a mixture of
curiosity with a slight uneasiness. For I had read

André
Theuriet.
not a few of his books[2] carefully and critically
at their first appearance, and in such cases—
when novels are not of the *very* first order (which, good
as these are, I think few really critical readers would allot
them) nor possessed of those " oddments " of appeal
which sometimes make more or less inferior books readable and readable again—fresh acquaintance, after a
long time, is dangerous. It has been said here (possibly
more than once) that, when a book possesses this peculiar
readableness, a second reading is positively beneficial
to it, because you neglect the " knots in the reed " and
slip along it easily. This is not quite the case with others :
and, unless great critical care is taken, a new acquaintance,
itself thirty years old, has, I fear, a better chance than an
old one renewed after that time. However, the knight
of Criticism, as of other ladies,[3] must dare any adventure,
and ought to be able to bring the proper arms and methods
to the task. For the purposes of renewal I chose *Sauvageonne*, *Le Fils Maugars*, and *Raymonde*. With the first,
though I did not remember much more than its central
situation and its catastrophe, with one striking incident, I
do remember being originally pleased ; the second has,

---

[1] Her girls are perhaps as good, but scarcely her men.
[2] This had *not* been the case—to an extent which I am puzzled to account for—with
those of M. Fabre.
[3] *Deformem vocant quidam*, as in other cases also : but that is because she has eyes
and they have none.

I believe, at least sometimes, been thought Theuriet's masterpiece; and the third (which, by the way, is a "philippine" containing another story besides the title-one) is an early book which I had not previously read.

The argument of *Sauvageonne* can be put very shortly. A young man of four-and-twenty, of no fortune, marries *Sauvageonne.* a rich widow ten years older than himself, and, as it happens, possessed of an adopted daughter of seventeen. He—who is by no means an intentional scoundrel, but a commonplace and selfish person, and a gentleman neither by birth nor by nature— soon wearies of his somewhat effusive and exacting wife; the girl takes a violent fancy to him; accident hurries on the natural if not laudable consequences; the wife covers the shame by succeeding in passing off their result as her own child, but the strain is too much for her, and she goes mad, but does not die.

This tragic theme (really a tragic ἁμαρτία, for there is much good in Sauvageonne, as she is called, from her tomboy habits, and, with happier chance and a nobler lover, all might have been well with her) is handled with no little power, and with abundant display of skill in two different departments which M. Theuriet made particu-larly his own—sketches of the society of small country towns, and elaborate description of the country itself, especially wood-scenery. In regard to the former, it must be admitted that, though there is plenty of scandal and not a little ill-nature in English society of the same kind, the latter nuisance seems, according to French novelists, to be more *active* with their country folk than it is with ours[1]—a thing, in a way, convenient for fiction. Of the descriptive part the only unfavourable criticism (and that a rather ungracious one) that could be made is that it is almost too elaborate. Of two fateful scenes of *Sauvageonne*, that where Francis Pommeret, the un-

---

[1] For instance, in Highbury or Cranford there might be scandal about a young bachelor's very late visits to a pretty widow. But the adult portion of the population, at any rate, would hardly lay booby-traps to trip him into a river on his return.

heroic hero, comes across Denise (the girl's proper
name) sitting in a crab-tree in the forest and pelting small
boys with the fruit, is almost startlingly vivid. You see
every detail of it as if it were on the Academy walls. In
fact, it is almost more like a picture than like reality,
which is more shaded off and less sharp in outline and
vivid in colour. As for the character-drawing, if it
does not attain to that consummateness which has been
elsewhere described and desiderated—the production
of people that you *know*—it attains the second rank ;
the three prominent characters (the rest are merely sets-
off) are all people that you *might* know. Denise herself
is very near the first rank, and Francis Pommeret—not,
as has been said, by any means a scoundrel, for he only
succumbs to strong and continued temptation, but an
ordinary selfish creature—is nearer than those who
wish to think nobly of human nature may like, to complete
reality. One is less certain about the unhappy Adrienne
Lebreton or Pommeret, but discussion of her would be
rather " an intricate impeach." And one may have a
question about the end. We are told that Francis and
Denise keep together (the luckless wife living on in spite
of her madness) because of the child, though they
absolutely hate each other. Would it not be more
natural that, if they do not part, they should vary the
hatred with spasms of passion and repulsion ?

Le Fils Maugars is not only a longer book, but its
space is less exclusively filled with a single situation,

Le Fils Maugars. and the necessary prelude to it. In fact,
the whole thing is expanded, varied, and
peopled. Auberive, near Langres, the place of *Sauvageonne*, is hardly more than a large village ; Saint-Clémen-
tin, on the Charente, though not a large town, is the seat
of a judicial Presidency, of a *sous-préfecture*, etc. " Le *père*
Maugars " is a banker who, from having been a working
stone-mason, has enriched himself by sharp practice in
money-lending. His son is a lawyer by the profession
chosen for him, and a painter by preference. The heroine,
Thérèse Desroches, is the daughter of a Republican

doctor, whose wife has been unfaithful, and who suspects Thérèse of not being his own child. The scene shifts from Saint - Clémentin itself to the country districts where Poitou and Touraine meet, as well as to Paris. The time begins on the eve of the Coup d'État, and allows itself a gap of five years between the first and second halves of the book. Besides the love-scenes and the country descriptions and the country feasts there is a little general society; much business; some politics, including the attempted and at last accomplished arrest of the doctor for treason to the new *régime*; a well-told account of a contest for the Prix de Rome; a trial of the elder Maugars for conspiracy (with a subordinate usurer) to defraud, etc. The whole begins with more than a little aversion on everybody's part for the innocent Étienne Maugars, who, having been away from home for years, knows neither the fact nor the cause of his father's unpopularity; and it ends with condign poetical justice, on the extortioner in the form of punishment, and for the lovers in another way. It is thus, though a less poignant book than *Sauvageonne*, a fuller and wider one, and it displays, better than that book, the competence and adequacy which mark the author, though there may be something else to be said about it (or rather about its illustration of his general characteristics) presently.

Le Don Juan de Vireloup, a story of about a hundred pages long, which acts as makeweight to *Raymonde*, itself only about twice the length, is a capital example

Le Don Juan de Vireloup and Raymonde.

of Theuriet at nearly his best—a pleasant mixture of *berquinade* and *gaillardise* (there are at least two passages at either of which Mrs. Grundy would require *sal volatile*, and would then put the book in the fire). The reformation and salvation of Jean de Santenoge—a poor (indeed penniless) gentleman, who lives in a little old manor, or rather farm-house, buried in the woods, and whose sole occupations are poaching and making love to peasant girls—are most agreeably conducted by the agency of the daughter of a curmudgeonly forest-inspector (who naturally regards Santenoge with special abhorrence). She is helped by her grand-uncle, a doctor of the familiar stamp, who has known Diderot's child, Madame de Vandeul (the scene, as in so many of the author's books, is close to Langres), and worships Denis himself. As for *Raymonde*, its heroine comes closer to " Sauvageonne," though she is less of a savagess : and the worst that can be said against her lucky winner is that he is a little of a prig. But, to borrow, and very slightly alter, one of Sir Walter's pieces of divine charity, " The man is mortal, and a scientific person." Perhaps fate and M. Theuriet are a little too harsh to another (but not this time beggarly) *gentillâtre*, Osmin de Préfontaine, to whom, one regrets to say, Raymonde positively, or almost positively, engages herself, before she in the same way virtually accepts the physiological Antoine Verdier. And the *dénouement*, where everything comes right, is a little stagy.[1] But the whole is thoroughly readable, competently charactered, and illustrated by some of the best of the author's forest descriptions.

One has thus been able to give an account, very favourable in the main, of these three or four stories—selected General character-istics. with no hidden design, and in two cases previously unknown to the critic, who has, in addition, a fair remembrance of several others. But it will be observed that there is in them, with all their merits, some evidence of that " rut " or " mould " character which has been specified as absent in greater novelists, but as often found in company with a certain accomplishment, in *ordonnance* and readable quality, that marks the later novel. The very great prominence of description is common to all of them, and in three out of the four the scenes are from the same district—almost from the same patch—of country. The heroine is the

---

[1] An old schoolmaster, whom Raymonde has deeply offended by upsetting his just-gathered mushrooms at the beginning of the book, and who is warmly attached to Antoine, turns out to be the girl's legal father—her mother, a disagreeable, handsome person, having been run away with twenty years earlier by another character who has passed hitherto as respectable husband and paterfamilias.

most prominent character and, as she should be, the most attractive figure of all ; but she is made up and presented, if not exactly *à la douzaine*, yet with a strong, almost a sisterly, family likeness. Far be it from the present writer to regret or desiderate the adorably candid creature who so soon smirches her whiteness. Even the luckless Sauvageonne—worst mannered, worst moralled, and worst fated of all—is a jewel and a cynosure compared with that other class of girl ; while Raymonde (whose maltreatment of M. de Préfontaine is to a great extent excused by her mother's bullying, her real father's weakness, and her own impulsive temperament) ; the Thérèse of *Le Fils Maugars* ; and the Marianne of *Le Don Juan de Vireloup* are, in ascending degrees, girls of quite a right kind. Only, it is just a little too much the *same* kind. And without unfairness, without even ingratitude, one may say that this sameness does somewhat characterise M. Theuriet.

There were some who did not share the general admiration, a good many years ago, of the dictum of a popular French critic on a more popular French novelist to the effect that, though it was his habit, in the articles he was writing, to confine himself to literature, he would break this good custom for once and discuss M. Ohnet. In the first place, this appeared to the dissidents a very easy kind of witticism ; they knew many men, many women, and many schoolboys who could have uttered it. In the second, they were probably of the opinion (changing the matter, instead of, like that wicked Prince Seithenyn, merely reversing the order, of the old Welsh saying) that " The goodness of wit sleeps in the badness of manners." But if the question had been then, or were now, asked seriously whether the literary value of *Le Maître de Forges* and its companion novels was high, few of them would, as probably have been or be able to answer in the affirmative. For my own part, I always used to think, when M. Ohnet's novels came out, that they were remarkably like those of the eminent Mrs. Henry Wood[1] in English—of course *mutatis mutandis*. They displayed very fair aptitude for the *business* of novel manufacture, and the results were such as, in almost every way, to satisfy the average subscriber to a circulating library, supposing him or her to possess respectable tastes (scarcely " taste "), moderate intelligence, and a desire to pass the time comfortably enough in reading them once, without the slightest expectation of being, or wish to be, able to read them again. They might even sometimes excite readers who possessed an adjustable " tally " of excitableness. But beyond this, as it seemed to their critic of those days, they never went.

Re-reading, therefore—though perhaps the consequence may not seem downright to laymen—promised some critical interest. I first selected for the purpose, to give the author as good a chance as possible, *Serge Panine*, which the Academy crowned, and which went near its hundred and fifty editions when it was still a four-year-old; and *Le Maître de Forges* itself, the most popular of all, adding *Le Docteur Rameau* and *La Grande Marnière*, which my memory gave me as having seemed to be of such pillars as the particular structure could boast.

I suppose the Forty crowned *Serge Panine* because it was a virtuous book, and an attack on the financial *Serge Panine.* trickeries which, about the time and a little later, enriched the French language with the word " krach." Otherwise, though no one could call it bad, its royalty could hardly seem much other than that which qualifies for the kingdom of the blind. The situations are good, and they are worked up into a Fifth Act, as we may call it (it occupies almost exactly a fifth of the book, which was, of

---

[1] Excepting some of the " Johnny Ludlow " stories, which were, I think, in their kind, better than anything M. Ohnet ever did to my knowledge—I may perhaps observe that the above notice was written, exactly as it stands, *before* M. Ohnet's death, but under the impression that the death had occurred. When it did, there were things in the obituaries which made me raise my eyebrows. That he was a " belated Romantic " had certainly never occurred to me; but I have no quarrel with the description of him, in another place, as a practitioner of the *roman bourgeois*.

course, dramatised), *melo*dramatic to the *n*th, ending
in a discovery of flagrant delict, or something very
like it, and in the shooting of a son-in-law by his mother-
in-law to save the downfall of his reputation. But the
characters do not play up to their parts, or each other,
very well, with the possible or passable exception of
the mother-in-law, and of one very minor personage, the
secretary Maréchal, whom M. Ohnet, perhaps distrustful
of his power to make him more, left minor. The hero
is a Polish prince, with everything that a stage Polish
prince requires about him — handsome, superficially
amiable, what the precise call "caressing" and the
vulgar "carneying" in manner, but extravagant, quite
non-moral, and not possessed of much common sense.
His princess Micheline is a silly jilt before marriage and
a sillier "door-mat" (as some women call others) of a
wife. Her rival, and in a fashion foster-sister (she has
been adopted before Micheline's birth), does things which
many people might do, but does not do them in a concatenation accordingly. The jilted serious young man
Pierre accepts a perfectly impossible position in reference
to his former *fiancée* and his supplanter, and gives more
proofs of its impossibility by his conduct and speech
than was at all necessary. The conversation is very
flat, and the descriptions are chiefly confined to long,
gaudy inventories of rich parvenus' houses, which read
like auctioneers' catalogues.

But the worst part of the book, and probably that
which at its appearance exasperated the critics, though
it did not disturb the *abonné*—or, more surprisingly,
the Immortals—is the flatness of style which has been
already noted in the conversation, but which overflows
insupportably into the narrative. M. Ohnet speaks
somewhere, justly enough, of "le style à la fois prétentieux et plat, familier aux reporters." But was he trying
—there is no sign of it—to parody these unfortunate
persons when he himself described dinner-rolls as "Ces
boules dorées qui sollicitent l'appétit le plus rebelle, et
accommodées dans une serviette damassée artistement

pliée, parent si élegamment un couvert " ? Or when
he tells us that at a ball " Les femmes, leurs splendides
toilettes gracieusement étalées sur les meubles bas et
moëlleux, causaient chiffons sous l'éventail, ou écoutaient
les cantilènes d'un chanteur exotique pendant que les
jeunes gens leur chuchotaient des galanteries à l'oreille."
This last is really worthy of the feeblest member of our
" *plated* silver fork school " between the time of Scott
and Miss Austen and that of Dickens and Thackeray.

In the year 1902, *Le Maître de Forges*, which was
then just twenty years old, had reached its three hundred
Le Maître and sixty-seventh edition. Six years later
de Forges. Fromentin's *Dominique*, which was then forty-
five years old, had reached its twenty-seventh. The
accident of the two books lying side by side on my table
has enabled me to make this comparison, the moral of
which will be sufficiently drawn by a reference to what
has been said of *Dominique* above,[1] and by the few remarks
on M. Ohnet's most popular book which follow.

One old receipt for popularity, " Put your characters
up several steps in society," M. Ohnet has faithfully
obeyed. We begin with a marquis unintentionally
poaching on the ironmaster's ground, and (rather oddly)
accepting game which he has *not* shot thereon. We end
with the marquis's sister putting her dainty fingers
before the mouth of a duke's exploding pistol—to the
not surprising damage of those digits, but with the result
of happiness ever afterwards for the respectable characters
of the book. There is a great deal of gambling, though,
unfortunately told in a rather uninteresting manner of
récit, which is a pity, for gambling can be made excellent
in fiction.[2] There are several of M. Ohnet's favourite

---

[1] *V. sup.* p. 277-280.

[2] The great scene in Mr. Disraeli's *Young Duke*, when that youthful nobleman loses,
what is it ? two hundred and seventeen thousand pounds, I think ; the brief but poignant
plucking of Mr. Dawkins ; the occasion in *Sans Merci* where the hero *will* not lead
trumps, and thereby, though not at once, seals his fate ; and a quite nice game at Marmora in Mr. E. F. Benson's *The Babe, B.A.* emerge from many memories, reinforced by
some of actual experience. Marmora *is* a nice game : with penny stakes, and three players
only, you may have five pounds in the pool before you know where you are. But I do
not know anything more really exciting than a game at which you guess how many
marbles the other fellow holds in his fist. The sequel, however, in which you have to
ask for an advance of pocket-money to settle your " differences ", is not so pleasant.

inventories, and a baroness—not a bad baroness—who has frequented sales, and knows all about *bric-à-brac*. Also there are several exciting situations, even before we come to the application of a lady's fingers as tompions. M. Ohnet is, it has been said, rather good at situations. But situations, to speak frankly, are rather things for the stage than for the story, except very rarely, and of a very striking—which does not mean melodramatic—kind. And it is very important, off the stage, that they should be led up to, and acted in by, vigorously drawn and well filled in characters.

To do M. Ohnet justice, he has attempted to meet this requirement in one instance at least, the one instance by which the book has to stand or fall. Some of the minor personages (like Maréchal in *Serge Panine*) are fair enough; and the little baroness who, arriving at a country-house in a whirl of travel and baggage, cries, "Où est mon mari? Est-ce que j'ai *déjà* égaré mon mari?" puts one, for the moment, in quite a good temper. The ironmaster's sister, too, is not a bad sort of girl. He himself is too much of the virtuous, loyal, amiable, but not weak man of the people; the marquis is rather null, and the duke, who jilts his cousin Claire de Beaulieu, gambles, marries a rich and detestable daughter of a chocolate-man, and finally fires through Claire's fingers, is very much, to use our old phrase, *à la douzaine*. But Claire might save the book, and probably does so for those who like it. To me she seems quite wrongly put together. The novel has been so very widely read, in the original and in translations, that it is perhaps unnecessary to waste space on a full analysis of its central scene—a thing not to be done very shortly. It may be sufficient to say that Claire, treacherously and spitefully informed, by her successful rival, of the fact that she has been jilted, and shortly afterwards confronted with the jilter himself, recovers, as it seems to her, to the company, and I suppose to the author, the whip-hand by summoning the ironmaster (who is hanging about "promiscuous," and is already known to be attached to

her, though she has given him no direct encouragement)
and bestowing her hand upon him, insisting, too, upon
being married at once, before the other pair. The act
is supposed to be that of an exceptionally calm, haughty,
and aristocratic damsel: and the acceptance of it is made
by a man certainly deep in love, but independent, sharp-
sighted, and strong-willed. To be sure, he could not
very well refuse; but this very fact should have weighed
additionally, with a girl of Claire's supposed temperament,
in deciding her not to make a special Leap Year for the
occasion. To hand yourself over to Dick because Tom
has declined to have anything to do with you is no doubt
not a very unusual proceeding: but it is not usually done
quite so much *coram populo*, or with such acknowledgment of its being done to spite Tom and Tom's preferred
one.[1]

Two more of "Les Batailles de la Vie" (as, for some
not too obvious[2] reason, it pleased M. Ohnet to *super-*
Le Docteur title his novels) may perhaps suffice to give
Rameau. a basis for a more general judgment of his
position. *Le Docteur Rameau* is, at least towards its
close, one of the most ambitious, if not *the* most ambitious
of all its author's books. The hero is one of those
atheistic and republican physicians who are apt rather to
embêter us by their frequency in French novels. He is
thrown into the also familiar situation of ascertaining,
after his wife's death, that she has been false, and that
his daughter, of whom he is very fond, is probably or
certainly not his own. At the end, however, things come
right as usual. Rameau is converted from hating his
daughter, which is well, and from being an atheist, which
is better. But, unluckily, M. Ohnet devotes several
pages, in his own peculiar style, to a rhetorical exhibition
of the logic of these conclusions. It seems to come to this.

---

[1] Another scene, which brings on the *dénouement* and in which Claire is again supposed to have the *beau rôle*, does not please me much better. Thinking that her husband
is flirting with the detested Duchess, she publicly orders her out of the house—a very
natural, but a rather "fish-faggy" proceeding.

[2] It has been, and will be, pointed out that he was in all ways studious to run before
the wind; and it was just at this time, if I remember rightly, that the catchword of "conflict" began to pester one in criticism. Perhaps this was the reason.

There is no God and no soul, because freewill is sufficient
to account for everything. But M. le Docteur Rameau
has willed, in the free-willingest manner, to hate his
daughter, and finds he cannot. Therefore there is a
God and a soul. A most satisfactory conclusion, but
a most singular major premiss. Why should there be
no God and no soul because there is (if there is) free-
will ?[1] But all is well that ends well: and how can you
end better than by being heard to ejaculate, " Mon
Dieu ! " (quite seriously and piously, and not in the
ordinary trivial way) by a scientific friend, at the church
of Sainte-Clotilde, during your daughter's wedding ?

La Grande Marnière does not aspire to such heights,
and is perhaps one of the best " machined " of M.
Ohnet's books. The main plot is not very
novel—his plots seldom are—and, in parts as
well as plots, any one who cared for rag-picking and hole-
picking might find a good deal of indebtedness. It is
the old jealousy of a clever and unscrupulous self-made
man towards an improvident *seigneur* and his somewhat
robustious son. The seigniorial improvidence, however,
is not of the usual kind, for M. le Marquis de Clairefont
wastes his substance, and gets into his enemy's debt and
power, by costly experiments on agricultural and other
machinery, partly due to the fact that he possesses on
his estate a huge marl-pit and hill which want developing.
There is the again usual cross-action of an at first hopeless
affection on the part of the *roturier's* son, Pascal Carvajan,
a rising lawyer, for Antoinette de Clairefont. But M.
Ohnet—still fertile in situations—adds a useful sort
of conspiracy among Carvajan's tools of various stations
against the house of Clairefont ; a conspiracy which
actually culminates in a murder-charge against Robert
de Clairefont, the victim being the pretty daughter of a
local poacher, one of the gang, with whom the Viscount
has notoriously and indeed quite openly flirted. Now

(margin note: La Grande Marnière.*)*

---

[1] The argument, or assumption rather, is all the odder because, on the one hand,
orthodoxy holds Free-will (if it accepts that) as a Divine endowment of the Soul : and, on
the other, serious Atheism is almost always Determinist. But the study of M. Ohnet
was probably not much among the Sentences.

comes Pascal's opportunity: he defends Robert, and
not merely obtains acquittal, but manages to discover
that the crime was actually committed by the village
idiot, who betrays himself by remorse and sleep-walking.
There is a patient, jilted lover, M. de Croix-Mesnil (it
may just be noted that since French novel-heroines were
allowed any choice at all in marriage, they have developed
a faculty of altering that choice which might be urged
by praisers of times past against the enfranchisement);
a comic aunt; and several other promoters of business.
It is no wonder that, given a public for the kind of book,
this particular example of it should have been popular.
It had reached its sixtieth edition before it had been
published a twelvemonth.

Sixty editions of one book in one year; three hundred
and sixty-seven of another in twenty; a hundred and
Reflections. forty-two of *Serge Panine* in five; sixty-nine of
Le Docteur Rameau in certainly at the outside
not more; these are facts which, whatever may be
insinuated about the number of an "edition," cannot
be simply put aside. Popularity, as the wiser critics
have always maintained, is no test of excellence; but
as they have also maintained when they were wise, it is
a "fact in the case," and it will not do merely to sneer
at it. I should say that the popularity of M. Ohnet,
like other popularities in England as well as in France,
is quite explicable. Novel-writing, once again, had
become a business, and he set himself to carry that
business out with a thorough comprehension of what
was wanted. His books, it is to be observed, are generally quite modern, dealing either with his own day or a
few years before it; and modernity has, for a long time,
been almost a *sine qua non* of what is to please the public.
They are, it has been said, full of situations, and the
situation is what pleases the public most in everything.
They came just when the first popularity of Naturalism
was exhausting itself,[1] and they are not grimy; but,

---

[1] The obituarist above mentioned, who thought M. Ohnet a belated Romantic,
thought also that he was "struggling against the rising tide of Realism." I do not think

on the other hand, they do not aim at an excessive propriety. Their characters are not of the best, or even of
the second-best class, as so often defined, but they are
sufficient to work out the situations without startling
inadequacy. The public never really cares, though part
of it is sometimes taught to pretend to care, for style,
and the same may be said of the finer kind of description.
The conversation is not brilliant, but, like the character,
it serves its turn. I once knew an excellent gentleman, of
old lineage and fair fortune, who used to say that for his
part he could not tell mutton from venison or Marsala
from Madeira, and he thanked God for it. The novel-
reading public,—that at least which reads novels by the
three hundred and fifty thousand,—is very much of the
same taste, and I am sure I hope it is equally pious.

I have quite a lively remembrance of the advent of
M. Édouard Rod, of the crowning of *Le Sens de la Vie*,
and so forth. That advent formed part of
the just mentioned counter-attack on Naturalism, in which, as usual, some of the Naturalist methods
and weapons themselves were used ; but it had a distinct
character of its own. Unless I mistake, it was not at
first very warmly welcomed by "mortal" French
criticism. There may have been something in this of
that curious grudge[1] against Swiss-French, on the part
of purely French-French, men of letters which never
seems to have entirely ceased. But there was something
more than this, though this something more was in a
way the reason, some might say the justification, of
the grudge. M. Rod was exceedingly serious; the title
of his laureated book is of itself almost sufficient to show
it; and though the exclusive notion of "the gay and
frivolous Frenchman" always was something of a
vulgar error, and has been increasingly so since the
Revolution, Swiss seriousness, with its strong Germanic
leaven, is not French seriousness at all. But he became,

Édouard Rod.

---

you would ever have found him struggling against rising tides, and, as a matter of fact,
the tide was already on the turn.

[1] Already mentioned in the case of M. Cherbuliez (*v. sup.* p. 447).

if not exactly a popular novelist to the tune of hundreds or even scores of editions, a prolific and fairly accepted one. I think, though he died in middle age and produced other things besides novels, he wrote some twenty or thirty stories, and his production ráther increased than slackened as he went on. With the later ones I am not so well acquainted as with the earlier, but there is a pervading character about these earlier ones which is not likely to have changed much, and they alone belong strictly to our subject.

Next to *Le Sens de la Vie* and perhaps in a way, as far as popularity goes, above it, may be ranked, I sup-*La Vie* pose, *La Vie Privée de Michel Teissier*, with *Privée de* its sequel, *La Seconde Vie de M. T.* These *Michel Teissier.* books certainly made a bold and wide separation of aim and subject from the subject and the aim of most French novels in these recent years. Here you have, instead of a man who attempts somebody else's wife, one who wishes to get rid—on at least legally respectable terms—of his own, and to marry a girl for whom he has, and who has for him, a passion which is, until legal matrimony enfranchises it, able to restrain itself from any practical satisfaction of the as yet illicit kind. He avails himself of the then pretty new facilities for divorce (the famous " Loi Naquet," which used to " deave " all of us who minded such things many years ago), and the situation is (at least intentionally) made more piquant by the fact that Teissier, who is a prominent statesman and gives up not merely his wife but his political position for this new love of his, starts as an actual supporter of the repeal of the divorce laws. To an English reader, of course, the precise problem would not have the same charm of novelty, except in his capacity as a reader of French novels. But, putting that aside, the position is obviously capable of being treated with very considerable appeal. The struggles of the husband, who *has* loved his wife—M. Rod had not the audacity or the strength to make him love her still—between his duties and his desires ; the indignant suffering of the wife; and most of all, the position of the girl who, by ill-fortune or the fault of others, finds herself expending, on an at first illicit and always ill-famed love, what she might have devoted to an honourable one, certainly has great capabilities. But I did not think when I read it first, and I do not think now when I have read it again, that these various opportunities are fully taken. It is not that M. Rod has no idea of passion. He is constantly handling it and, as will be seen presently, not without success occasionally. But he was too much what he calls his eidolon in one book, " Monsieur le psychologue," and the Psyche he deals with is too often a skinny and spectacled creature—not the love of Cupid and the mother of Voluptas.[1]

If he has ever made his story hot enough to make this pale cast glow, it is in *La Sacrifiée*. This is all

La Sacrifiée. the more remarkable in that the beginning of the book itself is far from promising. There is a rather unnecessary usher-chapter—a thing which M. Rod was fond of, and which, unless very cleverly done, is more of an obstacle than of a " shoe-horn." The hero-narrator of the main story is one of the obligatorily atheistic doctors—nearly as great a nuisance as obligatorily adulterous heroines—whom M. Rod has mostly discarded ; and what is more, he is one of the pseudo-scientific fanatics who believe in the irresponsibility of murderers, and do not see that, the more irresponsible a criminal is, the sooner he ought to be put out of the way. Moreover, he has the ill-manners to bore the

---

[1] The second part is occupied with two different but connected subjects. Suzanne, the first wife, dies suddenly, and the two daughters, the elder, Annie, quite, and the second, Laurence, nearly grown up—return to the custody of their Note on *La* father, and therefore to the society at least of his second wife, Blanche, *Seconde Vie* who, though of course feeling the awkwardness, welcomes them as well *de M. T.* as she can. The situation, though much *more* awkward, is something like that of Miss Yonge's *Young Stepmother* : but M. Rod makes it more tragic by Annie's death, partly in consequence of a love-marriage failing, through the lover's father's objection to the state of her family. The other subject is the gradual hankering of Michel after a return to political life, and his (consequentially inevitable) ratting from Right to Left. M. Rod brought into the matter direct reminiscences of the Parnell and Dilke cases, and possibly owed the conception of the whole book to them ; but he has, as is sometimes his wont, rather " sicklied it over " with political and other discussion.

company at dinner with this craze, and the indecency (for which in some countries he might have smarted) to condemn out loud, in a court of justice, the verdict of the jury and the sentence of the judge on his pet. Neither can one approve the haste with which he suggests to the wife of his oldest and most intimate friend that she is not happy with her husband. But this time M. Rod had got the forge working, and the bellows dead on the charcoal. The development of the situation has something of that twist or boomerang effect which we have noticed in *Michel Teissier*. Dr. Morgex begins by defending murderers; he does not end, but starts the end, by becoming a murderer himself, though one with far more "extenuating circumstances" than those so often allowed in French courts. His friend—who is an advocate of no mean powers but loose life and dangerously full habit—has, when the doctor warns him against apoplexy, half scoffed, but also begged him, if a seizure should take place, to afford him a chance of euthanasia instead of lingering misery. The actual situation, though with stages and variations which are well handled, arises; the doctor, who has long since been frantically in love with the wife, succumbs to the temptation—which has been aggravated by the old request, by the sufferings of the victim, and by the urgent supplications of the family, that he *shall* give morphia to relieve these sufferings. He gives it—but in a dose which he knows to be lethal.

After a time, and having gone through no little mental agony, he marries the widow, who is in every sense perfectly innocent; and a brief period of happiness follows. But his own remorse continues; the well-meaning chatter of a lady, who has done much to bring about the marriage, and to whom Morgex had unwarily mentioned "obstacles," awakes the wife's suspicion, and, literally, "the murder is out." Morgex confesses, first to a lawyer friend, who, to his intense surprise, pronounces him legally guilty, of course, but morally excusable; then to a priest, who takes almost exactly the opposite

point of view, and admitting that the legal crime may
be excusable, declares the moral guilt not lessened;
while he points out that while the wages of iniquity
are retained, no pardon can be deserved or expected.
And so the pair part. Morgex gives himself up to the
hardest and least profitable practitioner-work. Of what
the wife does we hear nothing. She has been perfectly
guiltless throughout; she has loved her second husband
without knowing his crime, and after knowing it; and so
she is " La Sacrifiée." But this (as some would call it)
sentimental appeal is not the real appeal of the book,
though it is delicately led up to from an early point.
The gist throughout is the tempering and purifying
of the character and disposition of Morgex himself,
through trial and love, through crime and sacrifice. It
is not perfectly done. If it were, it would land the author
at once in those upper regions of art which I cannot say
I think he attains. But it is a very remarkable " try,"
and, with one other to be mentioned presently, it is
nearest the goal of any of his books.

On the other hand, if he ever wrote a worse book
than *Le Silence*, I have not read, and I do not wish to

Le Silence. read, that. The title is singularly unhappy.
Silence is so much greater a thing than speech
that a speaker, unless he is Shakespeare or Dante or
Lucretius,[1] or at least the best kind of Wordsworth, had
better avoid the subject, avoid even the word for it.
And M. Rod's examples of silence, preluded in each
case (for the book has two parts) by one of those curious
harbingerings of his which are doubtfully satisfactory,
are not what they call nowadays " convincing." The
first and longest—it is, indeed, much too long and might
have been more acceptable in twenty pages than in two
hundred—deals with the usual triangle—brutal husband,

---

[1] A pleasant study, in poetic use of imagery and phrase, is the gradation from the
bare and grand Lucretian simplicity of *silentia noctis*, through the " favour and prettiness "
(slightly tautological though) of the Virgilian *tacitae per amica silentia lunae*, to the
recovery and intensifying of magnificence in *dove il sol tace*. By the way, *silentia* (for
the singular undergoes Quintilian's apology for the Latin -*um*) is one of the few instances
in which a Latin word beats the Greek. σιγή is really inferior.

suffering wife, interesting lover. But the last two never
declare themselves, or are declared; and they both die
and make no sign. In the second part there is another
triangle, where the illegitimate side is established and
results in a duel, the lover killing the husband and
establishing himself with the wife. But a stove for
tea-making explodes; she loses her beauty, and (apparently for that reason) poisons herself, though it does
not appear that her lover's love has been affected by the
change. In each case the situation comes under that
famous and often-quoted ban of helpless and unmanageable misery.

Nor can I think highly of *Là-Haut*, which is quite
literally an account of an Alpine village, and of its
Là-Haut. gradual vulgarisation by an enterprising man
of business. Of the ordinary novel-interests
there is little more than the introduction at the beginning of a gentleman who has triangled as usual, till,
the husband has, in his, the lover's, presence, most
inconsiderately shot his wife dead, has missed (which
was a pity) M. Julien Sterny himself, and, more unconscionably still, has been acquitted by a court of
justice, in which the officials, and the public in general,
actually seemed to think that M. Sterny was to blame!
He is much upset by this, and, coming to Vallanches to
recuperate, is rewarded later for his good deeds and sufferings,[1] by the hand of a very attractive young woman with
a fortune. This poetic justice, however, is by no means
the point of the book, which, indeed, has no particular
point. It is filled up by details of Swiss hotel-life: of
the wicked conduct of English tourists, who not merely
sing hymns on Sunday, but dance on wet evenings in
the week (nearly the oddest combination of crimes known
to the present writer); of a death in climbing of one of the
characters which is not in the least required by the
story; of the scalding of her arm by a *paysanne* in a sort of
" ragging " flirtation, and the operation on the mortifying

---

[1] What annoys him most of all is that he should have an uncomfortable feeling about
the woman " *comme* si je l'avais *aimée* ! " He had only, you see, done something else.

member by a curé who knows something of chirurgy ;
and of the ruin of some greedy peasants who turn their
châlet into a hotel with no capital to work it, and are
bought out, with just enough to cover their outlay and
leave them penniless, by the general *entrepreneur*. It
is a curious book, but the very reverse of a successful
one.

The centre, not by any means in the chronological
sense (for they were among his earliest), but in the
La Course à logical and psychological, of M. Rod's novel
la Mort. production, is undoubtedly to be found in the
two contrastedly titled books *Le Sens de la Vie* and
La Course à la Mort. The first, which, as has been
said, received Academic distinction, I approached
many years ago without any predisposition against it,
and closed with a distinct feeling of disappointment.
The other I read more recently with a distinct appre-
hension of disapproval, which was, if not entirely, to a
very large extent removed as I went on. It was strongly
attacked as morbid and mischievous at its first appearance
in 1885 ; and the author, some years afterwards, prefixed
a defence to his fifth edition, which is not much more
effective than such defences usually are. It takes something like the line which, as was mentioned above,
Mr. Traill took about Maupassant—that Pessimism was
a fact like other facts, and one was entitled to take it as
a subject or motive. But it also contained a slip into
that obvious but, somehow or other, seldom avoided trap
—the argument that a book is " dramatic," and does not
necessarily express the author's own attitude. Perhaps
not ; but the rejoinder that almost all, if not all, M.
Rod's books are " sicklied o'er " in this way is rather
fatal. One gets to expect, and seldom misses, a close
and dreary air throughout, often aggravated by an actual
final sentence or paragraph of lamentation and mourning
and woe. But I do not resent the " nervous impression "
left on me by *La Course à la Mort*, with its indefinitely
stated but certain end of suicide, and its unbroken soliloquy
of dreary dream. For it is in one key all through ; it

never falls out of tune or time ; and it does actually represent a true, an existent, though a partial and morbid
attitude of mind. It is also in parts very well written,
and the blending of life and dream is sometimes almost
Poesque. A novel, except by the extremest stretch of
courtesy, it is not, being simply a panorama of the moods
of its scarcely heroic hero. And he does not " set one's
back up " like René, or, in my case at least, produce
boredom like most of the other " World-pain "-ers. The
still more shadowy appearances of the heroine Cécile,
who dies before her lover, while the course of his love
is more dream than action, are well brought in and
attractive ; and there is one passage descriptive of waltzing which would atone for anything. Many people
have tried to write about waltzing, but few have done
it well ; this is almost adequate. I wonder if I dare
translate it ?

We never thought that people might be turning an evil eye on
us ; we cared nothing for the indignation of the mammas sitting
passive and motionless ; we hardly felt the couples that we jostled.[1]
Thanks to the cradling of the rhythm, to the intoxication of our
rapid and regular movement, there fell on us something like a
great calm. Drunk with one another, hurried by the absorbing
voluptuousness of the waltz, we went on and on vertiginously.
People and things turned with us, surrounding us with a gyre of
moving shadows, under a fantastic light formed of crossing reflections, in an atmosphere where one breathed inebriating perfumes,
and where every atom vibrated to the ever more bewildering sound
of music. Time passed, and we still went on; losing little by
little all consciousness except that of our own movement. Then
it even seemed that we came out of ourselves ; we heard nothing
but a single beat, marking the cadence with strokes more and more
muffled. The lights, melting into one, bathed us in a dreamy
glow ; we felt not the floor under our feet ; we felt nothing but
an immense oblivion—the oblivion of a void which was swallowing
us up.

---

[1] They should not have done this, and I do not think they did ; it was the couples
that jostled them. And even this ought not to have happened. The fastest waltzing
(I am speaking of the old *deux-temps*, which this must have been) conveyed an almost
uncanny extra power of vision, and at the same time of avoidance, to the right persons.
Indeed the first three lines of this extract have been objected to as base and inconsistent. I think not ; the common out of which you rise to the uncommon is worth
indication.

And doubtless it was so, as has been seen of many in the Time of Roses.[1]

To take one or two more of his books, *Le Ménage du Pasteur Naudié*, though less poignant than *La Sacrifiée* and with no approach to the extra-novelish merit of *La Course à la Mort*, starts not badly with an interesting scene, no less a place than La Rochelle, very rarely met, since its great days, in a French novel—a rather unfamiliar society, that of French Protestantism at Rochelle itself and Montauban—and a certainly unusual situation, the desire of a young, pretty, and wealthy girl, Jane Defos, to marry an elderly pastor who is poor, and, though a widower, has four children.

Le Ménage du Pasteur Naudié.

That nothing but mischief can come of this proceeding—as of an abnormal leap-year—is clear enough: whether the way in which the mischief is brought about and recounted is good may be more doubtful. That a person like M. Naudié, simple, though by no means a fool, should be taken in by a very pretty girl falling apparently in love with him—even though, to the general dangers of the situation, are added frank warnings that she has been given to a series of freakish fancies—is not unnatural; that she should soon tire of him, and sooner still of the four step-children, is very natural indeed. But the immediate cause of the final disruption—her taking a new fancy to, and being atheistically converted by, a cousin who, after all, runs away from temptation—is not very natural, and is unconvincingly told. Indeed the whole character of Jane is insufficiently presented. She is meant to be a sort of Blanche Amory, with nothing real in her—only a succession of false and fleeting fancies. But M. Rod was not Thackeray.

With two or three more of his later-middle books (it does not seem necessary to deal with the very latest,

---

[1] It may be added that the contrast of an earlier mazurka—in the slowness of which the pair had time to look at each other, feel each other, and otherwise remain in Paradise, but outside of the double Nirvana—is highly creditable. But I hope they *waltzed* to the mazurka. It is rather annoying to other people who are doing the orthodox step; but it is the perfection of the slow movement, which affords, as above, opportunities that do not exist in the faster and more delirious gyration.

which are actually beyond our limit, and could not alter the general estimate very favourably) the preparation of *Mademoiselle* judgment may cease. *Mademoiselle Annette* *Annette.* is the history of a "house-angel" and her family, and the fortunes and misfortunes they go through, and the little town of Bielle on the Lake of Geneva.[1] It is told, rather in M. Ferdinand Fabre's way, by a by-stander, from the time when the heroine was his school-dame and, as such dames sometimes, if not often, are, adored by her pupils. Annette dies at last, and M. Rod strews the dust of many others on her way to death. An American brother of the typical kind plays a large part. He is tamed partly by Annette, partly by a charming wife, whom M. Rod must needs kill, without any par-*L'Eau* ticular reason. *L'Eau Courante* is an even *Courante.* gloomier story. It begins with a fair picture of a home-coming of bride and bridegroom, on a beautiful evening, to an ideal farm high up on the shore of Leman. In a very few pages M. Rod, as usual, kills the wife after subjecting her to exceptional tortures at the births of her children, and then settles down comfortably to tell us the ruin of the husband, who ends by arson of his own lost home and drowning in his own lost pond. The interval is all blunder, misfortune, and folly—the chief *causa malorum* being a senseless interference with the "servitude" rights of neighbours, whom he does not like, by stopping, for a week, a spring on his own land. Almost the only cheerful character in the book (except a delightful *juge de conciliation*, who carries out his benevolent duties in his cellar, dispensing its contents to soften litigants) is a black billy-goat named Samuel, who, though rather diabolical, is in a way the "Luck of the Bertignys," and after selling whom their state is doomed. But we see very little of him.

The summing up need probably not be long. That

---

[1] This (which may be called M. Rod's novel-headquarters) occurs also not merely in *L'Eau Courante* but in *Les Roches Blanches*, a book which opens very well in a Mrs. Gaskell or Mrs. Oliphant vein, with the introduction of a new pastor, but ends much less satisfactorily, with a guiltless but not at all convincing love-affair between this pastor and the wife of his chief parishioner.

M. Rod was no mere stuffer of the shelves of circulating libraries must have been made clear ; that he could write excellently has been (with all due modesty) confessed ; that he could sometimes be poignant, often vivid, even occasionally humorous, is true. He has given us a fresh illustration of that tendency of the later novel, to " fill all numbers " of ordinary life, which has been insisted upon. But that he is too much of a " dismal Jemmy " of novel-writing is certainly true also. The House of Mourning is one of the Houses of Life, and therefore open to the novelist. But it is not the *only* house. It would sometimes seem as if M. Rod were (as usual without his being able to help it) a sort of *jettatore*,—as if there were no times or places for him except that

> When all the world is old,
>   And all the trees are brown,
> And all the sport is cold,
>   And all the wheels run down.

But there is something to add, and even one book not yet noticed to comment on, which may serve as a real light on this remarkable novelist. The *Scènes de la Vie Cosmopolite.* way in which I have already spoken of *La Course à la Mort*, which was a very early book, may be referred to. Even earlier, or at least as early, M. Rod wrote some short stories, which were published as *Scènes de la Vie Cosmopolite*. They include " Lilith " (the author, though far from an Anglophile, had a creditable liking for Rossetti), which is a story of the rejection of a French suitor by an English governess ; the ending of a liaison between a coxcomb and a lady much older than himself (" Le Feu et l'Eau ") ; " L'Idéal de M. Gindre," with a doubtful marriage-close ; a discovery of falseness (" Le Pardon ") ; " La Dernière Idylle " (which may be judged from some of its last words : " I have made a spectacle of myself long enough, and now the play is over "), and " Noces d'Or," the shortest and bitterest of all, in which the wife, who has felt herself tyrannised over for the fifty years, mildly retaliates by providing for dinner *nearly* all the things that she likes and her husband does not, though she effects a reconciliation with *pâté de canard d'Amiens*. I wonder if they ate duck-pies at Amiens in the spring of 1918?

The purpose of this postscript-account, and of the reference to *La Course*, should not be very obscure. It is clear that, at first and from the first, M. Rod's vocation was to be a prophet of discouragement and disappointment. You may be this and be quite a major prophet; but if you are not a major prophet your minority will become somewhat painfully apparent, and it will often, if not always, go near to failure. I think this was rather the case with M. Rod.

It is with reluctance that I find myself unable to give more than praise for admirable French, and "form"
Catulle in the strict sense, to the work in prose fiction
Mendès. of M. Catulle Mendès, sometime Gautier's son-in-law [1] and always, I think, his disciple. His early verse-work in the *Parnasse Contemporain* fifty years ago, was attractive and promising, though perhaps open to the exception which some took to the *Parnasse* generally, and which may be echoed here, *not* with that general concernment, but as to his own novel and tale-work. His late critical survey of modern French poetry was a really difficult thing admirably done. But his fiction leaves me cold, as Parnassian poetry did others, but not me. A friend of mine, whom I should have thought quite unshockable, either by principles or practice, once professed himself to me aghast at *Méphistophéla*. But M. Mendès's improprieties neither shock nor excite nor amuse me, because they have a certain air of being "machined." If anybody wishes to sample them at their very best, the half-score loosely and largely printed pages of "Tourterelle" in the volume entitled *Lesbia* will be no severe experiment. He may

---

[1] His wife for a time, Madame Judith Gautier, who died very recently, wrote in a fashion not unworthy of her blood both in verse and prose (part of her production being translations from Chinese), and was the only lady-member of the quaint *Contre-académie* formed by E. de Goncourt.

then take his choice of not going further at all, or of going further at the hazard of faring worse, or as well now and then, but hardly, I think, better.

I do not propose to add any further studies in detail to those already presented in this chapter. As I have (perhaps more than once) remarked, there are few periods of the century with the minor as well as major novel work of which I am better acquainted than with that of its last quarter. As I remember independently, or am in this or that way reminded, of the names of Jules de Glouvet; of at least three Pauls—Alexis, Arène, and Mahalin; of Ernest d'Hervilly; of the prolific Hector Malot; of Oscar Meténier, and Octave Mirbeau, and Jules Vallès of the Commune, of the brothers Margueritte and of others too many to mention, a sort of shame invades me at leaving them out.[1] Some of them may be alive still, though most, I think, are dead. But dead or alive, I have no room for them, and, for reasons also elsewhere stated, it is perhaps as well. The blossoming of the aloe, not once in a hundred years but all through them, has been told as best I could tell it.

Not shame but sorrow attends the exclusion of others, some of them, I think, better novelists than those actually discussed in this chapter—especially "Gyp" and MM. Anatole France, Paul Bourget, Jean Richepin, and "Pierre Loti." It would have been agreeable to pay, once more, suit and service to the adorable chronicler of the little rascal Bob and the unpretentiously divine Chiffon; to recall the delighted surprise with which one read *Le Crime de Silvestre Bonnard*, and follow the train of triumphs that succeeded it; to do justice (unbribed, but pleasantly seasoned, by some private gratitude) to the vigour and acuteness of *L'Irréparable* and its companions; to salute that masterpiece of Realism at its best, *La Glu*, and the

---

[1] And this shame becomes more acute when I think of one or two individual books, such especially as M. Henry Cochin's *Manuscrit de Monsieur C. A. L. Larsonnier*— a most pathetic and delightful story of a mental malady which makes time and memory seem to go backward though the victim can force himself to continue his ordinary duties, and record his sufferings.

more complicated as well as more pathetic history of *Césarine* ; and to re-discover the countries and the manners depicted for us from *Aziyadé* to *Pêcheur d'Islande*. But the *consigne* elsewhere laid down and experienced forbids it, and I think that *consigne* should not be " forced."

CONCLUSION

THE remaining pages of this book should be occupied partly with a continuation of a former chapter;[1] partly with a summary of the whole volume, the combination, almost necessary in all cases, being specially motived in this by the overlappings referred to above, and a word added on the whole *History*. Not only did Victor Hugo hold, to French literature as well as to French poetry, something very like the position [2] occupied by Tennyson and Browning in English poetry only, by covering every quarter of the century in whole or part with his work ; but there was, even in France, nothing like the " general post " of disappearances and accessions which marked the period from 1820 to 1860 in English—a consequence necessarily of the later revival of French. No one except Chateaubriand corresponded to the crowd of distinguished writers who thus made their appearance, at the actual meeting of eighteenth and nineteenth, with us ; and though, of course, there were exceptions, the general body of the French reinforcement did not dwindle much till 1870 onwards.

We noted that the first great development of the nineteenth-century novel was in the historical department, though many others made notable fresh starts: and we said something about the second development of the " ordinary " one which followed. It is this latter, of course, which has supplied the main material of the last third of the present volume, though (of course again)

[1] *V. sup.* " The French Novel in 1850."
[2] Called by some a " deadening " one. There was some very cheerful Life in that Death.

556

there have been many noteworthy and some great examples of the historical itself, of the supernatural, of the eccentric, and of many other kinds. But practically all who tried these later tried the ordinary, and a great many who tried the ordinary did not try the others. It is therefore on the development of the novel of common modern life that we must, at any rate for a little time, spend most of our attention here.

The fact of the change is indeed so certain and so obvious, that there is not much need to enforce or illustrate it, though it must be remembered that, on any true conception of history, the most obvious things are not those least worthy of being chronicled. Even Hugo, likely to be, and actually being, the most recalcitrant to the movement, comes close to modern times, and to such ordinary life as was possible to him, in *Les Misérables* and *Les Travailleurs de la Mer*. George Sand had begun as a sort of modernist; but by any one who can perform the (it is true not very easy) task of equating relative modernity, it will not be found that *Mlle. la Quintinie*, or even *Flamarande*, are more modern than *Lélia* or *Valentine* in the mere ratio of the dates. The ordinary life of the 'thirties and that of the 'sixties and 'seventies was no doubt different, but there is more than that difference in the books referred to. The artist is, consciously or unconsciously, trying to get nearer to her model or sitter. And this though George Sand was really almost as self-centred as Hugo, though in another way.

But it is, of course, in less idiosyncratic writers than these, who continued, and in others who began, to write at this time, that we must look for our real documents. Among the elder of this second class, Jules Sandeau's work is worth recurring to. He had sometimes gone a little earlier than his own time, and he had sometimes employed what is called—perhaps inconsiderately and certainly to some extent misleadingly—"romantic" incident in addition to purely novel-character and presentation. But his general manner of dealing reproduces itself, almost more than that of any of his contemporaries, in those novelists of the last quarter of the century who do not bow the knee to Naturalism: and one finds some actual recognition of the fact in dedications to him by younger novelists such as M. André Theuriet.[1]

But, look where you will, the lesson is unmistakable. Take Alexandre Dumas *fils*, beginning with a *Tristan le Roux* and ending with an *Affaire Clémenceau*. Take Flaubert's *Madame Bovary* and *L'Éducation Sentimentale*, in comparison with which *Salammbô* and two of the *Trois Contes* (the other is quite in the general drift) are obvious variations, excursions, reliefs.[2] Feuillet is practically (whatever may have been his early practice as a " devil "), when he takes to his own line, modern, and in a sense ordinary or nothing: Daudet the same. Naturalism *en bloc* would lose almost all pretence of justifying itself if it did not stick to the ordinary, or at least actual, though it may sometimes be a sort of transformed " ordinariness in abnormality." So great and so fertile a writer as Maupassant leaves us—except in his supernaturalisms—nothing at all that goes out of the actual probable or easily possible experience of a Frenchman of 1880–90. The four novelists who supply the bulk of the last chapter never outstep this. But since such indulgence in particulars may be thought mere driving at an open door, let us take the fact for granted, and turn to some consideration of its causes, results, conditions, features, and the like.

One of the causes is of such certainty and importance that a person, not indolent or prejudiced, might ask for no other. It is that sempiternal desire for change [3]— that principle of revolution, which is so much more certain than any evolution, and which governs human life, though it is always bringing that life back to the old places, " camouflaged," as they say nowadays, in a fashion that disguises them to the simple. The romance

---

[1] The better part even of M. Ohnet is a sort of vulgarised Sandeau.

[2] *La Tentation*, like others of the very greatest novels, is independent of its time, save in mere unimportant " colour."

[3] How little this change was one back to classicism—as some would have it—we may see presently.

of incident, historical and other, had had a long innings, and people were tired of it. But though this was undoubtedly the main influence, there were some others which it would be hardly judicious to neglect. It is true that the greatest of these were, in a fashion, only partial actions or reactions of the larger one already mentioned.[1] Beyle and Balzac, the latter of course with important " colours " of his own, and even the former with some modifications, had, as men of genius generally do, felt or found the spirit of change early, and their audiences helped to spread it. And yet minor impulsions might be indicated. It is a commonplace that from the days of the Napoleonic War to the middle 'fifties there were few great European events ; commercial progress, developments of colonisation, machinery, literature, and the arts, somewhat peddling politics,[2] and the like taking the place of the big wars and the grandiose revolutions that ushered in the nineteenth century. But these mostly meaner things themselves claimed attention ; they filled the life of men if they did not glorify it ; classes and occupations which had been almost altogether non-vocal began to talk and be talked about, and so the change again held on.

Lastly, of course, there was the increase of education : with which the demand for fiction, plentiful in quantity and easily comprehended, was sure to grow.

On the whole, however, the results concern us more than the causes. What is the general character of this large province, or, looking at it in another way, of these accumulated crops, which the fifty years more specially in question saw added to the prose fiction of France ?

The answer is pretty much what any wide student of history—political, social, literary, or other—would expect,

---

[1] The greatest of all—the direction and maintenance of the revolution under the inspiration of what is called Romance—must be again postponed for a little while.

[2] Of course the convulsions of '48 were ominous enough, but they seemed to be everywhere repressed or placated for a considerable time ; and if there had been a single statesman of genius besides Herr von Bismarck (I anticipate but decline the suggestion of Cavour) in the Europe of the next two decades, they might not have broken out again for a much longer time than was actually the case.

supposing, which is of course in fact an impossibility, that he could come to the particular study "fresh and fasting." Novel-writing in France, as elsewhere, became more and more a business; and so, while the level of craftsmanship might be to some extent raised, the level of artistic excellence was correspondingly lowered. It has been before observed more than once that, to the present critic, only Flaubert and Maupassant of the writers we have been discussing in these later chapters can be credited with positive genius, unless the too often smoky and malodorous torch of Zola be admitted to qualify for the Procession of the Chosen. But when we take in the whole century the retrospect is very different; and while the later period may suffer slightly in the respect just indicated, the earlier affords it some compensation in the other noted point.

There is, indeed, no exact parallel, in any literature or any branch of literature within my knowledge, to the manifold development of the French novel during these hundred years. Our own experience in the same department cannot be set in any proper comparison with it, for the four great novelists of the mid-eighteenth century, and their followers from Miss Burney downwards, with the Terror and the Political schools of the extreme close, had advanced our starting-point so far that Scott and Miss Austen possessed advantages not open to any French writer. On the other hand, the Sensibility School, which was far more numerously attended in France than in England, gave other openings, which *were* taken advantage of in a special direction by Benjamin Constant, and much earlier and less brilliantly, but still with important results, by Madame de Montolieu. The age-long competence of the French in *conte* and *nouvelle* was always ready for fresh adaptation; and at the very beginning of the new century, and even earlier, two reinforcements of the most diverse character came to the French novel. Pigault-Lebrun and Ducray-Duminil (the earliest of whose novels appeared just before the Revolution as Pigault's début was made just after it) may be said to have democratised the novel to nearly [1] the full meaning of that much abused word. They lowered its value aesthetically, ethically (at least in Pigault's case, while Ducray's morality does not go much above the " Be amiable and honest " standard), logically, rhetorically, and in a good many other ways. But they did not merely increase the number of its readers ; in so doing they multiplied correspondingly the number of its practitioners, and so they helped to make novel-writing a business and—through many failures and half-successes—to give it a sort of regularised practice, if not a theory.

Yet if this democratisation of the novel thus went partly but, as does all democratisation inevitably, to the degradation of it in quality, though to its increase in quantity, there were fortunately other influences at work to provide new reinforcements, themselves in some cases of quality invaluable. It has been admitted that neither Chateaubriand nor Madame de Staël can be said to have written a first-class novel—even *Corinne* can hardly be called that. But it is nearer thereto than anything that had been written since the first part of *La Nouvelle Heloïse*: while *René* and *Atala* recover, and more than recover in tragic material, the narrative power of the best comic tales. And these isolated examples were of less importance for the actual history—being results of individual genius, which are not imitable—than certain more general characteristics of the two writers. Between them—a little perhaps owing to their social position, but much more by their pure literary quality—they reinstated the novel in the Upper House of literature itself. In Madame de Staël there was more than adequacy—in Chateaubriand there was some-times consummateness—of style; in both, with whatever varnish of contemporary affectation, there was genuine nobility of thought. They both chose subjects worthy

---

[1] Nearly—but fortunately for literature—not quite. The jobbery and the tyranny which are inseparable from democracy in politics find room with difficulty in *our* " Republic."

of their powers, and Madame de Staël at least contented herself with ordinary, or not very extraordinary, modern life. But the greatest things they did, from the historian's point of view, were introductions of the novel to new fields of exercise and endeavour. Art and religion were brought into its sphere, and if *Les Natchez* and *Les Martyrs* cannot exactly be called modern historical novels, they are considerable advances, both upon the model of *Télémaque* and upon that of *Bélisaire*. And even putting this aside, the whole body of Chateaubriand's work, as well as not a little in Madame de Staël's, tended to introduce and to encourage the spirit of Romance.

Now the proposition which—though never, I trust, pushed to the unliterary extent of warping the judgment, and never yet, I hope, unduly flaunted or flourished in the reader's face—dominates this volume, is that Romanticism, or, to use the shorter and more glorious name, Romance, itself dominates the whole of the French nineteenth-century novel. If any one considers that this proposition is at variance with the other, that the main function of the novel during the period has been to bring the novel closer to ordinary life, he has failed to grasp what it might be presumptuous plumply to call the true meaning of Romance, but what is certainly that meaning as it has always appeared to me.

To attempt discussion, or even enumeration, of all the definitions or descriptions of Romance in general which have been given by others would not only be impossible in the space at command, but would be really irrelevant. As it happens, the matter can be cut short, without inadequacy and without disingenuousness, by quoting a single pair of epithets, affixed by a critic, for whom I have great respect, a day or two before I wrote these words. This critic held that Romantic treatment—in stage matters more particularly, but we can extend the phrase to fiction without unfairness—was " generous but false." *I* should call it " generous " certainly, but before all things "true." Nor is this a mere play upon the words of the original. It so happens that our friend the enemy has supplied a most admirable help. Legally, as we know, veracity requires " the truth, the whole truth, and nothing but the truth." I admit that the last clause will not fit Romance. She does give us something more than the truth, and that is her generosity, but it is a generosity which is necessitated by the fact that Romance is a quality or function not so much of nature essentially— though happily it is sometimes so by accident—as of Art, the essence of which is to require, whether it be art classic or art romantic, art of literature or art of design, art of sight or art of sound, something *added* to the truth —as that truth exists in reality.

Of what this addition is presently. But Romance, as I see it, insists upon and gives the truth and the whole truth of nature itself. Who is the greatest of Romantics ? By agreement of all but the purblind and the paradoxer, Shakespeare. Who is the truest and the most universal of all writers ? By consent of classic and romantic, at least of those of 'either kind who "count"—again Shakespeare. Let me say at once that, having early sworn allegiance to Logic, I am perfectly aware that a coincidence of two things in one person does not prove the identity of the things. But it proves their compossibility, and when it is found *in excelsis*, it surely goes near to prove a good deal more. Nor is one in the least confined to this argument from example, strong as it is. When you examine Classicism, which, whatever we may say or not say of it, will always stand as the opposite of Romance, you find that it always leaves something out. It may—it does in its best examples— give you truth ; it may—it does in its best examples— add something which is its own " generosity "—its castigation, its order, its reason, its this and that and the other. To be very liberal, it may be admitted that the perpetual and meticulous presence in it of " Thou shalt not " do or say this or that, is most conspicuous— let us go to the extreme of generosity ourselves and say, is only conspicuous—in its feebler examples. But there is always something that it does not give, and some of us think that there are not a few things which it cannot give. There is nothing, not even ugliness itself, which Romance cannot give, though there its form of generosity comes in, and the ugly in simple essence becomes beautiful by treatment.

I could bestow any amount of tediousness in these generalities on my readers if I thought it necessary: but having developed my proposition and its meaning, I think it better to pass to the applications thereof in the present subject.

Of the wide extension of aim and object effected by Romantic influence in the novel, as in other departments of literature, there can be little denial, though of course it may be contended that this extension took place not as it ought and as it ought not. But of the fact of it and of the corresponding variety introduced with it, the very pioneers of the so-called Romantic movement give ample proof. We have seen this even in the extremely inchoate stage of the first two decades; when the great definitely Romantic leaders made their appearance it was more remarkable still. The four chief writers who gave the Romantic lead before 1830 itself may be taken to be Nodier, Hugo, Mérimée, and Vigny. They stand in choice of subjects, as in treatment of them, wide apart; and just as it has been noted of Vigny's poetry, that its three chief pieces, " Éloa," " Dolorida," and " Le Cor " point the way to three quite different kinds of Romantic verse, so, confining ourselves to the same example, it may be repeated that *Cinq-Mars* and the smaller stories exemplify, and in a way pattern, kinds of Romantic prose fiction even further apart from each other. Always, through the work of these and that of Gautier, and of all the others who immediately or subsequently follow them, this broadening and branching out of the Romantic influence—this opening of fresh channels, historical and fanciful, supernatural and ordinary— shows itself. The contention, common in books, that this somehow ceased about the middle of the century, or at least died off with the death of those who had carried it out, appears to me, I confess, to be wildly unhistorical and uncritical. At no time—the proofs fill this volume—do we find any restriction, of choice of subject or conduct of treatment, to anything like the older limits. But the most unhistorical and the most uncritical form of this contention is the astonishing endeavour to vindicate a "classical" character for Naturalism. Most certainly there is "impropriety" in some of the classics and "impropriety" in all the Naturalists, but other resemblance I can see none. As for the argument that as Naturalism is opposed to Romance and Classicalism is opposed to Romance, *therefore* Naturalism is Classical—this is undoubtedly a very common form of bastard syllogism, but to labour at proving its bastardy would be somewhat ridiculous.

The fact is, as should have been sufficiently made good above, that Naturalism is not opposed to Romance in anything like the sense that Classicism is : it is nothing but a degradation and exaggeration at once of certain things in Romance itself. Nor do I think that there is the slightest difficulty in showing that every form of novel-writing which we have been surveying in this book—that the work of every one of those distinguished or undistinguished writers who have been, with or without regret, declined—is still essentially Romantic. It is Romantic in its inflexible resolution to choose subjects for itself and not according to rule; Romantic in its wise or unwise individuality of treatment; Romantic in its preferential appeal to emotion rather than to pure intelligence; above all, Romantic in its quest—often no doubt ill-guided and unsuccessful, but always more or less present—for that element of strangeness which, though invisible to many who live, is a pervading character of Life itself, and the presence of which it is the glory of Romance itself, from its earliest to its latest manifestations, to have recognised and to some extent fixed, in artistic representation. And so, I hope, that what has been discovered in this volume—in the way of pageant and procession even more than that of examination, though with something of that also—may have shown further progress towards—nay, actual attainment of, the goal which I ventured to mark out in the earlier volume as that of the novelist by the words, " Here is the whole of human life before you. Copy it or, better, re-create it—with variation and decoration *ad libitum*— as faithfully, but as fully, as you can."

Thesis - writing, however, is but dismal reading, unless (as Mrs. Scott told Jeffrey she hoped he was for the *Marmion* review) "you are very well paid for it." Nor do I, as I have previously explained, consider it a necessary part of history, though common honesty may require that the presence of a doctrine, behind the delivery of an account, should be confessed. I think the account itself should be sufficient to make good my point ; others may differ. But even if they do, some of them at least will, I hope, have found in that account some modicum of the amazing supply of rest and refreshment contained in the mass of literature we have been surveying.

On the two volumes together there may be a little more to say. I have touched, I hope not too frequently, on the curious pleasure which I myself have felt in reading again books sometimes unopened for more than half a century, sometimes read at different times during that period, sometimes positively familiar; and on the con- trasted enjoyment of reading others written long ago in all but a few cases, but not, as it happened, read at the time of their appearance. I am indeed inclined to lay much stress on the quality of re-readableness in a novel. Perhaps, as indeed is pretty generally the fact in such cases, a capacity of reading again is required in the person as well as one of being read again in the book. The late Mr. Mark Pattison was not a friend of mine, and we once had a pitched battle ; nor was he in any case given to borrow other people's expressions. But he was a critic, if he was anything, and he once did me the honour to repeat *verbatim*—whether consciously or not I cannot say, but in the very periodical where it had originally appeared—a sentence of mine about " people who would

rather read any circulating-library trash, for the first
time, than *Pendennis* or *Pride and Prejudice* for the
second." I think this difference between the two classes
is as worthy to rank, among the criteria of opposed
races of mankind and womankind, as those between
borrowers and lenders, Platonists and Aristotelians, or
Big- and Little-Endians.

But the vast library through which I have had the
privilege of conducting my readers does not exercise
any invidious separation between the two. I have read
a good many French novels—hundreds certainly, I do
not know that it would be preposterous to say thousands—
that I have not even mentioned in this book.[1] But I
have been a very busy man, and have had to read and to
do a great many other things. If I had had nothing else
to do and had devoted my entire life to the occupation
which Gray thought not undesirable as regards Marivaux
and Crébillon, I doubt whether I could have "over-
taken," as the Scotch say, the entire prose fiction of 1800–
1900 in French. On the back of one of the volumes
of fiction—itself pretty obscure—which I have noticed
in Chapter II. of this volume, I find advertised the works
of a certain Dinocourt, of whom I never heard before, and
who is not to be found in at least some tolerably full
French dictionaries of literature. They have quite
appetising titles (one or two given in the passage referred
to), and there are in all sixty-two volumes of them, distributed in fours, fives, and sixes among the several works.
Ought I to have read these sixty odd volumes of Dinocourt?
That is a moral question. That there *are* sixty odd
volumes of him, probably not now very easily obtainable,
but somewhere for some one to read if he likes, is a simple
fact. And there are no doubt many more than sixty

---

[1] I am prepared for blame on account of some of the absences of mention. Perhaps
the most provoking, to some readers, will be those affecting two industrious members of
the aristocracy : Mme. la Comtesse Dash—more beautifully and properly though less
exaltedly, Gabrielli Anna Cisterne de Courtiras, *Vi*comtesse de Saint-Mars—and M.
le Comte Xavier de Montépin. They overlapped each other in pouring forth, from the
'forties to the 'nineties, torrents of mostly sensational fiction. But I had rather read
them than write about them.

such batches waiting likewise,[1] and quite likely to prove as readable as I found M. Ricard.

I have by no means always felt inclined to acquiesce in the endlessly repeated complaints that the hackwork of literature is worse done in England than it is in France. But having had a very large experience of the novels of both languages, having reviewed hundreds of English novels side by side with hundreds of French as they came from the press, and having also read, for pleasure or duty, hundreds of older ones in each literature, I think that the mysterious quality of readableness pure and simple *has* more generally belonged to the French novel than to the English. This, as I have endeavoured to point out, is not a question of naughtiness or niceness, of candour or convention. I have indeed admitted that the conventions of the French novel bore me quite as much as anything in ours. It *may* be partly a question of length, for, as everybody knows, the French took to the average single volume, of some three hundred not very closely printed pages, much sooner than we took to anything of the kind. It is perhaps partly also due to what one of the reviewers of my former volume well called the greater " spaciousness " of the English novel, that is to say, its inclusion of more diverse aims, and episodic subjects, and minor interests generally. For this, while it makes for superior greatness when there is strength enough to carry it off, undoubtedly requires *more* strength, and so gives more openings for weakness to show itself. There are many average English novels which I should not mind reading, and not a few that I should like to read, again, while there are but few French novels that I should care to read so often as I have cared to read the great English ones. But I could read, for a second time, a very much larger proportion of average French fiction.

Of those books which are " above average " I have

---

[1] In the same place another novelist, M. Amédée de Bast, of whom I again acknowledge ignorance, advertises no less than *four* novels of *four* volumes each, as being actually all at press, *pour paraître à diverses époques.* Dryden says somewhere " in epoches mistakes." Let us hope there were none here.

tried to say what I thought ought to be said in the volume itself, and there is no need of a " peroration with *much* circumstance" about them. It is a long way—a perfect maze of long ways leading through the most different countries of thought and · feeling—from Atala dying in the wilderness to Chiffon doing exquisitely balanced justice to herself and the Jesuit, by allowing that while he and she were both *bien élevés*, he was *un peu trop* and she was not. It is not so far, except in time, nor separated by such a difference of intervening country, from the song of the Mandragore in Nodier to those muffled shrieks of a better-known variety of the same mystic plant, that tell us of Maupassant's growing progress to his fate. As you explore the time and the space of the interval you come across wonderful things. There are the micro-macrocosms of Hugo, where, as in Baudelaire's line on the albatross quoted above, he is partly hampered because he has come down from the air of poetry to the earth of prose ; of Balzac, where there is no such difficulty, but where the cosmos itself is something other than yours ; of Dumas, where half the actual history of France is *dis*realised for your delectation. On a lesser scale you have the manners of town and country, of high life and low life, of Paris most of all, given you through all sorts of perspectives and in all sorts of settings by Paul de Kock and George Sand, by Sandeau and Bernard, by Alexandre Dumas *fils* and Feuillet, by Theuriet and Fabre. Gautier and Mérimée make for you that marriage of story and style which, before them, so few had attempted at all, yet which, since them, so many have tried with such doubtful success. Once more in Flaubert and then for the last time, as far as our survey goes, in Maupassant, you come to that touch of genius which exalts the novel, as it exalts all kinds, indefinably, unmistakably, finally.

And this journey is not like the one great journey, and more than one of the lesser journeys, of our life, irremeable ; there is no denial, no curse, no fiend with outstretched claw, to prevent your going back as often as you like, wandering in any direction you please, passing or staying as and where you wish. It has been perhaps unconscionable of me to inflict so big a book on my readers as a cover for giving myself the pleasure of making and remaking such journeys. But if I have persuaded any one of them to explore the country for himself, by him at least I shall not remain unforgiven.

APPENDIX

DATES OF PUBLICATION OF NOVELS ARRANGED UNDER AUTHOR'S NAMES IN THE ORDER OF NOTICE HERE

(These dates are given subject to the caution stated under Addenda and Corrigenda for Vol. I., p. xvii of this present volume. It has not been thought necessary to add editions, etc., as was done in Vol. I.: almost all the books referred to being in common sale. For dates of the authors themselves, see Index as before. Those of some books merely glanced at are excluded to save room.)

Staël, Mme. de. *Delphine*, 1802; *Corinne*, 1807.

Chateaubriand. *Atala*, 1801, in the *Mercure*; *René*, 1802, in *Génie du Christianisme*, 1805; *Le Dernier Abencérage*, 1805; *Les Martyrs*, 1809; *Les Natchez* in *Œuvres Complètes*, 1826–31.

Paul de Kock. *L'Enfant de ma Femme*, 1812; *Gustave*, 1821: *La Femme, le Mari et l'Amant*, 1829; *Edmond et sa Cousine*, 1843; *André le Savoyard*, 1825; *Jean*, 1828. *Mon Voisin Raymond*, 1822; *Le Barbier de Paris*, 1826.

Ducray-Duminil. *Fanfan et Lolotte*, 1787; *Le Petit Carillonneur*, 1809.

Ducange, V. *L'Artiste et la Soldat*, 1827; *Ludovica*, 1830.

Montolieu, Mme. de. *Caroline de Lichtfield*, 1786.

Ricard, A. *L'Ouvreuse de Loges*, 1829–32.

Arlincourt, Vicomte d'. *Le Solitaire*, 1821.

Nodier, Charles. *Les Proscrits, Le Peintre de Salzbourg*, etc., 1802–6; *Jean Sbogar*, 1818; *Smarra*, 1821; *Trilby*, 1822; *La Fée aux Miettes*, 1831.

Hugo, Victor. *Han d'Islande*, 1823; *Bug-Jargal*, 1824–26; *Notre Dame de Paris*, 1830; *Les Misérables*, 1862; *Les Travailleurs de la Mer*, 1866; *L'Homme qui Rit*, 1869; *Quatre-Vingt-Treize*, 1873.

Beyle, Henri. *Armance*, 1827; *Le Rouge et le Noir*, 1830; *La Chartreuse de Parme*, 1839; *L'Abbesse de Castro*, 1832. First set of posthumous *Nouvelles*, etc., 1854 onwards; second ditto (*Lamiel*, etc.), 1887 onwards.

Balzac, H. de. · Most of the *Juvenilia* were written, alone or in collaboration, during the years 1821, 1822, 1823, and 1824, but the period of the whole extends to that of *Les Chouans* (originally *Le Dernier Chouan*), 1829. The dates of the rest, especially considering their frequent rearrangement, are too numerous to give. Those chiefly commented on in text appeared as follows : *Le Peau de Chagrin*, 1831; *Eugénie Grandet*, 1833; *Le Père Goriot*, 1834; *Les Parents Pauvres*, 1846–47.

Sand, George. *Indiana*, 1832; *Valentine*, 1832; *Lélia*, 1833; *Consuelo*, 1842–43; *La Comtesse de Rudolstadt*, 1844–45; *Lucrezia Floriani*, 1847; *Elle et Lui*, 1859; *Un Hiver à Majorque*, 1842; *La Mare au Diable*, 1846; *La Petite Fadette*, 1840; *F. le Champi*, 1849; *Mauprat*, 1837; *La Daniella*, 1857; *Les Beaux Messieurs de Bois-Doré*, 1858; *Le Marquis de Villemer*, 1861; *Mlle. la Quintinie*, 1863; *Flamarande*, 1875.

Gautier, Théophile. *Les Jeune-France*, 1833; *Mlle. de Maupin*, 1835; *Fortunio*, 1838; *Nouvelles*, 1845; *Jettatura*, 1857; *Le Capitaine Fracasse*, 1863; *Spirite*, 1866.

Mérimée, Prosper. (*Clara Gazul*, 1825; *La Guzla*, 1827; *Le Carrosse du Saint-Sacrement*, part of *Clara Gazul* originally, did not reach the stage till 1850.) *La Jacquerie*, 1828; *Chronique de Charles IX*, 1829. Most of the stories, including *Colomba*, appeared between 1830 and 1840. *Carmen*, 1847; *Dernières Nouvelles*, 1873.

Musset, A. de. Most of the stories noticed in text appeared originally after 1840 in the *Revue des Deux Mondes*, and were not collected till after his death in 1857. *Mimi Pinson* had been published in 1852.

Gérard de Nerval. Work noticed appeared sporadically, in many papers and some books, between 1828 and his death in 1855. The best edition of the *Œuvres Complètes* is of 1868.

Vigny, A. de. *Cinq-Mars*, 1826; *Stello*, 1832; *Servitude et Grandeur Militaires*, 1835.

Fromentin, Eugène. *Dominique*, 1863.

Sainte-Beuve, C. A. *Volupté*, 1834.

Bernard, Ch. de. *Gerfaut*, 1838; *Le Nœud Gordien*, 1838; *Le Paravent*, 1839. The rest between 1840 and his death in 1850.

Sandeau, Jules. *Marianna*, 1839; *Fernand*, 1844; *Valcreuse*,

1846; *La Roche aux Mouettes*, 1871; *Mlle. de La Seiglière*, 1851; *Sacs et Parchemins*, 1851; *Mlle. de Kérouare*, 1842; *La Maison de Penarvan*, 1858.

Sue, Eugène. *Le Coucaratcha*, 1832–34; *La Vigie de Koatven*, 1833; *Les Mystères de Paris*, 1842–43; *Le Juif Errant*, 1844–45; *Les Sept Péchés Capitaux*, 1847–49.

Soulié, Frédéric. *Mémoires du Diable*, 1837–38; *Le Lion Amoureux*, 1839; *Le Château des Pyrénées*, 1843.

Murger, Henri. [*Scènes de*] *La Vie de Bohême*, 1851; *Les Buveurs d'Eau*, 1855; *Adeline Protat*, 1853; *Le Sabot Rouge*, 1860. (Shorter stories at different dates between 1848 (?) and his death in 1861.)

Reybaud, Louis. *Jérome Paturôt*, Part I., 1843; *Jérome Paturôt*, Part II., 1848.

Méry, Joseph. *Les Nuits Anglaises*, 1853.

Karr, Alphonse. *Sous les Tilleuls*, 1832.

Beauvoir, Roger de. *Stories mostly* 1832–53.

Ourliac, Édouard. *Stories mostly* 1835–48.

Achard, Amédée. *Belle-Rose*, 1847.

Souvestre, Émile. *Les Derniers Bretons*, 1835–37; *Le Foyer Breton*, 1844; *Un Philosophe sous les Toits*, 1850.

Féval, Paul. *La Fée des Grèves*, 1851.

Borel, Pétrus. *Champavert*, 1833; *Madame Putiphar*, 1839.

Dumas *père*. *Isabeau?* [-*bel?* -*belle?*] *de Bavière*, 1835; *Le Comte de Monte Cristo*, 1844–45; *Les Trois Mousquetaires*, 1844; *Vingt Ans Après*, 1845; *La Reine Margot*, 1845; *Le Vicomte de Bragelonne*, 1848–50.

The sequels of *La Reine Margot* and the major part of the eighteenth-century series appeared between 1846 and 1850; *Olympe de Clèves* in 1852; *Les Louves de Machecoul* in 1859. Little of real value in novel later. The period of chief attack on him for plagiarism, *supercherie*, "novel-manufacture," etc., was 1845–48.

Dumas *fils*. *Tristan le Roux*, 1850; *La Dame aux Camélias*, 1848; *Antonine*, 1849; *La Vie à Vingt Ans*, 1854; *Aventures de Quatre Femmes et d'un Perroquet*, 1846–47; *Trois Hommes Forts*, 1851; *Diane de Lys*, 1853; *Affaire Clémenceau*, 1866; *Ilka*, 1895.

Janin, Jules. *L'Âne Mort et la Femme Guillotinée*, 1829; *Barnave*, 1831.

Flaubert, Gustave. *Madame Bovary*, 1857; *Salammbô*, 1862; *L'Éducation Sentimentale*, 1869; *La Tentation de Saint-Antoine*, 1848–74; *Trois Contes*, 1877; *Bouvard et Pécuchet*, 1881.

Feuillet, Octave. *Le Roman d'un jeune homme pauvre*, 1858;

M. de Camors, 1867 ; *Le Petite Comtesse*, 1857 ; *Julia de Trécœur*, 1872 ; *Honneur d'Artiste*, 1890 ; *La Morte*, 1886.

Daudet, Alphonse. *Le Petit Chose*, 1868 ; *Robert Helmont*, 1876 ; *Lettres de Mon Moulin*, 1869 ; *Jack*, 1862 ; *Tartarin de Tarascon*, 1872 ; *Le Nabab*, 1877 ; *Les Rois en Exil*, 1879 ; *Numa Roumestan*, 1890 ; *L'Évangéliste*, 1883 ; *Sapho*, 1884 ; *L'Immortel*, 1888.

About, Edmond. *Le Roi des Montagnes*, 1856 ; *Tolla*, 1855 ; *Germaine*, 1867 ; *Madelon*, 1863 ; *Maître Pierre*, 1858.

Ponson du Terrail, Pierre A. *Rocambole*, 1859 ; *Les Gandins*, 1861.

·Gaboriau, Émile *L'Affaire Lerouge*, 1866.

Feydeau, Ernest. *Fanny*, 1858 ; *Sylvie*, 1861 ; *Daniel*, 1859.

Droz, Gustave. *Monsieur, Madame et Bébé*, 1866 ; *Entre Nous*, 1867.

Cherbuliez, Victor. *Le Comte Kostia*, 1863 ; *Le Roman d'une Honnête Femme*, 1867 ; *Meta Holdenis*, 1873 ; *Miss Rovel*, 1875 ; *Samuel Brohl et Cie*, 1877 ; *Olivier Maugant*, 1885.

Barbey d'Aurevilly, Jules. *Les Diaboliques*, 1874 ; *L'Ensorcelée*, 1854 ; *Un Prêtre Marié*, 1865.

Cladel, Léon. *Les Va-nu-pieds*, 1873 ; *Crête-Rouge*, 1880 ; *La Fête Votive de Saint-Bartholomée Porte-Glaive*, 1872.

Champfleury. *Les Excentriques*, 1852 ; *Madame Eugénio*, 1874.

Goncourt, É. and J. Dates in text: from 1860 to 1870.

—— E. only. *Chérie*, 1884.

Zola, É. *Contes à Ninon*, 1864 ; *L'Attaque du Moulin*, 1880 ; The Rougon-Macquart books, 1871–93 ; " Les Trois Villes," 1894–98 ; " Les Quatre Évangiles," 1890–1903.

Maupassant, Guy de. *Boule de Suif*, 1880 ; *La Maison Tellier*, 1881 ; *Bel-Ami*, 1885 ; *Une Vie*, 1883 ; *Pierre et Jean*, 1888 ; *Fort comme la Mort*, 1889 ; *Notre Cœur*, 1890. Smaller Tales, 1880–93, and posthumously.

Huysmans, J. K. Contribution to *Les Soirées de Médan*, 1880 ; *Les Sœurs Vatard*, 1879 ; *Là-Bas*, 1891 ; *À Rebours*, 1884.

Belot, Adolphe. *Mlle. Giraud ma Femme*, 1870 ; *La Femme de Feu*, 1872.

Fabre, Ferdinand. *L'Abbé Tigrane*, 1873 ; *Norine*, 1889 ; *Le Marquis de Pierrerue*, 1874 ; *Mon Oncle Célestin*, 1881 ; *Lucifer*, 1884 ; *Taillevent*, 1894 ; *Toussaint Galabru*, 1887.

Theuriet, André. *Sauvageonne*, 1881 ; *Raymonde*, 1877 ; *Le Fils Maugars*, 1879.

Ohnet, Georges. *Serge Panine*, 1881 ; *Le Maître de Forges*,

1882; *Le Docteur Rameau*, 1888; *La Grande Marnière*, 1885.

Rod, Édouard. *La Course à la Mort*, 1885; *Le Sens de la Vie*, 1889; *La Vie Privée de Michel Teissier*, 1893 (2nd part, 1894); *La Sacrifiée*, 1892; *Le Silence*, 1894; *Là-Haut*, 1897; *L'Eau Courante*, 1902

Mendès, Catulle. *Lesbia*, 1886.

(*In a not inconsiderable number of cases a difference of* one *year will be found, from the dates as given in some reference books. This, which renews the elder trouble of " Old " and " New " Style, arises, probably, if not certainly, from the fact of the book having appeared late in autumn or early in spring, with a title-page, anticipatory or retrospective, as the case may be. The same thing occurs, of course, with English books ; but not, I think, so often. French books, moreover, unless I am mistaken, not infrequently appear with* no *date on title-page*)

INDEX

(This Index has been constructed on the same principles as that of Vol. I. But the full names, birth- and death-dates, titles, etc., of authors included in the former Index are not repeated here.)

THE END

Printed by R. & R. CLARK, LIMITED, *Edinburgh.*